B.Ed. GUIDE

B.Ed. GUIDE

[Based on UGC, NET, IGNOU and other Indian University Syllabus]

By

BHARTI SHARMA

ANMOL PUBLICATIONS PVT. LTD.

NEW DELHI - 110 002 (INDIA)

ANMOL PUBLICATIONS PVT. LTD.
4374/4B, Ansari Road, Daryaganj
New Delhi - 110 002
Ph.: 23261597, 23278000
Visit us at: www.anmolpublications.com

B.Ed. Guide

First Published, 2004

ISBN 81-261-1780-X

PRINTED IN INDIA

Published by J.L. Kumar for Anmol Publications Pvt. Ltd., New Delhi - 110 002 and Printed at Mehra Offset Press, Delhi.

SYLLABUS

B.ED. COURSE

PAPER-I : TEACHER IN EMERGING INDIAN SOCIETY

- Education: nature and meaning—its objectives in relation to the time and place.
- Education in the western context: with specific reference to Rousseau, Pestalozzi, Dewey, Russell, their impact on educational thought and class room practices, in term of progressive trends in education.
- Indian thought and its contribution to educational practices.
- Philosophy and education: significance of studying philosophy in understanding educational practices and problems.
- Major philosophical systems—their salient features and their impact on education.
  - (a) Realism with reference to Aristotle and Jainism.
  - (b) Naturalism with reference to the views of Rousseau and Rabindra Nath Tagore.
  - (c) Idealism with reference to Plato and Socrates.
  - (d) Pragmatism with reference to Dewey "Instrumentalism & Experimentalism".
  - (e) Humanism—Historical & Scientific and Buddhists.
- Child-centred education.
- Educational thinkers and their contribution in developing principles of education.
- M.K. Gandhi: Basic tenets of Basic Education.
- Swami Vivekananda: Man making education.
- Sri Aurobindo: Integral education, its basic premises; stages of development.
- Foebel: The play way method.

- Montessori: The didactic apparatus.
- Knowledge about the Indian constitution and its directive principles; various articles mentioned in the constitution that are related to education; meaning of secularism, social goals; democracy and socialistic pattern of society; meaning of the term "National integration and Emotional integration", factors contributing to achieve them; Economic planning and the meaning of five year plans.
- Sociological basis of education, Relationship between individual to individual and individual to society, in terms of Norms given by the existing social order; education as liberal and utilitarian, education as a tool of economic development, education as an agent of social change, education as a means of National welfare through the immediate welfare of the society, education and human resource development.
- Meaning of national integration and its need, role of teacher and educational institutions in achieving National Integration through democratic interaction, explanation of cultural heritage, contributions of different religions (Hinduism, Buddhism, Sikhism, Islam, Christianity and Jainism) for the same cause and human upliftment, equal communication.
- Meaning of a new social order, eradication of illiteracy, objectives of NAEP; provisions made and channels started for educating socially, culturally and economically deprived; Means and measures taken for equality of opportunities in terms of Castes, Tribes, Disabled, Gender and Minorities; Achieving a learning society in terms of distance education, green and clean society & povertyless society through planning the population and available resources, State's new programmes etc.

PAPER-II : DEVELOPMENT OF LEARNER AND TEACHING-LEARNING PROCESS

- **Nature of Psychology and Learners**

  (a) Psychology: Its meaning, nature, methods and scope; functions of educational psychology.

  (b) Stages of human development; stage specific characteristics and developmental tasks.

(c) Adolescence in Indian context—characteristics and problems of adolescents; their needs and aspirations.

(d) Guiding and counselling adolescents.

- **Learning and Motivation**

(a) Nature of learning; learning theories—Behaviourists (Skinner's), Information Processing (Rosger's) and Humanistic (Maslow's)

(b) Factors influencing learning and teaching process; learner related; teacher related; process related and content related.

(c) Motivation—nature, types; techniques of enhancing learners' motivation.

- **Intelligence**

(a) Nature and characteristics of intelligence and its development.

(b) Theories of intelligence; two factor theory—Multifactor Theory (PMA) and SI Model.

(c) Measuring intelligence—Verbal, non-verbal and Performance tests (one representative of group test and individual test of each).

- **Exceptional Children**

(a) Concept of exceptional children—types, and characteristics of each type including children with learning disabilities.

(b) Individual differences—nature; accommodating individual differences in the classroom.

(c) Learner centred techniques for teaching exceptional children.

UNIT V

- **Personality**—Definition, meaning and nature; development of personality; type and trait theories of personality.

PAPER-III : DEVELOPMENT OF EDUCATION SYSTEM IN INDIA

- Education in India during (a) Vedic, (b) Buddhist and (c) Medieval periods.
- Macaulay's minutes and Bentinck's resolution of 1835. Adam's report and its recommendations.

- Wood's Dispatch—1854.
- Lord Curzon's educational policy. Growth of national consciousness. National education movement.
- Recommendations of Indian Education Commission—1882, its influence on the subsequent development of education.
- Essential features of Sadler Commission Report—1917.
- Wardha Scheme of education—1937.
- Radhakrishnan Commission—1948.
- University Education Committee (1948-49).
- Secondary Education Committee Report (1952-53).
- Indian Education Commission (1964-66).
- National Policy on Education (1986).
- Revised National Policy (1992).

PAPER-IV : ESSENTIALS OF EDUCATIONAL TECHNOLOGY AND MANAGEMENT

- Definition of educational technology, distinction between hardware and software technologies. Their role in modern educational practices.
- Hardware technologies: Important accessories and their application—OHP, Still and Movie Projectors, Audio-Video recording instruments; TV, Computers, New technologies like e-mail; internet; etc.
- Use of strategies like teleconferencing, micro teaching, programmed instruction, CAI, language laboratory.
- Psychological uses for use of modern technologies—Cone of experience (Edger Dale), Multisemory Instruction—advantages.
- Developing programmed instructional material—linear, branching programmes, tryouts and validation etc.
- Meaning of guidance—rationale for guidance services, concept of counseling—directed and non-directed counseling.
- Organization school guidance services; use of community resources for school guidance services;

- Career guidance services; career information centre; career conferences;
- Personal guidance.
- Meaning of management in education—Managing men resources and materials. Implications for educational initiations.
- Managing curriculum, managing co-curriculum, managing school discipline, and managing physical resources.
- Evaluating institutional performance—Methods used—pupil evaluation, teacher evaluation, evaluation of institutional performance.
- Methods of teacher evaluation—use of pupil rating, peer rating, supervisor rating, community rating—ratings used for Institutional improvement.
- Accountability in school education—methods used for assessing accountability.

Contents

PAPER-I

Teacher in Emerging Indian Society

Q. 1. Explain the meaning of Education in Indian and Western context.

Ans. There have been variations in the very concept of education. Eastern and Western concepts have differed to some extent.

Indian Concept of Education. Education being an important social activity, its meaning has been changing through the ages due to change in social and physical conditions. Different educationists have interpreted it differently.

According to **Rigveda,** "Education is that which makes a man self-reliant and selfless." The Rigveda regarded creating confidence in the person as the only function of education whereas the function of education is unlimited.

The Upanishad explains, "Education is that whose end product is salvation." The Upanishad regards attaining salvation as the function of education whereas education develops a person physically, intellectually, socially, economically and culturally.

According to **Vivekanand,** "Education is the manifestation of Divine Perfection already existing in man."

According to **Tagore,** "Education makes man's life in harmony with all existence."

According to **Kautilya,** "Education means training for the country and love for the nation."

According to **Gandhiji,** "By education I mean an all-round drawing out of the best in child and man, body, mind and spirit."

Western thinkers have given following definitions:

According to **Aristotle,** "Education is the creation of a sound mind in a sound body." Aristotle has regarded the meaning of education complete by mentioning physical and spiritual development.

According to **Frobel,** "Education is unfoldment of what is already enfolded in the seed. It is the process through which a child expresses his internal abilities."

Frobel called education as a process through which internal abilities are expressed.

According to **Pestalozzi,** "Education is the natural, harmonious and progressive development of man's innate powers". Pestalozzi has talked about the development of innate powers whereas education also brings about personal, social, moral, cultural, economic, national and international development.

According to **T.P. Nunn,** "Education is the complete development of individuality so that man can make an original contribution to human life according to his best capacity."

Nunn and James have also stressed individual and social development but their definitions are also vague.

According to **James,** "Education is the organisation of acquired habits of such action as will fit the individual to his physical and social environment."

According to **Bossing,** "The function of education is conceived to be the adjustment of man to his environment, to the end that the most enduring satisfaction may accrue to the individual and to the society."

Bossing has emphasised individual and social aspects but did not make clear the meaning of education.

According to **Dewey,** "Education is the development of all those capacities in the individual which enable him to control his environment and fulfil his possibilities."

According to **Redden,** "Education is the deliberate and systematic influence exerted by the mature person upon the immature through instruction, discipline and harmonious development of physical, intellectual, aesthetic, social and spiritual powers of human being."

Redden has not considered the non-formal and economic aspects of education.

According to **Ruskin,** "Education does not mean teaching people what they do not know. It means teaching them to behave as they do not behave."

Ruskin has mentioned the function of education only to make man a social animal. He has not bothered for other aspects.

After studying the interpretation given by various educationists, we can classify the meaning of education into two categories—Narrower and Broader. In the narrow sense, education is regarded as equivalent to instruction, imparted in school or college. Education is believed to begin with the entrance of a child to the school and end with his departure from the university. Education includes those specific influences which are brought to bear upon the child with a definite purpose in a pre-planned, suitable, and methodical manner, by parents, teachers and other members of the community, for the preservation of the cultural heritage. According to this view education is limited to classroom teaching and readymade materials. Education is given in a formal way, under set and controlled conditions and environment. It is pre-planned and is given by teachers in the classroom.

According to **J.S. Mill,** Education in its narrower sense means, "The culture which each generation purposely gives to its successor in order to qualify, to keep up and to improve the level attained. Thus education becomes a purposeful activity which is planned deliberately for the purpose of the child's individual and social development. This activity is organised through the school as the chief agency of education.

According to **Dumvile,** "Education includes all the influences which act upon an individual during his passage from the cradle to the grave."

According to **Lodge,** "In the wider sense, all experiences are said to be educative. Even the bite of mosquito and the taste of water melon experiences have a directly educative effect on us." The child educates his parents, the pupils educate their teacher. Every thing that we say, think or do educates us.

In this wider sense life is education and education is life. Whatever broadens our horizon, deepens our insight, refines our reactions and stimulates our thoughts and feelings educates us. Life is a long process of education and education is synonymous with the act of living.

Analytical Meaning of Education

Education is the Harmonious Development of Child. Education is the harmonious development of the child. Through education all aspects—physical, mental, spiritual and moral are developed.

Education is the Development of Innate and Acquired Powers of the Child. Every child has innate capacities. Education helps in developing those natural qualities of the child. It peovides every person with the opportunity of developing according to his capacities.

Education is a Dynamic Process. Education is a dynamic and progressive process. It reconstructs a new and better social pattern according to the changing needs of time, place and society.

Education is a Process of Adjustment with the Environment. Education helps the individual in making adjustment with his own self, parents, peers and society etc.

Education is a Life Long Process. It starts in mother's womb and ends in tomb. The sequence of learning through experiences goes on up to death.

Q. 2. Critically examine various individual aims of education showing their importance and limitations.

Ans. Some of the most important individual aims of education are:

1. The Knowledge Aim. Knowledge is power. Achievements of all kinds are made possible only through knowledge. An ignorant man can do nothing for himself or for anyone else; and is like an animal. Knowledge is basic for living a rich and happy life. It is for this reason that many educationists consider imparting of knowledge to the people as an important aim. That is why all the schools have graded syllabus for children of different ages and classes. Different subjects are taught in the schools as different aspects of knowledge.

In fact acquisition of knowledge is the nucleon around which most of the activities of the schools in the whole world revolve. Most of the teaching strategies developed for teaching aim at imparting knowledge alone. The examination systems in all countries measure, by and large, only knowledge. In fact, education and knowledge giving have become synonymous. Teachers, students and parents all think that good education and good schools are only those which make their children knowledgeable.

There is no doubt that knowledge-giving should be considered an important aim of education. In the past many philosophers like Plato, Aristotle, the Sophists and many others emphasized this aim very much. Comenius said that an ideal school should impart knowledge of all subjects to all men and women. Knowledge and intellectual development go together; and cultivation of intelligence is an importance of education according to Bertrand Russel. Bacon's slogan was "all knowledge for all", knowledge was virtue for Socrates. To Cicero knowledge was a means of mental development. Even the development of other aspects of human personality is dependent largely on acquisition of knowledge. Thus, it is an important aim of education to impart knowledge. But where are we wrong?

We commit a serious error when we accept and say that it is the only aim of education, when we say that nothing else is important. Knowledge alone is not enough and sufficient for living a happy and complete life. Knowledge is a tool which has to be used for achieving many more things. So these many more things should also be brought within the purview of aims of education. Hence, the right way is to say that among many aims of education, knowledge aim is also very important.

2. Harmonious Development Aim. It means harmonious development of child's personality. Child's personality is one word but many things. Intellectual and cognitive development is one aspect. Emotional development including emotional control is another. Feelings, attitudes, interests, values etc., also fall within this component of emotional development. Similarly, development of skills, desirable habits and actions constitute still another aspect of personality development. Adjustment to the environment and many social behaviours come under this. Equal development of all these aspects, balanced development of these, is considered an aim of education. If it happens that a person is very knowledgeable, but socially maladjusted, this would mean a lap-sided development of the personality. Education should provide opportunities to all children for developing all aspects or their personalities.

3. Vocational Aim. This is also known as the 'bread-and-butter" aim of education. Thus no doubt should be considered an important aim of education. It simply means that education received by an individual should enable him to earn his bread, should enable him to get a job, some work that pays him sufficient money regularly so that the individual is able to buy bread, clothes, house, and other things necessary for living a decent and comfortable life. This has led in many countries, to a slogan by the people and educators which is "job-oriented education". Vocationalization of education is another dimension of the same. Gandhiji's basic education concept had this implication. When he said that true education should be, for the boys and girls, a kind of insurance against employment, he meant to emphasize vocational aim of education.

Again, although we all accept that vocational aim is very important, yet we commit a mistake when we say that it is the only aim to which education should cater. We should always think that along with vocational aim there are other aims which are equally important. We should neither ignore or belittle the importance of vocational aim, nor we should consider this only important aim. Nehru struck the balance between vocational and cultural aims of education when he said that cultural and vocational or productive aspects of education both are essential. "Everybody should be a producer as well as a good citizen and not a sponge on another person," said he. Mahatma Gandhi also emphasized the same point when he said that body, mind and spirit all should be developed by education. Although many philosophers from the ancient times to the present day have insisted upon the satisfaction of the soul belittling the importance of vocation in life, yet their view can not be the conscious of opinion. These should be taken as the extreme views and one-sided opinions. The majority of the people in the world feel that education should make individual self-dependent and capable of earning their livelihood. An educated man without a job or some work to earn is a curse, a blot on the system of education.

4. Complete Living Aim. This aim means that education should enable the individuals to live a life which is full and complete. In other words it means preparing the individuals for life. Living a full and complete life means exercising and using all capacities and abilities in the interest of one's well-being. Keeping good health, developing a sound mind and using it for the benefit of life's amenities, enjoying life and enriching it culturally, living like a good citizen and gainfully employed may be considered some important features of full or complete living. In other words it is the same as harmonious development of personality. According to this aim education should enable the individual to carry out all necessary activities of life successfully. He should be an enlightened citizen and an efficient man. Herbert Spencer seems to be the advocate of this aim. It is in a way laying an emphasis on liberal education which emphasizes teaching the pupils everything that is needed in life. It may be termed as life-centred education or education for life.

The main difficulty with this aim is how to define "completeness of life". When is life complete? Even it is possible to define completeness of life it becomes more difficult to identify what will make it so.

5. The Moral Aim. This aim lays stress on the ethical development of the people. Character-formation and learning of social and moral values are the focus of this aim. Gandhiji termed this as "purity of heart". Vivekananda's "man-making" function of education also means the same thing. Dewey said "all education forms character—moral and mental". This, in other words, means emphasizing the moral aim of education. Raymont also considered "cultivation of strength and purity of character" as an important aim of education. Herbart said "the whole work of education could be summed up in the concept of morality." All the idealist philosophers supported the moral aim as an ultimate aim of education. National Policy on Education of 1986 also said that education should be made a "forceful tool for the cultivation of social and moral values".

There can be no gain saying that education should teach morality to children. It is an universally accepted aim of education. But, the difficulty with this aim is how to define character and morality, what are its behavioural components, are these behavioural components acceptable universally, does morality help the individual in actual situations of life, is there any standard way of teaching morality. These questions have no set and unambiguous answers. Morality is good, but very difficult to be taught, particularly in today's materialistic world. Yet, the aim cannot be scored out simply for these difficulties. In a democratic country where the assumption is that the human being is perfect and given the freedom he will make the best use of it in the interest of the society and his own interest, it becomes still more important to teach morality to people. Education alone can play this role.

6. Aesthetic Aim. This aim emphasizes that education should develop in the pupil an aesthetic sense which means a taste for good and beautiful things. They feel that excellence of taste and fairness of feeling can form the basis of good character and genuine morality. By developing in the child sensitivity to what is beautiful and excellent ideals may be generated which play an important role in being a moral person. Aesthetic development is, in fact, a part of the education of the whole man. It is a sort of emotional training. In the past the Athenians considered this important. They aimed, through education, to develop a well-rounded individual, one whose physical, moral, intellectual and aesthetic powers were developed. For developing aesthetic sense of the child the educators stressed that while teaching pupils love of beauty and art should be fostered. The students should be presented with a large variety of art forms such as paintings, drawings, beautiful sceneries both real and painted, songs, poetry, etc. They should be taught to appreciate them and realize the beauty inherent in them.

7. Individual Happiness Aim. Happiness is essentially the purpose of all that an individual does in life. He goes to school, tries to build good health, tries to get a job, serves well, does something which brings him name and fame. All these activities of his are goal-directed. This goal is to derive happiness out of them. Happiness is the basic goal-life. It is asserted, therefore, that education should help the individuals in achieving this goal. All educators have considered health and well-being of the child important and that education must cater to this. For this reason athletics and games form a part of the curriculum of education in every country. For the same reason it is also emphasized that knowledge of the laws of health and right living and knowledge of laws of bodily grace and harmony should be taught to the children in the schools. Happiness of the individual very much depends on sound mind and sound body. So recreational activities should be included in the curriculum.

8. Education for Leisure. This aim asserts that children in the schools should be taught to utilize their leisure time such as their holidays, summer vacation and week days constructively for enjoyment and developing their potentialities. This may add to their happiness and development of creative powers. The educators, for this reason, plead that provisions for hobby centres, recreation centres, social service camps, scouting, NCC etc., should be made in which students can participate and use their leisure time fruitfully. Thus, there are a number of educational aims which fall within the category of individual aims of education. They are said to be individual aims because they all focus on the life of the individual. All round development of the individual is their only concern. They are all complimentary and should not be considered competitive.

Q. 3. Throw light on the aims of education in the present modern Indian Society. Give suggestions to achieve these aims.

Ans. Different ideologies such as political, social, economic, religious, psychological, scientific and philosophical and present problems affect the aims of education. Aims of education are laid down keeping them in view. To know this problem it is essential to throw light on various conditions, which are as follows:

Economic Conditions. In India economic conditions are not good. India is a country where large number of people are under poverty line. There is no equitable distribution of wealth, which increases the gap between rich and poor. Unemployment is increasing day by day. We are not economically independent.

Social Conditions. Social conditions of India are also badly affecting the Indian society. Many social evils are prevailing in Indian society such as dowry system, illiteracy, early marriage etc. Diversity of religion, caste, culture and language is assuming the form of serious problem.

Political Conditions. Political environment is also becoming polluted day by day. India wants such leaders who can guide people in right directions. Indian electorate are not educated, they are unable to choose the right people for governance. To preserve freedom is becoming a great problem. The existence of freedom is in danger.

Religious Conditions. India is a secular state. Here all religions have equal importance. But it is pity that people do not understand the meaning of religion, they are misusing the concept of religious freedom. There is lack of religious toleration among people due to which anarchism is increasing. It has become a great danger for national integration.

On the basis of these conditions, the aims of education have been patronised by different commissions from time to time which are as follows:

AIMS OF EDUCATION OF MODERN INDIAN SOCIETY

After independence, democratic view point was adopted. At that time education made its contribution and tried to bring prosperity in country. According to Rajendra Prasad, "India has to choose for herself a culture that derives inspiration from what is noble in our ancient culture and at the same time does not ignore the demands of the present age."

Aims of Education According to University Education Commission, 1948

Pandit Nehru had Observed: "Great changes have taken place in the country and the educational system must also be in keeping with them. The entire basis of education must be revolutionised."

According to University Education Commission, 1948, the aims of education are as follows:

(a) Development of leadership

(b) Preservation and transfer of culture

(c) Vocational efficiency

(d) Emphasis on human and spiritual training

(e) Development of democratic qualities in school

(f) Character development

Aims of Education According to Secondary Education Commission, 1952-53

This commission has stated that education which is national in character must develop in its citizens habits, attitudes and qualities of character and equip them to bear the burden of life in the changing economic structure.

According to Secondary Education Commission aims of education are as follows:

(a) Development of democratic citizenship

(b) Development of sense of eartriotism

(c) Development of vocational efficiency

(d) Development of personality

(f) Development of leadership

Development of Democratic Citizenship. It is a challenging responsibility with education to carefully train every citizen for democratic citizenship. Such a training develops following qualities:

(a) Clear Thinking. A democratic citizen should have the understanding and the intellectual integrity to distinguish truth from falsehood and facts from propaganda. Education should train the child for this purpose.

(b) Clearness in Speech and Writing. This quality is essential for successful living in democracy which is based not on force but on free discussion and persuasion.

(c) Receptivity to New Ideas. Education must aim at broadening the intellectual horizon of young scholars to enable them to accept new ideas that can help in strengthening democratic forces.

Development of Sense of Patriotism. Another important aim which the secondary school must foster is the development of a sense of true patriotism. True patriotism involves a sense of appreciation of the social and cultural achievements, a readiness to recognize its weaknesses and an earnest desire to serve one's country.

Development of Vocational Efficiency. Education must aim at increasing the productive or vocational efficiency of young students.

Development of Personality. Education should develop literary, artistic and cultural interests of the students. These are necessary for self-expression and for the full development of human personality. For this purpose subjects like art, craft, music, dance etc. should be included in the scheme of studies.

Aims of Education According to Indian Education Commission, 1964-66

According to Dr. Radha Krishnan, "It is my earnest desire that the Commission should survey all aspects of educational system at all levels and give suggestions that may help the educational system in progressing at all levels.

According to Kothari Commission, "One of the important social objectives of education is to equalise opportunity, enabling the backward or underprivileged classes and individuals to use education as a tool for improvement of their social and economic condition".

The most important and urgent reform needed in education is to transform it, to relate it to the life, needs and aspirations of the people and thereby make a powerful instrument of social, economic and cultural transformation, necessary for realization of the national goals. For this purpose the commission has suggested the following objectives of education:

(a) Increasing productivity.

(b) Social and national integration.

(c) Acceleration the process of modernisation.

(d) Developing social, moral and spiritual values.

These objectives are discussed below.

Education for Increasing Productivity. Though India is a land of vast resources, yet it has not become self-sufficient. For this purpose, the resources must be exploited and education must be related to productivity to increase national income. In order to create a link between education and productivity the following programme has been suggested by Kothari Commission:

Science Education. Science education must become an integral part of school education and ultimately some study of science should become a part of all courses in the humanities and social sciences at university stage also. The quality of science teaching must also be improved considerably so as to promote a deep understanding of basic principles, to develop problem solving and analytical skills and to promote the spirit of enquiry and experimentation.

Work Experience. In the programme of relating education to life and productivity, work experience must be introduced as an integral part of all education general and vocational. To commission work experience implies participation in productive work in school, in the home, in a workshop, on a farm, in a factory or in any productive situation. All purposeful education should include study of languages, humanities and social sciences, study of mathematics and natural sciences, work experience and social services.

Work experience is a method of integrating education with work. In the present education system work experience and social services have almost been totally neglected. Along with other elements of education work experience should be greately emphasised for the following reasons:

(a) It will bridge the gap between intellectual and manual work.

(b) It will decrease the over academic nature of formal education.

(c) It will make the entry of youth into the world of work and employment easier by enabling them to adjust themselves to it.

(d) It will relate education to productivity and also as a means of social and national integration.

Vocationalisation. Every attempt should be made to give a vocational bias to secondary education and to increase the emphasis on agricultural and technological education at the university stage. This will surely bring education into closer relationship with productivity. In the modern Indian society which is heading towards industrialisation, it is essential to considerably expand professional education at the university stage, especially in agricultural and technological fields.

Education for National Integration. India is a land of diverse social groups. Unity and harmony among these groups is the basis of national integration. Social and national integration is an important objective of a national system of education. The Commission has suggested the following steps for strengthening the nation through education.

The Common School System. The present educational system in our country instead of bringing social groups and classes together is tending to increase social segregation and class distinctions. The schools for the masses (generally maintained by the government) are of poorer quality than those run by private bodies. Good schools are not within the reach of a common man's pocket. This is one of the major weaknesses of the existing educational system. In the opinion of the Commission, "If our educational system is to become a powerful instrument of national development in general, and social and national integration in particular, we must march toward the goal of a Common School System of public education." The common school must be opened to all children irrespective of caste, creed, community and economic or social status.

— It should charge no tuition fee.

— It should maintain a good standard of education in order to meet the needs of average parents so that they may not ordinarily feel the need of sending their children to other expensive schools.

Social and National Service. Social and national service should be made obligatory for all students at all stages. It should form an integral part of education at secondary school and university levels. This programme will prove an effective instrument for building character improving discipline, inculcating a faith in the dignity of labour and developing a sense of social responsibility, if it is organised concurrently with academic studies in schools and colleges. The following are the main forms of organising such a programme:

(a) At the primary stage this programme should be developed in all schools on the lines of Basic Education.

(b) At the lower secondary stage social service should be made compulsory for all students for thirty days a year, at the higher secondary for twenty days and at the under-graduate stage it should be made obligatory for all students or sixty days a year, to be done in one or more stretches. Every educational institution should develop a programme of social and community service of its own in which all students must be involved for the periods as indicated above.

(c) Labour and social service camps or N.C.C. should be organised in each district as alternative forms of such service for those students for whom no other programmes of social service have been organised in their own institutions.

PROMOTING NATIONAL CONSCIOUSNESS

India is a land of different castes, peoples, communities, languages, religions and cultures. The main role of our schools, colleges and universities should, therefore, be to enable our students to discover 'unity in diversity' and in this way, foster a sense of national solidarity and national consciousness among them. This can be done by—

The Promotion of Understanding and Re-evaluation of Our Cultural Heritage. This can be achieved by the well-organised teaching of language and literature, philosophy, religion and history of India and by introducing the students to Indian architecture, sculpture, painting, music, dance and drama. Holiday camps and summer schools on inter-state basis, can also be organised fruitfully, for breaking down regional and linguistic barriers.

Creation of a strong faith in the future towards would involve an attempt to bring home to the students, the principles of the constitution, the great human values, referred to in its preamble, the nature of the democratic and socialistic society.

Education for International Understanding. There is no contradiction between national consciousness and developing international understanding. Schools should promote international outlook through the study of humanities and social sciences, simultaneously with developing national consciousness.

Democratic Values. The educational programme in schools and colleges should be designed to inculcate democratic values, such as scientific temper of mind, tolerance, respect for the culture of other national groups etc. This will enable our young citizens to adopt democracy not only as a form of government but also as a way of life.

Education for Modernization

In a modern society stock of knowledge is far greater, the pace of its growth is infinitely quicker and social change is very rapid. This needs a radical change in the educational system. Education in a modern society is no longer concerned mainly with the imparting of knowledge or the preparation of a finished product but with the awakening of curiosity, the development of proper interests, attitudes and values and the building up of such essential skills as independent study and capacity to think and judge for oneself, without which it is not possible to become a responsible member of a democratic society. Therefore the process of modernization will be directly related to the pace of educational advance. Education brings modernization in following ways:

(a) The way to modernize quickly is to spread education.

(b) By producing educated and skilled citizens.

(c) By training an adequate and competent intelligentsia.

(d) By bnging a radical change in the method of teaching and in the training of teachers.

Education for Social, Moral and Spiritual Values

The expanding knowledge and the growing power which it places at the disposal of modern society must be combined with the strengthening and deepening of the sense of social responsibility and a keener appreciation of moral and spiritual values. For this purpose, active measures should be adpoted to give a value-orientation to education. These measures are:

(a) The central and state Governments should introduce education in moral, social and spiritual values in all institutions.

(b) The privately managed institutions should also follow the same steps.

(c) Some periods should be set apart in the time table for this purpose.

(d) University department should undertake preparation of special literature for this purpose by students and teachers.

(e) For this purpose, a syllabus giving well chosen information about each of the major religions, should be included as a part of the course in citizenship or general education to be introduced in schools and colleges.

We may say that education is the most vital force which can help in the realisation of national objectives. While keeping in view the best features of the modern European culture and civilization, the Commission did not ignore the essential characteristics of our ancient culture and civilization as well as the needs and aspirations of our present day society. It is for the first time that we have been given an integrated picture of Indian education in all its wide and diverse dimensions.

Q. 4. Write a critical note on Rousseau's Theory of 'Negative Education'. What are its limitations?

Or

Explain the educational thought and class-room practice in term of progressive trends in education by Rousseau.

Or

How far is it correct to say that Rousseau is the father of modern educational theory and practice?

Or

What do you understand by "Naturalism" in education? What tendencies in the present day Indian education you ascribe to the influence of Rousseau's thought?

Ans. In modern times, we make use of a number of progessive methods of teaching and a variety of audio-visual aids, to make classroom teaching effective and attractive. But upto the seventeenth century, there was no systematic organisation or arrangement for imparting education to children. Schools in those days were very few and those that existed, were the terror of pupils and the slaughter-houses of mind. They followed no methods and used no aids. Every teacher had his own methods to follow. Severe punishments were given to pupils and all types of rods, canes and sticks were used for this purpose. The early educators, if any, "had confined their education to the training of the governing classes of the community and until the time of Comenius, it was only idealistic. There were many who could hazard the suggestion that all in their childhood be instructed in learning, in their own native tongue." During the seventeenth, eighteenth and the nineteenth centuries a number of educationists were born who, in fact, revolutionised education, Rousseau, Froebel, Montessori and Dewey are the most prominent among these.

Rousseau (1712-1778), was the great educator of the 18th century and one who belonged to the new school of education. Rousseau's life was greatly influenced by the prevailing atmosphere of society in France, his native country. In the beginning of the 18th century, the privileged classes in France, flourished at the cost of the poor and the helpless. Hypocrisy, artificiality, cruelty and despotism of the privileged classes, led to discontentment among the common people. However, in the later half of the 18th century a new era of 'Equality, Liberty, and Fraternity,' began in France which revolutionised the entire French society. Rousseau and Voltaire were the pioneers of this new era. It was a result of these new ideas that in the sphere of education also many new changes found their way. Children began to be treated well, properly understood and humanly educated.

1. Rousseau's Philosophy and Concept of Education. Rousseau's Philosophy goes by the name of "Naturalism". The keynote of his philosophy was to have a "Natural State, a Natural Man and a Natural Civilisation". He felt that all ills and miseries in the Modern world were due to a departure from the previous "State of Nature". He declared, "Everything is good as it comes from the hands of the Author of Nature (the Creator), but everything degenerates in the hands of man." He believed that child was essentially good but was made bad when he came in contact with society and its environment. He contended that "man in society is born, lives and dies in a state of slavery. He is fettered by our institution, which drags him away from his good nature." So Rousseau pleaded, "Leave the child alone. Let him be a natural man rather than a civilized man. Let him have a state of nature rather than artificial surroundings that stunt his proper growth and arrest his natural development." Thus Rousseau preached for a life according to nature—which was simple and real and free from all customs, traditions and conventions. He, in fact, wanted to educate the child for manhood and not for citizenship.

It should, however, be clearly understood that by Natural State and Natural Man, Rousseau did not mean the primitive social order and the savage man. He believed that human institutions were one mass of folly and contradictions. To regain the old vitality and happiness, human society should give up the present artificial modes of life and revert to the natural state. He favoured natural civilization, free from all artificial and rigid barriers that pollute the goodness of our nature. The Natural man of Rousseau's conception was a fully developed Man enjoying social life, without being carried away by the passions and prejudices of society. Reason was the only guiding force in producing natural Civilization and Natural man by Natural State also he meant 'a simple farming community or state, without the evils of large cities, corrupt rulers, social classes and luxury. His Natural Man is a true man, who is 'governed and directed by the laws of his own nature rather than those of social institutions. Natural powers, emotions and reactions are most trustworthy as basis for action, rather than reflections or experiences that come from association with society.' The catch-words of Rousseau's 'Naturalism' were freedom, growth, interest and activity. And all these words are the life and soul of modern progressive education.

2. Three-fold Meaning of Nature. Rousseau made use of the word 'Nature' in a very wide sense. He gave three-fold meaning to it, namely:

(a) ***Isolation from Society.*** Rousseau advocated that children should be saved from the evil influence of society. They should be isolated from society and brought up in contact with the beauties and wonders of nature. This, however, does not mean no-education. It simply signifies a non-social education *i.e.* an education which is not based on meaningless traditions and formalities of society. For Rousseau, society was not natural, but an artificial product, the outcome of a contract and evil. Nature and society, thus, become opposed to each other. Nature is accordingly, defined 'negatively to society'. It is a preventive education saving the child from the evil influences of society.

(b) ***Instinctive Make-up of the Child.*** Instinctive make-up means the native instincts, tendencies and capacities of the child. Rousseau believed that learning takes place when the child is free to develop and grow according to his natural impulses. So education must start from the child's instinctive tendencies and should be based on the same because these tendencies are more reliable bases of education than experiences, gained from society. According to Rousseau, "Education is no longer a procedure, artificial, harsh, dull, unsympathetic and repressive of all natural inclinations. It is, on the other hand, an organic growth. It is a development from withim."

(c) ***Contact with Natural Phenomena.*** Education according to child's nature, must be provided in natural environment. Rousseau himself was a great lover of nature, mountains, streams, sun-rise, sun-set, solitude and country life. He, therefore, recommends contact with hills, streams, plants, trees, animals, birds and physical forces of all kinds. One who is brought up and taught in natural environments automatically becomes a 'natural man' He follows nature and obeys, the voice of his own conscience.

3. Three Source of Education. At the outset of his book "Emile" Rousseau states that education comes from nature, from men and from things. In other words, the problem of education is the relationship of man to his physical and social environment. Explaining these sources of education, he says, "The internal development of our organs and faculties is the education of nature; the use we are taught to make of that development, is the education given by men; and the acquisition made by our own experience on the objects that surround us, is our education from things." In other words, by education from nature, he meant development according to the child's natural endowments and capacities. By education from men, he emphasised the importance of social environment, teaching how to make use of that development. By education from things, he understood physical environment, helping to gain experience by ourselves. He says that the harmonious development of these three factors constituted an ideal scheme of education.

Such harmony in education is possible by subordinating the education of men and things to that of nature because we have no control over nature. We must, therefore, direct the other two, to ensure cooperation of these three factors for imparting ideal education.

4. Rousseau's Aims of Education. Before Rousseau's time, the aim of education was either spiritual or social or vocational, Efforts were made to mould the child into the artificial forms of conduct, satisfactory to the judgment of adults in society. The child was trained to speak, think, act as a miniature adult without any consideration of his natural instincts and interests. Rousseau revolted against this wrong concept of education. He believed that education was a life-long process, which began from birth and ended only with the end of life. It was development from within and not an imposition from without.

So Rousseau's aim of education was the attainment of fullest natural growth of the individual leading to balanced, harmonious, useful and natural life. The real aim of education is to help the child to live his life. He says, "To live is not merely to breathe. It is to act, to make us of our organs, senses, our faculties and of all those parts of ourselves, which give us the feeling of our existence."

This general aim of education was split up by Rousseau, according to the nature, at different stages of human development.

(i) In infancy *i.e.* from birth to the age of five years, the aim of education is to develop a well-regulated freedom. For realization of this aim, he recommends purely physical education in an atmosphere of perfect liberty.

(ii) In childhood *i.e.* between the age of five and twelve, the main aim of education is to provide the child with the strength which he needs for the attainment of well-regualated freedom. So at this stage also no formal education is recommended, but the continuance of the same physical care and natural education, Rousseau's advice for this period is, "Exercise the body, the organs, the senses and powers and keep the soul lying fallow, as long as you can."

(iii) In boyhood or pre-adolescent period *i.e.*, from twelve years to fifteen years, the aim of education is "to acquire such knowledge which may satisfy the wants of the child and must be functionally useful". This is the period for intellectual education—the period of instruction, labour and study.

(iv) In adolescent period i.e. from 15 to 20 years, the aim of education is the training of heart, to make the child loving and tender-hearted so that he may live peacefully in social relationship. In this period religious, moral and social education is recommended. In the previous periods, the child has already developed physically and intellectually. He must now grow emotionally, aesthetically, socially and morally. The sex instinct, which is suficiently developed by this time, is to be sublimated by re-directing it to the love of some noble idea and by keeping the young person occupied in work and activity.

5. Role of the Teacher. Rousseau assigns a very minor place to the teacher in the educative process. He is not called an instructor but only a guide. His main responsibility is to motivate the child to learn. This he can achieve by exploiting the innate tendencies of the child. He must possess a profound understanding of the child's nature and be able to control his emotional reactions. He is not to impose any rules of control upon the child. He is to allow him perfect feedom and guide him properly.

6. Rousseau's Theory of Negative Education. As we have already stated, Rousseau believed that everything is good as it comes from the Author of Nature. Everything degenerates in the hands of man. By saying so, he meant that child is good; but it is society that makes him bad. So he advocated that first education should be purely negative. The child should not be taught the principles of truth and virtue but guarded against vice and error. In his own words, "I call a positive education one that tends to form the mind prematurely and to instruct the child in the duties that belong to man. I call a negative education on that tends to perfect the organs that are the instruments of knowledge and endeavours to protect the way for reason, by the proper exercise of the senses."

The following are the chief characteristics of his theory of Negative Education:

(a) No Time Saving. According to Rousseau, in childhood no time should be saved. It should rather be lost. Let the child run, jump and play all day long. In all these activities he will have a continuous reconstruction of experience which is nothing but education, pure and simple. Time lost on play and recreational activities in childhood, is not lost but profitably gained. Childhood is not the time for intellectual pursuits.

(b) No Book Learning. Rousseau says, "I hate books because they are a curse to children. They teach us to talk only that which we do not know. Instead of making the child stick to his books, I keep him busy in the workshop; his hands will work to the profit of his mind." Rousseau felt that ready-made material found in books, was of little advantage. Let` children gain knowledge by their own efforts and through different types of experience.

(c) No Habit Formation. In his own words, "The only habit which the child should be allowed to form is to contract no habit at all." Young children should not be made slaves of rigid habits. They should be left free in all their activities. If any habits are to be formed in childhood, let them form natural habits.

(d) No Social Education. In Rousseau's time, society was corrupt to the core. So he wanted children to be isolated from such a society and to educate them in the midst of nature till their power of reasoning and judgement is perfected, with which they are in a position to protect themselves from the evils of society.

(e) No Direct Moral Education. Rousseau is not in favour of direct teaching of morals. Let the child be left free to act and learn what is right and wrong, by the consequences of his own actions. He says, "Much more harm than good is done by your ceaseless preaching and moralising." He further says, "Inflict on the child no sort of punishment and never make him ask your pardon. As there is no moral quality in his actions, he can do nothing wrong.

(f) No Formal Discipline. Rousseau is in favour of free and positive discipline for children. Let the children suffer natural consequences of their own actions without the intervention of humam beings to protect or punish and in this way they will set themselves right. If a child breaks a window pane, let him sit in the cold wind that gushes in, as a result of his folly. If he climbs a tree, let him fall down and learn not to do so again.

(g) No Sticking to Traditional Precedure of Education. Rousseau was greatly disgusted with the prevailing social, political, economic, religious and educational conditions in his country. So he said, "Follow the reverse of the current practice and you will almost do right." He challenged the traditional procedure of education saying, "Give me a child of twelve who knows nothing at all. At fifteen I will restore him to you, knowing as much as those who have been under instruction from infancy, with the difference that your scholar only knows things by hearts, while mine knows how to use his knowledge.

It will, thus, be clear from his theory of Negative Education that many of its principles have been accepted by the modern educators. No doubt, at times, Rousseau went to the extreme. But it was natural and he had to eradicate wrong social practices like a reformer by focusing public attention to those practices. His play-and-activity principles in a child's education, his free and positive discipline, his advice against formal book-learning and his principle of no direct moral instructions of children, have all been incorporated in modern educational theory and practice. However, it is his theory of natural consequences which is not acceptable and dependable at all times.

Q. 5. Discuss John Dewey's views of an Ideal School.

Or

Discuss Dewey's ideas on democracy and education and their bearing on Indian Community.

Or

Compare and contrast the educational philosophies of Rousseau, Froebel, Montessori and Dewey.

Or

Evaluate Dewey's contribution to education, bringing out the orientation it has brought about in the aims and methods of school education.

Ans. John Dewey (1819-1952) was a famous American philosopher, psychologist and educator. Being brought up in rural environments, he realized from the very beginning that traditional methods of instruction were not at all effective and that social contacts of everyday life provided effective, dynamic and unlimited learning situations. These very ideas formed the foundation of the educational theory, formulated later by him. His outlook on education reflected the Industrial Revolution and the Development of Democracy. He believed in the dynamic nature of things and values. So he changed with the change in ideas, as a result of experience and experimentation, and finally emerged out as a Pragmatist. Today, he stands in the front rank of the world educators. His works on education are a great source of inspiration and hope and help in developing our experimental and scientific attitude of mind. Perhaps no other educator has written so much on educational problems as John Dewey.

1. Dewey's Philosophy—Pragmatism. Dewey's Philosophy represents a happy blend of naturalism and idealism because it is based on the evolutionary concept soft Darwin and Pragmatism of William James. Like Darwin he believes that world is still in the process of making and that life in this world is an every-changing and self-renewing process. Like William James, he believes that whatever useful is good and whatever good, is useful. Truth is also that which works, which fulfils our purposes and satisfies our desires.

For John Dewey there are no eternal and absolute values. All values change with time and space. Man is the creator of his own values. What is true today may cease to be true tommorrow. Man's life is a series of experiments and purposeful action. "Everything is provisional, nothing ultimate. Knowledge is always a means, never an end iteslf." It is purely instrumental. Hence the title of Dewey's philosophy is "Instrumentalism".

Then Dewey believes that knowledge and thinking are closely associated with action. They are tentative plans of action. They have to be tested by action and by knowing the result of their being acted upon. He affirms, "The essence of pragmatic instrumentalism is to conceive of both knowledge and practice as means of making good. It does not imply that action is higher and better than knowledge and practice inherently superior to thought. Constant and effective interaction of knowledge and practice is something quite different from an exaltation of activity, for its own sake. Action, when directed by knowledge, is method and means, not an end. The aim and end is the securer, freerer end more widely shared embodiment of values in experience, by means of that active control of objects which knowledge alone makes possible."

Further-more, he is convinced of the organic relationship between the individual and the society, to which he belongs. He is conscious of both the physical and the social environment. Self can neither grow in solitude nor in natural surroundings. For his proper growth an individual must live both in natural (or physical) environment and (human or social) environment. Man is not a solitary self but an individual, who lives with the rest of mankind. "He is a citizen, growing and thinking in a vast complex of interactions and relationships."

Lastly, Dewey holds that barriers of creed, religion, language, nationality and colour have divided humanity and separated man from man. These barriers must be broken to establish harmony between individuals and groups, and ensure the process of human growth. To him, growth stands for the "being process" and not for the "done product". Not perfection as a final goal, but the ever enduring process of perfecting, maturing and refining, is the aim of living. He further declares, "The bad man is one, who is beginning to deteriorate, to grow less good. And the good man is one, who is moving to become better." This is the function of education to break the barriers of separation and bring men and nations together for establishing a happier and nobler world.

2. Dewey's Educational Theory and Aims. About the importance of education, John Dewey writes, "What nutrition and reproduction are to physiological life, education is to social life. Education is a social necessity. It is a means of social continuity of life. It is a means by which a person is helped to have useful and helpful experience." All this he said in the light of the rapid changes in social and economic life of his own time.

Defining education, Dewey says, "Education is development of all those capacities in the individual which will enable him to control his environment and fulfil his responsibilities." It means that education extends the limits of human possibilities. It is progressive both for the individual and the society. Thus education, to John Dewey, is a bipolar process. It has two sides, the psychological and the sociological; neither of the two can be subordinated or neglected.

The psychological side is the study of the child, with all his inclinations, instincts, endowments and interests. It forms the very basis of education. The sociological side is the social environment in which the child is born, lives and grows for society. On a further analysis of his educational theory, we find the following four fundamentals:

(i) ***Education as Growth.*** Growth is the real function of education. It, therefore, must lead to growth. But growth is not directed towards any pre-determined goal or end. The end of growth is more growth and so the end of education, more education. An individual is a changing and growing personality and education is to facilitate that growth. It is, therefore, the duty of the teacher to provide opportunities for proper growth by arousing the instincts and capacities of children and by providing to them the solution of those problems which make the children think.

(ii) ***Education as Life.*** Dewey believes that education is not a preparation for life. It is life itself. "Life is a by-product of activities and education is born out of these activities." School is now taken as a miniature society which faces problems, similar to those faced in life outside. For education, pupils should be made active participants in the social and community life of the school and thus trained in co-operative and mutually helpful living. They should be encouraged to face actual life problems in the school and gain varied experiences. As our children are required to live in a democratic society when adults, they must experience same life in the school.

(iii) ***Education as Social Efficiency.*** Man is a social animal who continuously draws energy, strength, knowledge, experience and attitudes in a social medium. As a social being, he is a citizen, growing and thinking in a vast complex of interactions and relations." He owns character and mind, habits and manners, language and vocabulary, good taste and aesthetic appreciation, to his interaction with the social consciousness of his community. When as an individual he shares such rich resources of a good

society, he should also be ready to give back to that society and thus help other members to develop. It is the function of education to teach him this give-and-take process and make him aware of his social obligations. Education must transform the immature child into a social human being. It is in this sense that education becomes a social process and social efficiency becomes the aim of all education.

(iv) ***Education as Reconstruction of Experiences.*** According to John Dewey, experience is the only source of true knowledge. One experience leads to further experiences and each new experience calls for the revision, modification or rejection of the previous experiences. In this way the old pattern yields palce to a new pattem. Dewey says, "We should so regulate the learning and experiencing activities of the young, that a newer and better society will arise in the end." Therefore, there is a need of continuity of experiences, helping man to grow physically, mentally, socially and morally. Education must create environments for the promotion of continuity of experiences. Dewey, therefore, conceived of education as a process, involving continuous reconstruction and reorganisation of experience. He says that education is by experience, for experience and of experience.

(v) ***No Fixed Aims of Education.*** However, being a pragmatic education, John Dewey has no fixed aims of education. He believes that since physical and social environments are always changing, aims of education must also change. They cannot be fixed for all times to come. Thus, he revolted against the traditional aims of education—namely: the moral aim, the disciplinary aim and the knowledge aim etc. of the nineteenth century. He rejected the very idea of education as preparation for future life and said that education must cater to the present needs of the child rather than the future because the child is not interested in the unknown future. He therefore, said that educational aims must be restated and re-formulated in the light of the rapid social and economic changes in present day life.

3. Dewey's Ideal School. Dewey was dissatisfied with the existing system of education. In his opinion, the Industrial Revolution, the development means of communication and transport, various discoveries and inventions of science and ideals of democracy, had brought about extra-ordinary changes in social life. As such, an ordinary school had not been able to keep pace with these changes. It could not give the present day child an exact idea of the social, political and economic life of the community around him. It is, therefore, that social education is not connected with his daily life. John Dewey wanted to bridge this gulf between school life and home or social life, outside the school.

4. His Concept of an Ideal School. Dewey considered ideal school as an enlarged ideal home. In this home, the child learns to subordinate his interests to the general interest of the household. Here he learns the habits of obedience, regularity, hardwork, cooperation, sacrifice, fellow-feeling, patience, and discipline. In the ideal school, teachers play the same part as parents at home. Being better equipped than home, the school must provide ideals, high and noble, and worthy of being pursued and lived upon. These ideals are quite in conformity with the ideals of society which the school is required to serve.

Then the ideal school of Dewey's concept, is a society in miniature in which real life experiences of the community are provided on smaller scale. It is an activity school, wherein ample opportunities are provided to the child to construct his experiences, under the scientific guidance of teachers. In this ideal school, the child learns by doing and by actual participation in purposeful and intelligent activities. These activities include cooking, sewing, wood-work, weaving as well as other occupations and violations. Thus the schools provide various types of social, economic and moral experiences of practical utility.

5. Scheme of Education. Dewey outlined a definite scheme of education, according to the stages of mental development of the child. These stages were:

(a) Play period from 4 to 8 years of age

(b) Period of spontaneous attention from 8 to 12

(c) Period of reflective attention from 12 onwards.

In the Play Period, the child studies the life and occupations of the home. Then he studies larger social and community activities on which his home-life depends. Finally, he learns about the development and significance of other occupations and inventions. In the last year of this period, he also learns reading, writing and geography.

In the period of spontaneous attention, the child understands the difference between means and ends. He is able to act for the solution of practical problems of life. At this stage he is also taught social studies with a view to make him understand how man achieved his purposes under various conditions in different periods of history.

In the period of reflective attention, the child is grown-up enough to raise new problems and find out their solutions. At this stage he acquires definite skills and arts so that after leaving the school, he should adjust himself as a useful and efficient member of society.

6. Curriculum. Dewey's curriculum is not a mere scheme of studies. Nor is it a list of subjects. It is an entire range of activities and experiences, because to him subjects are only summaries and recapitulation of human activities. Dewey does not recommend any ready-made curriculum. He rather wants the curriculum to grow out of the pupils own impulses, interest and experiences. It consists of activities and projects, leading to reconstruction and re-organisation of experience. Thus he makes occupational activities or crafts, the core of school curriculum. He also includes moral, aesthetic and religious education in the curriculum. But this education is also imparted through parctical experiences and not through "chalk and talk lessons," in the classroom. In his opinion, "Purposeful activity and a curriculum comprising standard factors of social life, would give the children more interest and insight, through the functioning of intelligence and will, in the achievement of self-control and the appreciation of social values."

7. Dewey's Contributions and Influence. John Dewey is, by far the most original thinker in the field of educational philosophy. He stands in the front rank of the educators of the world. It is under his influence that today we find freedom, happiness and friendliness in American schools. Dewey is a philosopher of the present dynamic age, which is dominated by the forces of science, technology, industrialism and democracy. He has made an original approach to the problems, confronting man to-day and has offered sound solutions for them. To educators, he has given a new progressive outlook and called it life itself. He has also given new aim of education, new curricula, new methods of teaching, new role of the teacher and new concept of discipline. In fact, he glorified every aspect of education that he touched. His watch-word, "Progress more and more progress; growth, unlimited and illimitable," has given a new impetus of education.

Rousseau glorified the individual at the cost of society. This was not a balanced approach. Dewey fused both the psychological and the psychological aspects of education. He said that education is impossible without social medium. Education must proceed by the participation of the individual in social relationship, with other persons. Children should, therefore, be acquainted with social institutions and industrial processes by creating the same environment in the school and by actual living and working.

Another great contribution of John Dewey is democracy in education. Democracy stands for providing equal educational opportunities to all. It thus, stands for free universal education. It emphasises education through cooperative and shared efforts, in a social medium, to secure the best for the individual and the society. It also emphasises the breaking down of social, national, religious and economic barriers between man and man, group and group, and nation and nation. So John Dewey says that it is the school which can contribute a lot in this direction by training young children in experimental thinking and democratic cooperation.

Then, his Project Method is the practical outcome of his philosophy. It is based on "learning by doing and experiencing". This method encourages pupils to learn through self-effort and creative activity in real life situations. It is based on the fact that different branches of knowledge are not separate. They are studied separately for the sake of convenience alone. It incorporates integration and correlation of activities and subjects. It upholds the dignity of labour, favours social discipline and stresses problem solving, in place of cramming and memorisation.

Let us conculde with the words of R.R. Rusk:

"In education we cannot but be grateful to John Dewey for his great services in challenging the old static cold-storage ideal of knowledge and in bringing education more into accord with the actualities of present day life. The general principle, underlying the developments in his philosophy and his application of these in education. Appears to be that both philosophy and education should reflect the main currents of contemporary thought and incorporate the techniques that have so signally contributed to modern material and social progress."

Q. 6. What is the distinctive purpose and business of Philosophy?

Or

What is the function of Philosophy?

Or

What is Philosophy?

Ans. The traditional view of philosophy is that its business or aim in knowledge of Being or Reality, which is more comprehensive, fundamental and ultimate than the knowledge which can be provided by the organs and methods at the disposal of the special science, for according to this view, with the possible exception of matter; Science deal with what is temporal, changing and contingent while philosophy aims at knowledge of that which is eternal and inherently necessary. Its (Philosophy) knowings are so primary and final that it alone can give sure support to the claims of truth put forward by the lesser form of knowledge.

Since the business of philosophy is with ultimate reality behind and beyond the phenomenal world, the possibility of knowledge, the conditions of knowing before knowing, takes place, becomes the chief problems of philosophy.

Dewey's conception of philosophy widely differs from this. He does not believe in two levels of beings: the phenomenal level and the ultimate level, 'Dewey is out to abolish all dualism in ontology, and epistemology, science and philosophy.

Dewey's conception is that philosophy is not outside of and above all other human pursuits, cultivating in secrecy and silence a remote, stacked-off pressure of its own. Philosophy is and works within the open and public domain of all human activities, one among others, differentiated by its scope and function, but in no way set apart.

The scope' of subject-matter of Philosophy, as described by Dewey can be represented in the form of three concentric circles. The first area, bounded by the innermost circle, is occupied by reflective thought, by logic or what logic or Dewey now calls Inquiry. In the second area are the typical modes of human experience, such as the practical or utilitarian, the aesthetic, religious, socioethical, scientific. Philosophic inquiry here concerns itself with analysing what these modes of experience are and particularly, with discovering their inter-relations, how the practical or utilitarian developes with scientific, the scientific into aesthetic and vice versa.

The third area is that of the socio-cultural world. The social world raises such questions as "the Value of research for social progress: the bearing of psychology upon educational procedures: the mutual relation of fine and industrial arts; the adjustment of religious aspirations to scientific statements, the relation of organisation to individuality."

The significance of Dewey: conception is not, to be found in the mere extension of the range, significant as that is. It is to be found in the inter-relations of the three areas, that they are functional distinctions, discriminable divisions within one inclusive field of experience, the boundary lines being neither fixed nor impermeable, marking off, but not insulating any one from any of the rest.

Philosophy is an enterprise of reflective thought and can only deal with problems in a reflective or intellectual way. But when each bundle of actualised problems labelled with its own bag of epistemology, ethics, logic, aesthetics, social philosophy, are treated as if each constituted a separate and distinct substantive realm, as being the original and primary subject-matter of inquiry, philosophy instead of prospering as a reflective enterprise, degenerate into a mere process of untying each bundle in some way and tying it again in another.

Reflective inquiry, philosophic or otherwise can handle and actual condition that is a problem only transforming it into an intellectual form. An architect engaged on the problem of remodelling a house uses a blue print. The blue print is an intellectualised form of the actual house. An architect does not substitute his blue print for the house; he does not consider the blue print as constituting the original and primary subject-matter of his inquiry and he does not think that he changes the house when he changes the blue print although changing the blue print may be all that he professionally contributes towards the consummation of that final end.

In philosophy blue prints have taken the place of the actual house. This substitutions in philosophy has resulted in vain disputes and arid verbal jugglery. It has led to a diseased formulation of philosophic problems. Dewey distinguishes between problems in 'General' and the 'General Problem'. The problem of e.g. knowledge in General, i.e. 'Is knowledge prossible'? is a disceased formulation of the problem of developing a general theory of knowledge. It is just as intelligent for a philosopher ask 'Is knowledge possible' as it would be for a scientist to ask 'Is motion possible'. There are specific cases of motion and scientific inquiry experiments with these specific cases. There is no 'motion in general' and hence no 'problem in general'. But there is a general problem of theory of motion, which for the scientist consists in Central laws of motion. The general laws are not proved valid by evaporating out of scientific existence, specific cases of motion, but their validity rests on their ability to explain or account for the specific cases. Similarly there are specific cases of knowing. There is no knoweldge in general and hence no problems of knowledge in general. But there is the general problem of knowledge, which consists in finding general conditions in knowledge.

Thus a philosophic generalisation must satisfy the same requirements as a scientific generalisation. The philosophic task is to reach generalisations that meet specific conditions. It is true that generalisation of the nature of the reflections process certainly involves elimination of much of the specific material and contents of the thought situations of daily life and of critical science. Quite compatible with this, however, is the notion that it seizes upon certain specific conditions and factors, and aims to bring them to clear consciousness not to abolish them while eliminating the particular materials of particular practical and scientific pursuits, (i) it may strive to hit upon the common denominator in the various situations which are antecendent or primary to thought and which evoke, (ii) It may attempt to show how typical features in the specific antecedents of thought call out diverse typical modes of thought-reaction; It may attempt to state the nature of the specific consequences in which thought fulfils it careers.

There is thus no conflict between the philosophic concern with the general or generic and interest in the specific. Where philosophic activity eliminates the specific entirely, it gets into insoluable problems.

Philosophy if it is to escape being confined to the futile world of blue prints must adopt empirical method so that its activity is in continuous functional connection with socio-cultural and scientific world. All philosophic problems have empirical fathers who can be empirically traced, located and identified. An insoluable problem in philosophy is an intellectual disease which can be caused by tracing back the problem as it appears in philosophy backs to its origins in the primary subject method of experience and finding out how, in the course of its intellectual genetic history, it got that way. Again the prevention against a insoluable problem and futile and frustrated philosophic activity consists in working back and forth between the narrow and large fields of the technical study of the intellectualised problems in philosophy and the socio-cultural, and scientific world that generate those problems. A working back and forward between the three areas of problems called by Dewey 'double movements'. This "double movements" is both corrective and cummulative. It tests the increment in our field by transferring into method of work in another field. Again it functions to uncover new clues for different fields.

To sum up Philosophy has at various times been set up as a separate and peculiar science, sin genesis. This according to Dewey, is not true. Philosophic problems arise out of the common matrix of experience. For philosophy to solve its own intellectualised problem it must move into the common field of problematic situations. The solution of problems in philosophy can be reached only by working back and forth between the technical or private domain of philosophy and the final or public domain of socio-cultural experience.

Q. 7. Discuss the relationship of Philosophy and Education. How do this function interact with each other?

Or

Discuss the concept and functions of philosophy. What is its relationship with education?

Or

"Philosophy is the science of sciences" if we accept this definition of philosophy as given by Comte, how will it benefit us in performing our educational tasks?

Or

Discuss the relation of philosophy with Education.

Or

What do you understand by philosophy of education? How does it influence the field of education?

Ans. Philosophy as a field of knowledge deals with three things (i) reality (metaphysics), (ii) knowledge (epistemology) and (iii) problems related to values (axiology). What is reality? What is the purpose of creation? What are time and space? These are some of the questions that are answered by metaphysics. It is the main branch of philosophy. It discusses three aspects of reality e.g., the world, the self and the God. Epistemology examines different methods to achieve different types of knowledge. Axiology is mainly concerned with value. It is a science of value. It concerns itself with problems such as what is value, what is good, what are fundamental values? and so on.

Reality, knowledge and values are very much the concern of education. All problems of education, finally get concerned with these. What knowledge should be imparted to pupils, what values should be learnt by them, exactly is the reality to which education should be made to conform are questions which can be answered in several ways depending upon the kind of philosophy one believes in. Different views about reality, knowledge values etc., have been expressed by different philosophers. There is no philosophy. There are several schools of philosophy. Within each school there are several philosophers who have contributed to the thoughts on that philosophy. These have influenced the theory and practice of education also.

1. Philosophy of Education. Education is said to be the dynamic side of philosophy. It means philosophy tells what education should be and what it should aim at, but education implements that or practices that. Education is the purposive influence to be brought upon the pupils. But what kind of influence this ought to be has to be decided prior to any atempt on making it real. Who should do this? How should it be done? Philosophy of education helps in solving these problems.

2. Different Philosophy of Education have described the content and methods of education in different ways. This is so because each one of them makes different assumptions about human nature, knowledge, ethics, morals and values. For example, idealists consider man a spiritual being, a supreme creation of God who is regarded by them as the source of all knowledge. So they consider values of life absolute and unchanging and recommend that education should make all-out effort on teaching these values. To the naturalists material world alone is real and so all values exist in nature, in living close to nature. So they recommend that goals of education and methods of education should be determined by the nature of the child. Like that other philosophies of education also differ in their philosophical views and corresponding aims and methods of education. Thus, philosophy of education means a specific point of view on aspects of education. Dewey, for that reason, said that "philosophy is the theory of education in its most general phases". It is philosophy applied to education. There are several aspects of education like the aims, the curriculum, the methods, the discipline, the values to be taught, etc. Philosophies of education present specific ideas about each of these. Thus, it may be said that they constitute different foundations on which the superstructures called education are raised.

3. Philosophy of education is a critical method of approaching education and its various elements. It is true that there are certain well-defined philosophies of education but apart from these views, underlying them is essentially a spirit or method of approach to education, the philosophical way of thinking and appraising educational matters. Thus, philosophy of education is a way of looking at various aspects of education. In other words it may be

regarded as a general theory of criticism of education. It is a reflective approach to education leading to "wisdom".

4. Philosophy of education is a rational way to taking decisions in the field of education, a rational process to solving problems. Instead of taking decisions about what to teach, how to teach on *ad hoc* basis without any rationale underlying them, philosophy of education makes it possible to provide sound and reasonable basis.

5. The main problems of philosophy of education are aims and ideals of education, analysis of pupil's nature, relations of education and state, analysis of knowledge and curriculum, methods of teaching, place of the school in the society, relationship of education to social system, education of religions, etc. Critical evaluation of these from philosophical point of view constitutes the subject-matter of philosophy of education.

Determination of educational values of largely, a function of philosophy of education.

How Does It Influence the Field of Education. Philosophy of education influences almost all the aspects of a country's educational system. Particularly, it influences the following aspects:

1. Relationship between the State and Education. Depending upon the philosophy a country believes in there are rigidly controlled and free schools. In the totalitarian states the schools have to teach what the state wants with strict discipline and rigid schedule enforced in them. In democratic countries there is ample freedom for the schools.

2. Philosophy of Education Influences the Aims of Education. The aims and ideals of education, too, are determined by the philosophy of education a country believes in. Different philosophies of education have different views on education. A country that tends to believe in the philosophy of idealism will stress on creating a spiritual environment in the school as that pupils develop spiritual values and attain self-realization. Naturalism will like to see that the child is made to learn from nature in a natural way and realizes his potentialities. Pragmatism does not accept any universal or eternal and preconceived aim of education. Like that aims of education are necessarily influenced by the philosophy of education.

3. Philosophy of Education Influences the Curriculum. What should be taught in the schools is also influenced by the kind of philosophy of education a society supports. Various philosophies of education advocate differing views on curriculum. Naturalism, for example, lays stress on subjects that help in self-expression and self-preservation. It advocates teaching of basic sciences, physical and health education. Idealism emphasizes teaching of higher values through ethics, religion, art and subjects of humanities. Pragmatism focusses on child-centered curriculum consisting of activities and based on child's experience.

4. Philosophy of Education Influences Teaching Methods. Methods of teaching, too, are influenced by the philosophy of education a society adopts. A system of education based on naturalism stresses learning by doing, learning through experience and learning through observation. Societies which tend towards idealism prefer to have a system of education which prescribes rigid methods of teaching such as lecturing and prefer learning through imitation, memorization and discussion. Pragmatism stresses problem solving and project methods of teaching.

5. Philosophy of Education Influences Theory and Practice of Discipline Also. The concept of discipline and its practice also are influenced by the philosophy of education. To naturalists discipline is to be learnt by natural consequences. The child enjoys maximum freedom. Self-discipline is preferred to external control. The idealists on the other hand wish to enforce discipline through cultivation of higher values, moral and religious teachings and strict control over the child. In the scheme of the pragmatists, there is no place for punishment and discipline is learnt through moral training which is based child's experience gained through various kinds of school activities and programmes.

In the same way several other aspects such as the place of the child in education, the importance of the teacher, preparation of textbooks, etc., are influenced by the philosophy of education adopted by a system of education.

Q. 8. Discuss the influence of Philosophy on different aspects of Education.

Ans. INFLUENCE OF PHILOSOPHY ON DIFFERENT ASPECTS OF EDUCATION

1. Philosophy and Aims of Education. Every educational system must have some goals, aims or objectives. These act as guides for the educator in educating the child. In fact, we cannot think of any process of education without specific aims and objectives. Bode says, "Unless we have some guiding philosophy in the determination of objectives, we get nowhere at all." These aims of education, in different countries, are determined by the aims and ideals of life which the people of those countries have at that particular time. The aims and ideals of life, in their turn, are determined by the philosophy of the time. It is, therefore, that aims and ideals of education vary with the different philosophers. It is the philosophy of the time which determines whether the aim of education should be moral, vocational, intellectual, liberal or spiritual. In the words of Rusk, "Every system of education must have an aim and the aim of education is relative to the aim of life. Philosophy formulates what should be the end of life while education offers suggestions how this end is to be achieved." The philosopher struggles hard with the mysteries of life and arrives at their solution after mature reflection and thinking. He then suggests ways and means of dealing with them. Thus he lays down ultimate values and explains their significance to the community. In this way, he tries to convert people to his own beliefs and philosophy. These ultimate values, as formulated by the philosopher, become the aims of education for that community. The training of the younger generation, according to those aims and values, then lies on the shoulders of the educator in the field. He selects the material for instruction and determines the methods of procedure for the attainment of those aims. In this way, the entire educational programme proceeds with its foundations on sound philosophy.

2. Philosophy and Curriculum. Curriculum is the means through which we realise the aims of education. Naturally, therefore, our educational aims determine the curriculum of studies. But aims of education, in their own turn, are determined by philosophy, as we have noted above just now. So we can say that philosophy also determines the curriculum. As is the philosophy so will be the aims of all education and courses of study. Thus they are closely inter-related. It is philosophy and courses of study. Thus they are closely inter-related. It is philosophy which will decide why a particular subject should be included in the curriculum and what particular discipline that subject will promote. Thus, as Briggs has put it, "It is here (in curriculum) that education seriously needs leaders—leaders who hold a sound comprehensive philosophy, of which they can convince others and who can direct its consistent application to the formulation of appropriate curricula."

It should be clearly noted that curriculum is not fixed for all times. It changes in accordance with the aims of education determined by philosophy. It is, therefore, that curriculum differs with different schools of philosophy, according to their own beliefs. The naturalists advocate the selection of subjects according to the present needs, interests and activities of the child. They insist that adult interference should be reduced to the minimum and that the child should grow up in a free atmosphere. They are, therefore, of the opinion that curriculum should include subjects which are useful for the present life situations, experience and interests of the child. Those subjects must, in no case, be included in which the child is not interested at all. The idealists, on the other hand, approach the problem of curriculum from the point of higher values in life rather than from that of the child or his present needs. Their emphasis is on the experience of human race as a whole. They, therefore, advocate that curriculum should be graded in such a way as may enable that child to march gradually towards self-realization. The pragmatists emphasise the principle of utility in the choice of subjects. They are of the opinion that only such functional subjects should be included in the curriculum as are useful to the child in the present day world. The curriculum should give knowledge and skills which the child requires for his present as well as future life as an adult. Only that bookish knowledge which stuffs the mind with abstract ideas, is condemned as it does not equip children to face the real problems of life. Instead, curriculum should consist of subjects which may improve the health, vocational efficiency and social fitness of the child. Realists also put greater premium upon the vocational education.

Thus, we conclude that philosophy not only influences the curriculum, it also determines the subjects of study that meet its requirements.

3. Philosophy and Text-books. Text-books are important instruments, through which the aims of education are realised. In the selection of text-books, therefore, there is as much need of ideals and principles as in the choice of subjects. Those who select text-books, must have a standard of judgement, which should enable them to select the right type of books. This standard is supplied by philosophy.

Again, a good text-book must reflect the prevailing values of life, fixed by philosophy. If it does not, it is out-of-date and inappropriate. An appropriate text-book, therefore, must be according to the accepted ideals of the society as a whole. Then and only then its will be able to serve its desired purpose.

In the case of text-books also, there is difference of opinion among the different schools of philosophy. While the naturalists are in favour of illustrations, pictures and diagrams for capturing the interest of children, the pragmatists are satisfied only with the objective statement of generalization in a logical order. The idealists, on the other hand with the text-books should reflect the individuality of the author. They are in favour of the subjective presentation of the subject-matter so that there may be interaction of the prosonalities of the author and the reader.

4. Philosophy and Methods. Method is the procedure through which the aims of education are realised. And as we have already noted, aims of education are subject to the philosophy of life. It is, therefore, that there is close relationship between philosophy and methodology of teaching.

Every philosopher formulates his own methods of teaching, according to his own philosophy. It is, therefore, that different schools of philosophy have laid down their own methods of teaching. The naturalists emphasise the child-centred methods of teaching. They recommend proper motivation and effective use of illustrative aids to capture and maintain the child's interest in the lesson. The idealists believe that teaching is essentially an impact of the teacher's personality on that of the pupil. They recommend discussion method, rote-learning and a meditation in a cordial atmosphere. The pupil is expected to obey his teacher and have full faith in him. The pragmatists advocate that teaching is possible only in a social medium. So they recommend project and problem methods of teaching in which the pupils are engaged in a useful activity of their own choice and interest. Thus, we can say that all the methods of education that have come into vogue, have been the result of one philosophy or the other.

5. Philosophy and Discipline. Like curriculum, text-books and methods, discipline, too, reflects the philosophy of life, accepted at a particular time. It is mainly governed by the aim of education. In ancient India when salvation was the chief aim of education, stress was laid on a strict type of discipline. The student was required to lead a life of austerity and self-denial. In medieval ages when despotic system of government was established, a very harsh and strict discipline was advocated and practised. "Spare the rod and spoil the child" was the maxim for the guidance of teachers. In the present age of democracy, however, the concept of discipline is totally different. Whereas in the past, perfect order and silence prevailed in the educational institutions, now we insist on self-government of students and free discipline.

Different schools of philosophy also differ in their concept of discipline. While the idealists are in favour of punishment for maintaining order in the class, the naturalists advocate perfect freedom to the child. They believe in discipline by natural consequences. The pragmatists, on the other hand, emphasise social discipline, which is maintained by the proper direction of the pupil's natural impulses through cooperative activities.

6. Philosophy and Teacher. Teacher is the back-bone of the entire process of education. It is, therefore, essential that the teacher's philosophy of life should be in perfect consonance with the philosophy on which the educational system is based. To be a successful teacher, he must know his subject, his pupil, the society and the philosophy of education. A teacher in a Basic school, who has no faith in and no regard for the Gandhian way of life, will never prove to be a successful teacher.

The naturalists insist that the teacher should never interfere with the free activities of children. He is simply to set the educational environment and that is all he is expected to do. Then his role is a negative one. The idealists advocate that the teacher's role should be that of the head of a family. Pupils should be inspired by his personality and develop full faith in him. According to pragmatists, the teacher is not to impose anything on the pupil. He is simply to provide opportunity to his pupils for activity and learning.

7. Philosophy and Evaluation. Evaluation is the pivot of educational system. Goals or aims are only cherished desires which decorate the reports of education commission. Curriculum also remain confined to booklets on syllabus. It is evaluation alone which gives an exact idea of what has actually been achieved at the end of a particular period or stage as a result of the teaching-learning experiences, provided in the classroom. Evaluation is also the process of determining the extent to which the aims and objectives are being attained. Again, the maintenance of good educational programmes and the improvement of techniques and procedures of education also require good evaluation. It is, therefore, that there is a close relationship between objectives, learning experiences and evaluation. Object-ship between objectives, learning experiences and evaluation. It is, therefore, legitimate to ascertain how far our evaluation programme is in conformity with the philosophy that has determined the aims and objectives of education, its curriculum and its methodology. It was this judgement that led the educationists in many progressive countries to search for the philosophical analysis which proved very helpful in thrashing out the issue and in overhauling the entire system of examination. The term 'examination' which was mainly based on essay and which measured only the factual knowledge retained by the pupils, was replaced by the new term 'evaluation' which takes into account the growth of the child as a whole individual and in his total environment. It is also this philosophical analysis which is responsible for the movement of objectivity in the field of relationship between philosophy and valuation.

8. General Impact of Modern Philosophies on Education. The nineteenth and the twentieth centuries have witnessed a radical change in the educational practices as a result of some common elements in all the modern philosophies. Firstly, education has been psychologised. Instructions have become paedo-centric or child-centred rather than book-centred. Individual differences have been recognised. Secondly, the principles of activity has gained ground. Learning by doing has been the common watch-word. Thirdly, the social discipline has been recognised as a potent factor of educational development. The child is to be trained for community life. Fourthly, democracy has been recognised in most of the developed or developing countries as the guiding factor of educational practices. Fifthly, there has been a metamorphis in the social structure of each country. There is shift of emphasis from rural to urban, joint family to individualism, capitalism to socialism and spiritualism to materialism. New concepts of citizenship, social life and political life have emerged. Westernization has taken place rapidly, and there is a scientific outlook on all matters of life. There are new business and professional practices. Hence there is need for a new type of education which can meet the existing demands of life. Man is a socialised being, and so the current social philosophies have their bearing or education. To cite one example, the restless adolescents of today cannot be treated in the same nanner as they were treated during the last century. The concept of discipline in education has undergone a radical change.

Conclusion. We can now conculde by saying that philosophy, life and education are intimately linked with one another. For the successful harnessing of education, for the good of life, for the good of individual and for the good of society, it stands in need of direction. This direction is provided exclusively by philosophy, which is the mother of all sciences and to which education is very intimately related. In fact, philosophy and education are two sides of the same coin. While philosophy is the contemplative side, education represents the dynamic side. In the words of Rusk, "From every angle comes a demand for a philosophic basis of education. There is no escape from a philosophy of life and philosophy of education." Education, therefore, is the dynamic side of philosophy. It is an active aspect of philosophical beliefs and a practical means of realising the ideals of life. Without wisdom and philosophy, education is irrelevant. In the words of Whitehead, "Wisdom is the fruit of balanced development. It is this balanced growth of individuality which should be the aim of education to secure....when you understand all about the sun and all about the atmosphere and all about the rotation of the earth, you may still miss the radiance of the sunset."

Q. 9. Write an essay on impact of realism on various aspects of Education.

Ans. REALISM IN EDUCATION

Realism was born as a reaction to excessive idealism.

Characteristics of Realistic Education

The chief characteristics of realistic education are given below:

1. Based on Science. The supporters of Realism emphasized the importance of useful and purposive education. They advocated the inclusion of scientific subjects in the curriculum and in place of academic and artificial education, they laid stress on the natural education which gave birth to Naturalism. Thus, the emphasis on scientific education is the first characteristics of realistic education.

2. Emphasis on Present Life of Child. The second characteristic of realistic education is to make the present life of child as the focal point of educational system. As we know the fact that Realism was born as a reaction to excessively Idealism, it opposed the academic education of mere ideals and values and emphasized the immediate real and practical problems of day to day living which only can promote individual goods and welfare.

3. Emphasis on Experiment and Applied Life. The third characteristic of racialistic education is emphasis on experiments, experiences and application of knowledge learnt. It lays great stress on learning by doing, by developing creativity and urge of political work in children so that they are able to solve their immediate practical problems and lead a real successful life.

4. Opposition of Bookish Knowledge. Realists decry mere academic, theoretical and bookish knowledge which develops only rote memory and encourages cramming. It does not enable the child to understand the realities of external things and natural phenomena. According to Realists, education should inculcate in the child an understanding of both the thing and the environment. Thus, the slogan of realistic education is 'Not words but things'. Such type of education promotes intelligence and a sense of judgement which the bookish education does not do.

5. Emphasis on Training of Senses. The sixth characteristic of realistic education is to train and develop the senses of child.

Unlike Idealists who impose knowledge from above, Realists advocate self-learning through senses which ought to be trained. These senses are the gateways of knowledge and develop by use and experience.

6. Limited Freedom of Child. Realistic education realizes the prime importance of child. Hence, according to Realists the child should be given full freedom to develop his self according to his innate tendencies. But this freedom should promote self-discipline and self-control. In other words, the child should procced from ignorance to knowledge slowly but surely through his own efforts and self-discipline.

7. Equal Importance of Individuality and Sociability. The seventh characteristic of realistic education is to emphasize equally the individuality and sociability of the child. Thus, the aim of realistic education is to develop both the individual self and the society of which he is an integral part. Bacon clearly asserts that realistic education develops the individual on the one hand and on the other hand tries to develop society through the development of social consciousness and sense of service of the individual.

AIMS OF EDUCATION

The following are the aims of realistic education:

1. Preparing the Child for a Happy and Successful Life. The first aim of realistic education is to prepare the child to lead a successful and happy life. Thus, education should be such that the child is able to love his problems of life successfully and lead a happy life promoting the welfare of society as well.

2. Preparing the Child for a Real Life. The second aim of realistic education is to prepare the child for a real and practical life. Realists believe in the reality of knowledge of external material world gained through senses. Thus, they wish to prepare the child for the real life of material world.

3. Developing the Physical and Mental Powers of Child. According to Realism, mind as well as the physical organs together constitute an organism composed of matter. Hence, according to this ideology, the third aim of education is to develop the physical and mental powers of the child so that with the help of his developed intelligence, discrimination and judgement, he is able to solve all the problems of life successfully.

4. Acquainting the Child with Nature and Social Environment. According to Realism, a child is related both to the external Nature and the social environment. Hence, the fifth aim of education is to provide the child full knowledge of both the society and the external Nature so that he is able to strike a balance between the two.

5. Imparting Vocational Education. According to Realism, education should be of practical utility of child. Since the problem of livelihood is main problem of life these days, so according to this ideology, the sixth aim of education is to provide vocational education to the child.

6. Developing and Training of Senses. Resists believe that unless the senses of the child are developed fully well, he will not be able to have full knowledge about the external world. Thus, the fourth aim of realistic education is to develop and train the senses of the child through varied experiences.

CURRICULUM

Realists insisted that only those subjects and activities should be included in the curriculum which prepare children for actual day to day living. Accordingly, considering the real situations, conditions and circumstances of the present day life of human beings, realists emphasized to give prime place to Nature, Science and vocational subjects whereas secondary place to Arts, Literature and Languages. It is to be noted that Realists have recommended about thirty subjects for the curriculum. They have also advocated free choosing by the children from among these subjects. At the same time they have made clear that teaching of mother-tongue is the foundation of all development and vocational subjects which are essential for livelihood. Hence, the essential subjects in the curriculum should be language and vocational subjects.

METHODS OF TEACHING

Traditional system of education gave to the child only bookish knowledge which was purely academic and wordy. Hence, it failed to prepare the child for real life. Realists changed that system of teaching to gaining knowledge through senses according to the child's nature and capacity by way of observation and experience. Emphasizing that objects are real, the Realists insisted to impart knowledge of objects and external phenomena through senses. In their opinion, objects should be first shown and allowed to be handled if need be arise and then only they be interpreted and explained to the child.

Bacon, the famous Realist introduced the inductive method in the process of education. According to this method the object is shown to the child first and then its interpretation is done. In addition to this, the child does his own observation, experimentation and derives conclusions. In short, the child does self-learning to a great extent by employing inductive method.

Milton advocated learning by travelling. John Locke also spoke of tours, observation and learning by experience as powerful means of education. Some Realists also propounded many maxims of teaching which discourage rote memorization and prescribed instead learning by observation and experience.

ROLE OF TEACHER

The role of teacher according to Realists is neither as high and important as the Idealists advocate nor so negligible as the Naturalists speak out, it is fairly important. The teacher, according to Realists, is expected to have full knowledge of the content and the needs of children. Not only this, he must also be capable to present before children the content in a clear and intelligible way by employing psychological and scientific methods. It is the duty of teacher to tell children about scientific discoveries, researches and inventions by others in various fields of knowledge. He himself should also be engaged in some research work on experimentation. At the same time he must inspire children to undertake wide and close observation and experimentation themselves so that they are able to find out new facts. Not only this, the teacher must understand well the amount of knowledge to be provided to each child at a specific time.

DISCIPLINE

Realists emphasize moral and religious education of the child. For this type of education, discipline is essential and a pre-requisite condition. But what type of discipline? The upholders of this ideology decry repressibilities discipline. They advocate self-discipline to effect smooth adjustment of the child with external environment, the teacher only inspiring and encouraging sympathetically. According to Coummnis the school should be like the lap of mother full of affection, love and sympathy. In short, Realists advocate a synthetic form of impressionistic and emancipator forms of discipline.

SCHOOL MANAGEMENT

Realists have different views about school. Some Realists do not feel any need of school at all. They prescribe wide travelling, tours and teaching by private tutors as the best means of education. On the contrary, other Realists emphasize the importance of school and class teaching. They regard school as a mirror of society reflecting its true state of affairs. As such, the school should not only include, in its work, all the activities going on in society, but it should also be well-furnished and equipped with all the necessary aids and device for effective observation and experimentations by children. According to them, the school is an agency which meets the needs of the child and the demands of society as well. Insert, it is school only which provides for the fullest development of the child according to his nature and needs.

Q. 10. Discuss the principles, aim of education, curriculum, teacher, discipline, school, students related with Realism.

Ans. **PRINCIPLES OF REALISM**

The principles of realism are as follows:

Material World is True. This philosophy considers materialistic world as true which we see directly. Moor has said, "Existence is perceiving." This world is a combination of matters. Matter is true. It is real. Therefore this world is also real. Spiritual world is thought-oriented, thus it is unreal. Soul and God is a figment of imagination and mind is just a thing of the world.

Man is Supreme. Realism considers man as the supreme creature of the material world. The ultimate aim of life is to live a peaceful life after acquiring the knowledge of things.

Universe is not External. Realists believe that universe is not external. There is law that governs the universe and the law is supreme since it is through this law and order that cohesion prevails.

Emphasis on Present Life. Realism lays emphasis on the present life and behavioural (practical) aspect of man. It opposes the ideals. It has no concern with the ideals and rules of past and future.

Senses are the Gateway of Knowledge. According to realism whatever sensation we get while coming in contact with objects through our senses is the only reality. This philosophy considers senses as the gateway of knowledge. We receive knowledge by seeing, smelling, touching and tasting. This knowledge is real.

Realism and Philosophy

Metaphysics. This world is made of many materials. Material world is true and real. It is directly visible to us. Whatever is beyond this is unreal. Soul and God is a figment of imagination. Matter is dynamic. Mind is matter-oriented.

Axiology. Realism believes in the material-oriented world. Realists search for beauty in the natural beauty. They have no faith on eternal values, because they consider spiritual world as a figment of imagination. They believe that beauty is the reflection of nature. They stress on the practical aspect of the present. Man is the maker of his destiny. It does not believe in the pre-determined values.

Epistemology. Realists consider senses as the gateway of knowledge. This material world is real because it has existence, this existence is felt through senses. Therefore, it is real and true.

Realism and Aims of Education

Realism recommends the following aims of Education :

Preparation for Real Life. The aim of realistic education should be such that the child is able to solve his problems of life successfully and lead a happy life. Realists believe in the reality of knowledge of external material world gained through senses. They want to prepare the child for the real life of material world. Spencer recommends, 'complete living' as the aim of education.

Training of Senses. The aim of education is to develop and train the senses of the child through varied experiences. Realists believe that unless the senses of the child are developed fully well, he will not be able to have full knowledge about the external world.

Physical and Mental Development. Aim of education is to develop the physical and mental powers of the child so that with the help of his developed intelligence, discrimination and judgement, he is able to solve all the problems of life successfully.

Social Development. To ralism, a child is related both to the external nature and social environment. The aim of education is to provide the child full knowledge of both the society and the external nature so that he is able to keep a balance between the two. Aim of education is the social development of the child.

Scientific Outlook. Realism considers the 'development of scientific attitude' as an important aim of education. It aims at the development of the habit of reasoning, independent thinking and judgement among the pupils.

Vocational Development. Realism lays emphasis on material comforts and facilities. Attainment of material happiness is possible through a vocation. Therefore, we must make a child self-sufficient by developing vocational skills in him so that he may live a happy life by fulfilling his needs.

Realism and Curriculum

Curriculum is a means of realising the aims of education. Realists insisted that only those subjects and activities should be included in the curriculum which prepare children for actual day to day living. Accordingly, considering the real situations, conditions and circumstances of the present day life of human beings, realists emphasized to give prime place to Nature, Science and vocational subjects whereas secondary place to Arts, Literature and Languages. Knowledge must be given through the medium of mother tongue so that the child is in a position to solve his daily life problems and make his life happy. Hence the essential subjects in the curriculum should be language and vocational subjects.

Realism and Teacher

Realism recognises the teacher but does not attach much importance to the personality of the teacher like Idealism. The teacher is supposed to put the facts as they are in their real form. He should present the knowledge in an effective and intelligible way. He should create opportunities for observation and experimentation. He should be well versed in the psychological methods, techinques and skills of teaching. Realists insist upon the training of teachers before they engage themselves in the teaching work in an effective way.

Realism and Methods of Teaching

The realism is opposed to the traditional methods of teaching. Realists stress the use of objective and scientific techniques. They support inductive-deductive experimentation, tours, self-experiences, use of audio-visual aids and other methods of teaching. In their opinion objects should be first shown and allowed to be handled if need be and then only they be interpreted and explained to the child. This encouraged the use of audio-visual aids in education. They are the supporters of correlation method.

Realism and Discipline

Realism emphasizes moral and religious education of the child. For this type of education, discipline is essential condition. Realists advocate self-discipline to effect smooth adjustment of the child with external environment with the teacher only inspiring and encouraging sympathetically. To Comenius the school should be like the lap of mother full of affection, love and sympathy. They advocate a synthetic form of impressionistic and emancipatory discipline.

Realism and School

According to Comenius, 'schools are true foregoing places of men'. Realists emphasize the importance of school and class teaching. They regard school as a mirror of society reflecting its true state of affairs. School should also be well furnished and equipped with all the necessary aids and devices for effective observation and experimentations by children. According to them, the school is an agency which meets the needs to the child and the demand of society. It is school only which provides for the fullest development of the child according to his nature and needs. Not only this, school is the only agency to provide vocational education to prepare the child for some livelihood.

Contribution of Realism in Education

Aims. Vocational efficiency is an important aim of realism which is relevant even to-day.

Curriculum. Realism gave a comprehensive curriculum and attached great importance to science which is approriate in the present age.

Method. Realists emphasised inductive method. They advocate the principle of correlation between various subjects.

Discipline. They advocate a synthetic form of impressionistic and emancipatory forms of dicipline.

Student. They give important place to student.

School. They accept the necessity of school.

Teacher. Teacher should have full knowledge of the content and the needs of children.

Evaluation of Realism

- Realism accepts the real needs and real feeling only. It does not belive in imagination, intense emotion and sentiments. These also are the realities and genuine needs of the individuals.
- Realism emphasizes scientific subjects to the neglect of arts and literature. This is creating imbalance in the total curriculum.
- It gives undue importance to the need of material world and neglects spiritual world.
- Realism emphasizes exclusively on facts and realities of life. It does not give any importance to ideals and values. Denial of ideals and values often creates helplessness and pessimism which retard growth and development of the individual.

Q. 11. What do you understand by Naturalism as a philosophy of education? Discuss the concept of freedom and discipline according to the philosophy of Naturalism.

Or

Discuss the main contributions of Naturalism in modern educational thought and practice.

Or

What are the contributions made by the philosophy of Naturalism to education?

Ans. Although no system of education in the world may be found such as wholly operating according to the tenets of the philosophy of Naturalism, yet education in general throughout the world has been greatly influenced by it. In a sense the contributions made by naturalism to education are many. Some of the most important of these are as follows:

1. Paidocentric Movement. A natural consequence of the philosophy was that education was made paidocentric, *i.e.*, child-centred. It constantly emphasized the nature of the child as the focal point of all aspects of education. The child was put in the forefront and all other things such as the educator, the books, the curriculum, the school, etc. were thrown into the background. This tendency was called by John Adams as the paidocentric tendency in education. This conception emphasized that education is not preparation for life but life itself. Children should live like children and enjoy life. Education should be guided by the nature of the child. They take it for granted that the child is basically good. Rousseau himself said, "Eveything is good as it comes from the hands of the Author of Nature, but everything degenerates in the hands of men." The child is good, but he should be protected from a degrading environment. The child is desirable for his won sake. He should not be burdened with restrictions and made miserable. Allow him to develop naturally. These views constitute an important contribution of naturalism to education.

2. Education was Psychologized. This was another contribution made by the naturalists to education. When the naturalists stressed the nature and the natural development of the child, they immediately entered into the arena of psychology as it raised the question 'what is child's nature, what is natural development, and so on'. Thus, a psychological tendency was developed in education which forced educators to view every aspect of education from psychological point of view. It was emphasized that education must study the nature of the child and should adapt itself to this nature. Rousseau may be considered the pioneer for introducing the psychological tendency in education. He was the first person among the naturalists to say that education should follow the child's nature. Rousseau's ideas were, then, put into practice by Pestalozzi, Herbert, Froebel and several other educators. This emphasis in education generated a lot of new ideas and approaches in the field of education. Research in child psychology gained momentum. Educational psychology assumed greater importance. Methods of teaching and curriculum construction began to be considered from psychological point of view. McDougall made valuable contributions to child psychology. Psychology of individual differences came into prominence. It was considered desirable to make education flexible in view of specific differences in the nature of children. Psychoanalysis assumed still greater importance by bringing unconscious nature of the child into the picture.

3. Playway Method of Teaching. Naturalism made a very great contribution to teaching method at the early stages of education. Playway method was exclusively the contribution of naturalism. Even this method is considered important by educationists. The psychology of playway method was made explicit by Rousseau and several other naturalists. It was emphasized that all learning should take place in the spirit and by the method of play. Play reveals the child's nature most clearly. It is considered nature's mode of education. To James S. Ross "Playway in its manifold forms in the outstanding general method of creative education and it is essentially naturalistic." It is a method of teaching which includes all methods of learning which foster the spirit of joyous spontaneous creative activity. At Neill's Summerhill school children play all the day if they want to as childhood is playhood. Playway method has become the ideal of all infant schools. Montessori, Froebel and A.S. Neill developed methods of educating children which prominently use playway method of teaching-learning. In fact invention of playway method was a great contribution of naturalists to education.

4. Principle of Self-Education. This was another contribution to education made by naturalism. Rousseau's negative education was another name for child's self-education. He emphasized that it is child's natural development which should form the basis of child's education. For natural development self-education was the only means. The naturalistic educator should leave the child to himself. He should be there to only observe the child, not to give him knowledge or information. He should only provide an environment in which the child undergoes certain experiences and learns through them on his own.

5. Principle of Direct Experience of Things. Learning by doing or learning one's own experience is considered important even today. This was first emphasized by the naturalist philosophers. Rousseau said, "Give your scholar no varbal lesson; he should be taught by experience alone." Direct observation of things around and direct contact with the persons of object were considered important for this reason. It was stressed that science, instead of being taught through lectures, should be taught through experimentation in the laboratory; Geometry by actual measurement of the places around and geography by taking the pupils to various parts of the country. Similarly, the child should be taught concepts of responsibilities, duties and obligations by direct experience of social life. For this reason it was insisted that the schools should have practice of self-government in which students can participate and learn through their own experience, self-discipline, self-control and self-regulation.

In this way the naturalists were responsible for most of the revolutionary ideas in the field of education that are accepted widely even today.

Q. 12. Discuss "Naturalism" as a philosophy of Education highlighting its views on aims, curriculum, method of teaching, place of the child and the teacher in education and discipline.

Or

What do you understand by Naturalism as a philosophy of education? Discuss the concept of freedom and discipline according to the philosophy of Naturalism.

Or

Discuss essential features of an educational system based on Naturalism.

Ans. Naturalism has been described to have three forms (a) Naturalism of physical science which has little to contribute to education, (b) Mechanical naturalism which regards man as a machine and has given us the behaviourist psychology, and (c) Biological naturalism which is founded on the notion of evolution and is most important of all forms of naturalism. The materialistic explanation of the word was the ground of naturalism in education. According to naturalism the ultimate reality is nature which is material. The naturalists are empiricists and believe that all knowledge is acquired through sense organs. They believe in living according to nature. "Follow nature" is their slogan. Be natural is their motto. They hold that nature has made all persons different. The most important modern naturalist thinkers are Rousseau, Bacon, Hobbes and Herbert Spencre.

1. Naturalists View on Aims of Education. According to Rousseau education means "natural development of organs and powers of the child". He said child's first education should be negative which means avoiding teaching of virtue or truth to him. He was against imparting any education to the child in early years of life. Development of body, development and strengthening of every part of the body and making the child grow healthy and strong was considered the most important aim of education during infancy. Then, developing child's sense organs and personality were considered important during childhood and adolescence. Development of emotions and sentiments leading to development of moral and social qualities including religious sentiment was emphasized at the level of the youth between 15 to 20 years. Thus the aim of education according to Rousseau was bodily, sensory, mental, social and moral development of the individual. Herbert Spencer (1820-1903) another modern naturalist, in his book 'Education' (1961) enumerated the following aims of education:

1. Self-preservation which means growth and development of both the body and the mind.
2. Earning a living.
3. Upbringing of children which means making the students successful parents in future.
4. Development of citizenship through scientific study of history.
5. Teaching the individuals how to utilize their leisure time by teaching them painting, music, sculpture, poetry, recreation.

And all these subsidiary aims must ultimately aim at "preparing the child for complete living".

2. Views on Curriculum. Rousseau was against any kind of curricular teaching or learning upto twelfth year of life. He was against any kind of verbal lesson on history, geography, or even language. He was also against teaching of morality. This was his concept of negative education which suggested that child's mind should not be stuffed with information of different kinds. So he objected to the use of any text-books for education of the young child. Giving to the child a chance to learn everything through direct experience and observation is what was stressed by him by way of child's curriculum. Even morality was to be learnt by the child through natural consequences of his own action. Thus, upto the childhood stage no curriculum of any kind was needed. Formal curriculum consisting of education in natural science, language, mathematics, woodwork, music, painting, social life, and some kind of professional training was suggested to be introduced at the adolescence stage. Rousseau, however, said that books do not give knowledge, they only train one to talk. So he emphasized that curriculum for adolescence should be based on active work than on books. The youth should, however, by taught history, mythological stories and religious stories with stress on moral and religious education. Spencer also, like Rousseau prescribed the formula of returning to nature as the basis of all learning. Providing an environment, to him, was enough of the curriculum. Learning by consequences was considered enough, although he said that in case of dangerous consequences the child should be fore-warned. In order to realize the aim of complete living Herbert Spencer prescribed physical education which was considered necessary for good health. In the words of Monroe Rousseau was the first person who proclaimed that "education finds its purpose, its process, its means wholly within the child life and the child experiences".

3. Views on Method of Teaching. Rousseau was against the oral and theoretical methods of teaching which was pursued in his time. Instead he recommended playway method of teaching learning. Real education to him was self-education acquired through experience and observation. Two great principles of teaching which he stressed were *(i)* learning through self-experience and *(ii)* learning by doing. Naturalism, thus, stands for a kind of teaching which is not dependent so much on schools and books, as on the "manipulation of the actual life of the educaned". Its watchword is "Back to Nature". Herbert

Spencer was the naturalist who enunciated several principles of teaching such as:

(i) Proceeding from easy to difficult situations and experiences.

(ii) Proceeding from indefinite (vague) to definite (clear) meaning; theredy that the teacher should make child's knowledge which is vague, clear and definite.

(ii) Proceeding from known to unknown which means the new experience to be given should follow the one which the child has already undergone.

(iv) Conforming to the stages of development which means that the method of teaching should be suitable from the point of view of the characteristics of child's development. For very young children playway is the most suitable method.

(v) Proceeding from concrete to abstract which means concrete things and experiences should be presented first and abstract ones after them.

(vi) Proceeding from experimental to rational knowledge. It means that the child should, first, be allowed to experiment with things around. This will prepare him to acquire and retain rational knowledge given in books.

(vii) Create interest in learning by using audio-visual aids, charts, diagrams etc., in order to concretize knowledge.

Thus, playway, experience and experimentation are the most desirable characteristics of teaching method according to naturalists.

4. Views on the Place of the Child in Education. In Naturalist child is the measure of all things, the centre around which revolves every aspect of education. Naturalists' view of the child is very close to that of Wordsworth who said 'child comes from heaven trailing clouds of glory'. They are interested in the child as he is rather than as he will be. To them adult standards of behaviour are not at all important for being followed by the child. They conceive of childhood as something desirable for its own sake and expect children to be children before they become men and women. Hence, they abhor all kinds of restrictions to be imposed on children in schools. They recommend that the nature powers and inclinations of the child should be allowed to develop freely with a minimum of guidance. The naturalistic educators allow the child to follow the lines of his natural interests and to have free choice of activities with no interference or thwarting. No knowledge, no development of any kind (social, moral or religious) should be forced on the child. "These the child will forgo for himself. He knows better what he should learn, when and how he should learn it" (James S. Ross). Rousseau's negative education advised to leave the child largely to himself.

5. Views on Discipline. Discipline, according to Rousseau, is learnt by the child as a consequence of his actions. It can not be imposed on him by the teacher. Naturalists did not support the idea of punishing the child for ensuring discipline. Rousseau said that consequence of child's action was enough and natural punishment. Oral teaching of morality through lectures and preachings was against the naturalistic philosophy. Left to himself the child will learn better discipline. This was their belief. Rousseau and Spencer both had the same views. In fact Rousseau's conception of education was it is "the process of development into an enjoyable, rational, harmoniously balanced, useful and hence natural life".

Q. 13. What is Idealism and what is its contribution to Education?

Or

Discuss Idealism with particular reference to aims, teaching methods, curriculum, teacher, discipline, school, student and basic principles.

Ans. MEANING OF IDEALISM

Man has two facts—Spiritual and Material. When the emphasis is on the realization of spiritual life, it is called idealism.

Idealism is the oldest theory of philosophy. It reflects in the complete history of philosophy. It is born out of Plato's 'Theory of Ideas'. According to this, the ultimate supermacy is of ideas. The word idealism has been derived from the word idea. It should be taken as that of ideas and not to be confused with philosophy of ideals. Plato and other idealism philosophers believed that only ideas are permanent. Idealism holds that the essential nature of man is spiritual which is revealed in mental, religious and aesthetic areas. To them spiritual world is more important than material world. This spiritual world is a world of ideas and feelings. To idealists 'Mind and Soul' are more important rather than Matter and Body. These ideas art eternal and unchanging.

The important definitions regarding idealism are as follows:

According to **Dutta,** "Idealism holds that ultimate reality is spiritualism."

According to **Ross,** "To Idealistic Philosophy spirit is the essential world stuff and true reality is of a mental character."

Supporters of Idealism—Protagonists of idealism are Plato, Socrates, Kant, Hegal, Green, Gentile, Vivekanand, Mahatma Gandhi and Dayanand.

Idealism and Philosophy

Metaphysics—Idealism is concerned with the Natue of Reality. For Idealist Ultimate Reality is of the Nature of Mind. Universe is the idea of the division of reality. The visible universe does not exist of itself, its existence depends upon the real world of mind or spirit. Spiritual world is the reality and true. Man is different from other creatures due to his spiritual power. Man is the grandest creation of God.

Epistemology. For Idealists truth can exist only in the 'Real world of Ideas'. To arrive at truth man uses the methods of reasoning and intuition and through his mind trascends his physical impressions and gets some insight into the real world. Through logic and reason man discovers the pre-existent truths of the physical world and gains some insight into the ultimate truths of the world of ideas.

Axiology. Idealism believes in Truth, Goodness and Beauty. These values are eternal and permanent. To this philosophy God is truth, beautiful and good. It emphasises faith in God, character building, social responsibilities and other values.

Fundamental Principles of Idealism

Fundamental Priciples of Idealism are as follows:

- Idealists believe that spiritual world is real and the ultimate truth whereas the material world is transitory and mortal.

- They hold that the order of the world is due to the manifestation in space and time of an eternal and spiritual reality.
- To them, ideas are the ultimate reality. They are eternal and unchanging.
- To idealists man is more important than material nature. It is because man can think and experience about meterial objects.
- The spiritual or cultural environment is an environment of man's own making. It is a product of man's creative activity.
- Idealism believes in spiritual values. They are Truth, Beauty and Goodness. The realization of these values is the realization of God.
- Idealists give full support to the principle of unity in diversity.
- To them God is the Supreme Force which is omnipotent and omnipresent.
- Idealists insist upon the fullest development of the personality of an individual. Human personality is of supreme value and constitutes the noblest work of God.

Idealism and Aims of Education

The following are the aims of education according to the philosophy of Idealism:

Self Ralization. Idealism considers self-realization as an important aim of education. Self-realization involves full knowledge of the self. The aim of education is to enable man to become his truest self. Human personality is of supreme value and constitutes the noblest work of God. Every individual life has got the possibility of becoming a perfect pattern after his own self.

According to **Ross,** "The aim of education is the exhaltation of personality or self-realization, the making actual or real the highest potentialities of the self."

Spiritual Development. To idealism the aim of education is to develop the child mentally, morally and spiritually, Teacher should so organize education as to develop the child spiritually. To them truth, beauty and goodness should be encouraged more and more. The more an individual realizes these ideals the more spiritually enlightened he will be.

Character Formation. To develop morality in man is an important aim of education. Man is essentially a moral being. Idealism emphasises character building and character formation. The process of education must lead to the deepest spiritual insight to the highest moral and spiritual conduct.

Preparation for Holy Life. To Froeblel "The object of education is the realization of a faithful, pure and holy life." Idealists uphold that education should create such conditions and provide an environment which are conducive to the development of spiritual values in a child. Good ideals will lead a child towards self-realization and prepare him for a holy life.

Preservation and Enrichment of Cultural Heritage. To idealists the aim of education is to acquaint the child with the cultural heritage so that he conserves, promotes and tansmits it to the next generation. Our cultural heritage is of great value and worth. This cultural treasure belongs to the whole humanity and it is the prupose of education to preserve, develop and transmit it in all corners of the world.

Intellectual and Physical Development. The aim of education is to ensure the intellectual development and rationality of the child so that he may develop his innate and creative powers and thereby achieve his goal and seek adjustment with the environment. The aim of education is to ensure physical development of the child also. Sound mind lives in a sound body. Physically developed students can easily achieve their goals of life.

To develop the Feeling of Integrity. Idealists give full support to the principle of unity in diversity. They believe that implicit in all the diversities is an essential unity. This implicit unifying factor is of spiritual nature. The underlying divine force is God which is omnipotent and omnipresent. On the basis of caste, sex, colour and religion there are differences in the society, but God is present in all humanity. Feeling of unity is developed among the students through education.

Development of Moral Values. The aim of education is to develop morality in students. Education should develop the will power of the child so that he may be able to follow the good and avoid evil. This power can be developed by the correct appreciation of truth, goodness and beauty which are the highest moral values.

Universalization of Education. Idealism is in favour of universalization is of education so that an ideal society may be established. Every child must have an access to education. In idealistic society, no exception should be made in the education of children. It should be universal because all human beings are equally the children of God.

Idealism and Curriculum

Idealistic curriculum is thought-oriented and it stresses on those subjects which are related to the spiritual world. It provides for the training and cultivation of moral, intellectual and aesthetic activities.

For the asethetic and moral development Herbart gave prime importance to subjects like history, fine-art, music, poetry, ethics and religion.

For intellectual development of the child literature, language, science, social studies and mathematics are included in the curriculum.

Ross holds the view that man can develop spiritually only when he is physically fit and healthy. This philosophy insists on a sound mind in a sound body. It is essential to keep the body in a proper working order through physical activities. Hence this philosophy insists subjects related to care of body and skills, intellectual, moral, aesthetic and religious activities in the curriculum.

B.B. Bogoslovasky in his 'Ideal School' has given the new scheme of Idealistic curriculum construction as follows:

The first is the universe division an enlarged science department in which students study the inanimate forces of nature, the origin of our solar system, the development of life and the entire background of human drama, the second section deals with the civilization division which offers an inclusive study of social sciences. By civilization means all the activities, achievements and institutions of humanity which control our environment, and provide the necessities of life.

Security and comfort, food, clothing, shelter, technology, communication and government are all within the field of civilization. 'Culture Division' includes philosophy, art literature, religion etc. The fourth is the 'personality division' which offers study of physical, physiological, emotional, and intellectual factors that shape and determine the human personality.

Nature of Idealistic Curriculum is cleared through the following diagram :

Curriculum

Truth (Intellectual)	Goodness (Moral)	Beauty (Aesthetic)
Mathematics, Language, Science, Geography, Philosophy	Religion and Ethics	literature, music and art

In nut shell we can say that idealistic curriculum insists on values and ideals.

(a) It gives more importance to religion, ethics music and art.

(b) This curriculum is thoughtful-centred curriculum. In this only those subjects have been emphasised which are helpful in the personality development.

(c) This curriculum lays more importance to those subjects which reflect the achievements of human culture and civilization.

(d) It includes the subjects relating to social, spiritual, intellectual, moral, religious and aesthetic activities.

(e) According to Horne "Information will become knowledge, books will become tools and best ideas will become ideals."

Idealism and Methods of Teaching

The ultimate goal of the teacher is the attainment of the aim(s) of education for his pupils. Therefore, whichever method is appropriate should be practised. After all, method is a means and not the end. Teaching methods should be chosen according to the nature of ends and means. The teachers have also to put their maximum efforts in formulating the aims. They should select any method keeping in view the content or nature of learner, or the educational objectives.

Idealists consider themselves creators and determinaters of method, not devoters of some one method. An idealist has adopted different methods according to the needs such as Socrates followed Question method, Plato developed Dialectic method, Aristotle initiated Deductive-Inductive method, Hegel followed Instruction method and so on.

Most of the idealists considered Lecture, Discussion and Questioning as the best methods of teaching.

Froebel developed the methodology of play which is known as kindergarten. He regards the school as garden and the teacher as a gardener, whose main function is to tend the little human plants under his charge, very carefully, and thus help them to grow to beauty and perfection.

There is a regulated and directed freedom for teachers in Idealistic methods of teaching. A teacher remains active, in teaching. To Butler, "An Idealist teacher is the creater and determinater of independent teaching method. He is not slave of any method." Idealism has advised the teacher to follow the method of teaching according to his convenience. To Horn, "The aim of teacher is to develop the personality of the child. For fulfilling this aim, the teacher should select the teaching method." Teaching methods followed by Idealistic philosophy are as follows:

Question Method. Socrates followed Question method. In this method effort is made to draw out right answer from the students by putting questions.

Dialectic Method. Plato developed dialectic method to develop the knowledge of the students.

Deductive and Inductive Method. Aristotle initiated inductive and deductive method. Today this method occupies an important place in teaching learning.

Lecture Method. This method is followed to enrich the knowledge of the students.

Kindergarten Method. Froebel developed this method. It is used for small children. It is known as Play Method. It is essential for the physical and spiritual development of the child.

Text-Book Method. In this method more emphasis is given on the reading of text-books.

Instruction Method—Hegel followed this method wherein teacher gives instructions to the students.

Discussion Method. Teacher and students discover the truth through discussion method.

Imitation Method. This method is followed in Gurukul. In case of imitation the teacher sets before students some models and directs them to observe and try to reproduce them. The pupils are expected to follow the examples of great personalities and imbibe some of their good qualities.

Drill and Repetition Method. Pestalozzi advocated practice and repetition method in order to evaluate the knowledge of the students.

Idealism and Discipline

Idealism believe that there can be no spiritual development of the child without discipline. They give importance to impressionistic discipline in comparison to repressionistic discipline. They assert that the teacher should gain respect from the child by his affectionate and sympathetic behaviour and then motivate him by his praiseworthy ideals. Idealist believe in guided freedom and strict discipline. Children must endure a restraint on freedom. Self insight and self analysis are the main disciplinary factors. Teacher's guidance is essential. The discipline is not to be imposed on pupils. The teacher has only to help them to develop self discipline through that self knowledge. To them freedom is not means but it is an end. Idealists are the supporters of self discipline. They are not in favour of militant disciplne. They want to combine humility, courtesy, obedience and subordination in discipline. This approach signifies effective discipline.

Idealism and Student

Idealists have imagined an ideal student. To Bogoslovasky, "The student is a finite person, growing, when properly educated into the image of an infinite person." Idealists give more importance to thoughts and secondary place to student in the educational process. They consider a child under the control of the teacher. Teacher is the maker of his destiny. A student must obey his teacher. The order of his teacher is supreme for him and he must follow it. Other directions may be ignored. A student must have qualities like respect towards his teacher. The relationship between teacher and taught must be positive and congenial.

Idealism and Teacher

According to **Gentile,** 'Teacher is a spiritual symbol of right conduct'. Teacher leads a child toward absolute perfection. That is why he is considered as pilot of God in perfecting man. He provides to the child the knowledge of his cultural heritage. He is the priest of man's spiritual heritage. He tells the child the way to reach God. He is a living ideal. Children imitate him. His personality therfore must be ideal. He acts as a friend, philosopher and guide.

According to **Aurobindo,** "The first principle of true teaching is that nothing can be taught. The teacher is not instructor or task master; he is helper and guide. His business is to suggest and guide and not to impose. He does not impart knowledge to him; he shows him how to acquire knowledge for himself. In idealistic philosophy the teacher has a very important role to play in education as he has to lead the pupil from darkness to light and he has to help him in development of his personality.

Idealism and School

School is a place where the capacities of logical thinking, reasoning and evaluating of the child are progessively sublimated and developed by the teacher. According to Idealism spiritual ideals and values are achieved through proper guidance of teacher given in school.

- Idealists lay more emphasis on the inner aspect of the school and less on its building.
- Such schools are based on ideal principles.
- Idealism incorporates the principle of simple living and high thinking.
- Idealism has imagined such an ideal school where a child is equipped with spiritual and human qualities.

They want to develop in child love for the nation, humanism, love of God and religion through school.

Contribution of Idealism to Education

Idealism has contributed to education in the following ways:

(a) Aims. Idealism emphasises individual and social aims of education. It gives importance to the aim of self-realization which leads the child towards perfection and enables him to realise the self.

(b) Teacher. Idealism has emphasised the position of teacher as Guru. The teacher has been described as a living ideal and co-worker with God. He humanises the child and develops high ideals and values in him.

(c) Child. Idealists want to develop eternal values in the child so that he may become an ideal human being.

(d) Curriculum. Idealism paves the way for the construction of a systematic curriculum.

(e) Discipline. Idealism stresses on self discipline. Idealists want to develop child's personality through discipline.

Q. 14. What is the role of educator according to idealism? Explain idealist educational method.

Ans. IDEALIST ROLE OF THE EDUCATOR

Idealistic pattern of education grants the highest place to the educator, and conceives of the educator and educand as two parts of an organic plant. The educator creates a specific environment for the educand's development and provides guidance so that the later may progress towards perfection and a rounded personality. The most precise explanation of educator's role is manifested in Froebel's Kindergarten pattern of education, in which the school is treated as a garden, the educand as a delicate plant which requires nurturing and the educator as the cautious gardener. Although even in the absence of the gardener the plant will continue to grow and will inevitably follow the laws governing its nature, the gardener has a certain significance in that he has the skill to develop plants. He may be unable to change a rose into a cabbage, but he certainly can contribute his mite to the plant's development. His efforts help in achieving perfection in this development, a level of perfection which would otherwise have been impossible. The educand plays a parallel role in the school. He can guide the educand appropriately because he knows the rules which govern the latter's development into a process leading to perfection and beauty. Ross explains, "The naturalists may be content with briars, but the idealists want fine developing which may be denied to him." Clearly, the idealists attach much more value to the educator than do the naturalists. Adams opined that both the educator and educand are two parts of the intellectual universe both of which should be considered equally important. The educator inspires the educand to realize the ideals of truth, goodness and beauty and guides him along the path to its realization.

Idealist Educational Methods

Turning to methodology in education, idealists suggest that the method must be oriented to achieving the complete development of all innate abilities of the child and to train him for self-realization. In Rivers' words, "The process of education in childhood consists, or should consist, in the direction of innate or instinctive tendencies towards an end in harmony with the highest good of society of which the child is an active member. Idealists believe in a harmony between individual and social objectives. The child must be provided with a liberal environment for his development and his education should be related to present experience. One finds, therefore, that many elements of the idealist methodology are common with those of the naturalist, realist and pragmatist methodology.

The idealist methodology in education lays special stress on the three following processes—

1. Instruction. The term instruction, as used here, implies educational instruction which is believed by Herbart to be essential to education. But instruction does not mean that the child mind should be stuffed with various scraps of information. It implies a modification and a refinement of the child's mind. For this it is essential that the educator must provide sympathetic guidance. The idealists believe that training of all kinds must be provided in the school.

2. Activity. Like the naturalist methodology, the educational methods recommended by the idealists also are based on activity. The child must learn through doing. Although the child can learn much by asking questions after lectures in the school, creative activity is much more important. This creative activity should be natural, continuous and progressive. This helps in moving towards self-realization, because it encourages the child to manifest his innate tendencies. Through mental activity the child learns cheerfully and happily and this also helps in the development of his personality. Besides, by these means the child learns rapidly. Hence, the idealists also stress that instruction should be active.

3. Experience. Idealist methodology also lays considerable strees on experience. Every educand must base all his education on his own experience. The educator's task is not to stuff his own experience in the educand's mind but to provide the latter some insight into his own experience. The guidance given by the educator helps to manifest many frustrated and repressed tendencies and drives of the educand. Independence is an essential pre-requisite for experience. For this reason the idealist believes freedom to be an essential part of education but it must be remembered that this freedom is not absolute, but controlled and guided.

It is evident from the foregoing account that idealists believe the experiences of both the educator and the educand to be of great importance. Both of them should be active and they should indulge in the mutual exchange of experience so that they can progress. The teaching method should be such that the child should recognize it as a mode of self instruction.

Q. 15. What is humanism? What are its implications in education?

Ans. Humanism implies both a human and a humane approach to educational problems, human in the sense that human nature (including likes, dislikes, interests, aptitudes etc.) should not be suppressed by religion in favour of an ascetic ideal and a narrow dogmatic interpretation of the world; humane in the sense that the nature of the child and its growing mind should not be suppressed by cruel discipline, teachers and rigid methods of teaching.

Humanism is a revolt against theology, church and dogma.

In simpler words we can say that when human world and human being become the concern of philosophy the result is humanism.

It also means studies of humanities.

It also means reasonable balance of life.

It is a philosophy, the centre of whose studey is man. Man is the measure of everything.

Implications in Education

The aims of humanistic education are:

(i) **Broadly Educated Man.** To produce a broadly educated man possessing a well rounded personality who could assume leadership in church and state.

(ii) **Accomplishments.** To produce men who should have a wide range of accomplishments. They should be able to express themselves in poetry, song, dance etc. All men should be physically and mentally healthy.

Jacks says that according to Humanists human perfection must be final objective.

CURRICULUM

The main tenet of humanism, *i.e.,* education for all and child is the centre of all education and the broad aims of education reflect on the type of curriculum. Hans says that the humanistic curriculum had in it the 'real' studies so that those could light the minds of children since it was the pupil who came first or got priority—method and theory later.

(i) Accordingly, curriculum included the study of old classics of Greeks and Romans since early humanists considered these to possessing profundity of content, literary style etc. and they believed that all the values such as wide leraning, all round development, life of action, qualities of artistic enjoyment could be achieved by teaching Greek and Roman literature. In comparison with literature and classics, they gave slight attention to mathematics, natural history, music etc. etc. and much less attention was given by them to the vernaculars in their curriculum. They believed that if history and ethics is to be studied—we should study those as a part of the work of the old classical writers.

(ii) Training for Good Manners such as modesty was also stressed.

(iii) Physical Education was also included in their curriculum and there was due place for it. It aimed at producing a new brave class of people.

Academician J.B. Florin and his Humanistic Curriculum. In the 18th century Florin asserted, "Philosophy and the sciences ought to be made the principal study of young persons." He classified all subjects of instruction into three groups: (i) Relation of man to nature, (ii) Relation of man to himself, and (iii) Relation of man to other men.

He advised a ten years course for the ages seven to seventeen presuming that the boys would enter his academy with a fair knowledge of writing and reading. The subjects included all branches of mathematics, history, applied sciences for the first group; Latin, French, Italian, Grammar, Rhetoric, poetry, drawing, music and exercise for the second group; History, politics, economics and biography for the third group.

Method of Teaching

(i) It was Erasmus who had left in writing about the method. He had tried the old methods in teaching literature and he told us, "Do not give the personal account of the author—rather appreciate the work of the author." We should talk about his style, about his vocabulary etc. rather become personal with him.

(ii) Talking about difficulties in the way of learning, humanists say that the teacher should give few simple directions to overcome difficulties. Do not hurry because learning comes easily when the proper statge is reached. Avoid difficulty which can be easily ignored. Postpone things.

(iii) Next item in the method of humanistic education was to set exercises for the matter taught. It should not be literal reproduction. The subject should be reproduced. He did not favour taking notes. He would encourage memorisation, understanding and reproduction. The substance be memorised. Let the child understand critically and then reproduce. The maxim was:—Understand—Arrange—Repeat.

(iv) For mature students, early humanists recommended lectures and debates. Independence and individuality were introduced in learning of lessons. It was a protest aganist verbalism and cram work.

Other Features

(a) Discipline. Humanists believed in discipline in the schools. It was a discipline of kindness than of vindictiveness. There was an appeal to pride and ambition in the child rather than to rigors of punishment.

(b) Role of Teacher. It is the teacher who is the chief agent in this enterprise of sensible integration and success or failure depends upon his outlook and methods. If he lives a unified life himself, he will help his pupils to find a unity in the multiplicity of their experience, but if he is to do all this, he will require different type of training.

Q. 16. Discuss Pragmatism with particular reference to aims, teaching methods, curriculum, teacher, discipline school, student and basic priciples.

Or

What is Pragmatism and what is its contribution to Education?

Ans. Pragmatism is midway between Idealism and Naturalism. It is an American philosophy typical in nature and practical in approach. The term pragmatism is derived from the Greek word 'Pragma' which means activity or the work done. Pragmatism is also known as Experimentalism because pragmatists believe experiment as the only criterion of Truth. It is noted that the fundamental start of Pragmatism is change. In this sense, no truth is permanent. It is always changing from time to time, from place to place. To them only those ideals and values are true which result in some utility to mankind in a certain set of circumstances, place or time. It is intimately connected with human life and human welfare, that is why, it is called as a humanistic philosophy of life.

Idealism is psycho-centric, Naturalism is neutro-centric and Pragmatism is anthropo-centric, according to which, man's own experiences are the centres of reality and truth. Idealist looks before and after and pines for what is not, naturalists look to present needs and problems and have no concern for future, Pragmatist looks here and now.

Idealist constructs a transcendental ideal which is beyond man's realisation. Naturalists follow the principle of struggle for existence and survival of the fittest. Pragmatists are practical people believing in finishing the book here, solving the problem now, making the social contact immediately, striking the business deal at once. Whatever they wish to do, they examine its utility and do it immediately.

Idealists live in the world of ideals. Naturalists live in the lap of nature. Pragmatists live in the world of facts. Pragmatism makes 'activity', 'engagement', 'commitment', and 'encounter' its central theme.

Different philosophers and educationists have defined pragmatism as follows :—

According to **Prett,** "Pragmatism offers a theory of knowledge, a theory of truth and a theory of reality."

According to **William James,** "Pragmatism is a temper of mind, an attitude, it is also a theory of the nature of ideas and truth, and finally it is a theory of reality."

According to **Ross,** "Pragmatism is essentially a humanistic philosophy maintaining that man creates his own values in course of activity, that reality is still in making and awaits its part of completion from that future."

According to **Dr. Prem Nath,** "The nature of Pragmatism is naturalistic, its duration is scientific and practicable and its aim is social and humanistic."

Pragmatism is definitely a foreign ideology. In modern times, the introduction of pragmatism to human life was first done by American philosopher G.S. Pearce in 1878 A.D. He asserted, "our beliefs are really the rules for action". Due to inhuman cruelties in England, thousands of the oppressed people migrated from their native countries in Europe to America. The new way of thinking led them to new types of activities and new ways of learning by doing and by consequences and experiences.

Forms of Pragmatism

There are different types of Pragmatism which are as follows:

Biological Pragmatism. According to this the capacity of a human being is valuable and important which enables him to adjust with the environment or which makes him able to change his environment according to his needs and requirements.

Humanistic Pragmatism. According to this 'whatever fulfils one's purpose, satisfies one's desire, develops one's life, is true.' It maintains what satisfies the human nature is only true and real.

Nominalistic Pragmatism. It emphasises on the concreteness of an idea. When we do an experiment we come across future solutions. Its basis is concrete. It results in some visual solutions.

Experimental Pragmatism. According to this whatever can be experimentally verified is true. That principle is true which can be verified as true by experiment.

Supporters. Perce, William James, Kil Patrick and John Dewey were the supporters of Pragmatism.

Characteristics of Pragmatism

Characteristics of Pragmatism are as follows:

Faith in Democracy. This philosophy believes in humanism which is in accordance with democracy. Pragmatism shows its deep faith in democracy, as democracy is a way of life and a spirit of sharing experiences.

It does not believe in eternal values. Man makes his own values. Values change according to the change of time. They are relative. There is nothing in the name of eternal values. Truth is that which works, which serves some purpose and is useful to a man. Truth is man-made and the values of life and truth always change.

It is a Revolt against Traditionalism. This philosophy is a midway between Naturalism and Idealism. It neither believes in the established beliefs nor in the objective interpretation of naturalism. It lays emphasis on the practicability of thing and activity.

Principle of utility. Pragmatism believes in the priciple of utility. Utility is the measure of a view point. The thing which gives satisfaction is useful. According to this only those ideas and things are true which have a utility for man.

Thought in Subordinate to Action. Pragmatism sees thought as intrinsically connected with action. It gives supreme position to action.

Pragmatism and Philosophy

Metaphysics. Pragmatism regards the material world as true. It regards human being as the supreme person. He is a social being and his development is possible only in the society. To it this world is the combination of different elements. It considers truth as chaugeable. Truth is man-made. There is a change in its form and concept. Pragmatism believes in the power of God if the existence of God is helpful in the growth of human being otherwise not. It lays stress on action and its consequences. It considers reality as a process of the completion of a task.

Axiology. Pragmatism does not believe in eternal values. Man himself creates values. Values are not predetermined. Pragmatists consider consequences as the basis of selection of all types of values. If the values are useful their sellection is appropriate otherwise not. In the context of religion, Dewey has said, 'God is active relation between Ideal and Reality, They consider the use of intelligence in the solution of problems.

Epistemology. Pragmatism considers experience as the source of attaining knowledge. Human being receives knowledge through experience based activity and ideas by acting and reacting with human environment. Pragmatists consider experimental methods as the best means of attaining knowledge. To them problem, selection of problem, data collection, hypothesis and experimentation are the steps of experimental method. Truth is the outcome of expected consequences through this method.

Principles of Pragmatism

Principles of Pragmatism are as follows :—

Pragmatism believes in the power of God if the existence of God is helpful in the growth of human beings otherwise not. It recognises the importance of human power. The essence of human life is humanity. The world is like a laboratory where man solves his problems. In it means are more important than ends.

Stress on Social Values. Pragmatists uphold social and democratic attitudes and values. Pragmatism holds that man is a social being. He is born in society and all his development takes place in and through society.

Principle of Utility. Pragmatism is a utilitarian ideology which holds that the reality of a principle lies in its utility. Any idea or thing which is useful to us, is proper and right. In case it is of no use, it is improper, wrong and untrue.

God is not Absolute. To the Pragmatists God is not infinite, absolute and immortal entity as the idealists proclaim. To them, God and Soul are not immortal and infinite. These entities as well as the religion are useful to human beings only when they serve usefully to develop human personalities, otherwise Pragmatism shows an attitude of indifference towards moral and spiritual ideals and values.

Emphasis on Activity. The greatest contribution of Pragmatism to education is the principle of learning by doing. It lays great emphasis on activity rather than on ideas. It holds the view that ideas are born out of activities. Man is active by nature. He learns by his activities.

Problems are Motivating Force. According to Pragmatism, human life is like a laboratory wherein each individual undertakes various experiments to solve the problems which confront him in course of his growth and development. The success of the experiment is a search of truth. Hence problems are the motivating force for the search of truth.

Past is Dead. According to Pragmatism past is dead and gone. It is of no use to think and talk about what is dead and gone. To it each individual has to solve the problems of his present and future life. Hence present and immediate future are of great value to an individual.

Importance to Human Intelligence. Pragmatism gives more importance to human intelligence and mental capacity which brings about harmonious and progressive adjustment with environment which results in human welfare and happiness. It is against old customs and traditions. It believes in realities of life.

Faith in Pluralism. This philosophy is pluralistic. It takes "life" from naturalism and 'Psyche' from mentalism and evaluates and explains God, nature and man. It is just in the middle of naturalism and idealism.

Pragmatism and Aims of Education

All Round Development. Education ensures all round development of the child. The child must develop physically, mentally, socially, morally, and aesthetically. The aim of education is for development. To Dewey, "Education has no aims, only persons have aims." Therefore the aims of pragmatic education are chageable".

According to **Ross,** "The general educational aim of the pragmatists is just the creation of new values. So the main task of the educator is to put the educand into a position of developing values for himself."

Adjustment. Pragmatic education is flexible. Therefore it wants to develop a child as a dynamic and flexible intellectual so that he may adjust with the changing environment and ensure his progress by controlling it. It wants to enable a child adjust mentally for the present and future by making him as the centre of education. The aim of education is 'to direct the impulses, interests and abilities towards the satisfaction of the left needs of the child, in the environment.

Social Efficiency. Pragmatism wants to develop social efficiency in the child through education. Education wants a child to stand on his feet by providing him vocational efficiency so that he may fulfil the needs of his family and society besides his personal needs. Thus, social efficiency tries to enable him to adjust with the society.

Reconstruction of Experience. As every individual is required to solve many diverse problems in his life, the aim of education should also be the formulation and cultivation of a dynamic, adoptable, resourceful and enterprising mind. It is with such a mind that original and creative thinking is possible which will enable a person to cope successfully with the varied situations of life.

Pragmatism and Curriculum

Pragmatists want to construct such a flexible, dynamic and integrated curriculum which helps in the development of the child. According to pragmatism only those subjects, activities and experiences should be included in the curriculum which are useful to the present needs of the child and meet the future expectations of adult life as well. Knowledge, of languages, hygiene, physical training, history, geography, mathematics, science, agriculture and professional subjects is compulsory. The main purpose is to help the child more and more in his development in all the fields of human activity. Only those activities and experiences in which the child takes interest should be included in the curriculum. The curriculum should consist of such varieties of learning experiences which promote original thinking and freedom to develop social and purposeful attitudes.

According to Pragmatism knowledge is one unit. It cannot be divided into water tight compartments of separate subjects. Teaching of various units should be closely inter-linked and co-related so as to form right concept and proper understanding in the children.

Pragmatism and Methods of Teaching

Pragmatism is opposed to the traditional methods of teaching. It favours child-centred, scientific and psychological and active methods of teaching. Pragmatism has contributed significantly to the methods of teaching. Pragmatists laid stress on learning through activities and the real life situations. Their main methods are Project method and Problem-solving method. Through these methods a child attains knowledge by solving his practical problems. These methods are experimental and creative.

These methods lay emphasis on learning by doing and learning through experience. Both the teacher and taught remain active. Pragmatism does not merely insist upon practical activities but tries to provide real life experiences and real life situations so that the child gains the required insight and capacities to face and solve the problems and challenges of life successfully. To it only that method is most effective which employs correlation and integration of all subjects, activities and experiences.

Pragmatism and Discipline

To Dewey discipline is a sort of mental state in the formation of which social conditions play a major role. Pragmatism condemns enforced discipline and advocates social discipline based on child's interests, activities and a sense of social responsibility.

Pragmatism advocates the merging of play with work. This merging of play and work will develop interest and a sense of purpose in the child to do his work with joy and eagerness without interfering with the work of others. This mental condition will infuse in him seriousness, sincerity and consideration for others. He will develop self-confidence, self-reliance, co-operation, sacrifice, sympathy and fellow-feeling for others. With the development of these social qualities he will develop a sense of social discipline and moral obligation towards self and others.

Hence according to pragmatism, the school should provide purposeful and conducive experiences to the child in a free and congenial atmosphere, which helps him becoming a true citizen in the real sense. Such activities create in children virtues like mutual respect, toleration, self-control and originality. This helps him in the training of character formation and establishment of self discipline.

Pragmatism and Student

Pragmatism gives an important place to the child. The aim of education should be to prepare the child for the society so that he can become responsible citizen and succeed in life. This philosophy stresses child-centred education. There are three aspects of child's personality—Biological, Psychological and Social. Pragmatism lays emphasis on social aspect. This philosophy considers a child as an important part of educative process. It does not want to impose external ideas upon the child. It is in favour of giving him academic freedom. It wants to educate the child in social envionment.

Pragmatism and Teacher

According to pragmatism teacher is a friend, guide and philosopher to the child. He must educate the child in social environment so that he may attain social efficiency. There must be positive relationship between teacher and taught. His behaviour towards children must be sympathetic. His attitude should be democratic and child must have academic freedom. His function is to suggest problems to his pupils and to stimulate them to find for themselves solutions which will work. His emphasis is not on the knowledge as arranged and systematised in the text-books. He wants the children to do one experiment or to have a particular experince. 'Doing' is more important than knowing. Like Socrates the Pragmatist teacher wants "his pupils to think and act for themselves, to do rather than to know, to originate rather than to repeat."

Pragmatism and School

John Dewey maintains that school is a 'Miniature Society' here a child gets real experiences to act and behave according to his interests, aptitudes and capacities. Pragmatists ragard school as a social institution where the child gains real experiences of actual life which develop in him social sense and a sense of duty towards society and the nation. Group games, working in laboratories and studying in libraries with others are the various activities and experiences which inculcate in children social qualities, social attitudes together with a spirit of mutual help and cooperative activities. In this way, according to Pragmatism the school is not a centre of education alone but it is also a community centre of various activities and experiences.

Contribution of Pragmatism in Education

Aims. It lays more stress on social and vocational efficiency.

Teacher. It gives important place to teacher.

Student. It stresses on child-centred education.

Teaching Method. New teaching methods is the contribution of pragmatism.

Curriculum. It lays more stress on experience and learning by doing.

Evaluation of Pragmatism

Opposition of Pre-determined Ideas. Pragmatism opposes pre-determined ideals and values. They are man-made and change according to the changes in circumstances, time and place.

Opposition of Eternal Truth. Pragmatism does not have any faith in eternal truth. Pragmatists believe that if the result of an activity is satisfactory then it is true otherwise not.

No Fix System of Education. Pragmatism provides academic freedom to every institution which leads them no where. Pragmatism gives no fixed ideal to education. Such an education is bound to be fruitless.

Emphasis on Material and Negation of Spiritual Values. There is no room for spiritual values in pragmatism. It gives more weightage to material values. Without spiritual values, we can not achieve happiness, contentment and peace of mind and can go astray.

Laxity in Discipline. Pragmatism allows full freedom to the child which is not proper at the school stage and it leads to serious chaos and confusion.

Condemnation of Formal Education. Pragmatism advocates that all knowledge should be acquired through direct personal experiences. But knowledge is so vast and the span of life so short, that it is quite impossible to receive all knowledge through direct experiences. Hence acquiring all knowledge needs personal experinces and formal education both.

Negation of the Past. Pragmatism gives undue importance to the present. It ignores both past and future. The study of past is important to understand the present. Also there is need to link the present with future.

Pragmatism is a Method Only. Pragmatism is not a philosophy of life but only a method of education, growth and development. In the words of William James. "There is absolutely nothing new in the pragmatic method. It is just empirical attitude. It has no dogmas and no doctrines save its methods."

Pragmatism believe in Pluralism which is not proper.

Merits of Pragmatism

Project Method. Project method is a gift of pragmatism. Through this method child attains knowledge by solving his practical problems. He performs the problematic acts in natural conditions. This method lays emphasis on learning through experiences.

Importance of Child. Opposing bookish knowledge and formal education, pragmatism lays great stress upon the development of child's individuality by his own efforts. This makes education child-centred.

Emphasis on Activity. The principle of learning by doing is the main contribution of pragmatism. Children are active by nature. It emphasises on the activity of the child. It prepares the child for future life in a very effective manner.

Revolutionised the Process of Education. This philosophy has infused life and zest in contribution. The concepts of 'New

Education', 'Progressive Education' and Activity-centred curriculum which have changed the education outlook are the contribution of pragmatism.

Social and Democratic Education. Pragmatism infuses in a child a spirit of freedom, initiative, equality and also a sense of responsibility in relation to rights and duties of a citizen. This develops in the child love for democratic values and social efficiency which bring harmonious adjustment and development of personality.

Progressive Attitude. Pragmatism emphasizes the qualities of freedom initiative, expression, conducive experiences, congenial environment, purposeful creativity and development of human values for the welfare of whole mankind.

In the words of Rusk. "It is merely a stage in the development of a new Idealism that will do full justice to reality, reconcile the practical and spiritual values and result in a culture which is the flower of efficiency."

Pragmatism is an attitude and a way of living which, opposing the old doctrines of Idealism and Naturalism, inspires the individual to look ahead and create new values for an unknown future so that he leads a better, happier and a richer life.

Q. 17. Explain the Educational Philosophy of Gandhiji.

Ans. His Life and Work. Gandhiji, the Father of the Indian Nation, the apostle of Truth and Non-violence, was born on the 2nd of October, 1869 at Porbandar in Kathiawar. Gandhiji's mother was a saintly woman. She had a strong influence on his life. After studying Law in England, he started practice in Bombay, but he could not earn sufficient to live on. He went to South Africa. His experiences in England, India, and South Africa made him bitter against the British Rule. What he did for the liberation of the country is known to all of us. At present we are concerned with his Educational Philosophy.

Background of His Educational Philosophy

There are three important elements in the background of his educational philosophy:

1. His philosophy of life.
2. His dissatisfaction with the British System of Education.

3. His educational experiments at Tolstoy Farm, Sabarmati and Sewagram Ashrams.

1. His Philosophy of Life. He had Faith in God. All things move due to God. To him God is every thing—"Life Truth, Light and Love". Other important principles of his life were Faith in Truth, Ahimsa—Creed of Non-violence, and Dignity of Labour.

2. His Dissatisfaction with the British System of Education. British System of Education did not suit to the Indian Socio-Economic conditions. Teeming millions of Indian were wrought in ignorance, superstition, intertia and illiteracy. This education is not related to life. It makes the Indians foreigners in their own homes.

3. His Educational Experiments at Tolstoy Farm, Sabarmati and Sewagram Ashrams. In these Ashrams, the inmates, living and working together, adopted certain codes. All the inmates were to work with their hands. There was no servant. Every job was performed by the inmates. Gandhiji found that manual work has great virtues in its trail. One can learn and can also be self-sufficient. These experiments encouraged him to put forward important principle of the education philosophy *i.e.,* earn while you learn.

His Educational Philosophy. There is a general tendency among educationists and laymen to identify Gandhi's educational philosophy with Basic Education or Wardha Scheme of Education. Basic Education is, no doubt, an integral part of Gandhi's educational philosophy but it is a scheme or programme of education not synonymous with Gandhi's philosophy of education, which aims at bringing about a revolution in the hearts and minds of men all over the world. Basic Scheme is primarily meant for children between 7 and 14 years of age.

Concept of Education. According to Gandhiji, "By education, I mean an all-round drawing out of the best in child and man—body, mind and spirit." The aim of education is not literacy. Gandhiji laid emphasis on the development of the whole personality. Education which draws out the best or Truth consists in the development of the mind and body with a corresponding awakening of the soul. "True Education", says Gandhiji, "is that which draws out and stimulates the spiritual, intellectual and physical faculties of the children."

Aims of Education. Aims of education are implied in the very meanings of education. He has given two sets of aims—*viz.* immediate and ultimate aims of education.

(a) Ultimate Aim. Ultimate aim of education is identical with the goal of life, which is 'Self-realisation'. Self-realisation is the realisation of the self proper. True education should result not in the material gains but in spiritual uplift.

Gandhiji laid great stress on religious education which teaches fundamental virtues of truth, love, justice and non-violence. According to Gandhiji, "Like without religion is life without principles." Gandhiji is also of the opinion that God could be achieved not by returning into jungles but by living in a society and serving it. He preferred to call a student "Brahmachari", a searcher after God.

Selfe-realisation can take place through self-control, character and abstinence.

(b) Immediate Aims. Immediate aims, include 'bread and butter aim', the cultural aim, the harmonious development of all powers, the moral or character development aim, and sociological aim.

1. Bread and Butter Aims. This is also called utilitarian aim. It is due to this aim that he gave the principle of 'self-supporting education'. The educand should not only be made capable of earning his own livelihood in later life after school but also during the schooling. The child must be an earning unit who must be self-sufficient right from the beginning of the education of the child. This aim is really an important aim of even modern education.

2. Cultural Aim. Cultural aim refers to the refinement of the personality. Mere knowledge is not enough. Education should lead to that quality of mind which may be reflected in daily conduct. Speech, behaviour and manner must be refined. Culture brings in humility and frankness. Education should not take Indian children away from its own culture. There is a need of synthesising cultures so that one could inherit world cultures. This aim enables the students to assimiliate and appreciate other cultures.

3. Harmonious Development Aim. Harmonious development or perfection of nature is another aim that Gandhiji advocates. Harmoniously developed person is that who adjusts to his life and environment. He laid greater emphasis on the development of 3 H's *i.e.,* Head, Heart and Hand than on 3 R's *i.e.,* reading, writing and arithmetic. Present system of education leads to unbalanced development.

4. The Moral or Character Building Aim. It is the chief aim of education. The central purpose of education is to build character. If choice is to be made between character and other things in life, then every thing else can be subordinated to the former.

Man must be a man of word. He must be ready to do something for the humanity at the first call to this conscience.

5. Sociological Aim or Training for Citizenship. Gandhiji reconciled the individual and social aims of education. In democracy the first slogan is 'Educate your Masters'. Thus Gandhiji advocated 'Universal education'. Every member of this Samaj should be educated so that he could uplift it. He must have qualities of a good citizen. Essential qualities are—spirit of courage, self-sacrifice and industry.

Curriculum. Gandhian curriculum includes following subjects:

1. Basic craft which may be agriculture or spinning and weaving or card-board work and mental work.
2. Mother tongue both as a language and as medium of instructions.
3. Arithmetic/Mathematics: More emphasis is to be laid on numerical and geometrical problems connected with craft and community life.
4. Drawing, Painting and Music.
5. Domestic science for girls at higher stages. At lower stages same for boys and girls.
6. Social Studies.
7. General Science.

Methods. Gandhiji framed teaching through physical and mental activities. Activity is the starting point of his teaching. Gandhiji advocated teaching through a method.

Craft. Correlated knowledge should be given through a craft.

Discipline. The spirit of non-violence should prevail in the school. Love and truth should be the basis between the teacher and the taught. Self-discipline is the only discipline worth the name.

Basic Education. Gandhiji's philosophy is reflected in Basic education. The four features are:

1. Education should be free and compulsory for all children between the age group 7-14 years.
2. Mother tongue should be the medium of instruction.
3. Education should be craft-centered.
4. Education should be self-sufficient.

Q. 18. "Gandhian philosophy acted as a spearhead of a silent revolution in the economic, social and the political field." Discuss.

Or

Make an estimate of Gandhian philosophy of education comparing it with that of Pestalozzi, Rousseau, Froebel, Montessori and Dewey.

Or

What is the philosophy of Nai Taleem? How does it change the whole structure of our educational system?

Or

What are the most important characteristics of the educational philosophy of Mahatma Gandhi? How do you compare his educational philosophy with naturalism, idealism and pragmatism?

Ans. Education, to Gandhiji, was a means to achieve perfection of individuality on the one hand and an instrument of service to the nation on the other. Thus, individual and social both the aims of education were considered by him equally important. "By education I mean an all-round drawing out of the best in child and man—body, mind and spirit", he said. This in other words meant development of the whole child, the whole personality of the child. Harmonious development of all the aspects of human personality such as physical, intellectual and spiritual was emphasized by him as an individual aim of education. Emphasizing the social aim of education he said that the individual has a responsibility to work for the welfare of the whole society. "Willing submission to social control and restrain for the sake of the well-being of the whole society" were considered by him important attitudes to be developed in the people through education. Good of the individual and good of the society were inter-dependent. So education should be both for the child as well as for the state.

Education, to Gandhi, was something more than literacy. Though he did not belittle the improtance of vocational aim of education, self-realization and knowledge of the Ultimate, God were considered the ultimate aims of education. Emphasis on vocational aspect led him to say that education has to be self-supporting, a theory which culminated into his system of basic education.

Cultural refinement of human personality through education was also considered important by Gandhiji. But, it was Indian culture that was emphasized by him. Culture, according to him was in quality of the soul which was reflected in all aspects of human behaviour. For achieving this kind of cultural refinement he emphasized the study of the Geeta and the sacred books of all other religions.

Gandhi attached much importance to character education and moral development of the child through education. This would mean to him development of such qualities in the individual as purity of personal life, self-restraint, service of humanity, courage, strength of conviction, righteousness and sense of responsibility. The attitude of "Ahimsa", non-violence was the supreme value to be developed in the people through education.

The ulitimate aim of education according to Gandhiji is the Self-Realization. All other aims are important as they lead to self-realization. Self-realization, to him, means realizing that the ultimate reality, the Truth is the universal soul, some unknown supreme power and that the man is only a spark of that which fuses with that supreme ultimately.

The Curriculum. Gandhiji considered elementary education the most important phase of the educational system. He, therefore, expressed his views only about the curriculum of primary stage curriculum. About this stage he said that intellectual development alone should not be emphasized. The curriculum should be so designed that it caters to the development of all the aspects of child personality. Physical, social, moral and spiritual development, too, are important. Hence, there should be provision in the curriculum for activities, experiences and subjects of knowledge that can help achieve these developments also. He, then, suggested to make the curriculum activity centred by introducing teaching of some craft like spinning, weaving, handicraft, book craft, art, agriculture, pottery etc., whichever is close to the child's life in his environment. Besides, he recommended that mother tongue should be the medium of instruction at this stage. It was also suggested by him that mathematics, social studies, drawing and music should necessarily included in the curriculum. General science including biology, chemistry, physical science, hygiene, nature study, physical education and general knowledge of astronomy were also recommended to form the basis of the curriculum. He also suggested that upto class V boys and girls should be subjected to the same curriculum. But, after that girls should be taught home science instead of general science.

Method of Teaching. Gandhiji once wrote in Young India (1921) that "schools and colleges should become almost, if not wholly, self-supporting". He, then emphasized that teaching should be done through arts and crafts, work and play, voluntary activity and self-choosen activity.

Gandhiji said that the method of teaching should be such as it provides to the child freedom, a chance to come into closer contact with the teacher, a chance to be an active investigator, observer and experimenter.

Craft-centred teaching and correlation method may be said to be the most important ingredients of the educational method Gandhiji suggested. Correlation method would mean relating the knowledge, of each subject being taught to the craft on the one hand and to the child's life on the other. Gandhi, emphatically, demanded that craft should be made the center of all education, centre of the school life. The idea, afterwards, found an expression to the Basic Education System which was introduced in all the states of the country.

COMPARISON WITH NATURALISM, IDEALISM AND PRAGMATISM

Some writers have tried to put labels on Gandhiji as a naturalist, an idealist and a pragmatist. In fact we find elements of all these three philosophies in his views on education. But, basically, he was an idealist. His emphasis was on character formation and spiritual development of the child. He himself lived a spiritual life and stood for higher values throughout his life. The good of the society, according to him, was contingent upon the goodness of each individuals. The perfect and spiritually developed individuals alone could constitute an ideal society. So he emphasized that education should lead the individual to self-realisation, realization of God and should develop in him attitudes of self-control, social service, ahimsa, sacrifice righteousness, brotherlihood. These are all higher values like the idealistic he also emphasized that education should be used to cultivate these moral and spiritual values in the people.

There are elements of naturalism and pragmatism too found in his educational philosophy. He considered the child an important element in the process of education and emphasized, like the naturalists, that education should conform to the nature of the child. The child should be allowed freedom. He should be taught in natural environment for "drawing out the best in the child". Like the naturalists, he also said that education should aim at the development of all aspects of child's personality. Activity, play, experimentation and own experience as the strategies of education were emphasized by Gandhiji also like, the naturalists. He also considered books as the means of imparting knowledge to young child unimportant. Thus, several ideas of naturalism are found expressed in Gandhiji's educational philosophy also. Yet, it can not be said that he was a naturalist only.

Some elements of pragmatic philosophy may also be seen in Gandhiji's educational philosophy. His emphasis on making education self-supporting and preparing individuals for vocation, craft-centred education, activity centrd, teaching, learning through child's own experience and experimentation, correlated teaching clearly brings him closer to the pragmatists.

Q. 19. Explain the basic principles of Vivekananda's educational philosophy.

Ans. VIVEKANANDA'S EDUCATIONAL PHILOSOPHY

Swami Vivekananda ranks among the greatest educationists of the world. Here in the following lines, we discuss the basic principles of the philosophy of education:

1. Only study of books is not education.
2. Knowledge lies hidden in the mind of man. He uncovers and develops it by his own efforts.
3. Concentration is the key of all knowledge. For this, practice of Brahamcharya is very essential.
4. Purity of thought, speech and deed is self discipline.
5. Education should develop the child physically, mentally and spiritually.
6. Education should foster spiritual faith, devotion and self surrender in the individual and should full development through service and sacrifice.
7. Education should develop character, mental powers, intelligence and inculcate self confidence together with self-reliance.
8. Religious education should be imparted through sweet impressions and fine conduct in preference to books.
9. Boys and girls should receive the same education.
10. Specially women should be imparted religious education.
11. Mass education schemes should be formulated and launched.
12. Provision for technical education should be made so that industrial growth leads to the economic prosperity of the nation.
13. Teacher is a friend, philosopher and guide. He should sympathetically bring out the latent knowledge in a child by inspiration and motivation.

14. There should be an intimate relationship between the teacher and the students.
15. All those subjects should be included in the curriculum which promote the material and spiritual advancement of a child.

Meaning of Education

Education is not the mass of informations which are inserted by force into the mind of a child. According to Swami Vivekananda if education meant information only, then, libraries could be the greatest saints of the world and Encyclopaedias had become seers and rishis. In his own words—"Education is the manifestation of perfection already reached in a man."

Aims of Education

According to Swami Vivekananda the following should be the main aims of education:

1. The Aim of Reaching Perfection. The prime aim of education is to achieve fullness of perfection already present in a child. According to Swamiji all material and spiritual knowledge is already present in man covered by a curtain of ignorance. Education should tear off that veil so that the knowledge shines forth as an illuminating torch to enliven all the corners by and by. This is meant by achieving fullness of the latent perfection.

2. Physical and Mental Development Aim. The second aim of education is the physical and mental development of the child so that the child of today, after studying Geeta, is able to promote national growth and advancement as a fearless and physically well developed citizen of tomorrow. Stressing the mental development of the child, Swamiji, wished education to enable the child to stand on his own legs economically rather than becoming a parasite on others.

3. Moral and Spiritual Development. According to Swami Vivekananda, a nation's greatness is not only measured by its parliamentary institutions and activities, but also by the greatness of its citizens. But the greatness of citizens is possible only through their moral and spiritual development which education should foster.

4. Character Development Aim. According to Swamiji character develoment is a very important aim of any education. For this, he emphasized the practice of Brahamcharya which fosters development of mental, moral and spiritual powers leading to purity of thoughts, words and deeds.

5. The Aim of Development Faith in One's Ownself, Shraddha and a Spirit of Renunciation. All through his life Swamiji exhorted the individuals to keep full confidence upon their powers. They should inculcate a spirit of self surrender, sacrifice and renunciation of material pleasures for the good of others. Education should fosts, all these qualities in the individual. He gave this call to his countrymen. "Arise, awake and stop not till the goal is achieved."

6. The Aim of Searching Unity in Diversity. The ture aim of education is to develop insight into the individuals so that they are able to search out and realize unity in diversity. Swami Vivekanandaji has further asserted that physical and spiritual worlds are one, their distinctness is an illusion (Maya). Education should develop this sense which finds unity in diversity.

7. Religious Development Aim. To Swamiji religius development is an essential aim of education. To him, each individual should be able to search out and develop the religious seed embedded in him and thus find the absolute truth or reality. Hence he advocated the training of feelings and emotions so that the whole life is purified and sublimated. Then only, the capacities of obedience, social service and submission to the teachings and preachings of great saints and saviours will develop in the individual. Education should foster this development.

Curriculum

According to Swami Vivekanand, the prime aim of education is spiritual growth and development. But this does not mean that he did not advocate material prosperity and physical well-being. He feelingly advocated the inclusion of all those subjects and activities, in the curriculum, which foster material welfare with spiritual advancement. For spiritual prefection Swamiji prescribed Religious, Philosophy, Puranic lore, Upnishads, Company of saints and their preachings and for material advancement and prosperity he recommended Languages, Geography, Science, Political Science, Economics, Psychology, Art, Agriculture, Industrial and Technical subjects together with Games, sports and other Physical exercises.

Methods of Teaching

Swamific prescribed the same ancient spiritual methods of teaching wherein the Guru and his desciples lived in close association as in a family. The essential characteristics of those religious and spiritual methods were as under:—

1. To control fleeting mental faculties by the practice of Yoga.
2. To develop the mind by concentration and deep meditation.
3. To gain knowledge through lectures, discussions, self-experience and creative activities.
4. To imitate the qualities and character of teacher intelligent and clear understanding.
5. To lead the child on the right path by means of individual guidance by the teacher.

Place of Child

Like Froebel, Vivekanand emphasized the education to be child centered. According to him the child is the store and repository of all learning material and spiritual. Like a plant a child grows by his own inner power naturally. Hence advising the child to grow naturally and spontaneously, Vivekanand asserted—"Go into your own and get the Upnishads out of your own self. You are the greatest book that ever was or will be. Until the inner teacher opens, all outside teaching is in vain."

Place of Teacher

Swamiji believed in self-education. According to him each of us is his own teacher. The external teacher only guides and inspires the inner teacher (soul) to rise up and start working to develop the child. Hence discussing the role of teacher Swami Vivekanand said—"Teacher is a philosopher, friend and guide helping the educand to go forward in this own way."

Education of Masses

In the times of Swami Vivekanand, education was not available to the common people. It was confined to the well to do persons only. The poor, the miserable and the lowly placed used to strave and die for hunger. Swamiji yearned to improve the condition of the masses and thus advocated mass education as the only way to achieve any improvement in individual as well as society. Swamiji exhorted his countrymen to know—"I consider that the great national sin is the neglect of the masses, and that is one of the causes of our downfall. No amount of politics would be of any avail until the masses of India are once more well educated, well fed and well cared for."

Q. 20. Discuss the meaning and aims of education as they emerge from Vivekananda's Educational Philosophy.

Ans. Swami Vivekananda was born in 1863 in Calcutta of a famous advocate of Calcutta high court. Narendra Dutta was his childhood name. From the beginning he was interested in religion and philosophy. But, he was totally transformed after a meeting with Rama Krishna Paramhans in 1888. Since then he had been a wandering monk. In 1893 he went to attend a World's Parliament of Religions at Chicago. His views on education are found scattered in his lectures delivered at many places in India and abroad which are, now, available in printed from titled as Collective Works of Swami Vivekananda.

Meaning and Aims of Education. To Vivekananda education was a man-making process which would mean arousing the people to an awareness of their own worth, dignity and responsibility, making them the source of all the strength and sustenance of society, creating a society which will provide a healthy milieu for the development of character and personality of all its children.

Educational philosophy of Vivekananda and the aims of education together with the concept of education are founded on Vedanta philosophy, particularly the Advaita philosophy which says that in the lowest worm as well as in the highest human being the same divine nature is present. "The whole object of Vedanta philosophy is, by constant struggle, to become perfect, to become divine, to reach God and see God". The belief of this philosophy is that every human being is spirit (Atma), the soul which is immortal, evolving up or reverting back from birth to birth and death to death. Swami Vivekananda only reinterpreted the basics of Vaidik philosophy in the context of 20th century man and the society.

Swami Vivekananda had great faith in education to him, this was the basic means for achieving human excellence and solving national problems. He said there are no problems which can not be solved by that magic word "education". He defined education as the "development of faculty, not an accumulation of words". To him education was meant for the training of individuals "to will rightly and efficiently". He further said that the education that does not help the common mass of people to equip themselves for the struggle for existence, which does not bring out strength of character, a spirit of philanthropy, and the courage of a lion is not worth the name. Real education, to him, means that which enables one to stand on his own leg.

Vivekananda stressed the need to educate the millions of our common people to revitalize Indian culture of the day. A nation is advanced in proportion as education and intelligence spread among the masses. National development rests upon the goodness and greatness of men; and goodness and greatness of men are determined largely by education.

Education for "total human development" was the vision of Vivekananda which, he believed, could be achieved by refining and processing of in eternal human energies through the science of man in depth (Adhyatma Vidya). Philosophy, the science, the art and studies of various other fields of knowledge could help nations in achieving this goal. Through education nations have to unfold the humanistic and divine possibilities lying hidden within their people and raise the levels from which their consciousness handles their external, natural and social environment. True education is that which does this.

Vivekananda was deeply spiritual and intensely human. His message is the message of humanism. But his humanism has a deeper content. He said that education which gives us intellectual energy must also give us humanistic impulse and its energy of character. If man's education combines thsese two energy sources he will become tremendously powerful, well educated, full of hope, endowed with a firm mind and will, and strength of muscle and nerve. Vivekananda said "We want our education to turn out millions of such young people enjoying that unit of human bliss."

Although Swami Vivekananda was an idealist and a spiritualist emphasizing realization of divinity in man, yet he was fully aware of the need for national development to be achieved through education.

He stressed education for democracy and said that strengthening of democracy was possible only through education. The strength of a democracy was seen to lie in its alert and patriotic citizens who could be produced and developed through education. All institutional education, socio-political education in a democracy, he held, should therefore be designed to produce citizens who are free, responsible, and politically aware, who feel to belong to the country in which they live, who are sensitive to what happens around them. Education should produce such enlightened democratic citizens. Thus, Vivekananda, emphasized education for democracy and citizenship. He, however, was in favour of creating an ethical basis of democratic politic through education. He stressed the need for developing democratic tolerance in the people and a sense of being truly free which could be fulfilled by properly organized and rightly conducted education.

Thus, Vivekananda's educational philosophy had two major components of aims—one the individual aims and second the social aims. Under individual aims of education he emphasized total human development including physical, mental, social, cultural and spiritual development of the child. He did not leave out even the vocational development aim. In a way he stood as the embodiment of man-making education. Under the social aims of education he stressed education for citizenship and democracy, education for national integration, education for the poor and education for women, education for strengthening the whole society. In a way he stood for nation-building education.

But, these two aspects were not considered by him as separate and independent. He brought a fine systhesis between the individual and the social aims of education when he said "they alone live who live for others; the rest are more dead than alive."

Q. 21. What should be our approach to the curriculum, methods of teaching and the place of the teacher in education in view of the educational philosophy of Vivekananda?

Ans. Vivekananda did not make deliberate and specific suggestions about what subjects should be taught in the school, in what way, and what the place of the teacher should be in education.

However, it is possible to draw inferences about these aspects of education from his philosophy.

APPROACH TO CURRICULUM

Vivekananda held that all knowledge secular or spiritual is in the human mind. Man only discovers it within himself. It is pre-existing and is manifested in man. Knowledge is eternal. Like fire being present in the wood, it is pre-existing in the human mind. It does not come from outside. It is all inside. Man only brings it out, discovers or unveils. Soul is reservoir of all knowledge. Man takes the cover of the soul and finds that all knowledge is there. "All knowledge that the world has ever received comes from mind, the infinite library of the universe is in your mind. The external world is only the suggestion, the occasion which sets you to study your own mind. The falling of an apple gave the suggestion to Newton and he studied his own mind. He rearranged all the previous links of thought in his mind and discovered a new link among them, which we call the law of gravitation. It was not in the apple nor in anything in the centre of the earth." Thus, Vivekananda considered the curriculum just as the massive suggestion, a series of stimulations only to bring out what is there in the mind of the child. All subjects, studies and activities should be treated as a series of stimuli. These, according to him may constitute his cultural heritage found in the form of history, art, poetry, paintings, Vedas,, Upnishadas, sacred books of all religions, language, stories about India's glorious past.

He was an idealist and a spiritualist and, hence, emphasized teaching-learning of such subjects which could be the powerful source of the development of higher values and child's character. But, on the other hand, being a staunch nationalist and an aspirant for nation's economic progress and prosperity emphasized teaching of science and its all branches. He was in favour of Western technology and engineering being taught in Indian institutions as it was necessary, through them to eradicate poverty from the society. He was of the opinion that the schools should produce self-reliant individuals who can earn their living after finishing their education. Hence, it seems, he suggested that vocational courses should also form a part of curriculum crafts may be taught along with other subjects. The curriculum for girls may include "needlecraft, cookery, child-rearing, and other uselful subjects.

Methods of Teaching

With regard to teaching methods Vivekananda was of the view that children should be made to learn themselves. As all knowledge is within them and learning is only a function of their mind, they should only be made active.

The teacher and the curricula should act only as stimuli. This shows that he was against child's cramming of pieces of information. The child should not be a passive recipient of knowledge.

Discussions with the teacher was considered most important a method of teaching-learning by him.

Meditation and concentration were also considered important by him as through them developed the mental powers of the child.

It was also emphasized by him that the teacher should encourage children and develop in them self-confidence for learning.

Thus, along with the teaching the teacher was advised to develop in children those qualities which are necessary for learning. The learner must be able to control the internal and external senses. He should control his lower nature and concentrate on learning.

Q. 22. Discuss, in brief, the contribution of Sri Aurobindo to educational philosophy and educational practice.

Ans. Born in Calcutta and educated in England from the age of 7 years to 21 years Aurobindo was a top notch idealist, a unique philosopher who attempted to synthesize matter and spirit, science of the West and Vadanta of the East. To him the aim of life was to attain "Divinity" through "Integral Yoga" (development of inner self) and "Dharma" (perfection of Outer life). He said that every living being is a form, a part of the Universal Consciousness and one can come into contact with this "true" self through yoga and meditation. His assumption about life was that divinity in potential from is inherent in some amount in every individual. Realization of that is the goal of life to which education should contribute. Following are said to be the contributions of Sri Aurobindo to educational philosopher:

(i) Meaning and Aims of Education. Though not much is spoken about education by Sri Aurobindo, significant ideas may be inferred about education from his philosophy. Since he was a spiritualist who saw everything in the universe rooted in the soul. They wanted education also to be rooted in the soul and "founded on the rock of the Divine", aiming at the purity and spiritualization of human life. Thus the aim of education according to Sri Aurobindo seems to be spiritual development of the individual and the society both. The spiritual aim "regards man not as a mind, a life, and a body, but as an soul seeking for divine fulfilment." Education, to him, must lead the individual to realize that "it is the some supreme force that is active in the universe. He held that physical science being necessarily in complete in the range of its inqudiy can not help much in understanding the occult movements of the Force. Hence, he seems to have been in favour of spiritual education all through the human life.

Spiritual development of the individual was emphasized by Sri Aurobindo. Education could be a tool for this development. Knowledge was unavoidable in this context. But, all these could not be the end in themselves. Education, knowledge and its related aspects were considered only the means for the ultimate fulfilment of the individual. He said emphatically that the individual should learn not to multilate or destroy his "ego", but should learn to expand it out of its limitations and lose it in something greater. Thus, to Aurobindo education is not only for the individual and his developments. Individual development was, perhaps, seen by him as a means of the development of the total mankind. He said that the individual should "learn to fulfil himself in the fulfilment of mankind". He wanted that human society, human friendship, love, affection, fellow feeling all must have spiritual basis, a pure foundation instead of being founded on the ego. This requires, according to Sri Aurobindo, a "transmutation of the very substance of human nature." Education must play an effective role in this transmutation.

"The first natural aim of the individual must be his own inner growth and fullness and its expression in his outer life; but this he can only accomplish through his relations with other individuals" and the humanity at large. This view of Sri Aurobindo emphasized the ideal of human unity. It may be inferred from this that education should aim at the development of the total humanity by developing each individual separately. The individual and the whole mankind can never be separated for achieving this objective.

Sri Aurobindo emphasize five aspects of education each relating to a specific aspect or human personality. These are physical education, education of the vital, mental education psychic and spiritual education. They are complimentary to one another and should be taken up simultaneously. This is known as the principle of integral education.

(ii) Contribution to Human Development. Another contribution of Sri Aurobindo was in the field of human evolution, upward movement of man from matter to spirit. To grow is the inner urge of the Divined in every one. Sri Aurobindo firmly stood for the change in man from the vital and the mental to the spiritual order of life, transference of man's centre of living to a higher consciousness, so as to enable him "to become himself", "to exceed himself", to realize that he is divine potentially. The secret of this evolution is to Sri Aurobindo, is not the intellect and will; rather it is the spirit which is higher then the reason. He calls this development a form of free-self-rule, a development from within rather. Then a repression of his dynamic and vital being from without. Through "Yoga" (Integrated Yoga) of Sri Aurobindo this upward ascent of the individual may be possible. The law for the individual, according to Sri Aurobindo, is to perfect his individuality by free development from within. Education should be made an effective tool for promoting this process of human evolution.

(iii) Contributing to Principles of Teaching. Sri Aurobindo once said that nothing can be taught. This principle implies that learning and knowledge are a function of child's own will and effort. Nothing can be imposed on him from outside. Hence, instead of teaching, it should be child's own self-learning.

He again, suggested that teaching should mean only to provide the most relevant experiences and most conducive environment to the child which can cater to his physical, mental, social, moral and spiritual development.

Freedom to think for himself, freedom to realize what the reality is, freedom to experiment with the Truth should essentially be allowed to the child. This is the greatest principle of teaching-learning.

(iv) Contribution to Curriculum Development. Though specific suggestions about should be included in the curriculum have nowhere learn made by Sri Aurobindo inferences about this can be drawn from what is being followed at the Ashram School at Pondicherry. The curriculum includes physical and health education, teaching of academic subjects, vocational education, cultural activities, psychic and spiritual studies, education for international understanding. The emphasis, however, is on moral and spiritual development.

(v) Views About the Teacher. About the teacher's place in child's education Sri Aurobindo's position was that of a pragmatist. He had to be there very much on the scene but only as a guide, a helper. He is not there to impart knowledge, but only to help the child know how he can perfect his instruments of knowledge. He helps the child in knowing what knowledge is and how he can acquire that.

To sum up, the whole purpose of his teachings was "that man can achieve an extension of consciousness beyond the mental principle he will continue to be trapped by the dilemmas which beset him." Education, to him, must prepare the individual for this transformation. "Integral Yoga" was suggested by him to be the most practical and effective way of child's education for this purpose. It is only in Yoga that the psychological knowledge essential for attaining extension of consciousness and divine life exists.

Q. 23. Discuss Philosophy of Rabindra Nath Tagore. What are its implications in Education?

Ans. Rabindra Nath Tagore was born on 7th May, 1861 at Calcutta. He was the fourteenth of the fifteen children of his parents.

He had unhappy schooling. He composed poems till his death on 7th August, 1941.

He own Nobel Prize in Poetry. He was a great thinker also.

HIS PHILOSOPHY

Tagore as an individualist, naturalist, Idealist, humanist—all these rolled into one. We shall presently examine his philosophy.

1. Tagore as Individualist. Tagore was out and out an individualist. He believed in the right and freedom of the individual to shape his life as the individual desired. Everyone knows that no two individuals are alike—so why bind all of them with the same rope? It was thus in the development of the individual that Tagore wanted the unity of the mankind. With the development of the individual the Creator will be realised by the individual. Some of us are likely to misunderstand Tagore. The development of individual is compatible with the growth of the social units! This is not to be forgotten.

2. Harmony with all Things. The basic principle of the philosophy of Tagore is "harmony with all things," harmony with nature, harmony with human surroundings and harmony in international relations. The highest education is that which does not merely give us information but attains our life in harmony with all existence.

3. Tagore as Naturalist. Tagore's naturalism is based on the Indian belief in fundamental unity of creation and man's kinship with nature. The essential fact is that this world has a vital meaning for us and we have to know it, was connot ignore it, we have to establish a contact with it. This way, we shall be happy. When a man does not realise his kinship with the world, Tagore says, "he lives in a prison house whose walls are alien to him." He loved nature immensely—the moon, the stars, the hills. Nature had deeply moved him—had stirred the poet in him.

4. Tagore as Spiritualist (Spiritualism of Tagore). Tagore's naturalism as described above, paves the way for spiritualism. Music is an aid to the process. He started the Shantiniketan school to give spiritual culture to Indians. His belief was that every Indian should attain spiritual perfection.

5. Tagore's Humanism. According to Dr. R.L. Ahuja, the humanism of Tagore has two aspects: the actuality of individual joy and suffering, and the reality of a world—culture of humanity as its background. He worked unwearingly, to relieve the distress due to flood and famine in his own villages of Bengal. Equally untiringly did he endeavour to spread to the four corners of the world the message of the coming together of the races of mankind, of universal humanity.

(i) Tagore's Conception of God is also Human. To quote him, "He is there where the tiller is tilling the hard ground and where the pathmaker is breaking stone." This is the high point in Tagore's philosophy.

(ii) Tagore's Conception of Universe is Purely Human. All values have their origin in man. Truth is realised through man. Beauty is felt as such by man. He says, "Reality is human and even Truth is human.

6. Tagore and Cultural Cosmopolitanism or Internationalism. Rabindranath Tagore was an internationalist. He looked at the world as a whole. He was for unity of mankind and its brotherhood. He hated distinctions, made on caste, creed, sex. He was for the unity of soul between East and West. Thus in conformity with his culture and philosophy, he advocated a synthesis between East and West, so that the East should give its best to the West and in return assimilate the best that Western civilization can give it. He faced the both—East and West. He was grateful to both—East and West. His University is "Visva Bharti". It is very much international.

7. He belived in spontaneous expression and creativity of the child. This again supports the first point in the philosophy—individualism.

8. Tagore believed in truth; beauty, peace and non-violence. He was also a lover of art, painting and music.

Educational Philosophy of Tagore

His educational philosophy sprang up from two sources:

(a) hatred towards school.

(b) love of nature.

To quote, "Tagore's philosophy of education is therefore, a result of the memory of his school days, when the school resembled an educational factory, lifeless, colourless, dissociated from the context of universe, within base white walls staring like the eye balls of the dead."

His contributors revolve round the two above.

Concept of Education. Education to be real must be of the whole man, of the emotions and the senses as much as of the intellect. Man in the fullness, said Tagore, is not limited by the individual but overflows in his community. And so in his school, alongwith training in individual initiative and self-reliance, equal emphasis was laid on community service.

Nor is education a plant that can be made to grow as an exotic variety in the hot house. If it does not strike roots in the soil and adapt itself to the natural environments, it has little value for the people as a whole.

In short, education according to Tagore meant development of the individual. It meant enrichment of personality and education should be Indian one and not borrowed from the West.

Aims of Education. The aims of education according to Tagore are:

1. Emancipation and Perfection of Man. About this Tagore says, "The highest education is that which does not merely give us information but makes our life in harmony with all existence." He aims at the emancipation of man from all kinds of bondages. He aims at a perfection not only of body or mind but also that of soul. It is the fullest growth and freedom of soul. In order to achieve that aim in his endeavours he makes education as broad based as possible.

2. Moral Development of the child is the second aim of education according to Tagore. Tagore attached for more significance to moral values in education than for mere results of science which produced a system and physical power.

3. Unity of Truth. Another object of education, according to Tagore, was that of giving man the unity of truth. He says that physical, intellectual and spiritual life are one and we must give this idea to the children. This way harmony will prevail and when we do not do this, there is a break between the intellectual, physical and spiritual life.

4. Education should develop international outlook is another aim.

5. Education should be Creative. Tagore does not want education to be mere informative but desires that it should be creative also. He says, "The great use of education is not merely to collect facts, but to know man and to make oneself known to man."

Of course, education is to develop one physically. It should be utilitarian too.

Curriculum. Tagore was a naturalist and also an idealist and he wants things of beauty and nice virtues to be taught in the curriculum. He lays stress on those subjects which make a child full and rich in knowledge. He also wants them to appreciate truth, beauty and goodness. This guides us towards the curriculum. Subjects recommended by him to be taught are: History, geography, nature study, language, science. Activities or finer subjects will include music, art, poetry, dancing, dramatics.

He was very particular about Music and Drama. Music is essence of life and drama releases the children's tensions and anxieties.

Methods of Teaching

Methodology. Rabindranath Tagore does not believe in routine methods of teaching. He broke new ground in the methodology of teaching. His belief is not in routine methods of teaching. Even at the outset, to quote Dr. R.S. Maini, when he opened his new school, he declared that the ordinary routine methods of teaching were not to be expected in his institution. To quote Tagore, "Those who still require an artificial method of feeding in their lessons, who need constant watching and goading from their teachers will find themselves out of place in Vishwa Bharti." He rejected mechanical methods of teaching. These methods were uninspiring. Tagore wanted the boys to progress at their own rate without being goaded by others. Tagore points out, "When I was young I gave up learning and ran away from my lessons. That saved me and I owe all that I possess today to that courageous step taken when I was young. I fled the classes which gave the instructions, but which did not inspire. One thing I have gained, a sensitivity to the touch of life and of nature who speak to me."

What then is his method?

It is clear that his method of teaching is method of freedom in teaching as well as learning and, therefore, does not like the lessons being forced upon the children.

Secondly, it is activity method. He wants teaching-learning to be a joyous adventure, full of thrills, wonders, surprises. It could be Heuristic approach. Let the child find out through activity. It is also sense training through and through. It is also naturalness in teaching. School is not to be a factory and learning has got to be enjoyable.

His approach is Gestalt approach. He believes that children learn their lessons with the aid of their whole body and mind, with all the senses fully active and eager. He thus believes whole methods of teaching rather than in part methods.

He also believers that child's mind is quite sensitive and it will pick up things of its own.

Discipline. Tagore does not want that we should be harsh to children. They should be treated with all symapthy and consideration. Discipline was never, in fact, a serious problem for Tagore.

Tagore says that if the atmosphere is good, discipline problems will not arise. It is only control that breeds in scandals and indiscipline. So where there is freedom—no question of indiscipline. He also believes in self-discipline. He wants children to experiment but not in indisciplined manner.

Tagore recognizes that the boys are full of enthusiasm and when they find opportunities for self-expression, they may be little uncontrollable. He could rather enjoy the children expressing themselves freely in their outbursts of playful spirit which may seem uncontrollable, but not tolerate the repression of the child with no freedom to expand. Therefore, after analysing the psychological cause of indiscipline, he gave the children unrestricted freedom to do whatever they liked. This way, many psychological complexes are eliminated and "naughtiness" seldom occurs.

Further, man should be disciplined through art. Tagore discovered that the secret of maintaining discipline lies in the development of integrated personality. It is basically discipline of freedom.

Role of Teacher. Role of teacher is important. He is the Guru. He is to guide the students. He is to keep them on the track. He is also to keep in contact with them. Teacher is also to remain learner throughout his life. He who fails as a learner, fails as a teacher.

Vishwa Bharti University at Shantiniketan

To give his ideas and ideals a practical shape, Tagore founded what is now known as Vishwa Bharti University at Shantiniketan (Rly. Station Bolpar in West Bengal). It is an international university for Tagore believed in internationalism very much. Vishwa Bharti means a place where universal knowledge is given or gathered. In fact, Vishwa Bharti University has grown out of an ashram founded by father (Maharishi Debendra Nath Tagore of the Brahmo Samaj Fame) of R.N. Tagore in 1863. Since 1921, it is recognised as a university. It is said that India needs more such type of universities.

Why of Shantiniketan? The Vishwa-Bharti University at Shantiniketan was opened with the following aims:

(i) To bring learned people from East and West together.

(ii) To promote internationalism.

(iii) To help Indians create.

Tagore said that our knowledge was second-hand knowledge. There was nothing original in it. At Shantiniketan, all freedom will be given to create.

(iv) Lastly, to provide for the fullest development of man.

The Main Faculties of Vishwa-Bharti University

1. Vidya Bhawan: It is school of research. Here research is carried on in all languages and in Indian Philosophy.
2. Patha Bhawan (Just ordinary school).
3. Teacher's College.
4. Hindi Bhawan.
5. Industrial Training School.
6. Music and Drawing School (Kala Bhawan).

Other Features of Vishwa-Bharti

1. It is located in natural surroundings.
2. Classes are held in the open under the trees.
3. More stess is laid on teaching and learning of music, art, drama, poetry.

4. Unlike Gandhiji, Tagore did not lay much stress on manual work. He stressed on something fine and delicate. He did not reject manual work altogether.
5. Atmosphere is homely, prayers are sung and due stress and place is given to extra curricular activities.
6. Individual attention is paid to each and every student.
7. Students themselves make rules and run the university.

In fact, what Tagore said is fully practised here. Students work hard here.

Q. 24. Explain the Froebel's educational philosophy.

Or

Compare and contrast the educational systems propounded by Rousseaus and Froebel.

Or

State how the Kindergarten of Froebel provides proper environment for all children, adopted to their needs, interests and abilities.

Ans. Froebel (1783—1852) was a great educator of Germany. He also had a neglected childhood and boyhood, and so he had to roam about from place to place, learning, studying and trying various professions. He also started his own schools in Switzerland and Germany but these could be flourish for want of proper finances and because of official restrictions. He, however, brought out his world famous books on education during this period which include "The Education of Man", "Pedagogies of Kindergarten", "Mother Plays and Nursery Songs" and "Education by Development". These books mainly deal with the education of children, below the age of seven years.

1. His Philosophy. Froebel's philosophy is of absolute idealism. He mainly pressed two great things, namely, his 'idea of unity in diversity' and his 'theory of development'.

With regard to the former, he viewed this whole universe as a unity from God—the Absolute. In his book, "The Education of Man", he remarked, "The whole world—the All, the Universe—is a single great organism in which an eternal uniformity manifests itself.

This principle of uniformity expresses itself as much in external nature as in spirit. Life is the union of the spiritual with the material. Without mind of spirit, matter is lifeless, it remains formless, it is mere chaos. Only through the entrance of the spiritual into the material, does the cosmos originate....Every creature, object is matter, informed by spirit....God is the presupposition, the condition of their existence. Without God, they would not exist. God is the only ground of all things. God is the all-comprehending, the all-sustaining. God is the essential nature, the meaning of the world. He further says, "All things have come from the Divine Unity (God) and have their origin in the Divine Unity. The Divine affluence that lives in each thing is the essence of each thing."

With this belief Froebel formulated the principle that there is unity of man, nature and God. Men must be aware of this Absolute Unity of Universe. The real purpose of education was "to expand or develop the life of an individual until it comprehends this existence through participation in all-pervading spiritual activity."

Regarding his theory of development, he said that there is an absolute goal towards which all things are growing. This absolute goal is realized through the presentation of symbols, representing the various aspects of the Absolute. These symbols are called "gifts" which we shall discuss later.

Development can be produced only by the exercise or use of faculty; physical, mental or spiritual. If mind is to be developed, it should be exercised and so is with the development of the body. Effective development is possible only if the exercise arises from the thing's own activity. "Each individual must develop from within, self-active and free, in accordance with the eternal law, because full development comes only by spontaneous self-activity". Froebel advocates balanced and unified development of body, mind and soul.

2. His Concept and Aims of Education. To Froebel, education is growth from within. It is a development by which an individual realizes that he is one unit of the all-encompassing unity. "It is development by which man's life broadens until it has related itself to nature; until it enters sympathetically into all activities of society, until it, participates in the achievements of the race and aspirations of humanity." Education is to unfold the child's innate powers and awaken his spiritual nature so that he may have a spiritual union with God.

Regarding the functions of education, Froebel remarks, "Education should lead and guide man to clearness, concerning himself and in himself, to peace with nature, and to unity with God. It should life him to a knowledge of himself and of mankind, to a knowledge of God and a nature and to the pure and holy life."

As regards the aims of education, Froebel wants all-round development of the individual, so that he may be able to express the spiritual, the Divine, that slumbers in him. Like Rousseau, Froebel education should lead to moral improvement, religious uplift and spiritual insight. Then the child will be able to realise that he is component of all-pervading spirit, which is Absolute Unity.

Finally, education should enable the child to enter sympathetically into all activities of society and participate freely in its achievements and aspirations.

3. Froebel's Kindergarten. Froebel, however, attached great importance to education in the child's early life. He thought that if the education of pre-school years was not properly reformed, no tangible improvement could be made in school education. This led him to establish a school for small children between the ages of three and seven. This school was named "kindergarten" or the *garden of children*. The chief characteristics of the kindergarten are:

(i) Self-Activity. Self-activity is spontaneous in which the child carries out his own impulses and movites. Such activity directs the growth of the child along the lines of racial development. So it merges the individual spirit with the spirit of humanity. Self-activity, in fact, is self-realization through which the child comes to know of his own nature as well as the life around him. Thus, self-activity not only fills the gap between knowledge and action but also gives joy, freedom, contentment and peace of mind. Self-activity is promoted through song, movements and construction.

(ii) Creativeness. Child is creative by nature. If he is given some material, he will at once try to create new forms and combinations with that material. "Since God created man in his own image, man should also create and bring forth like God," Froebel also believes that every man's mind, soul and hand are inseparable, although they are independent parts of him. Mind and soul express themselves through physical activity and expression. It is, therefore, that thinking must express itself in doing, otherwise education will reman unproductive.

(iii) Social Participation. Froebel believes that man is essentially a social animal by nature. It is the primary instinct of man to live in the company of other persons. So unlike Rousseau, he emphasised the social aspect of education and advocated that home, school, church, vocation and the state, should all provide opportunities to children for social participation. By participating in co-operative activities, the child not only receives physical traning but also intellectual, social and moral education.

4. Methods of Teaching in the Kindergarten. Froebel's Kindergarten is a miniature state for children in which they move freely and joyfully, of course, with due consideration for each other. There are no books prescribed. The entire school programme gives training in self-expression through song, movement and construction. Out of these three, the child automatically learns the proper use of language. But these three modes of expression are not generally separated from one another, but they often go together, so that the entire process may become one organic whole. For instance, when a story is told or read, it is expressed in a song, dramatised in movements and gestures and finally illustrated by construction work from blocks, paper, clay, drawing or other material. Through such a procedure, "thoughts are stimulated, imagination vivifies, hands and eyes trained, muscles coordinated, and moral nature strengthened."

5. Teaching Through Songs. In the Kindergarten, education is generally imparted through songs. It is, therefore, that songs are included in the daily school programme. All the songs, selected and included by Froebel, are about the common objects of life. They relate to nursery games and satisfy some physical, intellectual or moral needs of children. These are arranged no accordance with the development of the child. Each such song has three parts *(i)* a motto for the mother's guidance *(ii)* a verse for singing to the child and *(iii)* a picture illustrating the verse. There are in all fifty play songs of this type. Besides these play-songs, Froebel also devised such nursery rhymes, as "Jack and Jill", "Humpty Dumpty" and "Cyndrella". The main aim is to enable the child to use his senses, limbs and muscles and to make him familiar with the objects, around him.

6. Teaching through Gifts and Occupations. Gifts and occupations of Froebel are the most conspicuous contribution to the methodology of nursery education. Gifts are simple educational toys which are presented to the child in a definite order, without charging their forms. The child is given the freedom to handle them in any way, he likes.—While gifts signify the material, occupations represent activities which are suggested by that material and which can be continued with its help. Gifts are in the shape of wooden balls of different colours, wooden spheres, cubes and cylinders of different types and sizes. Additional gifts are in the form of wooden squares, triangles, tables, sticks and rings. Occupations include activities like construction with paper, clay, wood and materials.

It may, however, be noted that gifts and occupations have a definite purpose behind them. They train the senses of sight and touch. They give the idea of size, form and surface. They also develop the number sense and artistic consciousness. In this way they facilitate further instruction in Algebra, Geometry, Trigonometry and Drawing. And as Rusk says, "By his methodological arrangement of the gifts and occupations, Froebel nevertheless founded a new type of educational institution and although his system too readily lent itself to formalism by later generations of teachers who had not the spirit of the natter, it ameliorated the lot of countless children."

7. Teaching Through Play. About play, Froebel remarks, "Play is the characteristic activity of childhood. It is the highest phase of child-development—of human development to this period, for it is self-active representation or the inner-representation of the inner form, inner necessity and impulse. Play is the purest, most spiritual activity of man at this stage and at the same time, typical of human life as a whole—of the inner, natural life in man and all things. It gives, therefore, joy, freedom, contentment, inner and outer rest and peace with the world. It holds the source of all that is good."

It is through play that the child discloses his real self and clearly indicates his interests. So Froebel gives a prominent place to play activities in his Kindergarten system. He has rather based the educational process in early years on play. He utilizes play for cultivating in child the habits of action, feeling and thinking. Courage, instinct and motivation are also developed through play. But Froebel's play activities are all very well-directed and guided by the teacher.

8. Other Subjects of the Curriculum. Besides spontaneous self-activity and play activities, Froebel has also recommended manual work, nature study, natural sciences, languages, art and religious instruction. About the inclusion of manual work, Froebel says, "Scholastic education of our times leads children to indolence and laziness and a vast amount of man-power remains undeveloped and is lost. Manual work is necessary condition of the realisation of pupil's personality; through it, he comes to himself." Nature study creates a sense of wonder and admiration in the minds of children for the work of God and, therefore, he believed that it would result in religious uplift and spiritual insight. Natural sciences including Mathematics, which gives an insight into the laws that govern human life. Languages establish the inner living connection among the diversities of things. Art activities like singing, drawing, painting, clay-modelling, wood-work and leather-work provide the soul with opportunities for expression in those outward forms.

9. Role of the Teacher. Teacher in the Kindergarten acts as a gardener, whose function is to see that young plants (small children) under her care, grow according to their own natural course of development. Froebel compares young growing children with plants and, therefore, he asks the teachers to let the children grow and develop in accordance with their natural endowments. He says, "The tree germ bears within itself the nature of the whole tree. So the development and formation of the whole future life of each is contained in the beginning of its existence."

So the teacher is instructed not to distort the natural endowments, powers and tendencies of children by undue and wilful interference in their activities. The teacher is simply to redirect the child's growth to natural direction when she feels that the child is going astray. According to Froebel, education is controlled development so it is the duty of the teacher to control this process.

10. Discipline. Discipline, according to Froebel, is not a set of rules and regulations, imposed upon children. It is a way of living and doing which gives children a strong will. In the Kindergarten, discipline is of protective and co-operative type. Spontaneous and play activities, games and strories, art and crafts, gifts and occupations, all provide sound physical and mental training to children and teach them discipline.

11. Contribution of Froebel to Educational Theory and Practice. Froebel's Kindergarten system attracted the attention of the educational world to the proper education and training of pre-school-going-age children. Although this stage is the most important stage of child development, yet its education was so far neglected altogether. The Kindergarten system soon became very popular throughout Europe and now it has firmly established itself in the shape of reformed nursery schools throughout the civilized world. Froebel has really shown the right road to further advance. His main contribution to educational theory and practice is as follows:

(i) ***Emphasis on Nursery Education.*** As we have stated above, it was Froebel who greatly emphasised the importance of pre-school education. He often said, "All school education was yet without a proper initial foundation and until the education of the nursery was reformed, nothing solid and worthy could be attained." He was a great lover of young growing children. So he made a minute study of their nature, aptitudes, interests and endowments and then gave to the world a theory and practice of education for the pre-school period, which had very largely been neglected so far.

(ii) ***Respect for the Child's Individuality.*** All the modern educators have a great respect for the child's individuality. They consider the school as a "temple where they are to pay homage to the individuality of the child". But it was Froebel who first realised the value of "discovering and developing individuality by means of initiative, execution and co-operation in the educational process." It is in the wake of Froebel that modern educators recognise the child's individuality and work it out by means of the child's own initiative and effort.

(iii) ***Self-Activity in Education.*** Although the concept of education as a process of learning through self-activity is not original, yet Froebel by making spontaneous inner activity of the child as the very basis of all learning, attached a new value to the native capacities of children in scheme of studies. He said that children were not only receptive of knowledge, they were also very active in the expression. So at the pre-school stage they should be allowed to see, handle, arrange, rearrange, make and unmake things themselves.

(iv) ***Learning through Arts and Crafts.*** Modern progressive schools fully recognise that creativeness is a great insentive to work and to learn. So the child is made to create and construct things with his own labour and effort. In Basic education also a great stress is paid on learning through arts and crafts. It was Froebel, who was an early advocate of the inclusion of manual work in the school curriculum. In "The Education of Man," he says, "Manual work is a necessary condition of the realisation of the child's personality. Through it he come to himself." So he included various arts and crafts like drawing, painting, wood-work, leather-work, clay-modelling, paper-cutting, card-board work and embroidery etc., in pre-school education.

(v) ***Sociological Aspect of Education.*** By laying stress upon activity and social participation and by transforming school into a miniature society where children develop the power of doing things in a social atmosphere, Froebel brought sociological aspect of education into limelight. It is this aspect which is greatly emphasised in modern education. Froebel wanted education to fit the individual for full life within the group, so that he may adjust himself properly to his physical and social environment. For this purpose, he recommends that primary virtues like co-operation, sympathy, fellow-feeling and responsibility be developed in children in the school community. So Froebel is looked upon as the father of sociological trend in education.

(vi) ***Play-Way in Education.*** Modern educators stress that children should be taught through play-way. It was Froebel who based all the early education of the child on play by identifying play and work as one. This doctrine of play forms the centre of mordern education and has had the greatest influence on educational theory and practice. In modern progressive schools, the project and other new methods as well as all types of experimental and creative activities are based on play-way.

(vii) ***Emphasis on Sense-Training.*** For sharpening the intelligence of pupils, Froebel emphasised sense-training, against merely verbal instruction. Since senses are the gateways of learning, their training must form the first step in the child's education. Froebel's gifts and occupations are especially devised for training the senses of children.

(viii) ***Inclusion of Nature Study in Curriculum.*** Froebel gave new stimulus to the aims and methods of teaching Nature Study. He regarded the study of nature as a means of realising the presence of the all-pervading Diving Spirit, in the Natural phenomena. It is, therefore, that he recommends the study of nature page to page, as a living expression of Divine life. He main aim of including this subject in the school curriculum was moral and religious uplift of the child, by coming into contact with nature.

Thus, we can conclude by saying that Froebel's Kindergarten system aims at the complete development of the individual child. "It is by far the most original, attractive and philosophical form of infant development, the world has yet seen." This is the only reason why this system has now spread in all the progressive countries of the world.

Some critics of Froebel say that tiny rots of three or four years cannot undertand his philosophic principle of "Organic Unity". Then symbolism involved in gifts is also too difficult to be understood by immature brains. Furthermore, there is no correlation in the subjects and activities in the Kindergarten system. Everything is taught in isolation. Another defect pointed out by them is that Froebel stresses the sociological aspect to the neglect of the child's individuality.

Q. 25. Discuss the basic principles underlying the Montessori Method of Education. What is the philosophy behind this system?

Or

Make a comparison of the method of infant education, advocated by Froebel with that adopted by Montossori.

Or

Describe the main contributions of Madam Montessori to the science and art of education.

Ans. Madam Maria Montessori (1870—1952) was an Italian lady-doctor, who later became a world famous educationist. She entered the field of education through her interest in mentally deficient children. She studied those childen very intensively and reached the conclusion that mental deficiency was due to dullness of senses and that if their senses could be properly trained, those children could acquire some knowledge. Ans she actually succeeded when she tried the experiment. This lead her to employ that very method on educating normal children and she achieved far better results. Thus, her approach to education is scientific and rational as against that of Froebel's metaphysical. She is the originator of the 'Montessori Method'.

1. Concept and Aims of Education. According to Madam Montessori, "Education is the active help given to the normal expansion of the life of the child." She said that every child is different from others, physically as well as mentally. Each has peculiar powers and endowments. So the child's individuality must not be crushed or suppressed through collective teaching. Each child should be paid individual attention and allowed to progress at his own pace. Education should enable each child to adjust himself to his immediate environment. She wanted that each child should develop from within and not from without. Education should guide the process of unfolding the hidden powers of the child in a way that he becomes what he is destined to become.

2. Principle of Montessori System of Education. The important principles of the Montessori System are:

(a) ***The Principle of Individuality.*** As we have stated above, Montessori believed that each child has got his own peculiar interest, aptitude, capacities and endowments. He can, therefore, develop them in his own peculiar way and at his own rate and speed. Thus, individual differences must be recognised both physically and mentally. She says, "The child is a body which grows and a soul which develops. Such a mysterious thing should neither be marred nor stifled. Educational activities should be so planned that a child's individuality must be unfolded to the full." So she recommends observation of each child, proving him the environment, suited to his individual normal growth and thus educating him individually.

(b) ***The Principle of Sense-Training.*** Like Rousseau and Froebel, Montessori also stresses that senses play a very important part in a child's education because these are the gateways of knowledge. She believed that mental deficiency was due to the dullness of senses, and, therefore, proper training of senses was necessary for acquiring knowledge. From a study of children she realised that senses of children were particularly very active between the ages of three and seven and a such, a lot of learning could take place during this period. She, therefore, devised graded apparatus for providing sensations of weight, colours, sound, touch and temperature etc., and this enabled children to discriminate between different stimuli.

(c) ***The Principle of Self-Education.*** Montessori believed that self-education was the best method by which a child can learn in his own way and of his own speed, without any interference from outside. Knowledge gets a new meaning altogether when it is self-sought and self-caught. She, therefore, stressed that we should never goad on the dull child and check the bright one. In case of error, she recommended the use of Didactic Apparatus, which controls every eorror and helps the child to correct himself automatically. This apparatus enables even dull and defective children to receive education. In fact, it is a substitute for the teacher.

(d) ***The Principle of Liberty.*** For self-education, children should have an atmosphere of freedom and liberty. This principle of liberty has come out of her concept of education as development. It means that as education is concerned with the unfolding of the child's nature, his innate faculties and latent potentialities. The child must be allowed maximum freedom to unfold himself without any check or hindrance. Thus, freedom is the most suitable medium for the development of human personality. So she says, "The school must permit the free, natural manifestation of the child if he is to be studied in a scientific manner. The method of observation is established upon one fundamental basis—the liberty of the pupils in their own spontaneous manifestations which necessitates independence of action on the part of the child.

3. Practical Working of Montessori Method. Froebel called his school "Kindergarten" or "The Children's Garden". Montessori called it "the Children's House". It is the place where children are taught in homely atmosphere, which is very congenial to the development of pupils individuality.

"The children house" is a many-roomed school with a nicely laid-out garden. It has separate rooms for study, lunch, manual work, games, amusement and rest etc. All these rooms are properly equipped and furnished. These are looked after by the children themselves, who not only clean and dust them but also lay the tables and set the chairs. The Montessori school has no fixed time-table because class is only a unit of organisation and not a unit of teaching. There are no punishments and rewards. The child's sense of achievement is the only rewards and self-development is the greatest pleasure. Each child is free to choose his own activities, interest and inclinations.

For children below the age of six, three types of exercises are given in a Montessori School:

(a) ***Exercise for Practical Life.*** In Children's House, pupils are given exercises for practical life. They are taught how to wash their hands and clothes, how to sweep the rooms, dust the furniture, set the tables, clean their nails, brush their teeth, polish their shoes and comb their hair. Exercises are also given to train children in movements, necessary for dressing and under sing themselves. It is, in fact, a training in liberty, for freedom. According to Montessori, does not consist in having others at one's command to perform the ordinary services, but in being able to do these oneself and in being independent of others.

Montessori has also devised certain formal gymnastic exercises, which develop coordinated movements in the child. For these exercises she has also devised special apparatus. Muscular education and training is given through walking, holding objects and hand-work, Rhythmic exercises are also provided. These exercises not only make children healthy but also give them training for practical life.

(b) ***Exercises for Sense-Training.*** Montessori attached more importance to sensory training than learning, thinking or reasoning. She, therefore, devised apparatus for providing exercises in sense-training. The Didactic Apparatus sharpens the pupils' senses and accelerates learning. The varied material includes blocks, cylinders, paper, cabinets; coins, tables, pencils and wools of different colours, boxes, balls, cubes, rods, and water of different temperatures. This material is meant to give perception of size, form, weight, touch, hearing and colour etc. The sense of touch is developed by presenting water at different temperatures to the child. Sand-papers of graded roughness are also used for this purpose. Perception of size is developed through handling a series of wooden cylinders of varying heights and diameters. Series of blocks and rods of graded diameters are also used for this purpose. Sense of hearing is developed through boxes, containing pebbles and other sound-producing material. Sense of weight is cultivated through blocks and tables of wood of varying weights. Colour sense is trained through samples of wood of different colours, arranged and graded according to the depth of colour, as we have already stated under the 'Principle of Self-education'.

(c) ***Didactic Exercises for Teaching 3R's.*** After sensory training, children are taught reading, writing and arithmetic.

In her system writing starts before reading. For this purpose, she depends upon the psychological principle of "Transfer of Training". In her own words, "Preparatory movements could be converted and reduced to a mechanism by means of repeated exercises, not in the work itself, but in that which prepares for it."

(i) Teaching of Writing. The procedure of teaching consists these steps:

(a) ***Recognition of the forms of Letters.*** For this purpose, letters of the alphabet are cut in sand-paper and pasted on cardboard. The children are asked to pass their finger over these letters. In this way they gradually learn to manipulate a pencil. The same exercise is then practises with closed eyes.

(b) ***Learning of Phonetic Sounds.*** While the pupils are tracing out letters, the teacher tells them their sounds, which they are asked to reproduce. This prepares them for reading.

(c) ***Control of Pen.*** Then the pupils are asked to place the metal frame on a piece of paper and draw a line round it with a coloured chalk. The same thing is repeated by placing the metal inset. In their way, two figures are produced on the paper. The intervening figure is then filled up with another piece of chalk. While making upward and downward strokes, the pupils are not allowed to move their pencils or pieces of chalk, outside the outline. Thus they learn the necessary control of pen.

(ii) Teaching of Reading. About reading, Montessori says, "Reading is the interpretation of an idea from the written signs and not merely breaking at print. Until the child receives a transmissions and of ideas from the written word, he does not read." Her material for reading consists of slips of paper or cards, on which words and phrases are written in bold scripts. The child is given a card, containing the name of a familiar object. He tries to utter the sounds and then repeat them faster and faster. When the child is able to pronounce the word correctly, he is asked to place the card under the object, whose name is written on it. Similarly sentences, describing actions or expressing commands are written on paper or card-board. The child selects a card, reads it mentally and does the action contained in it.

(iii) Teaching of Arithmetic. After sufficient writing and reading, Montessori wished that children should be introduced to the four fundamental rules of arithmetic. But there is no originality in the methods of teaching arithmetic as advocated by her. It is the same old procedure of teaching by means of coloured beads, numerical rods, wooden spindles, sand-paper numbers, simple boxes, printed shells and such other attractive material as could be made available. Thus addition, substraction, multiplication and division were taught. The device, generally used, was the 'Long Stair'. Consisting of a set of ten rods, varying in length, from one to ten decimetres. Each rod was divided into a number of parts, painted red and blue respectively.

4. Place of the Teacher. Montessori recommends "consciously controlled and systematically directed" education for young children. This control and direction is to be provided by the teacher, who should be an expert guide and excellent organizer. The teacher in Montessori system is called a "directress", who should be well-versed in child psychology. Montessori says, "The broader the teacher's scientific culture and practice in experimental psychology, the sooner will come for her the marvel of unfolding life and her interest in it. The teacher must allow full freedom to the child and not to interfere with his activity. She is simply to observe and intervene only when absolutely necessary. She is to act as a stage director in this self-educative process. Virtues and not words are the main qualifications of the teacher. She should be partly a scientist, partly a doctor completely religious."

5. Montessori's Contribution. Dr. Maria Montessori's work has considerably influenced modern educational theory and practice, especially in case of children at nursery school stage. Her gospel of love, respect and sympathy for the child has been accepted all over the world. Her system of child education has become so popular that the word "Montessori" became synonymous with "child". All values her system have been absorbed and put into practice by the modern nursery school. Her main contribution is as follows:

(a) ***Scientific Concept of Education.*** Dr. Montessori started life as a doctor and, as such formulated her method of teaching young children in the light of her experience and experiment.

She gave us observation, experimentation and other scientific methods in education. She never insisted on material and method as the last words in the field of child education. She rather gave a scientific approach to education by breaking away from old traditions.

(b) ***Emphasis on Individual Teaching.*** As against collective and class reading, Montessory stresses individual treatment of each child. Because of individual differences in physical and mental make-up, each pupil should be observed, studied and handed in a different manner. Thus, like the modern educators, she made child as the "unit of teaching" in place of class.

(c) ***Psychological Approach to Education.*** Like Froebel, she has also given emphasis on sense training, which is based on psychological principles. By introducing exercises for practical life, she has enabled children to meet everyday situations themselves. She has advocated auto-education in an atmosphere of freedom and in the spirit of play. She has also emphasised child's development from within through his own efforts. All these principles have made *learning* more important than *teaching*, which is universally accepted today.

(d) ***Love and Respect for Small Children.*** Montessori often said that child-education was the most important problem of humanity. It is, therefore, that it should receive the best attention of the Government and the public. In her own words, "The child's soul which is pure and very sensitive, requires our most delicate care". For her "child was God, her school was the temple and deity of the temple was the essence of childhood." The profound love for children, that she had compelled her to travel from one corner of the world to another to start institutions for them, based on her system. She also stayed in India from 1939 to 1951 and conducted a number of training courses for teachers in her system of child education.

(e) ***Learning Through Exercises.*** The most conspicuous contribution of Montessori is the Didactic Apparatus, which she devised for imparting sense training, muscular co-ordination and instruction in 3 R's. It was really a new experiment to teach writing before reading, but the experiment was successful in actual practice.

6. Limitations of her Method. In spite of such a unique contribution to the field of child education, the Montessori Method also suffers from certain limitations. *Firstly*, she has neglected play activities of children, which are most valuable in a child's education. *Secondly* she gives too much stress on Didactic Apparatus. In fact, her entire method rests upon this apparatus. Exercises with this apparatus, as recommended by Montessori, are so limited that a child cannot express himself fully. *Thirdly*, she has neglected social factor in the education of children. She looks only to individual development. This is the reason that in Montessori method there is a little of music songs, dramas, dances and group activities, which are all so essential for social training. *Lastly*, her method is very costly. Teachers of the concept of Montessori are not available to majority of our schools, especially in villages. So this method is not suited to Indian conditions.

6. Special Role of the Teacher. In her system of education there are no *teachers* because they do not teach. They are simply *directors* because they direct and guide the movements of children. They only provide the proper environment and material at the right moment and then observe auto-development of children. Thus, in Montessori system, the child is more active than the teacher. He learns by participating fully in the reading-learning processes. Thus, the teacher has to play a different role altogether. "Instead of facility of speech, she has to acquire the power of silence, instead of teaching, she has to observe, and instead of the proud dignity of one who claims to be infallible, she assumes the venture of humanity."

Montessori Versus Froebel. Both Montessori and Froebel have oganised schemes of educating pre-school age children. Both of them consider education as the process of unfolding. Both lay stress on self-expression and self-activity in an atmosphere of freedom. Both advocate play-way methods of imparting education. Both respect the child's individuality and have profound love for the child. Both are in favour of sense-training for sharpening the intellect of children. Both recommend self-education on the part of the child, with his own efforts, while teacher should be in the background, to play the part of an observer and a guide. Both are idealist thinkers. To Montessori, child was God, while Froebel wished education to lead and guide a man to unity with God.

However, there are also certain points of difference between these two educators. While Froebel's theory is based on metaphysical, assumptions, Montessori's method has a scientific background, and, therefore, her approach is based on practical considerations. *Secondly* in the kindergarten, the children are taught in groups while in the Montessori, individual work and individualism is emphasised. *Thirdly*, kindergarten, social training is one of the basic principles. It is imparted through movement, plays, action songs, group activities and cooperative occupations. *Fourthly*, Froebel advocates a good use of stories, fairy-tales, fables, songs, dramas and poetry for stimulating the imagination of pupils. Montessori neglects altogether the training of imagination in her system. *Fifthly*, in Montessori system, writing, reading and arithmetic are provided, while there is nothing, of the sort in kindergarten. *Sixthly*, in Montessori, sense training is provided through Didactic Apparatus while in kindergarten, it is given through gifts. *Seventhly*, while in Montessori, daily life activities are given prominence, in kindergarten, manual activities like clay-modelling gardening, wood work, paper-cutting, etc. emphasized, *Eighthly*, teacher in a kindergarten school is like a gardener, looking after tender plants. She is to guide children's activities and may interfere when they go a stray. In a Montessori school, the teacher is simply to observe children, handling didactic apparatus. *Lastly*, kindergarten system can be introduced in any infant school without much difficulty as gifts can be got prepared locally according to needs. It can therefore be medium of mass education. On the other hand, the Montessori Method cannot be applied in that Didactic Apparatus. Moreover, teachers with knowledge of experimental psychology and laboratory procedure are not available.

Q. 26. How is Constitution a Source of Values?

Ans. Values are derived from the constitution, culture and religion of a nation and country. Indian values are determined by the Indian constitution, Indian culture and Indian religion.

What is a Constitution? A constitution is a fundamental legal document according to which the government of a country functions. It is the basic law which defines and delimits the main organs of government and their jurisdiction as well as the basic rights of the citizens. A Constitution, thus, is superior to all other laws of the country and no law can be enacted which is not in conformity with the constitution.

A government looks after law and order in a society. It does so by making laws and maintaining order. But a government cannot make laws and administer a country according to its own whims and forces. Every government has to function in conformity with basic law of the land. The Constitution contains those laws which act as the source according to which the rules and regulations of governing a country are framed.

A democratic government is one in which the citizens participate in the functioning of the government, directly or indirectly. It is a government in which the government's powers are limited and clearly spelt out. Conversely, it is also a government under which citizen's rights are also given clearly. Now, how are these limits placed on the activity of the Government? This is done by what is called a constitution.

A Constitution is considered the source of powers and authority of government. It lays down precisely what the powers of a particular government agency are, what this it can, or cannot do. The idea is to minimize confusion and conflict of operation between the various organs of the government. A constitution is concerned with two aspects—the relation between different organs of government; and between the government and the citizens. More than anything else a Constitution is an instrument of controlling the abuse of power by the government. That is why the Constitution is a very important document.

INDIAN CONSTITUTION

Preamble. "We, the people of India, having solemnly resolved to constitute India into a Sovereign Socialist Secular Democratic Republic and to secure to all its citizens: Justice, Social, Economic and Political; Liberty of thought, expression, belief, faith and worship;

Equality of status and of opportunity; and to promote among them all Fraternity assuring the dignity of the individual and unity and integrity of the Nation; in our Constituent Assembly this twenty-sixth day of November, 1949, do hereby adopt, enact and give to ourselves this Constitution".

The Preamble sets out what the objectives of Indian government the kind of value system the Constitution wishes to set up in India. It declares India a sovereign state. Sovereignty means absolute independence, a government which is not controlled by any other power. When India was under British rule, it could not be called a sovereign country. Besides, the Constitution provides for democratic society in India. Here every citizen enjoys equal political rights. The country is governed by the elected representatives of the people. There is no state religion of India. The state does not favour people of any particular religion. The citizens are free to follow and practise the religion of their own choice. The Constitution also declares socialism to be one of the objectives. The ideal of equality remains incomplete if it is restricted only to the political sphere. It must extend to social and economic life too. The Preamble declares India to be a Republic. It means that the haed of the state is not a monarch, but a president indirectly elected by the people.

Secular Government. The government under the Indian Constitution has to be secular. This means that the government must not formulate policies which discriminate between various religious communities which live in India.

Universal Adult Franchise. Indian constitution establishes a system of universal adult franchise. Under this system, every Indian citizen above the age of 18 years has the right to vote and participate in choosing the government.

Building a Just Society. Indian constitution has one part dealing with the fundamental rights and fundamental duties of the citizens. Another part contains provisions which are called directive principles of the state policy. These are instructions which the Constitution gives to the States (the government at both the central and the state level) for achieving a just society in India. Indian Constitution, also, has several provisions which seek to protect the interets of those people who have been traditionally poor and socially deprived, the

Scheduled Castes and Scheduled Tribes and Other Backward Classes of Citizen (OBCs).

Emergency Provisions. Finally, Indian Constitution also foresaw that there could be situations of danger when government could not be run as in ordinary times. To cope with these difficult times, it lays down some emergency provisions. In case of national emergency fundamental right can be restricted.

Fundamental Rights. The Indian Constitution mentions some of the most important rights of the citizens. These are called fundamental rights. These rights, are fundamental in two different ways. First, the Constitution gives us these rights. and guarantees them because it believes that the rights are necessary if citizens are to act properly and live democratically. Secondly, effective procedures for the enforcement of these Fundamental Rights have been guaranteed in the Constitution itself. A citizen has the right to go to the court of law if he/she is denied these rights. The Constitution is their guarantee.

This Constitution guarantees to six fundamental rights. Apart from these rights, the constitution also mentions some 'Directive Prniciples of State Policy', and a list of fundamental duties of Indian citizens.

To understand the fundamental rights it is necessary to know about the directive principles and the fundamental duties.

Indian Constitution guarantees to Indian citizens six fundamental rights. These are:

(i) Right to equality;

(ii) Right to freedom;

(iii) Right against exploitation;

(iv) Right to freedom of religion;

(v) Cultural and educational rights; and

(vi) Right to Constitutional remedies.

Directive Principles of State Policy

The name Directive Principles of State Policy, shows that these are actually directions given by the Constitution of the state to adopt policies, which would help to establish a just society in India. The aim of these instructions is to create proper economic and social conditions in which citizens of India can lead a good life. The idea of democracy need not be only a political idea. It can also be exended to the social and economic life of the people. Some of the principles are in the form of social and economic rights, for example, the right to work, the right to free and compulsory education of children up to the age of 14, right to equal wages for equal work; or the right to an adequate livelihood. These rights are not fully enjoyed by all Indian citizens today. The government has to try to provide conditions under which these can become legal rights of citizens. Unlike fundamental rights the rights mentioned in this part are not justiciable. The Constitution, however, tells the state, *i.e.*, whoever runs the government that it must not forget these long term aims, and it should try to achieve them in reality. If the government makes a law to enforce any of these principles it cannot be questioned in a court of law on the grounds that it violates any of the guaranteed fundamental rights. Indian Constitution mentions that the state should strive to give the right of work, right to education, right to assistance from the government in case a citizen is unemployed, sick, retired, or disabled. It should try to give free legal aid to poor people; so that poor people, who suffer greater injustices in society, can also go to courts and defend their rights.

All the Directive Principles, however, are not concerning social and political rights. Some of them are instructions to government in other matters. For instance, the constitution says that state should try to prevent concentration of wealth, it should ensure that workers in factories can have a share in decision-making. It instructs the state to promote and look after the interests of scheduled castes and tribes. The state is asked to promote cottage industries. It is instructed to protect forests, the wild life of the country and ancient moments.

Fundamental Rights and Directive Principles

Fundamental Rights are justiciable. They can be enforced by courts. The government cannot take away these rights. But the provisions of Directive Principles are not ineffaceable by courts of law. If a citizen is out of work, he cannot get a writ from the courts of law. If a citizen is out of work, he cannot get a writ from the courts of law. If a citizen is out of work, he cannot get a writ from the courts directing the state to give him work. But if he is jailed by the policy without reason, he can go to the courts. And the courts will direct the government to free him. The government must obey courts' order.

Fundamental Duties

Fundamental Duties have been incorporated by the forty-second Amendment of the Constitution, with the purpose of making citizens partriotic, help them to follow a code of conduct that would strengthen the nation, protect its sovereignty and integrity of India.

(i) to defend the country and render national service when required,

(ii) to promote the common brotherhood of all people in India and renounce any practice derogatory to the dignity of women,

(iii) to value and preserve the rich heritage of the nation's composite character,

(iv) to protect and improve natural environment and have compassion for living creatures,

(v) to develop scientific temper, humanism and spirit of inquiry,

(vi) to safeguard public property and abjure volence, and

(vii) to strive for excellence in all spheres of individual and collective activity.

Q. 27. Explain the nature and aims of democratic education.

Or

What should be the national objectives of education in India?

Or

What should be the aims of self education in a democratic country like India?

Ans. The Education Commission (1964-66), said that the development of values such as a scientific temper of mind, tolerance, respect for the culture or other national groups, etc., will enable us to adopt democracy, not only as a form of government, but also as a way of life. This clearly shows that in a democratic country like India the first and the foremost goal of education should be development of democratic values. Indian democracy is made by the people who profess different religions, speak different languages, belong to different races, castes, classes and communities. keeping in mind these and several other characteristics of Indian democracy following should be the most appropriate goals of education:

1. Development of Democratic Values in the People. These values apart from those given above include a spirit of large-hearted tolerance, of mutual give and take, of the appreciation of the ways in which people differ from one another. No education is worthwhile if an educated man does not translate these values in his behaviour and no democracy in that case can survive for long. Hence, education has to make deliberate and planned effort on development of these values in the people.

2. National Integration. It means harmonizing religions, language, caste, class and community differences as they exist in India causing social tensions. It is essential that the people of India in spite of these differences live peacefully and cooperatively and utilize their varied talents for the enrichment of the national life as a whole. Education through various programmes and tailored curricula should make efforts to develop in the people such attitudes and values. It is difficult but possible. These changes include realizing the importance of knowledge and education, learning various social skills, developing scientific attitude, computer literacy considering science and technology important, and so on. The Commission (1964) said that, "The most important tool in the process of modernization is education based on science and technology." But, the Commission, further said "Modernization, if it is to a living force must derive its strength from the strength to spirit."

The Secondary Education Commission (1952-53), has formulated three social or national aims of education. These are:

1. Development of democratic citizenship.

2. Improvement of vocational efficiency.

3. Development of leadership which means training pupils for discharging their duties efficiently.

Ishwar Bhai Patel Committee (1977), also reiterated the importance of development of citizenship as a social or national goal of education.

The Adiseshiah Committee Report (1978) formulated the following goals to be achieved through education:

1. Removal of unemployment.
2. Removal of destitution, *i.e.*, poverty.
3. Rural Development.
4. Adult literacy.

All these foregoing aims are social or national objectives to be achieved through education. They are the tasks completion of which is imperative for strengthening the society. These aims have been discussed here with special reference to India. Hence, they may be considered national goals of education or ducational aims of national development.

Our schools should develop a strong tradition of striving to generate a sense of national unity and national consciousness, in the pupils. This can be achieved as suggested by the National Commission on Education (1964-66), by *(i)* making pupils understand and revaluate our cultural heritage and *(ii)* by the creation of a strong driving faith in the future towards which we aspire. The first may be promoted by well-organized teaching of the language and literature, philosophy, religion and history of India as well as by introducing the students to Indian architecture, sculpture, painting, music, dance and drams. Faith in future would involve an attempt to bring home to the students the principles of the Constitution, the great human values contained in preamble of the constitution.

3. Development of Physical Resources through the modernization of agriculture and rapid industrialization should also be an important aim of education in a democracy like India. To achieve this purpose education should be linked with productivity, science should be made a basic component of education, work-experience should be considered important, vocational education should be expanded, scientific and technical education should be improved.

4. Development of Human Resources should be considered still more crucial an aim of education in Indian democracy. This aim implies changes in the knowledge, skils, interests, and values of the people as a whole. In a democracy the individual is an end in himself and the primary purpose of education should be to provide him with the widest opportunity to develop his protentialities to the full, through social reorganization and empahsis on social perspectives. Cultivation of essential values in the people, development of dedicated and competent leadership and educated electorate are essential for strengthening democracy. Education, therefore, must develop such human resources needed for the defence of Indian democracy.

5. Development of Social, Moral and Spiritual Values. In a democratic country like India it is inevitable to inculcate social, moral and spiritual values in the people. Knowledge in the absence of essential values may be dangerous. The success of democracy, its strength and stability are contingent upon people's developed sense of social reponsibility and a keener appreciation of moral and spiritual values. Hence, education must make efforts on developing these values in the people. Nehru in his Azad Memorial Lectures (ICCR, 1962) said "Material riches without toleration and compassion and wisdom may well turn to dust and ashes."

Q. 28. How can education be used to establish democracy in India? Discuss the views of secondary education commission and Indian universities commission in this connection.

Or

Discuss the provisions of Education in Indian Cosntitution.

Ans. EDUCATION FOR DEMOCRACY IN INDIA

Democracy in India. India is not merely a modern democratic state but a country which is traditionally inclined towards democracy. A democratic constitution was adpoted after independence. In 1938, Jawahar Lal Nehru had said, "The Indian Constitution seeks to establish a popular government in the country on the basis of democratic principles outlined earlier. For this every citizen must participate in the administration, through his right to vote and to be elected. Every individual is guaranteed and given equal status and opportunity, because no one is discriminated against on the basis of religion, race, caste, cummunity, sex, or on any other grounds. The government is responsible to the people and its elected representatives."

Provisions in Indian Constitution. In order to achieve this objective of democracy, education is as necessary in India as anywhere else, a truth which the Indian people have been quick to realise. In the words of F.W. Themes, "Education is no exotic in India. There has been no country where the love of learning had so early an origin or has exercised so lasting and powerful an influence. From the simple poet of the Vadic age to the Bengali philosopher of the present day there has been an uninterrupted succession of teachers and scholars." Not only did the Indian constitution accept the ideals of democracy, it considered education the prime responsibility of the state. In Article 45 of the Constitution it has been stated that every state must arrange for the provision of free and compulsory education to all children upto the age of 14, within ten years of the date of inception of the Constitution. After the achievement of independence, a new phase began in the history of education. Articles 29 and 30 of the constitution give fundamental rights to every individual in connection with education and cultural development. According to article 20, every Indian national living in any part of India will have the right to maintain his own specific language, script and his culture. No person can be refused right of admission to any educational institution, established by the state, by reason of religion, race, caste, language or any other similar consideration. According to article 30, every minority community will have the right to establish and maintain educational institutions of its own choice, irrespective of whether the minority is a linguistic or religious one. The state will also not refuse aid to any sucy institution created by a religious or linguistic minority. Articles 45 and 46 determine the policy for education as part and parcel of the directive principles. According to article 45, the state will make every effort to provide free and compulsory education, within ten years, to every child below the age of 14. According to article 46, the stage will pay special attention to the educational and economic interests of all backward classes, especially the scheduled castes and scheduled tribes. It also entrusts the state with the duty of protecting such tribes from social injustice and exploitation of every kind. The Indian Constitution laid the foundation for a federal government in which the functions of the state government have some duties with respect to education. It has been realised that there must be coordination between the central and state authority on education for a balanced development of the country. The modern Indian state is a welfare state whose objective is the complete development of its people. This welfare can be achieved only through education. Little surprise therefore if all the leaders of the nation stress the importance of education as a first step to improving the future of the nation.

VIEWS OF SECONDARY EDUCATION COMMISSION

The democratic ideals which the existing educational policy is trying to achieve have been outlined most precisely in the Secondary Education Commission's explanation of the objectives of education:

1. Development of Democratic Citizenship. The success of democracy depends largely upon the people's awareness of their rights and duties and the extent to which people fulfil their responsibilities. Education aims at developing this ability in the people, because education teaches the man to think and distinguish between right and wrong. He can understand social, economic and political issues, and reflect on the possibility of solving such problems. He can decide upon the political party or the leadership which should be entrusted with the task of forming a government and undertaking administration. He does this after thinking on the problems facing the country and considering the ability of each group or leader to face such problems. He can express his ideas and suggestion through lectures, essays, articles, etc. He can organize new movements or constitute various kinds of committees to solve the problems facing the country. It is the duty of the state to insist upon a syllabus which can be expected to generate such democratic awareness among the children being educated.

2. Training in Skilful Living. Democracy can be said to have succeeded only if it translate the democratic ideals to its society. And, for this, socialization of the individual through education is essential. It is desirable to develop such social qualities as collective feeling, cooperation, discipline, tolerance, sympathy, brotherhood, etc., in the individual. Education must also aim to create faith in social justice and the willingness to rebel against injustice. Education helps people in adjusting to each other, and the educated individual is generally tolerant and liberal. Although he may differ from other prople in their opinions, he has the ability to adjust to such people because he can understand their attitudes. Hence, education is the only means of removing the obstacles in the path of democracy and also of achieving some adjustment between people who differ from each other in respect of language, race, caste, religion, sixe, etc.

3. Development Vocational Skill. The Secondary Education Commission has pointed out that another aim of education is to develop some vocational skill in the educand. No nation can progress in the absence of economic progress. The first duty of the state is to provide a system and means of education which imparts some vocational and professional skills to the educands so that they can earn their livelihood at the same time as they contribute to the nation's economic growth. The country urgently needs skilled craftsmen, engineers, doctors, teachers and administrators. For this, specialized colleges are required. Every child should be given the right to choose a profession of his own liking, and he should be given the opportunity to acquire the highest training and education in this profession.

4. Development of Personality. The success of a democratic society also depends upon whether mature men and women form the majority or minority in its population. Democracy can succeed only if most of its members have developed mature personalities, because a mature person has gone through physical, mental, social, ethical and spiritual development. Hence, education should aim at the development of all aspects of the educands' personality through various kinds of training. Keeping this in view, most schools and colleges now provide many kinds of extra curricular training, which supplements all that is taught as part of curriculum.

5. Developing Leadership. The success of a democracy depends upon the capabilities of the leadership. The democratic government is a decentralized government, and for that reason it requires skilled leadership at many different levels of administration. The democratic government is run by the elected representatives of the people, who should be possessed of special qualities. Expert leadership is required for development and progress in every sphere—political, social, economic, artistic, scientific and cultural. Education should aim at evolving such leadership, because without doing this education cannot make any real contribution to democracy, for then it is leaving unfulfilled one of its important responsibilities. The element of leadership can be encouraged through many kinds of curricular and extra curricular activities in schools and colleges.

Apart from these objectives of education laid down specifically by the Secondary Education Commission, it is desirable to reflect upon some other objectives, which have significance in view of the fact that India is a democracy. In fact, the aims of education vary a little bit with the level of education—the primary, secondary and university education—a fact which has been recognised by the different education commissions established from time to time. The aim of education, at the primary level, is to develop the child's mind by presenting the fundamental elements in the various areas of knowledge, and also to give him an opportunity to develop all his abilities—physical, mental, moral, motor, creative imagination, etc. At this stage attention should be paid to physical development no less than mental development, but attention must also be paid to the burden such an education places on the child. The education imparted should not become a burden.

At the secondary level, attention should be focused on discovering the interests and abilities of every adolescent, and then developing such abilities. Education should be concerned not merely with the general welfare of society but also with the self-realization and personal development of each individual.

Recommendations of Indian Universities Commission. The Indian Universities Commission has laid down the following objectives of university education in the country:

1. Providing leadership in politics, administration, professions, industry and commerce;
2. Training intellectual leaders of culture and creating inventors;
3. Causing spiritual development in the educand;
4. Protecting the culture and civilization of the country and instilling the youth with the ideals of this culture; and
5. Discovering the inherent qualities of individuals and developing them through training.

Q. 29. What is the need for Democratization of Education? Explain impact of Democracy in Education.

Ans. It is only in recent times that democratic principles and values have entered the field of education. The credit of this revolutionary change goes to the American educationist Johy Dewey. He emphasized that in a democratic society, educational planning should be done in such a way that each individual member is made capable to shoulder social responsibilities efficiently and discharge them effectively and profitably. According to him, edcation should inculcate in the individuals the sense to welcome needful changes in the social structure and reoriented one's behaviour smoothly to the ever changing social milieu. The impact of this philosophy has brought about revolutionary changes in the thinking about educational planning and schemes of public education have begun to emphasize the provisions of the education of the masses so that general people become conscious about their rights and duties, about their individual and social responsibilities and about their national and international obligation. As the democratic rule is by the people for the people, they should be made to understand their obligations and to discharge their duties intelligently. Hence, in all democratically ruled countries, more and more emphasis is being laid upon free, compulsory and universal education.

IMPACT OF DEMOCRACY ON EDUCATION

The impact of democratic tendency on education is evident on the working of the following elements:

1. Provision of Equal Oportunities and Recognition of Individual Differences. In a democratic set up, each child is a sacred and valuable entity of society. As such, equal opportunities are made available to one and all for their fullest development. In this connection the principle of individual differences is given proper recognition and therefore each child receive proper support according to his interests, aptitudes and capacities to develop his individuality to the fullest extent.

2. Universal and Compulsory Education. In democracy, the reigns of government remain in the hands of the people. Hence, common people must be so educated that they develop themselves as responsible and dynamic citizens conscious of their rights and duties, fully conversant with their national and international obligations, well aware with the government procedures anti-administration processes.

3. Provision of Adult Education. Under the influence of democratic tendency, in different countries, emphasis is being laid upon adult education, women education and education of the mentally retorted and physically handicapped. Schemes are under operation in our country also for the effective education of the adults who constitute a bulk of our entire population. Night-schools, short-term-courses, one day schools and the schemes are being launched to solve this stupendous problem.

4. Free Education. The principle of universal and compulsory education involves free education to all irrespective of their social or monetary status. Hence, education is now regarded as the birth right of each child irrespective of colour, caste, creed and sex. In almost all democratic countries, education has been made free up to a certain standard. In addition, education of the physically and mentally handicapped is also receiving proper and increasingly effective attention.

5. Child Centred Education. Democratic way of thinking emphasizes the importance of each child as sacred individuality. Hence, educational schemes and plans are so structured that each child receives full attention and full facilities to develop his individuality to the fullest extent.

6. Methods of Teaching. Under the impact of democratic tendency, method of teaching are undergoing revolutionary changes. Old, traditional and mass education methods are being gradually replaced by individual attention methods. Nothing is now enforce or thrust in by force. Self-learning devices are encouraged and such methods are promoted which motivate children to pay attention and learn by their own efforts. Such wholesome and welcome environment is created wherein children search for truth, gain knowledge by their own efforts and learn by their own experience.

7. Social Activities. Bookish and academic activities are not over-emphasized in schools now-a-days. Proper attention is paid to social, cultural and co-curricular activities, so that children develop in a wholesome way and gain more and more social experience.

8. Importance of Individual Attention. As discussed above, each child receives individual attention. His family background, his own interests, likes and dislikes, his needs and capacities are fully taken care off in all plans of educational development, the purpose being to achieve the maximum development of personality.

9. Student Unions. Student unions and student welfare associations are formed in institutions to promote student welfare in all spheres with the aim of achieving balanced, dynamic, efficient and socially motivated personalities.

10. School Administration. To inculcate in children the sense of self-discipline and self-administration, their association with school administration is being welcomed. Such schemes are being formulated in various institutions where student participation in actual educational and school administration is a fact.

11. Respect of Teacher's Personality. Democratic philosophy respects teacher as a very dynamic and effective agency of social change for social progress. Thus, teachers are now made to participate more and more in curriculum construction and educational planning. Side by side, they are allowed to experiment freely in respect to methods, techniques and devices of teaching as well as materials which aid teaching prcedures and processes. Not only this, more and more plans are being laid and worked out for increasing the professional competency of teachers.

12. Intelligence Tests. Schemes of intelligence tests are under operation in various institutions all over the world to evaluate the mental capacity, growth and achievement of children. Diagnostic tests are proving very useful for this purpose.

13. Physical Health of Children. To promote physical well-being of children, facilities for games and sports, gymanzia, medical tests and medical help are being provided freely and on an increasing scale. Medical check up, advice and medicines are now provided to the needy.

14. Co-operation between all Agencies of Education. In a democratic set up, all the agencies of education co-operate actively for the development of children. Hence, under the influence of democratic tendency, schemes are being formulated now-a-days to establish co-operation between all the agencies of education namely—family, school, community, church and state.

15. School. School is now regarded as a centre of promoting national consciousness and international understanding. Education for dynamic citizenship is associated with education for national and international understanding, amity and fellow-feeling. Thus, school is now regarded as a miniature of society.

Q. 30. Discuss the meaning and scope of Sociology of Education.

Or

What is meant by sociological tendencies in education? How does it influence the various aspects of education?

Ans. Dualism has always been a popular view with the philosophers. It is quite natural also, for we always live in two worlds, namely, the world of things and the world of our own inner experience. Some philosophers have considered the inner world and the individual more important, while a few others have stressed the world outside the individual, *i.e.*, the environment or the society. Rousseau, for example, focussed on the individual while Dewey emphasized the social setting in which the individual has to live. Rousseau was the fore-runner of psychological tendencies in education. Dewey may be considered a pioneer to shift the emphasis to sociological tendency in education. He maintained that philosophy must be described in terms of the problems with which it deals and which originate in the conflicts and difficulties of social life. He defined the problem of education as "...the harmonizing of individual traits with social ends and values." He considered education a difficult process because effective coordination of psychological make-up of the individual with the demands of the social environment was, to him, extremely difficult. He lamented that such a coordination in the schools of his time was ignored. It was held by him that the process of mental development is essentially a social process. He said that "man is a social being who attains mind and self only when nourished in social experience." By "social" he meant individual's social adjustment to the group or to contemporary social realities. The business of education, as emphasized by Dewey, was "habituation of an individual to social control, sub-ordination of natural powers to social rules." Thus, social efficiency aim of education was emphasized which appealed to many people of his times as it was more in line with democratic thinking of nineteenth century. The great social change emerging from the nineteenth century industrial revolution in Europe may also be considered responsible for the origin and development of sociological tendency in education. The pragmatic philosophy of education also emphasized the social aspect of education for it believed that socially oriented minds alone could forge a better state of society, one in which human wants are fully satisfied.

Thus, the sociological tendency has its origin in the philosophy of Dewey, the pragmatists and the nineteenth century social change resulting from the industrial revolution and acceptance of democracy as a form of government and a way of life. The tendency emphasized the social aim of education. Its watch words are "education for social service" which means that education should be directed in a broader more elastic way to the good of the community. It emphasizes that the individual must be trained to be unselfish, to put the needs and desires of others before his own. Prof. Bagley in America said that, "Social efficiency is the norm against which educational practice must be judged." He, further, emphasized that social efficiency aim of education ought to have the position of primacy in a rational theory of education. The activities of the individual should be valued with reference to his social obligations.

The sociological tendency in education focussed on the interaction between the individual and the social milieu in which he lives. Education, according to this tendency, was defined as reorganization and reconstruction of this interaction so that the child learns what is socially desirable. Dewey said that education should develop individual's ability to "share in the experinces of others and thus, widen the individual consciousness to that of the race." Emergence of a new branch of knowledge known as sociology in the first half of the nineteenth·century contributed significantly to this aspect of the sociological tendency in education. Study of human relations in the schools was emphasized. Scientific study of the process of interaction of persons was considered important. Study of education in relation to social needs and social change was emphasized. Several new trends emerged in the field of education as a result of sociological tendency in education. The relationship between the school and the society, relationship between the school climate and education of the pupils, education as an instrument of social change, influence of various social groups on education, education as related to social mobility of the people in the society, etc., many issues figured for discussion and for being resolved. The aims, content, method and other aspects of education were also affected by this tendency.

The Relationship between Education and Society. Sociological tendency in education made several thinkers in the field of education to discuss and classify the relationships between education and society. Education was considered as a sub-system of the larger society. The character of society and social changes taking place must influence the system of education also. It was emphasized that these social changes and emerging social needs must be rejected in the theory and practice of education also. This point was very mush emphasized by Dewey in his book, "The School and Society" wherein he said that while proposing to bring about a change in education the social point of new should always be kept in mind, otherwise it will be considered merely an arbitrary fad. "Education for the society" emerged as the focus of educational thought.

Education and Politics. The relationship between education and politics also was emphasized as an aspect of sociological tendency in education. Education for democracy was, particular emphasized. Democratic aims of education, democratic methods of teaching-learning, democratic organization: of the classroom and the school, democratic discipline, etc., were several new concepts which were extensively discussed.

Education and Economic Factors. Sociological tendency in education forced the educational thinkers to analyse and see how economic factors affect education. It was realized that economic factors are important constraints of educational activities. How they affect education and how education affects the economy of the society were some of the themes which emerged for discussion. A new kind of thinking began in the field of education.

Cultural Aim of Education. The sociological tendency in education resulted into a greater stress on cultural aim of education. It was emphasized that education help in the transmission of cultural heritage.

The Curriculum. Sociological tendency in education resulted into a ranged approach to curriculum construction. These views took the form of sociological principles of curriculum construction. It was emphasized that the curriculum should conform to the conditions, problems and needs of the society. A functional curriculum which could serve the needs of the society was said to be the need of the hour, curriculum for international understanding, curriculum for citizenship, curriculum for vocation, etc., were the ideas about curriculum which gained popularity as a result of sociological tendency in education.

The Method of Teaching. In the context of method of teaching, the sociological tendency resulted into considering the classroom and the school as the society-in-miniature. Hence, it was emphasized that teaching should take help of the principles of group dynamics. Group methods of teaching, group discussions, social interactions, group planning, group activities, project method, etc., were considered important.

Thus, sociological tendency in education tried to approach education, its purposes, methods, content and other aspects from the point of view of the society and sociological forces working within it.

Q. 31. Analyses the impact of democracy on various aspects of Education.

Ans. IMPACT OF DEMOCRACY ON VARIOUS ASPECTS OF EDUCATION

In the following lines we are throwing light on the various aspects of education in a democratic set up:

Democracy and Aims of Education. In a democracy, the aims of education are as under:

1. Development of Democratic Values. The success of democracy does not depend upon Legislative buildings and massive structures of Parliament houses, but it rests upon the quality of the citizens devoted to democratic values. As such, the prime aim of democratic education is to promote in children a sense of devotion to democratic values. No book teaching can achieve this aim unless children are provided with opportunities to practise democratic norms and standards of behaviour. In fact, a child learns to live democratically by living democratically.

2. Development of Vocational Efficiency. For the success of a democratic set-up, economic contentment of citizens is a must. An indigent and poor person can be a victim of all kinds of allurements, inducements and exploitation by the resourceful and the powerful. Hence, the third aim of democratic education is to develop vocational efficiency in children, so that they are able to become self-reliant and serve the nation as much as possible.

3. Development of Interests in Children. The third aim of democratic education is to develop useful and worthy interests in children. Interests form character and enrich a child's life. Hence, the famous educationist, Herbart has insisted upon the fullest development of diverse interests. To achieve this aim, children should be provided with various and varied opportunities to participate in diverse activities and programmes in all fields of human life. If a large number of worthy interests are developed in children, they will be happy, well-balanced and efficient as citizens.

4. Development of Thinking Power. The fourth aim of democratic education is to develop thinking power of children. In fact, children of today are citizens of tomorrow when they will be confronted with all kinds of problems in political, social and economic fields. Education should develop in children the capacity to think clearly and take decisions confidently.

5. Development of Social Outlook. Development of social outlook is the sixth important aim of democratic education. This aim emphasizes upon, the fact that children should be imbued with the sense that they are the integral parts of society, the welfare of which should be their ideal. Not only this, they should learn to live and die for the nation. Education should develop this sense of service and sacrifice making them learn the sacredness of obligations and duties for the welfare of the nation to which they belong.

6. Development of Sound Habits. The fifth aim of democratic education is to develop sound habits in children. Habits are the sources of good or bad conduct. Hence, education should develop good habits in children from the very beginning to make democracy a successful venture.

7. Development of Leadership. The seventh aim of democrat education is to develop leadership qualities in children. For this, education should instil in children the leadership qualities from the very beginning. They are the future citizens who will have to shoulder the multifarious duties and reponsibilities of their nation in all areas. Their character, strength of will, insight, courage of convictions, clarity of thinking and decision-making will be the foundations on which the national edifice will go up and up.

8. Development of Harmonious Personality—The eighth aim of democratic education is to develop the individuality of a child into balanced and harmonious personality. In the modern world of strife, stress and strain a balance and harmonious personality can only seek and find adjustment with the surroundings. Hence, education should develop character, dynamism ans social outlook for this purpose.

9. Development of National and International Feelings. For the success of democracy, the ninth aim of democratic education is to develop in children the sense of ardent nationalism and devotion to international brotherhood. It may be noted that the two are not contradictory. On the other hand, they are mutually complementary and supplementary. In fact a nation cannot exist in isolation. All the nations of the world are mutually inter-dependent. Hence, education should foster the sense of inter-dependence, international good-will and fellow-feeling.

10. Training for Citizenship. Democratic education should impart of children training in dynamic and healthy citizenship. For this, education should instil in children—*(1)* Capacity to understand and solve the diverse problems of the country, *(2)* Capacity to distinguish between propaganda and reality, *(3)* Capacity to think and decide about issues, *(4)* Economic efficiency, *(5)* Consciousness of one's rights and duties, *(6)* Capacity to shoulder responsibility, *(7)* Development of diverse interests, *(8)* Sense of service and sacrifice,

(9) Good use of leisure hour, *(10)* Development of human qualities as love, sympathy, fellow feeling, co-operation, sense of nationalism and internationalism, *(11)* Healthy and dynamic outlook about problems, good behaviour and respect for moral values.

Curriculum. In a democratic country curriculum construction is done with the purpose of realizing democratic values. Hence, those subjects, activities and programmes are included in the curriculum which instil and promote healthy attitudes, dynamic habits, insight and understanding so that children are able to lead successful lives as happy citizens. The bases of such a curriculum are as under:

1. Diversified. Democratic curriculum is divisively to suit the needs of all children with basic differences of interests and aptitudes. Class-room activities, games, sports and other co-curricular activities bear an imprint of variety to suit various needs of children.

2. Achievement of Social Aims. While constructing a democratic curriculum emphasis is laid upon social aims and values. In other words, development of social sense in children is kept in view. As such, student activities, associations, corporate programmes and fellowship programes are liberally provided.

3. Emphasis on Local Needs. Democratic curriculum is constructed on the basis of local needs and available resources. It may be changed according to the needs of time, place and local requirements.

4. Flexibility. Democratic curriculum is flexible to accommodate various needs and requirements which are in a state of constant change. A portion of it is made compulsory in the form of co-curriculum and diversified subjects are made optional for children to choose according to their interests and aptitudes.

5. Emphasis of Activity. Democratic curriculum is laid on the foundation of an important principle known as learning by doing. It is through practical work and activities that development of mind and intelligence is fostered. Instead of enforcing and compelling cut and dried ready-made concepts into the minds of children, they are allowed to search for truth through their own experiments and experiences. This is real learning. It develops confidence, foresight and far-sight, the three important ingredients of wisdom.

6. Provision of Vocational Needs. Democratic curriculum very well meets the needs of vocations, professions and economic requirements of a region or the whole country. This enplanes the country to develop economically.

7. Place for Leisure Hour Activities. Democratic curriculum also contains such relevant and useful activities in which an individual can profitable indulge leisure time. Thus, it ensures the total development of personality.

Discipline. Discipline is the corner-stone of democracy. But democratic discipline does not believe in respiration or compulsion. It advocates self-discipline. In schools where democratic set up is in vogue, the following ideas are emphasized for fostering and developing self-discipline:

1. In democratic schools the headmasters, the teachers and the administrators are not despots or police officers. Instead, they are friends, philosophers and guides. Through their friendly and affectionate behaviour, they mould the behaviour of children and thus promote self-discipline by creating a congenial and cordial atmosphere.

2. In democratic schools, such activities and programmes are structured which cater to the interests and needs of children. This develops self-discipline among children.

3. In the administration of a democratic school, children participate actively, discuss problems and decide them freely. They, thus, feel their integral and intimate relationship with the school and feel internal kinship with its progress and development.

4. In democratic schools full freedom is given and opportunities provided for each child to develop his individuality to the fullest extent. Hence, no problem of indiscipline arises at any time.

5. In democratic schools, students unions, students parliaments and all kinds of student organizations are encouraged for the benefit and development of children. They learn self-government, co-operation, fellow-feeling and other human qualities together with qualities of self-discipline and leadership.

6. In democratic schools, the sense of rights and duties is instilled in children. They, thus learn self-control through social

service and social consciousness. Nothing is imposed on them from above. They discuss, decide and carry out the decision with perfect co-operation and cordiality.

Teacher. In a democratic set up a teacher is a friend, philosopher and guide. He often works as a social reformer. Such teachers process the following qualities:

1. The teacher is devoted whole hearted to the ideals and values of democracy. Hence, he tries to impart the same faith to children through gently persuasion and affectionate rapport.

2. The teacher regards every child as a sacred legacy to society. Hence, believing in the principle of individual differences he allows every child to develop his individuality to the fullest extent according to his interests, aptitudes and capacities.

3. The teacher tries to solicit maximum co-operation from the guardians, parents and other social agencies for the greatest possible development of children as dynamic and socially oriented citizens of the future.

4. In a democratic set up, a teacher lays greater stress upon environment rather than on heredity. Hence, he tries to structure such a wholesome environment for the child that fullest development is naturally achieved.

5. In a democratic set up, each teacher is fully conscious of his rights and duties towards society. Hence, he tries to instil the same sense of responsibility in children and also to make them capable and intelligent citizens of tomorrow.

6. Each teacher is well-versed in knowledge of his subject and has full academic competency to make children develop physically, mentally, morally and spiritually so that they are able to shoulder national and even international responsibilities in times to come.

Q. 32. Explain Socialization. How is it realised in family and school? Discuss the role of teachers in the process.

Ans. Socialization is a social process, and it has been variously defined. Some of these definitions are the following:

V.V. Akolkar. "The process of adoption by the individual of the conventional patterns of behaviour is described as his socialization, because it occurs on account of his integration with others and his expression of the culture which operates through them."

E.A. Ross. "The development of we feeling in association and the growth in their capacity and will to act together."

E.S. Bogardus. Socialization is, "The process whereby persons learn to behave dependably together on behalf of human welfare and in so doing experience social self-control, social responsibility and balanced personality.

Socialization then, is process by means of which the individual learns to behave according to the social traditions and conventions. The human child has a remarkable capacity to imitate others, and hence he develops according to the environment into which he is born. Man, being a social animal, tries to win the appreciation of the group in which he lives and hence he naturally tries to imitate the culture of that group. It is through socialization that he is transformed from the animal into the human, and it is socialization which gives—him a balanced personality. The social aspects of the personality is no less inportant than the individual aspect. Socialization teaches him to retain control over himself in the interest of others. It evolves a we feeling or community feeling in him and there by invests him with a sense of responsibility.

The Process of Socialization

Individuals influence each other by imitation, suggestion and sympathy, besides which the process of socialization is furthered by many social institutions. Man is the product of many social processes such as praise and blame, cooperation and conflict, submission and ascendancy, and these forces create the individual's personality. Education is the most potent agency of socialization available to society.

FACTORS OF SOCIALIZATION

1. Socialization in the Family. The family plays a very significant part in the individual's socialization because the child spends his early formative years in the home. He learns much by observing the people around him, by imitating them, by indulging in activities which win their approval and avoiding those which bring their disapproval and immediate punishment. It is the family environment which can create good habits in him, because the child's moral code is conditioned by the system of reward and punishment which prevails in the family. And, it is also in the family that criminal tendencies are first generated. In their book *New Light on Delinquency and its Treament*, Healey and Bronner have pointed out that juvenile delinquents are frequently found in those families in which the fulfilment of social relationships has been hindered at one time or the other. Freud and other psychoanalysts have demonstrated that the child remains throughout life whatever he is made out to be in the family. In his *"Psycholocial Factors in Marial Happiness"*, Termann has theorised that only those individuals can enjoy marital bliss whose own parents had been happy and contended. In the preface to *'Women of the Street'*, a depth study of the prostitutes of London, it has been commented that the problem of prostitution is, in reality, a problem of the relationship between the children and parents.

The family plays a very significant, perhaps the most significant role in the individual's development. Freud and other psychoanalysts believe that the impressions made upon the child's mind at home determine the child's personality as an adult, for in childhood, the child's mind is very flexible and susceptible to any influence. The parents' love for the child makes a deep impression on him. And, although it is true that exclusive love and affection have detrimental effects, the complete absence of affection creates complexes in the child's mind, which later disbalance his personality. His personality is also influenced greatly by the behaviour of his brothers and sisters towards him. Adler, the famous psycholgist, has stressed the fact that the order of the birth of children in the family distinctly and separately influences the personality of each child. The eldest child's mental make up differs from that of the last. Besides, all great thinkers and philosophers have admitted the importance of their mother's love as far as their personality development is concerned. In India, people often gauge the personality of a young marriageable girl by observing her mother. And, as far as marriages are concerned, more attention is paid to the prospective bridegroom's parentage than to his own personality, for the family makes a lot of difference.

The family's influence does not end with the individual's entrance into adolescence, for even then the influence continues.

Complete absence of control often results in moral degeneration among the young people, while excessive control manifests itself in repressed personalities and narrow minds. Only reasonable restraint and freedom can help the individual to develop a balanced personality. After marriage, the individual's personality is also exposed to the influence of his partner's personality, his or her health, mental attitudes, family background, physical beauty, attainments, etc. The ability to beget children or not is another factor which plays a significant role in the individual's personality development. In fact, considerable literature has been devoted to the subject of family's influence upon the personality by sociologists, psychologists and anthropologists.

2. Socialization in the School. After the home, the child is exposed to the school which also influences him, for the school is nothing less than a miniature society to him. It socializes him, gives him an opportunity to manifest his qualities, instincts, drives and motives, and helps to develop his personality. For the child, the educator's personality and character provide a model which he strives to copy, thereby consciously or unconsciously moulding his personality. This is ture only of those teachers who succeed in arousing in the child's mind an attachment and love for themselves. Every little action, every movement, speech, etc. imprsses itself on the child's mind. On the other hand, he is often repelled by some teachers, and he wants to contradict them through every act. This repulsion may be conscious or unconscious, but it drives the child away from such a teacher. The child is attracted by the other teacher who wins his sympathy, and it is from this teacher that the child wants to win praise and appreciation. He fears the frown of his teacher, he imitates him persistently. Apart from the teacher the child is also influenced by his colleagues, and his status and role in his school groups plays a large part in determining the status and role he is to occupy in society in later life. During the process of education, the child's personality develops under the impact of the other personalities with whom he comes into contact. In the school the child is disciplined. He is aware that disobedience brings immediate punishment, but too strict a system of discipline restricts the child's mental growth and may even drive him to criminal activity. On the other hand, complete absence of control may either make him liberal, free and independent or impulsive and impish.

In this manner, the human personality is profoudly influenced both by the home and the school, of the two, family influence lasts for a longer time and is more comprehensive.

Q. 33. Discuss individual and social aims of education. Explain with same examples.

Or

Individual and social aims of education are two sides of the same coin. Discuss.

Ans. Apparently it seems that individual and social aims of education are two rival camps, two rival claims of the individual and of the society. All educational aims tend to lay stress on either the one or the other. But the difference is merely one of emphasis and a synthesis of the two is possible if the extreme view of these is avoided.

The extreme view of social aims of education originates in the totalitarian philosophy of the state which says that the state is an entity over and above the individual citizen, superior to him in every way and transcending all his desires and aspirations. Hence, it follows, the aim of education should be the GOOD OF THE STATE. In the interest of the good of the state, it is argued that the state has a right to determine and dictate what shall be taught and how it will be taught. Similarly, who will be taught what is determined by the consideration that how best he will serve the state. From the primary stage to the University the children should be taught that the state or the society is absolute.

The extreme view of individual aims emerges from the philosophy of individualism which emphasizes the individual rather than the society. Expressed in T. Percy Nunn's words it says that "nothing good enters into the human world execpt in and through the free activities of individual men and women, and that educational practice must be shaped to accord with that truth." This is an attempt on asserting the importance of the individual and safeguarding his indefeasible rights. Hence, it stresses that the aim of education should be to secure for everyone the conditions under which individuality is most completely developed. Except this ideal of developed personality, according to this extreme view, there is no other aim of education. Nunn claimed that laws of nature would support this aim. In a slightly different way it means "self-realization". Thus development of "individuality" and the "Self" is the only aim of education according to the extreme view of individual aims of education.

These two extreme views as such have no possibility of any compromise or synthesis. But, in their moderate form a synthesis is possible. If both these aims are interpreted and understood slightly in different ways, they may appear to be the one and the same thing. And this way of understanding them alone is more, positive and realistic more so in a democratic country like India.

Synthesis. If instead of "education for the state" we say, "education for social service" or "education for citizenship" emphasizing the good of the community only on the one hand and "spiritual individuality" instead of only "individuality" or "self emphasing the importance of the development of the responsible man" the compromise between the two becomes possible. If we believe that the greatness of a society or the state is an outcome of its democratic institutions and responsible citizen the two aims appear just one as one can not take rise without the other. It is the virtues of the individuals that make a society or the state great and glorious. The interests of the state are enhanced by the development of virtue and wisdom in the individual and individuals find their best chance of self-development in the service of the state or the society. It is a fact that only in a social medium man's individuality can be fostered and personality exalted. The individuality of a person or his so called personality can be expressed and understood only in social terms. The very concept of individuality will be meaningless without a reference to what he is expected to be in relation to his society. A charming personality, for example, means what the society means by being charming how the society defines and describes it. As Nunn puts it "man's nature is social as truly as it is self-regarding". Thus as Ross has expressed it "the individuality is of no value and personality is a meaningless term apart from the social environment in which they are developed and made manifest." Self-realization can be achieved only through social service and social ideals. At the same time social ideals of real value can come into being only through free individuals who have developed valuable individuality.

Professor Bagley of America tried to synthesize these two aims into one by saying that education should aim at developing "social efficiency" in the pupils. It was defined by him as consisting of three components: *(i)* economic efficiency, *(ii)* negative morality and *(iii)* positive morality. This point of view stresses that all the activities of the individual are to be valued with reference to his social obligations. On the other hand social institutions exist only to make the individual life better, fuller, richer, happier, more secure and more fruitful.

Thus, there should not be any conflict between the social and individual aims of education. They are the two sides of the same coin, self-realization and social service are complimentary to each other. They can not be separated and pulled apart. If one single heading, theme or title has to be found for both of them, it may be "Welfare Aim of Education", meaning, thereby, seeking welfare of the individual as well as of the society, the state through education.

Q. 34. What do you mean by National Development?

Or

What is the role of planning in economic development? What role does education play in national and economic development?

Ans. The term National development is very comprehensive. It includes all aspects of the nation. It is dynamic and revolutionary development.

National development is the total effect of all citizens' forces and addition to stock of all physical, human resources, knowledge and skill.

National development is growth plus change; change in turn is social, cultural, and economic. It is qualitative as well as quantitative.

Development is brought by human beings, who participate actively in the process of change. Therefore, development and change are interdependent.

The most effective means for the development of human resources is education, which helps in the progress and prosperity of a country.

U.N.E.S.C.O. report has established the fact that there is a close relationship between educational advancement and national income. Advanced countries of the world are spending about 10% of their national income on education and this investment gives them returns in the form of development of the country. A country may have many resources but they will be of no use, if the people are ignorant and can not utilize the resources properly with proper planning.

Distribution of income and employment are the important parts of the economic growth.

The Primary goal of economic growth is to increase the welfare of the people. Welfare may be increased by producing more goods and services and distributing them more equally among the people. Production of goods and services can be increassed by the better and fuller utilisation of all the productive resources and by increasing the capacity of resources by research and development.

In 1971 U.N.O. gave the following factors for national development:

(1) Equal living standard for all.

(2) Equal share of all in profit.

(3) Equal distribution of income and capital.

(4) Expansion of facilities regarding education, health, shelter and social welfare.

(5) Preservation of environment.

Meaning of Economic Development. Economic Development of a nation means increase in national income. Economic development is the backbone of the progress, freedom and prestige of a nation. Economic bankruptcy leads to social backwardness, political corruption and psychological imbalances.

According to **John Vaizy,** "Economic development comprehensively, is the total effect of the development of labour force, the accumulation of physical capital and additions to the stock of knowledge and skills available in the country."

According to **Professor Marshall,** "The economic development at any time is the name given to the capacity of working on the part of national labourers by means of natural resources of the country."

According to **C.L. Anand,** "Economic development means the proportion of national income that is developed to the physical investment."

According to **Prof M.V. Matur,** "Our goals of development on the economic side imply building up a socialistic society through planned growth in which both the public and private sectors could contribute their mite.

Sometimes economic development and national development are interchangeably used for each other, although there is little difference between the two. When we refer to economic development, we refer to only quantitative change and development in the country like increase in agricultural production, increase in industrial production, increase in employment opportunities, increase in national and per capita income etc. But when we talk of national development we consider the broader meaning of the development where we include both quantitative as well as qualitative changes or development in the country like raising the level of education, removal of social, taboos, structural, social and economic changes, compulsory elementary education, promotion of women education, economic freedom of women, equal working opportunities to women, scientific and rational approach in place of traditional and superstitious approach towards solving various problems that people come across in life.

Following are the different approaches with regard to national and economic development:

1. The Sociologist's Approach. According to sociologists national development is possible only if social changes take place along with economic changes and they go together.

2. The Economist's Approach. According to economists economic development is the pre-condition for national development. They consider increase in production, increase in per capita income and increase in national income as some of the indicators of economic and national development.

3. The Psychologist's Approach. According to the psychologists national development is a psychological process. It takes place only it people of a country are ready to adopt new ideas and new ways of doing things. Change in psychological aspects like change in attitude of the people and competitive spirit among people and excelling in competition etc., are essential for national development.

4. The Political Scientist's Approach. According to political scientists national development is a political process. They are of the firm belief that national development is not possible without political consciousness and maturity. Existence of democracy and secularism is essential for national development.

ROLE OF PLANNING IN ECONOMIC DEVELOPMENT

Planning is a part of our life. It is a process of 'thinking ahead' in determining needs and fixing goals, action plans, strategies and resources to achieve the said goals. We plan at every step and moment of our daily life. After independence the need for planning was realised to modernise India and in 1950, the Planning Commission was set up and in the same year educational planning was introduced as a part of socio-economic planning. Educational planning is the main tool in the hands of the perspective planners to achieve the ends of economic growth. For fast economic development, improvement in human quality is essential which is possible by educational planning only.

There is close relationship between economic development and planning. No country can develop its economy without proper planning. It is the basic necessity in any social activity. We have to plan prudently and carefully at every step to economise resources, to avoid wastage and to achieve maximum output.

According to Planning Commission of India. "Planning is a way of organizing and utilizing resources to the maximum advantage in terms of defined aim."

According to **Gregory,** "Planning in general may be sufficiently defined as an attempt to organise resources for the attainment of chosen ends. It is, in other words, purposeful action."

According to **Dickinson,** "Planning is an organisation which is connected with production, distribution and consumption."

According to **Kothari Commission,** India is facing the following main problems in its economic development which can be solved by planning:

1. Problem of shortage of foodgrains.
2. Problem of unemployment.
3. Problem of political instability.
4. Problem of social and national integrity.

Proper planning helps us in the following ways:

It results in better employment for better educated and trained persons, who help in more production.

Proper planning helps in making major technical, economic and political decisions.

Planning encourages people to make new innovations and inventions to develop technical know how and scientific advancement for practical purpose and increasing production.

Planning promotes divison of labour and better use of machinery to increase production.

Planning helps in proper manpower planning.

Planning and economic productivity are positively highly co-related.

Planning is an integral and essential part of the development process.

Planning helps to think of future needs of the country.

Planning improves the quality of manpower and raises the national income. It prepares the people for agriculture, science, industry and community life etc. It removes ignorance and illiteracy and helps in the development of scientific attitude for progress. For national/economic development to take place, we must ensure the fulfilment of following essential conditions.

Removal of Scarcity of Capital. Paucity of capital is single most important reason of national backwardness and therefore the need is to augment capital supply by forming additional capital through cut in consumption and promotion of savings and investment in the country.

Industrialisation. For economic and national development, it is essential that ratio of industrial to total output should be increased. This is possible only if we set up large scale industries and increase the production of cement, paper, coal, electricity, power, iron and steel, textiles etc. This requires speeding up the process of industrialisation.

Inferior Quality of Human Resources. Low efficiency of labour, lack of education, malnutrition, bad health, lack of training, obstacles in occupational mobility are big hindrances in economic and national development. Adequate supply of labour, training facilities and technical knowledge are essential to increase the productivity and efficiency of human resources.

Fuller Utilisation of Human, Material and Natural Resources. Economic and national development is possible only if we ensure optimum utilisation of men, materials and natural resources. The vast army of unemployed and uneducated people can be used for the creation of infrastructure in our country like construction of roads, bridges and houses and slum clearnce in villages and in urban areas.

Technological Development. Technological development is the key factor in economic development. Technological development implies new and sophisticated machines, modern technology, reformation in production methods and adoption of new methods of production in agriculture, industry and service sectors of the economy ensuring greater efficiency, cost reduction. higher profits, more competitiveness in home and overseas markets. Technological development needs constant research and development and increasing expenditure on education, training and research and development.

Widening of Market. Natural resources themselves can not lead to economic development. For natural resources to assume economic value, the complementary factors must be available in adequate quantity and at economic price and there should be sufficient demand for the resultant product. The need, therefore, is to increase the demand or widening the market for final products.

Population and Economic Development. There is close relationship between population and economic development. Size and quality of population greatly affects the economic development of a country. Larger the size of population lesser is the per capita income and better the quality and smaller the size of population, higher the per capita income. Size of population here refers to total population, composition of population in proportion of working force, proportion of males, females, children and old people and the rate of growth of population *i.e.*, the net addition in population year after year. Quality of population refers to factors like education, training and health of people. Only the optimum size and high quality of population can bring sustained increase in real per capita income over a long period of time resulting in economic and national development.

Role of Planning. Planning is the most important tool in economic development. Planning ensures most efficient use of scarce economic resources in desired directions ensuring highest growth rates in minimum possible time, speeding up the process of economic and national development.

Structural Changes. In underdeveloped countries like India an essential condition for economic development is change in whole structure of society. In this regard there is an urgent need to reduce the size of population and proportion of population engaged in the agricultural sector, to bring land reforms, to expand non-agricultural activities and the proportion of people engaged therein and to optimally utilize all available resources.

Lack of Enterpreneurship. For economic development to take place, it is essential that there is good number of enterpreneurs who are ready to take the risk of setting up industrial ventures in the country. But unfortunately in underdeveloped countries like India the societies are traditions and customs bound and are divided on the basis of castes and creeds. In such a scenario, government can come forward and play the role of entrepreneur besides creating environment for private enterpreneurship.

Creation of Favourable Environment. Favourable atmosphere and environment is very important factor for economic development. Social, religious, legal and political institutions should act in a manner that they create favourable environment for economic growth. People must have a desire for economic progress and they must devote themselves for it, otherwise no amount of resources can ensure economic development.

Role of Education in Economic Development. Among all the economic and non-economic factors of economic development, education is perhaps the most important one. It has been observed historically that education provides the strongest base to economic development of a country. It has been seen that those nations which have made huge investment in terms of education and human capital have emerged very strong and those who have neglected education have lagged behind in economic race. History is the witness to the fact that Japan, England, Russia, U.S.A., Germany etc., have made all round progress only through the medium of education.

In India, during British rule, education was only theoretical and its practical aspect was not given due weightage. In Gandhiji's basic system of education, the importance of education was realized for the first time and effort was made to make it the basis of economic and national development. It was linked to life and became a means of satisfying the essential needs of life. However, this system was incapable of solving post independent burning problems facing the country. Therefore our government tried to link it with productivity and stressed the practical aspect of education. Keeping this in view, Kothari Commission emphasised the vocational education and considered educational expenses as investment in education. It included work experience in curriculum and education came to be linked with life.

Education is an important instrument for bringing change in the society. There is close relationship between education and economic development. Adamsmith and Marshall have already recognised the relationship between education, prosperity and development of mankind. John Wezy has described this relationship as chicken and egg relationship. Harbison and Myers called this relationship as flower and seed relationship. Kothari Commission has also stressed the need for linking education with productivity, considering education to be the most important factor in economic development. Education contributes directly and indirectly in economic development. Its direct contribution is in the form of increase in production and productivity, increase in employment opportunities, mobility of labour and increase in superior labour force. On the other hand its indirect contribution is in the form of family planning, development of national values, development of saving habit, formation of right attitude towards life etc.

Education can make following contributions in the national and economic development:

- Education acts as infra-structure for economic development.
- Education helps in the development of human resources through investment in education.
- Education helps in developing work-values. It develops dignity of labour.
- Education promotes technological revolution.
- Education develops scientific or problem solving attitude.
- Education removes gap between manual and mental labour.
- Education results in proper exploitation and utilization of national resources and also helps in the development of economic resources.
- Education helps in formulating national plans for economic development. Formulation of plans is possible only by experts in different branches of education. For example a person having good knowledge of agriculture can only formulate successful plan for agricultural development and only a good educationalist can draw good educational plans.
- Education promotes entrepreneurial abilities like risk taking and managerial skills etc.
- Education not only helps in increasing national income but also helps in equitable distribution of income and wealth in a country.
- Education promotes industrialization through technological development, mechanization, new discoveries and inventions.

- Education helps in better planning and policies of economic development. The implementation of plans can not take place in the absence of proper knowledge.
- Education motivates people for change. It also helps in increasing production by evolving new methods and techniques by training people in different skills and by implementing these methods in our own institutions and conditions. It thus not only makes people mobile but provides job opportunities in different places and areas.
- Education raises the aspiration level of people. Thus higher ambition promotes higher standard of living.
- Education converts human resources into human capital. It helps in the development of skilled manpower. It prepares manpower to work in different fields through proper training and education. It thus not only makes people mobile but provides job opportunities in different places and areas.
- Education creates proper atmosphere for economic development through widened outlook and multiple abilities etc.
- An educated man can better take care o his own interests and get out of exploitation by others. Thus education evokes the people's conscious against social and economic exploitation.
- Education helps in bringing social change by breaking social taboos, old traditions and superstitions.

Till now education was treated as an end only. Now it has been proved that education acts as a means also. Education is an investment in human resources as investment in steel or coal. Therefore, education must be given high priority in investment sector.

Q. 35. What is National Integration? Why is it needed? How will you educate for National Integration?

Ans. It we wish to retain our hard won freedom, national integration has to be our natural tune. In this integration lies our strength, dignity and hope for future progress. The basis of National Integration is emotional integration. It is through training of mind and heart, that a sense of oneness among the people of the country can be inspired. By emotional integration we mean a feeling of national pride and faith in the nation's greatness. When the emotions are conditioned by the idea of national loyalty and are directed towards national welfare, the result is national integration. It is a feeling among people to share certain common objectives, ideas and giving them high share over smaller. It is feeling of oneness which transcends all groups of cultural differences and connects the different religions, castes and linguist communities into a compact whole.

According to **Pandit Jawaharlal Nehru,** "By emotional integration I mean the integration of our minds and hearts, the suppression of feelings of separatism."

Emotional integration brings about an emotional synthesis of diverse elements. With the development of this national consciousness, all individuals forget about their selfish interests, personal or group motives, pursue national ideals, contribute to national aspirations and solve all the national problems with all sincerity and devotion. India is also a nation and we all people, belonging to diverse religions, castes and groups, are its inhabitants. Thus it is a joint responsibility of us all to defend the freedom of our nation.

Nationalism. An individual is an integral part of his nation. An individual is for the nation, the nation is not for the individual. Isolated from his nation, the individual loses his identity, his existence even. Hence every individual is duty bound to uphold the integrity and strength of his nation and offer his best co-operation in its advancement.

Nationalism is that feeling which inspires all big or small units of a society to raise above the narrow self-centered activities and work in unity and co-operation for national development. It is an aggressive, dynamic-social organisation interlinked with threads of unity and propagates the ideology and policies of national government. Nationalism is not mere love of one's place of birth. It includes the essential constituents namely love and regard for the history, culture, religion, language and traditions of the nation. In short, nationalism means whole-hearted devotion to nation, sense of duty together with obligation and unquestioning faith in its glorious future based on its present well-being and prosperity.

According to **Humayun Kabir,** "Nationalism is that which depends upon our feelings towards the nation."

There are two concepts of nationalism—Narrow and Broad. When a country is interested only in its narrow limited interests, it is known as narrow nationalism. My country right or wrong is the spirit behind narrow nationalism. This concept is full of dangers and shortcomings. Broader concept of nationalism is related with emotional integration. The whole world is now so intimately inter-connected that no national can dare live alone and the development of a sense of world citizenship has become just as important as that of national citizenship. In its broader sense, it means bringing about economic, social and cultural differences within tolerable range.

Meaning of National Integration. National integration is unity in diversity. It means a feeling of oneness. It implies social, political, economic, linguistic and cultural unity. It is the development of a mental climate that would help react in terms of oneness, irrespective of the region, language or religion of the people concerned. It means a heaven of freedom where the world has not been divided into fragments by narrow domestic wells. It is based on feeling of oneness, common ideals of life and a common code of behaviour. It implies confidence in antion's future, deep sense of values and obligatioin of citizenship, mutual understanding and respect for the culture of different sections of the nation.

Need for National Integration. National integration is the feeling that binds the citizens of a country. Its aim is to put individual's best efforts for the optimum growth, prosperity and welfare of the country as a whole. It does away with inter-state, inter-linguistic, inter-religious and inter-cultural differences. It promotes a spirit of tolerance and respect for the view-point of other cultural groups. To Kanungo, "Every country at every time needs national integration but India needs it the most."

India's passing through a critical period these days. The integrity of India is in danger. Therefore Indians will have to act carefully. In India national integration is needed due to following reasons:

Threat of Foreign Aggression. National integration is vital for India's survival especially at a time when the country is under the threat of foreign aggression and internally the people are divided on the basis of castes, religions, regions, communities, languages and races.

For the Development of National Character. National integration is an essential element for the development of national character. These days there is lack of national character. Corruption is increasing day-by-day. We are sacrificing national interests for the sake of money. National character can be formed only when we have the feeling of national integration.

For Success of Democracy. India is a democratic country. National integration is an essential pre-requisite for the success of our democracy. It is a basic need for the success of democracy, otherwise, the fissiparous tendencies in the country may lead to serious consequences.

For Diversity. National unity is essential for any country at any time. There is unity in diversity in India but now unity is in danger. Therefore, national unity is essential in order to maintain the eternal value of unity in diversity.

For Peace. National integration is essential for keeping peace at national and international level. Modern age is the age of science. It has changed the whole world in a family. Every nation is dependent on one another. Therefore, scientific achievement should be used for constructive work in order to provide peace to humanity. This feeling can develop only when we have the thought of national integration.

Obstacles to National Integration. Following are the obstacles in the achievement of National integration:

Casteism. The germ of casteism is cutting the roots of the Hindu society gradually. It has so compartmentalised this society into Brahmans, Kshatriyas, Vaishyas and Shudras that the people of one caste don't mix up freely with the people of the other castes. Casteism is fully exploited during elections. Such a situation creates bitterness and tension.

Communalism. Communalism divides the people having different religions. In india, people belong to different regligions like Hinduism, Islam, Christianity etc. It were these forces which led to the partition of our country in 1947. Even in free India, these fanatics spread the rumours of mal-treatment to the minority groups which results in ill feeling and creates tension. Communal riots are taking place in the country. It has become a serious threat to national unity.

Provincialism. It is a very big obstacle in the way of our national progress and national integration. Every person loves his/her province but he/she should not forget that nation is greater than the province. The inhabitants of one province should not look upon those of another province with hatred and feeling of inferiority.

Linguism. Language is the connecting link for the people. It is an important means of national unity. India is a country of many languages. This has led to much dissension and destruction. Separate provinces were demanded on the basis of languages and were formed too.

Economic Disparities. The growing gulf between the haves and the have-nots is also responsible for bringing about fissiparous tendencies in our Indian society. The ways of life and the standards of living of the lower and upper classes are so different that there can be no meeting point between the two.

Frustration in Youth. The young generation of today is getting frustrated because it sees no future for it. The ghost of unemployment haunts their youth all the time. This results in agitations, strikes, raising of slogans, destruction of public and private property, looting, arsoning and other such anti-national activities. There is scant respect for teachers, leaders and law. There is unrest, indiscipline and lack of values in the students of today.

Political Disparities. Unfortunately in India, the political disparities are increasing day-by-day. Political parties are organised in the name of community, language and province etc. which is a serious threat to national integration. Changing of parties time and again, making politics an arena of "Aya Rams'' and 'Gaya Rams', creates political instability in the states. In some states the political changes are so rapid that the administration comes to a virtual standstill. This creates frustration in the people.

These are some of the factors which put hurdles on the way to national integration. The history of India shows that India has always existed as one nation despite all these diversities. In fact, the Indians believe in unity in diversity and they have shown themselves as a nation during the three aggressions on them after the attainment of independence.

Education for National Integration. Education is a powerful means of bringing about national integration. In the words of Dr. Radha Krishnan "National integration cannot be built by brick and mortar or with chisel and hammer. It has to grow silently in the minds and hearts of people and the process by which it could be achieved was by education."

Education alone can develop the feeling of nationalism in the masses and it has to accomplish this task compulsorily. Without the active co-operation of education we shall not be able to defend the structure of the nation.

Objectives of Education for National Integration. The objectives of education for national integration can enumerated as below:

- To train the emotions for developing an emotionally integrated personality.
- To develop attitudes, dispositions, values and tolerance.
- To equip students with an intimate knowledge of the different aspects of the country, including the events which led to freedom.
- To encourage all studies and activities which lead to greater understanding between communities and states.
- To create a feeling that the country and its resources belong to the citizens who thereby acquire certain rights and privilegs alongwith corresponding duties and responsibilities.

Q. 36. Discuss the place of religion in education. Keeping in view that ours is a secular country.

Or

"No boy or girl can be counted as properly educated unless he or she has been made aware of a religious enterpretation of life." Discuss.

Or

"In a democratic set-up the importance of religious education cannot be minimised." Comment.

Or

"Religion and education are natural allies. Both recognize and have to do with spiritual as aganist an exclusive attention to the physical and material." Discuss the statement bringing out the importance of religion in an educational system.

Ans. THE NEED FOR RELIGION

In the beginning, the idea of Roligion might have been a divine inspiration, the basis of which might have been logic personal belief. Now the modern advanced religious belief developed in men in a subject for research. To day one may wonder how the modern religious concepts come to imagination? In the beginning the nature of religion has quite liberal, but today it has become narrow; Superstitions have crept into it. Some people hold different views regarding the same religion. Science has hoped in removing many superstitions, fears; doubts and orthodox views from religion.

Today if Dharm (religion) is taken in a wider perspective, man can create conditions of peace, hope, love, sympathy and contentment by bringing an end to frustration, mental-tensions, quarrels, unjealousy, discontentment and discomfort. Faith in religion can lead the world to brotherhood and peace. Religion establishes human values, cultural traditions; ideals and moral understanding in human society. Religion in India pervades throughout the whole life of an individual. Here we have many religions.

Relation of Religion to Human Life. The most developed period from the view point of religion has been the Vedic period when religion was considered as a basis for human life and source of inspiration for virtuous conduct. Since then religion has been inspiring people to follow the right path, improve their conduct and imbibe human virtues. It is possible that certain superstitutions, conservation, frustrations, fears and doubts might have crept into religion due to some ignorance. Self-confidence has always been with man in the form of religion. Religion by adding to the human qualities, has made man capable of self-confidence, self-reform, self-realization, self-discipline, self-reliance and self-development.

True Meaning of Religion. Vedas are the oldest books. Vedas are the repository of all knowledge. Here in religion has been described in its wider perspective. According to the Vedas, the efforts, which inspire man for various conduct and develop human qualities, fall in the category of religion. Hence, than in characteristic of religion is inspiration for virtuous conduct. The modern word 'Religion' can not be a synonym for 'Dharm', bacause 'Dharm' has been considered as all-pervading in Indian scriptures. All activities from rising in the morning to sleeping a night and death and actions after death are all included in 'Dharm'. In fact, whatever qualities a person acquires are his Dharm. Here qualities mean human qualities which are universal.

In Islam 'mazhab' is a way of imparting education for virtuous conduct. According to the philosophy of this religion, 'namaz', 'Roja' and 'Haj' are considered, a method for creating universal love and feeling of neighbourhood. To give some benefit to the society or social service are considered as a part of this religion.

Religion and Sects (Belief). Some narrow minded people evince unnecessary opposition by equaling religion with sects. We should clearly understand the meaning of religion and sects. Religion is taken in the wider sense which means spiritual development of human society through the welfare of mankind. In other words; religion means human religion which every society is prepared to accept. A sect (belief) is a specific religious view point of a group of persons. That is the individual belief of the persons of that group, based on the wider values of religion. It is not necessary for other sects to accept that belief. Hindu religion accepts the opinion of Vedas, Islam that of the Quran and Christians of Bible. Hindu Dharm has been divided into Buddha sect, Jains, Sikh, Vedic (Sanatan and Arya Samaj) according to the different methods to philosophers and thinkers of these sects, although all these sects are parts of Hindu Dharm. Some agitators and diplomats propagated it as different religions in order to create faction in Hindu Dharm. The idea behind this propaganda was to cut of the organisation and unity of Hindu Dharm. It is amazing that some Hindus also accepted the sects as different religions.

Islam Dharm has its original form the word 'Salm'. 'Salm' means peace which has been interpreted as knowing God peacefully and surrendering the self before Him. This is the true nature of Islam. Whenever some one seeks the shelter of God, forgetting his vanity and pride, he attain all-round development and divinity is rediated from his personality. In Christian religion, christianity was formed from the word 'christos' which means 'bathed in Divine wisdom'.

Thus christian religion extends that divine wisdom which creates brotherhood, love, sympathy and tolerance in the human society.

Vedic religion, is based on Vedas, 'Ved' means knowledge. Hence Vedic Dharm means that scientific knowledge which by recognising the existence of 'Inner self' and 'Supreme self' *i.e.* 'Antaratma' and 'Parmatma', develops human qualities like, non-violence, truth, humanism, love and compassion, etc.

Thus religion is a source of morality. Science can be of great help in this direction, but science devoid of religion is meaningless. Religion is all-pervading and Universal. So it should be included in education.

Mis-use of Religion and Violence. Due to ignorance and superstitions some universe followers of religions have strangulated humanity and have committed great atrocities. The reason for such violent attitude is misinterpretation of religion. These religions hypocrises of violent nature committed so many atrocities on humanity that man began to hate religion. These committing oppressions in the name of religion were non-vedic (unwise) and selfish. Religious reformers born from time to time led the people to the right path and presented the true nature of religion. Buddha, Mahavir, Shankaracharya, Dayanand, etc., were such great personalities. In the Western countries Rousseau and Locke suggested to save education from wrongly interpreted religion. Corrupt practice, in various religious bodies in the name of religion created hatred for religion.

Relation Between Religion and Education. Religion and Education are closely associated with each other both are of spiritual tendencies. Spiritual, material or physical urge are dealt with by religion as well as by the education. "Both seek to emancipate man, not from contract with his environment, but from slavery to it." As has already been discussed, *education creates certain values of life and help in the modification of behaviour*. It gives certain mouldings to the life, while religion beautifies the life by cultivation of truthful heart with the moral and spiritual values.

In this way religion and education have different ways but the same aim of achieving God through cultivating three absolutes truth, and goodness.

Religion must be given a suitable places in the curriculum because it is the core of our culture and 'heritage'. Gentle given a fine statement in regard to the place of religion in the curriculum.

He Writes. "National cultures have never been more conscious than now of the higher needs of the mind, needs that are not only aesthetic and abstractly intellectual but also ethical and religious. For a school without an ethical and religious constant is an absurdity." Thus, religion should find a suitable and proper place in the sphere of education. Education, according to Pestalozzi, is aimed at "natural harmonious and progressive development of man's innate powers." Wider education mean an education which broadens the outlook, awakens the inner powers and teaches us to respect all the religions. In this manner, a teacher should enable the pupils to cultivate religious attitude and mentality through education. Religion, in this sense does not mean merely a bundle of rites and of dogmas followed by symbols and emotions but it is applied to all that what noble. Religion and education with this collective and mutual efforts lead a person towards self-realization and self-understanding. Rousseau and Wordsworth believed in nature and education on the lane; of nature. The essence of their philosophy was to worship nature in practical way. In other words, we should obey natural laws and must follow the path traced by her.

Truly speaking, religious education does not mean something separable but pure, honest and beneficial. Education is nothing but religion, because both the religion and the education aim at harmonising the person to the ultimate truth. Religion is the pure form of education.

Education has been defined as "a process of development in which consists the passage of human being from infancy, to Maturity, the process by which he adopts himself gradually in various ways to his physical and spiritual environment." In this definition the ability of social adaptation means the development of the social qualities like cooperation, coordination among social groups and communities. This ability of the adaptation is religious, because religion in a wider sense says clearly that all are one. We are brothers and sisters borne of the same father. The same ideology of cooperation is found in this interpretation alike education. Therefore, curriculum construction should be based on the principle that education and religion are not the separate entities but they are one in nature and consequence.

What is man and what is God? These are the main problems dealt with by religion. These are the truth of a vital significance and are at the basis "of the whole structure of knowledge whether of fact or value, and deprived of them education as well as life is radically defective, without centre, balance or proper subordination of part to part."

The aim of education is all-round development of man. The same is the aim of religion. So because use of this common aim the corelation of education and religion quite natural. Now to include the various forms of religion in education, is a great problem. Some people due to their ignorance of the true nature of religion, do not and to give any place to religion in education, whereas some people want to give it an important place. Since earliest times in India, education and religion have been related to each other. With the break of this relation, indiscipline, violence and immorality have increased. According to Dr. Sarvapalli Radhakrishnan the reason for all vices and troubles pervading the world is want of morality which has been created due to education being not corelated to religion. Here in India there were those centres of education in which people from all parts of the world came to receive education. In Western countries also Movements were started for, educational organisation by correlating religion and education. Sunday School Movement, Religious Education Movement were some such movements in which the demand for integration of education and religion was asserted. The world has witnessed the evil effects of materalism. Hence it has rightly realised that humanity cannot be saved without relating education to religion. Now, the need for education integrated with religion is being felt throughout the world. Some politicians and economic groups do not think it proper to give a place to religion in education. In fact, if religion is treated as 'human religion' a revolution can be brought out in the improvement of education. Peace can be established in the world through a religion integrated education based on thinking of universal peace, universal-brotherhood and universal-good.

On the basis of the view point expressed above, it seems useful to impart religious education by integrating education and religion. But it is necessary to consder points both in its favour and against.

Q. 37. Discuss the arguments in favour and aganist Religious Education.

Ans. Those who want to separate religion and education, argue in the following way:

1. To give place to religion in education is not practicable, because children of all religions come to receive education in schools. In such a situation which religion is to be taught in a school? If one particular religion is taught in the school, the followers of other religions will not accept this position. It will lead to mutual ill-will quarrel and disturbance.

2. Religion education is generally based on preaching. So long as desired changes are not brought about in the environment and ideal examples are not presented till then good conduct cannot be spread through religious education. Hence mere teaching of religious doctrines in schools will not achieve the goal of education.

3. Doubts and mental conflicts are created in children as they cannot understand the abstract processes of sin virtue, reward and punishment as explained in religious educational schools.

3. Religious education emphasises, religious sermons and religious knowledge. But life is not conducted according to these sermons. Man cannot become virtuous simply by getting knowledge of religion. He become virtuous only when he puts the same into practice. This is not done in schools.

5. It is not possible for the modern teacher to analyse religious knowledge dispassionately because he may be faithful only to one particular religion. Consequently, the students will be incapable of understanding the true and obscure meaning of religion. It willl be better to analyse religion with the help of science but the teachers will not accept it because science may injure the personal beliefs. In fact, it will be difficult to get able and suitable teachers for religious education. It is a difficult task to correlate education and true human religion. Every teacher may not be capable of this.

6. We have already observed that religion means human religion through which human qualities should be developed. But history

bears testimony to the fact that humanity has been oppressed in the name of religion and in place of love, compassion, sympathy and cooperation, the feelings of enmity, hatred, jealously and opposition have grown. Such examples in the history of religion may create irreligious feelings in children.

7. Man imbibes 'religion' through self-realization. Self-realization is individualistic. Hence inclusion of personal elements in religious conduct is natural. In the school environment, collective and social tendencies are found. So personal view point of religion cannot be given importance. This view point may be suitable to those children who agree with that line of thinking but not to others who follow other view point.

Argument in Favour of Religious Education. There may be some strength in the above arguments. But this strength will be there only to the extent to which education is imparted on the basis one particular religions without understanding the true meaning of religion. Religion is universal, omnipresent and eternal. It is necessary to present its universal form. The following arguments may be presented in favour of religious education:

1. "All-round development of man is not possible only through physical, mental and intellectual development, as this requires, spiritual development also. Physical comforts alone do not provide real pleasure and peace. The more a man is absorbed in wordly pleasures, the more he is attached towards them. He tries to get the physical comforts of this material world through all possible means (even though in human action). He becomes prepared to commit atrocities and cruel actions. This disturbs world peace. Various subjects such as geography, science etc., lead to physical, mental and intellectual development, but they do not develop him spiritually. For spiritual development religion oriented education is needed. Only then the goal of an all-round development of the individual may be achieved.

2. Lack of religious faith in man is the cause of his troubles. All the vices of the world are due to irreligiousness and materialistic tendencies. Selfishness is the outcome of materialism which creates vices like enmity, jealousy and intolerance. Hence, religious education is necessary in order to get rid of inhuman tendencies.

3. We have said earlier that religious education becomes defective only when religion is teated in its narrow form. Religion is

not be identified with any sect or opinion. The essence of all sects, is the true religion. This religion alone can be named as human religion. If it is taught through education, the follower of any religion will not be ignored. It will be worthwhile to provide education in high human ideals which are adored by people of every religion instead of giving place to the rituals of different sects.

4. In such countries which are mainly religious, the religious education will be useful from educational point of view. Education based on religion will be easily understandable and interesting in such countries. India is one such country. But religion should not be taken into its narrow form. By adopting essence of all the sects, religious education should be given in its wider perspective.

5. The aim of education is all-round development of the individual in which development of character is the main aim. Religious education is the best source for character development. Today education being devoid of religion, the character of many of our youths is not what it should be. Evidently, religion is to be given due place in education for the sake of character development.

6. In the modern world scientific experimentalism, scientific invention, scientific thinking, intellectual and materialistic development have been continuously going on. Consequently, the progressive countries have achieved material affluence. But have these countries become happy and peaceful inspite their affluence? The two World Wars are the consequences of the materialistic selfishness. Humanity had to suffer due to the menace of these wars. Some people tried to bring peace in the world and efforts are still continuing. But world peace has not been achieved so far. The sole reason for it is the neglect spiritualism. The truth is that materialism and spiritualism should be integrated through religious education. That a hungry nation can survive with spiritualism alone, is not true. Along with physical hunger of soul should also be satisfied. Religious education alone can satisfy the hunger of sow. So it will be necessary to impart universal religious education in schools. One or two persons alone have not stressed the need of religious education. In India, Shri Syed Ahmed Khan, Radhakrishnan, Madan Mohan Malviya, Mahatma Gandhi, Dayanand, Ravindra Nath Tagore and Arvind and such other great men have advocated religious education. Smt. Annie Besant and Mira Behn, Mataji considered it necessary to integrate

education with religious education. While integrating education and religious education we shall have to keep it in mind that the religion to be integrated should be human-religion. Religious education should not be based on the belief of one particular sect.

Q. 38. Discuss the cautions in the teaching of religion.

Ans. An evaluation of advantages and limitations of religious education leads us to be conclusion that religion should be given a place in education. But religion should be included in such a way that the above mentioned defects religious education may be avoided. One of the objectives of religious education is self-realisation and to inspite virtuous conduct. It is necessary to make efforts in this direction. Self-realisation and virtuous conduct are inner-impulses. They can not be imposed on anyone. Sermons and instructions alone will not achieve religious aims. Moral development and virtuous conduct through religion is possible only when opportunities are provided for such behaviour. A religious atmosphere in schools can make it possible. The incidents are greatly influenced by the ideal behaviour of teachers. So the teachers themselves should present examples of ideal behaviour by leading a religious, moral and virtuous life. The teacher religion alone cannot create a religious atmosphere in schools. All teachers should cooperate in this process.

Religious education should be kept away from narrow mindedness. It will be better to give religious eduction based on logic, analysis and criticism, otherwise it may lead to superstitions fanatics, jealousy and narrow-mentality.

In schools, religion should not be taken as an end in itself. It is simply a means for all-round development of the individual. The schools are not to be made temples, mosques, or churches by titling religious education to a particular sect. Schools are not to fulfil the functions of religious institutions other the religious institutions should work as schools. If religious institutions make an attempt for the all-round development of children through spiritual development, they will certainly lessen the burden of schools. It is, therefore, necessary for the religious bodies to take the form of educational obligations to the extent possible.

Educational Functions of Religion. A man is attracted towards religion only when he is mentally, healthy and a sound mind are sides in a sound body. So it is the function of religion to co-operate in the physical development of children. In vedic religions behaviour the ideal of celibacy is for the sake of physical development. The child who observes restraint up to maturity and takes physical exercises for the development of body makes himself sturdy. This restorative power prepares him for household life and his regulated behaviour keeps him healthy till death. Some religious people think that good physical health creates a liking or worldly pleasures and happiness. So a person desirous of religious knowledge should not pay any attention to physical development. This is their fanaticise. Religion should first of all educate the individual for his physical and mental development. Body, mind and senses are means of inhibiting religion.

Religion should always mean performing of duties. To think only of the next world (Parlok) through religious knowledge and to forget this world (Ih-lok) is not fair. The first field of performing duties is this world Karma-Kshetra (the field of action) is another name for Dham-Kshetra (fields of religious). The man who succeeds in the Karma-Kshetra of this world is entitled to reach the other world (Parlok). Therefore, religion should prepare man for the Karma-Kshetra (field of action). The field of action of the individual is determined on the basis of his aptitudes. So religion should inculcate in the child the ability to choose his field of action according to his interest and aptitude and to get success engaging himself in it.

The basis of religion is knowledge. An ignorant person can not be religious. A person may be familiar with religion and religious behaviour after he has attained knowledge. The basis of religion are logic, analysis, observation, contemplation and freedom of thought. So the child should be provided opportunities for independent thinking, logic, meditation, analysis and observation with an open mind. The doubt of some persons that the child does not believe in religious facts on the basis of arguments, analysis, observation etc. is baseless. The permanent religious feeling is always based on perception. To have faith in religion without independent thinking, logic and analysis will be blind-faith and fanaticism.

Some people consider aesthetic sense and artistic sense as hinderance to religion. But this is not true. Satyam, Shivam, Sundaram (Truth, Bliss and Beautiful) and the bases for artistic and aesthetic senses. Satyam and Shivam are the bases of religion. A thing which is not true or for happiness cannot be beautiful. The carving of Jain idols in Ellora caves and Jatak stories connected with the life of Lord Buddha and their carving in Ajanta, the poetry of Sur, Tulsi and Mira and all considered unique for propagation of religious feelings. So religion should diffuse an aesthetic sense also.

Although it is true function of schools to develop the moral and character of the child, but religious institutions can bring about better moral and character development, if they pay attention in this direction. The very meaning of religion is to inspire virtuous conduct and virtuous conduct develops moral and ethical qualities. Today the country needs able and noble citizens. The religious institutions can fulfil their national duties by giving education virtuous conduct.

Thus, after studying the merits and demerits and functions of religious education we come to the conclusion that religion should be included in schools as a means of all-round development of children. Religious institutions can perform at least those educational functions which are difficult to be achieved in schools. Thus, it is necessary for schools and religious institutions to shoulder the responsibility of developing noble citizens.

Q. 39. Define Social Change. What are the various factors for bringing social change?

Or

Education is an important instrument of social change. Discuss.

Ans. Social means concerning society and change means deviation from existing pattern. In this sense, social change means change in the structure and functions of human society. In fact human life is not static. It is under a constant change in the ideas, attitudes and values of an individual. This changing process brings changes in the social structure and in other social attributes also. In fact, styles of living are changing so fast today that it is difficult to keep pace with the changing ideas, beliefs, life styles and material pursuits for more and more human welfare. This change in social structure is known as social change.

To understand the meaning of social change, it is essential to know the meaning of 'change' and 'society'. 'Change' means alteration of an item under consideration either in part or whole. It is a variation from previous state or difference through time. Therefore going by these two definitions we can say that social change is the change in social relations.

According to **Jenson,** "Social change may be defined as modification in the ways of doing and thinking of people."

According to **Davis,** "By social change is meant only such alterations as occur in social organizaton *i.e.*, in the structure and functions of a society."

According to **Ginsberg,** "By social change I understand a change in social structure, *e.g.*, size of a society, the composition or balance of its parts or the type of its organisation."

According to **MacIver and Page,** "Social change is the change in society. Society is a network of social relationship. Social relationships include social processes, social patterns and social interactions. Social change can be defined as change in social relations itself."

According to **Dawson and Gettys,** "Cultural change is social change, since all culture is social in its origin, meaning and usage."

Some scholars depict the process of social change in the following manner:

Change in the experience of individuals

↓

Change in the attitude of individuals

↓

Change in the social interactions

↓

Change in social relations

↓

Change in social structure

↓

Social change

On the basis of above definitions, we can say that any change in the social structure or its functions is a social change.

Social change is accepted as such only when the majority of individuals in a society accept it in their life, behaviours and beliefs.

In short, social change means replacing the old with the new in the society. It can be a modification of the old also if not total replacement. It can be a new mode of thought, a new attitude towards work, worship and wealth, a new behaviour pattern and so on. It can take various forms.

Different Aspects of Social Change. Social change is related with all types of changes related to society. It includes all aspects of society.

Economic Aspect. Change relating to industry, business, agriculture, productive process etc. comes in this aspect.

Political Aspect. It is related with change in administration and political power.

Moral Aspect. It is related with change in values and thoughts.

Scientific and Technological Aspect. It is related with change due to scientific and technological development.

Religious Aspect. It is related with change in religion and religious institutions as—Church, Temple and Gurudwara.

Factors Affecting Social Change. Social change is the product of the interaction of many factors which are as follows:

Geographical Factors. Change in the Geographical environment has great effect on human society. Climate is the only reason of rise and downfall of civilizations and cultures.

Geographical factors comprise all the inorganic (Non-living) phenomena which exert an influence on human life. Theoretically, such a definition would include even the physical state of other planets in our solar system. Practically, however, the geographic factors may be limited to the climate and its influences including temperature, sunshine, rainfall, relative humidity, prevailing winds and other climatic possibilities. Every man lives in particular geographical conditions which do affect the social life, e.g. social life of people living in plains is different from those living in hilly areas.

The inhabitants of West Bengal and other regions near sea depend more on fish for their food as fish are available in these areas in large number and at ease.

When natural calamities such as flood, drought, famine etc. uproot innumerable families, the individuals involved form new social relations which as a result bring about social change. Natural catastrophe encourages geographical mobility and people moving to a different place and culture adapt themselves to it.

Biological Factors. The important biological factors affecting social changes are: The plants and animals in the area and the human beings themselves. Man uses the available plants and animals according to his culture and traditions. He destroys the enemies like insects, poisonous plants, bacteria and dangerous animals with the best available means. The biological environment is dynamic and we find change in the climate, change in soil composition, drying up of lakes or streams etc. which spell the doom of some organisms and encourage new opportunity for others.

Psychological Factors. The psychology of human being may itself become the cause for social change. Man by nature loves change, desires to invent new things in every sphere and is always anxious for novel experiences.

As a conequence of this, attitude changes and rituals, customs, traditions etc. also go on changing in the society in a continuous manner. This does not imply that whatever is new is considered superior to the old. On one side man wants to preserve the good elements of what is old and simultaneously attends to what is new. In this process of interaction between the two tendencies change in social relationships takes place which leads to social change.

Technological Factors. Social change is brought about mainly due to the following technological factors:

(1) Development of new methods and processes of agriculture.

(2) Development of means of transport.

(3) Development of means of communication.

(4) Use of machines in industries.

Technology is nothing but applied science, which helps in bringing social change with the changing needs of the society. The development of technology has led to the establishment of factories, urbanisation and industrialisation. Therefore, new classes emerged.

People of different regions started migrating to industrial areas for want of work and stayed there which led to the mixing of different cultures. The increase in the number of educational institutions, facilities of bank, opening of new business centres and expansion of trade and commerce are also its products. As a result of industrialisation joint family system has broken and is fast being replaced by single family system.

Technological development has resulted into many material and non-material changes in our society such as:

— Abolition of untouchability and weakening of caste relationships.

— The manner of preparing our food, standard of living, decrease in the death rate, development of scientific attitude and emergence of new values such as equality, liberty, justice, secularism, brotherhood, co-operation and fellow feelings etc.

Cultural Factors. Culture encompasses values, styles, ideals, beliefs, traditions, emotional attachment etc. These affect the society to a great extent.

Main Factors in Bringing Social Change in India

The main factors of social change in India are as follows:

Science and Technology. Scientific and technological discoveries and inventions have caused several far-reaching social changes in the lives of people in developing as well as developed countries. Television, Films, Video, and other scientific inventions have completely changed our mode and style of living, modes of thinking and consequently social relations.

Sanskritization. "It is the process by which a low Hindu caste, or tribe or other group changes its customs, rituals, ideology, and way of life in the direction of high caste. Generally such changes are followed by a claim to a higher position in the caste hierarchy than that traditionally conceded to the claimant caste by the local community."

Social Mobility. Social mobility means position in social sphere. This mobility occurs in 'vertical' or 'horizontal' directions. It can be 'individual' or 'group mobility'.

Vertical mobility implies movements up the social or occupational ladder, accompanied by rise in status, position, income and economic condition etc.

Horizontal mobility means change in place without accompanying rise in social or economic status.

Indianisation. A glimpse of Indianisation is noticed in dress, meditation, religious songs, prayers, celebration of Indian festivals and customs. Integration with Indian culture and civilization is known as Indianisation.

Modernization. Modernization means the change in the values, attitudes, relationships, associations, social institutions etc. on the pattern of the so called modern culture of U.K., U.S.A., Japan, France etc. A country can evolve its own model of modernity as well by developing its own ideas on style of living and technology.

Secularization. Secularization implies rationality, differenciation, religious toleration, naturality, broad outlook and unorthodoxy. It implies that various issues in personal and social life are evaluated not from religious point of view but from utilitarian point of view.

Westernization. This is the process of social change in India by which the culture, traditions style of living and values are changing as the western culture considerably affected the Indian culture and society. Under the British rule the Indians have not only adopted the western technology and educational system but also they have accepted the western manners and habits in the matter of food, dress, social relations, mode of living, recreation and system of marriage etc.

Hinduization. The tendency and efforts of several tribal communities in India to enter the broadfold of the Hindu social structure are implied by this process. For example a section of the Bhil tribals has now bcome Bhil caste in Hindu social structure. By doing so they think that they have gained social status.

Urbanization. A significant feature of this change is the continuous migration from rural areas to the urban areas. This social change leads to the same problems as that of industrialisation. Urbanization leads to growth of towns, cities and urban centres, industrial towns, business projects, educational, commercial and trade centres and religious cities etc.

Industrialization. The spread of industrialization gives rise to crimes, strikes, prostitution, drinking, trade unionism and agitations. Other changes which take place due to industrialisation are: growth of educational institutions, banks and business centres, extension of roads and other civic amenities.

Planning and Law. Law also helps in bringing social change in the society. People have the tendency to oppose new changes in the society but they are forced to accept these changes if enacted as law. And then these changes become the part of their life, for example Zamindari system, privy purse, slavery, exploitation and untouchability etc. have been abolished by law.

Politicisation. There was politicisation due to leaders' political outlook, manifestos of political parties and awareness about the rights and duties of citizens, regional, national and international relations. The advancement of democracy, the spread of education and the mass media greatly promoted politicisation throughout the country resulting in vast social changes.

Role/Importance/Functions of Education in Social Changes

Education is an important instrument to bring social revolution Among all the instruments education is considered as the most powerful. Education for all, at all levels, and at all ages of children is the only remedy to bring about the desired social change in Indian society.

The relationship between education and social change takes a dual form—education as an instrument and education as a product. This implies that education as an instrument is used as a means for bringing about desired changes in the society and in the later case changes in the educational structure follows as a consequence of changes which have already taken place in the society.

There are three types of relationship between education and social change which are as follows:

1. Education as a Necessary Condition of Social Change. Historical experience of advanced countries has shown that for any social revolution education is the pre-condition. Illiterates remain satisfied with their existing conditions and feel that they are destined to be what they are. They never bother to exert to bring change in their present social and economic conditions. They are guided by orthodoxy, traditions and fate rather than by rationality in their actions. Education helps people to make them rational in their thinking and approach.

2. Education as an Outcome of Social Change. There is inter-dependent relationship between education and social change. On the one hand it brings change in social conditions. On the other hand it is influenced by social change, which means social change helps spreading education. Education follows social change. It has its place before and after social change. First come social changes and then teaching process is changed according to those social changes. Education system changes according to the needs of society.

3. Education as an Instrument of Social Change. Education as an instrument of social change means how education helps people to bring social change. Education changes the outlook and the tradition approach towards social and economic problems. It sharpens the skills and knowledge of the children. Technical education helps in the process of industrialization which results in vast changes in society. Education not only preserves the cultural traditions i.e., customs, traditions and values etc. of the society but also transmits them to the next generation. It also motivates the children to adopt new pattern in order to remain dynamic and forward looking. Education fulfils the needs of the society and propagates such ideas which promote social changes in all fields of life.

Functions of Education as an Instrument of Social Change

Education fulfils the needs of society and propagates such ideas which promote social change in all fields of life. In this way, education becomes a social process by means of which society moulds children according to its needs and approved patterns of behaviour. Functions of education as an instrument of social change are as follows:—

(1) Stabilizing Eternal Values. Education protects eternal values, saves them from pernicious effects of social changes and promotes their knowledge and acceptance in such a manner that inspite of social changes, people in general keep faith in these values. In our society such eternal values are of moral and spiritual nature. Education should protect, preserve and promote these values.

(2) Increasing the Areas of Knowledge. Education promotes in the individuals the capacity to increase the scope of knowledge more and more for their benefit. It opens new areas for investigations and researches, which bring about desirable changes in material as well as non-material aspects of culture. Thus education prepares ground for the advent of social change.

(3) Leadership Role in Social Change. Education provides leadership in social change. Education makes people capable to initiate and guide for needed social changes by fighting succesfully against social evils, customs and blind traditions. Thus people become capable for realizing their own true personality to the full and promote social welfare to greater and greater extent.

(4) Evaluation of Social Change. Education lays down the required standards and criteria of values with reference to which this process of evaluation takes place effectively, and only after that, desirable social changes are propagated wheres the undesirable ones discarded.

(5) Education Accelerates Social Change. Education tries to banish social evils, blind customs and traditions through various social reformation projects, political movements, social service schemes and also tries to bring in 'needed social changes and reforms'. For example, in India public movements and agitations against child marriage, forced widowhood, untouchability and social injustice resulted in desirable social changes.

(6) Education Prepares People Mentally for Social Change. It prepares the mentality of people to welcome and adopt desirable social changes easily. It may be noted that people will welcome and adopt any technique or pattern only when they become convinced of its utility and desirability. Education, thus structures a wholesome and conducive environment for these social changes to become acceptable to all.

It tries to remove the mental reservations and complexes in the minds of people which obstruct the progress of change.

Education provides necessary training in skills and occupations and thus produces the needed competent personnel for manning the different specialized jobs in modern industry, business, educational and research esablishments and other secondary associations.

Education is expected to change the values and attitudes of the people and to create in them the urge of the necessary motivation to achieve social class ascendency, social mobility and/or their sanskritization.

Modern education can mould people into enlightened, emphatic, risk-taking, thick-skinned, industrious and mobile personalities.

Education can be of immense help in bringing about democratization, secularism, national integration as well as economic prosperity and proper political socialization.

Education can cut down the thick roots of traditions, superstitions, ignorance and backwardness etc.

Education prepares the society for the initial cultural stock inherent in determined plans of modernization. Elvin Toffer's thrilling book 'Future Shock' tells us about it.

Education can prepare the society for the cultural imbalances that inevitably characterize the social transitional situation, and should endeavour to prevent, as far as possible, shocking conditions, and, during the long transitional phase, it can discipline the people to withhold immediate gratification in the interest of future inputs for the furtherance of the long-range plans of modernization.

Q. 40. Show your familiarity with Indian schools of philosophy and their implications in education.

Or

Explain the Indian thought and contribution to education practices.

Ans. The Indian schools of philosophy are:

1. Vedas (Vedanta).
2. The Gita.
3. Jainism.
4. Buddhism.

THE VEDANTA PHILOSOPHY

In the beginning, we had Vadas. The word "Veda" means knowledge. The Vedas are four—Rig, Yajur, Sam and Atharva. They contain hymns or Mantras.

These 'Mantras' stand explained in Upnishads. These Upnishads are known also as 'Vedanta' as it comes at the end of Vedas.

The Upnishads have two terms for ultimate realiy—The Brahman and the Atman. The "Brahman" is the ultimate source of the outer world and the 'Atman' the innerself of man. Both are complimentary. The subjective side is 'Atman' and the objetive side is "Brahman".

The "Brahman" is the supreme reality.

The 'Brahman' is the Absolute. It is called Sanchi-Ananda—pure existence, pure knowledge and pure bliss—all rolled into one. It is also Truth, Beauty and Goodness. These are the three values which Indians cherish the most and beauty being the highest value.

The Implications in Education

1. Perfect the Individual. It is said that the spiritual personality of the individual is the central core of the Vedanta philosophy. We must thus repeat the individual personality.

2. Teacher-Taught Relations. These relations are bound to be excellent if a student is to learn anything from a teacher.

3. The knowledge is to be acquired through detachment. The methods are Hearing, Reflection and Meditation.

4. The four ideals of life or the core of our culture are 'Artha', 'Kama', 'Dharma' and 'Moksha'. These are stressed by Vedantas.

HOLY GITA

Holy Gita is also called the 'Gospel of Humanity'. It is also called the Song Celestial. Its teachings are well known. Duty. Do your Duty. Do not expect any fruit. Duty itself is a reward in itself. It is Action which is important and only action will take you to salvation. And Fight the evil. 'Karma' is supreme.

Implications in Education

1. Act. Act now. Act boldly: Do not be despondent. Education should teach us to be manly.

2. Be of service to others.

3. Do your duty fearlessly and with devotion.

4. Renounce. Your only need should be 'Being needless'. No greed. But at the same time renunciation should not be of extreme type. And do not be over attached to the world.

To Conclude

"The Gita's message is for all men and women living in world doing all kinds of work. It shows a way of life by which people shouldering responsibilities can achieve all round success and happiness. The ideal of Gita is not only to produce great seers and sages but to produce also great warriors, statesmen, industrialists, artists and scientists. Anybody in any station-in-life can lift himself through his own self-effort."

JAINISM

Founder is Bhagwan Mahavir. Jainism is from "Jiva" which means to conquer.

It refuses to believe in God. It encourages a pessimistic outlook on life.

Main Points

1. Two aspects. There are two aspects of universe—Jiva and Ajiva—The conscious and the unconscious spirit. Jiva is expansion and contraction. It is life. Ajiva is divided into Kala, Akasha, Dharma, Adhara and Pudgala (motto).

2. Ignorance means slavery. Right knowledge is the act of liberation. Right faith, Right knowledge and Right conduct are the three pillars of Jainism.

3. Jainism believes in strict discipline. There are five vows—the last two are not for laymen; Ahimsa, Astega, Non-stealing, Celibacy and Renunciation.

4. Jainism is a religion of self-help. Jainism denies God. But every liberated soul is God.

5. Development of personality—individual and social are its aims.

The implications in education are:

1. One of the aims of education is obviously development of personality. The many sides of personality should be taken care of.

2. Right conduct should be always stressed.

3. Curriculum was based on three Ratnas—right faith, right knowledge and right conduct.

4. Memory is stressed.

BUDDHISM

Lord Buddha and his teachings are well known. We sum these up.

Three Fold Teachings of Buddha are:—1. The Four Noble Truths—There is suffering; There is a cause of suffering; There is a cessation of suffering; There is a way leading to the cessation of suffering.

2. The Eight-fold path to Nirvana are:

— Right Faith,

— Right Resolve,

— Right Speech,

— Right Action,

— Right Living,

— Right Effort,

— Right Thought,

— Right Concentration.

3. Dependent Organisation. All things hang between reality and nothingness. Each object of reality is relative. Everything is conditional, dependent. Everything is merely a link in its chain.

Implications in Education

1. You can achieve peace here and now. Teachers need not despair.
2. Buddhistic philosophy is pragamtic. Everything is in a state of flux. Nothing is permanent. Change is the rule of universe.
3. It is democratic. It encourages enquiry.
4. It believes in the teaching and learning of manual skills.
5. It is ethical. Our education should be ethic based.

Q. 41. Explain the meaning and importance of education and how you provide Environmental Education?

Or

Discuss the role of teacher in providing Environmental Education.

Ans. Environment is a word which describes all the external factors, influences and conditions which affect the life, nature, behaviour, growth and development and maturation of living organisms. Environment stands for all those circumstances which assert their influence on the human beings since birth to death. Whatever is present around us, above the land, on the surface of the earth and under the earth is environment. It covers the whole natural surrounding that is spread over around us. It includes vegetation, like trees, plants, animals, birds, forests, rivers, mountains, lakes and tanks etc. The environment has been playing an important role since times immemorial. Environment is of two types—Natural environment and social environment.

1. Natural Environment. Natural environment is related with nature which includes air, water, forests, land, minerals, animals, birds, etc. or organic and inorganic substances. All the components of the environment keep themselves in balance but man has polluted the environment by his ignorance and carelesseness.

2. Social Environment. The social environment is expressed in the action and reaction of social relationships. All the aspects of man's life are included in the scope of social environment *e.g.*, political, economic, religious, spiritual, physical and intellectual etc.

Importance of Environment

Modern age is the age of science. We have conquered nature. Attention was paid to available and new resources because of explosion of population and explosion of knowledge. The explosion of population has a direct effect on our ways of living. India is a vast country having a population of about 88 crores. The estimate is that by the beginning of 21st century the population will touch 100 crores.

In India explosion of population has given birth to various problems pertaining to environment. Our population depends upon the natural resources to meet their basic needs, particularly of fuel, fodder and housing material. It has led to deterioration in the quality of life. Man has cut off forests to satisfy his endless hunger and adopted artificial means of irrigation. The fertility of soil is decreasing day-by-day. As a result of increasing pressure of pupulation land is becoming limited. Cultivable land is decreasing due to increasing population, industrialisation and urbanisation. Increase in population leads to pollution of air and water and spread germs of many diseases. Apart from this, industrialisation has given birth to noise and smoke. It increases slum dwellings. It compels a large number of people to live in dirty surroundings having dirty lanes permeating bad smell. The smoke emmitted by cars, motors and scooters pollutes the atmosphere.

Increase in pollution has given birth to several diseases such as tuberculosis, deafness, heart attack and high blood pressure etc. The carbide gas factory at Bhopal made thousands of people blind. Pollution also creates mental diseases.

The tendency of urbanization also contributes to this problem at a rapid rate. The rural population started moving towards the cities and the cities went on expanding. Due to the housing problem the life of big cities became more complex.

According to the Report given by United Nations, 22350 lakh acres of land has become sterile because of soil erosion and saltishness. 2/3 jungles of the world have been cut down. 200 kinds of animals and birds have become extinct because of human carelessness. This tendency continues in all areas. If attention is not paid to this side the future of man will become dark.

These days man is moving towards the planet whereas humanity is moving towards the jungle. Insecurity, restlessenss and disorder prevail in the society because human beings have been intellectually polluted. If environmental education is given to future citizens in the present day schools by formal and informal methods, humanity can get rid of this danger. We find around us air pollution, water pollution, noise pollution, nuclear pollution, ecological imbalance and increase in heat and radiation. Today's environment is not pure and natural due to these pollutions.

- — For checking pollution, more and more parks should be created in order to make the environment healthy and clean.
- — Factories should find place at long distance from the dwellings.
- — Rivers are to be protected from dirty water and filth.
- — Vehicles are to be checked from emmiting smoke.
- — They should be fitted with silencers to reduce noise.
- — Drinking water should be drawn from greater depth and put in clean and well covered pots.
- — Vanmahotsav programme should be a continuous process.
- — Ways and means are to be adopted to check soil erosion.
- — Special cleanliness drives should be undertaken at regular intervals in the cities.
- — Milk dairies are to be established at the outskirt of the city.
- — No factory should be allowed to work in and around the localities.
- — There is need to take steps to prevent the spread of various diseases. In this, family planning should form an integral part of the whole scheme.

Methods of Providing Environment Education

There is dire need to educate people about environment balance. Earlier we did not bother about our environment and took it for granted. We are now worried when we see that ecological and environmental (Air , Water and Noise) imbalances have started to occur in our life and have started to take their toll.

It is imperative that we carefully manage our renewable resources of soil, water, plant and animal life to sustain our economic development. Over exploitation of these is reflected in soil erosion, siltation, floods, rapid destruction of our forests, floral and wild life resources. It is only towards the end of nineteen seventies that Ecology has caught the imagination of people—of planners and educationists alike. It is the time to wake up or face tragedy or catastrophe of unimaginable dimensions. We shall fall victims to chronic and fatal diseases.

Some suggestions to educate people in this directon are as follows:

1. Environment Education in Curriculum. Environment education should be included in the curriculum. At the primary stage environment studies should be correlated with the nature-study, social studies and health education. Form class 8th onwards, environment studies should be made a compulsory subject.

2. Environment Education Corners. In the primary schools environment education corners should be set up. The pupils should be encouraged to carry out projects like cleaning up the environment, cleaning up vacant spaces, parks, school compound, lawns and other physically polluted areas of one's surroundings.

3. Arrangement of Extention Lectures. Lectures on environment education should be arranged in schools and colleges. Today's children are the citizens of tomorrow. It is they who have to face the ecological imbalance. They must be warned of and educated abut impending disaster of ecological imbalance. For this, experienced persons working in the field of environment education can be invited for delivering lectures on different aspects of environment education.

4. By Arranging Discussions and Seminars. Students can be made aware about the ill effects of different types of pollutions through discussions and seminars which can be arranged in schools and colleges.

5. By Organizing Co-curricular Activities. Co-curricular activities can be more helpful and useful in this field. Education for healthy environment can be given effectively with the help of various co-curricular activities being organised in the school. Co-curricular activities like organisation of exhibitions, seminars, workshops, excursions, declamation contest, organisation of clubs etc. can help a great deal in this respect.

6. Publicity. Our general public and policy makers should be effectively exposed to environmental issues. We must broadcast talks over Radio, T.V. on these issues. Films can also be shown to make people aware of the need to maintain ecological balance. Posters can also be displayed. Hoardings at crossings can make people conscious of their duty in this regard.

7. Legislation. In view of disastrous effects of different types of pollutions, there is urgent need to adopt suitable measures to prevent air and noise pollution, over exploitation of fisheries, control of impact of mining on environment. A provision for taking over the treatment of industrial effluents by the Government and preservation of landscapes is also of special significance. Old legislations should be suitably amended and strictly enforced. In 1974, Government passed a law for the prevention and control of water pollution and set up a Cental Water Pollution Board.

8. School Magazine. Teacher can invite the students to write articles on pollution and its ill effects on the humanity. They can take part in essay competitions. The teacher can guide the pupils regarding the literature available in this field. He can arrange poster competitions, declamation contests, dramatisations etc.

9. By Encouraging Research in the field of Environmental Education. To control the problem of environmental imbalance, the need to encourage research today is stronger than ever before. Latest technology should be utilised in industries.

10. By Involving Students. Schools should take up cleaning campaigns, campaign against social evils like drug addiction, cleanliness of the surroundings, etc. The teacher should involve students in solving local environmental problems. The teacher should make the students familiar with their close relationship to the environment surrounding them and tell about its contribution for them.

11. By Celebrating Environment Day. To make students aware about environmenal problems and their ill effects, there is urgent need to celebrate environment day in schools every year. On this day students should be made to understand the use of protecting the environment. Tree plantation programme can be ganized and cleanliness drives can be taken up.

12. By Encouraging People Initiative. In order to create awareness about environmental problems and their bad effects people should be encouraged to take part in "chipko" like movements. Such movements can be launched from time to time in different parts of the country against indiscriminate felling of trees. These movements can draw the attention of the government as well as general public. We should give whole hearted support to such movements.

Teacher is an important means of process of education. Therefore when education plays important role in the formation of healthy environment, teacher can make as much important contribution. He is the architect of the future whom the children copy.

The responsibility of guiding the society lies on the teacher. He is the agent of social change and modernization. He can impart current information to the new generation and develop outlook towards new values. He can prepare the students mentally for the healthy environment. Its effect is not only there on the student community but he can expand his area.

Q. 42. Evaluate the New Education Policy will prove boon to us.

Or

New Social Order (Education Policy) is not capable to fulfil the needs and aspirations of the people and nation. Discuss.

Ans. **NEW EDUCATIONAL POLICY**

The need for National Education Policy was felt after 1947. Kothari Commission had recommended for National Education Policy in 1966 and for the first time Policy for Education was declared in 1968. Due to political instability during 1971-79, Congress has to leave power and the then Government also declared its own National Policy on Education. Again, Congress came into power and deceased Prime Minister Shri Rajeev Gandhi took interest in Education and declared his National Education Policy in 1986 and proposed an action plan.

This document was published in 1986. Honourable Governor of Gujarat, Mr. R.K. Trivedi expressed his views on this policy—"Considering the all round development of the country, the structure of Education Policy was erected. Education is not considered within four walls of the schools. Teaching is not limited to the curriculum but it is a source of developing national unity, cultural preservation and indication of moral, social and ethical values.

Education Policy provides a sound basis to National Progress. Every ruler in India gave preference to Education according to its need. Present Government declared its National Policy on Education. Following are the main features of National Policy on Education 1986:

1. Role of Education. Education is responsible for the all round development of the individuals. It is also responsible for cultural assimilation and provide strength to democracy, secularism. Education constructs the nation at every level, creates self-sufficiency and search new areas of development.

2. National System of Education. Though Education is a state subject, this policy provides a National System of Education, *i.e.*, 10 + 2 + 3 system.

3. Equality. This policy provides equal opportunities to all for education. Navodaya schools have been opened for socially and economically deprived but to talented children. Regional imbalances are also being removed.

4. Education of Scheduled Castes. Socially and economically deprived scheduled castes are the backbone of our society. They need proper development and place in the society. Scholarships, hostel facilities, adult education programmes are being introduced.

5. Women Education. New Education Policy gave special emphasis to Women Education. This statement owes that women are the keys to nation's progress. Education of illiteracy vocational curriculum, nutrition and child care courses, home management, etc., are given priority.

6. Education for Tribes. This policy gave main emphasis to the education of tribes. Residential Ashram Schools have been opened for them, scholarships for higher education are given.

7. Adult Education. Education Policy gave a programme for adult education to remove the illiteracy from the masses. For this, adult schools, libraries, distance education, T.V. programmes are being introduced.

8. Education for other Backward Classes. A large number of backward classes, minority classes have not been given any opportunity for education. These classes have a very crucial situation. They are socially and economically deprived due to their profession, but they usually linked themselves with higher varnas. Thus upper castes do not give them social sanction. Education is the only way to give them chance to co-operation with the society.

As far as the secondary education is concerned, vocationalization of it is introduced. At Higher education stage, autonomy will be given to good colleges.

Though, New Policy gave a new direction in the field of education in the light of national unity and development this is the preparation to welcome the 21st century. Life deal, family structure, social organisation, national consciousness are influenced by the scientific and technological advancement. Moral, social, ethical and human values need development. This is a felt need of our new policy. Common man is on the cross roads. He does not find his way to destiny. Growing population, expansion of social distances and economic disparities put some questions before the new policy. Those questions are as under:

1. Whether new policy will create class difference?
2. Is this policy competent to shape the socialistic society?
3. Will it be possible to make free and compulsory education to all the children upto the age of 14.
4. Reservation policy will not give the passage to new policy.
5. What will be the shape of future? This indication is not given by the policy.
6. How will this be helpful to reconstruct the nation?
7. Will social justice be possible through it?
8. Language problem is a very big problem before new policy?
9. No equality is possible through it.

Though these questions are before our policy makers, even then they are much hopeful to build new India. In the word of our deceased Prime Minister Rajeev Gandhi—"We will have to build our society, such a society where education must be honoured. Education does not end after learning school or college. It is a life long process. We cannot progress until our education be honoured and we could not face the challenges in future to save our country."

In the end past is gold, present is full of dust and future is indefinite. New Education Policy is the determination of youth. This will create a faith for future, develop our determination, thus distance will be dispersed.

Q. 43. Explain the provisions made and channels started for education to all socially, culturally, economically deprived, disabled, minorities, castes and tribes.

Or

Discuss the education imparted to disabled children of armed forces/SC/ST/OBC and minorities.

Ans. INTEGRATED EDUCATION FOR DISABLED CHILDREN

It has been established scientifically that disabled children with mild handicaps make better progress academically and psychologically if they study with the normal children. To integrate these children with others in common schools, a revised scheme of Integrated Education for Disabled Children was started during 1987-88. Under it, cent per cent financial assistance is given to State Governments/ UT administrations/voluntary organisations for creating necessary facilities in schools. Admissible items of expenditure are books and stationery allowance, transport allowance, uniform allowance, readers allowance (for blind children), escort allowance (for orthopaedically handicapped with lower extremity disabilities), equipment allowance and wherever necessary hostel charges. Besides, the scheme also provides, among other things, to meet cost of salary and incentives for teachers, setting up of resource rooms, carrying out assessment of disabled children, training of teachers, removal of architectural barriers in schools, development and production of special instructional material for them. Assistance is also given through the University Grants Commission to the selected universities/institutions to run training courses in special education for teachers of handicapped children. Training facilities are also provided by NCERT and four regional colleges of education. The scheme is at present in operation in Andhra Pradesh, Bihar, Goa, Gujarat, Haryana, Jammu and Kashmir, Himachal Pradesh, Karnataka, Kerala, Madhya Pradesh, Maharashtra, Manipur, Mizoram, Nagaland, Orissa, Punjab, Rajasthan, Tamil Nadu, Uttar Pradesh, Delhi, Andaman and Nicobar Islands and Daman and Diu. By the end of 1993-94 about 40,000 disable children in over 9,000 schools were covered under the scheme.

EDUCATIONAL CONCESSIONS TO CHILDREN

The Centre and most of the State Governments and Union Territories offer educational concessions to children of the defence personnel and paramilitary forces killed or permanently disabled during Indo-China hostilities in 1962 and Indo-Pakistan operations in 1965 and 1971.

During 1988, these concessions were extended to children of IPKF/CRPF personnel who were killed/disabled during action in Sri Lanka and children of the armed forces personnel killed/disabled in action in 'Operation Meghdoot' in Siachen area.

EDUCATION OF SC/ST/OBC

Pursuant to the National Policy on Education, the following special provisions for SCs and STs have been incorporated in the existing schemes of the Departments of Elementary Education & Literacy and Secondary & Higher Education:

(a) Relaxed norms for opening of primary schools;

(b) A primary school within one km walking distance from habitations of 200 population instead of habitations of 300 population;

(c) Abolition of tuition fee in all states in government schools at least up to primary level. Most of the states have abolished tuition fee for SC/ST students up to senior secondary level;

(d) Providing incentives like free text-books, uniforms, stationery, school bags, etc., to these students;

(e) The major programmes of the Department of Education, *viz.*, District Primary Education Programme (DPEP), Lok Jumbish, Shiksha Karmi, Non-Formal Education (NFE) and National Programme for Nutritional Support to Primary Education accord priority to areas of concentration of SCs and STs;

(f) Reservation of seats for SCs and STs in Central Government institutions of higher education including IITs, IIMs, Regional Engineering College, Central Universities, Kendriya Vidyalayas and Navodaya Vidyalayas, etc. Apart from reservation, there is also relaxation in the minimum qualifying cut off stages for admission in universities, colleges and technical institutions. The UGC has established SC/ST cells in 104 universities including Central universities to ensure proper implementation of the reservation policy;

(g) To improve academic skills and linguistic proficiency of students in various subjects and raising their level of comprehension, remedial and special coaching is provided for SC/ST students. IITs have a scheme under which SC/ST students who marginally fail in the entrance examination are provided one year preparatory course and those who qualify are then admitted to the First Year of the B. Tech. Course;

(h) Out of 43,000 scholarships at the secondary stage for talented children from rural areas 13,000 scholarships are exclusively reserved for SC/ST students, seventy scholarships are exclusively reserved for SC/ST students under the National Talent Search Scheme;

(i) SC/ST candidates are provided relaxation up to 10 per cent cut off marks for the Junior Resaerch Fellowship (JRF) test and all the SC and ST candidates qualifying for the JRF are awarded fellowship;

(j) 50 Junior Fellowships are awarded every year in science and humanities including social sciences to SC/ST candidates who appear in National Eligibility Test (NET) and qualify the eligibility test for lecturership;

(k) UGC provides relaxation of 5 per cent from 55 per cent to 50 per cent at the Master's level for appointment as lecturer for SC/ST candidates. The Commission has also reduced minimum percentage of marks required for appearing in the NET examination to 50 per cent at Master's level for SCs/STs;

(l) The Central Institute of Indian Languages, Mysore has a scheme of development of Indian Languages through research, developing manpower, production of materials in modern Indian Languages including tribal languages.

The Institute has worked in more than 75 tribal languages; and

(m) 146 districts have been identified as low female literacy districts to be given focussed attention by the Centre as well as States/UTs for implementation of programmes/schemes.

The allocation of Rs. 889.98 crore and Rs. 436.54 crore have been made under the Special Component Plan and Tribal Sub-Plan (TSP) for SCs and STs respectively. This accounts for 16.33 per cent and 8.01 per cent of the total outlay.

MINORITIES EDUCATION

In pursuance of the revised Programme of Action (POA) 1992, two new Centrally-sponsored schemes, *i.e.*, *(i)* Scheme of Area Intensive Programme for Educationally Backward Minorities and *(ii)* Scheme of Financial Assistance for Modernisation of Madarsa Education were launched during 1993-94.

The objective of scheme of Area Intensive Programme for Educationally Backward Minorities is to provide basic educational infrastructure and facilities in areas of concentration of educationally backward minorities which do not have adequate provision for elementary and secondary schools. Under the scheme cent per cent assistance is given for:

(i) establishment of new primary and upper primary schools, non-formal education centres, wherever necessary;

(ii) strengthening of educational infrastructure and physical facilities in the primary and upper primary schools; and

(iii) opening of multi-stream residential higher secondary schools for girls belonging to the educationally backward minorities.

Q. 44. 'Literacy can be expanded through Distance Education.' Explain.

Or

Explain Distance Education, its growth in India and advantages.

Ans. Peter says—'Distance education is a method of indirect instruction, implying geographical and emotional separation of teacher and taught whereas, in main stream education, the relationship between a teacher and student in class room is based upon social norms, in distance education, it is based upon technological rules.' Jack Foks stated the Distance education—'Distance education is a mode of learning with certain characteristics which distinguish it from the campus based mode of learning.'

GROWTH OF DISTANCE EDUCATION IN INDIA

About 25 years ago, correspondence education in India was started as a pilot project in the University of Delhi. The success of this experiment encouraged other universities to take up instructions through the distance education. By 1985, 31 universities adopted this scheme. About 40000 students at various levels were enrolled by the universities under this scheme. Though the universities are providing education through this media, but there was a great demand for an open university. As a result in 1985, the Govt. of India decided to set up Indira Gandhi National Open University. The focal points of this university are as under:

(i) to promote open university and distance education system.

(ii) to determine the standards of teaching evaluation and research in such system.

(iii) to allocate and disburse grants to colleges, whether admitted to its privileges or not, or to any other university or institution of higher learning as may be specified by the statutes.

Indira Gandhi National Open University is providing Degrees in B.A., B.Sc. and B.Com., Diploma Course in Distance education, Creative writing, Nutrition, Management, Local Self-Government, Library Science, Banking, etc.

Separate Radio and T.V. channels have been started to broadcast and telecast the educational programmes.

As a measure for implementation, the programme of Action has also favoured and recommended Open Universities System to provide higher education through non-formal channel. The main suggestions and recommendations of this Action Programme are given as under:

(i) Action Programme suggested the Open University System. This should be cost-effective, flexible and innovative.

(ii) Indira Gandhi National Open University has been established and is running effectively.

(iii) Non-formal education system should be structured on modular pattern.

(iv) Network of course be framed.

(v) Quality of programmes be ensured.

(vi) Minimum level of learning should be objectively assessed.

(vii) Separate Radio and Television channels be used for the use of distance education.

(viii) Financial Assistance will be ensured very carefully.

ADVANTAGES OF DISTANCE EDUCATION

National Education Policy, 1986 has rightly stressed that distance education will provide many opportunities for education and will lessen the burden of formal education. The advantages of Distance Education are as under:

1. Reliable. Distance education is reliable. It has the cost-effective alternative and new means of communication.

2. Education at Learners' Door. Distance education is the only way which provide the education to the learner at his door. It provides equal educational opportunities even to those who used to live in remote areas.

3. Beneficial to Adults. Distance education provides many benefits to adults. They may up-to-date themselves for the development of skills and knowledge.

4. Variety of Programme. Distance education provides variety programmes according to the needs of the learners.

5. Co-ordination. Distance education is the co-ordination of various educational factors, *i.e.*, general, basic, professsional, technical, life-long, inservice and expansion.

6. Learner Centred. Distance education is learner-centred, therefore, there is no doubt in its success.

7. Freedom. This system provides freedom to learner. A learner, learns according to his needs, conditions and facility.

8. Minimizing Pressures. Distance education minimizes the educational pressures caused by the explosion of population.

9. Educational Needs. Distance education fulfils the need of society through variety of educational programmes.

Distance education is still in experimental stage. Even then nobody will disagree that this system will be helpful to solve our educational problems and minimize the pressure of population over the traditional system of education.

Q. 45. Explain the relation of education and population growth.

Or

Describe population education as a new discipline.

Ans. EDUCATION AND POPULATION GROWTH

Education is an input fundamental to the success of economic development. In the last thirty years, primary education has increased three times, secondary education by six times and higher education by seven times. The number of universities has increased from 19 in 1950 to 118 by 1981. Despite the increase in number of educational institutions and their intake capacity, the number of illiterates has also increased from 38 millions in 1971 to 446 millions in 1981.

'Eternal vigilance is the price of democracy.' Illiteracy and ignorance hamper the successful functioning of democracy. Education enriches the human potential. According to Prof. Kenneth Bounding, "From the social and cultural points of view, the development of human resources helps people lead fuller and richer lives, less bound to supersition and unscientific beliefs. In short, the process of human resources development unlocks the door to modernisation."

Education has a bearing on population growth. This is clear from the following Table:

Literacy and Population Trends

	Rural Kerala	*Rural U.P.*
1. Female literacy	63%	10%
2. Birth rate	27 per thousand	40 per thousand
3. Death rate	7	18
4. Mean average age at marriage	21.7	15.5

Population Education

India seeks to establish an egalitarian society through constitutional means. Education has a dynamic role to play by including right values, beliefs and attitudes in children, who are the future citizens. They should be made aware of the trends in population growth, the gap between the available resources and increasing numbers, the negative effects of population growth on social and natural environment and the blessings of a small family.

Population Education is not a sophisticated name for family planning. It is not sex education, either. It expects the students to be sensitive to the problem of population explosion and how it affects the happiness and well-being of their future.

Goals of Population Education

Dr. Simmons observes—"Population education holds promise not only as means of diffusing information about population problems more pervasively in a given country than can be done by the channels ordinarily available to family planning programmes, but as a means for bringing about the desired changes in attitudes, behaviours and values in the next generation (which is almost here)." Dr. Sloan R. Wayland has given the following list of possible goals of Population Education for the individual's own personal behaviour-pattern and attitudes:

1. Acceptance of the small family norm.
2. Understanding that the size of the family can be controlled.
3. Acceptance of marriage at a mature age as a desirable pattern.

4. Appreciation of the advantages of planning, including health and economic gains from spacing and limitation in total number of children, and of the health, education and other opportunities for children that may be more adequately provided for in the small family.

Q. 46. Discuss the role of Education in eradicating of pollution.

Or

What is the role of Education in developing environmental consciousness?

Or

Explain the environmental consciousness regarding green and clean society (pollution free society).

Ans. ROLE OF EDUCATION

Before we discuss the role of education in the eradication of pollution let us keep in mind a few things like its impact on health, the radio-active waves, rise in respiratory and eye diseases, the growth in diseases caused by virus, the gastroenteritis diseases, various diseases relating to noise resulting in deafness, and other diseases of lungs and heart. The growing adverse effect on all types of vegetation cannot be ignored.

Now it shall be worthwhile to discuss the role of education in the eradication of pollution. Following are the measures if adopted in letter and spirit in the right earnest, may bear fruitful results:

1. New ways of looking at the environment so that its value can be reflected in the national accounts, better planning and legislation, more careful and wider use of existing and new environmental technologies, including the all-important environmental impact assessment—a way of appraising the effect of any proposed project on the environment before it is launched.

2. The new Environment (Protection) Act, 1986, is far better in approach than the earlier laws. The Water (Prevention and Control of Pollution) Act, 1974, and the Air (Prevention and Control of Pollution) Act, 1981, were weak and merely regulatory in character.

3. There is a section on hazardous industries and environmental disasters. Thus, hazardous industrial pollution is also covered. A hazardous substance is defined as "any substance or preparation which, by reason of its chemical or physio-chemical properties or handling, is liable to cause harm to human beings, other living creatures, plants, micro-organisms, property or the environment."

4. There are stringent measures to check hazardous pollution. Section 8 of the Act states clearly : 'No person shall handle or cause to be handled any hazardous substance except in accordance with such procedure and after complying with such safeguards as may be prescribed.' Section 6(f) empowers the Central Government to make rules for 'the procedures and safeguards for the prevention of accidents which may cause environmental pollution and for providing remedial measures for such accidents.' Morevoer, it is now mandatory for a person responsible for the discharge of any hazardous substance in excess of the prescribed norms to immediately inform the concerned authorities and to render all possible assistance. Earlier there was no such responsibility.

5. Vigilant citizens can initiate proceedings against an establishment that is polluting the water supply or otherwise ruining the environment. The penalties for defaulters have been made more stringent. The Water Act provided for a maximum imprisonment of six years and/or a fine upto a total of Rs. 5000; in the Air Act the limits were a maximum imprisonment upto three months and/or fine upto a total of Rs. 5000. The new Act provides for imprisonment of defaulters for upto a total of seven years and/or a fine which may extend upto Rs. 1 lakh.

6. However, there are some flaws even in the new Act. One, all power and authority is vested in the hands of the Cental Government.

7. **Stress on Ecological Balance.** Addressing the first meeting of the National Land Use and Wastelands Development Council on February 6, 1986, Prime Minister Rajiv Gandhi called for a nation wide "people movement" to protect the country's ecological balance. He suggested a time-bound land reclamation and afforestation programme. The approach to this problem could not be departmentalised or compartmentalised but had to "respond to the differing needs of every section."

8. **Strategy Needed.** Having experienced the ill effects of industrial development, it is high time a long-term strategy for environmental protection is evolved. In this respect, the Parthasarathy Commission has strongly pleaded for a Regional Development Strategy and a National Urban Development Policy with a view to contain metropolitan choas, for developing secondary cities and to ensure development of existing small and medium towns as well as establishing new ones, as part of a regional strategy generating employment and promoting decentralised urbanisation. In addition, a clear industrial location policy will ensure setting up of specific large industries at specific locations with a predetermined time-frame. It will ensure not only systematic industrial growth but also facilitate in taking measures for environmental protection economically and in a coherent manner.

9. Apart from increasing the forest wealth, the programme generates additional earnings to the Panchayats, more employment to labour, and it provides cheap fuel to the village poor. In Dhanoli, a village in Valsad district of Gujarat, social forestry has achieved remarkable progress. By adopting the scheme of raising village forests in only four hectares of land a net income of over Rs. 43,000 was generated.

10. All state governments, semi-government bodies and municipalities as well as social organisations have been propagating "grow more trees" campaign. To boost the idea of growing more and more trees, the government has taken up the project of "social forestry" on a large scale. The project aims at planting trees singly or in groups wherever they can be grown.

11. Social forestry not only prevents felling of trees but also tries to distribute the produce of the project directly to the people of the area. The scheme also aims at growing more trees and forests on unused land and promotes research in the science of trees and their varieties.

12. Community lands in villages are wasted and used only for grazing village cattle. This unproductive use of land yields the village panchayats hardly Rs. 4,000 to Rs. 5,000. But the same land, if utilised for a cluster of trees for which the Government provides free

seedlings, can fetch a much higther income to the panchayats. The Gujarat Government has decided to give 50 per cent of the net profit realised from the sale of village wood-lot to the Panchayat. Crores of trees are required to strengthen and support agricultural and animal husbandry, to combat pollution and to attract adequate rains and also to stop erosion of fertile soil.

13. **The Ganga Plan.** The Government of India has launched a Rs. 292-crore project to clean up the mighty Ganga, which has been greatly polluted as a result of the inflow of effluents and dirt from various sources. There are about 100 cities situated along the banks of the river, in the States of U.P., Bihar and Bengal. Nearly 4200 small and medium units are responsible for polluting the holy river. The Ganga Project is the largest and most ambitious of all the environment protection plans launched in the country.

14. The cleaning up work began at Rishikesh and Hardwar in September, 1985. Cleaning the Ganga is also in progress at Varanasi waterfront, which is heavily polluted. A Central Ganga Authority had been constituted under the chairmanship of the Prime Minister himself.

15. The wanton destruction of natural wealth, including forests, and the indiscriminate setting up of chemical industries endangers the lives of both human beings and animals. The greed for personal gain, the general decline in values, the knowledge that one can flout the laws with a vengeance and get away with it, or at worst to pay a small fine, have cumulatively rendered ineffective the agencies enstrusted with the duty of protecting the environment. There are poachers galore, but it is only rare that legal action is taken against such offenders.

16. In February, 1986 the Supreme Court directed the Union Government to examine the possibility of setting up environment courts. The court judgement in the Shriram Foods and Fertiliser Industries case may well provide a basis for action by the Government to safeguard the environment in areas where potentially hazardous industies are located. The court has in fact set out a framework for appropriate governmental action. It has also set up a monitoring committee to ensure that the expert bodies recommendations are implemented. Even more significant is the suggestion that measures

should be taken to educate the workers and provide early warning systems for the public.

While the increasing awareness and rethinking about the importance of preserving all aspects of the environment, including forests, clean air, and wild life is welcome, there is an urgent need for earnest implementation of declared policies. So far, the implementation has been poor and, consequently the environment has been deteriorating; forests, in particular, are disappearing at a disconcerting pace. It is time to recall the farsighted Chanakya's observation in the 4th century B.C. that "the stability of an empire depends on the stability of its environment." Strong and committed machinery is needed and it must have sufficient resources.

Ecology also has some effect on poverty. Undeniably, an ecologically and scientifically sound afforestation programme can provide a solution to the problem of India's poverty, if it is not based on the profit motive alone. More research is undoubtedly needed to evaluate the costs of monoculture based social forestry. Unless afforestation programmes are linked with the basic needs of the rural poor, they will prove economically counter-productive and ecologically disastrous.

Obviously, the plunder of what Nature has built over billions of years has to be stopped. We need a new life-style with environmental ethics as an integral part of it, not only for this generation but also for the future generations to live and enjoy the freedom of this planet and beyond. It is important in this regard to reduce the rate of population growth to one per cent from the present 2.2 per cent, as China has done. Industries generating high pollution shoud be moved out of the perimeters of cities. Environmental education should be made compulsory at every level of learning.

❑

PAPER-II

Development of Learner and Teachings

Q. 1. Explain the meaning of Educational Psychology and its different branches.

Ans. Educational psychology is an applied branch of psychology. It is made up of two words education and psychology. Education is the change in behaviour or modification in behaviour. Psychology is the scientific study of behaviour. Thus education and psychology are closely related.

Educational psychology is the application of psychological findings in the field of education. Educational psychology is the systematic study of the development of the individual within the educational setting. It helps the teacher to foster harmonious development of the student into a responsible and participating citizen, a sensitive and reflective human being, a productive and creative person.

Educational psychology is an applied discipline which combines the two different fields of education and psychology. It is the scientific study of human behaviour by which it can be understood, predicted and directed by education to achieve goals of life.

It is concerned primarily with learners and how they respond to various conditions they meet in school and life situations. It selects from the total field of psychology those facts and principles that have direct bearing upon the growth, learning and adjustment of children. More specifically, educational psychology is a study of human behaviour as it bears upon learning and teaching activities. It is an application of principles of general psychology to the problems of education.

In a layman's view, educational psychology is that branch of psychology which deals with the problems of education.

According to *Skinner*, educational psychology is that branch of science which deals with teaching and learning. According to *Crow and Crow*, educational psychology describes and explains the learning experiences of an individual from birth to old age. According to *Judd*, educational psychology is the science which describes and explains the changes that take place in individuals as they pass through stages of development from birth to maturity.

According to *C.V.Good*, "Educational Psychology is the investigation of psychological problems involved in education together with the practical application of psychological principles to education."

According to *Trow*, "Educational psychology is the study of the psychological aspects of educational situations."

It is concerned primarily with the study of human behaviour as it is directed under the social process of education.

On the basis of above definitions it can be concluded that educational psychology is an applied science which employs the principles and findings of psychology in the field of education.

The word Psychology is derived from two Greek words, 'Psyche' and 'Logos', "Psyche' means soul and 'Logos' means science. Hence the original or etymological meaning of Psychology is the science of soul. In due course the meanings of psychology have undergone many changes. From Science of Soul, it became 'Science of Mind', 'Science of Consciousness' and 'Science of Behaviour' which is its modern concept.

1. Psychology as a Science of Mind. Philosophers in the middle ages considered psychology as the science of mind. They used to distinguish between the mental and spiritual life of the individual. These philosophers, however, failed to give the exact nature and, force of the mind of the individual. Hence psychology the science of mind could not progress.

2. Psychology as a Science of Soul. The earliest definition of psychology was 'a Science of Soul'. Philosophers like Plato, Aristotle and Descartes interpreted psychology, according to this concept. In 16th century this meaning of psychology was rejected.

3. Psychology as a Science of Consciousness. In the 19th century psychologists like William James, William Wondt and others considered psychology as a science of consciousness. By consciousness the psychologists meant awareness or wakefulness. They, however, had different interpretations of the term wakefulness. As this definition of psychology had a very limited approach, it was not universally accepted.

4. Psychology as a Science of Behaviour. The latest and modern concept of Psychology is in times of behaviour. Behaviour is the resultant manifestation of both conscious and unconscious urges. Behaviour can be observed objectively and is a more suitable method of studying Psychology.

Modern Definitions of Psychology. Let us now acquaint ourselves with some of the definitions of Psychology:

1. 'Psychology is the study of human nature'. (Boring Lang Feld).
2. 'Psychology is the science of behaviour and experience'. (Skinner).
3. 'Psychology is the study of human behaviour and human relationships'. (Crow and Crow).
4. Psychology undertakes to make a scientific study of the individual considered as a unit as he really is in his dealings with other individuals and with the world.' (Woodworth).

The most acceptable Meaning and Definition of Psychology. It is in terms of behaviour. A lot of work has been done by psychologists in this field. Detailed experiments have been conducted on human behaviour. William Wondt established the first Psychological Laboratory at Leipzig in 1879.

Human behaviour is highly complex. All human beings do not behave in the same manner. They differ in abilities, likes-dislikes, interests, attitudes, emotions and sentiments. Why is it so? The science that answers such questions and studies human behaviour is called Psychology:

Classification of Psychology. Psychology can be divided into eleven branches—

1. General Psychology. It studies the behaviour of human organism in general. Its scope is very large but generally it studies normal organisms. It is the mother of all other branches of Psychology.

2. Abnormal Psychology. The scope of Abnormal Psychology is limited to the study of abnormal individual only.

3. Child Psychology. It deals with the development of behaviour of the child. The child is an adult in the making. He differs from the adults very much. "His life urges, his emotions, his sentiments, his intelligence and his aspirations all differ from those of the adult individuals. Therefore, Child Psychology is a fullfledged science in itself.

4. Adult Psychology. It studies the behaviour of adult humans. An adult is a mature person and his emotional, social and intellectual behaviour is not like the behaviour of a child. So it is totally a separate branch of Psychology.

5. Individual Psychology. It deals with the variation in human beings. No two persons are alike. They always differ in their behaviour according to their intelligence, race and sex. They also differ in behaviour in other factors such as interest, philosophy and education.

6. Social or Group Psychology. This branch of Psychology deals with the behaviour of individual as member of a group or mob does not act in the same way as a majority of the individual members would act individually.

7. Educational Psychology. It is the most important branch of applied Psychology. It is the study of the psychological aspects of educational situations. It is study of educational problems with reference to psychological facts. Psychology is science of behaviour and Education aims at modifying the behaviour in the most desirable way. But modification of behaviour depends on some fundamental psychological laws and limitations. Educational Psychology studies those facts and limitations. It covers the development of the child from early childhood to maturity, general facts of Psychology which may have any relation with the modification of the behaviour of the child, psychologized methods of learning, measurement of capacities, attitudes and interests and other problems of applied Psychology related to education.

8. Industrial Psychology. This is also a branch of applied Psychology. It is in fact Social Psychology with reference to work, individual as well as collective. Industrial work may be made more attractive and interesting and output of industry may be increased and improved if we exploit the finding of Industrial Psychology.

9. Para-Psychology. This is the latest development in the field of psychology. It deals with the problems of what happens to an individual after death.

10. Experimental Psychology. It studies mental processes and behaviour in laboratories with the help of experiments.

11. Comparative Psychology. It may be named as Animal Psychology also as it is a comparative study of the behaviour of man and various animals. Animals cannot express themselves. Therefore, we can study their behaviour with the help of experiments only. It is very difficult to do some experiments on human beings. Therefore, some of the experiments are first tried on animals and then the results are applied to human beings. The laws of learning, now applied with much success to pupils in schools, were discovered in this way.

Q. 2. Discuss the Nature and Aims of Educational Psychology.

Ans. NATURE OF EDUCATIONAL PSYCHOLOGY

Nature of educational psychology is scientific, as it uses scientific methods. Following are the essential elements of science :

1. **Scientific Method.** A science makes use of the scientific method.
2. **Factuality.** Science is the study of facts, the search for true facts.
3. **Universality.** Scientific laws are universal.
4. **Vaildity.** Scientific laws are also valid. They are valid at all times and in all places. They are found to be invariably true. They are open to examination at all times.
5. **Discovery of Cause and Effect Relationship.** Science studies cause and effect relationship, it searches for cause and effect relationship in its material. On the basis of such relationships it creates universal and valid laws.
6. **Prediction.** Science makes predictions.

On the basis of above criterea of science we find that educational psychology is a science as it possesses all the characteristics of being a science.

The nature of educational psychology is scientific as it employs scientific method in the study of behaviour of the learner in an educational environment. Educational psychology makes use of scientific techniques such as observation, experimentation, case history, interview and projective techniques. Thus, educational psychology as a science is systematic as its procedures are orderly.

Educational Psychology is Empirical and Factual

— It is a body of facts or information that has resulted from observations and investigations. Its conclusions are objective and unperjudiced.

— It is one of the applied branches of psychology. It studies the behaviour of the learner in relation to learning situation.

— It has developed a methodology by which investigations are made, information is discovered hypothesis tested and theories are derived.

— It is a positive science of human behaviour. Its function is to describe, control and predict human behaviour. Human behaviour is quite dynamic and unpredictable.

— It defines cause and effect relationship and on the basis of this knowledge it analyses behaviour of the learner.

— After establishing cause and effect relationships concerning the behaviour of learners it becomes possible for the educational psychologist to predict the behaviour of other learners. He can predict the development of learners in future.

It is clear that educational psychology is an applied and positive science of behaviour of the learner. Its subject matter is subtle, complex and varied. As the human behaviour is unpredictable, more variable and less reliable, viewing this concept, we can say that educational psychology is not a perfect science. Educational Psychology cannot claim the same degree of validity, accuracy, objectivity and exactness as claimed by natural science.

Aims of Educational Psychology

Aims of educational psychology are parallel with aims of education. Various views have been expressed by different thinkers about these aims as given below :

According to **Kuppuswamy,** "The aim of educational psychology is to use psychological principles for good teaching and learning."

According to **Garrison,** "The aim of educational psychology is to know the behaviour of the child and to prediet and control it."

According to **W. A. Kelly,** the following are the aims often subject to :

(1) To give an insight with teacher about the nature of child.

(2) Enlightening the teacher with the growth and development of the child.

(3) Helping the teacher in finding out ways means of social adjustment for the child.

(4) Imparting knowledge about the principle and methods of learning.

(5) Studying about the control of emotions and their educational importance.

(6) Giving knowledge about the character formation of the child.

(7) A study of the techniques of evaluation of various school subjects.

(8) A study of the psychological methods of investigation used in the field of educational psychology.

Charles Skinner has classified the aims of educational psychology as general and particular:

The Gerneral aim is to provide a body of organized facts and generalisations that will enable the teacher to realize increasingly both cultural and professional objective:

The particular aims are as follows :

(1) Creating confidence in the teacher to plan harmonious development of the child.

(2) Approaching the problems of children in a sympathetic and impartial manner.

(3) Planning education of children according to their age, ability and aptitude.

(4) Understanding the social problems of children and planning for their total social adjustment.

(5) Imparting knowledge to the teacher about the latest developments in the field of child psychology and various methods of teaching.

(6) Enabling the teacher to evaluate himself and his methods of teaching.

(7) Helping the teacher to understand and analyse the behaviour of children.

(8) Helping the teacher in solving the problems that may arise in the class-room.

In other words we can say that the general aim of educational psychology is to provide a body of facts and principles which will enable the teacher to enhance and enrich his own life and which will help him to bring about improvement in the quality of instruction, thus, equipping him adequately, both culturally and professionally and the specific aims are following :—

(a) To explain the nature and characteristics of the learner.

(b) To describe the nature of learning processes.

(c) To explain the manner in which these processes may be facilitated by the teacher, and in the light of these, to explain, how he or she should teach.

(d) "To assist in defining and setting up educational objectives and standards in terms of desirable behaviour (conduct, attitudes etc.) that ought to be the goals of all teaching efforts. If the teacher knows what the desired outcomes should be, he can set-up appropriate situations (curricular materials, teaching procedures etc.) for bringing about the wanted changes." (Skinner)

(e) To assist the teacher in the better adjustment of children and in the prevention of maladjustments.

(f) To help the teacher in defining and planning suitable guidance programmes, and functional forms of organisation and administration.

(g) To aid in developing a scientific problem solving attitude toward the problems of learning and teaching.

(h) To help in the evaluation of the outcome of the educational process.

Q. 3. What is the meaning of Educational Psychology? How is Psychology related to Education ? What is the importance of Psychology and especially Educational Psychology to the teachers and the parents?

Ans. Meaning of Educational Psychology. Educational psychology aims at applying general priniciples of psychology to educational practices. Educational practices are limited to one type of individuals, the students. It deals with a particular environment, the educational environment. In this way, the scope of educational psychology is delimited to particular set of individuals behaving in a particular set of environment.

Education has been defined in many ways. But all the educationists agree on this point that it is an attempt to modify behaviour of the educand keeping in view his balanced and harmonious development. According to *Drever*, "it is a process in which and by which the knowledge, character and behaviour of the young are shaped and moulded." Education is the direction and modification of the behaviour of the educand along certain specified lines.

Meaning of Psychology. Psychology is the science of behaviour. The psychologists seek to understand and explain how and why we behave. He tires to tell us how we feel, think and act, why we feel, think and act in a specific way. He studies the conditions that underlie behaviour and the phenomenon of its modification.

Relation Between Psychology and Education

(1) Education determines aims and ideals, and psychology decides which aims can be attained.

(2) Psychology deals with facts as they are. Education determines the standards to be achieved. Psychology tells the way of attaining these standards.

(3) Psychology helps the teacher to know the child and plan for the maximum development of the child, which is the ultimate goal of education.

Importance of Educational Psychology to the Teachers

1. Psychology Helps the Teacher in the Realization of the Aims of Education. The main aim of education is the harmonious and all-round development of the educand. Development comes from within and the inner potentialities must be understood and approached for the desired modification in the development of the child. The knowledge of Psychology helps the teacher to understand the inner potentialities which underlie the behaviour of the child. He can direct and modify the development of the educand quite efficiently if he knows Psychology.

2. Character Development. Educational Psychology helps a lot to the formation and development of character. The teacher comes to know the methods he should adopt in inculcating character traits, and moral principles among the children.

3. The Knowledge about the Child is as Necessary as that of the Subject. The educator will have to consider the mental processes of the child and not only the quality of knowledge which he is going to be put into the living mind. Psychology helps him in understanding 'John'. The teacher may be a great scholar but he will not succeed in teaching if he has no knowledge of the mental forces of the child.

4. Educational Psychology Proves Useful in the Methods of Teaching. Psychology has discovered many secrets about mental forces. Recent researches made in the field of psychology gives us valuable suggestions for the better methods of teaching and memorizing, for making desirable habits and eradicating anti-social tendencies. Psychology tells us how significant play and recreation are for the children and how play-way-methods turn the work of learning into an interesting play.

5. Educational Psychology can Change the Outlook and Attitude of the Teacher towards his Pupils. The knowledge of psychology will change the outlook and attitude of the teacher towards children. He will no more denounce his pupils on account of their undesirable behaviour. He will not hate the juvenile delinquent.

Instead of being fed-up with the backward child the teacher will be more interested in him. The problem child will no more be a problem for him but he will be simply a child with problems and the teacher will be ever ready to help him in the solution of his problems.

6. Educational Psychology Helps the Teacher in His own Mental Adjustment. A maladjusted personality can never be a good model for hundreds of developing personalities. He cannot solve his own problems and therefore he cannot help the children in this aspect. The study of psychology may help the teacher to readjust himself. He will know his own weaknesses and merits and will overcome his complexes.

7. Knowledge of Educational Psychology will Give a Scientific Attitude to the Teachers. The knowledge of psychology will make an educator more scientific in his educational practices and consequently he will be more and more objective and methodical in his work.

8. Psychological Measurements are Very Useful for the Teacher. Psychology has developed many reliable tests and instruments of mental measurement. These are providing to be extremely useful in the field of education. We can quite easily measure mental capacities, basic intelligence, temperamental attitudes and special inclinations of children and base their educational programmes on these findings. These measurements show that all the children differ in their eventual capacities and that every child is a unique being. The teacher can know that children with I.Q. below 90 cannot do well in medical, engineering, administrative or other similar vocations. But he knows that such young ones are not doomed if they cannot do well in intellectual callings. He can easily explore some other fields where such children can also flourish.

9. Educational Psychology and Process of Learning. Teaching and learning go side by side. All education depends upon the learning of new responses and the capacity of a human child to learn new responses. Educational Psychology discusses the nature of learning theories and types of learning for different age levels and situations. It tells that learning is not possible if the child does not cooperate in the learning process. Therefore, knowledge of Psychology becomes essential to a teacher to study all these problems.

10. Educational Psychology and Nervous System. The entire education depends on the function of the brain and nervous system. It becomes essential to teacher to study the nervous system which controls human behaviour. He must have the knowledge of sensory organs which are the gates of knowledge.

11. Individual Differences. No two persons are exactly alike. There is individual difference. Pupils always differ in their level of intelligence, aptitudes, likes and dislikes and in other propensities and potentialities. Different minds are to be trained by the teacher. There are gifted, backward, retarded, talented and handicapped children. All of them should not be treated in the same manner. So, the teacher should know their Psychology to satisfy them.

12. Educational Psychology and Play. Play is a natural tendency having great educational quality. Psychology helps in playgrounds also. Child finds outlet for pent-up feelings and energy through play. It also gives joy and pleasure to the pupils. Hence there is a great importance of play-way in education.

EDUCATIONAL PSYCHOLOGY AND THE PARENTS

1. Educational Psychology enables the parents to understand the process of development and growth of their children.
2. Educational Psychology acquaints the parents with the emotional, mental and physical needs of the children.
3. Educational Psychology impresses upon the parents for the necessity of providing wholesome environment to the children so that they lead a happy life and are free from anxiety.
4. Educational Psychology enables the parents to know that they should not take recourse to repression and punishment which adversely affect the mental health of children.
5. Educational Psychology enables the parents to observe keenly the behaviour of children. It enables them to control their habits.
6. The knowledge of Educational Psychology points out to the parents that they should show love and affection to their children. They should bear in mind the maxim, "Love the child and the child will love you. Hate the chiid and he will hate you."

To sum-up, Educational Psychology has revolutionised education. It has made education child-centred. It is only with the knowledge of Educational Psychology that it is possible for the teachers to render proper guidance, arrange the learning situations and plan the instructional programmes and other activities for the all-round development of children.

Q. 4. What is Psychology? Discuss its relationship with education.

Ans. Psychology has assumed an extraordinary importance in the life of an individual. Infact, every action of life, may it be home, school, neighbourhood or social gathering, is influenced by it. All communications between the teacher and students are based on the knowledge of psychology. Theories of intelligence, creativity and personality have been responsible for shaping and designing the educational system according to individual needs.

Psychology is the Science of Soul. The word 'psychology' comes from Greek words 'Psyche' and 'logos' where psyche means soul and logos means science. Thus, literally psychology means a science of soul. But this is not acceptable because of following criticisms :

(i) Nature, origin and place of soul is not known. It has no physical existence. It cannot be seen and heard. It has no weight and volume. It is a metaphysical cancept.

(ii) It makes psychology more of religion than of science because it is a theological concept and implies certain theories of religion and relationship to God.

(iii) Soul makes science speculative as it is not open to observation and experimentation and therefore not given to verification. So this definition of psychology is unscientific and hence this is descarded.

Psychology is Science of Mind. Alternatively philosophers evolved another definition of psychology as science of mind. Mind is a combination of sum total of mental processes and it stands for personal internal experiences of man, *e.g.*, pleasures and pains, hopes and wishes, dreams and desires. But this is also criticised on following grounds :

(i) It is subjective. We can know our own mind and not the mind of others. So it is half true.

(ii) Mind implies continuity and unity but it is lacking in abnormals, insanes and animals etc.

Psychology as a Science of Consciousness. Failing to define the nature of soul and mind, the psychologists defined psychology as a science of consciousness. The definition was considered too narrow as this did not include the unconscious and preconscious activities of mind. Freud in his psycho analytical theory described that mind consists of 3 states—preconscious, unconscious and conscious. About 9/10th part of behaviour is determined by unconscious and preconscious mind whereas only 1/10th part is determined by conscious mind. But in Freud's terminology, unconscious mind plays a major role in the development of personality of an individual. This definition was also discarded.

Psychology as a Science of Behaviour. Psychology was finally defined as the science of behaviour where the term behaviour carries a very wide meaning. According to **Woodworth,** "Any manifestation of life is is activity" and behaviour is a collective name of all such activities. It includes all types of activities such as cognitive, affective and conative. So behaviour refers to entire life activities and experiences of all living organisms.

According to **Watson,** "Psychology is the positive science of behaviour."

According to **Skinner,** "Psychology deals with responses to any and every kind of situation that life presents by adjustment activities."

According to **Bernard,** "Behaviour is an attempt of the organism to adjust to the multiple stimuli which impinge on it." Behaviour is classified in three categories according to its content :

(a) Cognitive Behaviour where it is dominantly knowing or thinking, *e.g.*, solving questions.

(b) Effective Behaviour where the dominance is of feeling, *e.g.*, the emotional experience of anger, fear, jealousy *etc.*

(c) Conative Behaviour where the dominance is of motor activity, *e.g.*, cycling, playing hockey *etc.*

According to **Crow and Crow,** "Psychology is the study of human behaviour and human relationship."

According to **Munns,** "Psychology today concerns itself with the scientific investigation of behaviour."

According to **Garrison,** "Psychology is concerned with observable human behaviour."

Thus, it can be concluded that psychology is a behavioural science which helps us to describe, understand, predict and control behaviour.

MEANING OF EDUCATION

Generally education is the modification of behaviour in desirable direction. The word education has been derived from Greek word 'educare' which means to 'bring up' or to 'raise' which means to shape the behaviour and habits in accordance with the needs of society. Education is therefore, development of desirable habits, attitudes and skills which help an individual to adjust in the society. In the process of education we try to modify the behaviour of an individual. This modification of behaviour helps his healthy adjustment in the society.

According to **Drever,** "Education is a process in which and by which the knowledge, character and behaviour of the young are shaped and moulded. Education therefore gives knowledge to the child, builds his character and modifies his behaviour."

RELATIONSHIP BETWEEN PSYCHOLOGY AND EDUCATION

According to **Aristotle,** "Education is the creation of a sound mind in a sound body."

According to **Pestology,** "Education is the natural, harmonious and progressive development of man's innate powers."

According to **Gandhiji,** "By education I mean alround drawing out of the best child and man, body, mind and spirit.".

The relation between psychology and education is very intimate. Psychology has been defined as the science of behaviour. It seeks to understand and explain behaviour in terms of mental and bodily activities. Its chief porblem is how and why we behave, how we think, know, feel and act and why we think, know, feel and act in the way in which we do. It tries to understand the conditions from which acts of behaviour arise and to arrive at general prinicples which govern behaviour so as to interpret, control and predict it. Education, as we have seen above, is an attempt to mould and shape behaviour. It tries to help young people to grow and develop along certain lines, to acquire knowledge and skill and to leran certain ways of thought and feeling so that they may be absorbed in adult social life. The science of psychology must be basic to such an attempt, for any influence on behaviour, to be effective, must be planned and worked according to the principles of psychology. Education, therefore, must be based on psychology and from the very first step which he takes to educate the child, the educator must depend upon psychological knowledge.

Education deals with young people and the conditions that promote or retard growth and development; it selects and strengthens those influences which promote healthy growth and tries to eliminate and weaken those which retard it. As a result of this study it formulates certain principles on which organisation and administration in schools should be based; it has to study the needs and interests of children and provide for their healthy satisfaction and expression; it has to devise effective methods of teaching so that children may learn more quickly and better. All this is not possible without a knowledge of psychology which explains how young people grow, what dominant interests mark the several stages of their growth, how they differ from one another and grow at different rates, how they learn new skills or acquire new knowledge, how they react to the influence of teachers and class-mates. Psychology is expanding repidly and our growing knowledge of the minds and behaviour of young people promises to be an effective guide in the solution of our educational problems.

The Education and Psychology are complementary to each other. Psychology is an essential element to education. Without its help problems of education cannot be solved. Both education and psychology are concerned with behaviour. Modern education is based and founded on psychology. The child is imparted education only after making a thorough study of his interests, aptitudes, intelligence and personality. Both are two distinct branches of knowledge but they are closely related.

According to **Jha,** "The process of education is entirely at the mercy of psychology."

According to **Davis,** "Psychology has made a distinct contribution to education through its analysis of pupils' potentialities and differences."

According to **Skinner,** "The entire range of behaviour and personality is related to educational psychology."

Psychology is the science of behaviour and education in its narrower sense is the modification of behaviour. The modification in behaviour can not be easily brought unless we know the science of behaviour. The teacher must know about the developmental stages, personality development and emotions of the students in order to be successful teacher. Unless the teacher is fully aware of psychological characteristics of the child, he may not be successful in bringing the desirable changes in the behaviour of students. This leads us to believe that education and psychology are intimately related to each other.

Below are some points which show how far education and psychology are related to each other :

(1) Education is concerned with aims, ideals and standards of life and psychology determines whether these aims are attainable or not.

(2) Education demands the teacher to know the child as well as the subject matter of instruction, where the psychology helps to know about the child.

(3) Psychology also helps the teacher to teach effectively undertaking effective and appropriate teaching techniques.

On the basis of the following points the relationship between psychology and education can easily be seen:

Psychology and Aims of Education. Psychology helps the educator in the realization of educational aims by helping him to bring out improvement in the quality of instruction by providing him ability and insight into the child's attitudes, ideas, aptitudes, interests and emotions etc.

Psychology and Teacher. Psychology helps the teacher to understand the learner, learning process and the learning situations. Psychology states that teacher should have sympathetic and affactionate attitude towards the learner. They should have genuine interest in the teaching profession.

Psychology and Curriculum. Psychology suggests that the curriculum should be integrated, flexible, co-related and child-centred. There should be different co-curricular activities in the school. Co-curricular activities are considered as an important part of education because they are important media for sublimation of instincts and for the development of personality.

Psychology and Methods of Teaching. Various methods of teaching like Project method, Heuristic method, Montessori method, Play-way method are based on sound psychological principles.

Psychology and Text Books. Psychology tells the teachers and the students that text books should be attractive, well illustrated and according to the mental level of the pupils. These may act as good aids to the learners.

Psychology and Innovations. Psychology has made significant contribution by introducing innovative ideas for improving the process of teaching and learning such as—Activity-centred teaching, Micro-teaching, Programmed instruction, Interaction analysis.

Psychology and Audio-visual Aids. Psychology states that to develop interest among students, teacher should properly use audio-visual aids. Use of audio-visual aids makes the learning easy, interesting and effective.

Psychology and Time Table. Time table is prepared according to the psychological principles. While preparing it, the teacher should keep in mind the relative importance of different subjects and their toughness and the fatigue of students.

Psychology and School Administration. Psychology helps in solving problems of administration by mutual discussion among various agencies of school. It provides a scientific basis for the supervision of instruction.

Psychology and Discipline. Psychology tells us the ways of dealing with problems of deliquent, backward, handicapped and gifted children and helps in maintaining discipline. It states that dicipline should be self-discipline, dynamic and constructive through participation in purposeful activity.

Psychology and Evaluation. Psychological tools help the teacher to evaluate the achievement of the pupils and suggests improvements in examination. Teacher can control, direct and predict the behaviour of students on the basis of research studies in class-room teaching.

Thus, education and psychology are closely and intimately related.

Q. 5. Discuss the Problems of Educational Psychology.

Ans. PROBLEMS OF EDUCATIONAL PSYCHOLOGY

1. Development of a Balanced Personality. The main problem that engages the attention of educational psychology is the development of a balanced personality in the child. And, generally speaking, a balanced personality is one in whom the intellectual, emotional, ethical and moral aspects are properly blended and synthesized, functioning properly.

2. Motivation. Often enough, the problems that are at the root of various adjustment defects are problems of motivation.

3. Increase in Understanding and Meaning. Another factor at the root of the motivation problem is sometimes a deficient understanding and an inability to comprehend the implications of the problems existing. It is to this end that the material chosen in teaching nowadays is such as is drawn from an environment with which the child is reasonably familiar and with which he is conversant enough not to be embarrassed by it. A simple example would be the creation of a model government within the class in order to explain the working of the actual government of the country to the student. In democratic societies the students usually understand the functioning of a democratic system in their student groups.

4. Individual Importance of Heredity and Environment in Individual Differences. The aim of education is the development of the child. Hence, one of the important problems facing the educational psychologist is the determination of the relative importance of heredity and environment in the child's development and in causing individual differences among children. Can education change the inherited qualities? Can children reach an adequate stage of development on their inherited qualities alone if they are placed in a common environment? Is it possible to make a child into anything on the basis of education irrespective of his heredity? These are questions of this nature that encourage and inspire the educational psychologist to make a comparative study of hereditary and environmental factors. For example, one important question is the extent to which intelligence can be developed through education regarding which educational psychologists have discovered numerous facts after much investigation.

5. Methods for Maximum Progress in Learning. Fundamentally, the process of education advances with learning. The most prominent question that interests the educational psychologist in this regard in what methods of learning can most facilitate learning and achieve the maximum progress? One such question could be—is there any conflict between imitation and creation? Should education pay more attention to the collection of factual details or concentrate on creative activities? Psychology has made considerable experiments with such methods as imitation, conditioned response, taril and error and insight, and has tried to discover the conditions that are best attened to the application of these methods, the coordination between the condition and method being productive of the best results.

6. Education of Emotions. The proper and adequate development of personality demands the proper and complete development of emotions. An absence of such education of emotions results in many mental diseases such as indiscipline, split personality, etc.

7. Measurement and Development of Intelligence and Attainment. Education develops intelligence and attainment. Educational psychologists search for and discover methods and measures whereby one can know how this development can be achieved and once it has been achieved, to know how much development in the child has taken place.

8. Individual Differences. Practical psychology is based on the fact of individual differences. Educational psychology, a knowledge that makes practical use of psychology in the field of education, finds out why and in what respects individual beings differ from each other. These differences are so obtrusive and well defined that the skilled teacher cannot function properly unless he can understand them. For example, the mental level of some individuals is so low that they can be taught even fundamental activities such as wearing clothes and eating only with the greatest of difficulty, while some children, precocious ones, are so intelligent and quick-minded that the normal teaching and study level of the class is not enough to occupy them so that they soon tire of it. Hence, the educational psychologist attempts to discover the limits, if any, of these individual differences, and even evolves methods for their measurement in exceptional children. The modern teacher discovers these individual differences and then makes efforts to help the children progress individually.

9. Problems Relating to Learning. Many of the problems of educational psychology are concerned with learning. The main among them are:

(a) nature of the process of learning,

(b) relation between level of maturity and learning,

(c) importance of individual differences to the speed of learning and limits of learning,

(d) internal changes taking place within the process of learning,

(e) relation between the methods of teaching and the results of learning,

(f) modes of evaluating the progress of learning,

(g) relative importance of the formal and informal methods of the education or learning,

(h) psychological effect of social conditions upon the learner.

10. Practical Problems. Educational psychology is no less a practical science than it is a theroretical one. Hence, in it one comes across many problems that arise before the teacher when he is teaching normally. Such problems would be—

(i) knowledge of the nature of every student and of the possibilities of his development,

(ii) individual and social adaptation necessary for adjustment in modern culture,

(iii) search for the fundamental psychological causes at the root of the processes of the learning and teaching.

As Educational Psychology progresses, it comes face to face with newer problems. In modern democratic societies, educational psychology is engaged in adapting education to democracy. And it has the services of psychology on the one hand and many other social sciences on the other at its disposal in the solving of any problems that it come across in such an effort. And it is on the solution of these problems that the future of democratic societies depends.

Q. 6. Explain the Socpe of Educational Psychology.

Ans. SCOPE OF EDUCATIONAL PSYCHOLOGY

Scope refers to the fields of operations, applications, topics, and subject matter with which it deals. Since educational psychology is an emerging and growing subject, its scope has never been fixed or static. It has always been changing its boundaries. As a result of new findings in the field, educational psychology has always been adding new dimensions to its areas of activity.

According to Crow and Crow. "Educational psychology is concerned with the conditions that affect learning."

According to Douglas and Holland. "The subject-matter of educational psychology is the nature, mental life, and the behaviour of the individual undergoing the process of education."

It has been correctly said by **Garrison** and others that "The subject matter of educational psychology is designed to enhance and enrich the lives of the learners and to furnish teachers with the knowledge and understanding that will help them to bring improvements in the quality of instruction.

The following areas can be included in the scope of educational psychology:—

Study of Stages of Child Development. Educational psychology studies the nature of growth and development and general charactristics of physical, mental, emotional and social development at the various stages, *i.e.*, at the stage of infancy, late childhood and adolescence.

Study of Heredity and Environment. Educational psychology studies the impact of heredity and enviroment on the student.

Study of Development of Various Aspects of Child. Educational psychology enquires how various modifications can be brought about in the behaviour of the child, how and and when do physical, social, emotional and language development occur in children, and how do various instincts make their appearance.

Study of Learning Process. Educational psychology also studies nature and process of learning, laws and methods of learning as well as factors of learning. Interest, attention, motivation, memory, habits and transfer of training play very significant role in leraning.

Study of Psychological Basis of Behaviour. It studies the psychological as well as the physiological behaviour of the learner. Psychological basis of behaviour are instincts, emotions, sentiments, suggestion, sympathy, imitation and play *etc*. Physiological basis of behaviour are nervous system and glands *etc*.

Study of Motivation. Educational psychology studies the nature, principles and techinques of motivation in eductional field.

Study of Individual Differences. Educational psychology studies individual differences and suggests ways and means to provide education to all types of pupils. No two individuals are alike. Individuals differ physically and psychologically. Individual differences are mainly caused by heredity and environment.

Study of Intelligence and Personality. Educational psychology also studies nature, development and assessment of personality and intelligence.

Study of Measurement and Evaluation. Educational psychology is helpful in giving newer and newer techniques and tests for measuring intelligence, personality, aptitudes, interests and achievements *etc.* It is educational statistics which helps us in measurement and evaluation.

Study of Exceptional Children. Educational psychology studies about exceptional children. It studies about backward, retarded, gifted and creative children and their adjustment problems with home, family and school.

Study of Guidance and Counselling. Child is like a book whose every page has to be studied by the teacher. The teacher has to guide and counsel the students at every stage. Educational psychology studies the nature and process of guidence and counselling.

Study of Group Dynamics. Educational psychology studies group dyanmics and group behaviour in class-room teaching and learning. It studies importance and effect of group on the individual. It also considers how an individual can modify the group life. It emphasises the role of groups in the education of children.

Study of Statistics. Educational psychology studies mean, median, mode graph, rank difference and co-relation.

A careful analysis of the subject matter of educational psychology reveals that it has three important centres—

1. The Learner. In this area, educational psychology examines the following:

(a) The study of the child, his abilities, aptitudes and aspects of motivation.

(b) Individual differences among children.

(c) Various stages of growth and development.

(d) Influence of various social agencies like home, school, neighobourhood *etc.,* on the child's presonality.

2. The Learning Process. In this area, the following aspects are examined:

(a) Nature of learning and how it takes place.

(b) Theories of learning and how maximum learning in the minimum time period can be achieved.

3. The Learning Situation. Under the aspect educational psychology examines the following—

(a) Nature of classroom management and discipline.

(b) Use of techniques and aids which facilitate learning.

(c) Methods of teaching children with individual differences.

(d) New techniques of evaluation and their effective use.

(e) Knowledge about educational and vocational guidance to be given by the teacher to the child.

Thus, it is evident that the subject matter of educational psychology is designed to enhance and enrich the learners and to furnish teachers with the knowledge and understanding so as to help them bring improvements in their quality of instruction.

Q. 7. Describe observation as a method of enquiry in Educational Psychology. How can it be made more effective?

Ans. Psychology is the science of behaviour. Mind as well as behaviour constitute the subject-matter of Psychology. Psychology like other sciences employs certain methods for establishing cause-effect relations. With the help of a planned procedure we try to discover the causes of phenomena that we observe and also we try to know the effects of those phenomena. Thus, methods employed in Psychology are attempts to find the responses of the given stimuli and stimuli of the given resonses. The methods of Psychology are—*(1)* Observation, *(2)* Experiment, *(3)* Introspection and *(4)* Psycho-analysis.

OBSERVATION

The main method of Psychology, as of all sciences, is observation. Observation is a regulated perception. To observe is to look at a thing closely and to take careful note of several parts and details. Observation of the behaviour of others is an important method of Psychological study. By observing their behaviour we know what is going on in their mind. We observe bodily behaviour—movement of the limbs, facial expression, heart-beat, breathing and the like. A man's anger is known from his clenched fist, loud voice, contoured face, gnashing teeth and quivering lips.

Aduantages

1. We have to study mind in general and this we can do through observation. We study the mental processes of other human beings by observing their behaviour when they are angry or happy or sad or wonderstruck.
2. It is helpful in studying the mental life and behaviour of savages, children, animals, abnormal people, the people whose language we do not understand and illiterate people suitable words to convey an adequate idea of their mental processes.

Disadvantages

1. We do not observe impartially. We not only perceive but apperceive. We think that other people and animals think and feel in same way as we do. We look at the world through coloured glasses.
2. Observation without the help of instruments is no doubt subjective, because the observer may unconsciously neglect those factors of the situation which he does not expect. Moreover, the human senses have only limited powers. The teacher cannot observe the actions of all the students in a class of even twenty and even if he can observe he cannot record every item. This defect can be considerably reduced if instrumental aid is taken.
3. The mind does not always manifest itself in observable behaviour. Cognitive processes such as thinking, reasoning and imagining *etc.,* have no counterparts in bodily behaviour.
4. The behaviour of a hypocrite defies all explanation. How would you explain crocodile tears of one who is out to deceive you.

Q. 8. Explain the experimental method of taking an example. What are the limitations of experimental method ?

Or

"Experimental method of enquiry gives the status of science to Educational Psychology." Explain the nature of experimental method in the light of above statement.

Or

Discuss the method of experimentation in Educational Psychology with its merits and demerits.

Ans. In every science, as far as possible, knowledge is obtained first hand. This knowledge is obtained systematised and organised. How is this knowledge obtanied? It is done through observation and experiment. To observe is to find a fact; to experiment is to make a fact. Experiment is observation under known and pre-arranged conditions. Observation is the general thing of which experiment is the special form. When observation is controlled and ceases to be general, we have an experiment.

The termendous growth of Psychology during the last fifty years is due mostly to experimental method. Until the late 19th century Psychology was not considered as a Science. It was regarded as a branch of Philosophy and the methods employed for Psychological investigations were those of Philosophy such as observation and introspection.

The first attempt of making experiments in Psychology was made by Wundt in 1879. He established the first laboratory at Leipazig in Germany. Experiments were made chiefly in the field of sensation, perception, association and memory. Later on, Germany and America took the lead and by 1894, a score of research laboratories started working. The last two decades have brought in important developments in technique, methods and trends in Psychology. In America and England there is a psychologist for every school. His task is to take care of the mental health of the children and this experiment is proving very successful.

It consists in the recognition of the inter-connection of the human organism and the external world. The essential principle of the method is to place a human individual in a certain situation and to note how he reacts therein. It is on the basis of his reaction in relation to the situation in which has been placed that the laws of objective Psychology have been derived. Woodworth expresses it as a stimulus-Response chain. (SR). 'S' is the stimulus presented to the individual or the situation in which he is placed and 'R' is the individual's reaction to the stimulus or the way in which he behaves in the situation. The essential task of Psychology is to take the course from 'S' to 'R' and to state the routes from 'S' to 'R' under various circumstances.

Experiment in Psychology is performed on a subject who is a living being. The living organism has got certain characteristics and the experimenter must take these into account both in the conduct of the experiment as well as in the interpretation of the results. The experimental psychologist has to depend on the co-operation of his subject, whether an adult or a child or an animal. He cannot lose sight of the time-honoured saying, "one man can take a horse to water but even twenty cannot make him drink", Woodworth has accordingly presented a modified formula in Experimental Psychology as follows:

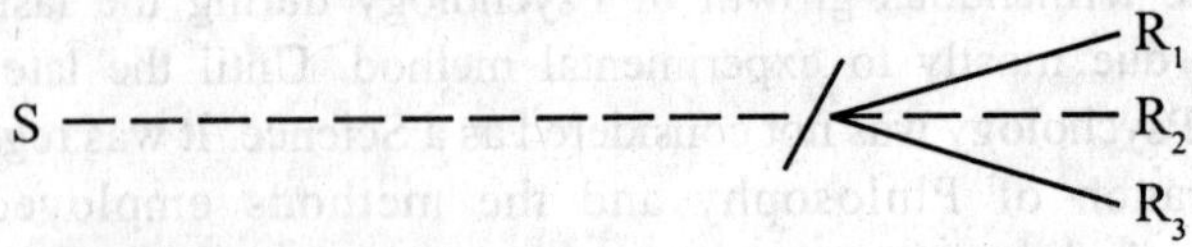

S—stands for stimulus ot situation.

I—stands for the individual (with his own initiative and urges).

R_1 R_2 R_3—stand for variety of responses.

STEPS IN THE PSYCHOLOGICAL EXPERIMENT

Broadly speaking the following steps are involved in a psychological experiment :

1. *Defining the Problem.* First of all the field of study is defined. The experimenter knows clearly which factors to control, which factors to change, what changes to observe and with the help of which material.
2. Selecting the subject or the individual on whom the experiment is to be performed.
3. Setting the material for observation.
4. Instructing the subject or telling him his functions during the experiment.
5. Observing the responses of the subject.
6. Getting introspective report of the subject. In psychological experiment we have to deal with living human beings and while stating the result of an experiment we must mention the reaction of the subject towards the experiment and his mental state during the experiment.
7. Anlaysis of the data obtained and interpretation of the data.

Problems Tackled. The following problems have been tackled in Experimental Psychology :

1. Sensation, sence training and preception.
2. Attention, its span and duration.
3. Memory and methods of memorising.

4. Laws of learning and transfer of training.
5. Habits.
6. Work and fatigue.
7. Imagery and association of ideas.
8. Thinking and reasoning.
9. Intelligence and its measurement.

Criticism. 1. Further, Experimental method has serious limitations when it is applied to Educational Psychology. While dealing with human beings it cannot be as objective as it is claimed by its advocates, because human behaviour cannot be controlled to that extent as is possible in the case of physical and chemical phenomena.

2. Secondly, human behaviour under controlled conditions is different from spontaneous behaviour. Therefore, the experimental findings should be cautiously applied to the spontaneous behaviour of human beings under normal and free conditions.

Concluding Remarks. It is not always possible for every teacher to experiment scientifically because of no special training in doing so and of lack of facilities for experimentation in schools. Yet he can adopt new teaching methods with better results.

1. New teaching methods suggested by Psychology should be tried.
2. Experimental Psychology helps the teacher in dealing satisfactorily with the backward, the deficient, the emotionally deranged and the delinquent child.
3. Experiments can also be carried on in the development of character and leadership. Schemes of self-government and of giving responsiblity to students can be tactfully introduced in schools.

Q. 9. What is the importance and utility of educational psychology for the teacher?

Ans. The contribution of educational psychology to the theory and practice of education is rich and varied. The knowledge of educational psychology is important as it provides teachers with some basic skills and guidelines to solve the problems of teaching-learning process.

Teaching is not every body's cup of tea *i.e.*, everyone cannot teach.

According to **John Adams,** "Teacher should know John as well as latin". It means teacher should know child and subject-matter. A teacher should know the nature, capacities, likings and aptitudes and attitudes of the child. Child is like a book, teacher should know each and every page of it."

Skinner's View, "The teacher needs psychology to bridge the lives of the young and the aims of education in our democratic society."

Kuppuswamy's View, "Psychology contributes to the development of the teacher by providing him with a set of concepts and principles."

Teaching is an art. Knowledge of educational psychology is very useful and indispensable for the teacher because it gives knowledge to the teacher.

Knowledge of Innate Nature. The child has got natural urges instincts, potentialities and propensities. These innate qualities are the "Prime movers" of his behaviour. The teacher who knows psychology can make his teaching very sucessful while keeping in view innate nature of the child.

Knowledge of Behaviour. Educational psychology assists the teacher in knowing the behaviour of the child at different stages of development. It also helps the teacher in understanding the physiological and psychological basis of behaviour, *i.e.*, nervous system, glands, instincts, emotions, sentiments, motives, play, intelligence, heredity and environment *etc.*

Knowledge of Guidance. It helps the teacher in giving guidance to the pupils by having an understanding of interests, abilities, aptitudes, achievements, problems, educational and vocational plans of the pupils.

Knowledge of Unconscious Mind. It helps the teacher in knowing the unconscious mind of the students and plays very important role in the development of the personality of the individual.

Knowledge About Himself. It helps the teacher to know about himself. He learns the psychology of being a teacher and acquaints himself with the traits of a successful teacher.

Understand Development Characteristics. Children pass through different stages of development as infancy, childhood and adolescence. These developmental stages have their own characteristics. If the prospective teacher knows the characteristics emerging at different stages of development, he can utilise these characteristics in imparting instruction and moulding their behaviour according to the specified goals of education.

Understand the Individual Differences. No two individuals are alike. The teacher with the knowledge of the kind of individual differences may adjust his teaching to the needs and requriements of the class and thus may be helpful in creating conducive environment in the schools where the students can develop their inherent potentialities to the maximum.

Understand the Nature of Classroom Learning. The knowledge of educational psychology provides a teacher the knowledge of learning process in general and problems of classroom learning in particular. The teacher by the knowledge of educational psychology can understand the principles of learning and various approaches to learning process, problems of learning and their remedial measures and also about factors affecting and guidance for effective learning.

Understand Effective Teaching Methods. Educational psychology gives us the knowledge of appropriate teaching methods. It helps in developing new strategies of teaching. It also provides us with the knowledge of different approaches evolved to tackle the problems of teaching at different age levels.

Understand the Problems of Childern. By studying educational psychology a teacher may understand the causes of the problems of the children which occur at different age levels and can successfully solve them.

Knowledge of Mental Health. By studying educational psychology teacher can know various factors which are responsible for mental ill health and maladjustment and can successfully help in mental hygiene.

Measurement of Learning Outcome. Psychological tools help the teacher to assess the learning outcome of the students and also to evaluate his teaching methods for required modification.

Curriculum Construction. Psychological principles are also used in formulating curriculum for different stages. Needs of the students, their developmental characteristics, learning patterns and needs of the society all are to be included in curriculum construction.

Research. Eductional psychology helps in developing tools and devices for the measurment of various variables which influence the behaviour and performance of students.

Helps to Develop Positive Attitude. The teacher training programme aims to develop positive attitude towards teaching profession and provides the prospective teachers with the necessary competencies to meet the classroom challenges. Training colleges provide the knowledge of organizing the subject matter in a sequential order to suit the needs of the class. The trainees are also aquainted with the techniques of motivating children for learning.

Understanding of Group Dynamics. Educational psychology helps the teacher to recognize the importance of social behaviour and group dynamics in classroom teaching learning.

Problem of Discipline. With the knowledge of educational psychology teacher utilizes the importance of indirect discipline rather than corporal punishment. It tells the teacher that discipline should be self-discipline, dynamic, positive and constructive through participation in purposeful activity. Pleasure and pain, reward and punishment, praise *etc.,* should be judiciously used. If the teacher is unaware of the principles of educational psychology he may be unable to solve the problems of his students and thereby fail to induce order and discipline among them.

School and Class Administration. Former autocratic method of administration in school and class has been charged by democratic way of life wherin the teachers and administrators are more democratic, co-operative and sympathetic and problems of administration solved by mutual discussion.

Use of Audio-Visual Aids. Educational psychology has helped the teachers to make use of various types os audio-visual aids in classroom teaching so as to make the concept more clear, definite and learning to last longer.

Time-Table. The knowledge of psychology is helpful to the teacher in preparing time-table. He should keep in main the relative importance and toughness of different subjects and level and index of fatigue of the students.

Use of Innovations. Activity-centred teaching, discussion method, micro-teaching *etc.,* are some innovative ideas adpoted to improve the teaching learning process.

Co-curricular Activities. Activities like debate, drama, games are given due importance alongwith theoritical subjects for the harmonious development of the personality of children.

Production of Text Books. Educational psychology has helped in planning of text books according to the intellectual development of children, their needs and interests at different age levels.

Undoubtedly the study of educational psychology may be very helpful to equip our prospective teachers with necessary skills to deal with classroom teaching learning problems.

Q. 10. Describe the constitution of educational psychology to teaching and learning.

Ans. **REVOLUTION IN EDUCATION INDUCED BY PSYCHOLOGY**

The extent to which psychology has produced into the field of teaching and learning education is so impressive that only the term revolution can be applied to it with any accuracy. In pointing to the changes in education caused by psychology. Ryan has written, "In many schools of today one finds an atmosphere of friendliness and happy activity. Much of the traditional formality, the forced silence, the tension, the marching is gone. Childern's voices are heard in the halls and class-rooms. The younger children come gaily down the stairways, naturally and relatively unestrained, the older boys and girls through the corridor or outside walk making their way to school rooms, shops, studios, libraries, laboratories and playing fields to tasks that mean something to them, that make demands upon their energies and their imagination, that often involve hard, difficult work, but work that they recognize as creative. Beauty of surroundings is considered a first, requirement in these schools—there are flowers about, brightly coloured murals painted by the children, attractive informal work rooms for the various groups....Art and music have begun to play the role that belongs to them as fundamental in education and life."

1. Child-Centred Education. In early times the teachers were mainly engaged in imparting various kinds of information to the children. In those times children were less the centre to attention, the school claimed more of their time. Today, it is the child who is the centre of attention in education. Every child is individually considered and treated. Efforts are always made to adapt the curriculum of study to the needs of the child with the result that the brilliant and dull witted children do not study the same subjects. Applied psychology has directed attention to the differing abilities and capacities of people. Such an attitude has made it possible for the teacher to gauge the special abilities of his wards and to make the best arrangements for the guiduance of individual children. The teacher of today not only must be acquainted with teaching but also with his students since his profession is now centred about the child and not about the subject or teacher. The consequence of this kind of reasoning is that what matters isn't the beauty, knowledge or ability of the teacher but the extent to which he succeeds in developing the personality of his students.

2. Process of Education. Previously, education was believed to be a comprehensive process that trained the individual, provided him with a moral character and made him more cultured. In psychology as it is understood today, the conception of mind has completely changed. Analysis has led to the discovery that many kinds of forces and mental activities take place within the human being so that for the development of the child it is ncessary to provide him with different kinds of programmes and subjects so that he may succeed in properly developing all his metal faculties and abilities. At present, variety is believed to be essential not only in education itself but it is equally held to be true that the eduaction of one individual subject includes many different activities and functions. The teacher should be aware of all these functions. It is only than that he can understand the difficulties of the childern in understanding the subject. If a child fails to memorize some one lesson, it can hardly be taken to indicate only a lack of effort on his part and no other cause. It is equally probable that he has a weak memory, or is not intelligent, or has no interest in the subject or that he is suffering from ill health. Learning is a complex activity and it is only through a complete knowledge of its various parts that one can diagnose the difficulty of a particular child in memorizing or learning a lesson. The teacher has no alternative but to attend to the activity of learning.

3. Reform in Curriculum. Psychology has also managed to bring about important variations and reforms in educational curricula. Now it is the mental age and not the chronological age of the child that helps to determine the course of study to which he is to be subjected. Intelligence tests reveal the mental age of the child. Different courses are devised for brilliant and deficient children. After the eighth or delta class, the curriculum is sub-divided into various parts such as literary, scientific, agricultural or art class. The child then has the opportunity of selecting his subject according to his interest and aptitude. Various extra-curricular activities are organized for the emotional and sentimental development of the child. These include picnics, dramatic societies, etc. Other programmes are organized in order to develop the qualities of leadership, public speaking, *etc.*, in the child. But no course of study or programme is foisted upon the child against his inclination. Inspiration is awakened in him according to his interests and his tastes. Education has now been made more interesting and appealing with the use of audio-visual aids such as television, film projection, *etc.* Many schools are also equipped with radio sets that provide both entertainment and information to the child. The use of analogies to penetrate the defences of the child is an inportant method in education. Childern who choose to study history are also taken to visit historical places. And even a glance at the curriculum of basic education makes clear the extent to which psychology has revolutionized education. And special curricula are also devised to meet the needs of adult education. They suit the psychology of adult individuals.

4. Discipline. Discipline has an important place in education. One of the aims of education is to instil respect for discipline in the child. But the recent discoveries of psychology have changed the ways and means in which discipline is taught. Previously physical punishment was one of the chief methods of teaching and imparting discipline in the children. The main motive behind the discipline was fear of physical violence and injury. But instead of injuring the body of the child it injured his personality by making it distorted. Psychologists attracted the attention of enlightened people to the injurious effects of physical punishment and also suggested alternative means of making children disciplined. One suggestive example is here described. The inmates of a hostel were given to indiscipline during lunch time. They threw morsels of food at each other and wasted much more. The warden made every effort to stop this nuisance used every means of arousing fear in the children but without success. He never discovered the name of the mischief makers and neither did the boys give up their behaviour. Some time later he was replaced by a new warden who resorted to psychological methods for solving this menace. He made an announcement to the effect that the best behaved table with the most seemly boys would win a flag that would entitle them to twice the normal ration of the most succulent food. The strategy took immediate effect and the indiscipline promptly ceased. The children seated at various tables were now busily engaged in trying to look more disciplined and seemly than all the others so that they now even prevented the more hardened and incorrigible boys among them from mischief. In this way, the warden took advantage of the psychology of children to effortlessly perform a task that had completely foiled all the effrots of the earlier warden with his shock and fear tactics. Nowadays it has become customary in schools to allow the children to adopt discipline rather than foist it upon them. At the college level it is from among the students that the prefects are chosen to create and maintain discipline among their fellow mates and to help the proctor in maintaining order within the college. Very recently there was a high level debate on the spreading indiscipline among university students in India and almost all speakers put forward psychological solutions because the problem of indiscipline is fundamentally and basically a psychological one. It need hardly be pointed out that the more a teacher knows of child psychology, the easier will it be for him to create discipline in the motley group with which he is faced in the class.

5. Education on Personality. The modern methods of education place great emphasis upon the education of personality. Education is now understood to mean something more than mere reading or writing, it is also understood to involve the development of personality. Many schools have resident psychologists who solve problems related to personality of the students and give advice to teachers and parents in this regard. At places there are also child guidance clinics, that make special efforts toward the correction and normal rehabilitation of problem children or juvenile delinquents. A study of psychology is an essential part of the curriculum of teacher's traning. In addition to these individual efforts most states and districts have a bureau of psychology whose functions are to solve all problems of students relating to their personality, to give personal guidance and to give advice to their parents and teachers regarding them. The truth of the matter is that the psychologist has become a link for the child's adjustment between the home and the school since such an adjustment helps to improve his personality. In the role of specialist his contirbution to the school has become indispensable.

6. Teaching Method. In the manner already described psychology has changed teaching methods lock stock and barrel. All new research aims at evolving teaching methods that induce the child to learn for himself and thus himself achieve his development. The means of a changed teaching method are radio, cinema, cultural programmes, debates and other competitions, picnics, visits to historical places, games, election contests, students' unions, etc. It is psychology that has contributed the Kindergarden and Montessori methods of teaching. Speical learning and teaching methods have been evolved for the use of blind, dumb and deaf children and mentally backward or handicapped children.

7. Individual Differences. In days gone by, the same curriculum was prescribed for all stduents in the class. The development of applied psychology led to the fact that different individuals differ from each other in respect of their interests, intelligence, ability, capabilities, *etc.* This knowledge of individual differences proved a variable source of revolution for education. Now-a-days the essential pre-requisite to guidance of an educational nature is a knowledge of the subject's ability and intersts. Choice of his curriculum and other extra-curricular activities is definitely governed by these individual differences.

8. Process of Learning. The experiments that psychology has carried on in connection with the process of learning have led to the discovery of many laws that economise of time and yet produce good results in terms of material learned. One example would be Thorndike's laws. It is the psychologist who has stressed the importance of reward and punishment in learning. Research in psychology has aimed at discovering the efficacy and inefficacy of the various methods of learning. The employment of the various methods of learning is improved and made more scientific by a knowledge of their qualities and drawbacks.

9. Mental Testing and Guidance. Mental testing and guidance are important factors in applied psychology. Psychologists have evolved scientific tests to measure intelligence and other abilities. Students can be guided in educational and vocational matters with the help of these tests. Now, education aims both at the complete development of the individual as well as his best possible adjustment to his vocation and of his vocation to his natural abilities. Teachers need the help of psychologists in either of these two matters. Psychologists solve the problems of students through personal guidance and inform them of the job they are best suited to through vocational guidance. In this way, the co-operation and co-ordination between the teacher and the psychologist in the field of education is on the increase.

10. Reform of Problem Children. One of the most notable contributions of psychology to education is the improvement and reform of juvenile delinquents, absconding children, morons, backward children, unsocial and problem children, and advice to their parents regarding them. To this end the state and district psychological bureau assist the educational institutions.

11. Extra-Curricular Activities. The aim of education is the complete development of the child so that mere book knowledge is insufficient to gain this end. In this connection many other programmes are included in the curriculum on the suggestion of psychologists apart from the normal theoretical knowledge.

In this manner, educational psychology provides the teacher with the means to attaining knowledge of the student's nature, capacity, characteristics, needs and motive. This knowledge is the equipment for him to modify his teaching methods sufficiently to attain the goal for education.

Q. 11. What do you understand by the term growth and development? Discuss in brief the various stages of human development. What are various educational implications. How can the school and the teacher help the child in his optimum growth and development?

Ans. Generally both the terms 'growth' and 'development' are used interchangeably though they differ in their meaning to a great extent.

The term 'growth' usually implies increase in size, weight, height, *etc.* It is in terms of growth is bodily features.

'Development' is a much broader term than 'growth'. It includes growth also in it. It refers to overall changes in the individual. Growth is one of its parts. Development includes changes in intelligence, understanding, attitude, interests, personality and character traits.

CHARACTERISTICS OF DEVELOPMENT

1. Development is the product of heredity and environment.
2. Development is a continuous process.
3. Development of various traits are correlated.
4. Development proceeds from general to specific.
5. Development can be predicted.
6. Rate of development is not even throughout.
7. Development follows a sequential order. It is a step by step process.
8. Rates of development of different aspects are different.
9. Every child has his own rate of development.

Various Aspects of Growth and Development. These can be named as follows :

(a) Physical growth and development.

(b) Intellectual or mental growth and development.

(c) Emotional development.

(d) Social development.

Various Stages of Development. Following are the various stages of development which have been commonly accepted:

Name of the Stage	*Period and Approximate Age*
1. Prenatal (Prebirth) Stage	From Conception to birth.
2. Infant Stage	From birth to three years.
3. Childhood Stage	From 4th to 12th years or to the on set of puberty.
(a) Prechild Stage	From 4th to 6th years.
(b) Early-childhood Stage	From 7th to 9th years.
(c) Later-childhood Stage	From 10th to 12th years.
4. Adolescence	From the on-set of puberty to the age of maturity (generally from 13th years to 19th years).
5. Adulthood	From 20th year or the age of maturity till the age of productivity—55 years.
6. Old age	From the end of productivity till death.

Educational Implications and the Role of the School. The teachers and parents should not expect a child to achieve something suddenly. They should provide suitable environment for the child for his proper development. The schools should provide different curricular and co-curricular activities so that these suit the students with their specific needs and traits. If a teacher finds any abnormality in the pattern of development of the child the case should immediately be referred to the guidance of counsellor. The teachers should provide learning materials and activities that will facilitate the development of different aspects at the proper time. If a teacher has the adequate knowledge of the rate of development of a particular child he can easily control the behaviour of the child. The school should realize the importance of individual differences while providing instructional materials and other activities. The child with the knowledge of child development becomes more practical and understanding. He knows what to expect from a child at a particular stage. Knowledge of development aids the teacher to find out learning readiness.

In a democratic climate of the school children display mutual understanding, tolerance, a sense of responsibility and disciplined conduct. A school provides suitable social environment for the development of a social beings who are socially efficient.

General Remarks. The characteristics, physical as well as mental, of all the stages as given above are too well marked and distinct that an infant is quite different from a grown-up child or an adolescent and similarly an adolescent differs from an individual of any other stage. The tastes and interest, and temperaments and inclinations, physical features and emotional attitudes of an individual of one stage differ from those of the individuals of other stages quite apparently and basically.

Still we cannot divide the whole life of an individual into distinct stages different from each other in watertight compartments. There is always a continuity of development in him from birth to adulthood. The child himself or his relatives and friends who come into contact with him everyday do not notice any abrupt and sudden change in him at any time. Growth is quite gradual continued and normal and it cannot be detected during the process of development.

It should also be noted that the characteristics of one stage are not entirely absent from those of any other stage. The difference lies in the prominence and domination of certain characteristics. The infant is imaginative and the adolescent again takes refuge in day-dreaming. But day-dreaming is not absent from the mind of an individual entirely at any stage. Similarly, other emotional impulses or intellectual trusts are, always there, but they are less or more prominent on different stages.

These changes do not appear in all the individuals in definite years of age. All children do not turn to be adolescent in the 12th year and all the adolescents do not develop to be adults in the eighteenth or nineteenth years of the age. Development depends upon many factors such as individual, physical features, sex, climate, social environment, food, habits and so many other environmental influences. However, an average individual is expected to develop at various stages at specific ages.

Q. 12. What are the differnt stages of development? Discuss.

Or

Discuss the development of children from the age of infancy to adolescence.

Ans. Different stages of development are as follows :—

(i) **Infancy,** from birth to two years.

(ii) **Early childhood,** from two to six years.

(iii) **Later childhood,** from six to twelve years.

(iv) **Adolescence,** from twelve to sixteen or sventeen years.

(v) **Adulthood,** after 18 years.

(vi) **Old Age,** period after the age of 58 years.

Infancy

It is a very improtant period of a child's life. It may be considered as the basis on which the future structure of a child's life can be constructed. This structure too depends on careful guidance and supervision.

According to **Ruth Strang,** "One can determine how a child stands in relation to life, a few months after his brith." "During the first two years of his life the child lays the foundation for his future."

According to **F. Goodenough,** "One-half of an individual's mental structure had been attained by the age of three years."

(a) Physical Development. It is the period of rapid growth in size and weight. The new-born child is 18 inches in size and weights about seven pounds. Changes in the proportion of the body are visible. The head which seems enormous of birth seems small now, as legs and trunk lengthen. The hands and the jaw develop. The muscles of the child also develop. He starts using his fingers by holding things, standing, walking and running.

(b) Emotional Development. He cannot show specific emotions like anger, fear, joy as the adults do. It takes time to develop them. As the children grow up and reach the age of two, there is differentiation of emotions. Anger is the most common emotion of this age and is aroused when adult force is used to restrict the freedom of the child. It is sometimes used as a device for gaining the attention of adults.

Children also show at this stage the emotion of joy. They express it on seeing familiar faces generally of adults and also show affection for parents and nurses.

(c) Social Development. The social development of the child essentially depends on the parents. If the parents are well inclined towards him, the child starts developing a healthy social personality; whereas an absence of such a relationship may injure his personality. He may develop anxiety, depression and feeling of insecurity.

Educational Significance of Infancy

1. The child at this stage should be provided wooden blocks and other play material which he may handle with ease and which do not require any special skill.
2. He should be given enough freedom in his movements. He should not be protected too much, otherwise he will not be able to develop his normal personality.
3. The child should feel secure in the family and the parents should treat him well.

Early Childhood—(from 2 to 6 Years)

(a) Physical Development. During this period the child attains height at the average rate of about three inches per year. At the age of six years he comes to have a height of 3 1/2 feet. The weight of the child also increases. The proportions of the body also change. The head grows very slowly. This is also the period of developing finer muscular co-ordinations.

(b) Emotional Development. At this age the child shows off his emotions. The young child will cry and throw himself on the ground, if his wishes are frustrated. He also fights with the children of his age. Another emotion of this stage is fear. The child is afraid of many things and situations as he develops his intelligence. He is also curious at this stage to know about the various things of the universe.

(c) Social Development. He makes friends with other children and tries to get on well with them. Sometimes he also quarells with his friends which is a normal form of behaviour. Children also disobey their parents which is also a healthy sign. "A child who never says no and always does as told is not growing satisfactorily."

Children also sometimes compete with each other at this stage. They also sympathise with each other in case of distress.

(d) Mental Development. He wants to know something about the universe. He is always asking questions. He also tries to handle the various objects of the universe and tries to understand them. It is after seeing and handling the objects that he builds up 'Concepts' about them. He is able to judge distances when he runs, walks and climbs.

He follows conversation. He also develops his vocabulary and expresses himself in short sentences. Children who have superior intelligence are able to express themselves well in comparison to average children.

(e) Moral Development. The child has no idea as to what is good or bad. He considers things good or bad as his parents explain to him.

Educational Implications of Early Childhood

Early childhood is considered to be "an ideal period for learning." **Watson** thinks, 'the scope and intensity of learning during this period exceeds that of any other period of development." The following points should be kept in view by the educator while planning the education of the child at this stage.

1. Proper Atmosphere. A healthy, peaceful and secure atmosphere should be privided for the child. This is necesary both at home and the school.

2. Proper Treatment. The child has to depend on others for the satisfaction of his requirenments. Hence he should always receive an affecticnate, sympathetic, and courteous treatment from others. An atmosphere of fear and repression will not allow the child to develop properly.

3. Developing the Endowments of the Child. A child takes birth with certain natural endowments. The educator should try to locate them and plan for their maximum development.

4. Satisfaction of Curiosity. Every child is curious to know the details of his social environment. The parents and the teachers should try to pacify this need of the child by answering the questions asked by him.

5. Developing Self-Sufficiency. The infant depends on others for the satisfaction of his needs. The child has to do everything himself. The educator should try to develop a spirit of self-sufficiency in the child and should provide him opportunities so that the child is able to dɔ most of the things himself.

6. Developing a Social Sense. Efforts should be made by the teacher to develop a rational social sences in the child. The Child starts developing a social sence by the end of this stage.

7. Encouraging the Instinctive Development of the Child. The child at this stage is guided by his instincts. The teacher should not try to suppress the instinctive development of the child. It should be sublimated in the best interests of the presonality development of the child.

8. Formation of Good Habits. This is considered to be the most flexible age of the child. Steps should be taken towards the formation of good habits by the child.

9. Learning by Doing. The child is active by nature. This ought to be satisfied through the use of activity method which advocates learning by doing.

10. Use of the Play-Way. Play is natural to the child. Let him play and learn. This will make learning easier and acceptable to the child.

11. Sensory Training. There are five senses of the child. These should be properly developed at this stage. This sensory training was also emphasised by Madam Montessori.

12. Use of Stories and Pictures. Children at this stage are interested in stories and multi-coloured pictures. They should be made to learn by using story telling method and with the help of multi-coloured prictures and charts.

Later Childhood—(from 7 to 12 years)

(a) Physical Development. The development is slow and uniform. The child at the age of 12 it about 55 inches in height, which means an annual increase of 2 to 3 inches. Boys are slightly taller than girls. Body proportions change considerably and the overall appearance of the child also alters. The nose becomes larger and the lower jaw also increases in size. Arms, legs and trunk increase in length and look thinner. This rather gives 'an ugly look' to the child. He also builds up fine muscular co-ordinations and improves many musculare and mother skills. Boys show superiority to girls and special interest in games and skills requiring physical strength, while girls are superior to body in skills involving the use of finer muscles, such as drawing, painting, sewing, etc.

(b) Emotional Development. The child now comes to have a control over his emotions. His emotional behaviour is guided by a rational expression. He is still jealous, may be of his younger borthers or his class-fellows. He may tease and make fun of those children who are the objects of his jealousy. He may be afraid of things but tries to look brave. His expression of joy is expressed by a smile. He satisfies his curiosity by asking questions from the teacher and by studying books.

(c) Social Development. At this stage the child is engaged in social give and take. Sometimes he is teased and bullied by others and he also teases and bullies others. He attaches great value to friendship and takes part in games and excursions. Now he is fairly independent in his behaviour. He moves with his friends and comes to have a 'group' spirit. Sometimes he may assume the leadership of the group as well. Boys and girls make their separate groups. The children also come to have a knowledge about their caste, religion bias and prejudices.

(d) Mental Development. Children develop their mental power by studying in the schools, reading books, and by visiting places. They develop their reasoning power, memory, attention and sensory discrimination during this period.

Children also judge their own actions and criticise the actions of others and in this way they come to have their own opinions. In religious and racial matters they take up the opinions of their elders. They also take up the aesthetic standards of their elders.

Their vocabulary increases by leaps and bounds. Now they are able to speak and write sentences of more than average length.

(e) Moral Development. To him the moral code is now determined by the group to which she belongs. He considers that stealing is generally bad. He judges the actions of others accrodingly. He has a strong sense of fair—play and justice. Sometimes conditions in the family play a very important role in determining these attitudes.

EDUCATIONAL IMPORTANCE OF LATER CHILDHOOD

This period of childhood is the time when the basic outlook, values and ideals of the child are finally shaped. Hence it is duty of the parents, teachers and the society to plan for their proper development. The School, however, has a very important role to play. The following points should be kept in view by the teacher.

(1) Proper Physical Development. Well-organised evening games and sports should be provided for children so that they are able to have a proper physical development. The teacher should see that every child takes part in these games. Morning physical training may also be organised for resident students. In the new educational pattern of 10+2+3, physical development is being highly emphasised by educators.

(2) Provision for Excursions and Scouting. Children start developing surplus energy at this stage. They are interested in adventure and roaming about here and there. It is, therefore, necessary that suitable provision should be made for excursions and outings for them. The scouting should be organized in the school to satisfy this need of the child.

(3) Proper Provision of Extra-Mural Activities. Hidden qualities have to be found out and properly developed. This is possible only if a large number of extra-mural activities are provided in the school. This will enable the child to choose those activities in which he is interested. In the organisation of these activities democratic ways should be adopted.

(4) Planning for Proper Social Development. Children develop the 'group spirit' at this stage. In order to direct it in the right channels it is necessary that group games on a group competition basis should be arranged. It is a period of competitive socialization. It is throguh these group competitions that the child will develop various qualities like discipline, self-control, sympathy and co-operation.

(5) Developing the Creative Instinct. Children want to create something new. This creative trend should be properly utilised for educational ends. The teacher should provide opportunities where children are in a position to satisfy their creative instinct.

(6) Proper Emotional Outlet. This stage, however, is considered to be a unique stage in the emotional development of the child. It is possible only if proper outlets for the emotional expressions of children are provided. The teacher should not try to suppress these outlets. He should try to redirect them in the right channels. He should place examples of greatmen of the world before them.

(7) Satisfying the Acquisitive Instinct. Children want to acquire those things which they like. If it is not properly directed they start stealing. They should, therefore, be encouraged to collect those things which have an educational value.

(8) Moral Training. The child at the age of eight years starts accepting the moral values of the society in which he lives. Therefore, it is necessary that some moral training should be provided. Instructions may be provided which have a moral value for the child. A democratic approach should be followed as morality is something which springs from the heart of the child.

(9) Learning Though Self-Activity. Children like activity. It comes to occupy a more important place in the educational system when it originates from the children themselves. Self-activity leads to self-expression, thus leading to self-realisation.

(10) Teacher's Role in Academic Development. The teacher has a very important role to play in the mental development of the child. His role may be in the following directions :

(a) Children are interested in language learning. They may learn two or three languages at this stage.

(b) Children should be encouraged to choose those subjects which have a functional value. Preference should be given to those subjects which are useful in life.

(c) Interests of children differ and change. Hence, it is necessary that their text-books should have different types of lessons. They may include advanturious stories, biographies of greatmen, drama, dialogue, etc.

(d) It is the duty of the teacher to make necessary changes in the curriculum and methods of teaching.

ADOLESCENCE STAGE
(Period From 12 to 16/17 Years)

The term 'Adolescence' is derived from the Latin word 'Adolescere' which means 'to grow to maturity.' This is a period lying between childhood and maturity. Thus, it is a period of change, when the individual is neither a child nor an adult. The changes which take place are physical, sexual, emotional, social, mental and moral.

A harmonious development of adolescence means full adult height, weight, stature and strength, and complete sexual maturity; the proper adjustment of the adolescent in the society; he also takes up his duties and responsibilities; the complete development of his mental powers and emotional stability and economic independence and professional competence.

Physical Development

Height and Weight. Growth is rapid just before and during the early years of adolescence. Both boys and girls develop their height and weight.

Bodily Proportion. Different parts of the body grow at different rates and reach their final size. Arms and legs grow longer and hands and feet grow much bigger.

Sexual Development. This stage is the development of sex maturity. The pituitary glands secrete 'gonadotropic' hormone which finally stops bodily growth and leads to sex maturity. The sex glands of male produce spermatoza which leads to the development of sexual growth. In the same way, female sex glands are called the ovaries which produce 'Ova' sex harmones.

Emotional Development. This is the period of increased and charged emotions as the instincts of the child attain maturity. His feeling also undergoes a great change. He is sensitive and easily offended. He feels he is all alone, unloved, and in a world which is hostile.

He is required himself to adjust to the new situations and behave as the new adult. He may face emotional difficulties. He is not able to control his emotions and this leads to temper outbursts. Sometimes he is happy and sometimes he is sad, sometimes he also suffers from emotional moods. He may also indulge in day-dreaming.

Love is also predominant feeling in this period. This is due to the development of sex instinct. This love may be of most selfless kind. Adolescents are prepared to sacrifice every thing simply to gain the love of another child. In the later period of adolescence this love is directed to the opposite sex. The adolescents also direct love towards great men, which is known as hero worship.

Social Development. At this stage the adolescent is self conscious and lacks confidence and is very modest. He wants seclusion. All these things disappear as he develops. He starts choosing his own friends and chooses them on the qualities they possess. Gradually he forms small group. He takes part in various social groups as a member of these groups. Thus he gains experiences which are valuable to him in adult life.

In this period adolescents also come in conflict with parental demands. They demand independence of action whereas their parents treat them as children and hence they come in conflict with them.

Moral Development. At this stage the child develops his critical ability and judgement. He also comes across various individuals and thus he does not accept religious principles without criticism. He becomes conscious of the idea of right and wrong.

Mental Development. At this stage the span of attention increases. Memory, reasoning and judgement also increase. He understands and appreciates, poetry, music, art, literature and mathematics.

Adulthood Stage (Period After 18 Years of Age)

Adulthood period is the longest of all the periods or stages of life. It is characterized by an all round maturity—physical, intellectual, emotional and social. At this stage the individual develops into a functioning member of the society and acts according to social and moral standards. He is self-reliant and accepts responsibility for this decisions and actions. He develops ability to think rationally and intelligently, ability to understand the world and to make maximum adjustments.

Old Stage (Period After 58 Years of Age)

This stage starts from 58 years till death. At this stage one spends one's most of time in worshipping social service and excursions.

Q. 13. Explain the principles of human development.

Ans. **PRINCIPLES OF HUMAN DEVELOPMENT**

Developmental psychology studies human development, the study starting not with the infant's birth but before it, while it is in embryonic form within its mother's womb. The child's development within the womb is a very important phase of his entire development. Hence, there have been origination in the form of a fertilized ovum. Gradually and continually, this fertilised ovum shows signs of structural development, the ovum cells multiply in number and increase in size. These cells are of two kinds, the germ cells and the somatic cells. The germ cells help the germ cell plasm to develop various physiological parts such as bones, muscles, nerves, etc. Beside changes in structure, the functions of the embryo also take on variety and complexity. Functional development occurs with the addition of new activities. While the human being is in the embryo, the structural and functional developments take place in the nature of two mutually supplementary aspects of total development.

Psychologists have divided the embryonic development of the being into several states. These states and a brief mention of them are given below:

1. Germinal Period. The period beginning with conception of the child and lasting for a period of two weeks is called the germinal period of the being's development. During this period of the being exists in the form of a fertilised ovum, not being given any external nutrition. The form of the fertilised ovum is that of an egg, and its cells are equally divided.

2. Embryonic Period. The period from the third to the eighteenth week of pregnancy is called the embryonic period, during which the embryo gets nutrition from its parent. As a result, its form undergoes rapid change. In the change there is a sac related to the ovum and it is situated between the cells that lie in between Omniotic sac and Yolk sac. In this the cells lying next to the omneiotic sac are called the ectoderm calls. The calls of the first kind prove of help in the development of the digestive and the respiratory systems, while the latter or second kind of cells lead to the development of the nervouss system and the skin of epidermis. The mixing of the two kinds of cells leads to the development of a new layer called the mesoderm. Development of the two kinds of cells leads to the creation of muscles and bones. Cell's structure which is originally flat and convex, gradually spread out. Every cell has its own peculiar position, and if it is changed, its characteristic features will also undergo some change. For example, if it would originally have developed into skin, it will develop into the muscles of the eye on changing the cells. Certain chemical substances are also of importance in the separate and individual development of the cells. These chemicals are called organizers. Besides these, the development of the embryo is influenced by the use of the light, electrical field, X-rays, and other chemical rays.

3. Fetal Period. In the development of the being, this state begins, with the eighth week, and in it a number of cells increase, following which their size improves. Change in this stage is very rapid.

As has been pointed out above, the child's development during pregnancy is characterized by two types of development, the structural and functional. The following two laws are accepted in respect of structural development:

(a) Law of Caphalocaudal Development. According to this law, in the development of the embryo, the development starts with the cephalic portion or the head and gradually proceeds to the tail portion. In this way, this law of development the direction of the bodily development. This law applies to growth as well as differentiation.

(b) Law of Proximo Development. According to this law, the progress in development is more rapid in peripheral parts situated in the centre.

In structural development, the structure of the nervous system is a very important one. In this development, the first layer of the ectoderm cell turns inwards to form the neural tube, the major protion of which, the spinal cord and the upper part develops into the brain. In the fifth week of development, the medulla, cerebellum and the mid-brain become distinctively visible. The nervous system develops very rapidly during the fetal period. Mucles, being to be formed even before the nerves and sensory organs. Almost all the sensory parts develop in the being before the delivery or actual birth. The development of vision starts with the second week, and continues even after pregnancy. Receptors concerned with olfactory reach maturity in pregnancy in the case of some children. Taste cells develop in the third month, that, is during the fetal period. Besides this, during pregnancy the being attains the power of felling sensations of pressure on the skin.

Q. 14. Write a note on social development of the child.

Or

What is the concept of socialisation? Discuss social development through various stages with educational implication.

Ans. **SOCIAL DEVELOPMENT**

The concept of social development *lies in the concept of socialisation*. To understand that, we have to understand socialisation.

At the time of his birth, a child is very selfish. He does not know about sharing his joys and toys with others. Round the age of two, he realises that he is just a little man in the complex order. Others also matter and that he alone does not matter. Giving and taking starts. This we call socialisation and social development. Social development never takes place *in isolation*. A child left in jungle will not be social. It is as a result of interaction that social development takes place. That is why schools exist. A man gone throught schooling is a better socially developed man as compared to one who never went to it.

Various authorities have also defined social development. Few are quoted below:

Freeman and Showel, "By social growth and development we mean increasing ability to get along well with oneself and others."

Hurlock, "It is attaining of social relationship."

In nutshell, socialisation means :

(i) contact with people—its beginning,

(ii) dealing with people and learning from them,

(iii) It is a conscious activity. It does not take place automatically.

SOCIAL DEVELOPMENT DURING VARIOUS STAGES

Babyhood. Boby deals with adults in his/her immediate environment. According to Mrs. E. B. Hurlock, the important patterns of his social development during this age are:

2nd month. On hearing a voice, the baby turns his head.

4th month. Stops crying when talked to and makes movements in anticipation of being lifted.

6th month. In touch with the adult 'talks' to adult.

2 years. The baby likes to do things independently and runs around for the adults—he can bring the newspaper lying at gate when asked to and when the baby is in mood. Learns to imitate adults.

Up to this age, babies indulge in what is known as parallel play.

EARLY CHILDHOOD (2—6 YEARS)

1. Becomes active members of the group. He participates in group activities.
2. 'Parallel play' activity is no longer there.
3. Social development during this stage depends much on his relationship with his parents. He can become *likeable* individual if relationship is not cordial he will become *assertive*.
4. He has many friends.
5. He shows preferences for friends.
6. His *patterns* of social behaviour are—*(i)* Aggression, *(ii)* Quarrels, and *(iii)* Selfishness.

LATTER CHILDHOOD (6—12 YEARS)

(i) This is called school going age.

(ii) The number of friends increases mainfold—permanent associations are formed. Social interaction is at its maximum.

(iii) The child is capable of dealing with many social situations.

Gang Age. Later childhood, social development-wise is also known as gang age. Formation of gangs is the peculiar feature of social development in this age.

Gang means small group or a spontaneous local group. It is formed by children themeslves. It is not authorised from outside.

Gang has a leader who issues commands.

Gang has a code of ethics.

Gang has secret language.

Gangs disband after sometime.

Girls gangs are smaller and firmer.

Gangs meet at a secret place or hide out.

Activitive. The activitives of the gang are mostly anti-social—teasing old men, bullying small children—stealing fruit from neighbour's garden, fights with other gangs, tearing posters, throwing stones in neighbour's courtyards etc. They also play cards and go to pictures together.

Sex Dfferences. It is at this age sex differences come in. Boys and girls become conscious of their sex and they tease one another.

(i) Social activitives depend upon sex.

(ii) They are conscious of social approval and disapproval.

ADOLESCENT AGE (12—16 YEARS)

1. Independence from Parents. The adolescent at this stage seeks independence from his parents. He is critical of them.

2. Peer Group Relations Assume Greater Proportions. The friends of child matter. It is the peer groups that shape the behaviour of adolescent. Company at this age matters.

3. Hetrosexual Relations. Boys begin to take interest in girls and vice versa. Both make themselvess attractive. Hence all sorts of beauty aids are used.

4. Friendships is a matter of mutual interest and not of nearness. Two adolescent brothers can have different friends.

5. Sentiments develop during this period.

Role of the Teacher in Social Development. The role of the teacher is very important in social development of the child. His role begins when the child enters the school. The following points highlight his role or educational implications of this topic:

1. Practice What You Preach. Teachers should practise what they preach. Things go wrong when they say one thing and do another.

2. Consistent Bebaviour. Teachers should be consistent in their social behaviour towards children. Inconsistency creates problems for them.

3. Opportunities. In schools and colleges, there should be maximum opportunities for give and take, for "hitting and being hit." Let there be maximum outings, camps, trips. It socialises the child. The teacher should be liberal in it.

4. Self Government in school will not only socialise the child but also make him responsible.

5. Avoid Harsh Discipline. Control will breed scandals. Understand it.

6. Mass Media (newspapers, magazines) which have bad influence (like some film magazines) on the development of child intellectually and result instunted. Social growth be not allowed to influence them. *Direct* the child along healthy lines.

7. Allow the child to display social responsibility. Let him receive guess at a function.

8. Parents and teachers should take children to parties. It socialises them.

Q. 15. Discuss the importance of Developmental Tasks. What facts help adjust?

Ans. IMPORTANCE OF DEVELOPMENTAL TASKS

The above discussion makes quite clear the importance of developmental tasks in the life of man. Briefly, their significance is as follows :

1. Direction to Individual. The list of tasks appropriate to various stages of life given earlier clearly shows to an individual what the society expects from him at various stages of life.

2. Prediction About Future. The knowledge of the developmental tasks tells a person in advance as to what physical and mental changes to expect in future. For example, the middle aged person who knows that will be his state of affairs after retirement, he can prepare in advance for all exigencies. He can save more or start side-business to be taken up fully later on. It is always difficult to make adjustment with new situations and this gives rise to great deal of tension. However, if one is mentally prepared for the change, difficulty will be less.

FACTS HELPING ADJUSTMENT

The development psychologists have found out certain facts which would help a man to make better adjustment. Following are the significant facts in this regard :

1. Childhood is the Foundation of Life. It is well said that the coming events send their shadows before. A strong foundation laid in the childhood will surely ensure happy and prosperous adulthood. It is generally found that the physical and mental characteristics observed in the childhood persist throughout. An honest child is likely to grow an honest adult. A study of fat adults has revealed that in childhood they were over-protected. As Alder has shown, alone child displays specific characteristics throughout his life. Similarly it also matters whether the child is first or last. The roles children play in their family later on determine their basic personality traits. If the experiences in childhood are positive and favourable the child grows into a healthy, moral and happy adult; but if these experinces are negative the child tends to develop abnormalities. The causes of a number of mental diseases are to be found in childhood experiences. The most important influence upon the child is that of his parents. If the child is taught to be tidy and clean, it develops in them a habit of cleanliness. Besides if there are some inborn defects in the children they can be best rectified in childhood. The child is a tender creeper. He must be zealously cared for and good habits inculcated in him. This will help him to become a healthy and moral adult.

2. Development is Dependent upon Maturity and Learning. In the past there was a controversy among the psychologists as to what is more crucial in the development—maturity or learning. Some opted for maturity and the others regarded learning to be the crucial factor. Now it is settled beyond doubt that there is an interaction between the two. It is also proved that in the absence of certain level of maturity there can be no learning. The interaction between maturity and learning can be seen in three ways. It tells us about individual differences. It tells us why some individual cannot learn beyond a certain point. Thirdly, we know what age is most appropriate for a particular type of learning. Educational psychologists have made special investigation in this regard. Upon the basis of these studies individual differences have been noted. No two persons are equal and same. Individuals therefore differ in tense in their reaction. A situation which may be ridiculous for some may be serious for others. Briefly, differ in their level of maturity and learning and they therefore have in different ways.

Q. 16. Write a note on character development and suggest a suitable scheme of Character Eduation.

Ans. To quote Professors Sharma and Narula, "Character is the end of all social development. It is the height of all that individual can think of."

Character formation thus is one of the most important aims of life. All systems of education in the world must meet at this point. Even Gandhiji stressed the importance of education building character or building of character through education.

Woe to the nation which has men and women of weak character.

What is Character? You talk to an Indian and ask him what he understands by character? His concept is a funny concept. Character to us is sex—sex-loaded or sex oriented or sex dominated. And bad character *is egg, meat and wine*! This is in fact not the exact or learned or psychological definition of character.

Various authors have tried to be fine character in their own way. Some selected definitions are given below :

Ross. Ross defines character as, "just organised self." You orgnise your instincts and sentiments.

Kolesnik. "It is acquired component of personality which inhibits impulses of an immoral or unsocial nature and disposes an individual to act in accordance with relative principles."

McDougall. "Character consists in proper organisation of sentiments."

Francis F. Powers. "Character is one's constancy in conduct trained, outer and inner, in conformity with group in which he lives."

Four representative definitions have been given above. The best definition comes from the pen of Cronbach when he says, "*Character is defined as the way you make choices*. How yours action affacts the welfare of others." This is the crux. At the same time, you do not have to sacrifice your interests. You have to be normally selfish.

Character thus is a stable organisation of needs/motives/ sentiments in relationship to others.

Marks of Good Character. (Test yourself!)

1. Consistency is the hallmark of character. He sticks to his stand.

2. Reliable. A good character is reliable. You can depend upon the person for his word.

3. Some Marks of Personality. Some known personality traits such as cheerfulness, optimistic (Netaji Subash Chandera Bose was the greatest optimist India ever produced) are found in men of strong character.

4. A man of good character is courageous. (Indiá suffers from this crisis!)

5. A man with good character is not influenced by the opinion of others. His decisions are his own.

6. He has strong master sentiment.

7. He has great powers of intellectual judgement.

8. He is emotionally responsive. He cannot sit still in a situation.

9. Simplicity is another mark of man of good character.

CHARACTER AND PERSONALITY

Personality is a bigger term. It includes character.

Personality is sum total of good and bad. Character is moral (good only) estimate of an individual.

FACTORS WHICH INFLUENCE CHARACTER

These are also known as determinants of character. As a result of survey of literature the various factors emerge:

1. Physical Factors Like Health. It is said that good food determines good health and good health determines good character. A man with good health has powers of resistance.

2. Intellectual Factors Like Intelligence. Intelligence helps to discriminate between good and bad. Intelligent man is fearless and truthful. These are hallmarks of character.

3. Social factors like home, sohool and other social agencies, Company influences.

4. Moral Factors Like Religious Education. Religious education is missing in Indian schools—may be because of this reason that immorality has increased in post-independence India.

5. Sex. Sex is another determinant of character. Females fall earlier or quicker to temptations.

6. Creativity. Creativity or ability to invent ensures good character of man. You are busy thinking and inventing. You have no time to waste it.

7. Will. Character is closely related to determination Will plays an important role in formation of character.

RELATIONSHIP OF INSTINCTS AND CHARACTER

Instincts are the movers of behaviour. They are innate dispositions. They form the basis on which character is formed, It is again not the raw instinct that leads to the formation of character but the sublimated form that leads to formation of character example. If sex instinct exists in one in raw form—uncontrolled form, it will make one a criminal, a sexual offender but if is sublimated, one can be a poet, a musician, and artist—sublimated form of instincts thus is the foundation of character.

LEVELS OF CHARACTER DEVELOPMENT

All leading authors have quoted from Croanbach in this connection. Various other views on development of character are also available but that is the popular version which is being discussed here.

There are five levels of character development:

1. Amoral Stage. This stage lasts up to first two years. The child is not aware of what is good and what is bad that is why this stage is called the amoral stage, *i.e.,* is not aware that his actions disturb others.

2. Self-Centered Stage. Then the second stage begins. The Child is aware that his actions sometime disturb others but it cannot help it. This stage lasts up to 8 years (2—10 years). The child knows that plucking flowers from neighbour's garden is not good but she/he does it.

Some children when they grow into adults remain fixated at this level. They live as misers.

3. Conforming Conventional Stage. This is the third stage. There is no age limit. Even adults operate at this level. The best example given by Croanbach is—while in Rome, do as Romans do. Why come in conflict with the society or with the established norms?

4. Irrational Conscientious Stage comes next. These people hold values of life clear emotionally rather than rationally. Best example—Yudhisthir from Mahabharta. People who stick to values emotionally are maladjusted. On the other hand, they are very happy.

5. Rational Conscientious Stage. This is the highest level of character development. Every one should try to operate at this level. Here the values of life are held clear rationally rather than emotionally. Example—Killing in war is bad but even then you are free to kill in self-defence.

Drever's Theory. Drever has divided the development of character into three stages. The basis of this development is Feeling. The three stages are :

(i) The stage of crude emotion,

(ii) The stage of sentiment, and

(iii) The self regard stage.

McDougall and others have also their own views.

EDUCATIONAL IMPLICATIONS

Both the S.E.C. (1952-53) and I.E.C. (1964-66) have laid great importance on the development or building of character. The S.E.C. has even suggested a scheme of character education. Kilpatrick, the American philosopher has also suggested a scheme of character education.

Some hints in this connection are as follows :

1. Teacher. Teacher himself should be man of sound character. Sound character is a matter of being caught than taught.

2. School Atmosphere. It is again the duty of the teachers working in schools to keep the school atmosphere as pure as possible. It is easy to preach but it is very difficult to practice. Whatever the preachings, teacher's actions in school be good, in mutual regard so that the atmosphere is not polluted. They should be fair in dealings with the students.

3. Sublimation of Instincts. It is the duty of teachers again to modify, sublimate, reform the instincts of the students. It is also the duty of the teachers to strengthen the determination of students.

4. Sentiment of Self-Regard should be developed in students.

5. Great Men and Their Lives. Teachers and parents should make their children familiar with the lives of great men. H.W. Long fellow—the famous English poet has remarked :

"Lives of Great Men, All remind us,

We can make our lives sublime."

6. Live Out Emotions. It leads to sound building of character.

7. Co-curricular activities and participation in these activities lead to building of character.

8. Celebration of Days. Important religious and social functions should be celebrated in the school. Through these we acquaint the students with moral and spiritual value of society.

9. Reward. Children when they carry out some good deed. Example helps.

10. Motivate children.

11. Strengthen Physical and Mental Health of Students. It plays a great role in shaping one's character. Someone has lightly remarked :

"If health is lost, something is lost.

If wealth is lost, nothing is lost.

If character is lost, everything is lost."

Nevertheless:

Character plays an important role in life. Without men of character, nation is doomed—personalities are incomplete.

Q. 17. Explain the characteristics of development during adolescent period giving out clearly the educational importance of this period.

Or

Write an essay on the special problems of adolescence.

Or

Is adolescence a period of "stress and storm"? Discuss. What are the psychological needs of adolescent which should be fulfilled to promote healthy adolescent development? Explain.

Ans. The English word adolescence is derivative of the Latin 'adolescere' which means to grow to maturity. This age begins from twelve and continues till the age of twenty. In the words of Jersild, "Adolescence is the period through which a growing person makes transition from childhood to maturity." Adolescence, in the opinion of most educational psychologists, begins between the age of 12 and 14 years. Compared to boys, girls enter the period of adolescence a couple of years earlier. According to Dr. Jones, adolescence is the recollection of infancy. It parallels the states of infancy and childhood in being patterned into two conditions, the first of growth and the second of maturation.

1. State of Growth. In this state, the adolescent is seen to be very active and unstable as well as disturbed. He gives the impression of being somewhat lost, and is subject to repidly, warying moods of dejection and elation, enthusiasm and deep lethargy, etc. The main thing concerning this period in life is that the adolescent is no longer a child but an adult, though the society in which he lives continues to treat him as a child. Secondly, he climbs down from the dizzy heights of imagination that he reached in his infancy and childhood and steps firmly into the real world. Both these factors engender in him a constant fear of reproof and criticism at the hands of others. He often becomes helpless and pitiable, shy and repressed. This does not indicate that the runs away from the real world, but that he tries to modify it according to his own notions. In efforts of this kind, relation and dejection are only natural, and it is for this reason that the adolescent is often seen wearing a look of anxiety.

2. State of Maturation. By the time he enters this stage, he has calmed down a bit and shown signs of stability. He carves a niche for himself in his society, and gradually his tendencies, habits and activities become stable and regular.

MENTAL CHARACTERISTICS OF ADOLESCENCE

In adolescence the individual is so transformed that he wears but inwardly he seeths with revolt and pent up anger which sometimes leads him to run away not only from school but even from the home a new and unrecognized look. Mental charges in this period of life find their best expression in the works of poets as they depict the mental states of young men and women. Adolescence exhibits the following mental characteristics generally:

1. Development of Mental Abilities. In adolescence the individual's nervous system becomes more strong with the result that his mental activities show greater tenacity and system. Ability to think, to solve problems, to differentiate and evaluate are some of the more prominent characteristics and abilities that he exhibits.

2. Sexual Development. From the psychological viewpoint, the most significant characteristice of the period of adolescence is sexual development. According to Dr. Jones, the repressed sexual force of infancy, that continued latent through the period of childhood, once again wakens and the individual passes through various stages of sexual development. The truth of the matter is, that even if it not the only tendency, sexual tendency is undoubtedly the most prominent and stable tendency to be found in adolescence. Hence, to disregard it is to make a fatal mistake as it is the most harmful form of negligence conceivable. The development in this sphere is so rapid that his entire personality appears to be coloured by it. Sexual development in adolescence finds its expression in attraction towards strangers, rather than towards parents as in the case infancy. It announces its presence even in such small activities as the young boy's anxiety and nervousness, biting of fingernails, putting a pencil in one's mouth, tying knots in handkerchiefs, etc. Both physical and mental teachings in this age can use the sexual tendency as an important force.

3. Hero Worship. Generally speaking, adolescence evince a strong tendency towards hero worship, though the criterion of heroism is not the same in all children. Possession of any quality that attracts an individual child the most is sufficient qualification for a man or woman to become its ideal. While one child may regard a wrestler as hero, another may profess allegiance to a scientist, yet another may be devoted to film personality or a political leader. In schools some teachers impress their students considerably with the result that they come to be tenderly and affectionately regarded by them, also being imitated by the tender children. Sometimes, this hero worship turns to love. It is not till considerably later that the young man turns his thoughts to his own heroic qualities, when he begins praising them. The tendency to hero worship can be turned to good account by inculcating a proper character and personality in the child's mind.

4. Religious Feeling. Many adolescents become positively and deeply religious in this period of their lives. One can often observe them loving God in some one image, talking to him, sacrificing themselves to him and praying to him. India is particularly productive of such specimens since, for one, the religious tendency is deeply ingrained in the people's mind, and for another, in Indian society young boys and girls meet great leaders and famous personalities on very rare occasions. While religious tendency protects the young inexperienced child from many bad habits, it sometimes helps in making him somewhat impractical. Teachers can help to create a healthy attitude towards religion.

5. Extroversion. In this period, the child once again regains his extrovert flambuoyancy, taking deep interest in his surroundings and other individuals, their activities and conflicts. In school, too, he likes to take part in all kinds of activities. And it is a matter of joy with him if he can spend the larger part of his time in the company of this friends. Various individuals become engaged in programmes of social service and welfare. In this manner does the adolescent announce the interest that he takes in the real world. This interest can be usefully explocited to ingrain, in him such useful qualities as self-dependence, self-determination cooperation, discipline, honesty and the quality of maintaining good relations with others or developing the social instinct. This is the age in which the foundations of good citizenship can be deeply laid.

6. Gregarious Instinct. Adolescents are always acutely desirous of being among their friends, of praising them and of improving their relation with them. Often, they form definite groups in which each adolescent has his specific status and a role to suit him. This status and role plays an important part in determining his status and role in adult life.

7. Lack of Stability and Adjustment. It has been pointed out earlier, too, that in his adolescence the growing individual is at the threshold of his life, although he is rarely if ever considered an adult by his serious. From the psychological point of view, he takes himself seriously enough not to consider himself a child and likes to be treated as an adult. Evidently, he shows considerable instability and lack of adjustment. His adaptation, to his environment is upset by such small considerations as the growth of pimples on his face or the presence of other small physical deformities. In fact, it is a stage in which he learns to lead adult life in every sphere and direction. Hence, the presence and continual development of problems is only natural. And these problems are susceptible to ready solutions if the seniors are prepared to extend their sympathetic cooperation and guidance.

8. Excessive Imagination. Although the adolescent is as much in this world as any other living being, yet he is prone to much imaginary flights into the world of fancy. The smallest thing can persuade him to temporarily abandon the world of reality and turn to the imaginary world. Such excessive imagination manifests itself in the strong tendency towards daydreaming, but some gifted children express their creative and aesthetic imagination through literature, music and painting, besides other arts.

9. Excessive Sentimentality. The adolescent is very sentimental and emotionally unstable, although at this age his mind is fairly well-developed. Of the many feelings that drive him, the strongest are the desire to win praise and self-respect, any injury to or repression of them leading to serious malformations and even open rebellion. Sentimentality can be turned to good use in developing culture qualities in the adolescent.

10. Personal Interests. In adolescence, as the individual develops both in mind and body, his interests vary. Progressively the boys and girls develop the interests of their adult counterparts. Girls show this development in such interests as the use of various cosmetics, efforts at appearing very beautiful, reading or taking interests in romantic novels, love stories, dramas or poems, participating in music, art and acting programmes etc. Boys manifest their approaching adulthood in the form of various active games, running around, doing acts to valur, developing a vocation that they are to pursue in their adult life. Both boys and girls task constant interest in their addled life. Both boys and girls like to mix with the other sex and maturing it to fruition through conversation, intimacy, letters and romance.

11. Development of the Mind. In adolescence, the mind develops rapidly. The cells of the nervous system increase rapidly and the chemical composition of the nerves also undergoes a change. In this way, the mind and the nervous system rapidly mature. In this period along with physical and mental development, practice helps to develop mental abilities. Linguistic ability also registers improvement during this period. In his adolescence the child develops the vocabulary that he possesses. His vocabulary reveals general intelligence. Mental development, too reaches its apex in adolescence. Despite the inevitable individual differences that are invariably persent, mental maturity achieves its completion normally by the age of twenty. Practice or experience contributes considerably to this maturation. Normally, the individual's intelligence continues on the same level or, on other words, even in different ages the intelligence quotient of an individual remains more or less the same.

Q. 18. What is adolescence? Discuss the stresses and strains experienced by adolescents. How can the teacher help adolescents to tide over their difficulties?

Or

What are the chief characteristics of the adolescent stage of growth? What are the physical, mental and emotional characteristics of adolescents? Enumerate some problems presented by boys and girls at this stage of their development and indicate how a teacher could deal with these.

Ans. The term adolescence is derived from the Latin word Adolescere, which means to grow to maturity. It is a critical stage of development which lies between later childhood and maturity, emerging from childhood and merging into adulthood. During this period of development great physical and mental changes occur. Therefore, the stage of development is a period of uncertainly when everything is in a ferment. Stanely Hall defined adolescence as "a period of great strain, stress and storm and strife".

Not a Sudden Growth. Adolescence in not a sudden spurt of growth. The new traits and tendencies do not appear suddenly. No individual sleeps at night as a child to get up as an adolescent in the morning. Growth comes in continuity. There is a continuity of development from infancy to early childhood, from early childhood to later childhood and then to adolescence. No two stages in the development are clearly marked off. Even the adolescent himself does not feel any sudden change. Endocrine glands were already working but they are more active now. However, sex glands now are active. This is a significant change in this stage and it affects the whole organism.

Time at the Advent of Adolescence and Duration. The physical signs of adolescence occur between the ages of 12 and 18 in India. But there are differences due to sex, climate, race and individual constitution. Generally boys grow to be adolescent in their thirteenth year while the girls in their twelfth year. The individual differences are always there. The duration of adolescence ranges between five and eight years.

Physical Charactristics of the Stage

1. Rapid growth.
2. Growth not uniform and proportionate.
3. Different rate of growth of boys and girls.
4. Increase in modern activities.
5. Sense of clumsiness.
6. More significant growth of reproductive organs.

Mental, Moral and Emotional Characteristics

1. Sex-consciousness.
2. Self-consciousness.
3. Imaginative Activity.

4. Development of Special Intellectual Interests.
5. Contrasting Mental Moods.
6. Revolt to Authority.
7. Moral Awakening—No Acceptance of Sermons without critical evaluation.

PROBLEMS OF THE STAGE

The adolescent is a problem-individual. There are many problems around him and he needs help and guidance for their solution at every step. The following problems are the most significant in this stage.

1. Excessive Energy. Adolescence is the stage of excessive energy. In-take of food is increased in this stage and general health is also improved. The result is excessive energy. The adolescent needs more activity for catharsis of excessive energy. Our traditional schools do not provide such physical activity. Consequently, the adolescent is restless. Various activities act as sublimation for the adolescents and they feel relieved.

2. Misunderstandings Concerning Sex. With the advent of adolescence the gonads come into activity for the first time. The appearance of secondary sexual characteristics is due to the same. They produce emotional upheaval in the adolescent. The first appearance of menstruai course or nocturnal emission bewilders and shocks the adolescent who is quite ignorant about it. The school should supply right kind of information regarding sex at this stage. Due to ignorance about sex, many promising personalities are doomed.

3. Aggressiveness or Withdrawal. When an adolescent cannot adjust himself with the world, he grows to be aggressive or withdraws from the field and his personality is arrested. If the conflict is too serious, he regresses. The school should provide ample opportunities to the children to express themselves properly. Cocurricular activities, scouting student self-government and changed methods of instruction can go a long way in enabling the adolescent to adjust himself with the world.

4. Rebellious Attitude. The adolescents are no more children. They should be recognized as young men and women in the school as well as in the home. Their craving for independence should be satisfied to some extent. They should be given some responsibility. They turn to be very obedient if they are trusted. But things do not work so smoothly in ordinary schools and homes. Their sense of independence and responsibility is seldom recognised. The result is rebellion against authority.

5. Physical Awakwardness. Most of the adolescents have the feeling of physical clumsiness. Consequently their movements stand to be awkward and unbalanced. They may be corrected in the playground and on the stage. Games and dancing will give them harmonious and balanced movements. Social service at the occasion of festivals etc. and practical work can help the children in this respect.

6. Excessive Day-Dreaming. Day-dreaming is normal at this stage but when it grows to excessive it may be injurious as far as development of personality is concerned. The teacher should note that the adolescents are active and busy in their studies and other aspects of school life. The children indulging in excessive day-dreaming should be encouraged tc be constructive and creative.

Role of the teacher in solving problems and proper physical, mental, emotional and social development of the adolescent :

1. Proper Physical Development. The teacher should plan for this aspect in the following manner :

(a) by organising various types of physical exercises, sports and games,

(b) by imparting a proper knowledge about physical and health education.

(c) by organising various types of extra curricular activities.

2. Proper Mental Development. The mental development of the adolescent should be according to the following lines :

(a) It should be according to the ability and aptitude of the pupils.

(b) They should study both arts and science subjects.

(c) Excursions to various places may be organised.

(d) Moderm methods of teaching should be used to teach various subjects.

(e) All the school teachers should try to impart him necessary guidance as and when required.

(f) They should be entrusted with responsibility so as to develop a feeling of responsibility in them.

(g) The teacher should keep in view that there are individual differences among students. Every child should be able to find out subjects of his choice.

3. Proper Emotional Development. The emotional development of the adolescent should be as follows :

(a) The teacher should try to sublimate the lower emotions of the child.

(b) A healthy emotional atmosphere should be maintained in the school.

(c) The teacher should try to avoid frustration among the adolescents.

(d) The teacher should pay due regard to the personality of every child.

(e) The adolescent should be imparted proper knowledge about sex. If this aspect is properly attended to it would lead to a better emotional development.

4. Proper Social Development. The social development of the adolescent may be as follows :

(a) He should have a knowledge about social relations and he should know the art of group-living. Various group activities may be organised.

(b) A right and rational attitude towards democracy should be developed in the school atmosphere. This would enable the child to develop his own philosophy of life.

(c) The Kothari Commission has emphasised the instruction of moral and spiritual values. We should try to impart a right and rational knowledge of various religions to the adolescent. Leaving him to his own resources would be dangerous for social development.

Q. 19. What are the emotional problems of adolescence? How would you solve them?

Ans. A Conflict between Empathy and Self-concern. The emotional problems of the adolescent are caused by his growth in the ability to interact with and respond to others accompanied by conflicting developments. On the one hand, he tends to develop a kind of self-concern; on the other, he becomes more aware of the needs and feelings of other peoples. The ability to understand the feelings of others is known as empathy. There is an inverse relation between self-concern and empathy. The greater the sense of self-concern, the less the empathy. The adults may not care at all about their self-concern and may not empathise with others, but adolescents do so. The adolescent behaviour is dogmatic. The adolescents show rigidity, narrowness and egocentricity while dealing with others. It is now thought that they develop these characteristics as defense mechanisms against feelings of insecurity and anxiety.

Insecurity and Anxiety are Caused by Thwartings. The adolescent feels a great deal of insecurity in his relations with others and particularly with adults. The society hopes and expects that he should behave like an adult but not too much like an adult. The adolescent is also eager to play adult behaviour but he does not know whether he has gone too far or not far enough. This state of affairs causes a sense of insecuirty and anxiety. The problem could have been solved, had the society placed before him definite standards of teenage behaviour.

The anxiety is also caused by the fact that the adolescent is living in two kinds of societies—teenage society and adult society. The behaviour that satisfies one irritates the other. Therefore, the adolescent is living constantly in a state of tension. Anxiety is caused also by a number of thwartings. Take for example sex. Autosexual behaviour is frowned upon in our society and sexual relations are forbidden to adolescents. Certain forms of sexual activity are punished by law and by adult society. This causes anxiety.

Sexual Problems. Ideally, the adolescent is supposed to wait until a certain age when economic independence has been achieved and marriage and subsequent monogamous, heterosexual activities are condoned. However, thoughout adolescence models for non-conventional behaviour are many and stimulation for sexual activity is generally strong.

The society imposes limitations on sexual experssion and creates problems for the adolescents. It regards even simple sexual urges as immoral and reprehensible. When the individual reaches his middle teens he is able to perform all the adult sexual functions. But society wants that he should postpone sexual expression, until marriage, There is freedom in print, as shown in many novels and stories. There is freedom also on the stage. Still most people speak of sex with embarrassment indicative of anxiety. Hence, the adolescents do not get clear answers to their problems regarding sex.

The sexual activity in the males is strongest during ten years and gradually declines after 20. This heightened male sex drive creates further problems for the adolescent boys. Although during these years, the desire of sexual activity is at its height there is no approved way in which it can be satisfied. The male adolescent tries to get some relief through masturbation. The solution of these sex problems becomes necessary in school and colleges. A compulsory programme of sex education has been suggested so that the adolescent may be better informed about sex and may be better able to discuss sex problem objectively and bravely.

Personal Problems. The adolescent is faced with many emotional problems. He does things which he later regrets. He wishes he were more popular but he finds himself ignored, isolated and rejected. He worries about little things but he cannot find answers to them. He wants to improve his prestige and position but fails. He needs to develop self-confidence but he is not given ample opportunities. He is easily hurt. He is not sure of himself. He hesitates to assume responsibilities. In short, he remains in a continual tense emotional state. Adolescence has, therefore, been regarded as the period of stress and strain.

Stress and Strain as Caused by Cultural Factors. The adolescent is subject to pressures. Many of his difficulties are caused by culture in which he lives. The conditions that culture imposes upon him are responsible for stress and strain. He feels that he does not belong, that he is different, that others view him with suspicion and hostility.

"In this world of human affairs" says Tagore there is no worse nuisance than a boy at the age of fourteen. He is neither ornamental nor useful. It is impossible to shower affection on him. If he talks with a childish lips he is called a baby; and if he answers in a grown-up way he is called impertinent. In fact, any talk from him is resented. Then he is at the unattractive growing age. He voice grows hoarse and breaks and quivers; his face grows suddenly angular and unrightly. It is hard to tolerate even unaviodable lapses in a boy of fourteen. The lad himself becomes painfully self-conscious. Yet at this age the lad most craves for recognition and love. But none dare openly love him for that would be regarded as undue indulgence. So with scolding and chiding he becomes very much like a stray dog that has lost his master.

Q. 20. Discuss the characteristics of physical growth and development of the adolescents and their educational implications.

Ans. Physical Development in Adolescence. If we study the growth curves of height and weight from infancy to adulthood, we find that growth in these physical aspects is rapid in infancy, goes down in middle childhood, and shoots up in adolescence. The adolescent not only increases in size or weight but all of his or her body alters; for example, there are changes in the internal organs and body processes and subtle alterations in the composition of the tissues. In males there is the deepening of voice, the growth of the beard and the ability to produce semen. In girls there is the development of breasts, changes in the uterine and the pelvic areas and the menarche. For both sexes we have the growth of the body hair particularly in the pubic and under-arm areas, changes in contours of face and body, and the eruption of new teeth. Most children exhibit pre-pubescent growth spurt and a marked increase in height and weight, especially during the month prior to menarche in the girls and the growth of public hair and the first ejaculation of seminal fluid in boys.

There are Changes in Proportions of the Body and in Organs and Tissues. For example, the legs grow relatively longer upto 15 years and then stem length increases slowly. In the childhood the whole body becomes slender but in the adolescence it begins to broaden again. The bones increase not only in size but also in number. The nose becomes so prominent that it perplexes the sensitive boy. The chemical composition of the bones also changes. Sexual maturing, which is the most complicated process of growth and chage at this stage of development, is the most prominent feature of adolescence. From 14 to 20 years of age there is a tremendous change in genital types, tests, overy, epididymis, uterine tube, prostatic urethra and seminal vesicles.

One of the Chief Characteristics of Physical Growth and Development of Adolescents is their Variability. For example, you will find in a certain class 50% of the girls having entered the pubertycycle whereas the remaining 50% has not done so. A girl at 13 looks partically a young woman but the other of the same age looks still a child. Such variability in the maturation rate is a striking feature of both sexes.

Effects of Early and Late Maturing on Behaviour of Adolescents. The early maturing boy, as we have said earlier, gets a good position among his associates. Since he is tall for his age, he becomes the leader of the group, and the teacher also assigns him a position of responsibilities. This fact creates many problems which he is not yet able to handle. Just at a time when he is trying to adjust to an enlarged physical structure he finds more disadvantages than advantages. The only advantage that he gets out of early maturing is that he gets a chance to learn adult roles earlier. The late maturing boy is decidedly at a disadvantage, because he is ignored or slighted both by girls and boys. As he is small in size and weak in body, he cannot take an active part in games and sports with other boys of the same age. The result is that feelings of inferiority begin to develop in him. He becomes submissive and withdraws himself from competition. Some late maturing boys and girls become noisy, and mischievous to attract the attention of their teachers in the class-room. Such a behaviour is not liked by the elders, and the age-mates also tend to become hostile to them. Like many other persons, who for some reason or other, are rejected by their group, the late maturers suffer from criticism hostility of their associates. Physiological differences are thus regarded as the main causes of behavioural differences in the early and late maturers.

Educational Implications of Physical Development in Adolescence. The understanding of physical growth and change throughout the school years is basic for an adequate understanding of the development of personality. Most schools tend to pay no attention to this psychologically important aspect of growth and development. To the adolescent his growth, now in this part of the body and now in that part of the body, may be awkward and puzzling, and often causing stress and strain. But if the parents and teacher do not recognise and realize the problems raised by physical growth and development, it becomes difficult to understand the whole conduct or behaviour of the grown-up boy or girl. The study of the physical growth of the adolescents is of very great importance to understand the psychological problems faced by them. For a boy or girl to be constantly growing and changing is indeed an experience often puzzling and presenting problems in rapid succession. The youngsters of both sexes are faced with manifold anxieties and embarrassments. In a boy's world, especially the physical size and strength, are so important that his slow or rapid growth, late or early maturing in comparison with that of his class boy's mates or associates may determine his position and prestige among them. The grown-up man or woman, when he or she recollects the changes in puberty in his or her adolescent years, he or she is torn by unpleasant recollections of the adolescent years. Therefore, education should give due importance to this stage of development.

Q. 21. What are the social problems of adolescents? How will you as a teacher help the adolescent to achieve social maturity?

Ans. Adolescence is a period in which a number of social problems crop up. The social contacts of the person expand from infancy to maturity. In infancy a child's social contacts are with one person, usually its mother. From the early childhood onwards the mother-child relationship normally expands as the child comes into contact with the other members of family. When the child moves outside his family circle, he establishes contact with other children of his own age. These children form his peer group. When he takes admission in the school the peer group expands because now the child is free to choose his own friends and associates. Here he meets his teacher. As he enters adolescence he becomes a part of the gang, whatever be the stage of development of other people from his social environment. Adolescence is the stage of development which produces a number of problems for the person. These problems arise out of the adolescent's adjustment with following social groups :

(a) family;

(b) school;

(c) associates of one's own sex; and

(d) associates of the other sex.

Social Problems Raised by the Parents. During adolescent years the boy or girl tends to develop interests for groups outside the family. The youngsters commonly have misgivings about the changes that are taking palce in their interests. On the one hand, they feel joy in being dependent upon their parents and on the other, the experiences with their peers are also pleasant. The peer group attracts them a greater force, because it offers them esteem and statur which is either lacking in the family or is not got there at all.

Parents generally complicate the problem by placing demands on the adolescent sons or daughters. When they come to know that the relationship between them and their children is about to change, when they find their children are becoming more rebellious, less responsive, and less involved in the life of the family they feel threatened. Every father or mother thinks that his son or daughter is a psychologcial extension of himself, and when the adolescent slips along into the outside world, he or she feels that he or she is losing a part of himself or herself. As the adolescent becomes more independent he needs not so much care, direction, and attention of his parents, which parents still think necessary for his existence and well-being. The emotionally insecure parents are unable to face and accept this fact. The adolescent may feel the need of parental love, care and attention at certain times, but he is so proud of himself that he does not want to accept these things. He looks upon any form of dependence as a sign of weakness. This is the reason why there is a conflict going on between the adolescent and his parents. The conflict is of the approach avoidance type; it is so because he wants love and direction, at the same time wants to be strong and self-sufficient enough not to need love and direction. The adolescent resolves such a conflict by making decisions which are not in his interest and defends them stubbornly and rebelliously in the face of all adult opposition.

The loyalities of the adolescent are now divided between the family and the peer group. This division causes tension and anxieties in the adolescent and creates differences between him and his parents. The struggle that goes on within the adolescent is seldom known to most parents. The struggle is caused by his attempt to live in accordance with a double standard composed of the expectations of his parents and those of his associates.

How to Solve Social Problems Raised by the Family. Social problems which have a root in the relationship between the adolescent and his parents arise because the two do not understand each other sympathetically. The parents believe in the efficacy of greater control and direction. Whereas the adolescent believes in less adult control and greater opportunity for independence. The adolescent wants more independence but he also wants his parents to tell him what to do. The parents want to give more direction and control but at the same time require him to think and act for himself. There is dilemma, and the inconsistency is not soluble and therefore it creates difficulties for both.

The mutual problems should be discussed by the parents and the adolescents frankly. It is very unfortunate what and whenever the two parties try to clarify the issues through discussions heated arguments are advanced by each to defend its own point of view.

The adolescent who is in conflict tries to seek social satisfaction outside the home, but he does not get sufficient success in his attempt. If he wants to become successful outside the family he should have emotional support and acceptance within the family.

Problems of Adjustment with the School. The average adolescent tries to run away from home, though economically and vocationally he is yet not able to leave it. It is the school where he can be away from home for a particular length of time in the day. It is in the school also where he can mix with associates in the study-hall, in the classroom, on the playground and on the streets. If the school does not organise social gatherings like excursions, outings, trips, and if there is no arrangement for social develpoment, the adolescent does not find the school a satisfactory place, consequently, he becomes a truant.

If the school wants that the pupils should find joy and satisfaction, pleasure and happiness it should organise social activities in its premises. These activities, if wisely directed, tend to develop social maturity in the adolescents. Maximum participation in co-curricular activities like evening games and sports, plays and dramatics and student councils will inculcate better social interests, skills and attitudes.

Social Problems of Adjustment with Associates of One's Own Sex. Why does a boy belonging to upper class or higher caste family not like to mix with the one of lower class family? Why is a particular boy not popular? Why does a boy like a particular boy and not others? These are some of the problems raised when the adolescent tries to mix with the associates of his own sex. So long as he is a child he does not have such problems. Children of different socio-economic status work and play with each other. But the social distance increases in the adolescence period.

In the society of adolescents there are many who are not popular, who do not belong, and who are occasional. It is strange to find isolates everywhere. Isolates are boys and girls who regard others their best friends but are disregarded by them. The adolescents who are thus rejected become quarrelsome or unduly sensitive. On the others hand, those who are liked seem to be cheerful, humorous and lively.

Social Problems of Adjustment with the Other Sex. The adolescence is the stage when interest in the other sex is developed as a result of certain physical developments. The perennial topics of conversation among boys or among girls are sex and the opposite sex. They try to learn about sex from each other; often, they do help each other but such help is fraught with difficulties. Hence, there is a need for sex education at this stage. It is this stage when the youngsters try to discover the other sex. At first the boys and girls do not know what to make of each other and how to get along together. The boy now sees the neighbour girl in a new way. She is now really a different person from what she was when both of them were of twelve year's age. If he develops healthy relations with her he is an a happy position. If he does not achieve a satisfactory adjustment to the other sex, he may have difficulties in marrige. He may have other social problems also. The boy who cannot establish happy relations with girls may withdraw from their associations. If he becomes too interested in the other sex and goes too far he may cause scandal. If the adolescent boy withdraws from association with girls he will become mentally unhealthy. Marriage becomes either impossible or likely to be unhappy for the introverted youngster who does not have healthy normal associations with the other sex.

Adolescent girls try to attract adolescent boys. The increasingly do thing which may catch and sustain the attention of the other sex. They are more active because of their ealier sex maturity. Many girls, who find the boys of their own age sexually not so mature and responsive, try to seek attention from older boys. As sex maturity among boys and girls occurs at different ages, in a complicated and rapidly changing social situation the adolescents find it difficult to make social adjustment with the other sex.

Education and Social Maturity. The teacher who has to guide the adolescent facing social problems will have to understand the social liabilities and assets. He has to find out the relationships between the adolescent on the one hand and his parents, the peer group, and the school on the other. The teacher has to make a close study of the quiet, commonplace youngster who is rejected by his group or the other sex. If the teacher wants to understand the adolescents and develop them socially he may do the following :

(a) Know the settings and backgrounds of the adolescents.

(b) Make an appraisal for their social status.

(c) Plan a broad social programme to meet the needs of all.

(d) Teach them an informal applied Social Psychology directly or indirectly.

The first step in helping the adolescent achieve social maturity is to gather information about his settings and backgrounds. It is, therefore, necessary that the teacher should try to find out whether or not a particular boy or girl takes part in social activities, whether or not he or she belongs to a team, a society, or a council. Early or late maturing, higher or lower socio-economic status of the family may be influencing his or her social maturity. The teacher has to investigate the causes of social maladjustment. He should then plan a social programme comprehensive enough to meet the needs of all adolescents. As some of the problems arise in the school environment, he may produce good social atmosphere in the school for adequate social development. But most of the social problems arise out of the school, in the family, in the group, in the relations with the other sex. To solve these problems an active co-operation of the parents and the society has to be sought so that desirable social adjustment may be fostered. Regular P.T.A. meetings, conferences between parents and adolescents, healthy associations of one sex with the other, active participation by both boys and girls in the school and community functions may go a long way in helping the adolescents achieve social maturity.

The teacher teaches his subject; the boys or girls learn it. But of greater importance than teaching and learning of the particular subject in the classroom is the development of social maturity. The first thing needed for that is a good-humoured, relaxed, friendly, social climate in the class. Where socialized activity programmes as group games, scouting and guiding, debates and dramatics, run regularly and where students take part in them freely, social maturity is developed as desired. Social adjustment or social maturity may be developed through a direct or indirect instruction in informal applied social psychology.

It is said that adolescents are inept and out-of-place socially. There is little doubt about it. Some adolescents do lack in social skills considered desirable by adults. This social out-of-placeness is, however, due to their lack of experience and self-consciousness. The educational implication of the fact is that adult judgment should be allowed to measure their aptness or ineptness in social skills. The adolescents should be provided with experience in social skills. When the youth is given a chance to express himself in the class, he expresses himself in the public.

Q. 22. Explain the meaning of Learning, its nature, main charactersitics and what are the factors which affect learning?

Ans. Learning pervades our life from cradle to grave. It is the phenomenon with which we come across in almost every walk of our life. It occupies an important place in the field of education. All educational processes appearing in formal, non-formal and informal contexts aim at development of learning. Learning influences our life at every turn, as parents in family, as the teacher in a school, as a friend in society, as a boss in an office, as a leader in a group.

Learning is not a thing that exists somewhere outside the individual. It is a process or product which results into some potential behaviours and capabilities or an activity which causes some change in the behaviour of an individual.

Learning means the modification of behaviour of an individual. It is said to be equivalent to change, modification, development, improvement and adjustment. It is not confined to school learning, reading, writing, typing, cycling, cooking but it is a comprehensive term which leaves permanent effect on the individual. While approaching a burning match stick the child gets burnt and he withdraws. By this incident he learns to avoid not only the burning matchstick but alos all burning things. Learning has been defined in many ways as follows:

According to **Walker,** "Learning is a relatively permanent change in performance that occurs as a result of experience."

According to **Jones and Simpson,** "Any change of behaviour which is result of experience and which causes people to face later situations differently may be called learning."

Garden Murphy, "The term learning covers every modification in behaviour to meet environmental requirements".

Woodworth, "Any activity can be called learning so far as it develops the individual (in any respect, good or bad, and makes his behaviour and experiences different from what that would otherwise have been."

Henry P. Smith. "Learning is the acquisition of new behaviour or the strengthening or weakening of old behaviour as the result of experience."

Kingsely and Garry. "Learning is the process by which behaviour (in the broader sense) is originated or changes through practice or training."

Pressey, Robinson and Horrocks. "Learning is an episode in which a motivated individual attempts to adapt his behaviour so as to succeed in a situation which he perceives as requiring action to attain a goal."

Crow and Crow. "Learning is the acquisition of habis, knowledge and attitudes. It involves new ways of doing things, and it operates in an individual's attempts to overcome obstacles or to adjust to new situations. It represents progressive change in behaviour.... It enables him to satisfy interests to attain goals."

Nature of Learning

1. Learning is the acquisition of new behaviour.
2. Learning is the process by which an activity originates.
3. Learning is the perceptual reorganisation of the situation.
4. Learning is the total reaction of total situation.
5. Learning is goal-directed activity.
6. Learning is universal in nature. Man is rational and he learns the most.
7. Learning is the change in behaviour as a reult of experience.

All Animals Learn

1. Learning is motivated by adjustment.
2. Learning is a never ending growth. We always aspire to learn more and more.
3. Learning is acquisition, retention and modification of experience.
4. Learning is process and product.
5. Learning is a life long process. It starts with birth and comes to an end when the individual dies.

MAIN CHARACTERISTICS OF LEARNING

Yoakman and Simpson have enumerated nine general characteristic of learning which we discuss below :

1. Learning is Growth. The word growth is generally associated with the body which is growing, but through the mental growth of the learner. Although it is latent yet we can perceive its growth. Through his daily activities the child grows both mentally and physically. Therefore, we say that learning is growth through experience.

2. Learning is Adjustment. Learning helps the individual to adjust himself adequately to the new situations. Children meet with new situations which demand solution. Repeated efforts are required to react to them effectively. Life is full of experiences, and each experience leaves behind some effects in the mental structure. These effects modify his behaviour.

3. Learning is Organising Experience. Learning is not mere addition of knowledge. It is not mere acquisition of facts and skills through drill and repetition. It is the reorganisation of experience.

4. Learning is Intelligent. Meaningless efforts do not produce permanent result. Any work done mechanically is without any soul. When a child learns something unintelligently, he is likely to forget it very soon. He does not assimilate but simply commits to memory. Only efforts made intelligently have lasting effects.

5. Learning is Purposeful. All true learning is based on purpose. Purpose plays a big part in learning. According to Ryburn, "This purpose is always connected with the use of some instinctive power, with the use of the energy with which we are endowed with birth." We do not learn anything and everything that comes in our way, in a haphazard manner. All schools activities should be purposeful so that the child should feel real urge for learning.

6. Learning is Active. Learning does not take place without a purpose and self-activity. In the teaching-learning process, the activity of the learner counts more than the activity of the teacher. The principle of learning by doing is the sole principle and has been recommended by all modren educationists. It is the basis of all progressive methods of education such as the Dalton, the Project, the Montessory and the Basic.

7. True Learning Affects the Conduct of the Learner. There is a change in the mental structure of the learner after every experience. By Colvin learning has been described as the "modification of the reactions of an organism through experience."

8. Learning is both Individual and Social. Learning is more than an individual activity. It is a social activity also. Individual mind is affected by the group mind consciously as well as unconsciously as individual is influenced by his friends, relatives, classmates, parents etc., and learns their ideas, feelings and actions. Social agencies like the family, church, film and gangs of playmates have a tremendous influence on the child and are always moulding and remoulding him.

9. Learning is a Product of the Environment. Environment plays an important part in the growth and development of the individual. Environment should be healthy and rich in educative possibilities.

FACTORS AFFECTING LEARNING

Learning is influenced by various conditions of life and school. Our attempts should be to create such conditions as are conductive to effective learning and which help students to make the most satisfactory adjustment to life. The following factors influence learning:

1. Hereditary Factors. Neither we can change nor increase hereditary endowment. Of course, we can use it and develop it. This differs in different individuals. Some are very rich in the matters of hereditary endowments while others are very poor. The native intelligence is different in individuals. Children vary also in particular abilities. The intelligent children can establish and see relationship very easily and more quickly. Our ability to learn and the rate of learning are conditioned by our heredity. Maximum use should be made of the hereditary endowment.

Attempts should be made to see to it that children get opportunities to use and develop their hereditary endowment.

2. Physical Conditions of Children. The physical conditions of children also affect learning. Bodily weakness, chronic illness, malnutrition, fatigue and bad health are a great hindrance in learning. The home conditions—bad ventilation, unhygienic living, bad light, overcrowding etc., affect the rate of learning and the general response of the child. Sometimes children have to walk long distances to and from the school and this also influences learning.

Physical conditions of the class-room are the other determining factors.

It may also be remembered that learning is affected by the physical teachers—their health, voice and speech.

3. Goals Set Before the Pupils. A definite goal should be set before each child according to the standard expected of him. Immediate goals should be set before small children and distant goals for older ones. It must be remembered that the goals should be very clear and the children must understand these goals.

4. Stimulation. Best learning takes place when the teacher is successful in arousing the interest of the students. "The guidance of the teacher is mainly a matter of giving the right kind of stimulus to help him to learn the right things in the right way", write Ryburn.

5. Association of Things. Thorndike points out that things which we want to go together should be put together as a part of one process. Then it becomes easier to make the students understand their connection.

6. Guidance and Instruction. Suitable guidance should be given to the students in selecting the best response to their environment. Demonstration is very helpful to teach various skills.

7. Emotional Conditions. Children should be praised when they show good results. This gives them encouragement to show all the more better results and they develop confidence, hope, self-reliance and self-respect. Sympathetic attitude on the part of the teachers gives stimulus and a sense of security to the students. We should discard our habit of fault-finding. This develops fear and feelings of insecurity and of inferiority.

8. Result of a Total Situation. Learning is affected by the whole situation. It is not always possible to estimate the result of one individual factor. Learning is fruitful and permanent if the total situation is related to life.

Q. 23. Describe various theories of learning and their educational implication. Describe conditioning as a theory of learning. What are its educational implications?

Ans. Psychologists differ at the nature of learning process. Accordingly they have propounded different theories.

Some of the important theories of learning are as follows :

1. Learning by trial and error.

2. Learning by insight.

3. Learning by imitation and observation.

4. Learning by conditioning.

1. LEARNING BY TRIAL AND ERROR

The chief exponent of this theory was *Thorndike.* He make many experiments on rats and cats. He concluded that an individual makes many random efforts to reach a goal. Most of his efforts go useless in his aim. By further trial and error he goes on eliminating useless movements and synthesizing useful ones. At last he reaches the aim. In further trials he need not repeat the useless movements. He will perform the activity quite easily in further attempt as he learnt to perform the real needed movements after eliminating the useful ones. His typical experience in his connection is given below :

The Cat Experiment. He shut-up hungry cat in a big cage. An attractive piece of food was placed outside the cage. The cat looked at the piece and tried to get at it. It extended its paws through the bars of the cage but the piece was far away. It tried every part of the cage but all its efforts failed. It thrust its nose through the bars but all in vain. There was a latch inside the cage. While it was making random movements its paw struck against the latch. The door of the cage opened. Next week the experiment was repeated. The cat made some random movements again but was successful in opening the door sooner than before. In the third or fourth trial there was no random movement. The cat pushed against the latch and went ouside. It learnt the method of opening the door by trial and error.

The experiment sums up the following stages in the process of learning :

(1) Drive. In the present experiment it was hunger and was intensified with the sight of the food.

(2) Goal. To get the food by getting out the box.

(3) Block. The cat was confined in the box with a closed door.

(4) Random Movements. The cat, persistently, tried to get out of the box.

(5) Chance Success. As a result of this striving and random movement the cat, by chance, succeeded in opening the door.

(6) Selection (of proper movement). Gradually, the cat recognized the correct manipulation of latch. It selected the proper way of manipulating the latch out of its random movements.

(7) Fixation. At last, the cat learned the proper way of opening the door by eliminating all the incorrect responses and fixing the only right responses.

Educational Utility. In solving problems of mathematics in the school and those of life in the world we do follow this method in many cases. There is a tendency in animal as well as in men to find out the solutions of difficult problems by trial and error method but the whole behaviour of man is not based on this sort of learning. Skills like walking, talking, running, swimming, cycling, reading and writing can be well explained by this theory. Pupils should remember the motto of 'practice makes a man perfect,' 'work hard' 'try, try again'.

2. LEARNING BY INSIGHT

Kohler and Koffka, were the chief exponents of this theory. They stressed on the totality of the process of learning. They took the process of learning as a synthetic activity which brings forth complete solutions of problems. They referred to the sudden appearance of solutions in many cases. Insight means penetration into the nature of things to find out the solution of a problem without necessary trial and error.

Experiment 1

In one of his experiments *Kohler* shut up his chimpanzee, Sultan by name, in a big cage. Out placed a banana at a considerable distance of the cage. Close the cage there were put two sticks—one of them a long one and the other a bit shorter. The shorter stick could be screwed into the long one. The long stick could not reach the banana but if the other one was screwed into it, the banana could be touched. Sultan tried to get at the banana. He tried the longer stick but it did not reach the fruit. The other was still smaller. He sat down and began to play with the sticks. But he was still brooding over the matter. Suddenly an idea flashed to him. He thrust the smaller sticks into the hole of the longer one and thus managed to get at the banana with the help of the combined sticks.

Experiment 2

In another experiment the chimpanzee was shut up in a room with unscalable walls. A banana was hanging with the ceiling. The animal was hungry. He jumped at the fruit but it was too high. He left the efforts and sat down. There was a box lying in the corner of the room. The animal began to play with the box. He then suddenly got up and pushed the box to the centre of the room below the banana, jumped from it and got the fruit.

Kohler says that learning is a question of perception and not mere motion-activity or mere trial and error. He insists that this sort of learning is very useful in difficult and complicated institutions.

In fact, man does not always learn through trial and error. He often learns through insight. Anyhow learning by insight is much superior to learning by trial and error and we should encourage the children in this process.

Educational Implications :

(a) Learning by insight leads to transfer of training.

(b) It saves time and energy because it is quick, efficient and permanent.

(c) It can be used while teaching lessons because the teacher can proceed from whole to part.

(d) The teacher can arouse the motivation of pupils psychologically in the class-room.

3. LEARNING BY LIMITATION AND OBSERVATION

We find that children learn much by mere imitation. They observe doing various things. They then try to intimate the same activities and learn many things in this way. Even in school the children learn reading and writing and many other processes by imitation, and most of our behaviour is imitated.

Thorndike put some cats in a cage and studied their behaviour as regards the process of imitation. He came to the conclusion that cats do no imitate. Therefore, he does not give value to this theory. But the apes of Kohler imitated. In fact animals differ in this tendency. There is no doubt in it that man learns a lot by initation.

4. LEARNING BY CONDITIONING

By conditioning we modify the behaviour of an individual in such a way that the response originally connected with a particular stimulus comes to be aroused by a different stimulus. The classical experiment of Pavlov will make the process of conditioning clear.

Pavlov was Russian psychologist. In one of his experiments he fitted a tube in the lower jaw of a dog. The dog was kept hungry and was offered food at a fixed time. Simultaneously with this act of offering the food to him, a bell was rung. It was natural that the dog secreted saliva when he saw the food. The saliva went into the tube and it was measured. The experiment went on for some days. After that the bell was rung one day but no food accompanied it. The dog secreted the saliva even then. It was observed that the saliva went on coming in the same quantity with the ringing of the bell for some days. The actual stimulus to bring forth the response, *i.e.*, the secretion of saliva, was the sight of the food but it was conditioned in such a way that another stimulus which ordinarily had nothing to do with secretion of saliva began to stimulate it.

Educational Implications. Most of the habits are conditioned reflexes only. Similarly, some sentiments are also conditioned reflexes. The school can exploit this mechanism to a great extent. The children learn to speak with the help of this process. Direct method of learning, the use of audio-visual aids, associating various subjects with incentives are based on this theory. It may be helpful in formulating principles regarding rewards and punishments. It is also useful in the learning of languages.

All the theories explained above help in the process of learning but man does not learn through any one of the theories exclusively. The child does learn through trial and error as the cats of Thorndike did but he does not stop there. Often he benefits from the power of insight but he does not stop there too. He observes and imitates others also—insects, animals, men and inanimate physical forces. Many times different stimuli combine to develop conditioned reflexes in him. He synthesizes all those modes of learning and goes on developing.

Q. 24. Explain S-R Conditioning Theories of Behaviourists.

Or

Explain Classical Conditioning Theory of Pavlov?

Ans. Beside the methods of limitation and insight another method of learning is conditioning. Many experiments have been done on animals in connection with conditioned response learning. First experiment was done by a famous Russian Physiologist Pavlov on dog around 1890. Pavlov made an opening in the dog's cheeks by operation so that drops of saliva from the salivary glands were collected in a test tube and the amount of saliva could be measured.

In this arrangement food is delivered to the dog through the window. A bell rings simultaneously or just before the food delivery. As the response to the food is conditioned with the bell, Saliva begins to come out from the dog's mouth on the ringing of the bell. Saliva from the dog's mouth is collected in a calibrated glass tube. This activates a recording mechanism through a lever and the experimenter is able to know the number of drops of saliva fallen and whether the salivation was regular or not.

What are the factors which are responsible for conditioning? Which elements are essential for is establishment? Factors controlling are given below in brief :

1. Effect of Motives. For conditioning the stimulus must have the capacity to produce the response. In Pavlov's experiment, the dog was hungry. Therefore it associated the bell with the food, not food with the bell. Thus, the motive has an influence on the learning of conditioned response.

2. The Time Relation of the Two Stimuli. The time relations of the two stimuli are very important in conditioned response learning. It is essential that the new stimulus (c s) is given before the response ends. The natural order is that first the new stimulus (c s) is given and then the old stimulus (u c s). In Pavlov's experiment the bell is given before the food and food is given before the response to the bell ends.

3. Absence of the Deserting Stimuli. Conditioning becomes difficult if some other stimulus is present with the two stimuli (CS and UCS); The lesser the distracting external stimuli are, quicker is the learning of conditioned response. In Pavlov's experiment, a sound proof room was used for this purpose.

4. Repetition of the Stimuli. Food is given to the dog after the bell for many such relations. If the dog gets the food always with the bell then it begins to salivate to the ringing of the bell only. But once the response if conditioned, the two stimuli need not be repeated together continuously. In Watson's experiment when fear to a hare is developed in the child, producing a loud sound suddenly in the presence of a hare once while was enough for the child to remain afraid from the hare.

Application of Conditioning

In general the conditioning becomes easier, the higher the species of the organism is. Thus, learning by this method should become easier in the case of human beings. But man is so complex an organism that stimuli which distract him and interfere in his learning are numerous. Inspite of this conditioning has a great importance in the learning of a child. Many of our responses are conditioned to particular things in childhood and these remain fixed even in the adulthood. For example, if a person of a particular appearance treated you badly in your childhood, your hate or fear response for that figure becomes conditioned and this response remains so in your adulthood for the persons of similar appearance. Conditioning technique is also used in the teaching of words meaning to children. The word 'Mama' is spoken to the child while pointing to 'Mama'. The child associates the sound 'Mama' with the figure of 'Mama' and begins to call her Mama. If the child cannot distinguish between different females in the family he calls 'Mama' to all persons of that figure. But when he is similarly told about other females, he learns to distinguish between them. Thus, whereas we acquire different responses to things, animals or human beings through conditioning, we also acquire the meaning of words through this process.

Pavlov wanted to prove that all learning is conditioning. Modern psychology does not accept this view. But no psychologist can deny the fact that conditioned response is a very important technique used in teaching many things to tamed animals. For example, if a bear is to be taught dancing to the sound of the drum, it is made to stand on a hot plate and the drum is sounded as the animal lift its feet. After sometimes it begins to lift its feet at the sound of the drum only.

Many examples of the application of this method can be given in daily life. At the time when the husband normally returns home, the wife expects her husband coming at each sound of the bell on the road. Your hand always goes to the right pocket for the purse though it is in the left pocket; because the purse has been taken out from the right pocket so many times that the activities of taking out purse and putting hand in the right pocket are associated with each other.

Another form of conditioning is negative adaptation. Negative adaptation means learning not to make a response. This is infact, a form of conditioning. It is very useful in the changing of habits. In negative adaptation a particular response in inhibited when a second response takes place. For example, if an adult male rat is given an electric shock as it reaches the female rats, it will gradually learn to go away from the female rats.

Conditioning starts very early in life. Even the child in the mother's womb is influenced by the sound etc., through this process. Learning by this technique increases till the age of four or five years. After that, with increasing age its importance gradually decreases because conditioning is interfered by many tendencies of the adult person.

Q. 25. Discuss Skinner's Operant Conditioning Theory.

Ans. Operant conditioning theory has been developed by American psychologist B.F. Skinner. The basis of operant conditioning is Reinforcement. The term 'operant' emphasises the fact that behaviour operates upon the environment to generate its own consequences. Operant behaviour is external. It can be observed. In operant conditioning a response occurs spontaneously in the absence of any stimulation with which it may be specifically correlated.

It differs from classical conditioning mainly on two issues, firstly in it 'operant behaviour' is conditioned whereas in classical conditioning 'respondent behaviour is conditioned. Secondly in operant conditioning the behaviour should get immediate reinforcement, it has to occur at least once before it can be reinforced. While classically conditioned reflex may have zero strength in the beginning respondent behaviour is internal and personal.

According to Skinner, "The whole behaviour is the result of operant conditioning. In every field of life, reinforcement brings changes. When any behaviour is reinforced there is more opportunity of repetition of that behaviour."

Skinner proposed two types of behaviour:

1. Respondent Behaviour. Respondent behaviour is known as S-R. type behaviour. There must be a known stimulus for evoking respondent behaviour such as jerking at the pinch of pin, salvation at the sight of food, to pulling of the hand back by touching hot objects. Such behaviour is known as Stimlus-Response (S-R. type) behaviour.

2. Operant Behaviour. Operant behaviour is not evoked by any known stimuli or cause. Whistling, movement in the class while teaching, jumping the chalk are the examples of operant behaviour. These activities occur without any reason. In such behaviour response occurs before than stimulus. Due to this reason it is known as Response—Stimulus (R-S type) behaviour. It is the consequence of behaviour that is quite fundamental in operant conditioning. If the behaviour is followed by pleasant consequences it will lead to its repetition and maintenance. In other words a behaviour must get due reinforcement for its proper conditioning or learning. In case if we want that particular behaviour should not occur, we may do well by ignoring it *i.e.,* not providing any reinforcement for its reoccurance.

Any stimulus that strengthens a behaviour is considered as a reinforcer. There are two types of reinfrocers. A stimulus whose introduction or presentation strengthens a behaviour may be said to be a positive reinforcer. Examples of such reinforcers are praise, money, food, medal, certificates etc. On the other hand, a stimulus whose removal strengthens a behaviour is considered as a negative reinforcer.

Negative reinforcement involves the concept of negative reward, the avoidance of which gives the individual relief from the unpleasant situations. Negative reinforcement strengthens desirable behaviour by withdrawing unpleasant consequences.

When a teacher announces in the class that those who will draw this picture here in the class will be exempted from home work. In this case home work is considered as an unpleasant task than exemption from it will be reinforcing.

One learns through the mechanism of operant conditioning. When a child pays regard to the guest at home, his parents praise him, they reward him and ask to do again. The behaviour that was operated on the environment by the child spontaneously without any specific reason now gets due reinforcement. It this way in operant conditioning, a behaviour just occured spontaneously, has almost all chances of its learning as a habit by the individual if it gets immediate proper reinforcement for its maintenance and repetition.

Experiment

Skinner conducted his experiment on pigeon *i.e.*, learning to dance in a specific way by a pigeon.

For this purpose he suggested to break the tasks into steps and providing reinforcement at the each step. For this purpose one can start from any desired simple response say turning its neck in the left direction by a pigeon. The initial response can be immediately reinforced by a small amount of grain for elicitating the other desired response *i.e.,* moving a step in the left direction and then taking round like dance, and thus leading it to learn to dance in a desired way.

Educational Implications

- In operant conditioning learning of a behaviour is dependent upon its consequences, therefore, it should be properly decided before hand the type of behaviour we want from the children. While the desired behaviour should be immediately and properly reinforced, the unwanted one should not get any reinforcement.
- It has suggested that the best way to get rid of an undesirable behaviour is to ignore it and reward the appropriate behaviour. This theory has disapproved the use of punishment (the weakening of a behaviour) in the process of learning in comparison to reinforcement (strengthening of the behaviour).
- Activities which provide satisfaction and reinforcement, help in quick learning.
- According to this theory, if the students are told about the results of the efforts then they can progress much faster.
- The most significant contribution of operant conditioning lies in its role towards the development of programmed

instruction material and systematic individualised approach to teaching through teaching machines and computer assisted instructions.

- With the help of this theory a teacher can give the desirable shape and direction to the behaviour of the students.
- This theory is helpful in improving the behaviour of mental patients, mentally retarded and problematic children. The desirable behaviour of these children is reinforced in the form of reward.
- This theory is not in favour of giving punishment to the children. Punishment makes the child rebellion and revolutionary.

Limitations

Mostly educationists and psychologists agree that operant conditioning is a practical approch to human behaviour and can be used in class-room teaching learning. The theory of operant conditioning has been criticised on the following grounds:

- Skinner denies the importance of genetic inheritance. To him all the behaviour is acquired during the life-time of the individual. He neglects innate endowment.
- This theory fails to account for spontaneity, curiosity and creativity in human beings.
- It is superficial and does not deal with the depths of mind.
- This theory daps into subjective explaination such as self reinforcement and thinking.
- This theory mechanizes the mental process and treats the organism like a machine.
- It dehumanizes learning process.
- It is antidemocratic, its result can be misused by direction.

Q. 26. Explain Thorndike's Trial and Error Theory of Learning or connectionist view point in learning. What are its educational implications?

Ans. Trial and Error Theory of Learning. For nearly half a century, one learning theory dominated all others in the U.S.A.

despite many attacks on it and the rise of its many rivals. It is the theory of E.L. Thorndike (1874-1949). This theory was given by him in 1898, in his book the *'Animal Intelligence'*.

The basis of learning accepted by Thorndike in his earliest writings was association between sense impressions and impulses to action. Such an association comes to be known as a 'bond' or a 'connection'. Because it is these bonds or connections which become strengthened or weakened in making and breaking of habits. Thorndike's system sometimes has been called a 'bond' psychology or simply 'connectionism'. As such it is the original S—R Psychology of learning.

To quote K.P. Pandey—Thorndike's theory of learning is based on the following three elements :

(a) The Stimulus element which involves an environmental event.

(b) The response element which indicates a behavioural act.

(c) The formation of a connection or bond which implies that every stimulus is linked with some kind of response and thus makes for the building block or structure of behaviour. Pandey in his book "Advanced Educational Psychology for Teachers" further states that the *formation of a bond* (S-R bond) is the key expression in describing the learning theory of Thorndike. When an oganism is said to have learned something, it is essentially the formation of a connection or bond between a stimulus and a response.

Connectionism has two phases :

First phase was before 1930.

Second phase was after 1930 because Thorndike made important changes later on the basis of experiments. We shall examine this theory as follows :

There are four characteristic features of Trial and Error Learnig :

1. There is some sort of a motive that arouses or sustains the activity. This motive may appear in the form of need, a problem or a goal. Essentially the equilibrium of the organism is disturbed and this impels the organism to react to the situation in an effort that comes to terms with it.

2. Several different kinds of responses are made.
3. Finally there is a progressive integration and establishment of the reaction by which the goal is achieved.
4. There is progressive elimination of superfluous unsuccessful or wrong form of activity.

The essential point in trial and error is the second point—the process by which the correct response is identified through tyring various responses until a solution which permits the attainment of goal is achieved.

The Puzzle Box Experiment. Thorndike studies the character of Trial and Error learning in a number of experiments on cats. A favourite device was his puzzle box used years ago by him for his studies of animal learning.

In one of the experiments`a hungry cat was placed in the box and the door was closed. A fish was placed outside the box. The cat was given 100 trials, ten each morning and each afternoon for five days. The cat was fed at the end of each experimental period and then was given nothing more to eat until after the next session. In after opening the door in any trial by jumping or by chance, he went in immediately to the food, he was allowed a small bite. A complete record was made of the cat's behaviour during each trial.

It may be mentioned that besides these cat's experiments which became so common and cheap, it has trained some classical experiments performed by Ebbinghaus on memory and by Brain and Harter on Telegraphy. But these experiments of Thorndike are different from Ebbinghaus experiments w.r.t. two points and those points are that of : (i) Motivation, (ii) of Reward and punishment. He aid that the world cannot ignore reward and punishment and motivational factors.

As early as 1913, Thorndike wrote, "Both theory and practice need emphatic and frequent reminders that man's learning is fundamentally the action of laws of readiness, exercise and effect. He is first of all an associative mechanism working to avoid what disturbs the life processes of the neurons. If we begin by fabricating imaginary powers and the faculties or if we avoid thought by loose and empty terms or if we stay lost in wonder at extraordinary versatility and inventiveness of the higher forms of lerning, we shall never understand man's progress or control of his education."

Criticism. A serious limitation of this theory is its lack of understanding. Thorndike did not consider understanding important. He merely assumed that it would follow as a natural result of well organised learning. He believed that insightful learning, though it did occur, was infrequent.

Educational Implications of Trial and Error Theory

1. Effect of Motivation. It is the most important factor in all learning. Motivate the child.

2. Exercise Patience. Learning by Trial and Error theory is always gradual. The teacher must exercise patience with the child if the child does not show any progress immediately in any learning situation.

3. Place of Exercise. Exercise has its own place in education and learning. Repeat, give a sufficient drill in some tests.

4. Make Learning Meaningful. Effect of belonging to a thing shold be exploited.

5. We must learn basis things needed for it in any learning.

6. This theory has drawn our attention to the principle of learning by doing. You will learn only when you do a thing.

Q. 27. Explain S-R Bond Theory of Thorndike.

Ans. S-R BOND THEORY OF THORNDIKE

One of the most accredited among all the current theories on the law of learning is the one presented by Thorndike, in America. Talking of its importance Tolman says, "The psychology of animal learning, not to mention that of child learning has been and still is primarily a matter of agreeing or disagreeing with Thorndike or trying in minor ways to improve up him. Gestalt psychologists, conditioned reflex psychologists, sign gestalt psychologists, all of us here in America seem to have taken Thorndike, overtly or covertly, as our starting point."

Thorndike first presented his theory in his book '*Animal Learning*' published in 1968. The clearest form of his theory is seen in the three volumed treatise '*Educational Psychology*'. His theory may be understood in a systematic way with the help of three major laws which are as follows :

1. Law of Readiness.
2. Law of Exercise.
3. Law of Effect.

Writing on the subject of the importance of his laws in the action of learning Thorndike says, "Both theory and practice need emphatic and frequent reminders that man's learning is frequently the action of the laws of readiness, exercise and effect." Accordingly, in Thorndike's opinion, man's learning takes place according of these laws.

He drew a learning curve for men and animals and concluded from it that usually the methods employed are similar in both classes of creatures. Until 1930, Thorndike laid particular emphasis on these three laws.

Law of Readiness

The law of readiness describes those situations in which the person who learns either invites the object of his learning or rejects it. Readiness include all those preparatory adjustments which immediately precede the action. Reminding the learning of his past experience mental preparation for the understanding of new things, deverting his attention towards the subject to be learned, the altering of the environment to suit the learning, are all included in learning. This readiness creates a desire for learning and turns the learners's mental attitudes towards the suject to be learned.

In Thorndike's the view law of readiness is active in three following conditions :

1. When a conducting unit is prepared to go into action, its work is quite satisfactory because nothing is done to alter its working.
2. When a conduction unit is forced to act while it is not prepared to do so its behaviour is of a nature calculated to excite anger.
3. The inactivity of a conduction unit which is ready to behave, may be unsatisfactory and any reaction may arise is connection with that deficiency.

Law of Exercise

The second law, of any consequence in human and animal learning is the law of exercise, which is based on the laws of use and disuse. The repeated application of an activity fixes it firmly in the mind while on the other hand no psyhological reference is intended. The relation is weekened through continuous disuse. Whenever there is an appropriate situation, the activity which is firmly entrenched might take place. This law, taking a cue from this universal experience, emphasizes repetition in the activity of learning. Repetitive application of the activity results in the formulation of a habit in the muscles and the nerve fibers of the brain so that there is a facility in its execution in time of need. The element of understanding in repetition was not adequately stressed in Thorndike's law of readiness. For example, it is a rule that if repetition in the memorizing of a poem is complemented by an attempt to understand and mutual relate the different stanzas, the learning may be affected with ease. Not so with Thorndike, who considered the mechanical repetition of learning individually sufficient. This type of memorizing becomes rote learning highly undesirable thing, and the forgetting of one line resuls in the forgetting of the rest while the recollection of the important makes a clear understanding of the subject-matter and constant renewal quite as important an constant repetition. Thus, Thorndike's mechanical repetition came in for a lot of criticism and he reached by effecting modifications.

LAW OF EFFECT

The meaning of the law of effect is the effect of learning in answer to question as the success or failure of learning has very significant bearing on the law now under study. Success brings with it satisfaction and along with it a strengthening of the relation of the facts. Failure increases dissatisfaction and the absence of the relation amount the facts weakness them. Thus, we may compare success to a reward or failure to a punishment and desire to repeat success or avoid failure or the inevitable antecedants.

In 1932, Thorndike propounded a new theory on the basis of his experiments about the law of effect, and this he entitled "Spread of effect." This novel theory postulates that by the activity of learning adjustments are not left unaffected. For example, the son of a businessman is ahead of his class in arithematic because he has already learnt some accountancy in connection with sales in the shop.

In 1935, Thorndike made some modification in the law of effect, based on experimental findings. He now said the influence of reward or punishment is not equivalent and neither it is paradoxical. The effect of reward is for more influential than that of punishment, the strengthening of associations due to reward is not paralleled by the demoralization caused by dissatisfaction as possible in order that he may learn with success . Encourage the child when he does some thing and congratulate him besides rewarding him with object of desires in order to bring desirable spirit in his learning.

IMPORTANCE OF THE MAJOR LAW

These major laws enunciated by Thorndike are of great practical importance. Very few of us realize the effect which reward, encouragement, praise etc., have on learning. These theories are of importance not only in the teaching of others but also in personal activity to be learned should be created in the learner, be it oneself or some other, because the learning will be greatly expedited. And the meaningful practice of the learnt activity will help its retention in no small measure.

SUBORDINATE LAWS

Other five subordinate laws were also mentioned by Thorndike in relation to the three major ones studied above. Though a methodical explaination of true laws as given by Thorndike his later expositions sometimes contain their description while at other occasions they are lacking in it. He does not consider these subordinate laws to be of equal importance with the three major ones mentioned above. These five subordinate laws are :

1. Multiple Response. The first subordinate law is called varied reaction. A person seeks to solve a novel problem placed in front of his in accordance with his instincts and learned behaviour, because his search in conditioned by these two. There are many multiform and diversified responses in behaviour which guide a person in attaining success and makes learning possible. The learner reaches the solution by the variation in the response.

If the activities are not multiform the person would never get the correct solution. The theory of learning by trail and error if founded on multipurpose response and diversified reactions. If a person adopts a particular method of approach but does not change it in case of failure and gives up his attempts or if nothing new suggests, that person will never learn anything.

2. Set or Attitude. This is the second law of learning. Learning is conditioned by the attitude and set of the creature. The response of a person in a specific situation is dependent upon his permanent adjustment in a particular culture. On seeing a figure or idol a Hindu child will bow his head but a Muslim will not pay any respect. Both these responses are affected simultaneously by current tendencies. In an extraordinary situation, the worshipper may even throw the status. The set or attitude decides not only the response of the person but also the object from which he will derive satisfaction or classification. A first class student cries on scoring 50 per cent marks, while a third class student feels delighted with the same score. The reaction of a student on scoring certain number of marks depends upon the set, attitude and the tendency present in him at the time.

3. Response by Analogy. This is the third law of learning and is called the law of assimilation. A person will respond in a manner similar to the one in which he has behaved previously if he finds that similarities between the previous situation and the new situations are none too numerous, the response will be similar of that in the first.

4. Prepotency of Elements. The fourth subordinate law of learning is the prepotency of elements. Every problem has some fundamental proponent element. The learner gets greater success if he bases his response on those elements, though this depends on the insight and capability of the learner. This kind of capacity is of great help in though learning. The insight, into a mathematical problems, of a student of this particular subject cannot be equaled by that of a student of languages into the same problem because the student of mathematics will grasp its fundmentals with consummate ease.

5. Associative Shifting. This is the first and last law of learning. The title quite obviously indicates that the position of the response of the learner shifts. This shifting is done in respect of the basic stimulus or some related associative stimulus. To take an example, a dog starts salivating when he sees food, and approaches the bearer with his tail wagging. The result of constant repetition of this phenomenon is that dog wags his tail on the mere perception of the man and the shape of dish. Thus, the response originally directed to the food is now aimed at the man and the dish because both these objects are associates of the main stimulus, the food. Thus, an associative shifting in the response is observable.

All the law subsidiary and main, presented by Thorndike are important in learning, both for the teacher and the student. They are applied comprehensively in education though all the pscyhologists are not agreed upon the truth and usefulness usevally attributed to them.

The above described laws of learning are not intended to convey the impression that Thorndike's attention was confined only to the laws. Actually, Thorndike paid even greater attention to the practical aspect education and made attempt to absolve the difficulties to the teachers and taught alike. Thus, Thorndike attended to the specific aspects of learning and did not rest content with a general description of the activity. He has mentioned many factors which may assist in learning but which are not implied in and cannot be derived from his laws of learning. For example, he has stressed the following five things which assist in the progress of learning :

(i) Interest in the work,

(ii) Interest in improvement,

(iii) Significance,

(iv) Problem Attitude,

(v) Attentiveness.

To these five. Thorndike added two which in his opinion, are not indisputable. These are absence of irrelevant emotion and absence if worry. In this way, he encouraged practical experience and measurements. He himself conducted experiments throughout his life and made continuous progress in his theory. He is fundamentally a behaviourist, not with-standing his acceptance of the effect of introspection of human being and he frequently used subjective words. He encouraged the psychological revolution in the field of education and emphasized the study of elements according to specific situation.

Q. 28. Explain the laws or principles of learning and their educational utility.

Ans. Thorndike formulated laws of learning. Laws of learning are divided under two parts—

(1) Primary law, (2) Secondary law.

Primary law of learning

Law of Readiness | Law of Exercise | Law of Effect

1. Law of Readiness. Readiness means a preparation for action. It is a kind of 'action tendency' aroused through preparatory adjustments, sets and attitudes. The fulfilment of this tendency is satisfying and its non-fulfilment is annoying. Thorndike employed physiological terms in describing this law.

Learning is a matter of interest. The learner must be made ready to learn. When a person feels ready to learn, he learns more effectively and with greater satisfaction than when not ready. There are some motives, desire or purpose without which no learning is possible. So, for learning the learner must be mentally ready.

Educational Implication. This law can be effective in the following ways—

(a) To arouse the interest and attention of the students by asking suitable questions.

(b) This law is useful in arousing curiosity of the students. Curiosity is indispensable for learning.

Motivation is an important factor for learning. It is also based on the principle of readiness. If the learner is properly motivated he will be ready for the work and apply his energies vigorously.

2. Law of Exercise. This law is known as law of practice or law of use and disuse. If any activity is exercised we come to have efficiency in doing it. If it is not repeated we soon forget it. It means repetition of an activity strengthens the nerve connections and on the other hand disuse weakens the bond. In short it can be said that law of exercise as a whole emphasises the need of repetition practice and drill work in the process of learning. Children learn spellings and pronounciation according to this law.

Educational Implications. In educational field this law can be effective in the following ways:—

It Leads to Formation of Habits. If good acts are repeated again and again then they become habit. So it is the duty of the teacher to see that children are given a great deal of practice in good activities.

Correct Pronunciation. It has to be learnt by practice and incorrect pronunciation can be unlearnt only by avoiding its repetition.

By Practice Handwriting can be improved. Bad handwriting can be improved by practice. For this the teacher can ask the students to do regular practice.

Bad Habits can be Eradicated. According to Dunlop Bata theory of learning, if the children are made to practice consciously, then they automatically tend to leave their bad habits. For example if a child is in the habit of thumb-sucking or nil-biting (chewing) then he should be asked by the teacher not to repeat this habit consciously. The underlying idea is that he will become conscious of this mistake and avoid the same in future.

Mathematics is dependent wholly on practice. Arithmatical tables, formulas and definitions can be learnt only with the help of practice.

The element of forgetfulness can be delayed or avoided because by practice the activities become deep rooted. So forgetting can be avoided to some extent.

Skills like music, painting, typing shorthand, athletics etc., can be developed to the maximum with the help of this law.

3. Law of Effect. Thorndike has defined this law as—"When a modifiable connection between a situation and response is made and is accompanied by a satisfying state of affairs, that connection's strength is increased, but when made and accompanied by an annoying state of affairs its strength is decreased."

It is also called as the Law of Pleasure and Pain or Law of Satisfaction and Annoyance. The word effect means the effective result of the activity. The child has to perform a number of activities. Every activity has its effect. Some activities end in pleasure and others end in pain. The activities which are associated with pleasure or satisfaction tend to be repeated again and again and the learning becomes more effective. Activities which are assoicated with pain, punishment or annoyance are not repeated and their strength is decreased. The entire system of rewards and punishments is based on this law.

Educational Implications. The educational utility of this law is as follows :

Theory of reward and punishment is based on this law. Reward should be given for desirable beahviour and punishment should be associated with undesirable behaviour.

This law is helpful in forming and developing the desirable sentiments in the pupils. Positive sentiments should be associated with satisfying state of affairs.

Problem Behaviour and Delinquent Behaviour can be improved by associating it with annoying state of afairs (punishment).

Interest is directly related to this law. Interest causes satisfaction and satisfaction promotes learning and better learning gives higher satisfaction. In the selection of subjects, books, hobbies games and curricular activities pupils prefer which is interesting to them.

Formation of good Habits. Good habits can be formed in children by assoicating them with reward, satisfaction or praise. Undesirable habits can be eradicated by associating them with punishment, dissatisfaction and blame.

Memory is also connected with the law of effect. Pleasant things are generally remembered better than unpleasant things.

Control of Emotions. With its help, the teacher can control the emotions of anger and jealousy of the students.

Some times it appears that a punishment is more effective than reward. Strong punishment brings about a desired attitude towards learning.

It is also found that it is human tendency to remember certain highly unpleasant incidents better than pleasant incidents.

SECONDARY LAWS OF LEARNING

Secondary laws of learning are as follows:

Law of Multiple Response. This law implies that when an individual is confronted with a new situation he responds in a variety of ways before arriving at correct response.

Law of Analogy. An individual responds to a new situation on the basis of the responses made by him in similar situations in the past. He makes responses by comparison or analogy.

Law of Associative Shifting. This law is also known as the conditioned response. A response may be shifted from one situation to another which is presented at the same time. In other words any response which is possible can be linked with any stimulus.

Law of Partial Activity. According to this law the learner has the capacity to select the important from the irrelevant element in order to determine appropriate responses.

Law of Sets and Attitudes. Learning is guided by a total attitude or 'set' of the organism. The learner performs the task properly if he has developed a healthy attitude towards the task.

Law of Recency. It means that whatever is recently learnt by the child is retained by him. The law may be defined as 'recent acts are lasting'. Hence students should revise their courses just before the examination.

Law of Primacy. Learning that takes place in the beginning is the best and lasting. It is a normal saying that 'First impression is the Last impression'. It implies that pupils should make the right start and should be serious from the first day. Teacher should impress his pupils from the first day of teaching. It seems the experiences that are acquired by the child at the primary stage have lasting effect.

Law of Intensity of Stimulus. To this law, if a stimulus is strong the response will be strong and *vice a versa*. Examinations present an intense stimulus to study and hence bear a positive effect on learning.

Law of Belongingness. This law shows that if a response belongs to a situation, the learning will be more effective. Connection between stimulus and response is natural. The teacher should create natural atmosphere in the class-room and appeal to the natural tendencies of the child.

FACTORS OR VARIABLES OF LEARNING

Maturation. Learning depends upon maturation. If the individual is matured to learn a particular activity, he will learn effectively. If the individual is no mature, learning will not be effective.

Readiness. If the learner is ready to learn a particular activity he will learn better and quickly.

Capacity. The greater the capacity for learning a person has, the better will be the learning.

Attention and Interest. If the learner is motivated to learn a particular task he will take more interest in the task with full attention and hence will learn that task better.

Memory. A learner who has good momory will learn quickly and effectively.

Mental Health. A child who is mentally healthy *i.e.,* free from frustrations, conflicts, anxieties and worries will learn better.

Motivation. Motives like reward, completion, level of aspiration, success and punishment etc., are powerful incentives to the learner for better learning.

Fatigue. Fatigue causes boredom and indolence and hence has negative effect on learning.

Food and Drugs. Food also affect learning. Poor diet, alchoholic drugs, tobacco and addictive items adversely affect learning.

Perception and Sensation. Perception and sensation are the basis of all cognitive learning. The stronger the power of perception, the greater the amount of learning.

Practice. 'Practice makes a man perfect' is a well known proverb. Learning is more efficeint when practice is distributed at intervals over a period of time when it is considered in one period as in cramming (Ebbinghaus 1885; Leuba and Hyde 1893).

Will. Will to learn is an important factor of learning, and it arouses, sustains and regulates the pattern of activity, and leads to better attention, better motivation and hence better learning.

Guidance. Guided learning is always better than unguided learning, Guidance saves times and energy of the learner, eliminates wastage and stagnation. But too much guidance should be avoided so that student many not learn the habit of remaining dependant upon teachers.

Timely Testing. Occasional and periodical testing motivates the pupils to be regular in their studies. If the pupils are regular in studies they can learn better. Moreover through tests the learner knows his exact achievement, his accomplishment and there is little scope for under-estimation.

Time of Learning. Experiments have shown that there are significant variations in learning efficiency during different hours of the day. It has been established that morning and evening hours are the best hours for study. During the day there is decline in the mental capacity due to noise.

Knowledge of Result. Knowledge of result particularly the specific knowlege of progress of the learner improves his performance, motivates him for greater learning and serves as an incentive towards increased effort.

Pleasantness of Task. Generally pleasant tasks are learnt quickly than the unpleasant tasks.

Vigorous Application. Slow learning is seldom efficient. Learning vigorously is a great asset and it pays much. The students should be taught to work whole heartedly. They must put their heart and soul while learning something.

Q. 29. Define Learning. Differentiate between Pavlov's classical conditioning and Skinmen's operant conditioning theory of learning.

Ans. I.P. Pavlov (1849-1936), an eminent Russian physiologist and a noble prize winner for his work on physiology of digestion, while experimenting on the gastric secretion in dogs observed that any stimulus frequently associated with the presentation of food aroused salivation. This observation led to the famous conditioned response theory of learning. The noticed that an incidental stimulus was sufficient to bring salivation. Then his attention was diverted to the possibility of producing saliva to an unnatural stimulus.

Likes trial and error, conditioning deals with certain basic principles of learning process. It holds that the formation of SR connection, its strengthening or weakening depends upon association between two things.

Presentation of a stimulus arouses a response in every normal organism. When you see a friend you welcome him, when you see a snake you run away from it. Sight of food arouses salivation. Here friends, snake and food are natural or unconditioned stimuli and responses like welcome, running away and saliva are natural or unconditioned responses.

However, when an unnatural or conditioned stimulus is frequently associated with a natural or unconditioned stimulus, the 'O' starts showing his conditioned response to the stimulus. The conditioned response here is equal to the unconditioned responses, *i.e.*, saliva. In other words, saliva is the natural response to food. If food is associated with bell for several trials, bell alone brings out saliva. In short, due the association between the unconditioned (Food) and conditioned stimulus (Bell) the 'O' responds to the conditioned stimulus (Bells) in the same way (Saliva) as he responds to the unconditioned stimulus. This is called conditioned response learning. In case of Pavlov's dog, bell is the conditioned stimulus (CS) and Saliva is the conditioned response (CR).

Conditioning is supposed to be a process by which a response (Saliva) is attached to a stimulus (bell) different from the one which originally elicits that response. In simple words, a response is said to be conditioned when some stimulus other than the already effective one comes to arouse of modify it for the establishment of a definite stimulus response connection. A non-effective stimulus, therefore, brings an effective response due to conditioning. This pattern of behaviour is observed when learning by conditioning is complete.

The nipple in the mouth of an infant in an unconditioned stimulus and sucking is an unconditioned reflex. But when the sight of the bottle produces sucking response in the baby, it is called conditioned response. Similarly, happiness at the sight of a friend's letter, fear for the doctor, crying at the sight of water, are certain examples of conditioned responses. When an injection needle pricks the muscle of the baby he cries out of pain. Next time when only he sees the needle or the doctor, he cries with the anticipation that the needle would now prick him again. Here the pricking of the needle is the U.S. crying is the U.R., sight of the needle is the C.S. and crying is C.R. Strengthening of the SR connection therefore depends upon the association between two stimuli.

CLASSICAL CONDITIONING

The conditioning technique developed by Pavlov is famous as the classical conditioning technique. The following experiment conducted by Pavlov on a dog is known as classical conditioning experiment. Pavlov made a minor surgical operation in the cheek of the dog to measure the rate of salivation. The animal was kept in a sound-proof room. During the experiment a servant was feeding the dog. Pavlov to his great surprise noticed that one day, only the sound of the footsteps of the servant made the dog to salivate. The very incident created such an interest in Pavlov that he devoted most of his time to study the phenomenon of conditioning.

To start with the experiment, when food was placed in the mouth of the dog, it brought saliva. On other occasions, only a bell was rung, but it did not bring any salivary response from the dog.

Then Pavlov rang the bell first and after an interval of 5 seconds placed the food in the mouth of the dog. In this first trial bell alone did not bring saliva until food was not placed in its mouth. Only after the repetition of bell-food sequence for several days, when the dog could connect the bell with the food and anticipated food at the sound of bell, did it salivate to the bell only, even before seeing the food. Pavlov noticed that the dog salivated to the presentation of bell only after several trials when learning by conditioning was firmly established. From this Pavlov inferred that stimulus response connection has been established. The dog has finally learnt to respond to the C.S. This technique of establishing a response to a conditioned or artificial stimulus is called classical conditioning process. Pavlov, in course of his many experiments, demonstrated that the dog can be made to salivate to any stimulus, however, unnatural and irrelevant it may be. This discovery of Pavlov made a significant contribution to the learning theory.

Pavlov's classical conditioning can be explained by the following pattern, which Pavlov used in his experiment on dog :

1. Natural or unconditioned stimulus (U.C.S.) food.	Natural or unconditioned response (U.C.R.) Salivation
2. Conditioned stimulus (C.S.)	—No salivation
3. C.S. (Bell) 5 seconds interval U.C.S. (food)	—Unconditioned response U.C.R. (Saliva)

Condition 3 is repeated for several trials until an association is established between bell and food (C.S. and C.R.)

4. C.S. (Bell)	—C.R. (Saliva)

In any classical conditioning experiment in the C.S., U.C.S. pattern, the C.S. should always precede the U.C.S. and the time between the two must be constant and very close in all trials. If the time gap is too large! Conditioning may not be established because lack of close temporal pairing of the C.S. and U.C.S. will not be able to establish the association between C.S. and U.C.S. While establishing the salivary response to a tone in one experiement the following observations were recorded :

No. of presentations of sound and feeding	*No. of drops of saliva in 30 seconds*
1	0
9	18
15	30
31	65
41	64
51	69

[From Munn, O.N.L. (1954) Psychology page 118, Time sequence in conditioning.]

In this experiment after 9 presentation of the C.S. and U.S. in close proximity, conditioning was established. It is also noticed from this table that the number of drops of saliva increased with number of repetitions of the conditioning process.

The strength of conditioning can be found out in terms of saliva and in terms of latency (the time elapsing between the bell and the saliva).

Time Sequence in Conditioning

Usually is conditioning technique the C.S. precedes the U.S. by a fraction of second. Sometimes it is almost simultaneous. As a matter of fact, about 3 seconds give the best result as studies show. It is also found that if we measure the effectiveness of conditioning, the strongest conditioning occurs with shorter latency period, i.e., near about 3 seconds.

The most vital point in Pavlov's classical conditioning technique is that food always follows bell irrespective of the salivation of the dog. Whether the dog salivates or not, does not matter. Food is always presented after bell with the lapse of a very short time interval.

Besides Pavlov, Bechterev, Waston and many more psychologists have conducted experiments on conditioning. Wever made respiratory conditioning to belt. Pavlov and his associates have observed certain important phenomena in conditioning which are discussed below.

Stimulus Generalisation

It is a tendency for the CR to be aroused by a similar stimulus other than the stimulus aroused in training. Generalization in conditioning occurs to a certain class of stimuli rather than to a specific stimulus. Pavlov noticed that when a C.S.C.R. bond has been established by conditioning, a stimulus which is similar to the C.S., can produce the same response and he called this stimulus generalisation. The more similar the new stimulus, the greater is the probability for generalization and *vice-versa*. If the dog is conditioned to salivate to tone, it will salivate to any type of tone like electric bell, worship bell, college bell, buzzer, ding dong bell and other sounds.

Watson in an experiment on the development of fear in children has demonstrated stimulus generalization. Albert, a small child, used to play with a rabbit without showing any fear. Watson produce a loud sound whenever the child started playing with the rabbit. After a number of trials, the child started showing fear towards the rabbit, associating rabbit with the occurrence of loud sound. Then the child showed fear in gerenal towards while furcoat, bunch of cotton and to all other stimuli having similarity with white rabbit. Stimulus generalization in conditioning happens usually more in childhood particularly when the child has not developed the capacity of differentiate between two stimuli. This is why, during infancy the baby considers every women to be his mother. This tendency of generalization Pavlov attributed to a spread of effects from the region stimulated to other parts of the organism.

Stimulus Differentiation

Differentiation develops out of generalization. Though in the beginning mostly generalization in conditioning is found, the organism can be conditioned to make a response only to a specific stimulus by appropriated conditioning procedures.

Suppose you want to positively condition a dog to a tone of 400 cycles and negatively condition to 800 or 1200 cycles. You present the reinforcement only after 400 cycles tone and do not present reinforcement when the other tones are presented. If this is done for several trials the dog will learn to discriminate between these tones eventually. In this case the animal is positively conditioned to 400 cycles and negatively conditioned to 800 and 1200 cycles. Since it is not given any reinforcement at 800 or 1200 tones, these are not reinforced.

Children gradually learn to differentiate one stimulus for another in their own environment. In the early period they consider any woman as their mother. But gradually, as they grow up, they differentiate their mother from other woman. The woman who fondles, nurses, feeds and takes every care of the child and sleeps with him is considered as his mother.

Discrimination in conditioning has certain utilities in learning. Though usually stimulus generalization facilitates learning making, it is easy and quick, sometimes it also inhibits learning, creates confusions misunderstanding and many emotional problems. Like Albert, if one is afraid of any stimulus which has some similarity with white rabbit, he will have many adjustment problems. Differentiation at this point can prove useful. It can overcome the interfering and inhibitory effect of stimulus generalization. At the same time, if the differentiation is pushed too far, it leads to experimental neuroses. Munn, therefore, remarks "Sometimes as the difference is reinforced and unreinforced, stimulation becomes too small for the animal to discriminate, a nervous breakdown occurs."

Experimental Extinction

Once a C.R. is set-up, if one goes on repeating it without giving reinforcement, it tends to be extinguished. Sometimes people ask, how can one eliminate a conditioned response once it is established? The answer to this is experimental extinction. The process by which a C.R. can be weakened and finally eliminated is called the process of experimental extinction. It is a process by which a well established C.R. is eradicated by repeating the C.S. without the application of reinforcement. Take the case of Pavlov's dog. After the dog has learnt to salivate to the sound of the bell, it will continue to salivate to the bell for a certain period, although food is not given after bell. However, after some such trials when the dog will see that no food is coming after bell, the connection between bell and food will grow weaker, the flow of saliva will decrease. At last, the dog will not salivate to the bell at all. The salivation will practically be zero which will indicate the operation of the phenomenon of experimental extinction.

Similarly, in a study of "The Eradication of a tactile conditioned reflex of man (Hull 1934) the shoulder region of the subject was conditioned so that is elicited a galvanic skin reflex. Vibration of this region was then repeated without presentation of shock. There was a gradual weakening of response and finally complete elimination". (Munn 1953).

Internal Inhibition

After the establishment of a C.R. if the reinforcement is not provided check to salivate becomes stronger and stronger. So much so that it becomes inter-natural in nature.

Internal inhibition is a kind of negative learning not to salivate and can be applied to Ebbinghaus's curve of forgetting. But when the inhibition becomes weaker it leads to spontaneous recovery like reminiscence in forgetting. The idea of Ebbinghaus's curve of forgetting was applied to the concept of internal inhibition. It was said that this check or block was something which is acquired, *i.e.*, learning not to salivate. The negative learning not to forget is also forgotton to the same extent. However, this extinction is only a temporary suspension of response because of an internal set.

Spontaneous Recovery

Pavlov was of opinion that complete or permanent extinction of a C.R. is not possible. When the experimentally extinguished response reappears again after a period, it is called spontaneous recovery. This concept can be compared with reminiscence in forgetting. In this process even without the presentation of food, bell produces a few drops of saliva. Pavlov noticed that once the flow of saliva was completely extinguished, after about 30 minutes of rest interval the dog again salivated to the C.S. without U.S. But if again no reinforcement is provided after the C.S., spontaneous recovery will grow weaker and weaker and would at last fail to reappear.

Higher Order Conditioning

In course of his experiments on dog, Pavlov found that once conditioning was firmly established, for further conditioning, he could use the conditioned stimulus as unconditioned stimulus. When the dog is conditioned to salivate to Bell, Pavlov used this Bell (instead of food) as a U.S. for establishing further conditioning. Pavlov was of opinion that a conditioned stimulus can be used in much the same way as an unconditioned stimulus. He stated that more elaborate forms of behaviour can be developed by the process of chain of conditioned response.

First order or original conditioning

Food	—	Salivation
Bell	—	?
Bell	—	Salivation

Second order conditioning

Bell	—	Salivation
Light	—	?
Light	—	Salivation

Third order conditioning

Light	—	Salivation
Colour	—	?
Colour	—	Salivation

The arousal of the same response, *i.e.*, saliva to light by frequently associating it with bell but without presenting the food is called second order conditioning, as it could conditions a second neutral stimulus.

Though Pavlov claimed that a third order conditioning can be possible in the same way he could not proceed after the second order in case animals. However, with human beings, all sorts of complex learning can be possible by the process of higher order conditioning, he asserted.

Negative Conditioning/Unconditioning

Otherwise known as backward conditioning or negative adaptation it is learning not to make a response. The 'O' by the technique of backward conditioning can be made not to show a response to a neutral stimulus. Thus, instead of U.S. (Food) following the C.S. (Bell), C.S. will follow the U.S., *i.e.*, reverse to the pattern of classical conditioning technique, food (U.S.) will be given first and Bell (C.S.) will be presented next with an interval of 5 to 6 seconds between each presentation. As the 'O' will get the reward first it will not have any motivation or need to make a response (to salivate). So the C.R. would not be strengthened. If at all there will be any salivation, it will be marginal.

Many of our bad habits like nail biting, bed wetting, moving the leg all the while, various ticks and mannerisms, thumb sucking, smoking, alcoholism, breast feeding in case of older children, irrelevant fears can be removed, withdrawn by negative conditioning. Various habit patterns can be broken by this procedure. Thus, negative conditioning has valuable implications in practical life.

Whenever the rat proceeds for food, if it get electric shock, it will avoid food. A child who is punished while entering into a river will avoid the river in future. Mann (1953) reports that is sexually mature male rat is given electric shock everytime is approaches a female rat, it soon avoids female rats. When cockroaches are given electric shock for running into the dark, they learn to go to the lighted place instead of approaching for darkness. Tigers of Sunderban (West Bengal) over the last decade have killed at least 650 persons officially and the unofficial record is about 1000. The forest department worried over the increase in human deaths introduced something which was new in India, the use of electrified dummies. These dummies which look extremely life-like have been placed at a few corners of the sanctuary. Officials explain that when the tiger attacks the dummies, it gets electric shock and this persuades it from further attacks on humans. The projects officials claim atleast an 80% reduction in the death rate due to this method of withdrawal conditioning.

When alcoholics are given to take alcohol containing a drug which produces violent vomiting, they develop aversion for alcohol. Similarly, for babies who do not give up breast feeding, quinine is smeared on the nipples and then only they develop aversion for breast feeding. Negative conditioning is, therefore, known as aversive conditioning.

Withdrawal Conditioning

Becheterev, another Russian physiologist and a follower of Pavlov, taking animal and human subjects, found that when the 'O' gets a painful stimulation in a part of his body, it withdraws from it. Withdrawal may take place from electric shock, beating or any painful stimulation. Bell or light is presented before shock. After some trials by seeing the light or hearing the sound of the bell the 'O' withdraws that specific part of the body where shock is anticipated.

Experimental Neuroses

In recent times, the phenomena of \neuroses has been studied by the process of generalization and differentiation. If differentiation is pushed too far the 'O' fails to discriminate between two stimuli, becomes completely non-adoptive and is unable to salivate to any stimulus due to conflict. Consequently, nervous break down occurs. The animal suddenly becomes wild. It resents the situation.

An experiment on circle and ellipse can be referred to demonstrate experimental neuroses. When the circle and ellipse became very much similar, the animal unable to discriminate became wild. Physiological changes in respiration, heart beat, blood circulation etc., took place. It showed abnormal symptoms and behaviour disorders.

In experimental neuroses there is a clash between positive and negative forces to or not to salivate. Anxiety neuroses is produced experimentally by this method.

The concept of experimental neuroses which threw light on various abnormal behaviours opened new avenues for research. Nessermen, Meyer and Sears have made such experiments on experimental neuroses.

Implications of Conditioning in Practical Life

The contribution of Pavlov to the psychology of learning can be said to be equally important like Freud's as Pavlov as advanced certain concepts like generalization, differentiation, withdrawal conditionings, unconditioning and experimental neuroses which have tremendous significance in life. In fact, Pavlov's discovery was so powerful that it became completely Pavlovian.

Conditioning works in every sphere of life. Bulk of learning in animals and children develops due to conditioning, language development and different habits, take place because of conditioning. Therefore, it became a key technique not only for physiology, but also for psychology, mental hygiene and therapy. Watson, therefore, remarked that the whole system oif behaviourism he has worked out in terms of habit.

When Watson found that habit is not as simple as he thought, he realized the role of conditioning in habit development. Thus, he remarked, "I had worked the thing out in terms of habit formation. It was the enormous contribution Pavlov has made and how easily the conditioned response could be looked upon as the unit of what we had been calling as habit. I certainly form that point on gave the master his due credit."

Observation of animal and human behaviour led Pavlov and Watson to believe that all our habit patterns, behaviours, attitudes, likes and dislikes, values, etc., can be attributed to conditioning. Conditioning also works as a technique for behaviour modification, elimination of behaviour problems. It is also very significant in emotional learning. Watson and Rayner (1920) believed that it is the only way by which emotions can be acquired. "Since fear or anxiety is a common symptom of mental disturbance we are led correctly to anticipate that classical conditioning figures in the development of such disorders".

Thus, the sort of dream which Pavlov had, came true to a large extent. Due to the practical implications of conditioning in life it has occupied a very prominent position in the learning psychology even today.occupied a very prominent position in the learning psychology even today.

Q. 30. Explain Kohler's Insight Learning Theory or Kohlers Insight Learning.

Ans. According to German Getalt psychology Kohlers learning is insight. Insight is a important constituent in the solution of problems and is found in the higher class of animals and human beings. It is the best method among the methods of learning.

According to Kohler a person can deduce the solution by insight if the perceives the situation as a whole. Kohler, prepared some simple problems for experiments with dogs, hens, monkeys and chimpanzees. In an experiment a hungry animal was released from the house while some food was placed behind the fence adjoining the wall. Both the dog and the hen trotted around in the vicinity of the wall but as soon as they found the way out they made their exist and reached the food. This perception of the change in the meaning of the wall in insight. Bofore the insight the wall was an insuperable obstacle, but after insight it was not longer an obstacle but an object necessitating of new relations, the discovery of new patterns and the fomation of new organisations.

The most famous experiments conducted by Kohler in relation to insight were those that were carried out on chimpanzees. Some bananas were placed outside the cage of a chimp called Sultan, who was then given two sticks so cinstucted that they could be fitted together. Sultan tried to pull the bananas with the sticks, an effort which he kept up for an hour, but he got tired of the attempt and gave it up for playing. While playing he brought the two ends together and suddenly he had an idea which resulted in his fitting the smaller stick in the hole of the bigger one. He then used the two together to draw the banana inward. The two sticks disintegrated but he fitted them together again. He then pulled in everything within reach as if he were trying out his discovery. The next day he took far less time to fit the two together. It is a peculiarity of insight that once the solution is learnt, it is not forgotten though its memory may become hazy with the passage of time.

The above experiments make it quite obvious that learning by insight has certain characteristics of its own. They are briefly as follows—

1. Insight is sudden.
2. Insight alters perception.
3. Old objects appears in new patterns and organisation by virtue of insight.
4. In insight understanding is more useful than dexterity of hands.
5. Insight is relative to the intellectual level. The higher species of animals including human beings have more insight than the members of lower species.
6. In Woodworth's opinion, insight is sometimes hindsight and at others it is foresight. The quote him, 'Foresight is seeing the way to the goal before taking it our perceiving the uselessness of a certain lead without trying it and hind-sight is observing that a lead is good or bad after trying it. When the whole situation is clear and above board, there is a good chance for foresight, but when important characteristics of the situation have to be discovered by exploration and manipulation, hindsight is the best we can expect.
7. Some psychologists any that learning by insight is associative learning. Insight appears suddenly after the manipulation of thought or objects for a small thought significant length of time.
8. If the pieces essential for the solution of the puzzle and present together when perceived, insight comes about earlier.

9. Previous experience is of assistance in sight, though its excess does not necessarily increase insight because organised perception too is an essential factor in learning.
10. Maturity also affects insight as evidenced by the smoother working of insight in older age than in adolescence.
11. The insight gained in particular circumstances is of assistance in other circumstances. A verbal formula is generally extracted by people learning by insight and this formula is capable of facile application to other circumstances.

The above mentioned characteristics of learning through insight apply both the human and animal learning. The solitary difference is the fact that a human being by virtue of his superior capacities of experiencing and understanding; observes relation between various objects quickly and sees the patterns concealed in them with alacrity. He is assisted in this by language. As a matter of fact insight occurs only when the learner perceives the related link hidden in the activity. The learning curve is altered suddenly due to insight. Insight is impossible in an extremely unfamiliar problem, because familiarity is very necessary for insight. A student of literature will have no insight in any scientific problem because he does not know even the a b c of science. When the subject of study becomes a part of life, insight becomes easier. History can be made alive by exhibitions, Geography by travelling and Arithmetic by shop accounts. Fimiliarity is also important besides the theoretical study.

One example of human learning by insight will suffice. A student of Arithmetic tries hard to solve a difficult problem of Arithmetic. He tries many methods but fails to secure a solution. He gives up and lays it aside or goes to sleep. After some time suddenly or when he is awakened the solution suggests itself and he notes it down in his note-book. When he is confronted with similar problems in the future, he will have no difficulty in solving them. The insight method is superior to imitation or conditioned response because both the later methods take more time. It is superior to trail and error in the following respects :

1. Trial and error emphasizes the acquisition of motor skill but in insight mental effort is stressed upon.

2. The person keeps an eye on the goal in trial and error and all activity is goal directed, but in insight it is the unconscious mind which exerts the most while the conscious activities are either very few or aimless.
3. While insight depends upon perception, trial and error depends upon sensory motor coordination.
4. Every new problem has to be tackled from the very beginening if the trial and error method is used. On the other hand, both generalization and differentiation are present in insight, which adds to the possibilities of transfer of learning and the use of old insight in the solution of novel problems.

Students will be permanently helped by the use of the insight method of learning in place of the trial and error method in their study and other daily activities. They will also be above to conserve their energy. Suppose that a person has to arrange furniture in a room. An average person will determine the position of the table by using the trial and error method and shifting the table from place to place. An intelligent person will take up a position from where the whole room in visible, and imagine all the possible positions of the pieces of furniture in an imagined framework of the room and then place the respective pieces accordingly. But this does not mean that trial and error method is not meant for the intelligent. But no means is this so. In many noval situations progress is not possible without it.

Q. 31. What is the psychology of teaching aids of learning?

Ans. To make learning very effecitve it is not only necessary to utilise the factors and techniques that facilitate learning, the teacher is to create certain conditions in the class-room that may imporve learning. These conditions are providing teaching aids, creating rivalry and co-operation, giving the knowledge of progress and success, praising or reprimanding and guiding learning.

Visual Aids. Visual aids make learning concrete and meaningful. Yoy may describe the physical features of the Indo-Gangetic plain, but motion pictures, filmstrips, maps, charts, diagrams, pictures would make your verbal description concrete. An additional meaning is attached to verbal instruction when teaching aids are used. These are simply supplementary devices and not the supplanters of what the teacher can do. The following are the uses of teaching aids :

Uses. (1) There is a belief that some students are eye-minded, some auditory-minded and some verbal-minded. Those who are verbal-minded can be easily taught through verbal instructions but for the rest visual aids are necessary. Whether the above belief is sound or not, whether pupils can be so sharply differentiated or not is not the question. The fact is that the more organs are used in learning, the more effective the learning sensory becomes. The abstract notions become easy to understand when they are presented through motion pictures or T.V. or such other teaching aids.

(2) Instructional aids provide substitutes to objects and situations that cannot be presented in the class-room. The science exhibition that is held at a far-off place cannot be brought into the science room but through a T.V. programme the whole of it can be viewed in a short period.

(3) Much of school learning involves symbols and abstractions. Language is conceptual. Arithmetic is even more conceptual. It means that the teacher who is teaching language or arithmetic will have to present varied experiences so that correct concepts may be formed. Instructional aids supply such vivid experiences.

Caution. Teaching aids are aids only. They are not to be so enthusiastically used that effort on the part of the learner is ignored. When a T.V. programme is viewed, precast and telecast work has to be done. The teacher has to connect the programme with the class work he has done previously or will do in the immediate future.

Q. 32. Enumerate the factors that affect Learning. What techniques are generally used to learn a material effectively?

Ans. There are factors that facilitate learning; for example, readiness, motivation, mental set, mental health and teacher's personality. Unless the child has reached a stage (readiness) of development and growth at which instruction becomes effective and before which instruction is relatively fruitless, we do not like to give him instruction in reading; unless we arouse (motivate) or accelerate behaviour or stimulate an activity towards a goal when there was previously no such behaviour, change in behaviour does not occur, unless the child has a temporary preparedness (mental set) to get instruction say is arithmetic, he does not learn it; unless the child's inner nature get free expression, and meets job efficiency and satisfaction, he does not succeed in learning; finally unless there is someone to mould or shape or influence child's behaviour there will be no learning.

So the factors that affect learning are :

1. Motivation. Motivation is at the heart of learning. It is *sine qua non* for learning. It arouses, sustains, directs and determines the intensity of learning effort.

2. Maturation makes speedy learning possible. The child who is physically and mentally mature learns a subject at a faster rate.

3. Physical and Mental Development of the child affects learning. The child who is mentally and physically not developed learns at a slower rate.

4. Home Conditions and School Environment affect learning.

5. Academic Ability of the Teacher Affects learning.

6. Meaningfulness of Subject-matter makes learning easier.

7. Teaching Methods facilitate learning children learn more by activity or by doing or by playway.

Then there are factors that make learning easy. Such factors that tend to promote learning are intent to learn, distributed effort over learning, capitalising whole and part learning, knowledge of progress, recitation, active recall, application of what is learned and activity. To make these factors that facilitate learning more effectively, we work have to improve learning conditions by giving audio-visual aids, by giving praise and reprimand, by arousing rivalry and co-operation and by guiding children properly.

Intent to Learn. The child learns what he intends to learn. When there is intent or purpose to learn, one learns rapidly and that learning is permanent. When children know what goals they are to achieve, and when they accept those goals, they become more active in the pursuit of those goals. The efforts they make are more intensive and better organised. The attention they play is more definitely focussed to the thing they are required to learn. Such learning is intentional or purposeful.

Distributed Effort. It is a simple fact that an hour spent everyday in learning a subject results is more thorough and permanent learning than the same number of hours, devoted to its study at the end of the term. Spaced or distributed effort at learning any subject results in more learning than a massed one. Spaced learning is also economical and effective. The reasons are given below :

1. Massed learning by sticking to a task for longer periods the child develops a tendency to inattentiveness. One's attention fluctuates if one tries to concentrate, on a job for longer periods.
2. Going back to a subject studied a week ago to better than studying and restudying it immediately.
3. Trying to do the same thing again and again within a short space of time is against the natural tendency to resist early repetition of an act.

It means that the study period should be short and not very long. But how short should the study period be? It depends upon the individual learner, the material to be learnt and the conditions under which the material is learnt. The more mature the individual the more capable he is for prolonged work.

In elementary school the length of the class period is kept 20 to 30 minutes and in colleges, even one hour period is short. If the material requires constant attention and is difficult to learn, shorter periods are more fruitful. In the summer we usually have shorter periods than in winter.

Long periods of study are not always fruitless. If the material is too easy, longer periods of study are recommended. It motivation is high, massed practice is useful.

The principle of distributed effort has a great significance for the time-table builders. It is convenient for the student to learn different subjects in different periods. If the child learns mathematics in the same period on successive days, the teacher can show him how the lesson builds today upon what was learnt yesterday. The idea of distributed effort demands carrying on the same task in the same direction in a period on successive days. The principle of distributed effort indicates that since in massed learning attention begins to fluctuate, individual lessons should have variety. Even in a lesson on mathematics some time may be devoted to explaining concepts and principles and some time to their application and the rest to reviewing what has been learnt a week or two ago in the same period.

Massed practice causes boredom and boredom causes errors. Hence, distributed effort is particularly advantageous in learning many motor skills like type-writing. Proficiency in simple motor activities can be achieved in relatively short practice periods once or twice a day until competence is gained. The practice periods for younger students should be shorter than those for the older ones. Between the periods of practice certain inner co-ordinations may take place as a consequence of previous practice and present themselves in the next practice period.

Overlearning. The repetition of some matter after it has been learned to the point of one successful reproduction is called overlearning. If learning a poem, means reciting it once, overlearning it would mean continued practice after reaching a criterion level. Overlearning may be defined as applying oneself to the acquisition of a skill or knowledge beyond the point at which one can say it has been learnt.

If we have a topic when it has been learned once, it is forgotten but overlearning makes it permanent. For example, if 5 repetitions of a poem are needed to recite it, 10 repetitions would fix it in the mind for a longer time. Overlearning makes initial learning thorough and permanent.

The question arises, 'How many more repetitions would make overlearning more effective? Would 30 repetitions of a poem make it permanent when initial learning to recite takes place in 10 repetitions? It is scientifically proved that effective overlearning takes place only when 50% to 200% additional repetitions are made. But these repetitions should not be simply unintelligent ones; they should involve reviewing the material just read, reciting to oneself, placing the material in a new context and reading similar materials in another context.

The educational significance of overlearning to the class-room teacher and the student is great. Students should be encouraged to review immediately the work they have just completed. Teachers should present material in a new context, make applications and hold class discussions.

Whole Vs. Part Learning. Memorization is not only facilitated by overlearning. It is also facilitated by the whole method which means that a long poem can be committed to memory by reading and rereading. If on the other hand, the poem or the passage is learnt verse by verse or sentence by sentence, it is learnt by the part method.

There are advantages and disadvantages of both these methods. A combination of these methods is suggested. When a child is required to learn a poem or a passage in prose, its meaning should first be made clear to him. Some part of it may be difficult, *e.g.*, some phrases may be hard to understand for the learner. These parts may be learnt by the part method. After that each part may be placed in total context. Such a combination of two methods may be little more time consuming, but it saves total times.

Which method should be adopted depends upon the nature and size of the material to be learnt and the intelligence of the learner. If the material is meaningful, whole method is advantageous; if the size of the material is short it is useful to learn it by part method, and if the learner is intelligent be learns a material by whole method more easily.

Recitation. Recitation again is a device helpful for retention. Recitation means repeating aloud a poem or a passage from memory. But recitation may be subvocal. Recitation, vocal or subvocal is useful to a student because it enables him to use the material before a lapse of time causes forgetting. It immediately motivates the learner by making the learner aware of the degree of success being achieved; it helps the learner to use it. It provides feedback to the teacher and tells him whether or not the class is understanding him. Recitation does not simply mean repeating what one has learnt. It also means placing the material in a different setting, applying it in a new situation, and viewing it is another perspective. The questions given at the end of a chapter in a book and meant to provide opportunities to recite.

Recitation to be an effective technique for facilitating learning should be more than restatement of the printed word. It should mean sensing of information in new context. Teachers can make this technique more effective by employing discussion or conversation or presenting problems before students so that they may make a functional use of knowledge.

Active Recall. While reciting one uses certain cues; for example, when we recite the subject-matter presented in a chapter we make use of the paragraph headings. These headings serve as cues for recitation. While recalling one has to recollect material without the help of such cues. For example, in completion type of items one has to recall because there is nothing to help him, but in matching type items one recites with the help of cues given.

Active recall is a challenge to the learner. It requires him to recollect, or reconstruct the material without cues, hints or guides. The more the amount of active recall used in learning, the greater is the speed, precision and permanence of learning, Once a student makes it a habit to recall actively what he has learnt, learning becomes easy to him. He notes headings, emphases, and illustrative material to make an active recall.

It means that teachers should advise children to be active and vigorous while studying a chapter. They should be encouraged to recall what is learnt just after learning it. The should be encouraged to seek answers to questions such as these, "What have we studied similar to this?" "How does it relate to our lesson of the last week?" A few extra moments spent in active recall will be more economical than re-reading the same material later.

Applying What is Learned. Application of what is learnt is a really useful technique to facilitate speed, precision and permanence of learning. Information is made functional when it is applied. Making applications encourages the use of learning. Making use of knowledge provides a purpose for learning and yields reinforcement.

The class-room teacher has in teaching as well as in testing situations, a very great scope for applying what is learned. After presenting principles in any subject-field, their applications should be encouraged. For example, after teaching theorems in mathematics, their application in solving problems may be stressed; after teaching rules of grammer, the teacher may emphasise on writing sentences and essays using those rules; after giving information in civics, he may lead his students to solve problems faced by the community.

Students can be encouraged to apply for themselves the knowledge gained in the class-room in student government, community projects, work experience.

Activity is Essential to Learning. By activity we do not mean simply muscular activity. One has to be mentally active if one wants to learn speedily, precisely and retain it permanently. When the child listens to the lecture given by the teacher he is mentally active, but he is mentally more active when he recites and discusses. Listening as a process may be derogated but here too the listener has to accept or reject the ideas presented. In a traditional school where the child sits and listens, he does not learn effectively. In a progressive school in which activity is involved in the learning process, there is a better learning, provided the acitivity is meaningful. Even where the school is not in a position to provide such an activity, children may be encouraged to make use of insight and understanding.

Q. 33. Clarify the concept of motivation and mention its types and theories.

Ans. Motivation plays a vital role in every sphere of life and various phases of activities. Our success and achievement in life depends on motivation. It is, in one form or other, always present at the root of all human activities.

Motivation is said to be the 'heart of learning,' 'golden road to learning' and 'potent factor in learning', as all learning is motivated learning. Adequate motivation results in promoting reflection, attention, interest and effort in the pupils and hence promotes learning. Learning cannot be successful, effective or efficient without persistent, purposeful and selective effort. So teacher's problem is a to discover, direct and capitalize upon these motives and develop interest for educational purpose.

Motivation is derived from the word 'movere' which means to 'move'. It is an art of inculcating and stimulating interest in studies and in other such activities in the pupils. It is the process of arousing action, sustaining activity in progress, regulating and directing pattern of activity.

Motivation is the combined action of desires and incentives, pushes and pulls. Like a machine, a person must have energy in order to behave. Motive provides the energy. High motivation means high drive. High drive means that organism is set to respond which it does not respond in the absence of stimulation. The two concepts *i.e.,* drive and incentives are important in defining motivation. If we are in a state of need, a drive is aroused that energizes and pushes us into action to seek the things that will satisfy the need. The incentive value of these rewards represents their pulling power. Incentive is primarily concerned with the objects, events and state of affairs, that people and rewarding or punishing and thus are motivated to achieve or avoid.

Definitions of Motivation

According to **J.W. Atkinson,** "The term motivation refers to the arousal of tendency to act to produce one or more effects."

According to **Maslow,** "Motivation is the universal characteristic of every organismic state of affair. It is constant, never ending, fluctuation and complex phenomenon."

According to **Good,** "Motivation is the process of arousing, sustaining and regulating activity."

According to **Woodworth,** "A motive is a state of the individual which disposes him of certain behaviour and for seeking certain way."

According to **Crow and Crow,** "Motivation is considered with the arousal of the interest in learning which is essential for learning."

According to **Lowell,** "Motivation may be defined more formally as a psychological of internal process initiated by some need, which leads to the activity which will satisfy that need."

This movtivation is concerned with the inculcation and stimulation of the learner's interest in the learning activities. It is the force which energizes a man to act and to make constant efforts in order to satisfy his basic motives. In fact motives are the dynamic force that energizes all behaviour. Motives are to two types—Primary motives and secondary motives.

Primary Motives are the biological or pshychological motives. These motives ensure the preservation of life. Hunger, thirst, sex, sleep, rest are the examples of these motives. They are inborn and innate. They are found in all organisms.

Secondary Motives are the psychological or social motives. The need for belongingness, need for security, desire of gaining status and recognition, power and achievement 'motive' are its examples.

On the basis of these definitions we analyse the nature of motivation as follows :

(a) It is a psychological and physiological phenomenon.

(b) It is the internal condition of the learner.

(c) It is helps in capturing attention of the learner.

(d) It helps the learner in the achievement of right responses and in the elimination of wrong responses.

(e) It makes pupils active and provides energy to them in the learning activities.

(f) It is an art of inculcating interest in the students.

(g) It is not an end but a means to reach the end.

(h) It is an helping aspect of learning.

(i) It clarifies the behaviour of the learner.

(j) It helps in the prompt acquisition of knowledge.

(k) It helps in the development of social qualities.

(l) It helps in developing sense of discipline in students.

Q. 34. Explain the Characteristics of Motivated Behaviour.

Ans. Characteristics of Motivated Behaviour. The analysis of place of motive in experience and behaviour as given above, clarifies the general characteristics of motivated behaviour. Roughly speaking, these characteristics are as follows :

1. Energy Mobilization. Even the most peaceful animal becomes frightening in times of emergency. This is due to the mobilisation of energy. This process of the mobilisation of energy is chemical as well as physical. It cannot be perceived directly, but when there is some difficulty in the instilling in him love towards good habits, hatred for bad ones, anger for injustice, curiosity towards nature, *etc.* Once there emotions are conjoined to the right object, his behaviour takes a good turn. Sublimation does not destroy the emotion, it only changes the mode of its expression. It achieves the necessary control while avoiding all the damage that is the inevitable corollary of repression. It also avoids the formation of emotional complexes. As psychoanalytic studies have revealed, most of the great poets, authors, scientists, leaders and saints could contribute to human well being only through the sublimation of their emotions. The compositions and creations of both Tulsidas and Kalidas clearly show the results of sublimation of their love for the opposite sex, as a result of which their sexual instinct was sublimated into love of God.

Attainment of the object of motive, it is seen in the form of extra energy. The animal tries to attain the object with as much power as is the urge of the motive behind it. A hungry dog takes the bread even while beaten. The labour which a student puts in to attain a first division in the examination is never seen in his ordinary life. Thus it is often observed that some of the persons brought up in the poor families are very persevering and laborious. Some men perform such inhuman action due to the sex urge which they would never do in ordinary conditions.

2. Variability. Motive has a goal, hence it continuously changes with the veiw of attainment of goals. A hungry cat closed in a cage tries new devices to open it. Sometimes it tires this way, sometimes that and this change of behaviour goes on till it succeeds in coming out of the cage. A man with the goal of earning money tries hundreds of ways for it. Sometimes he purchases a lottery ticket while at other times he is busy in some business. In fact, the motivated person goes on changing his ways till he arives at the way successful for the achievement of the aim.

3. Persistence. An animal cannot leave its work without achieving the goal of its motive. An animal wandering in search of food keeps on roaming so long as it does not get it. The fighting birds keep on fighting till either of them is wounded or runs away.

Sometimes some motivated actions go on for years. A young man in search of a job goes on labouring for several years till he gets a suitable one. A lover determined to conquer his beloved, does not leave her even in the face of great difficulties. Even in the motivated behaviour of insects and animals much patience and persistence is observed.

4. Restlessness for the Attainment of the Goal. the motivated behaviour is goal-directed. The restlessness observed in such a behaviour persists so long as the goal is not achieved. For example, the goal of hunger is food. Till the food is taken the restlessness disappears. The goal can be conscious or unconscious. Sometimes the man knows the goal of his motive, but at other times it is only after long efforts and trial and error that he knows the real object which will bring his restlessness to an end. The physical and the mental motives have physical and mental goals respectively.

5. Extinction of Restlessness After the Attainment of the Goal. The restlessness of the motivated behaviour exhibits itself in following ways of the fulfillment of some internal want or desire and extinguishes as soon as that want or desire is fulfilled. A thirsty animal roams in search of water. As it gets water it drinks it and the restlessness is gone. There are only two ways to get rid of the restlessness of the motive. Either the tension should be removed or it should be changed. The tension can be removed by the attainment of the object. Sometimes conflicts are observed due to tensions between more than one motives at the same time.

Q. 35. Explain the types of Motivation.

Ans. TYPES OF MOTIVATION

M.K. Thomson has classified motivation under two heads—

A. Natural Motivation

Natural Motivation is of the following five types—

1. Bodily Goals or Motivation. These motivations are nothing but bodily or physical needs, like hunger, thirst, sex, *etc.* Certain motivations are caused by physical activities such as respiration, throbbing of the heart, digestion, circulation of blood and working of the glands etc. These motivations are inborn and inspire a person to fulfil the needs of the body. By causing change in the glands of a person, it is possible to bring him to the normal situation. Such a situation will be helpful for the information of motivation.

Various experiments that have been done, put forward the conclusion, that in future, by physical and operational experiments and chemical activities, it shall be possible to bring about changes in the glands of the person. Such a change shall give rise to requisite of natural and required motivations.

2. Habit. Habit is a form of nature of a person. A good habit of a child shall be that which can bring about development in his character and help him in achievement of education.

3. Instinct Motivation. Instincts, as already said, are inborn powers and they inspire the physical organs of the individual to take to certain jobs. Unless a person has satisfied his instincts, he remains restless. Teachers, in order to provide for their satisfaction, should present a normal atmosphere for the students.

4. Feelings and Emotions. Pain and pleasure, joy and distress are the natural feelings and experiences of human nature. This aspect of the nature and the personality is very helpful in that system of education. Where an atmosphere is aimed to be created, which can bring about the development of the character of the students and help them to educate themselves. This aspect of the personality should be very cautiously handled, otherwise, it can have adverse effect.

5. Emotional Motivations. Those motivations, that inspire us to bring about the fulfilment of certain emotional needs, are called "Emotional Motivations". Emotions are awakened by the outside stimuli. These stimuli are part of the environment. The teachers should try to create such a healthy environment that the sublimation or motivation of the emotions may be possible.

Other than the above five Main Motivations, there are certain other motivations as well. These motivations are also part of natural motivations. It shall be wise to have an idea about them as well.

1. *Social Motivations.* Due to inspirations from social environment, a person takes to certain activities. These activities are guided by the emotions and the instincts. Normally certain motivations are awakened for the

fulfilment of social needs. They express themselves in the following forms—

(a) Gregariousness is a natural instinct of man. It is therefore natural for him to be guided by social motivations.

(b) Due to social motivations, a person takes up those jobs that are good from the point of view of the society or which are appreciated by the society.

(c) The man has a great social consciousness of getting a place of respect in the society or to get his Self-regarding sentiment fulfilled. Consequently he tries to do certain good things in the society.

2. *Individual Motivations or Motivations of Self.* Those motivations, that inspire a person to satisfy his personal needs are called individual motivations, beauty, knowledge, faithfulness, competition, ideal, hero worship etc., are personal needs. These needs inspire a person to fulfill his personal desires.

3. *Desires.* It is the duty of the teachers to create in the students, the desire to acquire knowledge and achieve success. Is the teacher succeed it is, he shall be achieving a great task.

4. *Recreation and Play.* Programmes of games and play are joyful for the students. In plays, elements of direct motivation are present. The elements can therefore, by very nicely utilised for imparting education to the students.

5. *Direction and Imitation.* Children have the tendency to imitate. If proper direction and examples are presented before them, they can improve the power of motivation. They can also lead them towards success.

6. *Appreciation and Self-expression.* It is natural for a man to be inclined towards such goods goals, that give him importance and greatness. Social appreciation is another form of this feeling. It is, therefore, necessary to provide students the opportunity to observe these things.

7. *Other Natural Motivations.* Other than these things, man is also anxious to have knowledge, love, faith, office, ideal, rest, leadership, achievement of wealth etc. It is quite possible to utilise all these motivations of the child in the field of education. It is clear, that in human nature there is enough material for Natural Motivation.

B. Artificial Motivations

Artificial motivations are of various types. These motivations are not present in the human personality. They are part of the environment or the society. It is useful for the teacher to know and use them. They are being given below :

1. Reward and Punishment. In the works of the school this serves as a very imiportant and useful motivation. It has the following accept as well—

(a) Punishment is a negative motivation. Sometimes it is not very useful for children.

(b) Reward is a positive motivation. Reward may be physical, social, or normal. It is very dear to the students. Teacher should try to use this motivation in such a way that the students may grow into useful future citizens.

2. Co-operation. It is also a strong motivation. The teacher can use it as a medium of education. In the Project Method of Education attempt is made to develop a spirit of co-operation amongst the students. This motivation can be well utilised.

Q. 36. Explain the functions of Motivation.

Ans. FUNCTIONS OF MOTIVATIONS

In modern educational psychology every possible effort is made to base the education of the child on its motivations. Modern education aims at the excitation of one or the other motivation in a child in order to make any and every kind of education natural and normal. Various motivations in a child are useful in education in the following ways :

1. Escape. In a child one finds the motivation of escape conjoined to the emotion of fear. The intelligent teacher arouses fear and a disgust towards bad things in the child. He also tries to prevent fear and escape from action in many unnecessary cases. Meaningless fears are thus eliminated.

2. Pugnacity. The instinct of pugnacity of combat is a universal motive. The most important fact that accelerates or excites it is restraint. A child whose means of locomotion are stopped by the simple expedient of being placed under restraint will go red in the face and cry at the top of its voice. Conflict starts the moment one removes a chick from the hen, or makes fun of an irritable individual or prevents an animal from fulfilling and satisfying its motivations.

The object of animal in turning pugnacious is to remove the obstacle preventing its progress or to defeat the obstacle. As long as the individual fails to defeat the obstacle or to remove it from his path, his internal, physiological and psysiological disturbance continues. The pattern of pugnacity or combat is not the same in all animals or individuals nor are the implements common to all. Animals having long nails or teeth use them in warfare. In most animals it is the male who is pugnacious. He combats the animals of different species, and other males of his own species for supremacy over the females or for food. It is possible that the instinct of the pugnacity is somewhat depressed by the female hormones. Human beings and some other animals are known to threaten before actually attacking. Proverbially it is the monkey who is the best exponent of this behaviour pattern. Some animals threaten by showing their teeth, others by making offensive noises while others show their ungentlemanly instants by hanging on their chests. Forms of pugnacity are modified by age, intelligence, social and cultural influences and social behaviours. The pugnacious motivation of cultured individual finds expression is more indirect manner. His animosity continues over the years, and his vengeance is achieved in many devious and indirect ways. Litigation is only a form of conflict and it is very common in cultured societies. In fact, it is difficult to believe that pugnacity is only an instinct or an internal motive whose single object is conflict or fight. The motivation to competition may be innate but the pugnacious motivation is activated only when the fulfilment of a motive is obstructed. Anger results in conflict but sometimes anger finds expression in more devious and uncommon ways. An employee who has been severely reproved by his employer is in no position to answer him back in strong language as he goes in fear of losing his job, but as an alternative he lets off his pent up feelings of anger on his wife and children. Sometimes our pugnacious instinct is satisfied when we see others fighting. The tension of conflict is also released and relieved when one plays games or sees others playing or fighting going on the film screen. Within the family the parents prevent many of the child's instinctive actions so that he develops feelings of animosity them. Children worry the parents so that the latter become angered. Children compete among themselves for the love of their parents.

3. Repulsion. The intelligent teacher does his best to develop the motive of repulsion in the child for unsavoury and undesirable expendient.

4. Sex. Sex motivation of a person may be turned into more acceptable outlets such as dancing, music, art, etc., by the teacher. And, particularly in the adolescent stage, this motivation can be restricted and moulded to provide the desirable development in the adolescent.

5. Parental Motivation. To this motivation is conjoined the emotion of pity. This motivation finds its expression in the older child's love for his younger counterpart and for other living beings.

6. Curiosity. Curiosity is the most important motivation from the educational viewpoint. It is a fundamental motivation without any definite biological basis. When any living being is confronted with any new or unrecognised object, it is natural for it to desire a complete knowledge or understanding of it. Curiosity in human beings is accompanied by the sense of surprise. Almost all individuals are desirous of knowing new things and new places. When a child is handed something it has not seen before, it will immediately turn it over and explore it to the best of its ability. The child is always ready with an unending list of questions. He never tires of asking questions even if the parents tire of answering them till he is forced to rebuff the child. If the child's curiosity is not suppressed it continues its exploration and questioning till it finally comes to know its surroundings to its own satisfaction. It is such children who turn into the best investigators and scientists when they maintain their curiosity intact in their adult circumstances.

Teachers who fail to arouse curiosity in their students regarding the subjects of study fail to achieve even a semblance of order and administration in their classes. To curiosity is conigined the emotion of surprise. An object or thing that surprises the child also arouses in him curiosity. Hence, if a teacher is intelligent he will create surprise in the child regarding the subject he wants to teach with the result that the child will become curious. Once this is achieved more than half the battle is won, since the child starts studying on his own once his curiosity is aroused. Besides arousing the curiosity of the child, the teacher also has to turn it in the required direction. For a child to develop curiosity regarding detective novels or matters of sex may be harmful to him as well as to his normal course of studies. Hence, the teacher must see to it that the child's curiosity takes desirable paths, such as good books and subjects. Being curious about the subject, the child will find interest in its perusal.

7. Self-Assertion. The motivation of self-assertion occupies an importance place in the child's character. To it is conjoined the sentiment of self-respect which helps the child steer clear of all undersirable activity and to concentrate only on the desirable one. In order to develop self-respect, in the child, the teachers must put before him examples taken from the child's own environment. If instead of punishing a child for his mistake, the teacher tells him that such foolishness is not expected of him or from one of his upbringing, then the child will abstain from repeating it. He will also be remorseful. Once the motivation of self-assertion is fully developed, the individual makes his own efforts to progress in life, since he does not want to live the life of an insect but wants to hold his head high in society.

8. Gregariousness. A child is gregarious by motivation and he naturally wants to remain with the group of friends. A child does not desire solitude. The teacher can make the best of this instinct and help in the social development of the child. The teacher should keep an eye on the various group tensions that develop within the school and also try to evolve healthy competition, co-operation and team spirit in the children. Blind faith in small groups may be turned to more productive channels when it is turned to love of country and philanthropy. In this way, the child becomes socially mature.

9. Self-Submission. Of course, the motivation of self-submission may prove to be a hindrance in the child's development but the sensible teacher can turn it towards himself and arouse feelings of respect for the teacher and a healthy regard for discipline in the child. Students are prone to accept teacher's mandate without questioning so that success in education becomes possible.

10. Food Seeking. The food seeking motivation may be put to much fruit if indirect use by the teacher as he can instigate the student to greater effort in his study by inspiring him with vision of success in his future livelihood. Young men are seen to work very hard as they are afraid for their bread at a later stage. The motivation of self-assertion also contributes to this process.

11. Acquisitiveness. A child motivity collects many odds and takes great pleasure in doing it. It gives him a feeling of possession and pride. In their tender age children are often seen collecting stamps, match boxes, cirgarette boxes and are often seen fighting to the better end for them. Within the bounds of the school, this innate tendency of acquisition can be put to constructive use. They can be guided to collect stamps, photographs, old coins and books etc. But in this process it is essential to see to it that the child does not resort to undersirable methods of augmenting his collection. In the school, the child's acquisitive tendency can be adequately exploited to create a small library or a collecting of odd bits, in which the child can retain possession over them and yet allow them to be used by all his colleagues.

12. Laughter. The motivation to laughter is accompanied by the emotion of enjoyment and relief. If the children are made to laugh in class they are more inclined to accept the teacher's suggestions. Hence, the sensible teacher can get the children to perform different tasks by arousing laughter and enjoyment.

13. Constructiveness. It is due to the motivation of constructiveness that the child is seen making and breaking many things. The teacher can teach the children to make many small objects of various kinds with clay, colours, wood, stones and small mechanical objects. This has the effect of aspiring children to much greater creative effort when they grow up so that they become scientists and engineers.

Q. 37. Define the theories of techniques of Motivation.

Ans. Theories of Motivation. The different theories of motivation are as follows:

Psychoanalytic Theories. Freud, Jung, and Adler were the chief exponents of psychoanalytic theories of motivation. Freud originally conceived of sex as a primary driving force in behaviour. He called this psychic energy the libido, later he spoke of the life instinct and the death instinct. Psychoanalytic theories put emphasis on the ego and the rational aspect of personality. The ego regulates the impulses of the *id*, that is, the primitive part of the unconscious, composed of instinctive cravings characterised by unrestrained pleasure seeking.

Murray defined need as "a construct which is a force in the brain, a force which organizes perception, appreciation, intellect and action in such a way as to transform in a certain direction in existing, unsatisfying situation." According to him, an unsatisfied need would arouse a person to work that would be sustained until satisfaction had been attained.

Behaviouristic Theories. Thorndike, Hull, Miller and Dollard, Mowrer, Spence, Skinner and P.T. Young are the chief proponents of behaviouristic theories. Concepts of motivation are largely governed by the principle of reinforcement. Behaviour is assumed to be purposive, and different theoretical concepts are employed to deal with the energizing and directive aspects of motivation. The classical form of behaviourism utilises a "drive reduction" concept, which regards the basic source of energy in the organism as undifferentiated drive.

Skinner 1953, exercises purely a functional concept of drive, stressing that no assumptions need to be based about internal energy source beyond recognition of the functional purposivism or goal directedness of behaviour.

In short was can say that this theory has the following main points—

(a) All behaviour is motivated in the sense that all behaviour is based on needs and drives.

(b) Needs may be biological or psychological, primary or secondary.

(c) All learning involves reward in the sense that only those responses that reduce need or drive are stamped in.

(d) Energy is the function of need reduction, or of functional reinforcements, its direction is accounted for by habits.

Physiological Theory. Lord Ruthford, William James and Morgan are the exponents of this theory. To them all explanations must be in physical terms. All science is physics or stamp collecting. They believed that the secrets of the mind are locked within the cells of the nervous system.

Cognitive Theories. Lewin, Heider, Festinger, Newcomb and Helson were the major proponents of cognitive theories. Cognitive theories of motivation centre on an understanding and anticipation of events where, by means of perception, thought, and judgment, we choose relative values that govern our behaviour. We build up beliefs, opinions, and expectancies, which regulate our goal-seeking behaviour.

According to behaviourists, man is like a machine which is governed by fixed principles and motivation of behaviour originating from physiological derives. The motivation is an urge which results from a stimulus which may be internal or external.

Maslow's Theory of Self Actualisation

Maslow defined that needs are arranged in a heirarchy. As one general type of need is satisfied, next higher order need will emerge and become operative. He divided needs into two broad categories; (a) Deficit needs and (b) Growth needs. The deficit needs include physiological needs such as hunger and thirst. Once these needs are fulfilled, the person seeks to satisfy safety needs. Under the growth need, there is one general need called self-actualization.

All the above mentioned theories should be taken to be complementary rather than contradictory.

Q. 38. How is Motivation helpful to a student in learning? Being a teacher how would you develop class-room Motivation?

Ans. Every teacher daily faces a number of behaviour problems. For the explanation of these problems, he has to turn to psychology of motivation. This is a great problem for teachers, parents, administrators and those interested in the improvement of performance and learning of people. Students in the class-room learning require constant motivation from the teacher so that maximum use of their talents may be made for their welfare and also for the welfare and progress of the society. A learner may be motivated for an action in a particular situation but the other learner may not be motivated in that situation and even the same learner may not be motivated under the same situation for any other occasion. The socio-economic condition, previous experience, age and social climate in the class-room all affect the process of motivation.

Psychologists have developed some common techniques which may be used by a class-room teacher to motivate children in their work. The teacher should not strictly adhere to only one theory of motivation but should make use of various approaches in his teaching keeping into consideration the individual differences among the students. Below are given some important techniques of the motivation in the class-room teaching learning situation.

Maturation. It is useless to attempt motivation in school learning if the learning assignment is too difficult for the child's readiness or his maturation. Maturation and motivation must be synchronized. Formal learning can occur only if the learner is psychologically, mentally and emotionally mature enough to understand and carry out the assignment.

Provide Real Life and Symbolic Models. Most of the learning in human beings is acquired through the process of observation and imitation. The teacher can influence the behaviour of his students by his attitude and ideal living written or verbal presentation and by use of audio-visual techniques.

Aspiration Level. It means the level of performance to which one aspires for future. The teacher must see that the activity of the class is in accordance with the aspiration level of the students. The level of aspiration depends on several factors like intelligence, parental relations and expectation from children. The teacher should organize the activity in such a way that students keep striving and give a promise of goal attainment.

Create Needs to Learn. The teacher must create psychological and social needs for learning in his students. The importance of class-room learning should be related to future life of the students. The students should be actively involved in learning task.

Setting of Goal. Motivation is goal oriented behaviour that leads to drive reduction in the organism. Goal setting is an important component of human motivation. Teacher should set goals both for individuals and the class which are attainable.

Respect for the Personality of the Child. Children as well as adults have their pride and self-respect. Any attempt to embarass or humiliate a child especially in the presence of his class-mates is likely to end in withdrawal. The teacher can accomplish a great deal in motivating school learning by appealing to age maximazation than by shaming and ridiculing the learner.

Self-motivation. Know of results, high aspiration and clear goals are the best preparation and incentive to self-motivation.

Setting a Good Example. The teacher is a very important person in the school and child's life, and his own personality influences the learning more than the methdods and materials of teaching.

Group Dynamics. Along with the teacher, his paymates, parents, relatives etc., and every person with whom the child comes in contact influences his behaviour directly or indirectly. Group dynamics offer the best means available for development of social skills essential for democratic living, better social understanding and preparing the individual for democratic citizenship.

Novelty. Every novel thing creates interest in the individual. Teacher must introduce novelty in to his teaching. According to Travers, one of the essential ingredients in energizing pupils in the class-room is the provision of materials that permit them to move into new fields of exploration. The subject matter should be presented in novel ways so that curiosity and interest of the students may be maintained.

Use the Principle of Pleasure and Pain. Pleasant experiences which give satisfaction are sought and painful experiment are avoided by the individuals. Thus the teacher must provide pleasout and satisfying experiences to his students so as to motivate students for further learning.

Use Praise and Blame. Praise and blame have different effects on individual students. Some students may be praised for minor achievement because of their limited abilities but others will be motivated by praise for more worthy accompalishment related to their high ability. Praise can be verbal, or symbolic in nature. Teacher should be cautions while using praise in the class-room. For each and every activity, children should not be praised. Blame should be sparingly used because it creates personality maladjustment. Successful use of praise and blame depends upon the students, their personality and prior learning experiences.

Use Rewards and Punishments. The teacher must occasionally administer reward and punishment in his class-room teaching. Rewards create interest in the students. They are motivated to get the reward. The teacher must use punishment very sparingly because punishment creates behaviour troubles. He may use reward of different types as material, symbolic and psychological.

Reward has a positive effect in motivating children for learing. The teacher must remain cautious that the reward should not become an end in itself but should create learning desire in the learner.

Competition and Cooperation. Teacher should stress friendly relation rather than rivalry. Competition should involve a degree of equality among the participants. Competition may be of 3 types—*(a)* interpersonal competition among peers, *(b)* Group competition, *(c)* Competition within oneself.

Like competition, co-operation is also a strong incentive for motivating children. Teacher should encourage active participation of all the students in the learning activites.

Knowledge of the Result (Feed Back). The knowledge of the performance of the learner works as a motivating force in learning task. Learning is faster and effective when the learners are provided with the knowledge of their progress. The teacher should provide proper feedback to the students to motivate them in learning.

Use of Effective Methods, in Teaching. In order to create motivation the teacher should use progressive methods based on psychological principles. The use of audio-visual aids and the services renolered by museum, library, visit of place directly helps the teacher in motivating his students.

There are many other techniques which have been successfully used like team teaching, discussion method etc. In spite of all the techniques referred above, the place of the teacher remains supreme, his teaching method, warmth and his techniques of handling class-room problems play an important role in the process of motivation in the class-room teaching.

Q. 39. Explain the Techniques of Motivating the Learners or Students.

Ans. TECHNIQUES OF MOTIVATING STUDENTS

1. Set Induction. It means the introduction of the lesson. It links previous knowledge with the present knowledge. It is known as the skill of introduction or set-induction skill.

2. Stimulus Variation. It means changing of gestures and positions by the teacher. If a teacher does not change his gestures and positions during the teachning process, it becomes bore and lacks in interest. Hence, it is necessary to provide the training to the teachers in the skill of changing the gestures.

3. Lecture. It is concerned with the effective presentation of the content. The teacher leaves his impressions by using many techniques and tactics through this skill. It is also known as 'Communication skill'.

4. Probing Questions. it is concerned with the questions to be asked about the content in more depth. It stimulates the cognitive development of the pupils.

5. Illustration. There are two teaching methods-continuous lecturing method and demonstration method. The pupil-teachers should explain the concepts through examples and by displaying pictures and charts. It is called the illustrating skills.

6. Closure. It means to finish some task, *i.e.,* in class the pupil-teacher exhibits various behaviours. If we divide these behaviours in smaller units, these are termed as 'skills'. When a pupil-teacher delivers lecture and sums up properly and in an attractive way, the skill is termed as 'Closure Skill'. The lesson remains ineffecitve in the absence of proper closure.

7. Skill of Explaining. It means—use of explaining or connecting links to link the statements or systematic information. When a teacher shows his behaviour while explaining the pupils about 'What', 'Why' and 'How' regarding some facts, principles and concepts, that behaviour constitutes the skill of explaining.

8. Increasing Pupil Participation. It is concerned with increasing pupil participation which means—'Pupils' direct behaviour which is observable. This includes both responses and reactions of the pupils along with their own new activities.

9. Skills for Class Management. Both—social as well as educational activties performed in order to create proper environment for learning in the class-room. The performance of these activities needs special skill. As these activities manage the class it is called 'Skill for Class Management'.

10. Use of A.V. Aids. It is essential to make the teaching task more attractive and effective. As its use also needs a skill, the training of using A.V. aids is also desirable for the teachers.

11. Use of Black Board. It is very essential in the class. Its use also needs special training. The necessary components of black-board work are clarity of handwriting, legibility and rationale of black-board work etc.

Q. 40. 'Motivation is a vital condition of learning.' Discuss the statement and suggest some ways and means by which school learning can be effectively motivated.

Ans. Motivation has been defined as impulsion to do something to satisfy a need. The stronger the need, the stronger the impulsion and stronger the motivation. Till the need is not satisfied the person remains in the state of tension. This state of tension forces him to do something to satisfy the need and reduce his tension. The need is satisfied by the attainment of a goal perceived by the person himself and learning results from action directed towards the attainment of that goal. An example will make the matters clear. The child, who has an appetite for candy, feels a need and if a challenging problem is placed before him to find out the candy which is hidden under a book placed in a shelf in an almirah he feels a kind of tension and is motivated to sereach it out. Till he does not discover the book under which the piece of candy lies, he remains in the state of tension. The stronger is the appetite for candy, and the stronger is the desire to find it out, and the stronger is the motivation to learn.

Other definitions of motivation and motives are given below :

1. Motivation is the process of arousing, sustaining and regulating activity.—Good
2. A motive is particular internal factor or conditions that tends to initiate and sustain activity.—J.P. Guilford
3. A motive is a state or set of the individual which disposes him for certain behaviour and for seeking certain goal.—Woodworth
4. Motives are conditions physiological and psychological within the organism that dispose it to act in certain ways.—McDougall

The Place of Motivation in Learning. Motivation, arouses, sustains, directs and determines the intensity of learning effort. Therefore, it is said that without motivation learning is not possible at any level. Motivation is at the heart of learning. It is *sine qua non* for learning. And no teacher who hopes to induce learning can ignore motivation. The central problem faced by the school involves motivational status of its students. Various ways and means that have been devised to motivate the students to learn are given below :

(1) Intrinsic and Extrinsic Forms of Motivation. Motivation has been classified as intrinsic and extrinsic. The intrinsically motivated child does an act, because the mere performance of the act pleases him and because its outcome satisfies him. For example, he solves a problem because he has a strong desire to do so and he does so whether his teacher requires him to do or not. He solves even the most difficult mathematical problems because finding a solution appeals to him as an end in itself.

(2) Intrinsic Motivation is a state of impulsion in which the learner wants to learn something for its own sake. The teacher, who impresses upon the child the idea that learning a particular subject has its own rewards, is using the most powerful weapon. If all our activities were intrinsically motivated we would have derived very great satisfaction in life. Very few learners learn a thing for its own sake. Hence intrinsic motivation is unrealistic in practice.

(3) Extrinsic Motivation is defined as a state is which a child learns something not for his own sake, but as a means of obtaining some desirable goal which is artificially related to the activity. For example, the child, who solves a problem in algebra or who does his home assignments not for his own sake but either to avoid his teacher's sarcasm, is extrinsically motivated. Many students learn a lesson or master a subject because they want to gain approval or prestige or regard from their teachers or their parents or their class-mates. In reality, most of the behaviour of children in schools or adults in general is extrinsically motivated. A boy, who wants to learn how to deliver a speech in the public both for his own sake and for the cup he will win, is in a fortunate position.

It is the function of school to help the child progress from his present status to a more advanced one by inducing him to learn something for its own sake but where intrinsic motivation is not possible sensible extrinsic motivation can be accepted as a substitute. The teacher may ask the child to accept something originally extrinsic as worthwhile and interesting to him for his own sake. For example, if the child wants to learn problem-solving in algebra, he may be asked to take interest in the solution of equations for its own sake. The child, if interested in the steps for their own sake and if strongly motivated to go through a series of such steps as may be helpful for the solution of the problem, will certainly achieve the desired goal.

Motivation whether intrinsic or extrinsic forces an individual to learn but there are conditions for its successful operation. Those teaching methods are found to be effective 'which pay a necessary regard to students' interests and experiences. Motivation is the art of stimulating interest in the pupil', says Thompson. Children learn the material which is related to their needs, concerns and environment. The teacher should start with the interest a child has and relate his school work to those interests so clearly and effectively that he may have strong desire to learn.

The teacher who wants to attract the attention of students should find out and make use of interests of his children. If the learning is to be permanent, mere arousal of interest is not enough; interest has to be sustained also. The children have to be led to keep on trying to learn and progress in a particular subject in spite of all kinds of difficulties, distractions and interferences. In simple words, the children should be led to persist in their goal. The more motivated they are in attaining the goal, the greater will be their goal persistence.

Ways and Means to Motivate Children. Let us examine the effectiveness of certain ways and means which school teachers use for motivating their children. Some of these are punishment, rewards, and prizes, success, approval and disapproval, praise and blame.

Experiments have been made to determine the effectiveness of these positive or negative means of motivation, and the results are given below :

Punishment and reproof are found relatively ineffective. It has been found that students do not improve when subjected to sarcasm, ridicule and public reprimand. The general opinion of students is that if reprimand is necessary it should be in private. If blame is to be administered it should be judicious. Judicious blame gives good results. It has been found by Hurlock that the progress of children, who were reproved and blamed in front of the class for their poor work, went down. He also found that the children, who were ignored for their good or bad work and who heard the praise or reproof of others showed no progess at all . There is another study by Brenner in which it has been found that neither praise nor blame was particularly effective. Praise or blame may be effective or ineffective according to the way it is administered, the conditions under which it is given, the reason for which it is offered and the interpretations made by the child.

Experimental Studies on Effectiveness of Rewards and Punishment. Rewards and Punishments have been traditionally used as particularly effective ways of inducing children to learn but experiments show otherwise. When an act helps in the attainment of goal it functions as a reward. On the other hand, when an act does not help in the attainment of the goal it works as punishment. Reward acts as facilitator, and punishment as inhibitor.

Throndike in his 'Law of Effect' has told us that the learner is more likely to respond to those stimuli which past experience has shown to be satisfying and does not respond to those ones which past experience has shown not to be satisfying. Following him educators generally believe that learning takes place when a motivated child is rewarded. Thorndike has advised school teachers that they should use as much reward as possible and conversely as little punishment as possible, because he believed that punishment would disorganise the learning process and lead to undersirable or at least unexpected learning. Thorndike thought that reward had a favourable effect on learning and he presumed that punishment had an unfavourable one. But experiments later have given confusing results. In a study under school-room conditions Klardu and Cohen found that these commonly used incentives are not as effective as has been supposed. Similarly, Forlans found after extensive experiments on the use of money as a motivating device in school, that rewards were not as effective as would be accepted. Rock, in his investigation for finding the influence upon learning of the quantitative variation of reward, concluded that merely telling a person that he is right is just as effective as telling him he is right and giving him money.

Knowledge of progress and praise or reward, when giving together, does not show significant benefits over the knowledge of progress alone.

Increase in size of reward or increase in the intensity of motivation has been found effective in learning. If the bonus is increased each time, students break their former records for performance. In other words increase in the reward accelerates the performance.

Forms of Rewards and Their Effectiveness. Rewards that motivate or accelerate performance are of three kinds :

(1) Material—a piece of candy, a sum of money, right to participate in student activities etc.

(2) Symbolic—gold stars, medals, honour rolls etc.

(3) Psychological—knowledge of progress, recognition of adequacy, growth towards adequacy etc.

Rewards, whatever their form may be, ensure safety, indicate esteem and satisfy needs of love and belongingness. In this way, by need satisfaction they motivate the pupil in his initial contact with an

area of knowledge. Bruner (1961), has criticised the giving of external rewards because they promote undesirable behaviour. The extrinsic motivations can be justified only on the ground that they lead to intrinsic motivation. For example, when one gets high marks, parental approbation or gold star because of standing first is his class, the knowledge so gained may become of interest (intrinsic) to the individual child and he may then pursus further knowledge after the lure of reward has ceased to exist. Rewards should lead students to learn activities outside the class-room. The real reward for reading is not the gold star but the desire to read further and enter into the realm of great thinkers.

Confirmation of Success. Success motivates the continuation of activity. 'Nothing succeeds like success' has practical implications for a teacher. School work should be so organised that every pupil has a chance to succeed at his level. No one activity in the school should be capitalised. One child may get success in the academic studies and the other may succeed on the playing field. Success comes through a variety of experiences and success so achieved helps the individual child to satisfy his needs of esteem, belongingness and self-actualisation. Success builds self-confidence and increases efficiency. It encourages pupils to set realistic goals.

If the child is to stay in the school, he should meet success at his own level. Special classes and remedial work may be organised for those who are unable to meet success in academic work. Cent per cent promotion policies may be adopted or curriculum may be transfrmed so that the learning material is made appropriate to his children's background and ability.

Praise. The teacher, who recognises the worth of deserved praise as a motivating device, sees his pupils clearly and understands them. As soon as the detects humour, leadership, curiosity, independence, artistic aptitudes and other human traits in his pupils he recognises them and praises them. In this way, he satisfies their need of esteem, belongingness and self-actualisation.

The effectiveness of praise as a motivating factor depends upon two things—it should be deserved and it should be given in an appropriate manner. Praise may be verbal or non-verbal. The examples of non-verbal praise are a nod, a smile, placing one's hand on the pupils's shoulders, stopping long enough to take a good look at what the pupil is doing.

Knowledge of Progress. Pupil's knowledge that he is progressing is an extremely effective way of motivation. Ask your chidren to correct their own paper, and make their own charts of progress; they will be stimulated to make further progess. Let children evaluate their work periodically; they will achieve better. Even if the teacher asks his students in the last few minutes of discuss what they have learned, they get the prompt knowledge of progress. Knowledge of progress gives satisfaction to status and esteem needs, and then, act as a good motivator.

Blame. In few cases blame works as a positive incentive. The success of awarding blame depends upon a variety of factors. It is better not to use it. But it is good to use it when it is deserved. The teacher should know and understand the indivdual child upon whom he is showing blame. It should not be given to the retiring student because it increases feelings of inferiority in him. It may be given to an extroverted child because he achieves more when blamed than when praised. The successful teacher watches the effect of praise or blame upon the individual child and sees his reaction. In no case a child should be ignored because by ignoring a child we stimulate him less than by either praising or blaming.

Level of Aspiration. Good teachers use appropriate tasks according to levels of difficulty. Level of aspiration is the degree of difficulty of a task that child will accept and strive for. For example, if the difficulty level be such that the child can stretch himself and strive for it he will be motivated to achieve it; but if the difficulty level is too great and the task is too difficult for him to achieve he will leave the field and if forced to strive to achieve it, he will show anger, disobedience and sulleness; and if the task is too easy, he will transfer his attention to other activities and if forced to achieve the too-easy-task, he shall be bored and hate it.

In the class-room situation the teacher should first form a valid estimate of the pupil's potential and the appropriate goals. The clues to the appropriateness of goal will be offored by the pupil's behaviour in terms of acceptance, rejection or withdrawal. Child's past records should be studied to set goal appropriate to the potential. The level of aspiration and the setting of tasks appropriate to it will serve as a motivating factor.

Q. 41. Explain Intelligence, its nature and types.

Ans. The modern psychologist has been taking more interest in measuring the intelligence than defining it. The processes of measurement and their result have helped us a lot in discovering the nature of intelligence.

Binet defines intelligence as "judgment or common sense, initiative, the ability to adapt oneself, to judge well, understand well, reason well". He stresses that "intelligence is a capacity to enable the individual to take and maintain a definite direction, to make adaptations for attaining a desired goal and to be able to criticise oneself and others."

Freeman defines intelligence as a capacity of successful adjustment in all sorts of situations. Intelligence tests lead us to this definition. But it is too general. Intelligence is more than the ability of adjustment.

According to Terman intelligence is an ability to think in terms of abstract idea.

This definition has also been criticised very much. No doubt 'to think in terms of abstract ideas' is a significant aspect of intelligence but this is not at all. All intelligent persons can deal with abstract ideas quite successfully but they can handle objects and concrete jobs also with the same success. Moreover, even insane persons think and talk in terms of abstract ideas but they are devoid of intelligence, because their ideas are not directed to some useful goal.

Tharndike is content to define intelligence as the power of "more association or connection forming ability". But this explanation is quite incomplete. Even feeble-minded powers have enough connection forming ability. They too can associate ideas to some extent.

In the words of Johnson intelligence is an "ability to solve the general run of human problems, to adjust to new situations and in short the ability to think."

Rexknight defines intelligence, as "Intelligence is the aggregrate activity of the individual to act purposefully, think relationally and deal effectively with the environment."

After analysing these definitions it may broadly be said that intelligence consists of the following mental traits :

(i) Ability to do the maximum in the minimum period of time.

(ii) Ability to think in abstract terms.

(iii) Ability to solve problems independently.

(iv) Ability to take benefit from personal and experience of other.

(v) A proper sense of discrimination and relationship between objects and persons.

What is Intelligence. This is perhaps the most difficult question over posed to psychologists. This question has not been so far satisfactorily answered inspite of various seminars and conferences. No body knows what is intelligence. The nature of intelligence is compared with the electricity. Everybody knows about the utility of electricity, but nobody knows about its nature. In the same way people know about the importance of intelligence, but they are unknown to its real meaning. Different psychologists have given different definitions to clarify the concept of intelligence. We can divide these definitions in three groups:

(1) Ability to Adjust. It means that intelligence is not to adjust but it is ability or capacity to adjust. This definition has been given recognition by following psychologists:

View of Burt. "It is the capacity of flexible adjustment."

View of Ross. "Conscious adaptation to new situation is Intelligence."

View of Stern. "Intelligence is the ability to adjust oneself into a new situation."

View of Woodworth. "Intelligence is an acquiring ability, it is capacity to acquire capacity."

(2) Ability to Learn. It means that intelligence is not to learn but capacity or ability to learn. In this regard views of various supporters of this definition are as follows:

Buckingham's View. "Intelligence is ability to learn."

Woodro's View. "Intelligence is an acquiring capacity."

Dearborn's View. "It is the capacity to learn or profit by experiences."

Thorndike's View. "Intelligence is the ability to make profitable use of past experiences."

(3) Ability to Carry on Abstract Thinking. It means intelligence is the capacity to carry on abstract thinking. This definition has been recognized by the following psychologists.

Spearman's View. "Intelligence is rational thinking."

Terman's View. "Intelligence is the ability to think in terms of abstract ideas."

Binet's View. "Intelligence is the capacity to think well, to judge well and to be self-critical."

It is very difficult to separate all these definitions into three separate categories. Wechsler's definition seems to combine and extend the above these groups of definitions. He says, "Intelligence is aggregate or global capacity of individual to act purposefully, to think rationally and to deal effectively with the environment."

Vernon classified all these definitions into three different approaches, namely—

— Biological Approach.

— Psychological Approach.

— Operational Approach.

Biological Approach. Man is an organism and his survival depends upon adaptation to the environment. This category of definition lays stress on adaptive nature of human beings. If psychology can be interpreted as a biological science, intelligence can be interpreted as an adaptation to the environment. This approach emphasizes that intelligence is the ability of an individual to adapt to new situation of life. From practical point of view, the biological concept is not useful in the study of individuals within a culture.

Psychological Approach. This approach emphasizes the role of both heredity and environment in the development of intelligence.

It is very difficult to isolate the relative effect of heredity and environment in the development of intelligence.

Operational Approach. Operational approach is important to understand the concept of intelligence in clear and definite terms. Scientific terms are not defined in terms of isolation but by stating the observable conditions under which the statement is true or false. Instead of defining the word itself it should be defined under conditions in which it occurs.

A close look at all the above definitions suggest that intelligence is the ability to do a thing. Intelligence is the capacity to acquire knowledge, but it is not knowledge. Intelligence is not thought but the capacity to think. Intelligence is not a skill but is a capacity to acquire skill. Thus the nature of intelligence may help us to desire a workable definition of intelligence in the following form—'Intelligence is the mental ability of an individual which helps him to cope with the new life situations effectively and efficiently.'

Types of Intelligence

Thorndike has classified intelligence into 3 categories namely—

1. Abstract Intelligence. It is the ability to understand words, numbers and letters and to use them effectively. Abstract intelligence is required in ordinary academic subjects in schools such as reading, writing an solving academic problems. The highest level of abstract intelligence is manifested in the thoughts of poets, philosophers and writers.

2. Social Intelligence. It is the ability of an individual to deal effectively and efficiently with his social and cultural environment. Social intelligence is revealed when a person is able to establish and develop desirable social relations in confirmity with his social and cultural norms.

3. Concrete Intelligence. It is the ability to understand and deal with things as in skilled trades or scientific appliances. This is also known as mechanical or motor intelligence. In education concrete intelligence is required in learning dances and participating in games and sports.

Characteristics of Intelligence

1. It is an endowment to the individual child, which has been given to him by nature.

2. It helps the child in the learning process and to achieve the goal of maximum learning in the minimum period of time.
3. It enables the child to proceed from concrete to abstract. It is in abstract terms that ideas remain in our mental make up.
4. It helps the child to acquire the capacity to profit from his previous experiences and the experiences of others.
5. Intelligence gives an insight to the child to evaluate the future and act according to the requirements of the situation.
6. It enables him to distinguish between the right and wrong, truth and falsehood, social and anti-social activities.
7. The child is able to face the future with success and solve the difficult problems of life.
8. There are very minor differences in the development of intelligence between boys and girls.
9. Though the development of intelligence is fixed by heredity, yet it is also determined by the environment as well. In a healthy environment the child is able to develop his intelligence better in comparison to a hostile one.
10. The development of intelligence proceeds from birth till the end of the period of adolescence.

Q. 42. Explain the various theories of Intelligence.

Ans. There are three theories of intelligence which explain the nature of intelligence :

1. Spearman's Two-Factor Theory. The English Charles Spearman (1904), who was the inventor and first user of factor analytic methods developed a two-factor theory of intelligence from his own experimental work.

The theory was expounded in his book *"The Abilities of Man"*. This book was published in 1927.

The essence of his theory in his own words was, "That all branches of intellectual activity have in common on fundamental function (or group of functions), whereas remaining or specific elements of the activity seem in every case to be wholly different from that in all the others." We can say that on the basis of this intelligence is composed of two factors—one 'g' factor and the other 's' factor. This 'g' factor is involved in all walks of life and 's' is a special factor which is exclusive and is shared by none. The Examples of 's' factor are : Artistic ability, 'Musical ability'. These 'special abilities' are independent of 'g' factor. There are 9 's' factors.

Spearman wisely refused to identify 'g' with intelligence or any other quality whose definition was controversial, he suggested that it depends upon the general mental energy with which each individual is endowed. The 's' factors he compared to a large number of mechanisms or Engines which could be activated by this energy. "S" are largely affected by education and training whereas 'g' is innate as well as ineducable.

The chief criticism that can be raised against Spearman's work is that he failed to allow sufficiently for types of abilities, which while less general that 'g', are certainly not specific. The reason was that he was unable to get at 'group factors' and his samples were small. Towards the end of his life, Spearman had begun to realize the existence of 'group factors' but could not formulate his views.

2. Thorndike's Multi-Factor Theory. E.L. Thorndike's multi-factor theory stands in sharp contradiction of Spearman's two-factor theory. According to this, intelligence is a name conveniently given to infinite number of specific abilities combined together. It can be stated that intelligence is the sum total of all the specific capacities with regard to every separate act. It also means that E.L. Thorndike denies the existence of a general factor. Intelligence is a host of highly independent factors. This theory was given to us in the beginning of the present century.

Types/Kinds of Intelligence. Thorndike concluded that there were three types of Intelligence :

(i) Social Intelligence of ability to understand and deal with persons.

(ii) Concrete Intelligence referring to dealing with things, as in skilled trades and specific appliances.

(iii) Abstract Intelligence or ability to understand and deal with verbal and mathematical symbols.

Abstract intelligence is the one that receives the greatest weight.

3. Thurstone's Group-Factor Theory. Intermediate between the theories of Spearman and Thorndike is the Group-Factor Theory or the P.M.A. (Primary Mental Abilities). Theory given to us by Thurstone.

It was in the year 1938, that Thurstone gave us this theory after giving 56 types of tests to students of Chicago University. All these results were subject to factor analysis. He concluded that in all these tests, seven types of factors were working. *i.e.*, Intelligence is composed of those seven primary mental abilities which are working in all tests. Thurstone does not believe in 'G' and 'S' theories. Thurstone concludes that certain mental operations have a common primary factor that gives them psychological and functional unity and also differentiates them from other mental operations. These mental operations constitute a group. A second group of mental operations has its own unifying primary factor, and so on. In all , there are seven such groups which cover the entire range of mental abilities. Each of these primary factors, is independent of others.

(1) V—Verbal (2) N—Number (3) S—Spatial (4) W—Word F—frequency (5) R—Reasoning (6) M—Memory (7) P—Perceptual.

Latest Views on the Nature of Intelligence. Thurstone's Theory has been a subject of lot of research. Two types of research have been made in this connection :

1st : Have these seven primary mental abilities no connection with one another? Is there no 'G' amongst them?

2nd : Are these primary mental abilities absolute? Are they not further reducible?

As far as the first question is concerned, answer has already been given that these are independent of each other. But recently some positive correlations have been found to exist between these abilities. It means that there is a general factor also. Thurstone admits this in a very clever way by saying there is a second order general factor. These positive correlations were more glaring as far as children were concerned.

Regarding the second question, lot of research has been done to determine their absoluteness. Even Thurstone and his associates now agree that these are not absolute. These abilities can be further split.

The splitting of erstwhile absolute abilities has led to another theory called the Hierarchy Theory, and P.F. Verson is connected with it. It was, however, Guilford who first of all split these abilities. He says that intelligence has got three dimensions—Products, Operations and Contents. Products are six, operations are five, contents are four and the multiplication of these, *i.e.* 6 × 5 × 4 gives us 120 factors which comprise intelligence. By 1968, 80 of these factors has been named.

The products are :

1. Units.
2. Classes.
3. Relations.
4. Systems.
5. Transformations.
6. Implication.

THE PARAMETERS

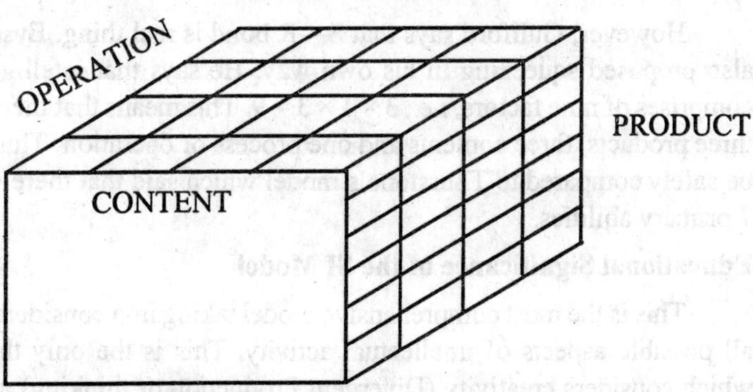

The operations are :

1. Evaluation.
2. Convergent Thinking.
3. Divergent Thinking.
4. Memory.
5. Cognitory.

The concepts are :

1. Figural.
2. Symbolic.
3. Semantic.
4. Memory.

The figure above indicates Guilford's model.

This is also known as SI (Structure of Intellect) model.

This model of Guilford is not basic model. It can be squeezed and expanded. When squeezed intelligence consists of only 18 factors (3 × 2 × 3 = 18) *i.e.*, instead of 6 products, we have the three; 5 operations can be reduced to two (example convergent and divergent thinking are one, memory can be deleted, evaluation is based on cognition and as such is one. As such five operations stand r' duced to two), and 4 contents to three.

When expanded by breaking, each of the products, operations and contents, intelligence is composed of 960 mental abilities, *i.e.*,

8 × 12 × 10.

However, Guilford says that S—R bond is real thing. Eysenck also proposed squeezing in his own way. He says that intelligence comprises of nine factors, *i.e.*, 3 × 1 × 3 = 9. This means that there are three products, three contents and one process or operation. This can be safely compared to Thurstone's model which said that there were 7 primary abilities.

Educational Significance of the SI Model

This is the most comprehensive model taking into consideration all possible aspects of intellectual activity. This is the only theory which considers creativity (Divergent Production or thinking) along with intelligence. Convergent production or thinking in the same model. At least there are two very significant educational implications of it.

1. In the present world, the body of knowledge is expanding very fast, forcing specialization even at the earlier stages of the educative process. We know already that special aspect of intellectual activity are involved in the different specialization processes, both academic and professional. We therefore need an *apriori* knowledge

about the specific ability of each student to place himin the right line of specialization. SI Model and analysis of the individual under its guidance can just pinpoint the individual's abilities and provide us a secure base on which his future learning is to be based. This sounds like the theory of 'Perfect Niche' in educational and vocational guidance where square pegs are placed in square holes and round pegs in round holes. Probably the fundamental human creativity and freedom will elude it, but surely this is so far the most scientific step as compared to previous attempts. We are aware that the theory of 'human multipotentiality is also there where an individual may capable of a group of jobs or activities, rather than a 'unilinear occupation', but in that cease his attainment on the various tests constructed on SI model should show corresponding results. After all the day psychology ceases to attempt to predict human behaviour, it will cease to be a science. Of course there are no such studies which can establish the empirical predictive validity of SI model. This can be carried out by testing young students on SI Model Tests. Predicting their future success on certain abilities, putting them on those trainings or educational streams and finally evaluating whether they come up to the expectations as held out by the test battery. It is very desirable if a control group is also studied alongwith.

2. When some students with adequate intelligence fail to learn, corrective teaching (also known as congnitive therapy) in that case first requires an accurate measure of his abilities, and some concrete steps for utilizing his strengths and developing him where he is weak. Merely a knowledge of IQ here is of little use. Only assessment made by SI Model tests can provide here an academically acceptable method of dealing with the problem. This can be a great diagnosis use of this theory.

Q. 43. How is intelligence measured? What are the kinds of intelligence tests? Briefly describe each and give their educational uses.

Or

Explain individual tests and group tests of intelligence.

Ans. Many attempts have been made to measure intelligence by various methods. The measurement movement has passed through various stages.

(i) Phrenological. Gall discovere phrenological approach to measure intelligence. Gall held that intelligence is directly proportional to the size of the head *i.e.,* the larger the head the greater is the intelligence of the individual.

(ii) Stage of Physiognomy. Physiognomy is the science of shape of features of the face. Features of face were taken to be an index of intelligence. According to this view it was held that an individual having sharp and bright facial features is an intelligent individual. But it was found that many students having bright faces did not fare well in the school. So this view was also rejected.

(iii) Brass Instrumental Stage. Psychologists tried of find out certain instruments to find intelligence known as aesthiesometer. With this instrument psychologists calculated Aesthiesometric Index of the skin. They held that the lower the Aesthiesometric Index, greater will be the inelligence. This view was also rejected because skin index (resistence) differs from individual to individual.

Modern Intelligence Tests

Psychologists have been interested in knowing the specific mental abilities of the individuals right from the beginning. Intellgience tests provide useful information about these mental abilities such as in academic, vocational, personal and counselling situations and in many diverse areas.

Inelligence tests have been divided into two parts :

– Classification on the basis of Administration.

– Classification on the basis of form.

On the the basis of Administration, these tests can be divided into two groups.

Individual Tests. The tests which are used to test only one individual at a time are known as individual tests. These tests are Binet Simon Test of intelligence and Terman Test of intelligence. In these tests examiners can pay more attention to the examince, he can observe and encourage him more closely during the test. They are preferred by psychologists in clinics and hospitals. These tests are time consuming and require trained examiner.

Group Tests. Tests or intelligence which can be administered to a large number of individuals (groups) at a time are called group tests. They can be verbal or non-verbal performance tests. These tests are preferred because they save time and do not require trained examiners. Army Alpha Test, Army Beta Test and Raven's Progressive Matrices are the examples of group tests.

Classification on the Basis of form

Verbal Tests. The tests in which language is used to give response to the question is called verbal tests, *e.g.*, A bird does not always have :—

(1) Wings (2) Feet (3) Bill (4) Nest.

Non-Verbal Tests. In these type of tests the language is used only in giving necessary instructions to the subjects. These tests involve such activities in which the use of language is not necessary. These tests include itmes on picture completion, picture arrangement, block design, object assembly and digit symbols.

Individual intelligence tests are further divided into two parts:

Individual Verbal Tests. Individual verbal tests are those tests which are administered to one individual at a time. Binet scale is the example of this test. Individuals are required to use language as well as paper and pencil for giving the responses. The test content is loaded with verbal material. Some of the verbal individual intelligence tests are as under :

Benet-Simon Tests. French psychologists Binet and Simon have done a pioneer work in the field of intelligence testing. In 1905, they published a scale of intelligence tests, known as Binet-Simon scale. In this scale some 30 tasks, from the simplest to the most complex, were prescribed in a serial order. The scale was prepared to test feeble-minded children. The scale contained tests for the age group of 3 to 15 years. There were 6 items in the test meant for each age. This scale was being extensively used in almost all the European countries—America, Canada, Australia, New Zealand, South Africa, China, Japan and Russia. Some of the items which were included in Binet's scale are as under :

At An Age - 3

(i) Points to nose, eyes and mouth.

(ii) Repeats two digits.

(iii) Enumerates objects in a picture.

(iv) Gives family name.

(v) Repeats a sentence of syllables.

At An Age - 4

(i) Gives own sex.

(ii) Names key, knife penny.

(iii) Repeats three digits.

(iv) Compares two lines.

At An Age - 8

(i) Counts from 20 to 0.

(ii) Notes omissions from pictures.

(iii) Gives day and date.

(iv) Repeats five digits.

At An Age - 12

(i) Composes one sentence containing three given words.

(ii) Names 60 words in three minutes.

(iii) Defines certain abstract words.

(iv) Discovers the sense of a disarranged sentence.

At An Age - 15

(i) Repeats seven digits.

(ii) Repeats a sentence of 20 syllables.

(iii) Interprets pictures.

(iv) Interprets given facts.

In 1916, Terman of Stanford University had given a revision. Terman made some modifications by avoiding certain draw-backs in Binet's test. He placed six tests in each age group from 3 to 10, eight tests at the age 12, six tests at the age 14, six at 16 and six at 18. In 1937, Terman revised the Stanford Binet Tests with the help of Merril and published the Revised Stanford Test. It became useful for the age range of 2 to 18 years. In Stanford-Binet scale 1960, language was used to the highest degree. In it certain items were deleted which were criticised to be out of date.

Individual Non-verbal Tests/Performance Tests. Individual non-verbal tests are mostly performance tests. In performance tests, the content is in the form of material objects and the individual's response depends upon what he does or perform. Generally, following activities are used in performance tests.

(a) To Fit Block in the Holes. The material consists of a board having holes and numerous blocks. The subject has to fit the blocks in the holes.

(b) Block Building. In these types of tests, the subject is asked to make a structure or design by means of blocks.

(c) Picture Completion or Picture Arrangement. In picture completion tests, the subject completes the picture with the help of given pieces cut out of each picture whereas in picture arrangement, the pictures are to be arranged in series from the given picture *i.e.*, Hally Pictorial Completion Test.

Bhatia Battery Test. The battery has been standardised by Dr. Bhatia to be used under Indian conditions with the purpose of providing differences and comparisons of illeterates and school going children, and for providing useful information for school going children as a supplement to verbal tests. The battery includes 5 tests each with its own sub-tests and time limit.

Minnesota Pre-School Scale. This scale is used to test the intelligence of the children in the age group of 18 months to 5 years.

Group Verbal Intelligence Test. The tests which necessitate the use of language and are applied to a group of individuals at a time come under this category. It includes the following tests:

Therman Group Test. It was prepared in 1920. It includes 10 sub-tests.

Army Alpha Test. This test was applied to the new recruits in the American Army in the First World War. It includes 8 sub-tests.

Army General Classification Test. This test was developed during Second World War to serve the same purpose as the Army Alpha. It contains nine(9) number of vocabulary, arithmetic reasoning and block counting items.

In India, many attempts have been made to construct group verbal intelligence tests. A complete list of standardized tests in

Indian conditions is available with NCERT, New Delhi. Some of the popular intelligence tests are :

- The Group Test of General Mental Ability (Samuhik Mansik Yogyta Pariksha) by Dr. S. Jalota.
- General Mental Ability Test by P.S. Hundal (Punjabi)
- Group Intelligence Test by Prayag Mehta
- Group Test of Intelligence prepared by Bureau of Psychology, Allahabad (Hindi).

Group Non-Verbal Intelligence Test

Terman Mcnemar Test of Mental Ability. It was prepared in 1941. It includes 5 sub-tests.

Army Beta Test. It was developed in World War I in U.S.A. The Army Beta includes tasks such as cube analysis digit symbols, geometrical construction, mazes and picture competition. This test was primarily prepared for use in military selection, however, it subsequently proved useful for civilian workers.

Raven's Progressive Matrices. The progressive matrices was developed in U.K. to measure Spearman's general factor of intelligence. The original test consists of series of sixty matrices involving abstract figures and designs. Each matrix contains a blank section and the subject (student) is directed to select the missing piece from eight choices.

Cattle's Culture Free Test. It is available for three levels—4 to 8 years, 8 to 12 years and high school to adult. Each series consists of 4 sub-tests which are series, classification, matrices and conditions.

Chicago Non-Verbal Tests. This test has been proved most useful for the young children of age 12 and 13 years. C.I.E. non-verbal group intelligence test (adopted in Hindi medium schools). It was originally prepared by J.W. Jenkins.

Intelligence is only an idea, and an abstraction. It is not a thing. Therefore it cannot be measured in the same way as we measure a piece of cloth, wood or temperature of our body. The measurement of intelligence is not as simple, valid, reliable and definite task as the measurement of a piece of a cloth or temperature of a body. In case of a piece of cloth and temperature of the body it is convenient to use the measuring instrument when ever we like, but is difficult to use intelligence test with the similar convenience. The administration and interpretation of intelligence tests require sufficient skill, labour and competency on the part of the examiner.

Individual Tests	*Group Tests*
1. They can be given to children as well as adults.	1. They cannot be given to young children below 9 years.
2. In this test one individual is tested at one time which makes them costly in terms of money, time and labour.	2. It is administered on group, in this way it saves time, money and labour.
3. The examiner here has a close contact with the subject.	3. The examiner does not have a close contact with the subject.
4. These tests are not objective and standardized.	4. They are objective and standardized.
5. Their administration, scoring and interpretation require trained and competent examiners.	5. The mannuals and instructions provided with these tests make their.

Uses/Advantage of Intelligence Test. Intelligence tests are widely used in schools and colleges due to following reasons :

(a) To Identify Individual Differences. On the basis of intelligence scores we can identify the individual differences among students and provide them individual guidance *i.e.*, we can advise students to select subjects keeping into consideration their intellectual abilities.

(b) Selection. Intelligence tests can serve a useful purpose for selecting students for different purposes *i.e.*—

– For admission to school.

– For awarding scholarship.

– For selection in jobs.

(c) Predictions. On the basis of intelligence test results, it is possible to predict the future academic achievement of a chiid because I.Q. remains constant. If the child is dull, his academic achievement is bond to be low and for this, planning can be done in advance, and the child can be advised to opt vocational courses.

Classification of Pupils. Children can be classified into various categories on the basis of inelligence tests. We have children who are of superior intelligence, average intelligence, dull and feeble minded. Children having the same I.Q. may be grouped together and constitute a class. This will endure the uniform progress and avoid educational wastage.

Detection of Various Types of Pupils. Various types of pupils *i.e.*, gifted and feeble-minded etc. can be detected with the help of intelligence tests. Moreover causes of backwardness, delinquency and problematic behaviour can be found.

Award of Scholarships. Scholarships may be given to suitable and appropriate students on the basis of intelligence tests. The Government of India selects some students for the award of scholarship or studying in public schools on the basis of intelligence and achievement tests.

Promotion of Pupils. Intelligence tests can be used to promote pupils.

Use in Research. Intelligence tests are used to a very large extent in educational and psychological research. For example, to find out the causes of delinquency, slow learning and maladjustment among children, intelligence tests are used to see the effect of mental abilities in these abnormalities. Intelligence tests specially individual tests are used for research with young children, emotionally disturbed cases and cases with special educational disabilities.

Use in Clinics. Intelligence tests are used in clinics and mental hospitals in order to find out how far the disease has impaired intelligence.

Use in Educational and Vocational Guidance. Every vocational and educational course pre-supposes certain levels of intelligence. On the basis of intelligence testing, we can guide the students, whether they should go for studies or adopt some vocational course.

Understanding Personality. Intellectual ability is one of the most important aspect of personality. Intelligence tests help us to understand the personality disorders among students. These are used to understand delinquent and problem children.

Use in Industry. Intelligence tests are very useful in industry *i.e.*, in selection of the employees in industries, in locating workers who require training and to study working conditions which lead to efficiency.

Use in Army and Civil Services. Since the First World War intelligence tests are extensively used in the Army. Army Alpha and Army Beta tests have been used on lacs of persons. Army General classification tests have been used on millions. In India, intelligence tests are used in the selection of army officers. Moreover, they are being used in various competitive examinations.

Use in the Study of National and Racial Differences. With the help of intelligence tests we can know the intelligence level of various races and nationalities. Intelligence tests scores show that I.Q., scores of Germans, Japanese and Americans are more than those of Africans and Maxicans.

Helpful in Assessment of Teacher's Work. Teacher's work can be assessed with the help of intelligence tests. When the achievement of the pupils in a subject does not correspond to the scores of intelligence tests, it indicates that the subject has not been properly taught by the teacher.

Evaluation of Methods and Material of Instruction. Intelligence tests are useful in evaluating the results of the experiments conducted by a school in the relative importance of different text-books or with a certain text-book with extensive reading material.

Limitations of Intelligence Test. There is shortage of standardised intelligence tests. Hence, we cannot predict the future success of the child in any educational course or vocation with great certainty.

- These intelligence tests are not reliable. They are not exact measures of intelligence.
- These tests are not accurate. They contain only a limited number of questions. This is a very crude method for measuring something as subtle and complex as intelligence.

- **These tests put premium on speed. Children who are original thinkers and who can give many original alternative answers are penalised.**
- Intelligence tests are inevitably culture bound and favour the children of well educated parents.
- Intelligence is comprised on many abilities and traditional intelligence tests measure only a few of these abilities. Many of the abilities which are an esssential part of intelligence are not measured by intelligence tests.
- Once the teacher knows the I.Q. of the child, he tends to see him through his I.Q. Thus, he becomes partial.

Q. 44. What are the uses and limitations (precautions) regarding use of intelligence tests?

Ans. Uses. The main uses of intelligence tests are as under :

1. For Vocational and Educational Guidance. For certain vocations, we need a certain level of intelligence. That is known by tests of intelligence. Intelligence tests arc very useful in educational guidance, *i.e.*, the child can select the subject in the light of his I.Q.—other than his aptitude.

2. Useful in Class-room Teaching. Intelligence tests are useful in class-room teaching. The results of intelligenc tests are of great help to a teacher in assigning work to individual students. They are specially useful in the early part of a teacher's contact with a particular class as an aid in making teaching effective by knowing the students's mental level and in conducting discussion.

3. Used in Clinics. Intelligence tests are used in clinics and in mental hospitals in order to know as to how far the disease has impaired the intellect.

4. Grouping. Grouping in the class-room is done on the basis of intelligence test results so that special classes be run for the weak and the brilliant.

5. For Knowing Individual Differences. Through intelligence tests, we can know about individuals in a class.

6. Scholarship. They are used for giving scholarships to the students.

7. Useful for Employers. Intelligence tests results are useful for employers and for Parent-Teacher Conference.

8. Useful to Individuals. Results of intelligence test are useful for the individual also. He can know about his performance in a particular field.

9. Research. Intelligence tests are useful for research.

10. Promotion. Also used for promotion of students to the next class.

11. For Knowledge about Self. Intelligence tests can tell you about your own intelligence and you can improve upon it.

Cautions while Using an Intelligence Test

1. The teacher must recognize that I.Q. (especially from verbal tests) is not a complete measure of a person's worth. It is an indication of only one limited type of ability. A person may have a good level of ability in many other non-verbal aspects of living, *i.e.*, mechanical, social, artistic and musical. A child whose score on scholastic aptitude test is low should in no way be rejected.

2. Verbal group tests of intelligence must be supplemented by other types of intelligence tests.

3. Results of intelligence tests should not be declared to the students in a way so as to label a particular student once for all with a particular I.Q.

4. In case it is suspected that the child was emotionally disturbed at the time of testing, results should be considered quite tentative.

5. An I.Q. of 70 should be interpreted as an I.Q. somewhere between 60 and 80.

Q. 45. What are the qualities of a good Psychological Tests?

Ans. Following are the qualities of a good psychological tests:

1. It is Reliable. A test is reliable only when the results remain constant whatever the environment or on different occasions. It also means consistency of the scores of the subject when tested again and again. If the results change, the test is inconsistent and unreliable. How to make a test reliable? There are three important methods :

(a) Tes/Retest Method.

(b) Split-half Method.

(c) Parallel Forms.

2. It is Valid. An index of validity shows the degree to which a test measures, what it purports to measure when compared with accepted criteria. The first esesential quality of a valid test is that it is highly reliable. If the reliability of a test is zero, it will not correlate with anything. A test that yields inconsistant results (low reliability) cannot correlate with a measure of another variable.

3. It is Objective. Objectivity means freedom from personal opinion or bias of the examiner. A good test is free from the linkages and personal whims of the scorer. Essay type examinations are not objective—personal opinion counts.

4. There is Ease of Administring and Scoring. Readymade keys are available for calculating result. Administration can be easily done. Directions are clear.

5. A Standardized Test in Less Time Counselling. We have the example of 3 hours essay type examination with us. It is just miserable to stand guard duty for three hours.

6. Norms. Class/age/percentile norms are available. This helps in quick comparison of results.

Some More Facts About Intelligence Tests

1. The correlation of intelligence tests scores with school marks is substantial (0.5 to 0.6 is average).

2. Previous school achievement gives correlation with later school achievement to be equal or higher than the correlation between intelligence and later school achievement.

3. Intelligence tests and achievement combined in a battery give still better prediction about future achievement.

4. Intelligence tests correlate higher with standardized measures of achievement than with school marks.

5. The degree to which intelligence tests are related to academic success depends upon the subject matter.

Q. 46. How is intelligence measured ? Explain chronological age, mental age and Intelligent Quotient (I.Q.) Explain why individuals differ with regard to intelligence?

Ans. All the individuals differ in mental traits as much as they do in physical features. Whatever the conception of intelligence, all the psychologists and educators and even common people have been believing since ancient times that there are various levels of intelligence. Some individuals are more intelligent than the others. We come across some men who are giant intellects and at the same time there are some unfortunate people who are devoid of intelligence and cannot count up to ten even after full maturity. Between the genius and the idiot there lie all grades of intelligence both above average and below average.

With the advent of the 20th century there appeared a ray of hope in this connection. The educational authorities of Paris were very much disgusted with the leakage of students in Primary Schools due to their backwardness in studies. They wanted to know the basic causes of the backwardness. The problem was entrusted to Alfred Binet, renowned medical practitioner interested in psychology. Alfred Binet worked on this hypothesis that children fail in studies due to poor intelligence. Now he wished to ascertain if the intelligence of such children who had left school was really very low and that of those students who were doing well in schools was quite up to the mark. There was no objective instrument of measurement of intelligence so far. There arose the need of some reliable objective tests. He endeavoured to create the same in collaboration with Simon.

Both the psychologists prepared the first objective test of Intelligence in 1911. After laborious experiments and thorough research, Binet reached the conclusion that no single performance could measure this faculty adequatly. Therefore, he included many small problems concerning various situations in his test. He soon discovered that intelligence develops gradually with age. Therefore, many tests suitable for many grades of children according to their age were constructed. They were tried on large samples and were standardized for various age levels.

Mental Age. Binet and Simon discovered that all children could not attempt the test standardized for their particular age level although a large number out of the same could do the same. For example, a nine-year old should be able to do the test standardized for his age group. But sometimes a child could not do well in it. He was then offered the test for lower age groups. Suppose he succeeded in a doing well in the test prescribed for the seven year age group. Then his mental age was declared to be seven years although his chronological age was nine years (chronological age is the actual age of the individual counted in days, months and years from the day of his birth). Similarly, a child of nine years could have mental age of nine, ten, eleven or more years.

All such individuals whose chronological age corresponded with their mental age were thought, to be normal or average in intelligence. All the individuals whose mental age was more than their chronological age were declared to be of supperior intelligence while individuals with less mental age were believed to be below normal in intelligence.

Intelligence Quotient. Terman gave a new concept of Intelligence Quotient to the world. Binet gave the mental age along with the chronological age of the individual. One could know the intelligence level of child by comparsion of both the ages. Terman went a step further. He multiplied the mental age with one hundred and divided the result by she chronological age. It gave intelligence Quotient (I.Q.). The formula is given below :

$$\frac{\text{M.A.}\times 100}{\text{C.A.}} = \text{I.Q.}$$

Suppose the C.A. of a child is 10 years while his M.A. is 12 years; then his:

$$\text{I.Q.} = \frac{12\times 100}{10} = 120$$

Why Individuals Differ in Intelligence? Individuals differ as much in mental features as they do in physical aspects. In fact, no two individuals are alike physically or mentally in the world. This difference is due to heredity as well as environmental influences.

Influence of Heredity. Let us take heredity first of all. As individuals differ in intelligence, therefore, their offsprings are not expectd to be similar. If both the parents are very superior in intelligence, their children are expected to be intelligent and similarly mentally weak parents beget dull children. If one of the parents is superior in intelligence and the other one is dull, the young ones will be mixed generation, some of them intelligent, others dull, still others in between and most of them having reverse influences in themselves in latent forms apt to influence the coming generations only. Due to this fact we come across some intelligent children whose parents both mother and father are dull. The heredity influence may be coming down from distant forefathers either from father's side or mother's. Ordinarily we do not find dull children with parents who are both superior in intelligence, or a genius born in the house of dullards.

Influence of Environment. Environment, too, affects intelligence tests although to a very limited extent. Injury to brain, constant bad health, long and continued emotional disturbances either impair intelligence or make it ineffective in life.

Q. 47. How are individual differences in intelligence measured? What is the importance of intelligence tests in giving guidance and counselling?

Ans. Measurement of Individual Differences. Individuals differ in intelligence. No two children can be quite similar in intelligence or in any other mental trait just as no two individuals can be quite the same is any physical feature. However, individuals, can be graded in large groups of intelligence level with small differences.

There are standardized tests for every age level. Every standardized tsts has many items to be attempted. The child to be assessed is given the test of his age level to do. It is then evaluated. Every standardized test has its own norms. There is no need of finding out the Mental Age first and then calculating the I.Q. From the marks secured by the child in that particular test his I.Q. can be found out directly with the help of its norms. Suppose a child of 10 years attempts a test standardized for the group of 10 years chronological age. He secures 70 marks in it. The norms will show what his I.Q. is in that case.

We can divide the tests in the following way :

Intelligence Tests

- Individuals Tests
  - Verbal
  - Mixed
  - Non-Verbal
    - Paper-Pencil Test
    - Manual Test
- Group Tests
  - Verbal
  - Mixed
  - Non-verbal
    - Paper-Pencil Test
    - Manual Test

1. Individual Tests. These tests are administered to one individual at a time. These cover age group from 2 years to 18 years. These are : *(a)* The Binet-Simon Tests, *(b)* Revised Tests by Terman, and *(c)* Mental and Scholastic Tests of Burt.

2. Group Tests. Group tests are administered to a group of people. Group tests had their birth in America—when the intelligence of the recruits who joined the army in the first World War was to be calculated. These are : *(a)* The Army Alpha and Beta Test, *(b)* Terman's Group Tests, and *(c)* Otis Self-administrative Tests.

3. Performance Tests. These tests are administered to the illitrate persons. These tests generally involve the construction of certain patterns or solving problems in terms of concrete material. Some of the famous tests are : *(a)* Koh's Block Design Test, *(b)* The Cube Construction Tests, and *(c)* The Pass Along Tests.

TERMAN'S CLASSIFICATION

On the basis of I.Q. Terman gives the following classification on American tests :

Near genius or genius	above—140
Very superior intelligence	120—140
Superior intelligence	110—120
Normal or average intelligence	90—110
Dullness	80—90
Borderline cases	70—80
Definite feeble-mindedness which has been further classified as under :	below 70
Morons	50—70
Imbeciles	25—50
Idiots	below 25

The Bombay-Karnataka Revision Tests. Dr. V.V. Kamat revised Binet's scale to suit Indian conditions and administered intelligence tests to 1,074 children and adolescents of all ages from 2 to 20 of both sexes. The locality selected for the experiment was the town of Dharwar in the Bombay Presidency. The children selected were fairly representative of the general population of Indian children. Dr. V.V. Kamat classfies Indian children as under :

Class	Range of I.Q.s
Near genius or genius	140 and above
Extraordinary	130—139.9
Very superior	120—129.9
Superior	110—119.9
Average or normal	99—109.9
Backward	80—98.9
Very backward	70—79.9
Borderline	60—69.9
Morons	40—59.9

Role of Home and School in Building the Personality. Psychologists now will agree that social factors are the most important in shaping our personality traits. The members of the family, playmates, school and class-fellows, society at large all these in a way determine and influence his personality.

(a) Home Atmosphere. Fundamental patterns of personality are formed during childhood. A congenial home atmosphere, with good relations between the parents and the child, is essential for a well-adjusted personality to develop. If parents provide a stimulating environment and a great degree of freedom, children will grow into strong, independent and self-reliant individuals. If, on the other hand, they are domineering and strict, children will be timid, lacking initiative and self-confidence. Over affectionate parents make children too dependent and overstrict ones make the too timid or too rebellious. Similarly disrupted homes often produce unstable, badly-adjusted personalities. The child has close emotional tie to each parent. Hence their quarrels cause serious conflict in his personality.

The position of the child in the family has much to do with the pattern of his personality. The only child, the youngest child, the adopted child, the favourite child, the only son in a family of daughters or the only daughter in the family of sons-grows differently and develops emotional attitudes which makes a difference to his or her personality. For example, the only child is likely to be pampered or over-protected. The parents give him extra protection and love and unknowlingly teach him to expect more from the social environment. The child grows self-centred, obstinate and less co-operative.

(b) School Atmosphere. The share and responsibility of the school in forming the personality of the child is equally important. The school makes the man in more than one way. It gives him more knowledge, more opportunities to think and reason and a broader outlook on life. It helps the emotional development, cultivates tastes and attitudes and offers material for building up ideals and aims in life. The schools of today have realised that mere instruction is not enough. They are providing opportunities for social competitive and co-operative work and experience. N.C.C., A.C.C., scouting games, social service leagues, co-operative stores, school banks, art clubs, hobbies, trips and the like give opportunities to the growing young people to dominate over some and yield to others, to play the role of leaders and followers as the occasion demands.

Q. 48. Explain the definition of Exceptional children, also discuss its types and needs of special education for such type of children.

Or

What do you understand by exceptional children? Discuss its different types and need of special education for such children.

Ans. The term 'exceptional' is defined in different ways by different people. Some refer to very bright child as an exceptional child while some refer the dull child as an exceptional child. Many times the term 'exceptional' is accepted to mean the handicapped child.

Gernerally it has been said that the child who has a physical handicap such as crippled condition, deafness, blindness or the child who deviates mentally being too bright or very dull *i.e.*, mentally retarted or the child that is maladjusted or emotionally disturbed is treated as an exceptional child.

An exceptional child is he who deviates from the normal or average child in mental, physical and social characteristics to such an extent that he requires a modification of school practices or special education services in order to develop to his maximum capacity.

In the words of Barbe, the word 'exceptional' refers to children who differ from the average to such an extent that their differences warrant some type of special school adjustment either within regular class-room or in special class. It includes both, those children whose differences make them unable to perform upto the level of average as well as those whose differences allow them to perform above the average.

According to **W.M. Cruichshant,** "An exceptional child is he who deviates physically, intellectually, socially and emotionally so markedly from normal growth and development that he cannot benefit from a regular class-room programme and needs special treatment in school."

Based on all the above definitions a definition can be worked out. A child is educationally exceptional if his deviation is of such kind and degree that it interferes with his development under ordinary class-room procedures and necessitates special education either in conjunction with the regular class or in a special class or school for his maximum development.

It is to be realised that the difference of exceptional children is only one of degree, they are more like other children and so should be treated first of all as children who need to express their individuality and then adjustment made to their difference.

Types of Exceptional Children

1. Intellectually exceptional — the gifted and creative
   — the slow learner
   — educable mentally retarded
   — severly mentally retarded
2. Physically exceptional — Imparied vision
   — Impaired hearing

— Impaired speech

— Crippled

— Brain injured

3. Emotionally exceptional — Delinquents
4. Multi Handicapped — Children who have more than one of the above defects.

Needs of Exceptional Children. Exceptional children need special education services which embody the three elements—

(a) Trained professional personnel—teachers, consultants, physiotherapists speech threrapists etc.

(b) Facilities including special building features, special equipment, special extra literary materials and special crafts.

(c) Special curricular content suiting different areas of exceptionality, mental retardation, giftedness, deafness, blindness, speech retardation, social and emotional maladjustment.

Special education is thus concerned with the identification of and provision for children unlike the average whether this be in the regular class-room, special class-room or in a combination of both.

Importance of Special Education

1. Exceptional children do not always benefit from regular class-room teaching. They need different treatment in learning. If not attended to properly, they may develop behavioural problems and so it is imperative to make special arrangement for their education.

2. The second need of organizing special education for mentally and physically handicapped children arises because they find it difficult to adjust in home and society.

3. Special education will solve the problems which exceptional children present in regular school programme.

4. Special education must meet both needs in its efforts to bring exceptional children to the maximum of their development potential and to prepare them adequately for a satisfactory life adjustment.

5. To meet the needs of an exceptional child, society must provide special facilities for their education.

6. Special education will give insight into the problems of exceptional children to parents, educators and administrators.

7. There are categories of children who cannot be educated with normal children, for example—deaf, dumb and blind children need special schools with different curriculum, methods of teaching and teacher for their education.

Identification of Exceptional Children

Exceptional children are those children who deviate from the normal children either to lower side or to the upper side. They are recognised on the basis of their characteristics.

Identification of Mentally Retarded Children

Mentally retarded children are those children who deviate from the normal children to the negative side in mental dimensions. They have sub-normal mental development. They possess limited intelligence and social inadequacy. It is generally believed that children who possess I.Q. below 70 are mentally retarded children.

Mentally retarded children lack originality. They depend on others for their work. These children are of slow understanding and their I.Q. is low. They can not adjust themselves in home, school and society. They have limited interests, aptitudes and choices. They are not easily bored with a routine. They are very poor in understanding verbal instructions. They can only think in terms of concrete objectss and stituations. They lack thinking and reasoning ability. They are socially as well as emotionally maladjusted personalities. They have deficient moral judgement. It is actually the lack of one's ability to adapt properly to the situation or environment due to some mental deficiency.

Identification of Gifted Children.

Gifted children are those children whose performance is remarkable and who are academically superior. Children of I.Q. above 140 may be called gifted or genius. Gifted children are superior not only in intelligence but also in physical, emotional, social academic and other intellectual characteristics of children of their age. They have sharp sense organs. They have better ability to organise, analyse, memorise, 'reason, judge and to reproduce things accurately than the normal children of their age. They have rapidity in learning and comprehension. They have good vocabulary. Their general knowledge is good. They have varied and wide interests. They love books, journals, news-paper, dictionary and encyclopaedia. They are more interested in abstract than in mannual activities. They are humorous, cheerful, liberal, genius and honest. They take active part in various co-curricular activities in the school.

Identification of Backward Children

Backward children are those children who do not keep pace with the class. They show inability to progress normally in the school work. They are weak in their studies and their studies and results of examinations are not upto the mark.

According to **Barton Hart,** "Backwardness in general is applied to cases where their educational attainments are lower than what they are capable of."

According to **Burt,** "A backward child is one who in the middle of his school is unable to do the work of the class below that which is normal for his age."

They are emotionally disturbed and suffer from inferiority complex. They face problems of social adjustment. They have got less friends. Their learning speed is slow. They have limited interests and choices. They do not take any initiative. They lack originality. Some students are weak in all the subjects. In some cases child is backward in one or more than one subjects but he is not backward in all subjects.

Problem Children

Problem children are those children whose behaviour in one way or other is seriously abnormal. They suffer from many types of behavioural disorders. They create problems of the parents, teachers and classmates. Stealing, teasing other students excessive rebellious attitude against discipline, shirking work, complexes, physical and mental deformity and bad character are the traits and symptoms of problem children. The harsh or lenient discipline in the home, presence of step father or mother, quarrels between father and mother, poverty, repression of sex instinct or curiosity instinct are the causes of problematic behaviour of the child. Repression leads to mental conflicts and mental conflicts are responsible for problematic behaviour. Efforts should be made to understand the problem children. Such children cannot adjust themselves in home, school and society. Parents and teachers should help them in adjustment. Affectionate and congenial atmosphere should be created in home and school. The child should be dealt with psychologically. Moral, religious and sex education should be given in scientific manner.

Identification of Delinquent Children

Deliquent children are those who deviate seriously from the norms of their culture or society and commit such acts which if committed by an adult would be punishable as crimes. These children violate the laws of land and commit offences like thefts, gambling, cheating, pickpocketing, murder, robbery, dacoity, destruction of property, violence, begging, kidnapping and other sexual offences. Society hsas due provision of punishment and often such children are kept behind the bars. Delinquents are made so by the uncongenial environment and social conditions. Delinquency is not inherited, it is the product of social and economic conditions. It is the result of uncongenial environment of family, school, neighbourhood and society. Inspite of his poor health, short or too big stature or some deformity which give rise to feeling of inferiority, dispose one to more aggression as a compensatory reaction and consequentaly one develops delinquent behaviour.

Delinquency is environmental and social disease. Delinquent acts are learned and acquired acts. No child is born as delinquent and delinquent behaviour is not the product of genes. Thus, delinquents are not specific type of human beings which are born with some specific innate, physical, mental of emotional characteristic. They are quite normal individuals with normal needs and desires. Like other normal children, they also want to love, to be loved and to satisfy the need of security and recognition etc. Denial of the satisfaction of these basic needs brings maladjustment and makes them hostile and rebellious. Delinquent behaviour should be considered a sort of reaction or resentment against the prevailing social and environmental conditions. It is an open revolt against parents, teachers or other social organisations which do not provide them the essential environment for the satisfaction of their basic needs and urges. Therefore, the delinquent child needs a very careful handling. Delinquency is a serious behavioural disease that needs planned attempts for its prevention and treatment.

Q. 49. What do you mean by a gifted child? Explain special characteristics gifted children?

Ans. In the words of Hillingworth, "By a gifted child we mean one who is far more educable than the generality of children are. The greater educability may lie along the lines of one of the arts, as in music or drawing, it may lie in the sphere of mechanical aptitude, or it may consist in surpassing power to achieve literacy and abstract knowledge." Paul Witty Ruth Strang, Havighurst and many other think that the term 'gifted children' should include all those children who give promise of creativity of a high order in a worthwhile line of human endeavor. They have superior ability that can make them contribute to the quality of living in society. Therefore, we include not only the intellectually gifted but also those who show promise in music, the graphic arts, creative writing, dramatics, mechanical skills and social leadership.

School children with superior learning aptitudes are frequently referred to gifted children. It is exceedingly important to develop all the capacities of members of this group in view of the fact that this group provides us with leaders for different walks of life.

Three Categories of Gifted Children. According to Terman, the students of higher intelligence may be divided into three categories :

1. Superior having Intelligence Quotient between 100 and 120.
2. Very superior having Intelligence Quotient between 120 and 140.
3. Near genius having Intelligence Quotient 140 or more.

Intelligence Quotient 120 may be regarded as the lower limit of the gifted.

Special Need for the Education of the Gifted. With the world locked in conflict between two ideologies, there is special need to conserve and utilize all available human resources. The gifted child is both an asset and a responsibility. He is an asset of incalculable value to society. His potentialities for good are difficult to over estimate. Our socio-economic structure, both national and international, demands leadership of the hishest quality and keenest intelligence. Where else may we look for this type of leadership except among those of intellectual superiority?

Society is injudicious in the extreme to neglect those children who possess the potentialities of high-quality leadership. It is the part of wisdom to prepare these boys and girls for the important social responsibility which will be theirs. Today we face problems of world magnitude which threaten the existence of society itself. Education is challenged to develop leadership for termendous tasks which lie ahead. Under such conditions, special education of the gifted is not only justified but is demanded by the lessons of history.

Why should we be Interested in the Gifted?

1. Democracy will be realized in its fullest sense when we recognize the full range of ability within our total population.

2. There is a limited pool of ability and special talent in every country. This must be identified and developed to save if from total loss.

3. Many gifted children languish, in educational institutions simply because they are not aware of their 'gifts' and the school programmes do not provide them enough motivation and challenge.

4. We need leaders for our business, education, research and government. These leaders are provided by this class of gifted children.

5. The gifted individuals have played an important role in the preservation and advancement of civilization.

Special Characteristics of Gifted Children

1. Physical Characteristics. They are physically sound and rather better than the normal children. Their faces are usually bright. They possess vigour and vitality.

2. Intelligence. Their intelligence is high. Their 'g' factor of intelligence is very strong. Some have a very strong group factor or 's' factor.

3. Inquisitive Nature. They are extremely inquisitive, and quick in understanding.

4. Varied Interests. Their interests are more varied than those of normal children. A geften child of eight may read novels, write long essays, study such subjects as history, geography, astronomy, grammar, physics and music.

5. Superiority in Academic Work. They are characterised by general superiority in academic work. Even in the elementary school, they do their best work on tests of reading and language 45% of Terman's group of gifted children, when he studied, learned to read before entering school. Regarding one child. Terman says, "As early as 21 months she read and apprehended simple sentences, by 26 months her reading vocabulary was more than 700 words.

6. Well Adjusted. As regards character and personality traits they are well-adjusted. Terman states, "Even in leadership and social adaptability traits in which gifted children are thought to be especially deficient, most studies show gifted children to be somewhat superior to children of the general school population."

Methods of Educating the Gifted

Rapid Promotion or Double Promotion. By this we mean more than one promotion during the course of the year. If a child shows an extraordinary achievement in onw class, he may be given a double promotion. The aim of this promotion is to place the gifted student in a setting suiting him most. But at occasions such promotions prove to be very deterimental to the child. The child may be a gifted in comparison with the students of his previous class but may not show the same progress in the next class with the stduents of different mental and physical make-up and this would result in his mental retardation in the new setting. Age, social maturity and health—all these factors should be given due weightage.

Homogeneous Grouping. According to this scheme, students with more or less similar background are grouped together in the same section. It is a common practice in some of the schools to group students into various sections *i.e.,* A, B, C, etc., according to the intellectual, physical and social interests of the students. This creates healthy competition and is very useful in large schools where classes can be divided into different sections.

Enrichment of the Curriculum. This implies that the gifted students be encouraged to study a variety of books and reference material. On the co-curricular side also provision for a sufficient variety of activities should exist in a school so that the students may develop various social and moral qualities of a high order. Triple Track Plan which introduces elasticity in the classification of the students is very popular in American Schools. According to this scheme the authorities prescribe a uniform syllabus for all. Average children cover it within the normal period, the dull in a large period and the gifted in a shorter period in comparison to average children.

Special Schools. In some of the advanced countries of the world, separate schools have been provided for such students. This system has been criticised on the ground that quite a large number of such students will be deprived of that practice in leadership which they will get in association with average children.

Brown feels that keeping these children as an integral part of the school is the factor most important in affecting their future personal happiness. They have to live in a world of mixed people—superior, normal, inferior, good, bad and indifferent—and they have every right and more need, to be prepared for that.

Summer Schools. These schools may be planned during summer vacations. These schools are being successfully tried in the U.S.A. Academically talented students are selected from different parts of the country on the basis of psychological, tests, interview and previous school record and are brought together for a special educational programme. The programme is intended to be very challenging and is planned under the expert guidance of a band of talented teachers. The students are provided with the best available books which they may consult for writing their project reports and for holding discussion in the class. Usually three areas— science including mathematics, social studies and literature—are covered. After the programme is over, the students return to their regular schools. Students attend summer schools so long as they do not complete their final school leaving examination. Such a scheme may also be planned in our countries.

Q. 50. Define a Backward Child, problems, causes and remedies for their backwardness.

Or

Define the types of Backwardness and the remedial programmes for such students.

Ans. Generally speaking, no mother or father is easily prepared to accept that their child is mentally backward. But modern intelligence test techniques have indubitably established that some children are mentally backward. A backward child is more in need of assistance than one with average or above average intelligence. Hence, in modern schools teachers are expected to pay particular attention to the weak students in their classes. A backward child, evidently, is one who has an intelligence quotient lower then the average child. In the words of Cyril Burt, "A backward child is one, who in the middle of the school career, is unable to do the work of the class below that which is normal for his age." In this way, the backward child falls far behind other children of his age in matters of study. In school, such children remain in the same class for many years, and fail to progress upward. Education psychologists have no single opinion on the intelligence quotient below which a child can definitely be called backward. Yet, generally psychologists classify those children as backward whose intelligence quotient falls below 85.

Problems of Backward Children

Children who are backward have certain problems that are peculiarly their own. Having a very low intelligence quoting, they require to be taught many things by others. A backward child cannot lead, he is more in a position to end the help and sympathy of friends and relatives. A child who is very feebleminded, having an intelligence quotient of 70 or less, cannot obtain education in the ordinary school, and has to be sent to special institutions. Emotional adjustment of the child is completely disintegrated if he fails in the same class time after time. In a class, teaching a approximates to the average level of students. Hence, it is only natural for the backward child to meet with failure.

Backward child also faces difficulties in social adjustment. In the group he does not easily grasp even the smallest thing, and rules of play have to be respected for his benefit. His colleagues naturally heckle him. It is possible, that a spark of leadership may be ignited in him if he communicates with those younger than himself but on the same intelligence level. But there he is unwelcomed since other children steer clear of him because of his physical superiority. Adults pay him little or no attention, instead he is scolded from time to time. In adolescence and adulthood, too, the situation of this child does not improve. Activities of the group are usually on a higher level, so that he does not fit in them either.

Causes of Backwardness

It is not even possible to recount all the various causes of backwardness, but the main causes are the following :

1. Physical Causes. Due to many physical defects and abnormalities, the child lags behind other average children. Such physical conditions would be weakness of the eyes, deafness or being hard of hearing, stuttering, being weak or crippled, etc. This also has an adverse effect upon his social adjustment.

2. Educational Immaturity. Physical and mental short commands in the child result in educational immaturity. Putting it differently, he has no adequate maturity to grasp the teachings is customary for his age leave.

3. Mental Defects. It has been indicated earlire that the backward child has a very low intelligence quotient as compared with that of an average child. Having a low intelligence, his other mental characteristics and abilities also do not compare favourably with the average child.

4. Emotional Factors. The child's social adjustment is defeated by his mental and physical abnormalities, and he meets with successive failures. He meets with criticism on every account. Hence it is natural for him to manifest anxiety tension, depression and there emotional factors. Sometimes though every other defect is absent, the child is backward in his class for no better reason than these psychological or emotional factors.

5. Atmosphere in the Home. One reason of backwardness can also be the atmosphere in the home. Proper development of the child cannot occur in a virulent family atmosphere. Hence, he falls behind children of his age group. And among the factors that contribute to the defective atmosphere in the home are constant quarrelling and fighting between parents and children, unbalanced diet, strict discipline, absence of all peace and calm, proverty, etc.

6. Lack of Interest. Sometimes, even though the child is free from all the defects and shortcomings mentioned above and even those that have not been mentioned, he falls behind the rest of the class for the simple reason that he cannot stir any interest in the various subjects being taught. This causes repeated failure.

7. Factors Concerning the Schools. The school can be a veriable storehouse of factors that inhibit the child's development such as inadequate method of teaching, uneducated teachers, undesirable atmosphere, inadequate curriculum, defective time table, disgusting relations between students and teachers etc. All these causes conspire to make even the average child look backward.

Selection of Backward Children

Modern schools are led to believe that the backward children in a class should be specially attended to. Hence the teacher must know how to distinguish and recognise a backward child. This can be done in five steps :

1. Discovering the Child's A.Q. Test in arithmetic, language and general knowledge can be used for discovering the child's A.Q.

2. Discovering. I.Q. Selecting children with an intelligence quotient below 85, their exact I.Q. should then be calculated.

3. Individual Intelligence Tests. Now the results obtained from the group intelligence tests should be examined for their reliability by obtaining results through individual intelligence tests and coinciding the two conclusions.

4. Case History. After all the above tests have been completed, the child's detailed life history should be prepared.

5. Rating by Teachers. Following this, rating by teachers should be sought concerning children who appear to be backward so that the results of tests are confirmed by educated insight.

Types of Backwardness

Backwardness may be of two types—general and specific backwardness. A situation when a child is weak in almost all the subjects in general is called **general backwardness.** But it sometimes happens that the child is good or at an average level in many subjects except one or two. This is **specific backwardness**. Specific backwardness in a particular subject is often due to weakness in a specific ability needed for that subject. *e.g.*, verbal or numerical ability.

The school authorities should face two facts :

(1) That children who are backward owing to low general intellect need to be grouped into speical class and not only taught at a slower pace than the average children but also given more concrete and practical curriculum.

(2) Children who are specifically backward in a subject say arithmatic, reading etc., need individual teaching in that subject and often it is necessary to start again from the very beginning.

Causes of Backwardness. The possible causes for turning a child into backward may be divided into two broad categories - internal, lying within the individual and/or external, lying in his environment.

(1) Causes Lying within the Individual Child. The child may become backward on account of the factors or things lying within his body structure as:

– Child may have poor health or suffer from physical ailments and chronic diseases etc., and it may obstruct him to harness the actual potential of his natural abilities.

– Child may suffer from some bodily defects like defective vision, faulty hearing, speech defects, left handedness etc. These defects or improper functioning of the body organs, particularly connected with sense organs, may prove a stumbling block in attaining what could have been otherwise expected from him.

– Child may not be utilising his intellectual powerss like power of concentration, reasoning, thinking, observation and imagination etc., as he should otherwise do for actualising his basic potential on account of some defects in his brain system or its functioning or on account of some emotional and psychological pressure generated as a result of his personal and social maladjustment.

(2) Causes Lying in the Environment. The external environment may also force the child to turn into backwardness like:

(a) Defective Home Environment. The uncongenial and improper environment prevailing in a family or home has a negative force in the educational progress of a child. Such negative factors present at one's home may be termed as:_

— Tensions, conflicts and quarrels at home between the parents and among the members of the family.

— Improper behaviour with the child due to over protection, negligence, jealousy, rivalry etc.

— Noisy environment and inadequate physical facilities for the study.

— Poverty, illiteracy and intellectual inferiorty of the parents or gaurdians.

— Over engagement of children in household activities or family occupation.

(b) Defective School Environment. Conditions prevailing in the school with regard to men and material facilities and the child's adjustment to the available school environment contribute much in the attainment of what is allowed to the child by his natural abilities. The adverse and unfavourable conditions and improper environment lead the child to educational backwardness. These unfavorable conditions and factors may be of the following nature:

— Lack of discipline and poor administration.

— Lack of trained and qualified teachers.

— Lack of material facilities like as of accomodation, furniture, library, laboratary, teaching learning aids and equipments, and other things helpful for co-curricular activities.

— Defective inter-personal relationship among the staff members and students.

— Lack of proper guidance and counselling services.

— Defective curriculum, uninteresting and wrong methods of teaching and lack of proper evoluation system.

— Indifference or improper behaviour of the teacher.

— Lack of proper attention for the regular attendance and supervision of the drill and homework.

(c) **Other Negative Social Influences.** Apart from the defective home and school environment there may be other negative influences and undesirable forces present in the surrounding school environment of the child. He may have an adverse and unfavourable neighbourhood, evil company of the playmates and other members of the society and day-to-day quarrels and disturbances perturbing his peace of mind. He may be tempted by what is available in his social environment and may pick up bad habits like smoking, playing cards, gambling, taking drugs, reading improper and cheap literature, seing too much movies, playing truancy at the school hours and watching excessive T.V. etc. All these things, perpetuated by the negative environment influences, are quite forceful to affect the whole life style of an individual child including ways of thinking, motivational process and habits of work and studies. These may divert his attention towards undesirable social activities in place of school studies and thus prove a potent cause for putting the child into educational backwardness.

Remedial Programmes of Education for Backward Children

Remedy and treatment of backwardness is always dependent upon the nature and extent of backwardness present in a particular child and the diagnosis of the probable causes for such backwardness. Since children may differ in terms of the nature, extent and possible causes of their backwardness, therefore it is unwise to plan for any uniform remedial education for all of the backward children. Every case of backwardness must be treated as a unique case and therefore be tackled with specific individual care and attention depending upon the nature and causes of backwardness. Let us illustrate some of such remedial measures.

For the cases where backwardness is caused on account of some specific physiological and sensory defects, the remedy lies in the proper rectification of these defects, for example a child suffering from defective eye sight, speech or hearing impariment may be properly treated for overcoming these defects.

For the cases where defective home environment plays a role in making a child backward, it may need the counselling of the parents or members of the family or placing the child into a suitable environment providing desired love, affection and security or providing necessary economic help, social and emotional support to the child and members of the family.

Evil effects of the neighbourhood and other social agencies need also to be checked. It should be well cared that the child should not fall prey of the bad company and unsocial elements. In case he becomes a victim, then effort should be made to get him freed from the evil influences.

School environment should also be so designed as to help the child in his proper adjustment. Most of the backward children are often victims of what goes inside the school. Therefore, teachers and school authorities must feel their duty to pay due love, affection and security to the children and help them in the proper actualization of their basic potential.

Provision of special classes for the backward children by putting them into small groups.

Provision of suitable co-curricular activities and practical experiences.

Provision of special coaching and proper individual attention for the removal of individual specific backwardness.

Provision of special curriculum for providing suitable learning experiences according to their needs and interests.

Provision of special suitable methods of teaching depending upon the nature of backwardness and abilities of the children.

Care for making environment of the school quite healthy and congenial for the task of effective teaching and learning by taking due notice of the cases of indiscipline, truancy and non-attendance.

Provision of maintenance of proper progress record and keeping the students and parents informed about the same.

Provision of regular proper checking of home work, assignments and project activities besides maintaining proper continuous evaluation of the teaching-learning task.

Provision of educational and personal guidance of the children.

Besides above mentioned remedial measures the teacher should, keep in mind the following remedial measures also :

1. Short and Simple Method of Instructions. Educationally backward children require short and simple methods of instructions based on concrete living experiences with concrete materials. Verbal instructions must be reduced. Excursions, play activities, dramatization or even games should be introduced specially for these children.

2. Retention of Self-Confidence. Habits of success must be developed if the child is to retain the self-confidence which is so vital for him/her. The teachers should lead him/her very slowly, making sure that each step is thoroughly mastered before the next is introduced.

3. Participation in Extracurricular Activities. The educationally backward children should be encouraged to participate in extracurricular activities of the school according to their interests and abilities.

4. Individual Attention. Individual attention should be paid to such matterss as health, social conditions, while teaching in the class. So also, there must be more of individual instruction than is necessary for normal children.

5. Desired Outcomes Must be Known. The desired outcomes should always be kept in mind. Interesting but important matters may be given brief attention, more energy should be expended on that which is important and essential. Certain abstract technicalities which characterize each subject should be excluded for the backward child.

6. Stimulation of All Senses. The class work must be stimulating to all the sense organs. The class teacher should seek the help of specialists, if prssible, to remedy the defects of speech, hearing and sight.

7. Teacher's Patience. The teacher must have great patience and a firm determination, never, to be discouraged while at the same time recognizing the child's limitations. Moreover the teacher must respect the child. If the teacher looks down upon the child as being inferior since the latter will not attain as the average child can, then the teacher cannot give the child what he/she needs and is likely to be doing her/him real harm. A backward child needs praise, continuous help, sympathetic consideration of his/her difficulties and sustained interest on the part of his/her teacher.

8. Free Discipline. In the education of backward children. discipline should be free as far as possible character training rather than mere intellectual tuition should be given greater importance than is actually given.

9. Special Organisation. When a number of backward pupils are found together, a class may be organised specially for them. Sometimes such children may be retained longer in lower grade or may be specially sent to lower grade for learning skills which they lack.

10. Time Table and Syllabus. In the time-table for the backward class, the old lines of demarcation between one subject and another should be dropped or cut across. The syllabus, to a large extent, will have to be planned in terms of projects rather than of subjects. The school should be so organized that there is plenty of activity and reasonable freedom of movement of the backward pupils.

11. Medical Check Up. A special medical check up should be arranged at the outset and facilities should be available for remeding the ailments or defects so discovered.

12. Specific Backwardness Treatment. In the case of specific backwardness in specific subject area, remedial teaching has proved vary useful. The co-operation of the specialists is highly necessary in dealing with specific backwardness.

Thus, by means of systematic observation, and interviews with the parents and also by administering the tests, the child's outstanding physical and mental characteristics should be examined; and the analytical study will be followed by a comprehensive and synthetic study which aims at reconstructing a detailed character sketch of a child as a living, growing, conscious individual.

Q. 51. Define Delinquency. What are its causes and also suggest remedies.

Ans. Juvenile delinquency is one of the most serious problems of our times. Everybody has his or her idea of what delinquency is but many of these concerns do not take us anywhere. As such, we need a clear-cut definition.

1. A juvenile delinquent is one who is a minor with major problems.
2. The best definition, "Delinquency is anti-social behaviour."
3. "An offender below the age of 18 years is delinquent."

This is the legal definition of juvenile delinquency.

According to CBI, Maharashtra among the states and Delhi among Union Territories top the list of Juvenile delinquents or child offenders.

The incidence of delinquency is rising amongst the girls also. You cannot simply say that it is common amongst boys only.

The forms of delinquent behaviour are :

(a) Loitering.
(b) Loafing.
(c) Pick-pocketing.
(d) Stealing.
(e) Gambling.
(f) Truancy.
(g) Sexual offences like eve teasing.

Causes of Delinquency

The causes of delinquency are several like :

1. Physical causes.
2. Psychological causes.
3. Economic causes.
4. Educational causes.
5. Political causes.

We shall have another approach like :

Various investigations have been conducted to trace out patent factors responsible for the onset of delinquent behaviour. With the greater use of scientific techniques combined with critical studies of delinquents, it has become quite clear that criminals are not born but made. This naturally leads us to trace the causes of delinquency in the environment around the child.

Four elements in the social situation seem to be of utmost importance in influencing the behaviour of delinquents—the home, the peergroup, the neighbourhood and the school, political order.

(a) The Home and Delinquency. Almost all research workers have accepted that homes of delinquents are characterized by discords, desertions and divorces. Such homes have been pointed out as one of the main causes of delinquency.

More damaging than the absence of parents is the presence of intrafamiliar tension. The poor child has divided loyalties, he knows not to whom he should belong. Consequently he withdraws. All such children are unloved insecure and ill-supervised from peergroups. These peergroups when highly organized turn into gangs. These gangs, later on, indulge in anti-social activities. Many investigators feel that fundamental causes of delinquency are to be found in the treatment accorded to a child by his parents, especially during pre-school years. The basic theme is rejection. When both the parents are alive, a poverty-stricken home presents tremendous handicaps to the rearing of children as well-adjusted individuals. The crippling compulsions of economic stringencies contribute to the unfulfilment of basic needs. Small families mean more delinquency.

(b) The Peergroup and Delinquency. To those in sore need of a substitute for family-love and group belongingness, the peer-group or gang presents itself as a kind of closely kint unit that will answer the purpose. Recognition achieved through being noticed in a particular group is a good substitute for being loved by a parent. The delinquent may dramatize himself as a hero before his person in the dangerous enterprises on which they embark. Here have will find the anti-social sub-culture patterns with which his feelings agree. In some of the big cities of India, there are criminal organizations and groups that get hold of orphans and teach them the art of pick-pocketing and stealing.

(c) Neighbourhood and Delinquency. The immediate environments of a child also affect the trend he will adopt in connection with his personality. It has been seen that more delinquents come from slums and thickly populated areas. A slum is not merely an aesthetically unpleasant place, it is an area loaded with dynamite for entire community. The newspapers that glorify crime focus the attention of children on crime and furnish them with rationalizations for any later misconduct. From newspapers, the children learn about inconsistent moral values of adults, of business dishonesties, of black-markets and political corruption. The neighbourhood furnishes the setting in which a child is educated.

(d) School and Delinquency. Although schools are playing an increasingly important role in the training of future citizens, they are also contributing in many cases to juvenile delinquency. The chief adverse element is the nature of the curriculum. Delinquents are typically non-bookish, non-verbal and non-academic individuals who do poorly in traditional school subjects. It is probable that young delinquents experience a great deal of frustration in the course of their school life.

Teachers also influence students through emotional atmosphere of their class-room. If they are harsh, domineering and authoritative, they arouse the aggressive hostility of the already rejected child who now finds himself rejected once more. Perhaps the worst teacher for the delinquent in the making is the one who not only cannot accept him but also takes the reaction to his rejection as a personal insult.

School discipline is sometimes administered as to be thoroughly unacceptable even to well-balanced normal children and adolescents. The effect on delinquents is disastrous and it stimulates them to even greater hostility to school.

(e) Democracy and Delinquency. Democractic order increases delinquency. Look at the extent to which things went before the emergency was declared in India. And then we boast of Youth Organisations. Without reflecting on any one, it is said that youth organisations legalise delinquency or delinquent behaviour. Moral pressure can help in curing this. Lawlessness is at its extreme now!

Remedies for Delinquency

It is important to detect the potential delinquents early to treat them before they become problems for the society. Public awareness regarding delinquency had not been fully aroused in India. It is hard to reform a delinquent because his mode of life is extremely satisfying. It provides him what he wants with least possible delay, it brings him prestige among his fellows, it permits him to punish those who have neglected and rejected him. Still various projects of individual and group-therapy have proved quite successful. The child guidance clinics can be established for dealing with delinquents. Juvenile Jail at Bareilly (U.P.) is one of the best in India. But prevention is better than cure. Naturally parents and teachers cannot be solely responsible for the prevention of delinqueney. The police, local authorities, the cinema, the newspapers and other literature, all have a part to play. However, parents and teachers can help in many ways.

Following are some of the suggestions in this regard :

1. Affection and Security. Accept a delinquent as a person in his own right. Give the child affection and security.

2. Early Treatment of Maladjustment. Watch for signs of maladjustment. Early treatment may prevent this maladjustment from taking a delinquent trend.

3. Variety of Experience. Provide a child with a variety of experiences, crafts, art, music, athletics, covering a wide range of difficulties and interests can serve the purpose.

4. Stable System of Values. Attempt to build up a stable system of moral and social values.

5. Handle Delinquents Firmly. When an out-burst of delinquent behaviour occurs in class, do not get disturbed, handle it objectively and try to get into the delinquent's world and see things from his point of view.**6. Ignore Minor Incidents.** Accept minor instances of bad manners without comment and provide opportunities for normal emotional responses.

7. Reject Delinquent Behaviour and not the Delinquent. Reject the delinquent behaviour without rejecting the delinquent. A small amount of genuine affection will often do more to help a boy rehabilitate himself than all treatments combined.

8. Improvement of Surroundings. Do what you can to change the conditions of home, school and community that seem to give rise to such behaviour.

9. Encouragement to Admit Faults. Encourage the child to talk about and admit the existence of anti-social tendencies.

10. Give Responsibility. Give a potential delinquent some post of special responsibility such as task of preventing other children from committing delinquent acts.

11. Educate the Child. Once a delinquent act has been detected, never pass it over. Make clear to the child that he has done wrong and, if necessary, punish him in an appropriate manner. But once any punishment has been given, accept the child again as the member of the community.

12. Minimize Temptations. Minimize the chances of a child's going wrong by putting the smallest possible number of temptations in his way.

Q. 52. How do you identify mentally retarded children? What are the causes of mental retardation? How should they be educated and adjusted with family, society and school?

Ans. Mentally retarded children are those children who deviate from the normal children to the negative side in mental dimensions. They have sub-normal mental development. They possess limited intelligence and social inadequacy. It is generally believed that children who possess. I.Q. below 70 are mentally retarded children. All children in the categories of idiot with I.Q. below 25, imbecile with (I.Q. 25 to 50) and moron with I.Q. 50 to 70 can be considered as mentally retarded children.

Characteristics of Mentally Retarded Children

The characteristics of mentally retarded children are as follows :—

- The areas of their interests, aptitudes and choices are too limited.
- They lack too much in the power of observation, thinking and reasoning and ability to generalize.

- They feel difficulty in shifting from one type of activity to another and are not eassily bored with a routine job.
- They are essentially slow learners. They take longer time to learn a skill.
- They are very poor are abstraction. They can only think in terms of concrete objects and situations.
- In comparison with children of their own age their rate of intellectual development is too slow.
- They are very poor at following general verbal instructions, unless these are repeated at frequent intervals.
- They are dependent and feel difficulty in managing themselves of their affairs.
- They are socially as well as emotionally maladjusted personalities.

Causes of Mental Retardation

Heredity. Heredity is one of the causes of mental retardation. The mental retardation factor of parents also affects the generation.

Nutritional Deficiency. Severe nutritional deficiency in the mother during pregnancy also brings mental retardation.

Factors Operative at the Time of Conception. Mental retardation may be caused by some defective genes in the chromosomes of one or both parents at the time of fertilization.

Factors Operative Inside the Womb of Mother. Abnormal, emotional and mental conditions of the mother during pregnancy, her severe illness and chronic infections, and the deficiencies bring mental deficiency.

Abnormal Conditions of Delivery. It is possible that at the time of delivery, due to use of some mechanical instruments child may receive head injuries. Such head injuries often cause mental retardation.

Premature Separation of Placenta. Premature delivery is also an important reason of mental retardation.

Glandular Disturbances in Child. Glandular disturbances in child-unbalances the growth and make them mentally retarded.

Education for Mentally Retarded Children

It is our duty to rehabitate these mentally retarded children and to make them self-sufficient on the following grounds :

Social Grounds. In order to make mentally retarded children the useful and the self-sufficient citizens of the society education should be imparted to them.

Democratic Grounds. India is democratic country and justice demands that a democratic government has to look to the needs of each section of the population.

Humanitarian Grounds. On humanitarian grounds education must be given to unfortunate mentally retarded children in order to make their life worth living. They have adjustment problems with family, school, society and themselves. Educational programmes for mentally retarded children are as follows :

Educate Parents. Most mentally retarded children remain at home. This is because the parents fail to understand their children. For this, parents have to develop right and positive attitudes towards bringing up their mentally retarded children.

Diagnosis. When it is suspected that a certain child is mentally retarded we should get him medically checked up for physical, sensory and neurological defects and follow the advice of the doctor regarding those defects or malnutrition. The degree of mental retardation should be got ascertained from the child guidance. This knowledge will determine to a greater extent the kind and degree of his rehabilitation possibilities.

Help in Understanding the Child. Parents must accept the fact that their child is mentally retarded. They need to face the problem courageously and with determination rather than blame or curse their fate. The child needs a sense of basic security and he can have it only through genuine acceptance and affection.

Parents should realise that the mentally retarded child may not reach the standards of a normal child according to his limited capacities. Besides this, parents need not worry about what the neighbours say.

Parents Attitude. In providing love and affection to the mentally retarded child the parents should not amount to over-protection or indulgence. They need to be sympathetic but firm and consistent in their disciplinary demands.

Often parents forget that such a child learns and develops at his own pace and that he is a slow learner. It is therefore no use comparing his achievements with those of other children who are normal.

Provide Opportunity for Work. The mentally retarded child can he encouraged to do various household works as washing the clothes, doing the house decoration, cooking, sewing, cutting, needlework, knitting or looking after domestic pets. He should be praised for his accomplishment whatever it may be. This will give him a sense of achievement. To increase his vocabulary and his power of observation and reproduction to be improved, he should be given ample opportunities of seeing things, places and persons such as shops, playground, post office, exhibitions, films, dramas, dances and historical buildings.

Individual Attention. Teacher should play individual attention to the child and take him in confidence. Individual attention is possible only if the size of class is small.

Special Schools and Clinics. Mentally handicapped children (who possess below 55 I.Q.) must be taught in special schools or they should be kept in mental hospital or clinic. There should be specially trained teachers or psychiatrists for such children.

Teacher's Attitude. Teacher should have sympathetic and affectionate attitude. They should teach from the point of view of handicapped children and put their best to bring out the maximum out of these children. They should help them to make maximum adjustment. They should not expect too much from them.

Special Time Table. Time table should be flexible. The duration of period should be short. Time table should be constructed keeping in view the needs of mentally retarded pupils. Their should be provision for more rest periods.

Q. 53. What do you mean by delinquency? Who is a delinquent child? What are the causes of delinquency? How will you identify delinquent children and what special treatment will you provide them?

Ans. Meaning of Delinquency. Delinquency in simple terms means anti-social behaviour.

Who is a Delinquent. When the anti-social activities of the child are so serious that he becomes the object of official actions, he is known as delinquent. These anti-social activities are not approved by the social order. The code of society does not allow those actions.

The child will be abnormal if he deviates from the normal standard of behaviour. He experiences difficulties to make proper adjustment to the environment. He fails away from the accepted standard of social behaviour. 'Problem child' is the other name assigned to such a child. He is called a 'problem child' bacause his behaviour is a problem for the school, for the home, for the society and even for himself.

A line of demarcation though not a distinct one can be drawn between the 'delinquent child' and the 'problem child'. The problem child may be said to be at the first stage in maladjustment and the delinquent child at the second. If proper care is not taken to handle the problem child, he may become the delinquent child.

CAUSES OF BEHAVIOUR PROBLEMS

(I) Heredity Factors

(a) Physical Conditions. There are many diseases which are inherited. T. B., epilepsy etc. are generally inherited. If parents suffer from these diseases, their children also suffer from these diseases. They are unable to adjust themselves to the accepted pattern of behaviour.

(b) Intellectual Factors. It is not uncommon to find children of low I.Q., whose parents too have low I.Q. Such children have a weak will and can be taken in very easily.

(c) Temperament Conditions. Unstable temperament of children may be ascribed to unstable temperament of their parents. They are easily provoked and are likely to misbehave.

Some psychologists hold that criminal parents produce delinquent children. They quote some studies based on various famous and notorious families. There is a classic example of the Juke family. As the ancestors of the family were notorious, hence most of the offspring happened to be delinquents, criminals and maladjusted. But recent research shows that delinquency is not an inherited trait although emotional traits and set-up are inherited to some extent. But how those emotions are to be trained and exploited, depends upon environment and education.

(II) Environmental Factors

Among the environmental causes we may discuss :

(i) Home Environment.

(ii) School Environment.

Home Environment

1. The Rejected Child. The unwanted and the neglected child does not grow as a normal child. A child robbed of all love, sympathy, affection and appreciation always find himself insecure and may develop hatred for the family and even for the society.

2. Defective Discipline. Too strict or too lenient parents having different standards of discipline have an unhealthy influence on their children. Overprotection of the child reduces his ability to meet the hard tasks of life. On the other hand, a rigid discipline deprives the child of independent thinking and may develop in him revolting tendencies.

3. Vicious Home Atmosphere. Constant quarrels between the father and the mother and hostile attitude of the step-parents have unhealthy effects on the life of the child. There is every likelihood of the child becoming immoral if one is immoral at home; criminal parents are likely to produce criminal children. All these factors hinder the natural development of the child. Shortage of accommodation and the sexual indulgence of the parents in the presence of young children lead to unhealthy sex practice.

School Environment

If the school discipline is too strict and if it is undemocratic, children will develop an inward aversion for the school. The defective methods of teaching, unsympathetic attitude of the teachers, lack of security, lack of recreational facilities, defective time table, defective curriculum etc., may develop hatred for the school.

(III) Insecurity at School

He feels insecurity due to many reasons. The child tries other avenues for self-expression and these may lead him to form delinquent behaviour.

Lack of Aptitude

A child may not acquire the ability to learn a particular subject. His performance in it may remain poor. He may lose his interest in it fully. Teacher will punish him for not doing home task in the subject and he may become maladjusted in school environment due to his incapacities.

REMEDIES FOR BEHAVIOURAL PROBLEMS

1. Pupil-Teacher Contacts. The modren educator believes in the dictim "prevention is better than cure". As the child enters the school he should be observed closely and if any sign of delinquency is detected, it should be checked very promptly. The teacher should always be mentally alert to develop mental alertness in the pupils. He should be sympathetic, pains-taking, appreciative and trusting. He should study the child carefully in and outside the school. He should try to learn him thoroughly. He should try to find out his home conditions as thoroughly as possible. This child must have the feeling that the teacher is interested in his welfare.

The teacher should be impartial and unprejudiced. He should try to develop in him a strong self-regarding sentiment.

The teacher should always remember that every child has his own problems and every problem should be tackled from the point of view of each individual. The teacher should be just and fair in this treatment.

2. Congenial Home and School Environment. *(a)* Mental disorders are created due to unfavourable home and school environments. If the child has become delinquent due to uncongenial home conditions, the teacher should guide the parents to adopt suitable methods of upbringing. Growth of the child's home environment cannot be improved, he may be shifted to a school having hostel facilities. *(b)* Sometimes the environment of the locality in which the home is suited is not congenial. The guidance counsellor in that case should suggest the parents of the child to shift their residence. *(c)* The child must be saved from the unhealthy influnece of his companions in or outside the school. If it is felt that the atmosphere of a particular school is not conductive the proper growth of the child, it is always desirable to withdraw the child from such school and put him in some other school.

3. Freedom and Self-Discipline. There are two great enemies of mental health; (a) Feeling of insecurity, and (b) feeling of inferiority. These two demons can be killed by a knowledge of mental hygiene. Unnecessary rules and regulations greatly upset the mental equilibrium of the child. A child who is given an atmosphere of freedom, develops initiative, courage, satisfaction and confidence. There is mental retardation due to severe punishment. Our philosophy of discipline must undergo a drastic change. The teacher should not be regarded as a policeman by the child. Hobbes writes, "The fool cannot be mended by flogging and he who flogs is the greatest fool."

4. Intellectual and Social Life of the School. *(a)* Pupils must be given ample scope for self-expression. The class should not be teacher-monopolised. Children must be provided opportunities to think and act independently. Methods of teaching should be adopted according to the individual needs of children. Activity methods *e.g.*, Play way, Project method, Dalton Plan etc., should be encouraged. Audio-visual aids develop interest in the lesson. Weak pupils must be given individual attention. *(b)* Creative activities must be introduced in school. They help to provide outles for the increased fund of energy in children. These activities are very much helpful in sublimating instincts. *(c)* Students must be taught how to use leisure hours most profitably and satisfyingly. Recreational activities would be very helpful. *(d)* The child should never be given an idea that he is a misfit, worthless and good-for-nohting. If the child fails repeatedly, he is haunted by such feelings. Our approach to promotions and non-promotions requires a radical change. The system should not be too much examination ridden.

5. Medical Examination. Children should be frequently medically examined and reamedial measures should be adpoted to safeguard the health of the child. Sometimes mental disorders are created due to defective physique.

6. Spcial Institutions. Some of the delinquents wil require special treatment. They should be sent to child guidance clinical. A great care should be taken in such cases that the child does not lose his self-respect and not mix-up with hardened delinquents. The parents have a special responsibility and under all circumstances their attitude should be of sympathy and not of hatred. In every town there should be welfare councils to guide the parents and the teachers about the handling of such children.

Q. 54. What is the meaning of individual differences? Discuss the causes and nature of individual differences.

Ans. No two pupils are alike. The differ from each other in hundred and one respects. They differ in age, sex, hereditray potential, intelligence, achievement, interests, aptitudes, needs—physical, social, emotional and developmental. If there are forty pupils in a class there are forty problems to solve, if the teacher wants to be effective. For example, one child may listen to the teacher's words of advice, the other may not be at all hearing them : one may be a hard worker, the other may be lazy and lethargic : one may do the home work quickly, the other may not submit it even after repeated warnings : one may be intelligent, the other may be mentally retarded.

Causes. Each child is a unique individual and differs from every other and presents individual problems. Individual differences among children are related to their developmental state at any time. The developmental state refers on the one hand to the level of maturation and on the other to the resultant of the process of growth and effects of experiences. The causes of individual differences are :

1. Difference in Growth Rate. Some children grow rapidly and some grow slowly. Some grow mentally at a faster rate, some at a very slow rate. Some grow physically and mature early; some grow late. The different parts of the organism grow at different rates. Each child has his own growth rate. The result is the variety of ages that a child possesses. The different ages that a child has at one time may be a chronological age, a mental age, an educational age, a social age, a dental age, a grip age, an organismic age and so on.

2. Difference in Socio-Economic Backgrounds. Some of the differences are caused by differences in socio-economic backgrounds. These differences are seen in pupils' reaction patterns. Differences in socio-economic backgrounds may lead to differences in diet, cultural opportunities, ideals, attitudes and adjustive actions or in family behaviour habits.

3. Interaction of Heredity and Environment. A large number of individual differences are caused by the intereactive process of heredity and environment. To each child heredity provides a potential and the dynamic forces of environment act upon that a potential in a different way. Let us illustrate how the interactive forces of heredity and environment produce differences in individuals. We may have for the sake of illustration one trait (intelligence) and at one end of the diagram we place the rod measuring the rate of mental matuirty (I.Q.).

There are three children of the same parentage X or Y each. The hereditray potential for these children A.B.C or for P.Q.R is the same being represented by the equality of height of the cones. But as environmental factors influence members' sets differently, the hereditary potential is realised in defferent amounts or degrees. With least stimulating environments only a part of the potential is realised (A, P) and with very stimulating environments we have full realisation of the potential (C, R) The differences between the six children are due to interaction of hereditary potential and the environment.

Physiological Differences. The layman and the scientist both realise and recognise that differences exist among individuals in the innate ability to learn. A certain, a mongoloid or a microcephalic does not learn with the facility of a normal individual. It is a fact though it may not be obvious that among the pupils who appear to be normal, there are also enormous differences in degrees of ability. These differences are attributed to basic physiological differences.

The basic physiological differences may be, for example, due to visual difficulty or hearing difficulty or other sensory disability or glandular dysfunction or dietary deficiency. A child who appears to be normal may be having any or some of these difficulties with the consequent impariment of learning. For example, visual difficulty which is evidenced by rubbing the eyes, learning forward to see the board, tilting the head, hearing difficulty which is displayed by turning one side of the head towards the source of sound, asking that questions be repeated, and other sensory difficulties like speech defects, inattention and listlessness cause individual differences in learning.

Teachers must recognise that some of the individual differences arise because of basic physiological differences. They must recognise that these differences exist and demand that teachers should not force all children to learn at uniform rate. When children begin to show indifference, failure, boredom inattention, tantrums, they indicate through these symptoms that teachers are expecting too much or too little from them. Pupils with sensory difficulties should be given differential treatment.

Q. 55. Explain the meaning of individual differences. How can a teacher use individual differences in education?

Ans. In education, even since the most ancient times, students have been differentiated on the basis of age as difference in age levels entitles the children to differing levels of education. As the child's age gradually increases, the subjects of his education can be made more complex and difficult. In addition to differences in age, another factor that was partly taken into consideration is the difference in levels of intelligence. Besides this, educational attainments were also considered to be important. In this manner, during the ancient and the medieval periods, individual difference was believed to be the capacity of attaining skills in a particular subject. In modern schools, other kinds of skills and abilities, and peculiarities of personality in individuals are also taken into considreation. According to Skinner, "Today we think of individual differences as including any measurable aspect of the total personality." From this definition of individual differences it is evident that it comprehends every aspect of the human personality, albeit all aspects that are in some manner measurable. Aspects of this nature can be many such as variability, conformity, difference in the rate of learning and development of mutual relationship between the various characteristics of personality, etc. In this manner, verious individual differences of physical and mental development, nature, rate of learning ability, specific abilities, interest and personality, etc.

INDIVIDUAL DIFFERENCES AND EDUCATION

1. Curriculum. In school, the curricu um should be modified to suit the needs of the dull children. Failure to achieve this adversely affects the development of all three kinds of children. Whereas the backward students start playing truant from school the brilliant children find the studies inadequate and turn their intellect to more perverses.

2. Limited Size of the Class. Keeping in mind the individual differences of the students, it is advisable that if they are to be taught properly, a class should not include more than 20 students. With 50 or more students it is impossible to teach them, keeping in mind their specific requirements.

3. Vocational Guidance. Different professions require some specific physical, mental and personality traits of the individual. Hence, knowing their peculiar mental make up and their tendencies the teacher can guide the students in the vocation that they should adopt.

4. Method of Education. It is never advisable or efficacious to use the same method of education in the case of all children. It should be varied to suit and conform to their individual differences and mental requirements.

5. Educational Guidance. Knowing the personal differences between his students the teacher can render them signal service by guiding them in their educational career. It is the teacher who can tell them the subjects they must choose to pursue in their higher studies if they are not to do violence to their natures.

6. Contribution of School, Family and Community in Education. Knowledge of differences among children determines that education in school is not completely sufficient since many differences are due to the family and community. Hence, according to modren educational psychologists, to attain the objective of all round development of individuals, prescribed by modren education, the co-operation of school, family, community and the religious institutins is sought.

7. Individual Training. Having knowledge of individual differences, now many methods of individual training have been devised. In America, the Dalton Plan, Project Method, Winnetka Method, Contract Plan and Activity Programme Methods have been devised for individual training. A brief resume of the various methods is given below—

(a) Dalton Plan. In this, children are not taught in class-rooms. They are given subjects that suit their interests and they are given a project that covers a period of 15 days to a month. Such treatment leads to the development of naturality, independence, co-operation and sociability etc.

(b) Project Method. In this the children are required to do work of every day requirements, such as cooking. stitching, furniture making, etc. And in the process of this work, they are taught novel things.

(c) Activity Programme. In this method, keeping in mind the interests of the students, activities are prescribed in order to define the curriculum. These activities are based on democratic principles. This helps to develop democratic notion in the children.

(d) Winnetka System. In this method, the student on his own tries to attain a cretain definite objective and the teacher offers very little assistance. Later on, through some tests, the extent to which the student has attained his goal is descovered.

(e) Contract Plan. In this, similar to the Dalton method, the subjects of study are determined and similar to the Winnetka method the student's progress is meassured through tests. In this manner it is a synthesis of the Dalton and Winnetka method.

It is evident from the above description that modern education makes proper arrangements for a child's education, keeping in view his peculiar nature and special abilities. In a democratic society every individual has the right to achieve a definite level of development. Hence, even more essential it is that individual differences be kept in mind while educating people of democratic countries.

Q. 56. Describe different types of Individual Differences.

Ans. TYPES OF INDIVIDUAL DIFFERENCES

1. Average Intelligence. The following brief description may serve to make individual differences a simple concept that can easily be grasped. Individuals are seen differing in considerable measure in respect of their general intelligence. It is not possible to send to schools children with an intelligence quotient of below 50. Children with intelligence quotients between 50 and 70 can learn only the very simplest tasks. Even the small schools trouble children whose intelligence quotient varies between 70 and 80. Children between 75 and 90 I.Q., are considered morons and they have considerable difficulty in progressing along with other children in their learning. Generally, 40 to 60 per cent of the children in schools have I.Q.s. varying between 95 and 105, being the children with average intelligence who form the basis for the formulation of the syllabus and curriculum as well as the method of teaching. Children who are either above or below this level of intelligences require special educational methods and conditions. Children with intelligence quotients varying between 115 and 120 are considered brilliant or intelligent.

2. Special Abilities. During the junior high school as well as the college stage, the individual's differences in respect of special abilities, in addition to the general intelligence, are also important since special professions and specialised fields of vocation all need certain specific abilities. Abilities of this kind are concerned with mental, artistic, personality or motor ability.

3. Differences of Background. In school the differences that the children exhibit are the outcome of their different families and their communities. Attitudes towards education and authority differ in each family, culture and class. Some of these attitudes are favourable while others are unfavourable to education. In either condition, the differences of attitudes results in differences among children. Besides these attitudes, the child's emotional, social, aesthetic and moral development is influenced by his family and the neighbourhood.

4. Alacrity in Learning. Difference in the quickness or alacrity in learning is visible not only in children of different ages but also among children in the same age group. This difference is dependent upon their maturity and educational background Differences in the alacrity of learning result in benefits accruing from formal education.

5. Mental Age. Children of differing ages as well as children of the same age show differences in their respective mental ages. Generally speaking, all students studying in the same class differ according to their mental ages. It has been observed that in the age of 6, differences in mental age range up to 5 years. Mental age and education are intimately related. The child's level of education is determined according to his mental age.

6. Motor Ability. The individual's movements of the hand and feet and other physical abilities are seen to be very individual, as they do not resemble another's to any great extent. Till the individual attains adulthood, his manual dexterity, rate of muscular movement and resistance to fatigue develops continually. In this manner, the same individual in different ages and different individuals in the same age group manifest considerable differences in manual dexterity.

7. Sex Differences. Makneimer and Terman discovered the following differences between men and women, on the basis of some studies:

(i) Women have greater skill in memory while man have greater motor ability.

(ii) Female handwriting is superior while men excel in mathematical logic.

(iii) Women show greater skill in making sensory distinctions of taste, pain, smell, etc., while men show greater reaction and consciousness of size-weight illusion.

(iv) Possessing greater linguistic ability women are superior to men in languages, similitudes, word building, compositions and use of long sentences etc. On the other hand, men are superior in physics and chemistry.

(v) Women are more susceptible to suggestion while there are three times as many colour-blind men as there are women.

(vi) Women are better then men in mirror drawing. Faults of speech etc., in men were found to be three times of such faults in women.

(vii) Young girls take interest in stories of love, fairy tales, stories of the school and home and day-dreaming and show various levels in their play. On the other hand, boys take interest in stories of bravery, science, war and scouting, stories of games and sports, scouts stories and games of occupation and skill.

8. Nationality. Many studies have led to the couclusion that individuals of different nations differ in respect of nature, physical and mental traits, interest and personality, etc. Such a difference is only natural since their cultural and geographic environment is distinctive.

9. Economic Situation. Economic differences are seen causing differences in the children's interests, tendencies and character, etc.

10. Difference in Respect of Development. Difference in development is in evidence not only in individuals of different age groups but also between individuals of the same age.

11. Differences Relating of Learning. In respect of learning, children manifest such differences as past experience and learning, ability in the use of various kinds of apparatus, rate of learning, interest in learning, etc.

12. Difference of Interests. As has been pointed out, the difference in sex leads to a difference in interests. Similarly, factors such as family background, level of development, differences of nationality and race, etc., cause difference of interests.

13. Personality. Differences in respect of personality have led psychologists to much study, and on the basis of this study individuals have been classified into many groups.

Concerning these classifications of the human personality, it should be remembered that although one specific person may exhibit the main broad characteristics of one class of personality, he cannot be said to belong to only that class of personality as the differences between various personalities are so subtle and minute that it is not scientifically feasible to divide them into classes.

Teacher's Advantage in Knowing Individual Differences

The objective of modren education is the complete development of the child. In this connection, the teacher has the following advantage to derive from a knowledge of individual differences:

1. This can help him to form the proper attitude towards the brilliant and the dull-witted students. It is only too evident that very good results cannot be expected from dull-witted or medicore students.
2. Any effort to bring all or a majority of the students in the class to the same level is futile since some 50 or odd percentage of them will in variably remain below this level.

3. Improvements in atmosphere, method of teaching, and the apparatus of education cannot lead to the satisfactory teaching of all students since their individual ability to learn differs widely.
4. Knowing the presence of individual differences the teacher is not perturbed at the failure of some of his students since such failure are only to be expected from below-average students.
5. The teacher does not come to expect successes that are impossible. Individual difference makes it clear that all aspects of the personality are mutually related and to develop any one aspect it is essential that all the aspects be developed.

Q. 57. What is the educational significance of individual differences in intelligence?

Ans. The individual differences in respect of intelligence were not known before 1900. It was assumed that intelligence was equal in all pupils and there were only a few who were abnormal when differences were recognised. Men and women, boys and girls were classified into different types and it was assumed that idiots and gensuses have minds different from others. It was discovered that the genius learns more rapidly and remembers better and is able to solve more difficult tasks and the idiot is incapable of doing the simplest tasks even. The notion that the very extremes of distribution constitute sharply demarcated types has been repeatedly refuted by scientific investigation. Some pupils are bright in most things and others are consistently dull. There are not two or three types of pupils: genius, dull and normal. The differences in intelligence are graded. Types exist only as hypothetical averages or as extremes of a continuous distribution.

Individual differences in intelligence are of three types—*(i)* individual differences in the unselected, homogeneous group, *(ii)* individual differences between groups (*e.g.*, between age levels, sexes, nations, races), *(iii)* differences within an individual. The educational significance of within-group differences is that we have to provide differing, stimulating environment to the gifted and the mentally retarded. The educational significance of between-group differences is to deal with them adequately wherever they exist. The nature of differences within the individual is to improve those qualities he is most gifted with.

Individual Differences Within a Group. For the sake of convenience we may hypothetically divide a group into slow learners, normal learners, mentally superior, bright, and dull and remember that :

1. The bright and dull achieve less under unfavourable conditions.
2. The mentally superior may succeed in their learning ability as far as interests and available educational facilities take them.
3. The slow learner will reach his limit of educability sooner than the normal or superior one. But if he is given the most favourable environmental background and learning conditions, he is enabled to learn more at his pace of learning.
4. The normal learner may achieve good success in schools if favourable conditions are provided.

Teachers and educators will have to remember that individuals evidently develop only the portion of their potential that is required by the environment. We should not let potential at any age to suffer underdevelopment as much as we can in our schools. We should understand that we are not succeeding in our schools because we are not doing out best to check under achievement. Children do achieve less than what their mental ability warrants them to achieve and it is a challenge to every teacher teaching in schools.

The Slow Learner. The I.Q., of slow learners is in most cases below 90 but there are slow learners in the range 90-110 and it is necessary for the teacher to deal properly with them because they tend to profit little from academic work done in the school and show comparative retardation in academic achievement. Recent studies show that such learners, though they reach their limits of educability sooner than the superior, are capable of learning more at their own pace if more favourable environment is provided.

Slow learners with repeated explanations, varied approaches and concrete explanations come up with absurd answers. Explanations, drills and demonstrations seem to have little effect on them. They require about three to four times as many experiences to consolidate learning as the bright or normal pupils do. Even with extra time and repetitions they reach the limit of their ability, buy they do learn in accordance with their mental age. It takes more time, more repetitions, more drill, more demonstrations and can become assets rather than liabilities in the society. The following are the suggestions to deal with them :

1. More repetition of facts in different contexts and drill on fundamentals.
2. To make learning concrete, more illustrations, demonstrations, examples, experiences to be given.
3. Effective motivation in the form of immediate rewards, short-term goals, praise, ecouragement.
4. Traits of punctuality, neatness and health to be emphasized.
5. School work to be related with the occupations the learners will take up as adults.
6. Very little criticism or sarcastic remarks to be given.
7. Illustrations to be simple and specific, examples to be given from daily life.
8. More schooling, more hours of school work and more years.
9. Promotion to be given on chronological age rather than on achievement. Grading to be done according to personality growth.

The present school system does schooling for the average and neglects the slow as well as the rapid learner. The bright ones are forced back and slow learners are dragged or left behind by declaring them as failures. The slow learner is the individual who is neglected because the teacher can do noting for him. He is ignored totally. But if the school wants, it can do something for him. We have, therefore, emphasized on more repetition, more illustration, more effective motivation, on no censure or blame and on cent per cent promotion so that social or emotional maladjustment may not arise.

Rapid Learners. Many words have been used to designate what we call rapid learners. The gifted. the genius, the talented and the creative are some of the terms used in psychology to designate those who stand at the top level or at one extreme end of the normal curve for intelligence. Gifted is a frequent designation and a certain specific I.Q. range has been alloted to those who are known as gifted people. Scores on intelligence testing ranging from 130 to 140 have been used to identify them. Others scores on special abilities or achievement have been used in conjunction. We have not used the word gifted purposefully here. The word gifted has greater relationship with the natural endowment which we call talent as in gift of the gab. It indicates talent, musical or artistic or of leadership and as such it is not connected with intelligence. The word 'genius' is also not appropriate so far as pupil-population is concerned, because here it is a bit meaningless term.

The class-room teacher has more to do a with rapid learner, that is, a pupil who finds school work rather easy, who is excellent in all school subjects, who loses interest in things in which his agemates are intensely interested, who is superior in character and personality traits as judged by tests or by teacher observers.

Suggestions of deal with a rapid learner we propose :

1. Enrichment of instructional programme: an abundant supply of books, laboratory equipment, illustrative material for he may select the one needed according to his personal aims.
2. School work to give a liberal background for later professional preparation.
3. Enrichment of daily life experiences and readings to expand and clarify them.
4. More of verbal descriptions and generalisation, less of repetition, study beyond that required for average or slow learner.
5. Emphasis on development of personality and character traits.
6. Skipping of grades commensurate with social and emotional development.

7. Emphasis on well-rounded development and expansion of interests.
8. More permissiveness, freedom and challenge than more prescription of work.

The gifted or the rapid learner is a challenge to the school because he sometimes asks questions which are annoying to the average teacher. If he does not get answers to these questions he becomes bored and his energies turn to undesirable acts. Some educators therefore suggest that educational programme for these pupils should be enriched. We have emphasized the development of character and personality in the fast learners because when success comes with little effort in competition with persons who possess less mental ability, the fast learner is apt to develop egoistic tendencies. Skipping over may be adopted with caution, for it may create problems of social adjustment. Since we want the gifted person to lead the average ones, he should proceed with them and not away from them.

Q. 58. How is the work of the teacher affected by the phenomenon of individual differences?

Ans. Individual differences should be recognised in all effective educational programmes. Education should make every individual capable of making his unique contribution to the society. The operational knowledge of individual differences and the realisation of their eduactional significance is the main principle on which all the most important practical problems of teaching, discipline motivation, and progress in learning depend.

Developing Self-Actualisation. Self-actualisation means one must be what he can be. The pupil with musical ability will practise music: the pupil with artistic taste will practise art: the pupil with methematical ability will practise mathematical problems off and on. All want self-actualisation. Hence the teacher, who aims at instruction to meet the need of self-actualisation, provides varied curricula and manifold student activities and plans for independent study. He gives them all information derived from tests and observations about their abilities and aptitudes so that they may be enabled to choose the skills or knowledge that they desire to obtain. The educational psychologists have long since been criticising the uniformity of curricula for it does not meet the need of self-actualistion.

Giving attention to individual differences means that the teacher or the school should have a wide variety of goals rather than the single goal of mastering subject-matter. We have but one goal in all schools and in all states; that is, we want our pupils to get a certain fixed standard of achievement in different subjects areas. Let us increase the number of goals and their variety and then alone will we be able to meet individual differences.

Eliminating Individual Differences. A worthy school system aims at eliminating individual differences. Special classes are provided for those whose differences are marked. Ability grouping seeks to place the pupil where he can perform with some hope of success. Remedial classes are organised in the week ends or in the summer or in the long breaks to correct academic deficiencies that are due to one or the other causal factor. Many young pupils get off to a good start. Instruction is adapted to individual needs and differences so that all are sure to get the fundamentals.

Developing Talents. The problem before the class-room teacher may be either to reduce individual differences or foster them so that uniqueness may be developed. Educators and psychologists have begun to think the other way round. They assert that while mass education is useful for disseminating knowledge, "education that really recognizes the individual holds forth the promise of self-realisation for pupils and improvement for society." No class-room teacher has accepted the principle as yet that it is his responsibility to develop difference if uniqueness is to be achieved.

Why should individual differences be developed? It is so because they are usefui to the society and to the individual. In the traditional society it was probably useful fore very one to be equaly in meeting his needs of food, shelter and clothing: but in the present complex social structure specialisation and uniqueness are essential not only for individual to survive, but for the society to exist continuously. One makes his contribution to the good of the society, as a whole, by becoming a doctor, the other by becoming a scientist, and so on. The contributing citizen and educated person has to be a high grade specialist with sound general education. Individual differences are also useful for the full development of the individual person. A man, who is a talented teacher or a gifted scientist or a renowned musician, gets satisfaction for himself through recognition of his special aptitude, faculty or gift. The function of the school therefore is to foster the talent or gift or special aptitude which a student has so that he may yield graciously and readily when a demand arises.

Q. 59. Explain the learner centred techniques for teaching exceptional children (creative).

Or

Who are creative children? What are their characteristics? How would you educate them?

Ans. Creativity is the capacity or ability of an individual to create, discover or produce a new idea or object including the re-arrangement or reshaping of what is already known to him. Creativity is universal. Everyone of us possesses creative capacity to some degree. Through creative expression something new is produced.

DEFINITIONS OF CREATIVITY

According to **Skinner,** "Creative thinker is one who explores new areas, makes new observations, predictions and inferences."

According to **Drevdahl,** "Creativity is the capacity of a person to produce compositions or ideas which are essentially new."

According to **Stagner,** "Creativity implies the production of a totally or partially novel identity.

According to **Gange,** "Creativity to be a form of problem solving which involves intuitive jumps or a combination of ideas from widely separated fields of knowledge."

On the basis of these definitions we find that the creativity means—'seeing or expressing new relationships. Creativity involves different traits or qualities like fluency, flexibility, originality, elaborations, sensitivity' etc.

Creative Children

The expressions of creative behaviour change from one educational level to another—the pre-school, elementary school, secondary school and higher education.

Creativity in Early Childhood

Children from 3 to 7 years old observe the following categories of 'creative' imagination:

(a) Revision of a single memory image.

(b) Improvisation of the theme from a number of images.

(c) Organisation on the nature of a composite from several images.

(d) Selection of various elements of aesthetic interest.

(e) Fusion of compositional elements in to a composition of high character.

Creativity in the Elementary School Years

Elementary school years are considered to be critical for the development of creativity :

(a) Greatest attention should be paid to creative writing and art.

(b) Walls of the school rooms and other places should be decorated 'by childrens' creativity.

Examples of outstanding creative achievements at a tender age are many. Newton spent his childhood making water clocks and windmill models. James Hillier constructed his first microscope as a boy. Pascal wrote his famous essay at 16, the greatest mathematician Karl Friedric Gaus performed his distinguished work at 15.

Creativity in the High School

Some of the manifestations of creativity during this stage are—

(a) Presenting an original paper.

(b) Winning a prize or award in competition.

(c) Compositional skills of a high order.

(d) Inventing a patentable device.

Creativity in Higher Education

Manifestations of creativity at this stage are—

(a) The college and unviersity level students have been found to produce almost all types of creative produces—inventions, books, monographs, and original articles.

(b) Quite frequently such expressions are available outside college or university requriements and activities.

(c) The writing of a thesis and starting a project.

(d) Organizing a group programme by college students may be treated as manifestation of creativity.

Characteristics of Creativity

(a) Creative is universal.

(b) Creativity abilities are natural endowments, they are capable of being nourished and nurtured by training or education.

(c) There is complete ego involvement in creative expression.

(d) Any creative expression is the source of joy and satisfaction for the creater

(e) Creative thinking has complete freedom for the multiplicity of responses choices and lines of action.

(f) Life as a whole presents enormous opportunities for creative expression as for scientific invention, composition of poems, writing of story and drama, painting, dance etc.

EDUCATIONAL IMPLICATIONS

The following steps should be considered for the promotion of creativity in students :

Freedom to Respond. Children should be encouraged to express their thoughts and feelings in as many media as they can. Teacher should encourage students to express themselves in a novel and original way.

Development of Original and Creative Thinking. Teacher should help the students in original and creative thinking. There should be free atmophere in the class for creative thinking. Strict discipline will perish the interest of the students.

Removal of Hesitation and Fear. Teacher should not be authoritative. The instincts of the child should be properly sublimated. Care should be taken to remove fear, shyness and prejudice from their minds.

To Provide Opportunities for Creative Expression. For the purpose of providing opportunities for creative expression, we can make use of the co-curricular activities in schools. Our social festivals, religious and social get-together, exhibitions etc., can also provide the opportunity for creative expression. A regular class-work can be arranged in such a way as to stimulate and develop creative thinking among children.

Develop Healthy Habits. Self-confidence, industriousness, self-reliance are some of the qualities that are helpful in creative expression. Teacher should develop healthy habits and good qualities among students. They should be made to stand against criticism of their creative expression.

Using the Creative Resources. Children should be encouraged to use creative resources of the community. They should visit and see creative art or scientific and industrial creative work. Creative artists and persons should be invited in the school for enhancing the span of the knowledge of the children.

To Set Self-Example. Teachers and parents must try to develop the habit of creative thinking among themselves. They should believe in change, novelty and originality, and experience the creative process themselves. Their teaching and their mode of behaviour must reflect their love for creativity. They can inspire children for being creative.

There are some hinderances in the promotion of creativity. Teacher should try to avoid them, only then children can express their creativity Kothari Commission has rightly said 'Destiny of India is being shaped in her class-rooms.

Encouragement to Rote-Memorization. These days our pupils do not make use of their talent and intelligence at all. They mostly depend upon help-books and thereby rote-memorization is encouraged. This stands in the way to creativity among our pupils.

Teacher-Centred Teaching. In our schools teaching is mostly teacher-dominated. The child remains a passive listener. Pupils become blind followers rather than creative thinkers. Such type of atmosphere in our class-rooms hinders in creative thinking.

Lack of Facilities. Our schools do not have adequate facilities for creative activities. Our class-rooms are mostly overcrowded, laboratories, workshops and play fields are not well-equipped. There is little scope of co-curricular activities like games, dramatics, debates, symposiums, excursions etc. All these are hindrances to the promotion of creativity.

Authoritarian Curriculum. Our curriculum is very much authoritarian in nature. It does not cater to the needs, interests and ability of the students and does not encourage creative thinking and development in the pupils.

Defective Examination System. Our examination system is defective. It does not encourage creativity and experimentation.

By removing these problems we can fulfil the dream of our Commissions, who have rightly said that the future of India is moulded and designed in the class-rooms.

Q. 60. Explain the concept of Personality, its elements and bring out its traits.

Ans. The word personality has been derived from the Latin word 'Persona', which was the mask which Greek actors wore while acting. This, however, is not the meaning taken in the modern word personality. Thus, personality is not a fixed state but dynamic totality which is continuously changings to interaction with the environment. Personality is known by the conduct, behaviour, activities, movements and everything else concerning the individual. It is the way of responding to the environment. The way in which an individual adjusts with the external environment is personality. Following are some definitions of personality :

Munn, "Personality may be defined as the most characteristic integration of an individual's structure, modes of behaviour, interests, attitudes, capacities, abilities and aptitudes."

Allport, "Personality is a dynamic organization within the individual of those psycho-physical systems that determine has unique adjustement to his environment."

Watson, "Personality is the sum of the activities that can be discovered by actual observation over a long enough period of time to give reliable information."

Woodworth, "Personality is the total quality of individual behaviour."

Gordon Allport, "Personality is the dynamic organisation within the individual of those psycho-physical systems that determine his unique adjustment of his environment of his environment." The personality is the organisation of internal and external activities. It includes the external appearances, qualities, aptitudes and capacities, etc. It is the result of the interaction of the individual with the environment. It is not a collection of the traits, but a particular organisation of them. It is the total quality of the individual's behaviour. Individual affects other individuals through his personality.

Elements of Personality

There are several factors that contribute to our personality. These factors have received greater or less importance at the hands of different psychologists. Here we shall discuss some of the important elements. These elements generally stated are :

1. Personal appearance.
2. Intelligence.
3. Emotional life.
4. Temperament.
5. Character and moral traits.

Some of these elements are congenital while others are acquired. The latter are determined by environment and education, the former are not so determined.

1. Personal Appearance. The size and shape of a person influences his personality. If a man is tall, of good physical proportions, and well-muscled, his personality is likely to be affected favourably. He is likely to be respected by his fellows and popular with them. A physical "deviate" on the other hand, has his own personality problems. By a 'deviate' we mean some one who varies or deviates considerably from the average. A person who is very small, very tall, too fat or too thin is a deviate. Being a deviate lessens the feeling of confidence and personal worth.

It is true that there can be a relationship between physical development and certain personal attitudes, especially in the case of deviates. But the fact is that no one can judge personal and intellectual qualities by physical appearance.

2. Intelligence. Intelligence is an inborn capacity to perceive the right thing, at the right place, at the right moment. It is the general mental adaptability to new problems and conditions of life. Intelligence is certainly an asset. It enables easy adjustment even under difficult circumstances and thus helps in building up personality. Intelligent people are able to adjust themselves to changing environments with great ease, efficiency and speed and hence they are said to have good personality.

3. Emotional Life. The core of an emotional experience is feeling. When feelings violent and the composure of our mind is disturbed we have no longer feelings but emotions. An emotion is thus noting but an intense and violent feeling. Emotions play a very important part in the individual and social life of man. They determine to a very great extent his physical and mental health. They also determine whether a person will be liked in the society or will be treated as a nuisance. Emotions are to be sublimated. They should not be repressed. Repressed emotions give us complexes which further lead to disintegrated or maladjusted personality.

4. Temperament. Man may be rational animal, but at times he is extremely emotional also. Intense and violent feeling is emotional long drawn out emotion is a mood. Mood when it becomes permanent influences our temperament. Temperament is partly physical and partly mental. Diet and climate also effect our temperament and temperament affects personality. Differed types of temperament have resulted in different types of personalities :

(a) ***Choleric Type.*** He is also known as the violent type. He is energeting, full of ambition and courage but easily excitable to anger.

(b) ***Sanguine Type.*** He is active, cheerful and optimistic in his pursuits.

(c) ***Melancholic Type.*** He is humble, sad, depressed and pessimistic.

(d) ***Phlegmatic Type.*** He is slow, dull and unemotional. He is also known as 'apathetic' or 'indifferent type.'

Cyril Burt holds that majority of the cases belong to the mixed-type. Thus, there is a considerable overlapping of these temperament.

5. Character and Moral Traits. Character is the sum of all those tendencies, which the individual posesses. It is the organisation of instincts and habits under the sentiment of self-regard. If this organisation is strong, character is strong. It it is weak, the character is weak. Character includes our sentiments and habits in the widest sense of the term. It is the product of the interaction of instinctive dispositions with the physical and social environment under the guidance of intelligence. Character and the personality of the individual are very closely related.

Role of Home and School in Building the Personality

Psychologists now will agree that social factors are the most important in shaping our personality traits. The members of the family, playmates, school and class-fellows, society at large all these in a way determine and influence his personality.

(a) Home Atmosphere. Fundamental patterns of personality are formed during childhood. A congenial home atmosphere, with good relations between the parents and the child, is essential for a well-adjusted personality to develop. If parents provide a stimulating environment and a great degree of freedom, children will grow into strong, independent and self-reliant individuals. If, on the other hand, they are domineering and strict, children will be timid, lacking initiative and self-confidence. Over affectionate parents make children too dependent and overstrict ones make them too timid or too rebellious. Similarly disrupted homes often produce unstable, badly-adjusted personalities. The child has close emotional tie to each parent. Hence their quarrels cause serious conflict in his personality.

The position of the child in the family has much to do with the the pattern of his personality. The only child, the youngest child, the adopted child, the favourate child, the only son in a family of daughters or the only daughter in the family of sons-grows differently and develops emotional attitudes which makes a difference to his or her personality. For example, the only child is likely to be pampered or over-protected. The parents give him extra protection and love and unknowlingly teach him to expect more from the social environment. The child grows self-centred, obstinate and less co-operative.

(b) School Atmosphere. The share and responsibility of the school in forming the personality of the child is equally important. The school makes the man in more than one way. It gives him more knowledge, more opportunities to think and reason and a broader outlook on life. It helps the emotional development, cultivates tastes and attitudes and offers material for building up ideals and aims in life. The schools of today have realised that mere instruction is not enough. They are providing opportunities for social competitive and co-operative work and experience. N.C.C., A.C.C., scouting games, social service leagues, co-operative stores, school banks, art clubs, hobbies, trips and the like give opportunities to the growing young people to dominate over some and yield to others, to play the role of leaders and followers as the occasion demands.

Q. 61. Describe the various methods of assessment of Personality.

Or

Describe fully, with examples, any one of the modern psychological methods of the assessing traits of Personality.

Ans. Assessment of Personality. The following methods and devices are used to measure personality and its various traits :

(1) Observation Method. The experimenter has simply to observe the behaviour of the individual. If he finds that good traits are present in his behaviour, he tries to know to what degree they are present in him. Thorndike's studies are famous in this line. To get one index of leadership, for example, we could merely count the number of elective positions which a student has held.

This device needs much time and is liable to error.

(2) Interview Method. For information which cannot be obtained through observation, investigators make great use of the interview. In such an interview, of course, the experimenter may use many supplementary devices. Used by trained and judicious, inquirer it can bring to light information which could be obtained in no other way. He may rely largely on rather simple discussion, basing his estimate on the answers to his questions and on the information volunteered by the person being interviewed.

The informal interview, of course, is no device for the untrained inquirer. He may miss much that is significant and may mis-interpret a good deal of what he observes. Secondly, the informal interview does not yield a quantitative score.

(3) Personality Questionnaire of Inventory. Personality, frequently is measured by questionnaries. Woodworth devised a "personal date sheet" in 1918, to determine emotional instability among soldiers. It had 116 questions, each to be answered by 'yes' or 'no'. Woodworth choose items relating to various physical symptoms, fears, worries, feelings and attitudes known to indicate mental or nervous disorders.

Some of the questions are—Do you usually feel well and strong? Does liquor makes you quarrelsome? Are you troubled with the idea that people are watching you on the street? Did you ever have a nervous breakdown?

A variation of the personality questionnaire is Sidney Pressey's Crossout test" to measure emotionality. On a long list of words the subject is asked to cross out those unpleasant to him; on another list those he considers wrong or unethical; on another items about which he worries. This test is generally used to get information about a person's emotions.

There are, of course, many objections to the questionnaires. The person taking the test may see through the questions and check the answer which he thinks will give him a good score rather than the answer which be regards as true.

(4) Performance Tests. Obviously persons may answer questionnaires wrongly or dishonestly and there lies a serious weakness of this kind of test. To avoid such errors, performance and behaviour tests are often used. It is possible to put a student in a test situation and to see how he actually performs. It is possible, for instance, to give him a test in which he has an opportunity to cheat and to determine whether or not he overcomes the temptation. He could copy from a neighbour's paper, change answers when scorring their own tests, 'peep' in a blind-fold game. Other situations tested stealing and lying impulses. Other performance tests are also used.

Allport and Vernon show that handwriting and other expressive behaviour like walking and reading, speed or ability to estimate areas and distances, show rather consistent personality patterns. Yet there is no evidence that anyone expressive movement, or in fact all of them together, relate very closely to personality traits.

(5) Projective Techniques. Most of the measuring devices discussed so far are designed to cast light not on the integrated personality but on various isolated traits of personality. Now we will discuss those tests which reveal an integrated pattern of personality. Prominent among these are the so-called projective techniques.

Meaning of Projective Techniques

This title is derived from projection, meaning reflection of one's own inner-self upon the external objects. Freud first used this word. According to him perception of the outer world is determined largely by the feelings, desires, fears, thoughts and ideas of the inner world which is unknown. This is based on depth psychology or the psychology of the unconscious. According to it the quality of personality is much affected by the unconscious motives and emotions. To test the whole personality we must have technique to measure this unconscious. Projective technique makes this possible. Through this technique is let out the hidden quality of the personality. This tells us as to what lise at the back of our conscious behaviour. When a person tells what a cloud looks like to him, or gives him his own interpretation of a picture containing people, he 'projects' into it something of his own personality. If he interprets several items in the same general way, this may reveal important trends of his thinking, attitude, interest and emotion.

Following are the devices used in projective technique :

(1) Dream Analysis. Dreams, according to Freud, are wishful-filling. The reperssed wishes of the individual come in a disguised form in dreams. Thus the analysis of the dreams of the individual reveal the type he is.

(2) Free Association. You give a casual word to the individual and ask him to give out all those words which come to his mind. A study of this chain of words will help us to assess his personaiity.

(3) Story Completion. An incomplete story is given to the individual and he is asked to complete the story in any manner he deems fit.

(4) Story Telling. The individual is asked to narrate stories which have been of special interest to him. This device is used to elicit the hidden and unconscious whishes, ambitions, fears, judgements, etc.

(5) Expressive Movement Tests. This is a technique to judge personality through :

(a) the handwriting of the individual,

(b) painting,

(c) picture completion test.

(6) Visual Tests. Out of the projective techniques the best known is the "ink blot test". The 'ink-blot test' was prepared by a Swiss Psychiatrist Herman Rorschach. It consists of ten cards, each containing a rater elaborate ink-blot. Five blots are in colour, five in grey and black. Those ink-blots are made by dropping some ink in the fold of a paper and squeezing the paper together. These blots suggest various pictures to different people, and since one is free to see almost anything in them, the reaction is supposed to indicate tendencies in the person. Subjects study one blot at a time and tell what each resembles. They can think as long as they like over each card. The examiner records their responses, then shows the card a second time asking the subjects to elaborate ambiguous interpretations and explain which parts of the ink-blots led to their responses.

Results are scored by three main criteria :

(a) Do subjects react to the whole blot, to a part or to a small detail?

(b) Do their responses involve movement, from colour or the three combined and is the form clear or blurred?

(c) Do subjects see human or animal figures or chiefly inanimate objects?

The complete scoring is quite complex, involving many factors beyond mere counting of responses. Seeing whole figures indicates high intelligence and ability to synthesize. A predominance of forms in motion, especially of human forms signifies vivid imagination. Great response to colour means impulsiveness, if not emotional instability. Setting mostly animals, and giving unoriginal responses in general, suggest lower intelligence. On the other hand, noting small unusual details indicates introversion and possible emotional conflicts.

A method somewhat similar to the 'ink-blot test' is the "Thematic Apperception Technique". In this method, the subject is shown a picture, for instance, of an older man taking hold of the arm of a startled woman. The subject is told that this is a test of the fertility of his imagination. He is asked to give a story into which the picture would fit. The resulting story is supposed to give some insight into the hopes, fears and needs of the subjects.

Limitations of the Projective Technique

1. There is a great dearth of standardised test.
2. These tests are to be administered with great care and that also by an expert. Everybody cannot use them.
3. They are more subjective. Scoring is difficult and exacting and interpretation is exceedingly complex.
4. There is no proof of their validity. Henry A. Murray of Harvard, himself the creator of several new projective methods, says that their validity is demonstrated with children but some doubts remain about adults. There are many other psychologists who say that these tests lack objectivity and their interpretation is without experimental verification. They feel that the validity of these tests is not yet established for normal persons.

Q. 62. Define the factors affecting the personality development.

Ans. FACTORS AFFECTING PERSONALITY

The important factors in which the origin of personality lies are:

(I) Heredity. It provides the child with certain endowments to start with. Hereditary factors may be summed as constitutional, biological and physiological factors:

1. ***Constitutional Factors.*** The constitution of an individual is an effective factor in determining the type of his personality. There can be 3 bodily types of personality—*(1)* short and stout, *(2)* tall and thin, *(3)* muscular and well proportioned. We are always impressed by an individual who has a muscular and a well proportioned body. Height, weight, physical defects, health and strength affect personality.

2. ***Biological Factors.*** The working of the nervous system, glands and blood chemistry determines our characteristics and habitual modes of behaviour. These factors form the biological basis of our personality. Adrenal gland, thyriod gland, pituitary gland and endocrine gland affect personality. Adler points out that personality defects lead to the development of inferiority complex and the mental mechanism of compensation. This aspect also includes the mental ability of the child. It is this ability which enables him to mould the social environment according to his requirements.
3. ***Intelligence.*** Intelligence is mainly hereditary. Persons who are very intelligent can make better adjustment in home, school and society than those who are less intelligent.
4. ***Sex Differences.*** Sex differences play a vital role in the development of personality of individual. Boys are generally more assertive and vigorous. They prefer adventures. Girls are quieter and more injured by personal, emotional and social problems.
5. ***Nervous System.*** Development of personality is influenced by the nature of nervous system.

(II) Environment. The sociologists emphasise that the personality of the individual develops in a social environment. It is in the social environment, that he comes to have moral ideas, social attitudes and interests. This enables him to develop a social 'self' which is another term for personality.

The important aspects of the environment are as follows :

(1) Physical Environment. It includes the influence of climatic conditions of a particular area or country on man and his living.

(2) Social Environment. The child has his birth in the society. He learns and lives there. Hence, the social environment has an important say in the personality development of the child.

(3) Family Environment. Family is the cradle of all social virtues. The first environment, the child moves in, is his home. Here the child comes in contact with his parents and other family members. His likes, dislikes, stereotypes about people, expectancies of security and emotional responses all are shaped in early childhood. The type of training and early childhood experiences received from the family play an important role in the development of personality.

Besides this, economic factors *i.e.*, economic condition of the family and the type of relations between the parents also influence the personality of the child.

(4) Cultural Environment. The cultural environment refers to certain cultural traditions, ideals, values etc., which are accepted in a particular society. All these factors leave a permanent impression on the child's personality.

(5) School Environment. Schools play an important role in moulding the personality of the children because a significant part of a child's life is spent in school between the ages of 6 and 20 years. In the school, the teacher substitutes the parents. The school poses new problems to be solved, new taboos to be accepted into the superego and new models for imitation and identification, all of which contribute their share in moulding personality.

In addition to the above there are many other social factors which influence the development of personality of a child which are as follows :—

(a) Language. Human beings have a distinctive characteristic of communication through language. Language is an important vehicle by which the society is structured and culture of the race transmitted from generation to generation. The child's personality is shaped by the process of interaction through language with other members of his environment.

(b) Social Role. The child has to play several roles like son, brother student, officer, husband, father, etc., throughout his life at different stages of his development. Social roles may be described as the process by which the co-operative behaviour and communications among the society members are facilitated.

(c) Self Concept. Self concept influences our personality development in two ways—*(1)* If other people hold high positive attitude towards us, this enhances our self and *(2)* If others hold negative attitude towards us, it creates feelings of worthlessness and may lead to self-defence or withdrawal from social situation.

(d) Identification. Identification is an important mechanism by which we try to imitate the physical, social and mental characteristics of our model. It is a very important relationship with others.

(e) Inter-personal Relations. Inter-personal relations among the members of a society are important means which help in the development of certain social personality characteristics like attraction towards others, concept of friendship, love, sympathy, hostility and also isolation which is a negative orientation.

(III) Psychological Factors. These include our motives, acquired interests, our attitudes, our will and character, our intellectual capacities such as intelligence *i.e.*, the abilities to perceive, to observe, to imagine, to think and to reason, These factors determine our reactions in various situations and thus affect our personality, growth and direction. An individual with a considerable amount of will power will be able to make decisions more quickly than others.

Thus, we see that hereditary, environmental and psychological factors contribute towards the development of personality.

Q. 63. Discuss the influence of hereditary and environmental factors of personality traits.

Ans. DETERMINANTS OF PERSONALITY

The factors affecting personality can be divided into two classes—

(1) Biological and (2) social. The biological factors affecting the development of personality are of three types : (1) Ductless Glands, (2) Physique, and (3) Body Chemistry.

BIOLOGICAL FACTORS

1. Endocrine Glands. Ductless glands send their secretions directly to the blood without ducts. Their secretions are called hormones. These hormones are responsible for many changes in the personality. Different glands secrete one or more type of hormones. A description of the effect of some of the ductless glands will show the extent to which personality is influenced by them.

(i) ***Pancreas.*** Pancreas send insulin to the blood. The amount of sugar in the blood depends upon the amount of insulin in it. When the deficiency of insulin, *i.e.*, sugar, is in the body the mental powers are weakned and the personality of the individual seems less balanced. His book is changed, temperament becomes irritated and fear increases.

(ii) ***Thyroid Gland.*** Thyroid glands has a very important function in the development of physical structures as well as mental development. If it is absent since the very birth the intellect of the child does not improve.

(iii) ***Adrenal Gland.*** Adrenal gland secrets adrenaline. Adrenaline has an important influence upon personality. Its excess creates the sexual triats in men or women. Its excess in women is responsible for the absense of the rounded contours and feminine voice. It organizes the organic capacities in the time of emergency.

(iv) ***Gonads.*** The secretion of the gonads *i.e.*, sex glands is an important influencing personality. Gonads secrete sex hormones. Sex hormones are very helpful in the increase of sex interest. In adolescence there is a special increament in sex hormones. Hence, changes are observed in the individuals according to their sex. In man one finds the manifestation of manual characteristics such as beard, moustaches, high pitch in voice etc. While in the female there is development of mammary glands and other womanly traits. The processes concerning pregnancy *e.g.*, mensas, pregnancy, the bearing of the child and maternal behaviour is very much influenced by the sex hormones.

(v) ***Pituitary Glands.*** The hormones secreted by the pituitary glans control other glands. The hormones secreted by the front part of the pituitary glands increase the activity of other glands as well. The hormones created by the back part of the pituitary glands control the blood pressure and the metabolism of physical growth. In the time of physical growth the bones and muscles of the individual grow speedily due to the activity of these glands. In its excess, the height can go even up to 7 to 9 feet. But because after excessive activity this glands becomes very much inactive, these very tall persons die at an early age. If the activity of the pituitary gland is very much dificient in the time of development, individual remains is midget, rough his intellect is normal and the physical structure is not un-attractive. It the activity of this gland is normal during he developmental period and becomes excessive afterwards the hands, feet, nose and lower jaw, etc., beome broad.

The effect of the hormones is influenced by the heredity as well as the environmental factors. But still the excess or deficiency in their activity created some changes quite apparent in the personaliy of the individual. It is not necessary that the excess of the excess of the secretion of any one of the particular glands should always show some special influence in the body *e.g.*, the excess of sex tendency should not always be supposed as due to the excess of the secretion of the sex gland, since different glands also interact upon each other due to which the activity of some is increased while that of others is decreased. The sex behaviour, for example, is very much influenced by social norms circumstances, habits and many other things.

2. Physique. Another important biological factors affecting personality is physical structure. It is seen in daily life that often the fat men are easy going and social, while the thin persons are self-controlled, irritated and un-social. While the thin persons are self-controlled, irritated and un-social. Thus, the physical structure has some relation with the temperament. But even the instances contrary to this rule are also existing. As a matter of fact, the relation of physical structure and the temperament has not been definitely established. More experiments are required in this direction. The experiments conducted so far have been mostly on college student. Before one arrives at some detinite conclusion, experiments must be conducted on adult persons as well. But even after that, the problem of the basis of co-relation remains un-answered, simply by co-relation the temperament cannot be taken as a result of physical structure. It should also be remembered in this context that the physical structure makes a difference in other behaviour towards a particular person. It is observed that our behaviour towards different individuals is modified, to some extent-according to their physical structure.

3. Body Chemistry. Another important biological factor affecting personality is body chemistry. In ancient times the difference of temperament was supposed due to differences of chemical elements in different men. Thus, the nervous personality was taken as the result of excess of nervous fluid. It was supposed that the sanguine persons have an excess of blood, the choleric persons an excess of bile, phlegmatic persons an excess of phlegam and the melancholic persons, an excess of spleen. This principle is not accepted in modern psychology, but still no psychologist denies the relation of personality with the proportion of chemical elements in the body. These chemical elements are two types. Some reach the body from outside while some are created in the body itself. Thus, the durgs have sufficient effect on personality. the behaviour of the drunkard is an example of such effect. Different types of intoxicating drugs have a clear influence upon the personality of the individual. The deficiency of different vitamins also causes some change in the personality. With the increase or decrease of the quantity of sugar in the body, the physical and mental state of the man is very much changed.

Besides the above-mentioned biological factors many other factors influence personaliy, *e.g.*, sex, intelligence, intellect and nervous system, etc. The difference in the sex of male and female create an essential difference in their personality, though it has been established that much of this difference is caused by social and cultural environment. Galton and Goddard believe that intellect is absolutely hereditary. The modern psychologists do not agree with this hereditary view through the influence of heredity is not denied. The environment affects intellect, but the development of intellect is ultimatly limited. The influence of special talents, as that of music, mathematics, etc., on human personality is very well-known. Like the intellect, the talents are also generally hereditary.

SOCIAL DETERMINANTS OF PERSONALITY

The environments of different individuals are very much different from one another and so also their effects, but the influence of environment on personality can roughly be divided into that of home; school and society. All these three play an important part in the development of personality.

1. Influence on Home of Personality. The environment of the home has a wide influence on the development of personality. This influence, as a general rule, is according to the patterns found in a particular culture. In the family the relation of child with the parents is the most intimate. The cultural development of the child is very much influenced by the behaviour of the parents *e.g.*, a child brought up in Indian family will be very much different in his behaviour than another brought up in western culture. But even in the same culture much difference can be observed in the parent-child relationship in different families *e.g.*, generally the child has a respectable place in Indian family, but all Indian parents do not sufficienlty love and sympathies with the child. In such circumstances much repression is observed in child's behaviour. He becomes an introvert and often enjoys in his dreams, day-dreams and imaginations things which are denied to him by his parents. The influence of the presence of the parental love is again not the same in the face of all children. A child may become aggressive while another may become submissive in the same circumstances. On the other hand, if the parents show excessive suffocation towards her child, the child may became an extremist and excessively dependent upon the parents. A child excessively ignored shows different types of conflicts in his personality. Children brought in the psychological clinics for the curse of defects of personality showed that an important cause of their defects was the behaviour of their parents towards them. According to segment. Fraud, the tendency to depend upon the parents in the childhood is manifested in the tendency to depend upon the leader in the adult age. If the child is allowed freedom in the matters concerning his belongings, food, clothes, books, *etc.*, he will develop a habit of free will, if all these are decided by his parents he will not get any opportunity to utilize his judgment and so become over dependent or submissive.

Parents are more powerful and efficient than the child. Hence, they are the ideals before him. The child wants to become like his parents. Thus, he establishes his identification with either of the parent and tries to follow his manners, ways and behaviour. The child also fulfils his frustrated desires through this identification. It has been observed that the little boy wears the big shirt of the father and walks proudly like him with a stick in his hand. This identification with the parents in the childhood is later on converted into the identification of the individual with the leader.

In the absence of affection and sympathy, the child often turns criminal. While discussing the causes of criminal tendencies. Heavy and Bronner had emphasized three factors: the effort to get rid of the painful circumstances, the tendency to revenge for the misbehaviour of the father, the efforts to satisfy the frustrating desires. Often the child has the curiosity as to from where the younger brother or sister has come. The answer to this question by the parents has an important effect on his personality. The child has a natural curiosity towards the sex tendency. Often the parents try to suppress his curiosity towards sex or they just rebuke when he asks such question. But the child in not silenced by this. He tries to enquire from the servants or friends in the house. But this leads to guilty conscience. The reaction in the parents about the every day matters in the family also effect the personality of the child. The relations of the mother and father among themselves also effect the personality of the child.

It has been observed that the behaviour of the eldest and the youngest, the elder or the younger is not the same in the family. Similarly, it has been found that the parent's behaviour towards them is not also the same. This has led the psychologist Alfred Adler, to emphasize the importance of birth other in the deevlopment of personality. The birth order of the child fixes the status in the family which decides his roles which affect his personality. The younger child is treated with affection by everyone, hence he becomes over dependent. The eldest child becomes self-sufficient and tyrant, because being the only child for sometime he dose not share his rights and things with others. The birth of another child in the family has an important influence on the child, since it takes away his monopoly in affection and sometimes he is neglected altogether. The above description of the child's problem based upon the conception of birth order has not been conclusively proved. The researchers have found similar conflicts in different birth orders. Adler has truly said that the individual develops his style of life from the pattern of his early lie in the family, but there are no grounds to suppose that this style of life remains un-changed in future.

2. Influence of School on Personality. School also has an important influence on the personality of the child. In school both the teachers and class fellows mould his personality, just as in the family the parents are ideals before the child so are teachers in the school. The child hates the cruel and strict teacher. On the other hand, he respects good and sympathetic teachers. The personality of the teacher and his behaviour towards the child both exercise important influence on child's personality. The child tends to identify himself with the teacher and tries to imitate his ways, manners and personality traits.

Besides the teacher the classmates and playmates exercise important influence on the personality of the child. These constitute a group in which every child has his own particular status and roles corresponding to it. One can see the leader, the dare devil and the scapegoal child in the group. The leader is the mind of the group. He plans adventures and games. The dare devil executes them while the scapegoat is left to receive the blame and consequent punishment. In different types of groups of children, different traits of leadership are required according to the purpose. Thus, sometimes the intelligent child leads while at other times the leader is theater devil. This particular role in the group determines the future role of the individual in a society. This, however, is not without exceptions.

3. Influence of Society on Personality. Society is a web of social relationship. These social relationships connect men and women with one another. These interpersonal relations influence and mould the personality of the individual. In the society each individual has some peculiar status and roles corresponding to them. For example, in Hindu community, members of different castes have different social status in society. The roles and function of an individual are determined by his status. This mechanism controls the behaviour of the individuals. Social control is further exercised by more, traditions, myths, legends, customs, etc. These determine the style of life of the individual. The individual cannot behave in the society as he likes. Society punishes the individual who breaks its norms. The fear of society is often more powerful than even the fear of heaven and hell or punishment by the state. Therefore, social norms influence been the ways and attitudes of the individuals. This ultimately influence his personality. The individual adopts the prevalent patterns of social behaviour. That is why one notices so much difference in the behaviour and personality of members of different societies. This however, does not mean that there are no individual differences in the same society. In fact, in every society one can find men and women who scarcely care for the social norms. But in every case, personality is affected by the social environment.

Q. 64. Discuss the charactersitics of an integrated Personality.

Or

Write a note on Traits of Personality.

Ans. One's material success is often thought to provide an index of personality. Consequently, having a good personality, in the opinion of many, is the same thing as being well-dressed and wealthy. In spite of the proverb, "The apparel of successful proclaims the man", dress is really of negligible importance, it does not constitute personality. Education, though valuable, is not strictly necessary. Some even hold that goodness is not essential, for they argue, while many great personalities have been saints, a large number have been great sinners; Beauty is an important factor, but by itself it is negligible. Personality is not the same thing as high birth. Many people with highsounding titles are unutterable bores.

There are certain basic qualities to be found in all men who rise above their fellows. Vitality or energy, which radiates outwards, impressing others with a sense power and dominance is one of these qualities. Good physical health is another. Intelligence is another *prerequisite*; other important qualities are courage, sincerity, diligence, tact, enthusiasm originality, enterprise and good judgement. A sense of humour is also a valuable asset, provided its possessor does not become cynical or does not treat life as a huge joke. Self-complacency, unobtrusiveness, quite self-assurance, modesty kindness and character are some additional traits of personality. Sociability, above all, is the most shining trait. The sixth sense called "the social sense" is the most important quality of all. The social sense is the ability to feel at home in any social situation is never overawed by people; he knows how to deal with his fellow beings, for he is acquainted with his foibles and weaknesses. A person possessing this trait may achieve promotion over his more talented workers, because he can handle men and situations better. Tactfulness, and social sense are not learnt from books, but from social interaction, from rubbing shoulders freely with fellow-companions.

Lack of vitality, indifferent health, dullness of wit, timidity, tactfulness, sluggishness, poor judgement, ostentation, selfishness, arrogance, self-disgust, ignorance, indiscipline, lack of originality and lack of enterprise and unsociability are grave defects and they unmake personality.

According to Woodworth, a personality trait is some particular quality of behaviour such as cheerfulness or self-reliance which characterises the individual. Personality is the product of these different traits, rather than a mere sum of separate qualities. It has some unity. For example a certain person is not merely cheerful and self-reliant; he is cheerfully self-reliant. Each individual has his own style or quality which is only roughly characterized by naming his traits. Judgment of personality will be better, if the judge observes the most revealing aspects of the individual, and if he has thorough experience in interpreting those aspects. By an interview a person can be judged in a short standardized conversational situation. Case study is a comprehensive analysis of a person based on all informaton about him, including his life history.

Personality Profile

The pairs of extremely contradictory qualities are called the "dimensions of personality." For example, honesty and dull-wittedness, persistence and waywardness, sociability and egotism ascendance and sub-missiveness, etc. A diagram can best indicate the personality profile of a person whose various traits of personality have been measured; it conveys an impression of the individual's high or low striding in general and of the evenness or unevenness of his personality.

Sociability is a tendency to behave sociably, to seek company and to participate eagerly in group activities. Ascendancy is to be masterful in any situation. A person, strong in both these traits, would naturally be a good leader. The individual's several traits conceived as tendencies or forces, interact and are combined in his behaviour. These measurements of personality are designed to locate individuals accurately in comparison with other individuals in various dimensions of personality. An integrated personality is one in which the several traits, interests, and desires are combined in an effective harmonious unity. This unity is more characteristics of mature adults than of children. Lack of integration of personality is clearly seen in certain mental disorders, and in extreme cases of double personality, multiple personality and "split personality." Measurement of personality is designed to locate an individual accurately in comparison with other individuals in various dimensions of personality. Rating scales provide a method for indicating intermediate degrees of a trait and permit averaging the judgements of two or more raters. Questionnaries are used to secure measures of traits such as trouble-finding ascendancy sociability, extroversion-introversion, and of interests and attitudes. If questionnaries are carefully constituted, they will be quite adequate, but their validity must be determined for each particular purpose. Situation tests are sample life situations in which certain traits can be observed best by any other test. Projective tests evoke imaginative responses which can be scored to reveal basic personality traits and patterns.

❐

PAPER-III

Development of Education System in India

Q. 1. Discuss the Education during Vedic Age.

Ans. The Vedic system of education very much emphasized the importance of discipline in the attainment of knowledge. This, however, was self discipline. In fact it was self-control which was realised by observance of rules of the Brahmacharya Ashram. The Parishads or the local academies were initiated by the king. Therefore, the scholars and the aspirants of knowledge gathered at the parishads with a perfect academic order. There was hardly any need for insisting upon rules and regulations as these were laid down by scriptures. No one questioned the scripture's command concerning discipline. Therefore, discipline was self-imposed as a part of self- culture.

Since Vedic age education had been put thus "The education is the source of knowledge which shows the real way in the various fields of life". This is approved by the Rigveda statement "If any one is greater than the other, that does not mean that he has extra bodily organs, but he is great because his intellect and mind have become enlightened and completed by real education." Education system of Vedic age aimed at proper and all round development of humanity.

Though Vedic education was carried on verbally, but there were two methods of Vedic education *(i)* in first the Rigvedic hymns were composed, and *(ii)* in second they were preserved. The first was based on the inward meditation, which enabled the formation of the hymns and second was based on outward learning method, which enabled the presentation of those hymns. The Rishis, who brought the hymns in spiritual beings were enlightened with the inner light and eternal knowledge. In Vedic age, they were recognised as 'Deva'. In Rigveda, Acharya Guru is called 'Agnipracheta' which means specially learned, Vishvavida, *i.e.* knowing everything (sarvagya), 'Satya-janma' i.e. one who knows every thing that is born, 'Vishwani Deva Yoyunani Vidvan' *i.e.* knowing everything, 'Dhiman Yanta' i.e. one who gives progress to intellect etc. These were the qualities attached to the 'Gurus'. Their boundless learning is proved with the fact that they composed the hymns and enabled the development of various knowledge and philosophies. It should also be noted that the symbols of Acharyas were Indra, Agni, etc.

In the beginning, Vedic hymns were the traditional heritage of the various families of the Rishis. Thus these hymns were verbally preserved in the families of Vamadeva, Attri, Bhardwaja, Vashishtha, etc.

Vedas occupy a very important place in the Indian life. The basis of Indian Culture lies in the Vedas, which are four in number—Rigveda, Samveda, Yajurveda and Atharvaveda. Scholars differ as regards the causes and time of the rise of Vedas. This remains still in mystery. Scholars are still trying to unravel this mystery. However, nobody doubts that they are the most ancient books of the world.

VEDIC EDUCATION

The Four Vedas. What are the Vedas? What have been their objectives? Why were they written? These questions are being debated since long. Many commentators have expressed their views on these issues. But the commentary written by *Sayan* is accepted as most authentic. He has explained the meaning of Veda in his book entitled Krishna Yajurveda. According to *Sayan* Veda in his book entitied Kri hna Yajurveda. According to *Sayan* Veda is a symbol of that thing through which one attains his objective and protects oneself against bad traits, undesirable things and behaviours.

Vedas have their own characteristic features. Through them we are able to know about the culture, civilization, life and philosophy of people in ancient India. Vedas symbolise the chief objective of human life which has been deliberance from this world of births and deaths. This objective has always been unchangeable. The Indian philosophy of life has never accepted life as purposeless. The deliberance of soul has been the chief objective of this philosophy of life from time immemorial. This fact is very clear from the study of the Rigveda.

Yajna (Sacred offering or religious sacrifice to Fire) occupied a very important place in human life during the Vedic period. In each and every sacred work some Yajna was performed. It will be wrong to regard Yajna as a tradition of ancient Indians. In fact, they were purposeful as experimental laboratories of great thinkers, teachers, philosophers, Rishis and Munis of the period. Through these Yajnas the learned saints used to realise the truth of human life. The great saints like Vashistha, Vishwamitra, Kanva, Narad, Atri and Gautam etc. realised the truth through their penances of which Yajnas were essential parts. The Rigveda, the chief of all the Vedas is the essence of their basic teachings and realizations.

Yajnas were not only experimental laboratories. They may be compared with those successful experiments through which man may obtain knowledge of even many practical spheres of life. The Yajnas were performed under the headship of Brahma.

The Curriculum of Vedic Education. Various subjects were incorporated in the curriculum of Vedic education. Grammar, rhetoric, astrology, logic, Nirukti (etymological interpretation of words) Manan the meanings of Vedic Mantras were developed and preserved were the main subjects. Vedang was the synonym of all these subjects taken together. The study of logic occupied a special place, because knowledge of any other subject was tested on its basis. Debates and discussions were organised for training in logic. Logic was regarded as the criterion for finding out truth and untruth. Logical discussion was usually organised between two scholars or two groups of learned persons. The main purpose of this discussion was to find out the truth and untruth and to make as assessment of the same.

Method of Teaching. Two methods of teaching were being practised during the Vedic period. The first method was Muakhik (Oral) and the second was based on Chintan (Thinking or reflection). In the oral method the students were to memories the Mantras (Vedic hymns) and Richayas (Verses of Rigveda) in order that they might not be changed wrongly and they might not be changed wrongly and they might remain preserved in their original forms. Under the oral methods those prosodies were thoroughly taught on which Richayas happened to be based. Special emphasis was laid on the various lines of a particular verse, their pronunciations and meanings. In the oral method correct pronunciation was specially emphasised. For this instruction in grammar and pronunciation was compulsory for all. The success of the oral method of the Vedic age lies in the fact that it could preserve the Richayas (Vedic verses) in their original forms down the ages.

Thinking method was another part of the teaching method. Through this an attempt was made to preserve the Veda Mantras (Vedic hymns) and Richayas (Vedic verses).

Manan was a higher method of teaching than thinking. Through Manan the meanings of Vedic Mantras were developed and preserved in one's own mind. This method was used to encourage the highly intelligent students. Just as in modern days teachers encourage intelligent students by guiding them to make research, similarly in ancient days 'Manan' (Reflection) was a method specially for highly intelligent students.

During the Vedic age the oral education was started in the family. The Rishis (Sage or ascetic) used to educate their children in the family through the oral method. They used to emphasise the learning of correct pronunciation. No new word was taught unless it was ascertained that the previously taught word was correctly learnt with correct pronunciation. The teachers were very particular about the correct learning of all vowels, consonants, rules of Sandhis (i.e., joining of words) and compound word (Samasas). Through the oral method one had to learn through hearing and the Veda Mantras (hymns) were learnt through hearing. Therefore, the Vedas were also called Shruti (that which is heard). It was after learning the correct pronunciation through hearing that the student was advised to follow the method (Chintan-Manan). From the above it is clear that there were two methods of teaching. The oral method meant for students of average intelligence and the thinking (Chintan-Manan) method was for those who were highly endowed.

Women Education. During the Vedic age women were given full status with men. They were honoured and respected in society. Therefore, women education was at its peak at the time. Women were regarded as a great source of power, peace, and knowledge for men. It was thought that without women, men could not progress. Therefore, girls during the Vedic period were taught like boys. No distinction was made between the two. The importance of women has been explained in the Vedas days 'Manan' (Reflection) was a method specially for highly intelligent who due to their deep scholarship and penance were regarded as Women-sages. Lopamudra, Apala, Ghosh and Vishwavara were some of the great women-sages who were held in high esteem.

Equal Right for Education to All. During the Vedic period educational right was given to all without any distinction of class and colour. There was no caste system then. According to one's capacity each one was free to receive education.

Q. 2. Explain the main features or characteristics of Vedic Education.

Ans. CHARACTERISTICS OF EDUCATION

Such terms as knowledge, awakening, humility, modesty, etc. are often used to characterise education in the Vedic period. Ancient texts refer to the uneducated person as an ignorant beast. Education is regarded as the source of light. The main features of Vedic education can be briefly enumerated as follows:

1. Knowledge, the Third Eye. Education is knowledge. It is man's third eye. This aphorism means that knowledge opens man's inner eye, flooding him with spiritual and divine light, which forms the provision for man's journey through life. Through education, the development of every aspect of human life becomes possible. Knowledge protects an individual like a mother, inspires him to follow the path of good conduct as a father does, and gives the pleasure that one's wife provides.

Education leads to the development of personality. The word 'Veda' originates from the root 'vid' which bears the meaning of knowledge. Sayana declares that the Veda is a means to the obtaining of the adorced that which is worthy of worship, as well as a means to the banishment of the underised, the evil. Knowledge of the four Vedas (Rigveda, Yajurveda, Samaveda, and Atharvaveda), along with the knowledge of Shruti, Smriti, etc., provided an individual, with new knowledge which broadened his inteclletual horizon.

2. Alms of Education. In the Vedic period, education had an idealistic form, in which the teachers (acharyas) laid stress upon worship of God, religiousness, spirituality, formation of character, development of personality, creation of an aptitude for the development of culture, nation and society. It is in this context that Dr. Altekar said that the objectives of education in ancient India were worship of God, a feeling for religion, formation of character, fulfilment of public and civic duties, an increase in social efficiency or skill, and the protection the propagation of national culture. These objectives and ideals took an individual along the path of spiritual development. In their fundamental form, these objectives and ideals were—

(i) **Emphasis upon Knowledge and Experience.** The Gurukuls laid emphasis upon knowledge and obtaining of experience. During the Vedic period, the practice of distributing degrees did not exist. Students exhibited the knowledge obtained through discourses and discussions conducted in a concourse of scholars.

(ii) **Spirituality.** In the Vedic period, Nature was regarded as divine and worshipped. During this period, many hypotheses concerning spirituality took birth. Knowledge came to be seen as the instrument of salvation. Fire sacrifices, fasting and taking of vows became a part of life. Education was given the objective of inculcating control over these aspects and learning right conduct based on them.

(iii) **Sublimation of Instincts.** Man is the virtual slave of the instinctive drives embedded in his psyche, and when he is obsessed by his senses, he often adopts the wrong path. The objective of education was to sublimate these instinctive tendencies, to turn the mind away from material knowledge, and centre it upon the spiritual world, thus establishing control over materialistic and base tendencies.

(iv) **Fulfilment of Duty.** Great importance was attached to developing such qualities as discipline, obedience, performance of hostly duties, rendering help to others, fulfilment of social responsibilities, etc. Through such education social skills were developed in the students. In addition, education was also provided for earning a livelihood, and for this, one or more skills were taught. Dr.

Mukerjee says that this education was not exclusively theortical or literary. It was related to one or the other manual skill.

(v) **Growth of Character and Personality.** The objective of education was the formation of character and personality of children. It was achieved through an appropriate environment, lessons on right conduct, and teachings based on the life, character and ideals of great persons. Education aimed at developing the virtues of self-control, self-respect, love, cooperation, sympathy, etc. in the students.

3. The Method of Education. During the Vedic period, the Gurukul method prevailed, in which the student lived in the house of the Guru, instead of living with his parents. Along with his colleagues, he led a celibate life and obtained education in the house of the Guru. Initially, in the Vedic period, it was the teacher who occupied the primary place, but in the later period, it was the student who occupied the central place in education, the process of education passed through the three stages of comprehension, meditation, memory and nidhi-dhyaasana. The Gurukuls were the centres of education, in which education was imparted only by individuals of character and ability. The student remained with his Guru for 12 years. There were parishads or committees to satisfy the student's thirst for knowledge. Congresses of scholars were also organised from time to time. In these, awards were also given to prominent scholars.

4. The 'Upnayana' Ritual. The word 'Upnayana' means to take close to, or to bring in touch with. A ceremony called the Uphayana ceremony was performed before the child was taken to his teacher. This ceremony was performed at the ages of 8, 11 and 12 for the brahmins, kshatriyas and vaishyas, respectively. The ceremony signalled the childs's transition from infancy to childhood, and his initiation into educational life. In this context, the term 'Upnayana' means putting the student in touch with his teacher. With the passage of time, the ceremony came to be confined to the brahmin class only.

5. Celibacy or Brahmacharya. Every student was required to observe celibacy in his specific path of life. Purity of conduct was regarded as of supreme importance. Only the unmarried could become students in a Gurukul. On entering student life, the student was made to wear a special girdle called a 'makhla'. Its quality depended on the caste of the student. Brahmins wore a girdle of moonj grass, the kshatriyas of string gut-taanta-and the vaishyas a girdle made of wool. The clothes worn by them were also accordingly of silk, wool, etc. The students were not allowed to make use of fragrant, cosometic or intoxicating things.

6. Alms System. The student had to bear the responsibility of feeding both himself and his teacher, this was done through begging for alms, which was not considered bad, since every domestic knew that his own son must be begging for alms in the same way at some other place. The reason behind the introduction of such a practice was that accepting alms induces humility. The student realised that both education and subsequent earning of livelihood were made possible for him only through society's service and its sympathy. For the poor students, begging for alms was compulsory and unavoidable, but even among the prosperous, it was a generally accepted practice.

7. Service of the Teacher. Every student was required, while residing in the Gurukul, to serve his teacher compulsorily. Any violation of the Guru's instructions was regarded as a sin, and subject to stern punishment. The student's duties included obtaining such daily necessities as water, a twig for brushing the teeth, etc., for his guru. The teachers also ensured that the students should not be distracted from their studies while performing such duties. During the vacations in which the student returned home he was not required to perform any service for the teacher.

The work of teaching began early in the morning. After performing their ablutions, students participated in some religious rituals, such as havans. Subsequently, they were put to the task of studying. In the afternoon, after partaking of lunch, the students returned to their studies. At sunset, some more religious rituals were performed. They denoted the end of the day's routine.

8. Practicality. The education of that period encompassed the necessary activities of life. Students were given education about animal-husbandry, agriculture and other professions. In addition education in medicine was also imparted. According to Dr. Alteker, the purpose of education was not to provide general knowledge about a variety of subjects, but to produce specialists of the best kind in various spheres.

9. Education for the Individual. In the Vedic period, every teacher devoted himself to the integral development of each student. He aimed at the physical and intellectual development of his wards. The maximum attention was devoted to the individual development of every student, but there was no provision for the education of the incapable and the handicapped, especially those who were lacking in mental and moral qualities or were known for moral turpitude.

10. Duration of Education. In the house of the teacher, the student was required to obtain education upto the age of 24, after which he was expected to enter domestic life. Students were divided into three categories:

(a) Those obtaining education upto the age of 24—Vasu.

(b) Those obtaining education upto the age of 36—Rudra.

(c) Those obtaining education upto the age of 48—Aaditya.

11. Curriculum. Although the education of this period was dominated by the study of Vedic literature, historical study, stories of heroic lives and discourses on the Puranas also formed a part of the syllabus. Students had necessarily to obtain knowledge of metrics. Arithmetic was supplemented by a knowledge of geometry. Students were given knowledge of the four Vedas—Rigveda, Yajurveda, Samaveda and Atharvaveda. The syllabus took with in its compass such subjects as spiritual as well as meterialistic knowledge, Vedas, Vedic grammar, arithmetic, knowledge of gods, knowledge of the absolute, knowledge of ghosts, astronomy, logic, philosophy, ethics, conduct, etc. The richness of the syllabus was responsible for the creation of Brahman literature in this period.

The foundation of the education imparted in this ancient period was inherent tendency or aptitude (abhivrati). It is written in the Atharvaveda "O Lord Indra! fill us with that ability which a father imparts to his son." It is also stated in the Sabra Bhashya, "How a child learns is apparent from the fact that the child of a Brahmin learns the vedic aphorisms while still at home. The imprint of these aphorisms upon his mind is indelible." Along with education, the performance of certain rituals was also regarded as essential. It was after these rituals that the child embarked upon a study of the subjects of his choice, though he was also required to study some others subjects. In this connection Sanat Kumar inquired of Naarad what he had studied. Naarad replied, "I have read the Rigveda, Yajurveda, Samaveda, Atharvaveda, the fifth Ved, history, the Puranas. I also know the Vedic grammar, the veda of the Vedas. I am also read in rules pertaining to service of one's father, arithmetic, the science of time, knowledge of gods, the absolute, ghosts, mertrics, etymology, astronomy, knowledge of snakes and 'devas', dance, music-recreation and creation of fragrance."

Q. 3. Explain the various aspects of education during the later Vedic Age and its objectives.

Ans. The Vedic period education ends near about 1400 B.C. After that Post-Vedic period education starts. This period regarded as of 800 years' duration. Hence, it ends at 600 B.C. The Post-Vedic period is also called as the Brahman or Upanishadic period. The period comes between the end of the Vedic period and beginning of the Jain and Bauddha religions. The basic aim of education during the Post-Vedic period has been the same as during the Vedic age. In both the periods the aim has been the salvation of the soul, but the method for attaining this goal has been different between the two periods. During the Vedic period the student used to attain the objective of education though penance while living with the Acharya (teacher) as a member of his family. During the Post-Vedic period Yajna replaced the penance and a number of procedures were prescribed for the same. During the Vedic period the penance was trovert, but during the post-Vedic age it became extrovert. Consequently, alongwith education importance of Yajnas increased. This led to the necessity of able priests for assisting in the perfomance of Yajnas. For this purpose four types of priests came in the forefront. They were known as Brahma, Udgata, Hota and Adhvarya.

OBJECTIVES OF THE POST-VEDIC EDUCATION

To attain salvation by realising the truth has been the aim of education, during this period. Only that education was regarded true which helped one to realise this supreme truth. According to the Upanishads 'truth' alone is the knowledge and the other worldly knowledge is untruth. The worldly knowledge was regarded as ignorance. Upanishads maintain that one cannot attain salvation through worldly knowledge because through this one becomes involved in illusion (Maya).

Upanayan Sanskar. Upanayan Sanskar was considered important both in the Vedic and Post-Vedic periods. This is evident at several piaces in the Rigveda. But different values were adhered to in the two periods. It was not necessary during the Vedic period to have the Upanayan ceremony before starting education. But during the Post-Vedic period Upanayan ceremony was considered necessary for starting education.

The word 'Upanayan' means to come near. In the context of education this word signifies that the student should come near the teacher for receiving education. The Upanayan ceremony became so important during the Post-Vedic period that it was usually regarded as second birth of the individual. For the Brahmans this became very important. Brahmans began to be called as Dvij (the twice born or born again). It was after the Upanayan that a Brahman boy could be called a Dvij.

Two births signify the worldly and the spiritual births. On the Upanayan occasion the Guru (preceptor) used to give him his Mantra (Advice). His spiritual life used to begin from this point. That is, from this day his education was started which ultimately led to his spiritual development in due course of time. The Upanayan ceremony is still in vogue in certain religious groups in the world, though in different forms.

CURRICULUM DURING THE POST-VEDIC PERIOD

During this period the curriculum included more subjects than during the Vedic age. Veda mantras (Vedic hymns and verses) were principally taught in the Vedic period. During the Post-Vedic period various types of literatures were produced pertaining to the different Vedas. In addition to religious subjects many worldly subjects were also included in the curriculum. This may be verified in the conversation between Narrad and Sanat Kuman which is incorporated in the Chhandogya Upanishad. During the Post-Vedic period the curriculum consisted of Vedas, History, Puranas, Grammar, Mathematics, Brahma-Vidya, Nirukti (etymological interpretation of words), astronomy, dance, music, etc., etc.

THE IMPORTANT PLACE OF THE TEACHER

During this period the teacher (Guru) enjoyed a predominant place not only in his Gurukul (seat of learning) but in the entire society. He was regarded as a great guide for all. To his pupils he showered all love and affection and used to teach them whatever he knew, but before doing this he always tested the deservingness of a particular pupil. The pupils were free to discuss points freely with the Guru. We find many examples of free discussion between the teacher and his taught. We may cite here an example from Brahma and his son Bhrigu. Brahma gave the Brahma-gyan, i.e., the knowledge of the ultimate or God in an outline form and advised him to perceive the same through thinking (Manan) and meditation. Bhrigu accepted this advice and realised God (Brahma) on the basis of the same.

In addition to the above three methods we find a mention of another method—Question-Answer System in the Upanishad literature. In fact, the entire Upanished literature is on the question-answer system. We do not find its practice in the Rigvedic period. Through this system difficult and abstract ideas were made simple. The terse-spiritual elements were explained through this system. Examples, stories and help of certain biographies were also taken in the system for elucidating certain points. This question-answer method was also successfully used by Socrates in Greece to explain abstract ideas.

DAILY ROUTINE OF STUDENTS

During the Post-Vedic period the Ashramas (Schools) were generally organised and run by Guru (preceptors). It was compulsory to adhere to laid down rules of discipline and conduct. No distinction was made between students in this respect. Everyone was required to observe celibacy. Rules of conduct were enforced keeping in view the physical, mental and moral development of students. Strict adherence to rules of conduct and discipline was an inseparable aspect of education in those days.

(a) Practical Education. Practical education consisted of three parts : 1. to beg alms, 2. to prepare fire for the Yajna-kund, and 3. to look after the animals and other fellow-beings of the Ashrama (School). Besides, the students were also expected to do some agricultural work.

There were varying aims of all these three aspects of practical education. Begging of alms was meant to teach politeness. Preparing of fire for the Yajna-kund signified mental development of students. Rearing up Ashrama animals and doing agricultural work were meant to make the students self-dependent.

(b) Mental Development. Hearing, thinking and meditation were the three parts of mental education. For full mental development all these three aspects were considered necessary. Thinking over the heard things and perception through meditation were the accepted methods of mental development. This is true even today.

(c) Moral Education. Leading a disciplined and controlled life is the real basis of moral education. Moral education affects the conduct of the individual. Only oral instruction cannot improve one's conduct. Therefore, observance of celibacy was considered necessary for good conduct.

DURATION OF EDUCATION

Duration of education during the Post-Vedic period was almost the same as in the Vedic age. This duration was of about twelve years, although the number of subjects of study were increased. However, there was no uniform rule for the duration of education. We find examples in which students continued to stay longer than twelve years for keeping the fire of the Yajna or looking after the animals and inmates of the Ashrama. Satyakam Jawal may be cited as an example in this respect. In the literatures of this period we find cases of many students who stayed in the Ashrama for more than thirty years.

THE TEACHER-TAUGHT RELATIONSHIP

During the Post-Vedic period teacher-taught relationship was of the ideal nature. The teacher was the protector of the student in all circumstances. He was fully respected by the student. He occupied a more dignified place than the father. The student was just like a son for the teacher who constently thought and endeavoured for his development. To render service to the teacher was the sacred duty of the student. The student was always ready to execute any command of the teacher with all humility. During this period especial attention was paid to the analysis of the essential truth. However, Yajnas still occupied a prominent place in the Ashrama. Rituals were attracted less importance, but the great significance of Yajna was still maintained.

THE TEACHER'S PLACE IN THE ANCIENT INDIAN SOCIETY

In the ancient Indian society the teacher always enjoyed a dignified place. During the Vedic and Post-Vedic periods the teacher's place was second to that of God only. He was more respected than the king in society. The Guru-Ashrama was known as the Gurukul (the family of the teacher) and the Guru was regarded as a Rishi (Sage) or Acharya (the one who practises what he professes). The Guru was given this significant place, because without him it was impossible to attain knowledge. The Guru was the guide and could help anyone to carve out his course of action. He used to bring light wherever there was darkness. Thus the people always felt his necessity whenever there was a difficulty in solving any issue or problem.

During the Upanishadic period as well, when self-study was considered as dignified the place of Guru in society remained intact. It was believed that no knowledge could come without the assistance from the Guru. In other words, it was believed that the attainment of salvation was not possible without the help of the Guru.

RESTRICTION ON TEACHERS

The teacher was expected to lead a life of penance free of worldly things. He, too, was required to follow all the rules of strict discipline, thinking and meditation which were prescribed for the students. We find many references to such a position in the Maitrayan Upanishad. After the demise of the Guru even one of his disciples could succeed him if his son was not considered worthy of the same.

SUPREME KNOWLEDGE

It was compulsory for the students to have full faith in the teacher. Only students were considered as deserving of attaining real knowledge of supreme truth who had full faith in the teacher. So the student was always in search of a real Guru for attaining real knowledge and the Guru wanted to find out a really deserving student who he could give all that he knew.

Convocation Address

After receiving education for twelve years students used to assemble near their teacher (Acharya) for blessings before going home. The Acharya on this occasion used to give some places of advice for happy and smooth running of their future life. The teacher used to tell them how to lead a life of householder (Grihastha), how to take care of the society and the nation and how to serve the humanity as a whole. The teacher used to tell all these in a ceremony which was known as Samavartan Samaroha like the modern convocation address.

Women's Education

Many changes were introduced in women education during the Post-Vedic period. This led to the fall of women education. During the Vedic age the women enjoyed equal educational rights. During the Post-Vedic period they were deprived of the social and religious rights. They were not allowed to participate in social functions. Now they did not enjoy the same status as before. Thus the path of their social and mental development was blocked. Ultimately the position of women in society fell down so low that the birth of a girl was regarded as a curse on the family.

But an upward trend again appeared in the status of women during the Upanishadic period. Now they were given social and educational rights again. Once again they were given equal status with men and many women bacame as learned as men. Many women became Acharya (Principal teacher-Guru) in Ashramas. The name of Gargi may be cited as an example.

EDUCATION AND THE VARNA SYSTEM OF SOCIETY

The Varna system in the Vedic age was based on one's work or duty (Karma). Members of a family used to engage themselves in different types of work (profession) and their work decided their varna. During the Vedic period one could choose a particular profession as he liked and accordingly his Varna was determined. But during the Post-Vedic period Varna came to be determined by birth. Consequently, the whole society was divided into four Varnas—Brahman, Kshatriya, Vaishya and Shudra.

Out of these four Varnas, the Brahmans occupied the supreme position and enjoyed more rights. Kshatriyas resented this superiority and a clash ensued between the two. Kshatriya were the winners in the clash and the administrative powers came into their hands. Gradually they established their kingdoms and principalities. Thus in the Varna system the Brahmans and the Kshatriyas became predominant. The Vaishyas and Shudras came into the lower groups. In this hierarchy Shudras were kept at the lowest order of society. In course of time the condition of Shudras fell down further and they came to be regarded as untouchables and they were denied all social and religious rights. Vaishyas remained superior to Shudras and they divided themselves into professional groups such as—goldsmith, blacksmith, potter, fowler, milkman and sweet-seller etc., etc.

However, the position of Varnas during the Post-Vedic period had not degenerated so much as it is found today. Than, its was possible to change one's Varna. One could marry a girl from a different Varna. The Vaishyas were permitted in the Rajya Surya Yajna upto some extent. Then, Brahmans also did not control the Yajnas. The marriages of Chyavan Rishi and king Shantanu and the religious rites performed by Vishwamitra (A Kshatriya) and other Kshatriyas bear a testimony to the above.

The Post-Vedic literature does not contain much about the education of Vaishyas and Shudras. Agriculture was the main occupation of Vaishyas during this period.

Shudras were given education by Brahmans. But the number of educated Shudras fell down day by day. According to Shatpaths, fisherman, snake-charmers and other alike professionals were some of the other students of Brahmans. Shudras were mostly engaged in manual labour in agricultural fields, grazing cattle and pottery. Some of them knew music and dance as well as we find even today.

Q. 4. Give a brief analysis of Vedic Education.

Ans. An analysis of the achievements of education in this ancient period indicates that the aim of education was to make the individual a useful and productive member of society. The educational achievements of this age were as follows:

1. Education emphasised the development of spirituality. The ashram system was adopted for paying of the individual's

debts towards the gods, his forefathers, his teacher and society.

2. The minds of the parents were first prepared to instill in them a desire for the education of their children. It has been said that those parents are the enemy of the child who do not teach their children.
3. Great attention was paid to the development of the child's character. Teachers laid stress on the integral development of the individual's personality.
4. Social skill was evolved through training in the fulfilment of duties.
5. Efforts were made for the preservation and propagation of the national culture.
6. While living in the Gurukul, the child imbibed education in a favourable environment.
7. A student was compelled to obey the ideals of the Gurukul. He had to shoulder the burden of existence through begging for alms. This practice developed humility and tolerance in the student.
8. Education was free. Its expenses were borne by the society and the king.
9. In developing the student's character, attention was paid to his nature, early experiences and impression, upbringing and circumstances.
10. Self-study (swaadhyaya) was considered more important.
11. The examination was oral one. The student was required to give oral answers in a congregation of scholars. If he satisfied them, he was given a degree or title. The consensus of the scholars' opinions was essential for obtaining such a title.
12. The medium of education was divine pronouncement, and the period of education, according to caste, was 48, 36, 24 and 12 years.
13. During this period, vocational education was also in vogue. Military science, agriculture, animal husbandry, veterinary

science, medicine, etc., were among the subjects taught. Chemistry was also taught. Arts and handicrafts were highly respected. Education in commerce was very popular.

Dr. A.S. Altekar says: Infusion of piety and religiousness, formation of character, development of personality, inculcation of civic and social duties, promotion of social efficiency and preservation and spread of national culture may be described as the main aims and ideals of ancient Indian education. The basic tenet of the ancient educational tradition was the paying of the social debt. Teachers took up this profession to pay off their debt to society. They enjoyed the highest social status.

Teachers should imitate their ancient forerunners, the gurus of old. They should treat their students as their own children and pay attention to their development. They should also maintain the highest standards in their own conduct because students are profoundly influenced by their teacher's conduct. Undoubtedly, education has undergone various changes because of changed priorities and beliefs. Now, we have the university system of education in which the hours of teaching are fixed and students are required to pay fees. But students' hostels remind us of the Gurukuls of ancient days. However, it is not these differences but the fact that the teacher of today is no longer respected, which catches our attention. In the past, the teacher was placed on a pedestal and revered. Hence, now just as the teachers should mould their own conduct, the students, too, should respect their teachers as they respect their own parents.

Thus, the propagation and spread of education should be in accordance with the individual's abilities. It is only then that the real form of education will actually blossom forth and demonstrate its real potential. Dr. Altekar has argued that from the Vedic period to the present age, the basic tenet of Indian education has been the view that education is Light. It is that source which gives us the truest guidance in the various spheres of life.

Q. 5. Explain the Buddhist System of Education.

Ans. BUDDHIST SYSTEM OF EDUCATION

The history of education in Buddha period is interrelated with the history of monasteries and 'Vihars' because there were no independent educational institutions or centres, other than those religious centres. Only monks and shramanas were authorised to impart education to the people. Thus, the monasteries and 'Vihars' took the place of sacrificial altars and as a result, these places became the centres of cultural life. Thus, the methods of these monasteries and 'Vihars' were the educational methods of that time. Rules and regulations of Buddhist monasteries and 'Vihars' were not framed by Lord Buddha. They had been taken from Hinduism and the various sects of Sadhus and nuns so they resembled 'vedic' systems.

Rules of Admission. Admissions into Buddhist monasteries were based more or less on the rules and regulations observed by Gurukula as in Vedic period. Like the students of 'Vedic' period, here also the students had to present themselves before the teacher to ask for the admission. Like the 'Upanayan', 'Pabbaja or pravrajya' is to go out. The boys went out of their families and joined the monasteries. Every one had the opportunity to undergo 'Pabbaja' and become a 'Buddhist' monk. After admission into 'Sangh' they could remain a monk. They had to change the former caste, dress, character, etc. Though theoretically, all the castes were allowed to get admitted into the monastery but practically and mostly the people of higher classes were admitted there. However, it is also true that some of the monks were derived from the lower castes. At the time of entering into the 'Sangh' the disciple must have attained the age of 8 years and during this period the new monk made his preparation for the sangh-life. Afterwards at the age of 20 years, he accepted 'Upsampada' and became full-fledged member of the 'Sangh'.

The System of Pabbaja. At 8 years of age, one could go to any 'Vihar' or 'Sangh' according to his own will. With head shaved and a yellow cloth in hand he went to the principal monk and requested him for admission in 'Sangh'. He thus surrendered himself fully. The monk caused him to put the yellow clothes on and surrendered to the three words of shelter in a loud voice—

I go into the shelter of Buddha.

I seek the shelter of Dharma.

I enter the shelter of Sangh.

After taking the above three vows, one became entitled to admission. No one could get admission into the 'Sangh' without the consent of his parents. Patients of infectious diseases like Leprosy. T.B., Eczema, etc. and Government servants, slaves and soldiers were not allowed to be admitted into 'Sanghs'. However, there was no discrimination of any kind on the basis of caste or creed.

Rules for the Students. Now the admitted student was called "Samner". He had to follow the following rules—

1. Not to kill any living being.
2. Not to accept anything given to him.
3. Live free from the impurity of character.
4. Not to tell a lie.
5. Not to use any intoxicating thing.
6. Not to take any interest in music, dance, playshow, etc.
7. Not to take food at improper time.
8. Not to speak ill of any body.
9. Not to use luxurious and scented things.
10. Not to accept the gifts of gold or silver, etc.

The ten rules were essentially observed by the new monk. The 'Upajsata' i.e., the teacher took all responsibilities up to the age of 20 years when he became mature and capable for accepting 'Upsampada'. For the teacher, he was 'Sadvi Biharak'. Lord Buddha himself taught that teacher should recognise his taught (Sadvi Biharak) as his son and the taught (Sadvi Biharak) should recognise the teacher (Upajsaya) as his own father.

Upasampada. After completing the education for twelve years, the 'Monk' had to undergo the 'Upasampada' ritual at the age of 20 years and then he became the permanent member of the 'Sangh'. There is also evidence that only such monks who had enough of spiritual knowledge were taken in sangh. They were directly given 'Upsampada'. Their 'Pabbaja' and 'Upsampada' both the rituals were performed simultaneously.

The method of performing 'Upsampada' was slightly different from 'Pabbaja'. It was similar to Vedic 'Samavartan' ritual with some difference. After 'Samavartan' the Brahamchari entered into family life but after 'Upsampada' he became a full-fledged monk, having no concern with family life. While Pabbaja was a ritual for a limited period, 'Upsampada' was permanent. It was for the whole life. Celibacy or chastity was considered essential for Brahmanic education. While among Hindus those observing celibacy for the whole life were; in 'Buddhistic' education it was a common feature. In this respect, Buddhistic education was more austere than Brahmanic education.

At the time of 'Pabbaja' the new monk of 8 years would go to the teacher and say with folded hands, "You are my teacher (Guru)". Thus, their relationship was established. The 'Upsampada' was performed before the entire 'Sangh'. Therefore, 'Upsampada' was given unanimously or on the decision of the majority.

Restrictions on Admission. In 'Buddhist' education also, like 'Vedic' education, the eligibility and the competence of the entrant was taken into account. A candidate could not be admitted into 'Sangh' in the following conditions:

1. Without the permission of his parents.
2. Patient of any infections or serious disease.
3. Convict of any serious moral sin.
4. Under any legal responsibility and who was not free from legal bondage.
5. Not found generous and laborious during the probation period, which sometimes was four or five days.

Thus Buddhist sanghs did not intend to destroy the family system. No one was admitted into 'Sangh' without the due permission of his parents. Similarly those who wanted to get rid of their social, moral and economic obligations were not admitted. Moreover, only those were allowed admittance who were healthy both mentally and bodily. Hence Buddhism spread rapidly and in an organised manner, in so many countries of the world.

The Qualifications of the Teacher. In Buddhist educational system much stress was laid on the efficiency of the teachers. This has been described as follows:

(a) ***High Moral Order.*** The teacher himself, must have spent at least ten years as monk. He must have the purity of character, purity of thoughts and generosity, etc.

(b) ***High Mental Order.*** Essentially the teachers was expected to be of a high mental order, so that he might teach his disciple the religion and nobleness and he may also successfully combat the wrong religious notions.

Duties of the Teacher. In Buddhist system of education, the teacher was responsible for the proper education and up-keep of the disciple. He had to fulfil the needs of the disciple during the education period. He had to treat them affectionately. He had to supply his disciple with all the necessary materials. He was responsible for their physical and mental development. At the time of sickness he would attend to the treatment and care of his students. The teacher taught them through question-answer, explanation and such other methods, so that the student might gain full knowledge and realise "Nirvan."

Daily Routine of the Disciple. Regular service of the 'Guru' (teacher), was essential in the Buddhist system. In morning the student would arrange for water, duetonic, etc. for the teacher. He would also look after his meal. He would cook the food, feed the teacher and clean the utensils. He would go out for alms with the teacher. After bath the students would get ready for the education. The teacher would impart education according to the system of the day.

Thus the disciple had to serve the teacher and keep the place tidy. His daily routine depended on the orders of the teacher. He was not bound to obey anyone else except his teacher. He could not take any service from any other person. nor could he go any where without the permission of the teacher. Thus the disciples used to live under the disciplinary control of their teacher.

Teacher-Taught Relationship. In Buddhist period like 'Vedic' period the relation of the teachers and the taught was close, affectionate, pure and good. Their duties were fixed and they used to fulfil them well.

The teachers used to lead a very simple life. They had limited needs. Being learned men of high character, knowing themselves and having self-control, they put the same ideals before their taughts. Huen Tsang wrote that the teachers living in 'Buddh Vihars' were great and eminent scholars. They put inspiring ideals before the students. They were paid very little for their personal expenditure. Prominent teachers of even a famous University like Nalanda, were often receiving for their expenses, money equal to three times being given to an ordinary student.

The duties of the disciple were settled. He was called the 'Sidh Biharak'. He gained knowledge while serving his teacher. The teacher took every care of his student. He did not let him suffer in any way. The disciples were also ready to serve teachers. If the disciple was aware of the mental troubles of the 'Guru' he used to amuse him by religious conversations and other means. While taking lessons, the disciples gained knowledge meekly. The teacher enlightened the inner sense of the students through different methods such as explanation, question-answer, lecture, etc. If the disciple had some doubts the teacher would try to remove those doubts. He could take help from other people of the 'Sangh' also if required.

In Buddhist period the position of 'Sangh' was above everything. If the teacher behaved against the honour of the sangh then the taught was duty bound to bring the defects of the teacher to the notice of the sangh. He would request for proper action against him. After the due penances, he could again request for his re-establishment. Thus the relation between teacher and the taught was based on high ideals in Buddhist period.

Q. 6. Explain the similarities and dissimilarities between the Vedic and Buddhist Educational System.

Ans. Similarities. There are various similarities and dissimilarities between the Vedic and the Buddhist educational systems. The following have been the similarities between the two:

1. The aims of education of the two systems have been same, *i.e.*, the salvation of the soul.
2. In both the periods education was imparted in a natural environment away from the noise and din of the city or village life.
3. The Brahmacharis (Students) of the Vedic periods and the Bhikshuks (monks) of the Buddhist period. *i.e.*, the students of two periods were required to lead a hard and disciplined life of similar nature.

4. In both the periods the students were required to observe non-violence.
5. The students of both periods used to go out daily for begging alms.
6. The students of both the periods were to follow similar rules of conduct.

Dissimilarities. The systems of education in the two periods had their own distinct features. We are hinting at these distinctly separate features below:

1. Education during the Vedic period was individualistic in the sense that the Brahmachari (i.e., student) received education by living as a member of the Guru's (Teacher's) family. Education in the Buddhist period was given in monasteries. Hence its form was collective.

2. Education given in a Buddhist monastery was more well organised, whereas education given in the Gurukul was not organised at all, as it was more dependent on the whim of the moment as the Guru thought appropriate.

3. In the Vedic period, the student lived in the family of his teacher (i.e., in the Gurukul). Therefore, the impact of the family life continued over him even after he left his parents' place. This feeling was licking in the students (Bhikshuks) of the monastery, as they lived away from their homes.

4. During the Vedic period the student (Brahmachari) was required to observe strict rules of disciplined life and had to undergo some type of penance. He was never allowed to enjoy worldly pleasures. But for the students (Bhikshuks) during the Buddhist period the rules of discipline were not so strict. They had not to undergo so much physical difficulties. They used to get their daily meals regularly and all arrangements for their clean clothing and peaceful living in the monastery were duly made.

5. Another difference between the Vedic and Buddhist educational systems may be seen in the two types of positions for the teacher in the two periods. In the Vedic system the teacher was almost autocratic, as his voice usually prevailed and every student (Brahmachari) looked towards him for guidance. In the Buddhist

system the whole pattern was democratic. In the Vedic system the teacher always enjoyed a superiority. It was almost difficult for a student to give arguments against his version on a particular thing, unless the teacher (Guru) himself inserted the student for the same. But in the Buddhist system after entering in monastery the student (the Bhikshuk) was always free to forward his views parallel to those of his teacher. In a monastery the difference between the teacher and the student was just that of knowledge.

Q. 7. Define the Levels of Education and Centres of Education during Buddhist Period.

Ans. Buddhist education came into existence in the 5th century B.C. Brahmans deprived the common people of their right to education, and hence the emergence of Buddhism granted the people the freedom to obtain education and to practice their religion themselves. Lord Buddha imparted to life a perfectly practicable form. Consequently, a practicable religion and a practical educational system became a variable to the common people.

It is undoubtedly true that though Buddhist education had an individual character, it was, in essence, based upon the educational system of the Vedic period. The Buddhists imparted education in Sanghas or collective groups. R.K. Mukerjee has pointed out that the Buddhist educational method is the method of Buddhist congregations (Sanghas). Just as the rituals of fire Sacrifice (yajnas) were the centres of culture in the Vedic period, the congregations of the Buddhist period were the centres of education and knowledge. In the Buddhist world, there was no opportunity for the individual to obtain education independently, away from his Sangha or congregation. Every kind of religious as well as worldly education was in the hands of Buddhist monks.

Levels of Education

During the Buddhist period, education had two levels—primary and higher levels.

1. Primary Level. the Jatakas stories indicate that during the Buddhist period, primary education took the form of worldly or materialistic education. Fa-Hien has also mentioned the existence of a system so general education. Children of six were admitted to this level of education.

2. Higher Level. Dr. Altekar opines that the Buddhists raised Indian's international stature considerably by the high level of education in their monastries since students from as far as Korea, Tibet, Java and other distant countries were attracted to them.

Centres of Education

During this period, some prominent centres of education sprang up. Their characteristics were their collective nature and their association with Buddhist Viharas or monasteries. There was no discrimination between students on any basis, some of these centres possessed an international reputation, proved by the fact that Chinese, Japanese, Tibetan and other sudents came there to receive education.

As already pointed out, there were many universities in India during the Buddhist period. It was a time when democratic feelings were evolving, and hence many famous educational centres came into existence. Wherever Buddhist monasteries or viharas were established, educational centres too emerged. Among the most notable universities to develop during this period were the universities at:

1. Taxila. Taxila was an important centre of education during the Buddhist period. It was then the capital of Gandhar. It had been founded by King Bharata after the name of his son Taxa. Being situated on the borders of this subcontinent, the kingdom was subject to frequent external aggressions. Because of this, the university in this kingdom developed on the basis of the family. Students started their education at the age of 16. The university provided education in numerous subjects, such as the three Vedas, Vedanta, Grammar, Ayurveda, the eighteen Sippas, military science, astrology, agriculture, commerce, treatment of snake-bite, (Sarpa-dansha chikitsa), magical charius (Tantra Vidya) etc.

2. Nalanda. The Nalanda university was situated in the State of Bihar, 40 miles south west of Patna and 7 miles north of Rajgraha. It was an internationally famed Buddhist centre of education. It became famous because it was the birth place of Sariputra the disciple of Lord Buddha. Emperor Ashok had a monastry constructed here. By the 4th century B.C. it had become a famous centre of education, and by the 7th century it became the foremost centre of education.

Kings of the Gupta dynasty took interest in the growth of the university. Buddhist monastries were constructed here by Kumar

Gupta, Narsingh Gupta, Baladitya, Buddha, Gupta, Vajra, and Harsha. Because of these monastries, the university continued to grow and expand. Its land was surrounded by a rampart at the entrance to which lived a profound scholar who administered an entrance test to the students desirous of joining the university. The university had eight large assembly halls and 300 rooms for study. It had been stated in Epigraphic India that the highest point of Viharavali kissed the clouds. The buildings of the university are a fine example of the engineering skill existing in that age. The remains of these buildings are sufficient to prove that the art of construction had reached a peak during this period. In addition to the buildings, the university had beautiful lakes, numbering 10, according to It-Sing. The university also had a massive nine-storied library which was divided into three parts, called Ratna Sagar, Ratnodadhi and Ratna Ranjaka.

Thirteen of its many monastries served as hostels for the students. In each room there were stone seats, space for keeping books and other facilities. The university possessed huge kitchens. 10,000 students lived and received free education at this institution. The university fulfilled all their needs of food, clothing, medical treatment, education, etc. 200 villages have been gifted to Nalanda. Apart from the income derived from them, the university also received sizable donations from the king and the people, who thus contributed their mite to education.

In Bihar, the Buddhist monks, teachers and students led a balanced, regulated and spiritualistic life, far removed from leisure and luxury. Students of this university carned great respect in many foreign countries. Students came from Java, Sumatra, Japan, China, Ceylon and other countries to receive education here. The staff of the university consisted of 1500 teachers. Huen Sang, in his travellouge, mentions the names of such renowned teachers as Chandrapal, Dharampal, Gunamati, Sthirmati, Prabhamitra, Gyanchandra, Sheelbhadra, etc.

Nalanda continued to serve, preserve and propagate Indian culture for 800 years. It was in the 12th century that this brilliant source of light was quenched by Bakhtiar Khilji.

3. Ballabhi. From 475 A.D. to 755 A.D., Ballabhi, in Kathiavar, was a famous centre of Buddhist education. Heun Sang visited

Ballabhi also in his travels. At that time, there were a hundred Sangaramas here. This university imparted education in politics, diplomacy, medicine and various other disciplines apart from religious education. Its students obtained senior positions in the courts of kings after completing their education. This university, too became the unfortunate victim of foreign invasion in the 12th century.

4. Odantpuri. Odantpuri had evolved as an educational centre before the Pal dynasty came into existence. The kings of this dynasty further developed this university. Its library was internationally known. 1000 monks received education here.

5. Mithila. Mithila had been a centre of Brahman education in ancient times, and when the Buddhist period came, it became an important centre of Buddhist education. It was here that a scholar named Jagdwara composed his renowned commentaries on such famous compositions as the Gita, Devi Mahatamaya, Meghdoot, Gita Govinda, Malati Madhava, etc. Vidyapati was born here. Apart from other subjects, Nyaya philosophy was also taught here. A student was deemed to have passed only after he had taken a difficult examination in Nyaya and Logic.

6. Vikramshila. Vikramshila was located on the banks of the Ganga in Magadha, Bihar. It was surrounded by a strong rampart. The teachers of this university were among the finest scholars of the day. Many important religious texts were translated into the Tibetan language at this university. Its administration was in the hands of a committee. Students were granted admission only after a test was administered to them at the gates. Among the famous scholars of that time who administered this test were Ratankar Shanti, Baghiswara Kirti, Naroha, Pargyakamnti, Ratna Vajra, and Gyana Srimitra. The university provided education in grammar, logic, philosophy, tantra, etc. It, too, was destroyed in the 12th century by Bakhtiar Khiji.

7. Nadia. Nadia was established at the junction of the Bhaghirathi and Jalangi rivers in the 11th century by the Sen kings of Bengal. Jayaleva's Gita Govinda and Shoolapani's Smriti-viveka were composed here. It was a centre of teaching in Nyaya and Logic. It retained its reputation even during the middle ages.

8. Jagdalla. Rampal had the town of Ramvati established on the banks of the Ganges in Bengal in the 11th century. He also had a monastry named Jagdalla established here. This soon emerged as a centre of Buddhist education.

Vibhutichandra, Dansheela, Shubhkara, and Mokshakara were some of the famous teachers of this university.

This period gave birth to distinctions of class and varna in the sphere of education, and it was in reaction to this that the Buddhist and Jain religions came into existence. Their system of education changed from the method of teaching by gurus to an institutional method.

Q. 8. Explain the education during Brahmanic age and its characteristics.

Or

Define the merits and demerits of Brahmanic age.

Ans. The educational structure in the Brahmanic Age was, to a very great extent, only a refined and developed form of Vedic education. However, during this age, various forms began to emerge in the institutions of education. Various institutions, such as shakha, charana, parishad, kul and gotra, began to emerge at the various levels of education. Besides the Upnishads, Aaranyaka, Brahman and other classical texts were created in this period. Famous ashramas or monasteries came to be established in the forests. It was in this period that the sutra literature was created, along with the development of the six systems of Indian philosophical thought—Samkhya, Yoga, Nyaya, Vaisheshika, Karma of Purva Mimansa, and Vedanta or Uttara Mimansa. A significant characteristic of this period is the determination of the syllabus according to the Caste and Ashrama system. However, the education of the Shudras and women suffered a decline.

The best mirror of any country or society is the literature, it produces. From the Vedic to the Brahman period, literature and additional literature continued to be created. Even in the Brahman period, education continued to be looked upon as the means to knowledge. It has the same objectives that Vedic education had. However, with the passage of time and a change in the needs of society, the importance attached to them underwent a change. In this period, the following objectives were ascribed to education:

1. Self-control
2. Development of character
3. Generation of sociability or social awareness
4. Integral development of personality
5. Propagation of purity
6. Preservation of knowledge and culture.

Education in this age continued to proceed on the foundations given to it during the Vedic period, but a certain rigidity and narrowness now marked its implementation. Education now aimed at equipping the student for the struggle for existence. After the upnayana or introduction ceremony, teachers imparted education to their students according to the latter's interests, tendencies and nature. Celibacy was rigidly oberved. Teachers paid full attention to the psychological make-up of their students while teaching.

Students lived in close contact with their teacher or guru in the Gurukul. But, restrictions had now been placed upon the receiving of education by Shudras. For social reasons, they were not considered fit to receive education. After Vedic education, there was a gradual increase in ritualism. The result was that shudras and women began to lose their place in the educational sphere. But, on the other hand, education became more comprehensive in this period, as it was closely associated with every aspect of life. Some of its general characteristics are:

1. Dominance of Religion. As in the Vedic period, education in the Brahman period also was dominated by religion. Students were given knowledge of religious activities. Numerous religious and cultural activities were organised so as to acquaint students with them.

2. Worldly and Other-worldly or Spiritual and Materialistic Education. During this period, education paid equal attention to spiritual as well as materialistic or worldly matters. Education comprehended the materialism of life.

3. Celibacy (Brahmcharya). Like the education in the Vedic period, education in this period also laid great emphasis upon celibacy. Students were expected to obey their teachers and indulge only in moral conduct.

4. Individualism. Because of the absence of collective education, the emphasis was upon the individual. Teachers paid attention to the personal development of individual students.

5. Physical Punishment. In the Brahman age, the practice of giving physical punishment to students was not prevalent. Such famous acharyas as Manu, Gautum, Vishnu opposed physical punishment because they considered it inhuman.

6. Method of Education. In the Vedic period, education was primarily oral. Students were made to memorise aphorisms and then elaborate them. But, by the advent of the Brahman age, the art of writing had developed, and so both oral and written education came into practice, though the emphasis was upon oral education. Bhojpatra, the bark of a tree, was used for writing. Teachers gave importance to purity in pronunciation. Education was conducted through discussion, answering of questions, removal of doubts, etc. Students were given continuous practice in the art of writing and for this they were required to copy manuscripts. Practical work was emphasized in such subjects as grammar, astrology, nyaya, medicine, etc. The students as well as the teachers themselves obtained informal education through the concourse of famed scholars.

7. Curriculum. In this age, too, primacy was given to the study of the Vedas. Among the subjects taught were grammar, arithmetic, geometry, astrology, economics, history, politics, agriculture, millitary science, nyaya philosophy, etc. A special feature of this period is that, as time progressed, two kinds of syllabi came to be prepared, one for the short-term and another for the long-term. In addition, clear and correct pronunciation of consonants and vowels was stressed. Students were also given knowledge of metrics and figures of speech. It was on this basis that learned commentaries on the Vedas came to be composed. The Pingal Shastra was composed for the teaching of matrics. Surgery had also developed by this time.

MERITS OF EDUCATION IN THE BRAHMAN PERIOD

Indian culture has developed through its system of education. This system was especially fruitful in propagating the ideas of love, truth, non-violence, religion, peace and world brotherhood. It also pointed out the path to salvation. It was also responsible for the creation and preservation of literature. F.E. Keay has expressed wonder at the fact that though divine texts were composed such a long time age, and that though it seemed impossible to preserve them intact, this was done, and is still being done today. The education of this period possessed the following features :

1. It paid the greatest attention to the child's physical and mental development.
2. It was conscious of the development of the child's character.
3. The gurukuls were situated at a distance from inhabited areas so as to prevent excessive contact between students and society.
4. In the teacher's house, there was an abundance of family feeling. Students did not suffer from the lack of any familial necessity.
5. The teachers imparted education without any discrimiation.

DEMERITS OF EDUCATION IN THE BRAHMAN AGE

Certain demerits stood, had crept into the educational system of the Brahman age. They were:

1. Dominance of Religion. Since education was dominated by religion, less importance was attached to material or worldly development. This dominance also led to an increase in an anarchic attitude towards religion among the students and prevented the growth of rational thought.

2. Emphasis upon Philosophy. Education during this period laid excessive stress upon the study of philosophy, since the purpose was to put the student onto the path to salvation through a study of philosophy. The result was the growth of an escapist attitude towards life.

3. Deprivation of the Shudras('s) Right to Education. During this period, the right to education became confined to the Brahmans, Kshatriyas and Vaishyas, because of the emergence of aristocracy. The Shudras were deprived of the right to education.

4. Faith in the Vedas. In this period, people came to have blined faith in the Vedas. They were convinced that only the Vedas were true. Consequently, the tendeney towards logical and rational thought was hampered.

5. Women Education. There is some evidence of education of women during the Vedic period, but during the Brahman age, this was neglected. In addition, women became the victims of many restraints.

6. Lack of Handicrafts. During this age, the caste system became characterised by rigidity and narrowmindedness. Those engaged in handicrafts came to be regarded as inferior. The consequence to this was that handicrafts gradually vanished from educational curriculum.

7. Absence of Synthesis. The education of this period was taking in synthesis. Instead, it laid emphasis upon profound scholarship in any one subject.

Q. 9. Discuss the salient features of Ancient Indian Universities with special reference to Nalanda University.

Ans. Seats of Ancient Indian Universities were either holy places or capitals of great kings because the private teachers began to congregate in these places on account of facilities they received for educating pupils. To the holy places like Banaras, Kanchi, Karnataka and Gangasagar pilrigims flocked in large numbers and made huge gifts to the teachers there. In the capitals kings and princes patronised them. Hence, there rose up centres of high learning at Kanauj, Mithila, Dhara, Kalyani and Tanjore. Certain kings provided villages to a set of Brahman teachers and colonised them.

These seats of learning were simply centres of education where lived many famous teachers and to which flocked students from all parts of the country. They did not possess colleges in the modern sense of the term nor university campuses. Nor were the teachers members of any one single institution like the professors in a modern university. Every teacher with his Pittiacharyas formed an institution. He admitted as many students as he liked. He taught them what they liked. Such was the form of the Taxila University, the most important seat of learning in Ancient India. It was founded by Bharata and named after his son Taksha.

Banaras was a seat of learning situated at a holy place. In the 7th century B.C., Banaras was the most important centre of Hindu learning. With the patronage of Ashoka, Sarnath in the outskirts of

Banaras became the seat of Buddhist learning. It did not organise any public institutions like the Nalanda University. In the 17th century A.D., Bernier says, "Banaras is a kind of University; but it has no colleges or regular classes as in our Universities but it looks like the school of the ancients, the masters being spread over the different parts of the town in private houses.

The universities and monasteries which belonged to the Buddhist order were Nalanda and Vikramshila. From the 10th century onwards, Hindu Temple colleges became prominent as seats of higher education. They were a natural reaction to the Buddhistic monastic universities. The Mathas of Acharyas continued the same tradition. Salotgi Temple College in Bijapur district in the 10th century A.D. was a centre of Vedic learning. Ennayiram Temple College in South Arcot was an educational institution of the modern type with 16 teachers on its staff teaching a predetermined curriculum. Other temple colleges were at Tirunukkudal and Tiruvorriyur, Malkapurram.

Nalanda University. Nalanda was the seat of Buddhist learning. It was built largely by Buddhist disciples, but Guptas, the orthodox Hindus also patronised it. The university had a plan of its own. Monastic buildings and stupas were arranged in a regular fashion round the central college which had 7 halls. It has 300 smaller rooms for lecturing work. The building were exceptionally high. The very name Nalanda has been derived from the word Na-alam-da insatiable in giving, implying that the university education in those days did not cram the mind with knowledge but created an insatiable thirst for it.

Rise and Fall. The date of its foundation is not known for certain. Though as a monastic seat it was founded long long ago, as a seat of learning it rose into prominence about 450 A.D. General Cunningham assigns the probable date of the founding of university from 425 to 625 A.D. The University began to decline during the 11th and 12th centuries when it was suppressed by Vikramshila and was finally destroyed by Muslim rulers in the beginning of the 13th century.

Student Body. Throughout these seven centuries of its existence Nalanda attracted students from all parts of India as well as from abroad. Students from China, Tibet, Bokhara and Korea came to Nalanda. For example, Fa-Hien, Yuan, Chwang, Itsing were Chinese and Hwni Lun, Hwuii Viah were Koreans. Budhdharma was from Bokhara. The standard of admission to the university was naturally very high. Watters says, "Of those from abroad who wished to enter the schools of discussion, the majority beaten by the difficulty or problems, withdrew: and those who were deeply versed in old and modern learning were admitted: only two or three out of ten succeeded."

Teachers. The standards of scholarship among the teachers were very high. They were not only famous for their piety, but were renowned for scholarship also. They were eminent for 'conspicuous talent, solid learning, great ability and illustrious virtues.' Saraha, the tutor of Nagarjun, Nagarjuna the founder of the school of Madhyamika Philosophy, Aryadeva the pupil of Nagarjuna, Arya Asanga and his younger brother Vasubhandu, Dharampala the famous logician and grammarian, and Silbhadra were some of the illustrious pundits of the University.

Administration. The university was controlled and administered well. At the head was the Abbot-Principal who was assisted by two councils, one academic and the other administrative. The chief Abbot was elected by the members of the Sangha on the basis of his scholarship, seniority and character. Local and provincial jealousies did not influence the election. The academic council regulated admissions, determined courses and assigned work to different teachers. The administrative council looked after general administration and finance. The officials of this council were in-charges of construction of buildings, and distribution of rations, superintendents of hostels, and revenue officers. The head (chancellor) in Hiuen Tsang's time was Silbhadra. In the middle of the 8th century A.D. Kamalshila was its head. Besides the Dwarpandit and the Abbot Principal there were two other important officers. The Karmadana was the sub-director of the university and the Stavira, the presiding priest.

Teaching Methods. The methods of teaching at the Nalanda University were tutorial as well as professional. Beal says, "They arrange every day about 100 pupils for preaching and the students attend these discourses without fail even for a minute." There was a close touch between students and professors. Itsing says, "I have always been very glad that I had the opportunity of acquiring knowledge from teacher personally." A great importance was laid on discussion and debate. "The brethren are often assembled for discussion to test intellectual capacity, to reject the worthless and to advance the intellect", says Watters, "the day is not sufficient for asking and answering profound questions. From morning till night they engage in discussion; the old and the young mutually help one another."

Library Facilities. Library facilities for self-study were abundant. A monastery without a library was like a castle without an armoury. From the Tibetan accounts mentioned by S. C. Vidyabhushan in Medieval School of Indian Logic we learn that Nalanda had a fine library situated in Dharmganj and was housed in three splendid buildings: Ratansagara, Ratnadadhi, Ratnarayaka. Ratnadadhi was nine-storied. Such spacious libraries met the needs of hundreds of teachers and thousands of students.

Subjects of Study. The curriculum at Nalanda was catholic; for example, the works of Hinayana and Mahayana schools of Buddhistic philosophy both were studied. It was not sectarian because it was not confined to Buddhism alone. Subjects like Hindu religion and philosophy were also taught there. Vedas, Vedanta and Sankhya philosophy were taught at the university with miscellaneous works. Subjects like grammar, logic, literature, astronomy and astrology, medicine which were of common interest were taught profusely.

Hostel Arrangements. Hostel arrangements were adequate. Satras were free-boarding hostels where students were supplied with necessaries out of the endowments to the university. Students were so abundantly supplied with clothes, food, bedding and medicine that they engaged themselves wholeheartedly in studies. For example, it is learnt that Hiuen Tsang received each day 120 fruits. 20 arecanuts, 20 nutmegs, an ounce of tack and peck of Mahasali rice. He was supplied with butter daily and other things that he needed.

The Crest Jewel of Buddhist Monasteries. Thus Nalanda had all the best qualities that a university should possess. It was an international educational centre when Europe was enveloped with darkness of ignorance and when even Arabs had no seats of learning. The hall-mark of the university was of such a great value that some persons usurped its name and, in going to and from, received honour in consequence.

Q. 10. Explain the main features of Muslim Education System.

Ans. Muslim education system was essentially religious in character. It was patronised by the Muslim rulers who held orthodox views regarding perpetuating Muslim faith in lands they invaded and settled. The educational institutions they founded became strongholds of Muslim orthodoxy. The sole aim of Muslim education became spread of Islam, perpetuation and preservation of Muslim culture.

Religious Orthodoxy. Spreading Islam was considered the most sacred duty of every Muslim citizen. The one, who disseminates and diffuses Islamic beliefs among the non-Muslims, vigorously, becomes Ghazi. Principles and beliefs of Islam could be best propagated through education. Thus convinced, the Muslim rulers and beneficiaries established Maktabs and Madarsahs where the study of Holy Quran became a prominent feature. These institutions were built near the Mosques where theological thinking could flourish to the maximum extent.

The Islamic laws, opinions, customs, and doctrines were subjects of study and all students were required to master them so that this knowledge could help them in bringing the non-Muslims under the fold of Islam. A spirit of religiousness was strongly imbibed among the Muslim youth so that he could serve the cause of propagating Islam hastily.

Royal Patronage. The Muslim sovereigns had a very keen interest in the education of their youths. So they founded schools, colleges, and libraries at places where they settled or brought under their rule. Stipends and scholarship were offered to the needy and deserving. Orphanages were raised to help the poor.

The Slave and Tughlak dynasties patronised education very much. They established Madarsahs (seats of higher learning) in their capitals. For example, Feroz Tughlak endowed thirty colleges and most famous of these was Madarsahi Feroz Shahi. It was a residential university established near Hauz-Khas. Professors and students were required to reside in the university and conduct researches at government expense. The ruler spent 36 lakh tankas every year. Lodis also did a great deal to serve the cause of Muslim education. But the greatest patrons were the Moghal emperors. The credit for organising school and university education on sounder lines goes to Akbar, the Great. Colleges at Agra and Fatehpur Sikri, in Gujarat and in other provinces were established on his initiative. Curricula were reconstructed and reformed. Hindus and Muslims were treated on equality basis.

Education Urbanised. The Muslim system of education was thus restricted not only to the concerned section of the society, but it did not spread outside the urban areas. It was round about the capitals where the Muslim people mostly lived and so it was in the cities or big towns that educational institutions flourished. No attention was paid by any Muslim rulers towards educating the masses that lived in the rural areas. By the end of the 15th century A.D. Muslims in India appeared a 'little more than an armed garrison in a foreign country.

Sectarianism. It was only in the days of Akbar that we have the state offering equal opporunities of education to all sections of the society. In all other sovereignties the education system was meant for the good of the Muslim people. Even when the doors of colleges were open to Hindus, they were not treated on equal footing. The Maktabs and Madarsahs were established to educate the Muslim youth in general—the youth that could help the rulers in governance and administration.

Secularism in Education. The object of Muslim education was attainment of worldly prosperity and social distinction. The education was therefore materialistic. The spiritualism of Ancient Brahminic education was just antithetic to Muslim system. Though highly religious, it was perfectly secular.

Stress on Persian as Medium of Instruction. Since Persian was the official language it was but natural that it should have been adopted was the medium of instruction in the schools and colleges. Even the non-Muslims tried to acquire mastery over it. With a view to entering government service, Hindus also favoured it. The eminent works of Sheikh Sadi, Gulistan, and Hafiz and other treatises of Muslim culture where studied and memorized. There were schools where Arabic, Urdu, and Hindi were taught but much attention was not paid to them by the Muslim rulers for their development. Arabic was studied as a compulsory subject only.

Maktab and Elementary Education. The word 'Maktab' has been derived from the Arabic work 'Rutub' which means 'he wrote'. Hence a place where writing was practised was known as maktab. This place become a sort of formal agency of education. It was generally situated near a mosque. Later on, reading and arithmetic also began to be taught there and thus a maktab became an elementary school.

The elementary education was given not only in Maktabs but in Dargahs and Khanquahas also. The very atmosphere of these elementary schools was religious and religious education was at the base of Muslim education. These schools were mostly single teacher schools. Maulvis were in charge of these schools. The education was free. The local community or the state financed the schools.

The admission to a Maktab was given to boys only. Girls were not permitted to go out due to Purdah system. However, Maktabs for imparting religious education were lodged in private houses in the town itself where elderly women taught them reading and writing. Holy Quran, Gulistan, Bostan, and books on morality were taught to them as they were taught by the Maulvis to their brothers.

Maktabs were open to Muslim boys only. Hindus were only allowed to send their sons there by a few kings, for example, Sikandar Lodi. But the treatment given to them was not good, so Hindus got elementary education in their own schools. The initiation ceremony, when a boy or girl was admitted to a maktab, took place when he or she was 4 years, 4 months, and 4 days old.

Madarsahs and Higher Education. The word Madarsah is derived from the Arabic word 'Dars' meaning a lecture. Madarsahs therefore were centres of learning where a scholar delivered lectures to the eager students. The teaching method at the Madarsah was oral. But students were encouraged to make self-studies in libraries established for that purpose.

A madarsah was an institution of higher learning equivalent to a modern college. A student after acquiring primary and secondary education in a Maktab proceeded to a Madarsah. Such seats of learning were scattered all over the country. Those at Agra, Jaunpur, Lucknow, Delhi, Lahore, Multan, Sialkot, Ajmer and Murshidabad were of great renown. To these, students flocked. Some of the seats of learning specialised in one particular branch of learning only. Others were established to teach literature, grammar, jurisprudence, logic, rhetoric, theology, metaphysics, law and medicine. Among those that specialised in learning in some special fields were the following Madarsahs : (a) Delhi School of Shah Waliullah specialising in Hadi (Traditions), (b) Farangimahal School at Lucknow specialising in jurisprudence, (c) Sialkot School in grammar, (d) Rampur School in medicine, and (e) Agra Madarsah in medicine.

Students to these seats of learning were admitted to become learned scholars in the special branches of learning. They were given a fixed daily allowance for their maintenance as we learn from the traditional Madarsahi Feroz Shahi. There was a close contact between the teacher and the taught. The teachers were required to reside in the college campus so that they could be available to the students at all hours. These colleges were financed by the state. Some noble personages also contributed to the maintenance of the madarsahs. The medium of instruction at all these colleges was Persian. Arabic was taught as a sacred language of the scriptures.

Female education in the Muslim period did not develop very much; yet there were some madarsahs for women. Miasuddin Khilji of Malwa had one such college at Saranspur which specialised in arts and crafts as subjects of study.

Initiation Ceremony. Just as we had Vidyarambha Sanskar or Aksharasrikarna which was an initiation ceremony at the commencement of primay education in the ancient Indian system, so we had Bismillahkhani or maktab ceremony for beginning the education of a Muslim boy. The age at which Vidyarambha Sanskar took place was generally five. Similarly, in the Muslim system the age was 4 years, 4 monts, and 4 days. It was performed on this day in case of Humayun.

The boy was dressed in the best clothes and was placed on a cushion before the members of his family. He was taught to pronounce the alphabet, the form of letters used for computation, the introductory part of the Holy Quoran, some verses from Chapter LV and the whole of the chapter LXXXVII. If the boy did not like to pronounce these, he was asked in pronounce Bismillah and with this his education was considered to have started. In the case of a girl student, a blessing known as Zafarshani was written for her on a coloured paper.

Discipline. Just as we had hard and strict rules and regulations governing the life of a student in the Gurukuls or in the Vihars, so we had very strict rules in maktabs and madarsahs. Pupils were generally well-behaved, morally strong and humble. Whenever a pupil was found breaking rules of conduct, he was punished adequately. The type and manner of imposing punishment was left to the discretion of the teacher. Sometimes students were inhumanly punished. The reason behind such a harsh treatment was not vangeance but correction and preservation of discipline among others. However, such punishment was not given to a Brahmachari or a Pabbajja.

The Teacher-Taught Relationship. In ancient India the teacher was treated by his student as father, king and God. He was to serve him like a son, suppliant and slave. No progress in knowledge was possible without serving the teacher. These traditions went on being observed. In the Muslim period also the student was always humble and polite to his teacher and served him whole-heartedly. The Maulavi always regarded the student as his son. He had a constant touch with him and thus influenced his personality development. There was "mutual reverence, confidence and communion of life."

Teaching Methods. In ancient India recitation and recapitulation were the two ways of leaning a material. Memorisation was resorted to. Learning in ancient times had to be at the tip of the tongue. In medieval times the student had to take recourse to rote learning. The child was expected to learn by rote Qalma and verses of Quran even though he did not understand them. Many of these things were above his understanding power. He was simply required to pronounce the verses correctly. The teacher in the Madarsahs used lecture method. Such, however, was not the case in ancient times when discussions and debates were adopted, as a rule, for acquiring learning.

Q. 11. Explain the merits and demerits of Muslim Education.

Ans. MERITS OF MUSLIM EDUCATION

1. Compulsory. Education was compulsory, specially for boys.

2. Co-ordination. There was proper co-ordination between religious values and material or worldly needs and well-being.

3. Character. Great stress was laid on character building.

4. Personal Touch. There was a personal touch between the teacher and the taught.

5. Incentives. There was arrangement for rewards and scholarships for meritorious and intelligent students. This provided an incentive to learning and education.

6. Literature. Under Muslim rulers, through educational system, a good deal of development of literature took place.

7. Curriculum. Curriculum included arrangement for the teaching of various subjects.

8. Practical. Great stress was laid on practical utility.

9. Free. The education during the Muslim rule was mostly free.

10. Writing of History. During this period, the tendency to write history was developed. This tendency was different from the tendency of the ancient India. It helped preservation of record.

11. Institutions. During this period, great attention was paid towards establishment of educational institutions. Prospersous people were encouraged to establish institutions.

12. Special Centres. There were centres of specialized education.

DEMERITS OF MUSLIM EDUCATION

1. Unsuitable. Unsuitability was characteristic of the institution of education.

2. Disbalance. Education of the Hindus was neglected. This brought about a disbalanced development of education.

3. Material. There was predominance of material considerations.

4. No Universal Education. There was no provision for universal education.

5. One-sided Curricula. There was too much emphasis on teaching Arabic and Persian. This led to neglect of other subjects.

6. Lack of Co-ordination. There was no co-ordination between reading and writing.

7. Lack of Psychological Basis. Muslim education lacked psychological incentives.

8. Evil Effects of Corporal Punishment.

9. Defective Curriculum. Curriculum was defective.

10. Indifference Towards Women Education.

11. Low Status of Teachers. The teacher-taught relationship was not ideal. The teacher did not occupy that position that he occupied during the Vedic period.

12. Wrong Methods of Teachings. Oral or verbal method of teaching did not help the consolidation of the knowledge.

13. One-sided Personality. In Muslim education there was no place for all-round development of the personality.

14. Lack of Individual Attention.

15. No Development of Reasoning. No encouragement to students to develop their power of reasoning.

Q. 12. Explain the background of Education during Muslim period, its characteristics, objectives and organisation.

Ans. With the emergence of Islam, the attention of Muslim kings turned towards India. Time was kind to them. It allowed them to settle themselves firmly in this country. After the Gulam, Khilji, Tuglak, Sayyed and Lodhi dynasties, Mogul kings established many educational institutions in India. This education, too, had its roots in religion. During this period, Indian art and culture came under the influence of Arab culture and civilization. It was only natural that the same political influence should also have made itself felt. In consequence, education too came under this influence. Islam had its origin between 570 A.D. and 632 A.D. Hazrat Mohammed collected his messages in the Holy Kuran, and this text came to be an instrument of social direction for the Muslim kings. During this period, these kings made arrangements for education in order to serve their own interests. Mohammed Gauri started his aggressions on India, but at the same time, he also had mosques and schools constructed in Ajmer to make arrangements for education in Islam and Muslim law.

His successor Kutubuddin also followed in his footsteps. The other rulers of his dynasty, Altamesh, Razia Begum, Nasiruddin, Balban and others also had mosques, maktabs and schools established with government aid.

Ferozshah Tuglak of the Tuglak dynasty made efforts for the propagation of education. One of the schools established by him in Delhi has been described as follows. The school was located in a large ground and a big building with massive towers. It was situated in a garden in which human skill harmonized with nature, thus creating an environment most suitable for contemplation and thought. Near the school was a lake, whose water shone like silver. The grand building of the school was reflected in its waters. It was an enchanting sight to see hundreds of students crossing the polished and soomth floors and congregating round their teachers. According to N.N. Law there were provisions for governmental aid and scholarships in these schools.

During the reign of Sikander Lodi (1489-1519), Indians, too, had begun to learn Persian (Pharsi). After obtaining knowledge of this laguage, they began to work in government departments. The Muslim rulers themselves felt the need for Hindu workers in the administrative sphere, and hence they made arrangements for the study of Indian languages. And, as a result of the contact between the Hindus and Muslims, Urdu, which was the spoken form of Persian mixed with Hindi, was evolved.

The Mughal rulers who followed the earlier Muslim rulers had relatively greater interest in education, and hence it was in this later period that education developed more adequately. Akbar authorised the translation of many important Indian texts, including the Mahabharata, the Ramayana, Atharvaveda and Lilawati, into Persian. Akbar's deep interest in education is high-lighted by Abul Fazal's comments in his famous work 'Aaiyene Akbari' to the effect that in every country, and especially in India, boys were kept in school for years where they were taught about consonants and vowels. Since they had to read numberous books, a large part of the boys' time was wasted. Emperor Akbar declared that each student should be taught to write the alphabet in various ways. Each student was required to learn the name of every letter (varna) within two days. Emphasis was laid upon imparting education in moral values, arithmetic, political arithmetic, agriculture, medicine, logic, and physical, mathematical and divine philosophy to every student.

Jehangir went so far as to enact a law that the property and wealth of any person dying without an heir would be utilized for the repair of schools and religious buildings. Shahjahan had a university established near the Jama Masjid. Auraugzeb did propagate Muslim education, but at the same time he destroyed Hindu schools and temples. He granted excessive facilities for Muslim students, but he accorded a low status to teachers.

After the collapse of the Mughal Empire, schools suffered a severe blow. Many such institutions closed down due to anarchy and lack of finances. According to Vakil and Natrajan—"It must be noted that while mosques, maktabs and madrassas sprang up with the spread of Mohammadan power and provided facilities for Islamic learning in different parts of the country, the Hindu system of education continued to prevail in pathashalas, maths and temples except where their work was disturbed or dislocated by Mohammadan inroads or invasions." One finds a lack of organisation in Muslim education.

In the Muslim period, education was founded on community basis. Hence, it is illogical to claim that the Muslim ruler sought to propagate education liberally. Whatever the extent to which they propagated education, it was motivated by their own objectives, selfish interests and ambitions.

Bernier, the famous French traveller who visited India during this period, observed that during the period which he had described, it was only natural to find deep and universal ignorance. Was it possible to establish suitably financially aided schools and colleges or other centres of education in India? Where would the organisers be found? And, even if they were found, from where would the students be obtained? He also observed the absence of individuals whose wealth was adequate for providing suitable aid to colleges. And, even if such individuals existed, he felt that no one had the courage to compel them to bring out their wealth for such an investment. He felt that even some individual did venture on such a foolish act, there was an absence of religious places, enterprises and offices with employment potential which could utilize the ability and science imparted to students, and thus serve as an inspiration for youth to be hopeful and to compete for future success.

CHARACTERISTICS OF MUSLIM EDUCATION

During the Muslim period, education developed so slowly that no notable characteristic of it ever emerged. Minor rulers had educational institutions established for the satisfaction of their interests. However, the following features can be noted:

1. Encouragement by the State. Muslim rulers took an interest in education, and so they provided aid to maktabs and madrassas. There were granted jagirs or landed property. Scholars were given places of eminence in the courts of kings. The rulers started giving aid to madrassas and maktabs being run in or along with mospues. Hence, their propagation of education was communal.

2. Religious Influence. The education of this period was profoundly influenced by Islam. Every Muslim sought education for the purpose of searching for knowledge and for religious purposes. There is direct evidence of the influence of Islam on the education of this period. Students were required to memorise the Koran. Importance was attached to study of Islam. This religious influence upon education was positive proof of the communal attitude of Muslim rulers.

3. Arabic and Persian. During this period, special stress was laid on the teaching of Arabic and Persian, which were made the media of education by Muslim rulers. Knowledge of these two languages was essential for securing employment in government offices. Consequently, Hindus too began to learn Arabic and Persian.

4. Materialism. Muslim education sought the spread of education only from the practical and materialistic viewpoints. Education in manual skills, sculpture, agriculture, medicine, etc., is proof of this. In addition to religious education, teachers tried to ensure that after receiving education, the child should become capable of earning his livelihood. Consequently, knowledge of military science, painting, sculpture, housing construction, manufacture of weapons, etc., was also imparted. Knowledge of such subjects was given to students directly and individually by experts through a system of apprenticeship.

5. Emergence of Urdu. The evolution of the new language 'Urdu' which emerged from the inter-mixing of Arabic and Persian, is the greatest contribution of the Mughal period. The importance that this language enjoys today is due entirely to the Muslim period.

6. Development of History-Writing. By initiating the writing of the history of their period, Muslim rulers helped to develop the art of writing history. Both Mughal and Muslim rulers commissioned the writing of the histories of their period or reigns. Among the most famous of these are Babar Nama, Akbar Nama, etc.

OBJECTIVES OF EDUCATION

The education imparted in the Muslim period had numerous objectives. Its prime objective was to create able employees for the political and administrative system. However, the objectives of education underwent modifications as the attitudes of successive rulers changed. The objectives of education during Akbar's reign were completely different from its objectives during Aurangzeb's rule. In general, Muslim education had the following objectives:

1. Propagation of Knowledge. Religious knowledge could have been propagated among the Muslims who had come to India or those who had been converted to Islam only through education. Hazrat Mohammad had said that knowledge is divine and without it salvation is not possible. He taught people the difference between duty and wrong actions, religious and irreligious deeds, and laid stress on the need for knowledge through education.

2. Propagation of Religious Laws. Education also aimed at propagating the major laws of Islam and the shariyats of the holy Koran. Islamic religion had evolved very specific moral criteria, and it was the purpose of education to propagate them. All these elements contributed to the achievement of Islam's social and political objectives and the strengthening of its laws and customs in this period.

3. Propagation of Religion. Religion was the basis of education, and hence the purpose of education was propagation of religion. Maktabs were established along with mosques. It was generally held that the propagation of Islam was synonymous with the propagation of religion and he who engaged in this became a martyr. It was for this reason that knowledge of Koran was imparted in the maktabs. Hazrat Mohammad had also declared that a proper and liberal education was the finest of gifts that parents could bestow on their children.

4. Strengthening the Administration. Another objective of Muslim education was to strengthen the administration. Muslim rulers believed that their administration could not be firmly entrenched in the absence of education, and hence they wanted to utilize the educational system for strengthening their own political position.

5. Wordly Progress. According to Jafar, the state encouraged the educated people in every conceivable way. The posts of Kazis (preachers) and Wazirs (ministers) were reserved for the educated. Besides, Muslim education also aimed at preparing the individual for future life. Many Hindus received the highest Muslim education and rose to high positions.

Centres of Education

The political organisation of the Muslim rulers was decentralised. The Mansabdars, kings, zamindars or landlords, etc., became dependent rulers of their individual areas after paying the requisite tax to royal treasury. These rulers had mosques constructed, and soon the mosques changed into maktabs and madrassas. During the Muslim period, Agra, Delhi, Jaunpur, Lahore, Ajmer, Bidar, Lucknow, Ferozabad, Jullundur, Multan, Bijapur, etc., became important centres of education.

1. Agra. Agra was founded by Sikandar Lodi. He had the town established as a centre of Islamic education, and it soon took the form of a university. Hundreds of madrassas in this town provided education in literature, mathematics, philosophy, medicine, etc. Later on, Akbar, Jehangir and Shahjahan also contributed to the development of education in this town.

2. Delhi. Delhi was renowned far and wide as a centre of Muslim education. Nasiruddin established the Nasaria Madrassas here. The Gulam dynasty also helped the spread of education in Delhi. During the reign of Alauddin Khilji, 34 famous scholars of Islam lived in Delhi. Feroz Tuglak had 30 madrassas established. Humayun opened madrassas for imparting knowledge of astrology and geography. Akbar, Jehangir, Shahjahan and Aurangazeb also established various madrassas for imparting knowledge of various specific fields.

3. Jaunpur. During the reign of Feroz, Jaunpur was a prominent centre of Muslim education. It had many schools imparting education in the arts, literature and other spheres of knowledge. The Sharkias made valuable contributions to the development of education. Sher Shah Suri himself was a student here.

4. Bidar. Bidar, too, was an important educational centre. Mahmood Gawan had a huge madrassas and a library established here. Later, Alauddin Ahmed contributed to the development of education.

In addition to the above centres, there were at least one maktab and one madrash in every village of Bijapur, Golkunda, Malwa, Khandesh, Multan, Gujrat, Lucknow, Sialkot and Bengal.

ORGANISATION AND SYSTEM OF EDUCATION

During the Muslim period, the system of education was organised in the following manner—

1. Bismillah. Education began with the performance of the ritual known as 'Bismillah', which was performed at the age of 4 years, 4 months and 4 days. It was similar to the Upnayan ceremony of the Vedic period and the Pabbaja ritual of the Buddhist period. On this day, the child was adorned with a new crown and sent to his teacher, the Maulvi, where the latter inaugurated the child's education with a recitation from the Koran. Affluent people had this ritual performed at home.

2. Maktab. Education began in the maktab, i.e., a primary school. The teachers called Maulvis taught the alphabet along with verses from the Koran. The child's primary education took place in these schools. Generally, most such maktabs were appendages of mosques. The child was taught writing, the Koran, namaz or prayer, azaan, arithmetic, drafting, conversation, letter-writing, etc.

3. Madrassa. Madrassas provided higher education to the students. They were aided by the government. Here higher education was imparted through lectures. There were arrangements for hostels in the madrassas. They were owned privately as well as by the state.

4. Syllabus. The syllabus of education in the Muslim period included such subjects as the holy Koran, the biography of Hazrat Mohammed Sahib, the history and the laws of Islam, Arabic and Persian, grammar, literature, logic, philosophy, law, astrology, history, geography, agriculture, Unani system of medicine, etc. There were provisions for teaching Sanskrit to Hindu children. Madrassas provided both religious and material or worldly education. Subjects of religious education included Koran, Islamic laws, history and Sufi philosophy, while worldly or material education consisted of grammar, language, literature, etc. There were some specialized centres for education in particular subjects.

5. Method of Teaching. Emphasis was placed on memorisation in addition to reading, writing and arithmetic. The most prevalent method was the oral. Individual attention was paid to students. The monitor system had been used in maktabs and madrassas.

6. Student-Teacher Relationship. During this period, relations between students and teachers were not marked by intimacy, but there were no doubts about sincerity and purity. Though teachers received a low salary, they had an important place in society. People respected them and bestowed faith on them. The teacher had a paternal attitude towards his wards. It was believed that the students who served their teachers made God happy. Despite this, there was nothing notable in this relationship. Aurangzeb is known to have insulted his teacher Mulla Shah Saleh.

7. Medium of Education. During the Muslim period, Arabic and Persian were the media of education. However, after the growth of Urdu, education began to be imparted though this language.

8. Reward and Punishment. There was a system of severe punishment to maintain order and discipline, but brilliant scholars were also rewarded.

Q. 13. Explain Lord Macaulay's contribution to Indian Education System.

Ans. LORD MACAULAY AND THE OCCIDENTAL POLICY

Lord Macaulay was great scholar and educationist of his period. He was a writer of great repute. He was a good orator and could influence others very easily. On June 10, 1834 he became a member of the Governor-General's Council and was appointed the President of the Committee of Public Instruction. He was a staunch supporter of the occidentalism and had come to India with new educational ideas. When he reached India, the occidental-oriental controversy was at its peak.

As the President of the Committee of Public Instruction, he placed his proposal for spending the sanctioned one lac rupees. In his proposals he vehemently criticised the Indian languages and the literatures of Sanskrit, Arabic and Persian. He declared them useless before English languages. He showed injustice and partiality in his uncharitable criticisms and remarked that the Indians themselves wanted to learn English. He argued that the Indians were not so keen to receive free education in Indian languages as they are to receive education in English even on payment of fees. In this context he quoted that letter of Raja Ram Mohan Roy in which he had advised his countrymen to learn English.

In favour of English he observed that ultimately the Company would be a gainer financially. If English was made the commercial language, India would have better foreign relationships with other countries.

Macaulay further argued that Indians should be taught English even if they showed no interest in it, because their regeneration was possible only through English education.

Macaulay considered that person learned who knew English and European culture. He regarded the learned persons of Sanskrit, Arabic, Persian and other Indian languages as ignorant. The existing learned persons in India were great fools in his opinion.

Macaulay did not choose to interfere in the religious affairs of Hindus and Muslims, but he suggested a common law for both. He argued that this law should be based on the religious principle of both Hindus and Muslims.

He advised to close the Calcutta Madarsa founded by Warren Hastings. He regarded the Benares Sanskrit College as more useful than the Calcutta Madarsa. However, he did not want that Indians should be given education in Sanskrit, Arabic and Persian. He wanted that Indians should be given education in English and English alone.

H.T. Princep was requested to give his views on Macaulay's observations. Princep was an orientalist and he opposed Macaulay's views. But Lord William Bentinck accepted Macaulay's recommendations. Thus a new chapter in the history of modern education in India began.

DECLARATION OF EDUCATIONAL POLICY OF BENTINCK

The Occidental-oriented controversy lasted for about twenty-two years. Ultimately on February 2, 1935, Lord Bentinck gave his approval to the policy advocated by Lord Macaulay. The substance of Lord Bentinck declaration was as below:

1. The British rule in India will propagate European science and literature in the country and the money sanctioned or to be sanctioned for education will be utilized towards this goal.
2. The old institutions will not be closed and the financial assistance already given to them will be continued. But neither the Government will give stipends to new students in the old institutions nor will be responsible for their education. But the teachers in them will be appointed by the Government.
3. The Government will not help in printing and publication of literature in Indian languages nor will publish them itself.
4. Whatever money is saved as a result of the above policy will be utilized for publishing and propagating European languages, literature and science.

The orientalists got a great set-back by Bentinck's policy. However, Bentinck's initiated a definite educational policy as the thought fit at the time.

END OF ORIENTAL–OCCIDENTAL CONTROVERSY

Bentinck, by his declaration ended the oriental-occidental controversy, but it still continued. He resigned in 1835 and left for England. He was succeeded by Charles Metcalf. But Metcalf, too, could not pacify the orientalists and occidentalists and the controversy continued in some form or the other. After Metcalf, Lord Auckland became the Governor-General. He was an able and sighted administrator. He studied the situation deeply and concluded the cause of reduction in financial assistance. The orientalist submitted a memorandum to him. He decided to give financial assistance to both the groups in order that their needs might be fulfilled. Thus he ended the controversy.

DOWNWARDS FILTRATION THEORY IN EDUCATION

During the British rule in India the downwards filtration theory was adopted in the country. Filtration means coming of something to the bottom from the top. Thus the filtration theory in education meant coming down of education or knowledge from the top to the bottom, *i.e.*, from the higher class people to the lower classes or the general people.

There were many reasons for adopting this policy. Different views have been expressed about this policy. Some people think that this policy was adopted because of the narrow-mindedness and selfish attitudes of the English who intended to educate only a few for getting clerks for running their administration. They adopted this policy also because they wanted to create an elite group which would be given high posts in the administration and this group in turn would influence the general public for accepting the British rule in the country. In fact, according to some persons, the main reason for adopting this policy was the meagre financial resources with the Company for educational purposes. The Company thought that it could not provide education to entire mass. So it decided to educate only a few. But this 'few' were the people of the higher classes, because they alone could catch up the opportunity for English education. The downwards filtration theory had the following three chief characteristics:

1. To educate only the high class people in order to give them higher posts in the administration with a view to strengthening the roots of British empire in the Country.
2. When the higher class people would receive English education their culture would be improved and the general public would accept them as their models. As a result, the lower class people would also be educated after being influenced by the higher class people.

3. To educate the higher class people who might undertake the responsibility of educating the general people.

Besides the occidental-oriental controversy, the Company had to face another problem during this period. This problem pertained to the education of the general masses. The Company was to decide whether to limit itself to the education of the higher class people alone, or to provide for education of all. The Company took no time in reaching a decision in this regard, as the Board of Director, gave-clear-cut directions in this context. Lord Macaulay explained the same by observing that "the aim of education in India was to anglicize the Indians through English education and to make black-coloured Indian English in their way of living, behaviour, thought, culture, traditions and morality", as such persons were likely to serve as the connecting link between the British Government and the general public. On July 31, 1837, Lord Macaulay again explained his point of view by stating that the purpose of the Company was only to educate the elite group which would educate the general public later—thus fulfilling the goal of educating the masses in general. In 1839 the General Committee of Public Instruction again repeated the stand that education would be given only to the higher class people who should shoulder the responsibility of educating their countrymen.

During the Company's rule Missionaries were encouraged to work in the field of education and they opened a number of schools and colleges for educating children of the higher class family. They thought that if they succeeded in educating the higher class people and converting them to their own Christian faith, these converted persons would preach Christianity amongst the lower class people. Evidently, the educational efforts of the Missionaries were religiously motivated and not politically. But only some lower class people could be influenced by these Missionaries and the bulk of the Indian population remained unaffected by them.

FAILURE OF THE DOWNWARDS FILTRATION THEORY

The purposes of the downwards filtration theory could not be fully achieved. It could have only a partial achievement in the sense that the British Government got a few educated Indians who could help in running the administration. But these few Indians could not serve as connecting links between the British Government and the general people. The English educated Indians could improve their culture and ways of living, by they formed a class of their own and drifted away from the general people. Thus the general public was in a way ignored by them as by and large they became more interested in making themselves richer and richer. As a result, education became concentrated only to those who had money. Thus the filtration theory really failed. There were two principal causes for its failure.

The first cause of the failure of the filtration theory was that too many English educated Indians came out in the field and it was not possible for the Government to give them suitable employment according to their expectations. This situation led to unemployment. For ending their unemployment, these persons opened some schools on the Western pattern. Thus a number of new English schools sprang up and the educational need of the people was met upto some extent.

The second cause of the failure of the filtration theory was that it created a feeling of self-respect, national honour and independence in the English educated Indians. These re-awakened persons could not be tempted by Government services and they took a vow to fight for national independence. For regenerating the people these enlightened persons began to spread education. Thus education ultimately reached the people.

However, the filtration theory continued its impact till 1870 somehow or other. But because of the aforesaid two main causes this theory could not achieved its objectives fully. It was only a partial success.

Private enterprises engaged in the field of education did a lot towards educating the people and creating in them a love for freedom. Thus the work for national regeneration and educational expansion began.

CONTRIBUTION OF LORD MACAULAY TO INDIAN EDUCATION

Lord Macaulay's Minutes ended the controversy going on, about the education system in India, for about 20 years. An Education policy was laid down. Following are the statements enabling the student to evaluate Macaulay's contribution to Indian Education.

1. Ending Anglicist Orientalist Controversy. In their book *"A Student's History of Education in India"* Nurullah and Naik say, "To call Macaulay a torch bearer in the path of progress, gives an exaggerated account of the role that he actually played." Lord Macaulay was not the first person who pleaded the cause of Western Education. He was not the sole founder of Occidentalist group, as these elements were working before his arrival in the country. These were started many years earlier by Christian Missionaries and men like Raja Ram Mohan Roy. Macaulay, however, ended the Oriental-Occidential controversy and laid the foundation-stone of modern education system in India.

2. Cause of Political Disorder. Some critics have called Macaulay responsible for Indian slavery. This is also not reasonable. Political disturbances could place in the absense of his education policy also, as many Indian students were studying in Mission Schools. The Indian Rulers, whose powers had been snatched away by the English Rulers had also assisted the political disorder to a great extent.

3. Ignorance. A learned scholar like Macaulay could not recall even the European scholars, who had praised Sanskrit Grammar, Philosophy and literature. He cracked jokes on it though he himself as ignorant about it. This charge of ignorance is irrefutable.

4. Denigration of Indian Languages. Some scholars had criticised Macaulay for denigrating Indian languages with malicious remarks, like calling them rustic, undeveloped and inefficient. Thus he had given a great blow to the development of these languages. However, as the chairman of the Society of Public Instructions, Macaulay said in his report of 1836, "We have much interest in the development of Indian languages. We do not see any reason that the order of 7th March checks us in our efforts and we had already paid attention to its improvement... the development of Native languages is our final aim and our all the efforts should be utilised in its cause." Hence, Macaulay cannot be blamed for denigrating native languages.

5. Religious Motive. Through English education Macaulay wanted to create, "a class of persons, Indian in blood and colour, but English in taste, in opinions, in morals, and in the intellect." Of course, his policy succeeded to a great extent. He did create a group of WOGS (Western Oriented Gentlemen) who would always co-operate with British rulers in exploitation of Indians. In a latter to his father in 1836, Macaulay wrote "Our English schools are increasing with leaps and bounds and now the condition has reached to a position that it has become difficult to accommodate the students. Hindus are much influenced with education. There is no Hindu, who may keep real faith in his religion after studying English. I have full confidence that if our education policy succeeds then no idolator will be left in Bengal. All this will be done naturally without any religious preaching and interference." This statement clearly unravels the sinister motives of Lord Macaulay.

Q. 14. Discuss the merits of the British Education System.

Ans. MERITS OF THE BRITISH EDUCATION SYSTEM

Just as British administrative system teemed with defects, yet the hardships resulting therefrom inspired the Indians to fight for freedom, in the same manner the British educational system was undoubtedly defective, yet it was this very system which enabled India to develop deep cultural contracts with other progressive countries of the west. Time and circumstances are the best Judges of everyting. The evolution of the British system of education through the conditions prevailing in India at that time, and through the clashes and conflicts between the old and the new, orientalism and occidentalism and between tradition and progressivism, proved a boon for India.

1. More Good than Harm. It would be improper to imprecate British education whole-sale merely on the score that it did not conduce to the individual or national development, because in spite of these defects the system had also some such qualities and merits which proved very beneficial for the country both directly and indirectly. Thus if we consider this system impartially and without the yellow in our eyes we shall find that this system did more good than harm to the country. Some people believe that the Indians were compelled to adopt this system and they lay all the sin at the door of Macaulay. But this is not the truth. The British Government always remained indifferent towards the proper planning of education in India so much so that Hastings, Minto, Princep and others opposed the introduction of English education in India, whereas liberal leaders of India, like Raja Ram Mohan Roy, worked with heart and soul for its establishment in the country. The efforts which Macaulay and Bentinck made for English education in India appear to have had their goodwill for the country. The English system which Macaulay recommended for India did undoubtedly deal blow to Indian culture and literature, but from the point of view of the prevailing circumstances, it was necessary to introduce such a system of education which would put an end to the diversity and disunity created by the differences of languages. For developing the country it was necessary to equip the Indians for taking part, like the people of other countries, in the quest for new knowledge as also to acquaint the Indians with the scientific discoveries and investigations so that they could also make their contribution to the scientific research in the world.

2. The British System Acquainted India with Western Knowledge and Sciences. During the last years of the eighteenth century India was in great throes due to political disintegration, social animosities, traditionalism and superstitions. It had neither become acquainted with the new ideas of the West, nor did it have the power either to preserve intact its ancient culture, literature and ideals or to help them advance. All the paths of progress in the country were be set with difficulties and clouds of pessimism overcast the firmament of India. It was English education which showed India a way out of the darkness created by these circumstances.

3. English Education Brought out a Reawakening and a Desire to Recapture Our Ancient Glory. Apart from acquainting us with the progress that the world had made as well as with Western knowledge and wisdom, the English system dressed up a new, in the English medium, the old stories of our ancient culture, literature, history and religion. All the treasures which we had forgotten and which had been destroyed by time, was given back to us in the English form by the kindness of such great men as Max Muller, Williams and others. These scholars gathered together the scattered threads that had gone into the making of the texture of our ancient history and culture and gave them an organic form. The critical investigations of these European scholars redirected our attention towards the glory that was India and inspired us to make deep critical study, and research in the field. This resulted into bringing in us a reawakening and instilling in us a keen desire to recapture the ancient glory. We were thus put on the road to progress.

4. English Education Broadened the Path of a Better System of Education and Government in the Country. The introduction of English as the medium of instruction did adversely affect our mother tongues, but nevertheless it was this very factor which indirectly induced us to develop our languages. Several languages were prevalent at the time of the introduction of English education, but apart from Sanskrit and Persian no other language was so developed as to be fit for being adopted as the medium of instruction. Besides, the English scholars and officers made philological studies of the various languages of the country and prepared dictionaries and grammar. They even published magazines and periodicals in these languages. All this might have been done from a selfish motive for the propagation of their religion; nevertheless, India will always remain indebted to them on this score. Grierson's 'Linguistic Survey of India' is for us the greatest gift of the English education. It is due to the scholarship and research work of English scholars that we have been able to develop our mother tongue to such an extent as to make it a medium of even university education today. Had English education not been introduced into India, we would have remained today totally ignorant of the Western scientific investigations and advancements. English education produced such scholars in India who are thoroughly soaked in Western knowledge and wisdom and trying heart and soul for the establishment of a better system of education and government in the country.

5. Development of Nationalism through English Education. Besides acquainting the Indians with the knowledge of the west and the glory of ancient India alongwith its literature and culture, English education also rekindled in the people the spirit of nationalism. It was due to this education that the pearls of ancient Indian thought and feeling were wreathed together and it was again due to the universality of the English language that we could acquaint the world with ancient wisdom of our country.

Due to the uniformity in the English educational institutions and in the syllabi of the schools, colleges and universities, such an intellectual class was produced which could consider the problems of the country with amity and unanimity. The nefarious spirit of provincialism could thus be put an end to. Apart from getting the facilities for an exchange of language and literature with other countries, India was enabled to understand the conditions of life in other countries as also to acquaint them with her own conditions. This had the result which Macaulay had foreseen in 1833 at the time of the renewal of the Charter of the East India Company. The wave of national awakening spread throughout the country and in all provinces the intellectuals who were the products of the English education became the leaders of the National Movement. Thus it can be maintained that the English educational system has the credit for the development of the spirit of nationalism, emergence of the national leaders and for paving the way for the success of Indian struggle for independence.

There appears to be no need for holding the brief for English educational system because it is due to this very system that English ethics, arts and crafts, laws and rules, literature, science and administrative system are still prevalent in India and are useful also.

Q. 15. 'Macaulay was the torch-bearer in the path of progress.' Comment on the statement giving the contribution of Macaulay to Indian Education.

Ans. When Macaulay landed in India on June 10, 1834 as the first Law Member of the Governor-General's Executive Council, a heated controversy was going on between two parties—the Orientalists and the Occidentalists. The Orientalists were in favour of educating the upper classes of the Indian people through the medium of their classical languages Sanskrit and Arabic. The Occidentalists favoured the use of English as the medium of instruction. The Orientalists believed that the progress and preservation of ancient Indian culture, literature and learning would be in the best interest of the people in the country. On the other hand, the Occidentalists wanted to spread the study of sciences and new inventions going on in Europe and held that Arabian, Sanskrit or Persian literature had no useful knowledge but abounded in only conservative and narrow ideas. The section 43 of Charter Act of 1813, had directed the E.I. Company to spend at least one lac of rupees yearly for the revival and improvement of litterature and the encouragement of the learned natives of India, and for the promotion of a knowledge of the sciences among the inhabitants of the British territories in India.

Lord Macaulay was appointed the President of the General Committee of Public Instruction and was asked to advise the government on the judicious expenditure of one lac rupees. Macaulay expressed his views and these are known as Macaulay's Minutes.

He interpreted the word literature as English literature and said that the Act did not bind or limit the government to Indian literature only. He felt that the phrase knowledge of sciences warranted the change as there was no science, worth the name, in India, neither in Sanskrit nor in Arabic nor in any other Indian language. He said that natives could be made learned through an English education as through an Arabic, or Sanskrit or Persian education.

Then he said that Vernaculars were so little development that the intellectual development of those classes of the people, who wanted to get higher education, could be effected only through some language other than the vernacular ones. So the choice lay between the classical languages and the English. But the literature in the Indian Classical languages was so poor that 'a single shelf of a good European library was worth the whole literature of India and Arabia'.

The claims of English were then put forward in the following words : "The claims of our own language it is hardly necessary to recapitulate. *(i)* It stands pre-eminent even among the languages of the West. *(ii)* In India English is the language spoken by the ruling class. *(iii)* It is spoken by the higher class of natives at the seats of Government. *(iv)* It is likely to become the language of Commerce throughout the seas of the East."

He said that English would bring renaissance in India just as Greek or Latin did in England or just as the languages of Western Europe did in Russia. He also remarked that natives are themselves desirous of being taught English and are not eager to learn Sanskrit or Arabic and the demand of the latter was maintained artificially through bounty money. As it was possible to make the natives of this country good English scholars, hence efforts should be directed towards that end. It was his firm belief that only through English education it was possible to bring about a class of persons. Indian in blood and colour, but English in tastes, opinions, morals and intellect, that education could filter down from them to the masses.

William Bentinck approved of Macaulay's Minutes and said, "I give my entire concurrence to the sentiments expressed in this minute," and he passed the following order: "His Lordship in Council is of opinion that the great object of the British Government ought to be the promotion of the European literature and sciences among the natives of India: and that all the funds appropriated for the purpose of education would be best employed in English education alone."

The order made a turning point in the history of education in India. It defined the aim and type of education. The objective of English education was promotion of Western Arts and Sciences. The medium of instruction to be adopted was English.

Charge Levelled against Macaulay

Many charges have been levelled against Macaulay, some of which are given below. He cannot be called a torch-bearer in the path of progess.

(1) It is said that Macaulay was responsible for initiating a new educational policy, *i.e.*, introducing European knowledge through the medium of English. He was not the originator of this system or policy. A vast majority of people were in favour of the policy. Raja Ram Mahan Roy and his colleagues, the new officers of E.I. Company, and the Christian Missionaries all wanted westernisation of education. The ground was ready. "It was Macaulay's job to add tich mineral to the soil." A large body of people have been reared. Indian in blood and colour, but English in tastes, in opinions, in morals and in intellect. A dawn of cultural renaissance had already begun to appear. Before Macaulay came on the scene public opinion for this educational policy had already gained momentum. It was for him to let the machine go. The Government was also eager to introduce English education in India. It needed English-educated cheap Indian servants. It wanted some connecting link of communication between the rulers and the ruled and no other language seemed to be better than English then.

To call Macaulay the torch-bearer in the path of progress would be unfair because it was not he alone who aroused in Indians the desire for English education. The desire was there. It had already been aroused and sustained because Indians saw the advantages that they could reap from English education.

(2) Macaulay is said to be responsible for spreading Western political ideas in India. When he left England for India he had said in the House of Commons 'that having become instructed in European language Indians in some future age may demand European institutions'. But before he arrived in India the movement had already started. Enlightened Indians were demanding a representative constitution. The influence of western ideas was to be seen in interesting reform like the trial by jury, liberty of press and the like.

(3) Macaulay is justly blamed for his recommendation about use of English as the only medium of instruction. He totally rejected Indian languages as crude and unsuitable instruments for expressing scientific and literary ideas. It was an act of his negligence because he saw before his own eyes that some of the vernaculars or other lauguages were being used as media of instruction for college education in Bombay Presidency and a book like Bible could be effectively translated in them. Macaulay did not care to know the fact that a number of Indian languages were in a flourishing state under the Moghuls and were well equipped. He was perhaps misguided by local persons that the adoption of Indian languages as media of instruction was inpossible. At a later date in 1836, as President of the General Committee of Public Instruction, he wrote, "We are deeply sensible to the importance of encouraging the cultivation of the Verancular languages."

It appears that Macaulay admitted the utility of vernaculars as the media of instruction. It also appears from the above statement that he did not want English to continue for a long period as medium of instruction. He wanted that Indian languages should supplant it, after becoming enriched. But the government misused the concession and English continued to be the sole medium of instruction till quite recently.

Many Indian languages were rejuvenated by 1850. A number of educationists had started protesting against the use of English medium as the sole medium of instruction. But the Government of India did not pay any heed to it. It, on the contrary, reprimanded the

Bombay Government when they tried to improve local language through Poona Sanskrit College. It was only in 1904 that Lord Curzon drew the attention of the government to this policy. "Ever since the cold breath of Macaulay's rhetoric passed over the field of Indian languages and Indian Textbooks the elementary education of the people in their own language has shrivelled and pined."

(4) Macaulay has been rightly criticised for his utter ignorance of Indian and Asiatic culture. 'A single shelf of good European library was worth the whole native literature of India and Arabia', was a harsh and snobbish statement.

"The question now before us is simply whether when we can partronise sound philosophy and true history we shall countenance at public expenses, medical doctrines which would disgrace an English farrier, astronomy which would move laughter in girls at an English boarding school, history abounding with kings thirty feet high and regins thirty thousand years long and geography made of seas of treacle and see of butter."

The above ridiculous remarks show the narrowness of his vision and limitations of the grasp of the problem. "His pronouncements", says James "are too glib, too confident, too unqualified and sometimes err against good taste." Macaulay wanted to cut Indians from their past heritage by forcing upon them a new language and a new culture and by snatching away from them their own. It did not occur to his mind at all that the urgent need of the then India was acquisition of knowledge of Western sciences and methods. Had he tried to give emphasis to the acquisition of scientific knowledge that West had so far amassed, India might have gained a lot.

(5) Macaulay believed that English would bring renaissance in India as Greak and Latin had done in England. Macaulay did not consider how limited this policy was. It appeared that he was making an effort to grow a temperate plant on warm plains. It may be possible for such a plant to survive under artificial environment but not to thrive. The fate of India was closely tied with the prosperity of Arabic or Sanskrit. He was also mistaken in the belief that English education would anglicise Indians thoroughly. India can assimilate others' cultures but cannot accept others' culture in the place of her own. Has not his firm belief, which he expressed in a letter to his

father that if his plans of education were followed up there would be not a single idolator among the respectable classes in Bengal thirty years thereafter, come wrong?

Q. 16. Highlight the defects of the English eductional system.

Ans. Following are the defects of English Educational System:

1. The Promoters of the System had no Intention to do any Good to the Indian People. Having assessed the utility and the efforts of the English educational system, we have now to consider its defects. The English system was introduced in India at a time when the country was under political serfdom and the relation between the English and the Indian people was that of the ruler and the ruled. It would not at all be wrong to affirm that the British never tried for the progress and advancement of Indians from that point of view which they would have adopted for their own country. The English system of education did not produce any direct or ostensible benefit; in fact, it proved beneficial only indirectly.

Form the view point of quantitative development of education, we find that during the last 150 years this system could give education only to 15 per cent of the country's population. This figure stands no comparison with those of other countries.

The Charter to the Company in 1813, and the Despatch of 1854 have to be referred to in this context. On a perusal of these we find that the aim of education adumbrated in these was to produce competent and loyal clerks for the Company and the propagation of western knowledge. To expect any good to the individual, society and nation from an educational system with such a narrow outlook is hoping against hope. We can, therefore, say that the English system simply nourished British imperialism and it was not introduced with any idea of the good for the people. All the benefit that accrued therefrom was the indirect result of the weakness inherent in the system. It was due to these facts that this education did not prove advantageous to the Indians from the point of view of quantitative or qualitative development or even the prosperity of the country.

2. The Educational System Contrary to the Requirements of the Indians. That educational system can be called suitable which helps in all-round development of the individual, the society and the nation. Some critics think that from this point of view the English system was useless, and this again, was the reason why the people did not adopt it. There was no room for the spirit of self-reliance in this system. Most of the British rulers thought that the education which inculcated the spirit of self-reliance would create in the Indians the feeling of independence and liberty and they tingled with awe at the very thought. Their object was to keep India in their clutches in order to destroy its accumulated glory, to plunder its wealth and thus to show off to other countries of the world their own glory and prosperity. Their educational system catered to this.

3. Wrong Methods of the Implementation of the English System. The ideals of English education system were undoubtedly nefarious but alongwith this the methods adopted for its dissemination were also bad. As a result of its propagation of old schools like Vidyapith, Pathshala, Madarsas and Maktabs which catered to the needs of the Indians were destroyed root and branch. Another serious defect was the downward filtration theory which unnecessarily prolonged the period of education. Consequently, this system of education could not be widely propagated and it remained confined to a particular class.

In this system English was made the medium at the cost of the Indian languages. It proved useful at the university level, but it became an unnecessary burden on the immature minds of the students of lower classes. Consequently, other languages became the scapegoat of English and the opportunities were also rare for acquiring new knowledge.

4. British Education Created a Gulf between the Educated and Uneducated and between the Old and the New. Another serious defect of the system was that it had the same ideals for its implementation in India as it had for England irrespective of the fact that there was a world of difference between the social, economic, moral and cultural conditions of the two countries. Hence this system of education could not prove beneficial to India.

The main reason behind the indifference of the British towards the Indian condition was their intense dislike or hatred for India and the Indians. They were undoubtedly wrong, yet they were after all the rulers of the land. This very feeling proved later on the cause of their own going away from India, but even before the awakening of India, it produced a class of Anglo-Indians who were English in ways of living but were Indians to all intents and purposes. Thus this system, instead of bringing about synthesis of Eastern and Western culture, created a wide gulf between the education and the uneducated, and the old and the new. If, on the countrary, Eastern spiritualism and Western materialism could have been synthesised with the practical sense of England and the spirit of detachment of the East, respectively, ways of a new knowledge would have emerged in the world.

5. The English Educational System did not Inspire any Reconstruction. Being Government-centred, English education was adopted by the wealthy classes only. It was overridden by the administrative machinery and as such the commonality could not adopt it. This educational system also worked on the principle of 'divide and rule' so much so that it ostensibly aimed at the spiitting up of the Indian nation. Hence this system was totally devoid of the feelings of reform and reconstruction and it remained incapable of turning out good citizens for the country and the society as a whole. In this way, it simply helped in the consolidation of the British rule and had no concern for the reconstruction of the country. It was difficult to draw from this system any inspiration for reconstruction, nevertheless some sparks were ignited by this very system and these later on flared up into a conflagration.

6. Neglect of Education by the Administrative Centres. Education department was not given much regard and attention during the British rule and the emoluments of the officers of this department were lesser than those of other departments. It was due to this that Englishmen of low calibre were appointed on these posts from whom no help in the progress of education could be expected. This department was put under the coutrol of a minister who did the work of his department during his leisure hours in a very careless and casual manner. Thus the education of the Indians continued to be overlooked and neglected during the British regime. There were also some competent and capable persons like Grant, Michael, and Sadler but apart from these there was no other officer in the department who could manage the work efficiently. This was the reason why the education department could not get the co-operation of others.

7. Different Policies were followed by Different Officers. The British Government did not give necessary attention to organising Indian education in a good manner and no well planned scheme could be formulated for its implementation and dissemination. Different policies were adpoted and followed according to the whims of the different officers. After the transfer of one officer the other one adopted his own methods. Due to these recurring changes in the policies and methods of the department the education of India could not make any progress, nay it declined day by day.

Q. 17. Define Macaulay's views on the Westernization of Education (1833-34).

Ans. WESTERNIZATION OF EDUCATION (1833-34)

On June 10, 1834, Lord Macaulay, who was a great scholar of English, came to India as the Law Member of the Company. He supported the views of Charles Grant, and believed that Eastern education was inferior. On his arrival in India, Lord Bentick made him the chief of the Public Instruction Committee also. His advice was sought regarding section 43 of the Charter of 1813 as well as about the expenditure of one lakh rupees. Macaulay was waiting for just such an opportunity. On February 8, 1835, he presented his historical 'Minutes' in which he made a bitter attack upon Indian literature and culture and vilified it.

Macaulay's Views

(1) In his elaboration of section 43, Macaulay included Engligh literature along with Sanskrit and Arabic literatures, and along with the Indian scholars of Sanskrit and Arabic, he also enumerated English scholars. He also gave complete authority to the Company for spending the grant.

(2) A supporter of western literature, he had this to say for Indian literature—"A single shelf of a good European library was worth the whole native literature of India and Arabia." (Macaulay's Minutes). From the same viewpoint, he also praised the English language, arguing that it was the most flourishing and useful of all European languages. He, who knew this language, could esaily obtain that vast treasure of knowledge which had been created by the most

intelligent races of the world. English was the language of India's rulers, and hence, the higher classes living in the capitals also spoke it. It is perfectly possible that English may become the language of the trade on Eastern seas. (Macaulay's Minutes).

(3) Macaulay attached importance to the education of the higher classes and thus emphasised the theory of Downward Filtration.

(4) In education, Macaulay laid stress on religious objectivity. As he put it, it was the duty of England to teach Indians what was good for their health, and not what was suited to their tastes. He implemented the theory of Downward Filtration. He opined that the English rulers should create a class which could mediate between the English and the millons over whom they ruled. He wanted them to be Indians by colour and blood, but English by interest, morality and intellect. But, because of this principle, the objective of an education in consonance with Indian society could not be achieved.

Lord Macaulay was very typical, sincere to his country. He always thought about the propagation of English language and culture. His ideas for India were full of prejudices. Some of them are given here:

1. A single shelf of a good European library was worth the whole native literature of India and Arabia.
2. It is possible through English education to bring about a class of persons, Indian in blood and colour, but English in tastes, in opinions, in morals and in intellect.
3. English stands prominent even among the languages of the west. Whoever knows the English language has ready access to all the vast intellectual wealth which all the wisest nations of the earth have created.

Macaulay's resolution was put into the hands of the leader of the Orientalists in the Public Instruction Committee, Mr. Princep who was the leader of the opposition, he reduced it to shreds with his arguments. Despite this, Lord Bentick, who was prejudiced against eastern systems of thought, supported Macaulay's educational views and declared an educational policy founded on it. This policy gave primacy to the propagation of European literature and science, suspension of scholarships for students, neglect of publication of Eastern literature, and the propagation of English literature.

Lord Bentick's acceptance of the educational policy enunciated by Lord Macaulay gave stability to the English educational policy. This was the first genuine educational policy adopted by the contemporary government. Different people held different views on Macaulay's policy, but, in general, he is accepted as the inspiration behind the new educational policy. At least, he removed the element of doubt in this sphere and helped the government overcome its uncertainty.

It is beyond question that Macaulay said many prejudiced and bitter things about India, but his arguments had a definite force, and as a result, English came to be the language of government usage. Macaulay's dream of giving rise to a race which was Indian in colour and blood but English in dress conversation, ideas and thoughts, came true.

Lord Auckland's Educational Policy

Lord Auckland succeeded Lord Bentick as India's Governor-General. Supporters of eastern education presented him with a representation opposing Macaulay's declaration. Lord Auckland agreed that the financial restraints upon oriental education were excessive. Consequently, he increased the educational grant for the orientalists, gave primacy to oriental studies, increased the number or scholarships for these studies, and made arrangements for printing and publication of oriental works. However, he also permitted the spending of more than one lakh rupees for the spread of English education.

During Lord Auckland's reign, Adam, who had been appointed by Lord Bentick to prepare a report on Indian education, had published his report. It was a comprehensive document, containing some valuable suggestions for bringing about a Renaissance in India. Unfortunately, nothing was done to implement his ideas.

Lord Hardinge's Declaration

In 1844, the then Governor-General, Lord Hardinge declared that priority in employment in the Company's organisation would be given to those who had received English education. As a result, the demand for English education increased, and education came to be directly linked with livelihood. At the same time, employment became more important than domestic crafts, which came to be neglected. Between 1833 and 1853, Bengal, Bombay, Madras, the Frontier areas, Uttar Pradesh, and Punjab witnessed the kind of growth in education which had not taken place in many previous years. Professional or vocational institutions providing education in medicine, engineering, law and other professions were established. However, at the same time, dissatisfaction with the Compay's working was also being expressed. These improvements in the educational sphere were no more than a drop in the ocean. Hence, in 1954, Wood's Despatch was enunciated.

In 1853, when the Company's Charter again came up for consideration and renewal, the need for a permanent and comprehensive educational policy was felt. The British Parliament asked the Select Committee to consider this question. After deliberation, the Committee declared that the spread of education in India was not detrimental to the Company's interests. At that time, the President of the Company's Board of Control was Charles Wood, who published his declaration regarding education on 19th July, 1854. It is referred to as Wood's Despatch.

Q. 18. Explain the Wood's Despatch on Education, 1854 and its main recommendations.

Ans. Sir Charles Wood's Despatch on Education, 1854. Sir Charles Wood, the President of the Board of Control in the coalition ministry of Earl of Aberdeen (1852-55), was a true product of the Palmerstonian era of English history. He was a firm believer in the superiority of Enlish race and institutions and sincerely believed that these institutions chould serve as a useful model for the world. Charles Wood showed a larger vision about education than most of the zealous educationists in India. In 1854 Wood prepared his comprehensive despatch on the scheme of future education in India. The despatch came to be considered as the Magna Carta of English education in India. The scheme envisaged a co-ordinated system of education on an all-India basis. The main reeommendations may be summarised thus:

(1) It declared that the aim of Government's educational policy was the teaching of Western education. "The education which we desire to see extended in India" wrote Wood in the despatch, "is that

which has for its object the diffusion of the improved arts, science, philosophy and literature of Europe, in short of European knowledge".

(2) As to the medium of instruction, it declared that for higher education English language was the most perfect medium of education. It also emphasised the importance of the vernacular languages, for it was through the medium of the vernacular languages, that European knowledge could infilter to the masses.

(3) It proposed the setting up of vernacular primary schools in the villages at the lowest stage, followed by Anglo-Vernacular high schools and an affiliated college at the district level.

(4) It recommended a system of grants-in-aid to encourage and foster private enterprise in the field of education. This grants-in-aid was conditional on the institutions employing qualified teachers and maintaining proper standards of teaching.

(5) A department of Public Instruction under the charge of a Director in each of the five provinces of the Company's territories was to Preview the progress of education in the province and submit an annual report to the Government.

(6) Universities on the model of the London University were proposed for Calcutta, Bombay and Madras. The constitution of the University provided for a Senate, a Chancellor, a Vice-Chancellor and Fellows—all to be nominated by the Government. The universities were to hold examinations and confer degrees. A university might set up professorships in various branches of learning.

(7) The despatch emphasised the importance of vocational instruction and the need for establishing technical schools and colleges.

(8) Teachers' Training Institutions on the model then prevalent in England were recommended.

(9) The despatch gave frank and cordial support for fostering the education of women.

The new scheme of education was a slavish imitation of English models. Almost all the proposals in the Wood's Despatch were implemented. The Department of Public Instruction was organised in 1855 and it replaced the earlier Committee of Public Instruction and Council of Education. The three universities of Calcutta, Madras and

Bombay came into existence in 1857. Mostly due to Bethune's efforts girls schools were set up on modern footing and brought under the Government's grant-in-aid and inspection system.

The ideals and methods advocated in Wood's Despatch dominated the field for about five decades. The same period also witnessed a rapid Westernization of the educational system in India. The indigenous system gradually gave place to the Western system of education. Most of the educational institutions during this period were run by European headmasters and principals under the Education Department. The missionary enterprise played its own part and managed a number of institutions. Gradually private Indian effort appeared in the field.

Q. 19. How have the recommendations of Wood's Despatch paved the way for the development of the present education system?

Ans. "Wood's Despatch is said to be the corner stone of Indian education. It is said to have laid the foundation of our present system of education." Says A.N. Basu, "The Despatch was a statesmanlike document wisely worded and wide in outlook and the suggestions contained therein were quite sound. It did lay out a plan for a comprehensive system of education for this country." The similar view has been expressed by Lord Dalhousie. It was a scheme of education for all India, far wider and more comprehensive than the local or the Supreme Government could have ever ventured to suggest.

The plan was comprehensive. It decided the structure of education in India. Previous to 1854 education was conducted on piecemeal basis. Now it had a structure: at the base of which were indigenous schools and primary schools and at the top were the universities. There was now a department in each province to look after the state of education. The system of education now started was well planned. It recommended the foundation of graded schools—Indigenous Primary Schools, Middle Schools, High Schools, Colleges, Universities—all over the country. It introduced the system of grants-in-aid and thus sought the cooperation of private enterprise in the field of education. It laid due emphasis on the education of girls. 'Our Governor General-in-Council has declared that the Government ought to give to the native female education in India its frank and cordial support.' It laid down foundation for vocational education which had been so far uncared for. Vacational education was to be encouraged hereafter because the government wanted to give employment facilities to the educated, and also because it hoped that vocationally trained persons would be more grateful to the Government. The Despatch is important for drawing the attention of the local administration to the improvement and expansion of mass education. The filtration theory was rejected. It is also important because it made certain compromises. It said that religious education shall not be compulsory. Compulsory religious education will not be encouraged at public expense though it permitted missionaries to avail of state help if they gave their pupils a freedom of absenting themselves from religious classes. It is also important because it laid emphasis on the teaching of Indian languages.

The Directors realised the importance of training teachers for the schools they wanted to open. So they desired through the Despatch to establish training institutions for teachers.

"The Wood's Despatch may be regarded as a fitting close to the second period in the history of education in India", remarked Nurullah and Naik. The first two periods being : (a) from the early days till 1812, and (b) from 1813-1854.

What follows after the issue of the Despatch marks the three periods : (a) from 1855-1920, (b) from 1921-1947, and (c) from 1947.

The Wood's Despatch is then the climax in the history of Indian education. What goes before leads to it: and what follows flows from its.

According to the Wood's Despatch the Departments of Public Instruction were created in all the provinces and they were required to advise the Provincial Governments regarding educational matters, to make a proper use of money received from the Central and Provincial governments, to inspect the institutions receiving grant-in-aid, to submit an annual report to the Government and to run and organise government schools and colleges.

The education departments framed the rules for grant-in-aid schemes and began to give financial support to privately managed schools. The Education departments now started secondary schools and encouraged the private ones by giving them sufficient grant-in-aid. More money poured into secondary education. The state established three Universities by 1857 on the lines of London university. The rapid increase in secondary education led to the starting of a number of colleges for higher education. Vocational education in medicine, law, engineering, agriculture, forestry and veterinary science was started. Thus the Wood's Despatch can be regarded as the foundation stone of Indian education.

Q. 20. Whatever has been the importance of Wood's Despatch in 1854, but to call it the Charter of Education now would be ludicrous. Discuss.

Ans. H.R. James called the Wood's Despatch "the Magna Charta of Indian education". The Magna Charta was the great Charter of English personal and political liberty obtained from John in 1215. A Charter is the written grants of rights by a sovereign. The Wood's Despatch was a written document which gave forth recommendations to improve education of the country. It was thus a sort of Charter giving Indians the rights of primary, elementary, secondary and higher education. It gave them rights for vocational education and for the education of girls. Had the recommendations offered by the Despatch been followed completely without any deficiency and had the suggestions been carried out entirely, the foundation for a national system of education would have been laid. But unfortunately this was not done. For example, if we examine the history of education in the period which followed (1854-1882) we find that the Education departments were established in the province but they could not promote the interest of education. Similarly, the system of grant-in-aid did not operate well because of the inadequacy of grants, the irregularity of its release, step-motherly treatment towards the privately managed non-Mission Schools, and complexity of rules. The Primany education also did not make much headway because the Government had little time to attend to the primary education, the funds were inadequate, and the money raised through educational cess was diverted to other channels. The university education similarly could not be improved because the universities remained for a long time examining bodies. Not teaching was done; no chairs were formed.

This shows that the suggestions could not be carried out in their entirety.

The result was that there was a lopsided development of education even after the publication of the Despatch. To regard the Despatch as the climax of Indian education would be unfair and to accept what James says would be against propriety.

We cannot regard the Despatch as the Great Charter because—

1. The state did not provide for elementary education as was required.
2. The government did not curb the proselytising activities of the missionaries. The policy of neutrality was not acted upon even for a long time after the Despatch.
3. The state did not stop the instruction in schools and colleges through the medium of English.

The Charter, if at all it was so, remained on paper. The expenses on secondary and higher education were not cut down : the funds for primary and elementary education could not be adequately provided. As a result, primary indigenous education suffered in comparison to secondary and higher education. The higher education also remained equally defective. There was no teaching in the universities. Indian languages could not find any place in higher education and were neglected.

The Depatch is said to have adopted the policy of religious neutrality. It declared that there would be no religious instruction and for an appointment to a government post one's religion would not be a bar. It did not happen so. The Bible remained in the libraries of the colleges and schools and no notice of the religious instruction imparted in the schools was taken of by the inspectors in their periodical visits. Christianity was indirectly forced upon the pupils.

The medium of instruction did not change. English occupied the same place as it did before. The result was that pupils had to cram the subject-matter, or had to use cheap notes to pass the examination.

Had the government adopted the ideal of universal literacy, we might have been justified to regard it as a great educational Charter but the Despatch itself did not regard it the duty of the state to educate every child. M.R. Paranjpe wrote in 1941, "It would be ridiculous to describe the Despatch as an Education Charter in the year 1941 whatever might have been its values in 1854." The same argument may be advanced for the present and it can be asserted that whatever has been the importance of Wood's Despatch in 1854 but to call it the Charter of Education now would be ludicrous. We have in the report of the Education Commission 1964-66 much more significant recommendations on the aims and objectives of nationalistic system of education, in the improvement of primary, secondary, and higher education, on the medium of instruction, curriculum, teacher training, female education, vocational education and religious policy.

The Despatch failed to place emphasis on character, initiative and leadership among students. It tended to shake the faith of the future generations in the native culture and civilization for it wished 'to confer upon the people of India the vast moral and material blessings which flowed from the general difusion of useful knowledge'.

The system was fitted to answer the needs of the British people and the British government in India because the knowledge that would be conferred on the Indian people would 'secure for the people of England a large and a more certain supply of many articles necessary for their manufacture and an inexhaustible demand for the produce of British labour'. The system of education that the Wood's Dispatch wanted to create in the country would supply the British government 'with servants to whose probity they might with increased confidence commit offices of trust'.

Q. 21. "Despite the directives contained in the Wood's Despatch (1854) that active measures of the Government should more especially be directed to convey to the great masses of people useful and practical knowledge, the progress of primary education remained slow for over a century after the Despatch." Discuss.

Ans. The East India Company till 1854 had made no efforts at the education of the masses. The general public was left uncared for in the matter of provision of educational opportunities. Sporadic attempts were, however, made by a few enlightened governors in their individual provinces. The Wood's Despatch (1854) unequivocally defined the objectives of the East India Company in the following words :

"It is our sacred duty to confer upon the natives of India the vast natural blessings which flow from the general diffusion of knowledge."

The Wood's Despatch and the Education of the Masses. Compelled by a sense of moral obligation to the masses the government thought of directing active and special measures to convey to the Indian public useful and practical knowledge. Changes in the policy and programmes of education were brought about. Departments of Public Instruction were opened in five provinces. The Despatch recommended to the government that more and more elementary schools should be opened in every district in each province, that indigenous schools should be encouraged and that scholarships to capable students should be granted so that they might go high up the educational ladder.

Hunter Commission and Primary Education. Despite the express directives for special expansion of elementary education in the country little progress was made. The reviews of the progress of education made during (1855-80) by the government emphasised the need for expanding the education of the masses. The Education Commission (1882-83) was especially required to make an enquiry into whether the government had actually neglected the primary education and how its condition could be improved. The Commssion gave valuable suggestions regarding the policy to be followed. It said that "the elementary education of the masses, its provision, extension and improvement should be the main part of educational system to which strenuous effort of the state needed to be directed in a still larger measure than heretofore. It recommended that the control of primary education should be entrusted to District and Muincipal Boards and the responsibility of meeting expenditure should be placed on different types of funds".

The Indian Education Commission made recommendations on all aspects of primary education for its speedy growth but the pace of progress remained slow because sufficient money did not come forth for its expansion and while additional funds were expended on higher education, primary education was allowed to starve. The pace of progress was checked during the next two decades that followed, especially because the masses were indifferent to education and standards of recognition of primary schools were so raised that the enthusiasm of indigenous effort was chilled.

Efforts by Gokhale. A great dissatisfaction gathered in a mass as the National movement penetrated and diffused itself in every sphere of life. The policital leaders found that even after 150 years of British regime only 6 percent of the masses could read and write. A voice was heard on the floor of the Imperial Council and it resounded:

"An illiterate and ignorant nation can never make any progress and must fall back in the race of life."

On March 19, 1910, a resolution was moved which ran as follows:

"That this council recommends that a beginning should be made of making elementary education free and compulsory throughout the country." But the motion was withdrawn. The small private Bill which Gokhale introduced the following year was rejected.

Harthog Committee and Primary Education. The Report of the Harthog Committee (1929) pointed out the sheer waste and ineffectiveness of primary education but no effective measures were taken to reduce that appalling wastage and stagnation. In 1937 the Abbot Wood report made futher recommendations to improve primary education. It said that the education of children in Primay schools should be based upon their natural interests and less upon book learning and that mother-tongue should be the medium of instruction throughout the high school and that the pre-service course of primary school teachers should be of 3 years' duration after the completion of middle school course. The same year another report was published, which enunciated the epoch-making scheme of basic education.

Congress Ministries and Primary Education. In 1937 Congress came in power in seven provinces. A scheme of free and compulsory primary education was introduced. The implementation of the scheme needed money and the provinces lacked resources; so basic scheme of self-supporting free primary education was evolved. But the Congress ministries toppled and the zeal for a 7 years' free compulsory education through some basic craft began to dwindle.

The growing dissatisfaction in the country and the realisation of the importance of primary education led the Government in 1944 to publish what is known as Sargent Plan. The plan was modest. It recommended for the introduction of a system of universal, compulsory and free education for all boys and girls between the age of 6 and 14 to be completed in not less than 40 years. The country could not wait for such a long time. The period of 40 years was too much to complete the plans: so in 1948 it was recommended that compulsory and free basic education should be introduced for children between the age of 6 and 11 and the target should be achieved by 1958.

The brief review that has been presented in the foregoing paras indicates that despite the directives contained in the Woods Despatch (1854) and the recomendations made by Commissions and Committees for the improvement of primary education no perceptible progress was made during the British regime that ended in 1947.

Q. 22. What reforms did Curzon introduce? Do you think that he served the cause of Indian Education better than any other Viceroy with these reforms?

Ans. Lord Curzon by nature was a benevolent autocrat and by training he was a diehard imperialist. He had an implicit faith in a strong rule. As soon as he landed in India he took up the programme of administrative reconstruction in education. He called an educational conference in 1901 at Shimla and appointed the Indian Universities Commission (1902) for bringing out changes in the university education.

He saw that Indian unversities had become out-moded. Though the London University had been reorganised in 1898, but Indian universities maintained the old structure and pattern. The expansion of higher education was too great for exising universities to manage, the pressure of work on them was so great that they could not discharge their duties well, and no university attached any importance to its real functions. So Curzon appointed the Indian Universities Commission to report upon any proposal that might be made for improving the constitution and working of universities and to recommend to the Governor-General-in-Council such measures as may elevate the standard of university teaching and promote advancement of learning.

The Commission made valuable recommendations on the reorganised model of London University and wanted to improve the existing system. The main recommendations were embodied in an Act, *viz.*, Indian Universities Act (1904). The Act introduced some welcome measures of reform long overdue. For example, it introduced efficiency in university administration by giving statutory recognition to the Syndicate, and by making the new Senate more efficient and manageable than the previous ones.

"It is true", say Nurullah and Naik, "that the act of 1904 by itself did not achieve much. But Curzon will still have the credit of having been the pioneer to start a new movement in university reform which slowly and laboriously, but nevertheless steadily has ever been progressing to its destined goal."

There was an appreciable change in the college education with a change in university education. A grant of 13.5 lacs given to colleges on the basis of their improved their teaching standards, and provided better facilities in the form of well-equipped libraries and laboratories.

The reforms in secondary education were not of less significance. The Government of India Resolution, 1904 laid down the educational policy of Curzon in clear-cut terms. So far as secondary education was concerned, the G.R. said, "The Government is bound in the interests of the Community to see that the education provided in the Secondary Schools is sound." For achieving this objective Lord Curzon substituted in place of the old policy of expansion the new policy of control and supervision. Stricter rules of recognition of secondary schools were framed. No student from an unrecognised school could appear at the Matriculation Examination after 1904. No unrecognised school could get government grant. The result was that all the secondary schools came under the control of the government. For improving the quality of instruction the G.R. 1904 made some very good suggestions. The work of improving instruction was to be entrusted to Inspectors, and the neighbouring government high schools were to be made exact models, and the teachers were to be trained.

It was Lord Curzon's government that for the first time said that Vernacular should be the medium of instruction in Middle Schools and even in high schools pupils should not be permitted to leave the study of Vernaculars, and that English should, in no case, be taught before a child attains the age of 13.

Lord Curzon's ideas about Primary education were very liberal. He said that the active expansion of primary education was the first duty of the state. The Government of India Resolution, 1904 laid down a clearcut financial policy for primary education. Primary education had a claim on provincial revenue and a still more predominant claim on the local bodies' funds. Hence, the G.R. laid down clearly that Boards should spend their educational funds for primary education alone. These bodies should submit their budget to the Director of Public Instruction through their Inspector.

The government advised the primary schools to apply simpler methods of teaching and to base instruction on rural needs. A distinction was also made as regards curricular for rural and urban primary schools.

Lord Curzon tried to reform other aspects of edcuation also. It was on account of his boundless enthusiasm for educational reforms that conferences for technical, agricultural, commercial education were organised; professional education in medicine, engineering, forestry, veterinary science and agriculture was expanded and improved; grants for professional education were initiated; and state scholarships for technological subjects were instituted.

For seven years (1899-1905) Lord Curzon went on toiling hard to reform every aspect of Indian education. He improved University, Secondary and Primary education. He fought vigorously for the cause of mass education and the vernaculars. There was no sphere in education which he did not enter, no space in which his reforming touch was not felt. "What Curzon achieved in 7 years' time would certainly have required twice or thrice as much time for any other man", said Nurullah and Naik. "Lord Curzon was the author of the great movement for educational reconstruction which started in the beginning of this century. He laid the foundation of the reform of Indian Universities which gathered momentum in later years. In primary education it was he who started a drive for expansion. Today it is these services that Indians remember."

Though the Indian opinion opposed his reforms, though his successors tried to revise his policies, yet it was his educational policy that was followed firmly. It was admitted by all that his educational reforms introduced a better system of education; proper control was exercised over private enterprise; universities were reorganised; secondary education was improved and a better organised system of primary education was evolved.

The attempts at reforming Indian education by Lord Curzon were not well-received. The Indian opinion considered his reforms sinister in intentions. People were suspicious of his motives. "He fell far short of the achievement which might have been his", says Cuningham, "had his temperament enabled him to win the sympathies of the people and enlist their cooperation in a congenial progress." The Indian public opinion wanted a free charter to private enterprise and Curzon curtailed it. His education policy was associated with his political ideas that started a violent agitation in Bengal. Swaraj in the freedom of development and unchecked expansion appeared to the people their birthright and therefore they did not cooperate even in his best efforts at reforming education.

Q. 23. What changes were brought about by the Indian Universities Act, 1904 in higher education?

Ans. When the recommendations of the Hunter Commission (1882) were implemented, a phenomenal growth of secondary and higher education took place; college and secondary education both expanded enormously. Government became wedded to the policy of laissez faire. It withdrew from direct management of many institutions. It loosened control and superivission. Two more universities grew up in the Punjab and the North-West Frontier Provinces. Towards the end of the country people started criticising expansion in higher and secondary education. Colleges and schools began undercutting each other. They began lowering fees and thus lowered their standards. These were the conditions when Lord Curzon landed in India.

It was during his Viceroyalty that education in India was critically reviewed and revitalised. According to Nurullah and Naik, "the Viceroyalty of Lord Curzon, the ablest but the most hated Viceroy that ever came to India was one of the most important periods in the history of India. Lord Curzon was the ablest Viceroy because he had the wonderful intellectual gifts, brilliant powers of expression, phenomenal engery, and boundless enthusiasm for work."

No sooner he landed India, than he took up the problem of improving education in the country. Education seemed to deserve the most important position in his scheme of administrative reform.

The first thing that he did was to call a conference at Simla in 1901 and then he appointed a Commission on Education, known as Indian Universities Commission which submitted its report in 1902. The recommendations of the Indian Universities Commission were incorporated in the Government of India Resolution, 1904. The publication of the G.R. was followed by the passing of the Indian Universities Act, 1904.

Lord Curzon was not satisfied with the condition of Indian Universities which were set up on London model by the Wood's Despatch. Though the London University had been remodelled in 1898, Indian universities went on following the old model. They were all examining bodies. The universities in India were all affiliating universities. The expansion in higher education since 1854 had been so great and so much burden was placed on each university that it was incapacitated to discharge its duties efficiently. The number of members in the Senate was large. And yet university teachers had no representation.

The Commission made following recommendations:

1. The existing universities should be reorganised as teaching bodies.
2. No new university should be set up.
3. The undergraduate work should be left to affiliated colleges and only advanced courses should be provided in the university campus.
4. The number of Senators should also be reduced and the period of their tenure should be 5 years at the most.
5. University and college teachers, renowned scholars and Government officials should get adequate representation in the senate.
6. The territorial jurisdiction of a university should be defined.
7. The number of members on the Syndicate should be reduced to 9 and to 15 in exceptional cases. All members should be elected.

8. Rules of affiliation should be strict and affiliation should not be granted to second grade colleges.
9. Every affiliated college should be under the control of a Governing Body which should pay attention to staff, library, hostel and buildings.

The Government of India resolution on Educational Policy was published on March 11, 1904. The resolution gave a historical account of education under the British rule prior to 1902 and discussed the defects of primary, secondary and higher education. The defects that were pointed our the field higher education were as follows:

1. The higher education was highly examination-ridden.
2. It was pursued exclusively for employment under the Government and not for its cultural value.
3. Students had little thinking power and depended on memorisation of facts.
4. The courses were mostly literary and not practical.
5. The thinking in Europe about purely examining universities had changed and hence universities should be first-rate teaching centres.

The recommendations of the Indian Universities Commission (1902) were incorporated in the Indian Universities Act, 1904 which limited the size of the senates, authorised teaching by the university, and imposed more close supervision on its work. The important changes brought abut by the Act were as follows:

1. The size of the Senate should be reduced. The number of fellows should be between 60 and 100 and that they should hold officer for only 5 years.
2. The three older universities, Calcutta, Bombay and Madras were to have 20 members on the Syndicate and the rest 15 only.
3. The territorial limits of each university were defined by the Governor General-in-Council.
4. The importance of Syndicate was enhanced. It was recognised as the executive government of the university.

University teachers were granted representation on the Sndicate.

5.. Government was vested with additional powers. It was required to approve the regulations framed by the Senate. If the Senate failed to frame regulations within a sepecified period the government was empowered to do so.

6. The functions of universities were enlarged. They could not appoint their new professors and lecturers, undertake research, hold and manage educational endownments, their own libraries, labortories and museums, and make regulations regarding the residence of their students.

The Indian Universities Act (1904) led to improvement in College education. Special grants were offered to colleges to improve teaching, equip libraries, and laboratories and provide hostel accommodation to students. A grant of 13.5 lakhs was equitably distributed among provinces with due consideration to the number of university students and the population. The Syndicate was recognised statutorily. The new Senate become more manageable.

Q. 24. Explain Hunter Education Commission (1882-83) and its impact on the development of Education.

Ans. Hunter Education Commission, 1882-83. In 1882 the Government appointed a Commission under the Chairmanship of W.W. Hunter to review the progress of education in the country since the Despatch of 1854. Another reason for the appointment of this Commisstion was the propaganda carried on by the missionaries in England that the education system of India was not carried on in accordance with the policy laid down in Wood's Despatch. The resolution appointing the Commission instructed the Chairman so to reorganise educaion in India that "the different branches of public instruction should, if possible, move forward together and with more equal step than hitherto. The principal object, therefore, of the enquiry of the Commission should be the present state of elementary education throughout the Indian Empire and the means by which this can be extended and improved". The Commission was not "to enquire into the general working of the Indian universities". Thus the Commission mostly confined its remarks to secondary and primary education. It visited all the provinces and passed no fewer than 200 resolutions. Its main recommendations were:

(i) It emphasised the State's special care for the extension and improvement of primary education. "Primary instruction" declared the Commission, "should be regarded as the instruction of the masses through the vernacular, in such subjects as will best fit them for their position in life." While private enterprise was to be welcomed at all stages of education, primary education was to be provided without reference to local co-oepration. The Commission recommended the transference of the control of primary education to the newly set up District and Municipal Boards. The local boards were empowered to levy cess for educational purposes.

(ii) For Secondary education, the principle was laid down that there should be two divisions—one, a literary education leading up to the Entrance Examination of the University and the other of a practical character preparing students for commercial and vocational careers.

(iii) The Commission recommended that an all-out effort should be made to encourage private enterprise in the field of education. To achieve that objective, it recommended the extension and liberalization of the grants-in-aid system, recognition of aided schools as equal to Government institutions in matters of status and privileges etc. The Government should withdraw, it was recommended, as early as possible from the direct management of secondary and collegiate education.

(iv) The Education Commission drew attention to the inadequate facilities for female education outside the Presidency towns and made recommendations for its spread.

The twenty years following the report of the commission saw an unprecedented growth and expansion of secondary and collegiate education. The marked feature of this expansion was the participation of Indian philanthropic activity. A number of denominational institutions sprang up in all parts of the country. Interest was kindled in Indian and Oriental studies apart from the pursuit of Western knowledge. Another development of the period was the setting up of the teaching-cum-examining universities. The Panjab University was founded in 1882 as 'the supreme literary, supreme teaching and supreme examining body". The Allahabad Univeraity was set up in 1887.

The early years of the nineteenth century was a period of growing political unrest and controversies in educational policies. Political developments acted and reacted on educational developments. The official view was that educational expansion had not proceeded on the right lines, that quality had deteriorated under private management, there was lot of indiscipline in schools and colleges and that educational institutions had become factories for the production of political revolutionaries. All these unhealthy developments were attributed to unregulated rapid expansion under irrespousible private enterprise. Nationalist opinion admitted the lowering of standards but emphasised that the Government was not doing its duty to liquidate illiteracy.

In his characteristics zeal for improvement of all branches of administration, Curzon sought to reconstruct education in India. He deprecated the 'too slavish imitation of English models' and Macaulay's colossal blunder in erecting an 'inverted pyramid' and prejudice against Indian vernaculars. He referred to the poor quality of teachers who were 'merely the purveyors of certain articles to a class of purchasees' and found fault with the examination-ridden system of education. His motives were mainly political and only partly educational. Curzon justified the increase of official control over education in the name of quality and efficiency, but actually sought to restrict education and discipline educated mind toward loyalty to the Government. The nationalist mind saw in Curzon's policies an attempt to strengthen imperialism and sabotage development of nationalist feelings.

Q. 25. Discuss the recommendations of Hunter Commission on Secondary Education and discuss their effect on it (1882).

Ans. The Hunter Commission was required to enquire into as to what should be the agency for the expansion of secondary education. It was also required to suggest measures for removing defects in the secondary education. Though there had been a remarkable progress in the period 1854-1882 so far as the growth of secondary schools in the country was concerned, yet many defects had crept in. English as a medium of instruction in secondary schools had by now acquired a place of dominance. The study of vernaculars was neglected specially after 1862 when students in High Schools were required to answer the question papers in English. Secondary education instead of becoming a preparation for life became a preparation for the university. Except Bombay, in no province there was any provision for vocational education at the secondary stage. The secondary school teachers were not adequately trained. There was an acute shortage of training institutions for them.

The first question 'what should be the agency for the expansion of secondary education' was answered with the following set of recommendations.

(a) "The government should gradually withdraw from the field of direct management of secondary schools and leave the expansion to private bodies through a system of grant-in-aid."

(b) "The duty of the government was to establish one high school in every district and after that the expansion of secondary education in that district should be left to private enterprise."

(c) "The government may establish secondary schools in exceptional cases, in place where they may be required in the interests of people, and where the people themselves may not be advanced or wealthy enough to establish such schools for themselves even with a grant-in-aid."

(d) "With a view to making private institutions popular they should not be required to charge fees as high as those of a neighbouring government institution."

To remove the defects of secondary education, the Commission suggested improvements in curricula. Secondary education so far had been purely academic with no provision for vocational education. Hence the Commission recommended bifurcation in the curricula. They said, "We recommend that in the upper classes of High Schools, there should be two divisions: one leading to the Entrance Examination of the universities, the other more practical character intended to fit youths for commercial and non-literary pursuits." This was not at all a practical proposal for the parents were not at all inclined to take advantage of such a system and hence educational system continued to remain academic and bookish.

The Commission's recommendations regarding the medium of instruction were frustrating. It recommended that in Middle Schools the use of vernaculars was preferable to English as medium of instruction and suggested that students should have some elementary knowledge of English also. The implications of this suggestion were that even in Middle Schools English should be taught. The Commission favoured the use of English. The most poisonous effect of the domination of English as a subject of study and as a medium of instruction continued to ruin the cause of education even after 1882. In almost all the provinces English remained the medium of instruction at the secondary stage. The dominance of English in the secondary schools continued to increse : and by 1902 the teaching of English came to be regarded as the prime object of the secondary course. "The study of Indian languages was consequently neglected", said Nurullah and Naik. It was in 1904 that Lord Curzon advocated the use of mother-tongue or vernaculars as medium of instruction upto High School stage and wished English to occupy the place of an optional subject.

The suggestions by the Commission regarding the training of secondary school teachers were rather half-heartedly given. Although the Wood's Despatch had laid a definite stress on the training of secondary school teachers in 1854, yet only two training colleges, one at Madras and the other at Lahore were by now esablished. There was an urgent need for such a training. The Commission recommended that students of training colleges should be examined in Principles and Practice of Teaching and the training period for graduates should be shorter than for others. The Commission recommended that the success in the examination should be a guarantee for permanent employment as a teacher in any secondary school, government or aided.

The Government of India accepted the recommendations of the Commission. It is difficult to understand why the Commission laid emphasis upon the use of English as the medium of instruction. The Commission's recommendations regarding the bifurcation of coures at the high school level was a step in the right direction. The emphasis on technical education as a part of general education was given by the Government of India after 1886 to meet the requirement of local industries. The main effect of the Commission's recommen-dations was that secondary education began to expand rapidly.

Q. 26. "The primary education of the masses its provision and extention should be the main function of the state." Discuss it with reference to recommendations of the Hunter Commission.

Ans. Wood's Despatch laid down that Government should provide education for those "who are utterly incapable of obtaining education worthy of the name by their own unaided efforts." It directed the government to concentrate its energies on primary education. Is also asked the state to withdraw itself from the field of higher education and attend to the general education of the masses. But the government neglected primary education altogether.

The Hunter Commission was appointed to enquire particularly into the manner in which effect had been given to the principles of the Despatch of 1854 and to suggest such measures as it may think desirable in orther to further carrying out of the policy therein laid down. So far as the progress of the primary education was concerned, the Commission was specially asked to enquire into whether the government had actually neglected the primary education and what the state of primary education was and how it could be extended and improved. It was especially asked to suggest how grant-in-aid could be further extended.

The main recommendations of the Commission on the different aspects of Primary education were as follows:

Policy. The Commission boldly acknowledged the importance of primary education by declaring "the elementary education of the masses, its provision, extension and improvement to be that part of the educational system to which the strenuous effort of the state should now be directed in a still larger measure than heretofore." The Commission laid down in clear-cut terms the state policy in connection with the promotion of Primary Education. The state should give its fostering care to the fullest extent. The aim of primary education should be the instruction of the measses and not an instruction leading up to higher education.

Administrations. In England the Education Arts of 1870 and 1876 had placed the responsibility of primary education on the

Country Council; so the Commission recommended that the control of primary education should be transferred to District and Municipal Boards. These boards should deal with the whole system of primary education, keep a careful watch over the educational needs of classes and communities and provide for all such needs either by creating new schools or by aiding existing ones. The government primary schools were also to be transferred to these Boards. In a nutshell, the entire responsibility of the administration of the Primary Education was placed on one body which was too weak to discharge its duties properly. A wiser step for the government would have been to assume the responsibility of primary education itself.

Finance. The Commission recommended "that primary education be declared to be that part of the whole system of public instruction which poses an almost exclusive claim on local funds set apart for education and a large claim on provincial revenues."

The Hunter Commission took a decisive initial step to place the responsibility of meeting expenditure on primary education on different types of funds. For example, the cost of direction, inspection and the provision of normal schools was made the first charge of provincial funds and the expenditure on Primary education was considered to have an almost exclusive claim on local funds (set apart for education) and a large claim on provincial revenues. Every District and Municipal Board was required to have a separate fund for Primary education and the government was to give grants to local boards at the rate of one-third of the total expenditure or 50% of the total assets. The grants to individual scools were to be made strictly on the basis of results. Giving grants on the basis of results was a mistake, as the system of payments-by-results had failed wherever it had been tried. It might make the shirking teachers work, but it reduced the whole educational system to grind-as-dust-rule.

Training of Primary School Teachers. The Commission felt the necessity of training primary school teachers through a network of normal schools widely distributed throughout the country. In order to make the Normal Schools function well they were assigned to one Inspector or the other. Cost, direction, provision and inspection of Normal Schools was the first charge of the provincial funds and Normal Schools were to be so localised as to provide for the local requirements of all Primary Schools whether goverment or aided within the jurisdiction of an Inspector.

Curriculum and Text Books. The Commission felt the need for broadening school curriculum by introducing subjects like the native methods of arithmetic, accounts and mensuration, elements of natural and physical sciences and their application to agriculture, health and the individual arts. But it did not advocate rigidity in curriculum planning and construction. It neither liked unformity in curriculum nor the use of text-books throughout India. Provinces were to be allowed full freedom in the use of text-books.

Thus the Commission made important recommendations on all the aspects of primary education for its speedy growth. But the progress of primary education was not satisfactory during 1886-1902 : the main reason for slow progress was the primary education continued to be neglected and sufficient money was not forthcoming for its full expansion. The government did not give adequate financial aid to local bodies and while additional funds were spent on higher education, primary education was allowed to starve. Initially, the government made some progress in the field of primary education but the pace of progress was checked partially because people who lived in the interior of the country were indifferent to education and also because the rules for recognition were made stricter.

Q. 27. What were the causes of slow growth of primary education in India before 1882?

Ans. The E.I. Company did not make any effort to educate the masses. Most of the Directors believed in the Downward Filtration Theory that education would descend from the higher classes to the lower ones. According to this famous doctrine education was to permeate the masses from above. Hence right from the start the E.I. Company educated the higher classes only and paid some attention to secondary or higher education. The education of the masses was completely ignored.

It was Adam (in 1835) who held up the cause of mass education and urged the government to revive and improve the indigenous educational system. He put forth very sound proposals but his recommendations were turned down because Macaulay was not prepared to help the indigenous schools and was in favour of diffusing western information amongst the upper and middle classes. The Court of Directors wrote back that when the educational needs of the upper and middle classes had been provided for, Mr. Adam's proposals might be taken up on a liberal scale with some fairer prospects of success.

Adam's report revealed the decaying condition of primary education in Bengal and Bihar but the Government showed a lip-sympathy only. Macaulay had pronounced the education is a luxury and is not meant for the masses. The state accepted his verdict. It did not cater to the actual needs of the country and left the masses to themselves.

The missionaries, who were, however, doing some service to the cause of primary education, were also not encouraged. No official patronage was given to them. During Lord Hardinge's time (1844) some 100 elementary schools were opened in Bengal but by 1852 most of them perished because the schools were purely vernacular and did not cater for the tastes of the people. There was a demand for English schools even in the villages and the introduction of fees was resented.

Lord Dalhousie made attempts to improve primary education and introduced in 1853 Adam's plan of popular schools with certain modifications in the light of Thompson's experience. But the progress was slow. In 1854 Bengal had 1400 and Bombay 1200 pupils in primary schools. The main reason of the slow progress was inadequacy of financial support.

The E.I. Company did very little for primary education. In 1854 there were 36,000 pupils in the whole of the country in government primary schools. The mission schools were, however, teaching thrice the number. The Wood's Despatch had advocated for expansion and encouragement of primary education. The Despatch did not desire that the state should take up the education of the masses as her sole responsibility. It only hoped that the state may help the indigenous schools, give them grant-in-aid, inspect, guide and improve them.

For raising funds to meet expenditure on primary education some states imposed a monthly fee which was highly resented. The raising of subscription from the public agonised it because of their general poverty. In 1859, Lord Stanley stressed the need for levying a local educational cess. This again raised controversies. Some provinces liked to follow the instructions of the Wood's Despatch and others followed Stanley's.

The main controversy centred round the school system and its finances. Some provinces tried to improve indigenous schools, encouraged private enterprise and opened government schools to serve as models; others relied on departmental or board schools and entirely neglected the indigenous schools: still others followed the via media, *i.e.*, encouraged the indigenous schools and established the government schools also. The result was that except in a few provinces indigenous schools were totally neglected and even rival institutions were set up to compete against them. Hence, many of them were either absorbed in the new system or were closed down. Siqueria says that percentage of boys attending the indigenous school fell down from 10% in 1820 to 2.5% in 1882.

The second problem was that of finance. As a result of the recommendations of the Despatch recourse had to be taken to local taxation. There were, prior to 1882, two types of local bodies—municipalities in towns and cities and district or taluka local boards in rural areas. The early municipalities had nothing to do with education and could not legally incur any expenditure for educational purposes. Hence they made no contribution to the cause of primary education. The boards in rural areas had been familiar with the idea of levying tax for educational purposes. Hence tax could be levied in rural areas. Local cess was levied in many provinces. But money raised through cess was diverted again into other channels as the government was little concerned with primary education.

Q. 28. What were the recommendations of Hunter Commission on Women and Muslim education and what was their effect on these aspects of Indian education?

Ans. The Hunter Commission made the following recommendations for the growth of female education in India because it realised that famle education had been till now in the most backward condition and needed urgent fostering in every possible way.

1. More liberal grants should be given to girls' schools and the grant-in-aid rules should be easier.

2. Money from local and Municipal Boards and Provincial funds should be spend in an equitable proportion on girls and boys schools.
3. Men and women who are interested in female education should be included in the management of schools.
4. Girls schools should be transferred to the control of Local Boards but a board which is not prepared to take the responsibility should not be compelled to do so.
5. Capable girls should be awarded scholarships so that they may continue their higher education.
6. School managers should provide hostels for women because girls find it difficult to attened schools far away from their homes.
7. Girls should not be charged any fee so that they may be attracted to get education. Charging of fees should be no condition for girls schools for getting a grants-in-aid.
8. Inspectresses should be appointed to inspect and guide girls' schools.
9. Curriculum for girls should be different from what it is for boys as the instruction which is useful for a boy may not be useful for a girl.
10. Girls should be encouraged to get professional training and training schools for female teachers should be started.
11. For women who remain secluded in zenanas from their childhood should be provided with zanana teachers.
12. Secondary schools may be opened for girls only where there is a demand for them.

The results of these recommendations was that in the period of next twenty years 1882-1902 the education of women made slow but steady progress.

Education for Muslims. The Commission also felt that the education for Muslims in India was not adequate. Their backwardness in this respect was alarming. There were very few English speaking Muslims in the country. The Government was desirous of getting the support of Muslim community and wanted to make them rivals of

Hindus and staunch supporters of their own rule. Hence the Commission made the following suggestions:

1. Special arrangements of Muslim education should be regarded as a legitimate charge on local, municipal and provincial funds.
2. Higher education for Muslims be liberally encouraged.
3. A system of special scholarships for Muslims should be established. Scholarships given in primary schools should be tenable in middle schools. Those given in middle schools should be tenable in High Schools and those given in high schools should be tenable in colleges.
4. In all schools a certain proportion of free studentships should be reserved for Muslim students.
5. As far as possible, Muslim teachers should be employed in those Muslim schools where instruction is given through the medium of Hindustani.
6. Muslims should be given proportionate government appointments.
7. The standard of teaching of Muslim primary schools should be raised.
8. For inspecting Muslim primary schools, Muslim Inspecting Officers only should be employed.
9. Association for the promotion of Muslim education should be encouraged.
10. Higher English education should be given to the Muslims.
11. Where such endowments are under the control of individuals and bodies inducement should be given to them by liberal grants to establish English teaching schools and colleges.
12. Educational endowments for the benefit of Muslims under government control should be utilised for that purpose only.

Q. 29. Give the essential features of Sadler Commission Report (1917-19).

Or

Why was the Calcutta University Commission appointed in 1917 and what were its recommendations?

Ans. In 1917 the Government of India appointed a Commission to study and report on the problems of Calcutta University. Dr. M.E. Sadler, Vice-Chancellor of the University of Leeds, was appointed its Chairman. The Commission included two Indian members, namely Sir Asutosh Mukerji and Dr. Zia-ud-din Ahmad. While the Hunter Commission had reported on problems of secondary education and the University Commission of 1902 mainly on the different aspects of university education, the Sadler Commission reviewed the entire field from school education to university education. The Sadler Commission held the view that the improvement of secondary education was a necessary condition for the improvement of university education.

The Commission reported that an effective synthesis between college and university 'was still undiscovered when the reform of 1904 had been worked out to conclusion' and the foundation of a sound university organisation had not been laid down. Further, it reported that 'the problems of high school training and organisation were unresolved'. Although the Commission reported on the conditions of Calcutta University, its recommendations and remarks were more or less applicable to other Indian universities also. The following were the main recommendations:

Recommendations. The main objective of the Commission was 'to inquire into the condition and prospects of the University of Calcutta and to consider the question of a constructive policy in relation to the question it presented'. The Commission discussed the main weaknesses of Higher Education in Bengal and offered the following recommendations:

1. All the teaching resources in the city of Calcutta should be organised so that the Calcutta University may become entirely a teaching university. It means that the colleges in Calcutta should be so grouped together that they may discharge the functions of a teaching university.
2. A separate teaching and residential university should be established at Dacca.

3. Other universities should be established and the older ones be recognised as teaching and residential. It means that mosfussil colleges should be so developed that new centres may gradually rise to become universities.
4. Universities should be freed from excessive official control. The government interference in the academic matters of universities should stop. Its control should be less rigid.
5. An academic council should be set up in each university to deal with all academic questions for example, those connected with the courses of study, examinations, and conferment of degree and research.
6. The senate and the syndicate should be replaced by the Court and the Executive Council respectively. This step would improve the administration of the university.
7. Teaching work and work connected with research should be organised under different departments and each department should have a head.
8. A full time and salaried Vice-Chancellor should be appointed to be the administrative head of the university.
9. Faculties, boards of studies, and other statutory bodies should be formed. Faculties should serve as Departments of teaching.
10. Honours courses should be instituted and they should be distinctly different from the Pass courses.
11. Tutorials and superior kinds of research work should be organised.
12. Provisions should be made for imparting instruction in engineering education, medicine, law, agriculture and technology. Thus, university education would cover practical and vocational studies as well as teachincal and industrial courses.
13. There was a need for coordinating agency. Hence an inter-University Board should be set up.

Q. 30. Discuss the Wardha Scheme of Education and the contribution of Gandhiji to the basic education in the country.

Ans. In 1937 Congress ministries assumed office in seven major provinces of India. Their main concern was to fight for the cause of national system or education in the country. The traditional education system or had been faulty in many respects. It was highly academic. It produced a gulf between the masses and the elite, the rich and the poor, the educated and the uneducated. Education was meant for those who could buy it. It was not everybody's birthright.

Gandhiji Contribution to the Cause of Primary Education. The two main items involved in the programme of establishing a National system of education were mass education and temperance. Both these items ran counter to each other. If a policy of temperance was to be pleaded for and implemented, there would be a marked decline in revenue. If mass education was to be pleaded for, it required a large amount of money—a trenmedously heavy additional expenditure on primary education only. The ministries were at the horns of dilemma.

Gandhiji came to their rescue at such a critical hour. He wrote in Harijan (July 31, 1937), "As a nation we are so backward in education that we cannot hope to fulfil our obligations to the nation in this respect within a given time during this generation, if the programme is to depend on money. In have, therefore, made bold, even at the risk of losing a reputation for constructive ability, to suggest that education would be self-supporting. I would therefore begin the child's education by teaching it a useful handicraft and enabling it to produce from the moment it begins its training. Thus every school can be made self-supporting, the condition being that the state takes over these products."

The same year in October an All India National Education Conference was organised at Wardha under the presidentship of Mahatma Gandhi and his ideas on national education were discussed and it was resolved that free and compulsory education should be provided to children for seven years (6-14) through mother-tongue and that the process of education throughout this period should centre round some form of manual and productive work and that all other abilities that were to be developed should be integrally related to the central craft chosen with due regard to the environment of the child. The conference expected that this system of education would gradually be able to cover the remuneration of teachers.

The Wardha Scheme. A Committee was appointed under the chairmanship of Dr. Zakir Hussain to design a scheme on the lines suggested by the above resolution. It submitted its report in 1938 which came to be known as Wardha Scheme of Education. The main aspects of this scheme of education were as follows :

1. a free and compulsory education for age group 6-14,
2. craft-centred instruction,
3. mother-tongue as the medium of instruction,
4. teaching of craft in a way that it might enable the school to meet the cost of education,
5. emphasis on manual work,
6. co-education upto 5th class,
7. education to be closely related to social and physical environment of the child, *i.e.*, to his home, his village, crafts, industries, occupations followed in his neighbourhood,
8. course in a basic craft, mother-tongue, mathematics, social studies, general science, art work, Hindustani music—all these subjects correlated with the basic craft,
9. little importance to be attached to examinations and text books.

A National Scheme of Education. The Wardha Scheme involves the basic principles of the National System of Education as perceived and conceived by Gandhiji. The scheme is known as a scheme of Basic Education because, (a) it is expected to form the basis of our national culture, (b) it provides the basic amount of knowledge which is essential for an average Indian child to have an intelligent insight into his environment, (c) it is related to the basic interests and needs of the child, and (d) it is correlated with the basic occupation of the community.

Basic education is regarded as the most valuable gift which Gandhiji bestowed to India. It is one of the 14 pillars of his programme for national reconstruction. A social revolution could be made possible by such a scheme of education which was expected to create a free, classless, egalitarian society which recognised dignity of labour as the most important value of life. Basic education unlike the traditional education would be universal, free and compulsory. It should be free because it would cover all costs of expenditure and there would be no problem of finance.

The Experiements in this National System of Education were started as early as 1938 just after its being adopted in the Haripura session of the Indian National Congress. But it was only after the attainment of Independence that Basic education could be considered as the national pattern of elementary education for children of 6 to 14 years of age.

Education in a basic school began to be imparted through the medium of work and activities connected with physical and social environment but it could not be adopted universally. A common syllabus from class I to VIII was recommended for the country as a whole and the differences between basic and non-basic syllabi were reduced to the minimum.

Q. 31. Discuss the recommendations of Sargent Committee on Basic Education. Why were the proposals not accepted then? What were its recommendations regarding Secondary Education?

Ans. In the year 1944, Sir John Sargent, the then Educational Adviser to the Government of India, prepared a report on the post-war educaional development on the request of the Central Advisory Board of Education. The report is known by various names; the scheme of Post-War Development in India. Report by the Central Advisory Board of Eduction, and Sargent Plan or Scheme. The aim of the Plan was to reorganise the entire system of education at a total cost of Rs. 313 crores and was to be carried out in 8 stages by means of 8 five year programmes. It aimed at attaining the educational standard of contemporary England within 40 years.

The First Comprehensive Scheme of National Education. The Sargent Scheme has been the most comprehensive scheme, so far presented by the Government for the development and expansion of Indian education. It presented a very detailed scheme of educational reconstruction from top to bottom, from primary to universities, and higher technical institutions. It touched every aspect of Indian education. 'It is the first comprehensive scheme of national education', wrote K.G. Saiyidin, "it does not start with the assumption that India was destined to occupy a place of educational inferiority in the comity of nations : it is based on the conviction that what other countries have achieved in the field of education is well within the competence of this country."

It is said about the report that it was not an original document. It was a patchwork of different reports published from time to time by the Central Advisory Board of Education to consider the different aspects of Indian educational problems. So far as the Basic education is concerned it is the summary of the useful suggestions made by previous reports and schemes including the Wardha Scheme. The scheme was not accepted because the time of 40 years was required to implement it and the educational public leaders did not like to lengthen the period of attaining mass literacy to such an extent. Had the scheme been implemented, at least some targets would have been achieved; the percentage of illiterates would have gone down. But the scheme was not given a fair trail and the reform in education was delayed. The main recommendations of the Sargent Report about Basic education are given below:

Recommendations Regarding Basic Education:

1. Provision should be made for free and compulsory primary or basic education for all children between the ages of 6 and 14.
2. The course of basic education should be divided into parts: Junior Basic and Senior Basic, the former to be given to all children between the ages 6-11 and the latter to be given to those who could not proceed to high school.
3. Basic Education should not be expected to pay for itself through the sale of articles produced by the pupils.
4. The basic craft to be taught should be suitable to local conditions.
5. Mother-tongue should be the medium of instruction of Senior and Junior Basic Schools.
6. The education imparted should be general and emphasis should not be laid on the teaching of 3 R's only.
7. English should not be taught in Junior Basic Schools. It can be taught in Senior Basic Schools only when the

Education Department of the Province gives its decision in its favour.

8. The standards of training, recruiting and conditions of service of teachers should be raised.
9. In place of external examinations there should be internal examinations and successful candidates should be awarded certificates.
10. Attendence officers should be appointed to introduce compulsion.
11. The Senior Basic Schools should provide for corporate living. Physical training, organising of games are essential to supplement the instruction given in the class room.

Recommendations Regarding Secondary Education. The main recommendations regarding Secondary education are given below:

1. Secondary education should be for 6 years for selected students between age 11 and 17.
2. Admission to secondary schools should be made on selective basis and only promising students, about 20% of the children, attending Junior Basic schools should be admitted to High Schools.
3. High schools shall be of two types—Academic High Schools and Technical High Schools.
4. Every child entering a High School remains there till the age of 14 compulsorily. Even after this period steps should be taken to see that children are not withdrawn from the school before the completion of the course.
5. Subjects in the Academic High School as well as in the Technical should be common; for example, mother-tongue, English, Modern Indian Languges, Indian and World History, Indian and World Geography, Science, Mathematics, Agriculture, Economics, Music, Art and Physical Training. The Technical High Schools should include Science, Wood work, Metal work, Elementary Engineering, Drawing, Book keeping, Type writing, Short

Hand, Accountancy, Commercial, Practice, and Domestic Science.

6. High School leavers should receive an education that will fit them for direct entry into occupations and professions.
7. High school education sould not be preliminary to university education and should be complete in itself.

Q. 32. Explain the Radhakrishnan Commission 1948 and the University Education Commission 1948-49. Its aims, teaching standards, examination system.

Ans. THE RADHAKRISHNAN COMMISSION (1948)

The Radhakrishnan Committee had lot to say about the University Education but it reviewed the secondary education in the country as well. It was this commission which remarked that "Secondary Education continues to be the weakest link in our educational machinery and needs urgent reform." It recommended:

(i) a twelve year secondary course instead of ten years,

(ii) that teachers' lot be improved,

(iii) admission to the university be after intermediate examination,

(iv) liberal grants and better teaching facilities be available.

THE UNIVERSITY EDUCATION COMMISSION, 1948-49

This Commission was appointed under the Chairmanship of Dr. Sri. S. Radhakrishnan. Experts from U.S.A. and U.K. were invited to serve on this Commission. A number of educationists of the country were also made its members. This Commission was appointed through a resolution of the Central Ministry of Education on November 4, 1948. In all there were ten members of the Commission. The Commission was required to study the problem of university education in the country and to suggest measures from its reforms keeping in view the needs and aspirations of the people. The then Minister of Education, Abdul Kalam Azad inaugurated this Commission on December 6, 1948 and gave it the necessary directions. The members of the Commission showed great interest in their work. They visited various universities in the country and studied their varying problems deeply. The Commission interviewed a number of university teachers and students for understanding their problems The Commission prepared a questionnaire and sent it to interested persons for obtaining their suggestions for reforms of university education. About 600 persons returned this questionnaire with their suggestions. The Commission submitted its report within a year. Below we are hinting at some of the more important recommendations of the Commission.

THE AIMS OF UNIVERSITY EDUCATION

The Commission has laid down certain aims of university education in the country keeping in view the past tradition, the present conditions and future prospects of the country. In this context the Commission took into consideration the personal interests of students and also of the nation. While defining the aims the Commission has been also conscious of the international obligations. We are giving below the aims of university education as laid down by the Commission:

1. The aims of university education should be to produce able citizens who can take up national responsibilites successfully in various fields. The university has to produce able administrators and suitable workers in various occupations and industries. The university has to provide leadership in the various walks of life in the best interest of the nation.
2. It is the duty of a university to preserve and develop the culture and civilization of the land. It is on the basis of one's culture that one may acquire self-confidence, self-respect and self-dependence. These virtues on the part of citizens will make the nation really very strong.
3. The university should generate new ideas and discard those which are likely to prevent the growth of the nation. For progress it is necessary to rise above supersititions. The university has to help the students to imbibe good aspects of their culture and to accept new values for all-round development.
4. The university should provide opportunities to acquire all kinds of knowledge.

5. The university has to educate the mind and soul of the student in order that he may grow in wisdom.
6. It is the responsibility of the university to create a consciousness in students for protecting the directive principles as to be laid down in the Constitution. The university has to make the foundation of democracy strong and it has to develop the spirit in students for ensuring equality, fraternity and social justice to all while maintaining the integrity of the nation.
7. The university has to develop the spirit of universal brotherhood and internationalism in students.
8. The University has to make new discoveries and inventions and it has to develop new original ideas in order to make the society strong.
9. The university has to instil moral values in students while making them well disciplined.

TEACHING STANDARDS

The Commission has attached great importance to high teaching standards. So the Commission has urged that the standards of teaching and examination should be so raised that our students may be equal to their counterparts anywhere in the world. The Commission has expressed regret that the prevailing standard of university is deplorable because of the fall of standard of intermediate education. Consequently able students are not coming for University education. Therefore the standard of university education has also fallen down. The Commission has given the following suggesions for improving university standards:

1. Only the intermediate passed students should be admitted to universities.
2. In every State a good number of intermediate colleges should be opened. If intermediate classes are attached to universities at some places, they should be shifted on separate premises.
3. Intermediate class students should be given opportunities for obtaining vocational education.

4. A degree college affiliated to a university should not have more than 1500 students in it. Similarly, a teachng university should not have more than 3,000 students.
5. A degree college should have at least 180 working days in a year.
6. The teachers should prepare their lectures more carefully and they should take special interest in tutorial work.
7. No book should be regarded as a text-book and in no course text-books should be prescribed.
8. Too many private students should not be permitted to sit at a university examination. A minimum percentage of attendance at lectures should be fixed for students. Students falling below this percentage of attendance should not be allowed to sit at the examination concerned.
9. For tutorial work suitable teachers should be appointed.
10. Provision should be made for good libraries and well-equipped science laboratories.

POST GRADUATE TEACHING AND RESEARCH

The Commission has given the following suggestions in this regard:

1. A close relationship should be maintained between teachers and research scholars. Admission to post-graduate classes should be governed by an all India examination.
2. Ph.D. scholars should be chosen on all India basis. The duration of research for Ph.D. should be at least two years. The Ph. D. research scholars should also have knowledge of allied subjects.
3. Ph.D. scholars producing good research work should be given opportunities for further studies. Such research scholars should be given fellowships and their selection should be made on all India basis.
4. The Education Ministry should grant stipends to those. D. Litt. and D.Sc. degree-holders who have evinced capacities of high order of research. No partiality should be made in the selection of such degree-holders.

5. D.Litt. and D.Sc. degress should be awarded only on original works.
6. Universities should be given adequate financial assistance.

THE CURRICULUM

The Commission has given the following recommendations for reorganising the university curriculum:

1. Knowledge should be considered as one whole. The courses of studies are only means of composite knowledge and they should not be considered as an end. Hence while drawing up the courses of study the connection and link between the varying aspects must not be missed. In other words, knowledge should be cultivated in its entirety. There should be a connecting bond between the general, intellectual and vocational education.
2. The courses of studies for universities and intermediate college should be reorganised on the above principles. Only then the defects of the existing system of education may be removed.
3. The relation between the general and specialised education should be defined in the context of its relevance to individual, social and professional benefit to the student.

PROFESSIONAL EDUCATION

Vocational education, teachers' training, engineering, technology and medical education may be included under professional education. The Commission has given suggestions for improving these types of education. Some of the more important suggestions are being given below:

Education in Trade and Commerce. The Commission has suggested that commerce students should be given practical instructions in institutions of trade and commerce for three or four years. Their education should not be only bookish.

Teacher's Training

1. Greater attention should be paid on practical experience and less on theoretical. Accordingly, the curriculum should be reorganised in a more useful manner.

2. Teachers of training colleges should have enough teaching experience in schools.
3. Higher degree in education should be given to those students who have already taught for a number of years.
4. Teachers of training colleges should do original researches in the field of education.

Engineering and Technology Education. The Commission gave the following suggestions about this:

1. Institutions imparting education in engineering and technology should be nationalised. They should not be allowed to be a property of some person.
2. More colleges of engineering and technology should be opened in the country.
3. The curriculum of these institutions should be diversified according to the needs of the country.
4. Provision should be made for higher researches in these institutions.
5. Greater importance should be attached to the acquisition of practical skill and knowledge in these institutions.
6. Provision should be made in these institutions for special researches for a high order in the field of technology.
7. These institutions should be free to manage their own affairs. They should not be controlled by the ministry and bureaucracy.

Education in Medicine. The Commission gave the following suggestions for the improvement of medical education:

1. Researches should be made in the Ayurvedic and Unani systems of medicine and they should be developed.
2. Greater importance should be attached to preventive methods and nursing.
3. Not more than 190 students should be admitted to a medical college within a year and not more than ten patients should be kept under a student.

4. Institutions for post-graduate medical education should be well-equipped with tools, medicines and experiened teachers.
5. Special training should be given to students for treating patients in rural areas.

Education of Women. The Commission has given the following suggestions for improving the quality of women education:

1. Education of women may be similar to that of men in certain aspects, but it should be different also in some others in view of their different nature and duties of life.
2. Greater facilities should be given for promoting women education.
3. Able and experienced teachers should be available to guide women in the selection of their nature of education.
4. Women should be well informed about their rights and duties pertaining to the society and nation.
5. It is necessary for women to receive education in domesic science.
6. In institutions where co-education is prevalent, special facilities should be provided for women.

Religious Education. The Commission has made the following suggestions in this regard:

1. Instruction in each institution should be begun with self-meditation.
2. Biographies of great religious leaders of various religions should be taught to the first year students of the graduate classes. In these, leaders like Swami Dayanand, Shankeracharya, Buddha, Jesus Christ and Prophet Mohammad etc. may be included.
3. Essentials of all religions should be taught to the second year students of the graduate course.
4. The third year students should be taught the essentials of philosophies and problems of religions.

MEDIUM OF INSTRUCTION IN UNIVERSITIES

India is a land of languages. The various States stand for their own regional languages. The Commission studied the difficulties involved in this sphere and has given the following suggestions for solution of the language problem:

1. Excepting Sanskrit any other Indian language should replace English as the medium of instruction at earliest. Sanskrit cannot be made the medium as it involves many practical difficulties.
2. The students of universities and higher secondary schools should be taught the national language alongwith English and a regional language.
3. Regional languages should be the medium of university education. Certain subjects at the university stage should be taught through the medium of national language.
4. The national language and the regional languages should be developed.
5. A Committee of scholars of all the regional languages should be formed for reconstructing technical terms in sciences. This Committee should be given the responsibility of writing standard text-books. These text-books should be translated into various languages under the supervision of this Committee.
6. The State Governments should provide facilities for teaching national language in universities, degree colleges and higher secondary schools.
7. Teaching of English should be continued in high schools and universities in order that the students are acquainted with achievement in other countries.

STUDENTS' WELFARE AND CHARACTER FORMATION

The Commission has given the following suggestions in this respect:

1. Admissions to degree colleges and universities should be on merits.

2. Scholarships should be given on merits only to the poor and deserving students.
3. The students should be given the necessary health facilities.
4. Sports, games and gymnasiums should be organised in various schools.
5. Two years' compulsory physical training should be introduced for students. The students taking training in N.C.C. and handicapped ones may be exempted from this.
6. Students' Unions should be made free of politics. They should be engaged in activities directed towards their physical, educational and character growth.
7. Provision of physical training should be made under the N.C.C. programme for educational institutions.
8. Good hostels should be constructed.
9. Students should be given opportunities to participate in the administration of schools, colleges and universities.
10. A students' department should be opened in each university and degree college.
11. An Advisory Committee should be opened in each educational institution for protecting the interests of students.

UNIVERSITY EXAMINATION SYSTEM

The Commission made a deep study of the problems pertaining to examinations and opened that examination system could not be abolished. But it has given a number of suggestions for its reforms. Some of the more important suggestions have been as below:

1. The Government of India should appoint a Committee of experts and educationists for suggesting reforms in the existing examination system.
2. An Examination Board of three members should be constituted in each university to do the following things:
   (a) To suggest reforms in the curriculum.
   (b) To guide teachers of degree colleges and universities for constructing objective tests.

(c) The Examination Board will assess the qualitative utility of various colleges and accordingly will suggest measures for their qualitative improvements.

(d) To prepare a questionnaire for psychological test of those students of higher secondary schools who are aspirants for university education.

The Commission gave the following suggesions for removing the defects of the existing examination system and advised that these suggestions should be accepted until a new system of examination is not evolved :

1. For any government service a university degree should not be considered as essential.
2. One-third of the maximum marks should be allotted to sessional works.
3. Only such teachers should be appointed as examiners who have at least five years' teaching experience.
4. For the three years degree course a number of examinations should be held from time to time. Only one examination for obtaining a degree is not enough.
5. The examination standard should be raised. This standard should be the same for all universities. At least 70 per cent for first division, 55 per cent for second division and 40 per cent for third division should be fixed.

ADMINISTRATION

The Commission has remarked that the university administration is full of defects and the same must be removed for introducing any reform. It has given the following suggestions for reforming the university administration:

1. The university education should be brought under the Concurrent list of the States.
2. The Central Government should have only limited powers on universities. It may have a say only in the determination of administrative policy, giving grants and facilities and guidance for national education.

3. The University Grants Commission should be organised. For its help a number of committees should be appointed. This Commission should be made responsible for assigning grants to various universities in the country.
4. A degree college should be recognised only if it fulfils all the conditions.
5. A good Managing Committee should be considered necessary for a degree college.
6. Each university should teach so the idea of an affiliating university should be rejected.
7. All government degree colleges should be merged into various universities of the area concerned.

FINANCE

The Commission has remarked that most of the universities in the country are suffering from financial stringency, so they cannot implement any useful scheme. Therefore each university should be given adequate financial assistance. The Commission has given the following suggestions in this respect:

1. The State Government should shoulder the entire cost of university education.
2. Recurring and non-recurring grants should be given even to non-government colleges. Definite rules should be framed for giving recurring grants. Only those colleges should be given grants which follow these rules.
3. Income-tax concession should be given to those persons and firms which give donations to educational institutions.
4. In addition to recurring and non-recurring grants others financial assistance should also be given to universities for implementing certain schemes.

UNIVERSITIES IN RURAL AREAS

Most of the universities in India are established in urban areas. So they cater to the needs of only urban people. So the Commission has remarked that 80 per cent of the Indian population falling in rural area is being deprived of the benefits of university education. Moreover, the university education is not patterned on the needs and aspirations of the rural people. Therefore the Commission has recommended that from now on new universities should be established in rural areas in order to meet the requirements of the rural people.

Q. 33. Evaluate the recommendations of the Radhakrishnan Commission with its merits and demerits.

Ans. The Commission has offered important suggestions for the improvement of university education in the country after studying very deeply the problems and inadequacies of the existing universities. The Commission has realised that the leaders in the various walks of life in the country have impact of university education on them. It cannot be denied that the Commission has placed before the country important suggestions for improvement of university education. However, we cannot overlook some of the demerits of its recommendations. Below we are hinting at the merits and demerits of the work of the Commission:

Merits of the Recommendations. The Commission has accepted that human welfare as the basis of university education. It is on this basis that the Commission has tried to harmonise the western and oriental cultures in its recommendations for reforms in the university education. In view of the 80 per cent of the Indian people residing in villages, the Commission has rightly recommended that new universities should be established in rural areas for meeting the requirements of the village people. Since India is a religious country, the Commission has recognised the necessity of introduction of some kind of religious and moral education in universities in order to control the violent waves of materials of the present-day civilization. The Commission has not given all importance to material progress only. It has recognised the need of the spiritual development of the youths of the day. In this context the Commission has rightly emphasised the importance of study of humanities and the development of the spirit of universal brotherhood. Thus, the Commission has tried to preserve and perpetuate the ancient Indian ideals of life in general.

The Commission rightly perceived the various inadequacies of the existing university education and drew the attention of the people towards them and has given important suggestions for meeting them.

The Commission has drawn our attention to the following defects of the university education in the country:

1. Education not effecting the harmonious development of students.
2. Continual fall of standard.
3. Lack of proper vocational education.
4. Unrealistic examination system.
5. Lack of feeling of responsibility on the part of students.
6. The difficult and useless curriculum.
7. Infiltration of the evil impact of various political parties in the universities.
8. Groupism for serving selfish interests.
9. Development of indiscipline in students.
10. Educational system having no direct relationship with life.
11. Frustrated teachers because of financial difficulties.
12. Lack of necessary equipments and buildings in universities.
13. Lack of suitable hostels, liberaries, reading rooms and laboratories. Besides, the Commission has hinted at many other defects also.

The Commission has defined the aims and objectives of university education for the first time. The Commission has tried to spell out the objectives of University education in such a manner that the students after graduation may not feel helpless in face of onerous duties of life. The Commission has rightly recommended for the enhancement of pay scales of teachers in order that better persons may come to teach in universities and may prevent the falling of educational standards. The Commission has emphasised the importance of advanced research and development of knowledge. It has decried the penetration of political parties and groupism in the universities and has given many suggestions for improvement of university atmosphere. The Commission has very rightly emphasised the need of the development of technical, vocational, medical and law education. Similarly, the Commission has given useful suggestions for reforms of teachers' education.

DEMERITS OF THE RECOMMENDATIONS

On the one side the Commission has given suggestions of far-reachng importance for reforms of university education in the country, but on the other it has ignored many aspects which needed more attention. For example, the Commission has not chosen to study deeply the problems of medium of instruction. It has just given some casual suggestions in this regard. Similarly, the problem of religious education has not been given that attention which it merited because of its great importance in a religious country like India. The Commission has not given much attention to the problem of women education. The importance of education in fine arts has also been ignored by the Commission. However, it will have to be admitted that inspite of all these inadequacies in the recommendations, the Commission has revolutionised the field of university education by its various suggestions for reforms of univerisities in our country. It cannot be denied that the universities in our country would have done their job in a much better way, if the various recommendations of the Commission were fully and properly implemented.

Q. 34. Discuss the problems of Indian Universities before 1948. What recommendations were made by the University Education Commission?

Ans. After the achievement of Independence in 1947, the national leadership set on foot programmes of social and economic reconstruction. Education being the chief instrument of social change, needed a revolution. The first steps taken in the direction of educational reconstruction were the appointment of a series of commissions to survey, study, review, and recommend improvements in different sectors and stage of education. Everyone wanted to have an educational system most suitable to the needs of the country. A more specific and detailed direction became inevitable to raise the quality of higher education and expand it.

Problem of University Education Before 1947. To look into the problems of Indian universities that had cropped up in the pre-Independence period just before 1947, the then University Education Commission under the chairmanship of Dr. S. Radhakrishnan was appointed. The Commission was required 'to suggest improvements and extension that may be desirable to suit the present and future need of the country'. It was felt that in the British regime, university education was unnecessarily restricted and confined to a limited sphere. Its main aim had become nothing but the preparation of students for passing examinations.

The country wanted a new system of higher education which could develop knowledge and critical thinking rather than mechanical passing of examinations. The old system was producing a large production of indifferently educated graduates of arts who could make no contribution to economic growth and national development.

The Commission surveyed the whole field of Higher education and its correlates. After surveying all the features and conditions of the old system of higher education, the Commission concluded that the general dissatisfaction with falling standards of teaching and examinations and with the conduct of university administration and control was justified. The Commission was happy to note the deep general awareness in the masses, of the significant role higher education could play in schemes of national development and national well-being. It was distressed to observe the inadequacy in the present position of higher education.

The problems of higher education that required an urgent and immediate solution were:

(a) determining of aims and objectives of higher education afresh because preparing students for passing an examination was no worthy aim,

(b) gearing up higher education to the man-power needs,

(c) improving administration and control of universities,

(d) financing of higher education in the country,

(e) improving the standards of teaching and research,

(f) improving the examination system so that proper emphasis may be laid on critical thinking rather than on mechanical memorisation,

(g) deciding a common medium of higher education throughout the country,

(h) introducing religious instruction in universities,

(i) providing professional education,

(j) examining the causes of student unrest and its remedies.

Aims. The Commission formulated the following as aims of Higher Education. These objectives were decided upon with due consideration to the needs of the country:

1. The Commission desired that universities should aim at providing leadership in politics, administration, industry, commerce, and various professions. They should be required to meet the demands of all types of higher education in literary, scientific, technical, and professional.
2. "Universities should be", said the Commission, "the training grounds and organs of civilization." They should train intellectual pioneers to bring about a social change. The country needed a new social order—an order based on equality, liberty and justice. University education should aim at 'the development of social, political, and economic democracy'.
3. The aim of university education should be the development of intellectual adventuresomeness in young men and women. They should be able to take up daring enterprises in reseach and scientific inquiry.

Improvement in the Quality of Education. To maintain higher standards of education the Commission suggested for the first time a new pattern of education. A minimum education of 12 years, the last two years being specially spent as preparatory to university education, were considered utterly necessary. The introduction of 3 year-degree course thereafter for the first university degree would make higher education comparable to such education in other advanced countries of the world. The boy or girl who gets admission to the university should be mature enough to carry on self-study and work in the well-equipped library and laboratory.

The enrolment in a university and in a college according to the Commission should not exceed a certain limit—three thousand in a university and fifteen hundred in a college. At the end of the Intermediate stage a number of diversified courses should be provided so that the undeserving students may get entry into various occupational institutions and deflection of this type may check overcrowding in the universities. "We cannot look with equanimity", said the Commission, "upon the present situation in which a large number of students who are obviously unfit for higher education enter the universities and swell the percentage of failure. It is likely that many of these would succeed much better if they took to an occupation requiring craftsmanship after 10 or 12 years of schooling."

Improvement in Teaching. Improvement in standards was not possible without improvements in teaching methods. The Commission suggested that lectures should be supplemented by tutorials, liberary work and exercises. These devices were necessary to make for fuller treatment of the subject-matter and they would be treated as things simply to supply deficiencies. In the first year of the three-year degree course as recommended by the Commission senior teachers, professors and readers should kindle interest for the subject in the new entrants.

Teaching and research are so related that one implies the other. Teaching without research becomes stale. Research without teaching has no value. Hence the Commission recommended that all university teachers should engage themselves in research.

The value of a text book as an effective tool of learning may be great in a school. The provision of quality text books may be an effective programme for raising standards of school education but the practice of prescribing text books for higher education, according to the Commission was not a healthy one.

Increasing Facilities for Research. The Commission stressed the importance of scientific research and post-graduate training. The undergraduate work is but complementary and a by-product. The major work of a university is research and post-graduate training.

With a view to increasing the standards of post-graduate training it was suggested that admissions to master-level courses should be selective and a close personal contact sould be maintained throughout the course between the teacher and the taught. Rules for admission to M.A. and M.Sc. degree should be uniform throughout the country. Master-level courses should not be considered as ends in themselves.

Master-level courses are merely meant to train research workers because they provide a scope, a purview for intensive study of a special field. The study of the field at master-level is of limited kinds. The depth and breadth of the grasp can be achieved by pursuing the course at Ph.D. level. Universities should provide facilities for conducting Ph.D. courses so that desirous students may achieve a fuller view of the subject studied.

Research work should be developed in all universities. A large number of research fellowships should be instituted in every university. Facilities for research should also be provided in those fields which have been neglected so far or which are still new born or developing. The Commission was distressed by the lack of facilities for research and the unhappy position as regards the award of scholarships and fellowships at the post-graduate and Ph.D. levels.

Development of Professional Education. By 'professional education', the Commission meant 'a preparation for exacting responsible service in the professional spirit'. The Commission regarded a less exacting preparation for a responsible service as vocational or technical education. A sense of deep social responsibility was regarded as the foundation of professional education. The Commission was distressed about and sorry for the fact that actual professional education had not been so far provide. The reason was clear. It had not instilled in the professional man that sense of social responsibility and philosophy by which he should live and work. For example, the teacher was a teacher by profession, but not by the philosophy of life he held.

Agricultural education seemed to be neglected at all stages and specially at the university stage. The Commission said that agricultural education should be recognised as the most important national issue and the study of agriculture in primary and secondary schools and colleges should be given a higher priority. Agricultural colleges should be established in rural areas. Round about them experimental farms should be established and developed extensively. The long-time agricultural policy of the nation should be determined by some Institute especially set up for this purpose.

Professional education for commerce was too academic. Ample opportunities should be provided for practical work in 3 or more kinds of firms. After graduation some students may specialise in a particular branch; for example, in accountancy, and get specific requisite training in that branch. The enrolment to M.Com. degree should be restricted. The post-graduate training in Commerce should be less bookish and theoretical.

Teacher training programmes needed reconstruction and change. Courses required remodelling. Practice teaching neede more time. The isolation of teacher-training institutions from the school practices should be broken. The teacher educators should have first experience of school teaching. For admission to master's degree in education some experience of teaching and research was essential.

The existing engineering and technological institutions are national assets; hence they should be assisted in all respects to grow. The number of engineering colleges should be increased. The schools for training foremen, draftsmen, oversers should be multiplied. At suitable places post-graduate courses should be established to train design or research engineers. The Commission thus made vey valuable recommendations for reforming education in agricultural, commercial, legal, engineering, medical and teaching professions.

Improvement in the Examination System. The Commission was sure that the examination system at the university level was very defective. "We are convinced that if we are to suggest one single reform in university education it should be that of the examinations." Examinations should not be abolished because they are very useful. Evaluation is an essential element of the educative process. Examinations as a tool of evaluation, if they are rightly designed and intelligently used, are a 'must'. The Commission suggested a scheme of internal evaluation that 33% of the total marks to be awarded in a subject should be reserved for the work done during the course of instruction. The Commission recommended that it should not be necessary to take an examination after a specified period of time, but work should be planned in self-contained units and some of these units should be examined before the expiry of that period. The university degree should be awarded only after the successful completion of all the units.

The Commission did not like the present practice of awarding a first class to those who secure 60% marks or above and a second class to those who get 48% or above. To raise standards of higher education, the standards of success should be elevated to 70% for a first, 55% to 60% for a second, and 40% to 54% for a third. In all post-graduate examinations a viva voice test should be conducted compulsorily. The Commission wanted to make essay type examinations more valid and reliable.

Student Welfare. "The student is not created for the university, but the university exists for the student", such was the nation about the relationship beween the university and its student body. It was the duty of the university to look after the welfare of student community. A young man, if he is capable, should get a chance to be admitted to any university. He should be given the courses he wants to take. He should be financially assisted if he is needy and deserving. He should be provided with facilities, of a thorough medical examination at the time of admission and periodical examination later. The university campus should be provided with good health services and facilities. For co-curricular activities, there should be a provision of gymnasia, playgrounds, equipment, N.C.C. and social service programmes. Unions should be set up in all universities but care should be taken that they do not involve themselves in political activities. A modified proctorial system may be established to look after the general welfare of students.

Q. 35. Discuss the recommendations and aims of the Secondary Education Commission (1952-53).

Ans. RECOMMENDATIONS OF THE COMMISSION

Aims of Secondary Education

The Commission has defined the aims of secondary education in the following manner:

1. To Produce Ideal Citizens. The Commission has realised that no nation can progress without a national feeling alongwith social feeling. Therefore, it has laid down that the aim of secondary education should be to produce such ideal citizens who imbued with strong national and social feeling are prepared to shoulder their responsibilites and duties and can easily offer any sacrifice for the sake of their nation. Such citizens should have co-operative feeling directed towards universal brotherhood. While describing the national spirit the Commission has sub-divided it into three parts:

(a) In the first part the Commission has explained the concept of national feeling. Then it has urged that the students of the country should have faith in the greatness and importance of culture of their country and they should feel proud of the same.

(b) In the second part the Commission suggests that the student should himself make a self-study and analyse his own positive and negative traits with a view to improve his character and personality.

(c) In the third part it has been emphasised by the Commission that one should be prepared to make any sacrifice for the nation.

2. To Develop Capacity for Earning Money. The Commission is of the view that after having received secondary education one should be able to earn enough for maintaining himself. For developing this capacity vocational subjects should be introduced in the curriculum.

3. Quality of Leadership. Secondary education should develop the quality of leadership in students. This quality is very necessary for the sake of democracy and for the development of the country as a whole.

4. To Develop Human Virtues. Man is a social animal. So he should have the spirit of co-operation, discipline, humility, love, kindness and the feeling of brotherhood. The curriculum must have such subjects which may inculcate these virtues in students. Science, literature, fine arts, humanities, music and dance are some of such subjects.

Duration of Secondary Education. The Commission has recommended that the secondary education should be for children between 11 to 17 years of age. It has divided this seven years' education into two parts—(1) Junior High School stage for three years and (2) High School for four years.

The Commission has recommended the introduction of three years' degree course. For this secondary education should continue upto the eleventh class and the twelfth class should be added to the first degree course (B.A., B.Sc. or B.Com.) of the university. Thus the Commission has suggested the abolition of intermediate colleges existing in some parts of the country.

The Commission has suggested the following changes in the secondary school curriculum:

1. To open multi-purpose schools according to the varying interests of students.

2. The multi-purpose schools should be opened near the industrial institutions. The students of these two types of institutions should learn from each other.
3. Agriculture should be made a compulsory subject for schools in villages.
4. In big cities 'technical area' should be established on the demands of the local public.
5. Home science should be made compulsory for girls and other subjects should be common for both boys and girls.

Medium of Instruction. The mother tongue or the State language should be made the medium of instruction. In this connection, the Commission expressed the following ideas also:

1. The students should be taught at least two languages at the junior high school stage.
2. The Commission has suggested that at the secondary stage a student should learn at least three languages, the national language, the mother tongue or the regional language and a foreign language.

Curriculum. The Commission has emphasised the necessity of reorganising the secondary school curriculum in order that the aims of education may be realised. In this connection the Commission wants that:

1. The curriculum should be recognised according to the interests of the students.
2. It should be determined for meeting the social aspirations.
3. It should be reorganised keeping in view the demands of the times and those of the country.
4. It should be so organised that the student's time and leisure may not be wasted.

Subjects of Lower Secondary Education. The Commission has suggested mathematics, general science, languages, social studies, physical education, art, handicraft and music etc., for this stage.

Subjects for Secondary Education. For this stage the Commission has suggested seven groups of subjects as below :

1. Humanities.
2. Sciences.
3. Agriculture.
4. Fine Arts.
5. Industrial subjects.
6. Commercial subjects.
7. Home Science.

Selection of Text Books. The Commission has opened that text-books should be selected on the basis of their merits and utility. For this purpose the Commission has recommended the appointment of a High Power Committee which will select books for all the classes. The standard of production, printing and paper used and pictures and illustrations incorporated and suitable content will be the basis of selection. In the opinion of the Commission the following persons will constitute the High Power Committee for selection of text-books:

1. A High Court Judge.
2. A Principal of some government educational institution.
3. A member of the Public Service Commission.
4. A Vice-Chancellor of a university.
5. Two eminent educationalists and the Director of Education of the State.

The Commission has further suggested that the text-book once chosen should not be changed soon.

In addition to text-books each school should have some such books which may impart general knowledge to students.

The teachers should also be provided with new literature and books in order to keep up their inerests alive.

Character Formation. Character formation is an important aim of secondary education. This is useful not only for the individual but also for the nation. In fact the character of the nation is reflected by the character of its citizens. Therefore, for raising the character of the nation the character of the students should be well formed.

Health Education. All the students should be medically examined at least twice a year. Full medical facilities should be available for ailing students. They should be given knowledge of health principles also.

Teaching Method. For improving the standard of teaching the Commission has suggested that the Central Government should appoint a Committee of Experts which should make research for finding out ways and means for improving the teaching methods.

Improvement of Teachers' Status

1. Trained teachers should be appointed to teach higher classes.
2. The policy of same pay for the same work and ability should be adopted.
3. Teachers should be given handsome salary in order that the society may respect them.
4. Teachers should be given pension, provident fund and life insurance benefits in order to give then some economic security. The Government should provide these facilities.
5. The children of teachers should be given free education.
6. Teachers and their dependents should be given free medical service.
7. Separate committees should be appointed for removing the difficulties of teachers.
8. The retirement age for teachers should be 60 years.
9. The teachers should not be permitted to take up tuition of students.

Training and Qualifications of Teachers. The Commission has suggested that for junior classes at least higher secondary school and for senior classes at least graduate teachers should be appointed. These teachers should be given two years training.

Management and Administration of Secondary Schools. The Commission has given the following suggestions in this respect:

1. The post of Education Director should be equivalent to the Joint Secretary of the secretariate and he should advise the minister in this capacity.

2. Central and State Committees should be organised for giving advice on secondary education.
3. The District Inspector of Schools should not only find faults with teachers but should also assist them in performance of their duties. They should solve their problems arising from time to time and should acquaint them with latest developments in the field of education.
4. The Secondary Education Board should be organised under the chairmanship of Education Director who should arrange for secondary education in his State.
5. A Board for teachers' training should be established.
6. New schools should be recognised only when they fulfil all conditions.
7. The State Government should organise a Committee for management and administration of schools. This Committee should be responsible for the management and administration of schools, but it must not interfere with the work of the Principal.

Finance. For this the Commission has given the following suggestions:

1. The Government should be responsible for providing vocational education.
2. Industrial education should be levied for the development of vocational and technical education.
3. The Centre should give financial aid to States for education.
4. No octroi and toll tax should be levied on goods purchased for education institutions.

Duration of Session and Leave

1. The school should be opened at least for 200 days a year.
2. The schools in rural areas should be closed at least for 7 days at the time of sowing and harvesting in order that the students may help their family in agricultural pursuits.
3. The number of holidays be reduced.
4. At least 35 hours should be devoted for teaching per week.

5. The principal should be empowered to decide, about local holidays and school hours.
6. The student should get at least 10 to 15 days' leave during a session. The summer vacation should be for two months.

Arrangement of Buildings

1. School buildings should be away from the hubub and noise of cities. They should be situated in peaceful atmosphere.
2. The school building should be adequately vantilated.
3. A class should not consist of more than 40 students.
4. There should be proper desks and chairs in the schools.
5. Each school should have a big hall where all the students may assemble for some group programme. This hall should be decorated with pictures of great national leaders of different walks of life.
6. There should be a well equipped reading room in each school where the students should get newspapers, periodicals, magazines and other literatures of general knowledge.

Q. 36. Analyse the defects of secondary education in the light of the findings of the Secondary Education Commission 1952-53.

Ans. Defects in Secondary Education. The defects of secondary education have been pointed out by a number of commissions. It does not prepare adolescent boys and girls for the pursuit of higher education adequately because, among those who take admission in the university, there is a great incidence of failure in the first year of the first degree course. The Secondary education is too academic and far removed from the problems of life and therefore it is incapable of fulfilling its second objective of equipping boys and girls to enter life confidently and earn their living. The defects in the school education as highlighted by the Mudaliar Commission are given below.

1. An Emphasis on Book Learning. The school education does not inculcate in the student the habit of thinking and clear expression. He is unable to reason and sole problems. His expression is weak. Neither can he speak nor write. The instruction is bookish. Answers are crammed. Examinations are passed. But no ability is produced for creative thinking and expression.

2. Neglect of Cocurricular Activities. The emphasis on book learning is so great that all students are supposed to be equally interested in studies. Cocurricular activities are neglected. Facilities for organising such activities in secondary schools are limited. There is paucity of funds. Curricular load is so heavy that teachers and students find time to engage themselves in group games, recreational activities, games and sports, debates and dramas.

3. Education One-sided. The school education is one-sided. It trains the intellect and leaves other aspects of personality undeveloped. It aims only at mental growth and development. Little attention is given to the social or emotional development of the child and the youth. It does not cultivate a sense of moral and social responsibility. It does not emphasise character-building. No efforts are made to cultivate interests, attitudes and values for a socialistic society. No arrangements exist for imparting moral instruction. Study of religious is lost sight of.

4. Education Unilateral. The school education is unilateral. Secondary schools are one-track schools. They prepare students only for the university. There is little scope for diversification of studies. Individual differences in needs, interests, aptitudes and mental abilities are ignored and all have to pass through the same straight jackets.

5. Teaching Methods Defective. The teaching methods are defective. In no secondary school you will find dynamic methods of teaching being followed. Though great efforts have been expended during the last two decades on familiarising school teachers with right techniques and activity methods through workshops, seminars and refresher courses, yet classroom teaching shows little improvement. Audio-visual aids, the radio and the T.V. have been provided to some schools generously, but their effect is insignificant. The average teacher suffers from a lack of professional preparation. Educational research on teaching methods suited to Indian needs is nowhere conducted. The existing educational system is rigid and does not encourage initiative, creativity and experimentation. The administrative mechinery is not at all concerned with diffusing new and dynamic methods of teaching.

6. Class Sizes Big. The number of pupils in each class in most of the secondary schools is too great. There is no teacher-pupil relationship, and hence no personal contact is possible. No improvement in methods of teaching is possible when a teacher is required to teach very large class every day and in every period allotted to him. Class sizes in schools where extension of buildings is not possible have grown formidably great.

7. Quality of Taxt-books Defective. The quality of text-books, teachers' guides and teaching materials is not satisfactory, Probably there has been no serious effort either on the Central or on the state level to produce good quality text-books. The top ranking scholars do no like the job. There are malpractices in the selection and prescription. The publishers who are interested in profits do to produce teachers' guides to accompany text-books.

8. Examination System Improper. The evils of examination system are known to everybody. These defects have been pointed out, time and again, by committees and commissions. The Secondary Education Commission (1952-53) devoted a whole chapter to surveying the limitations of the present examination system and suggesting ways of improvement. The movement of examination reform that started after the publication of the report does not seem to have the desired impact on objectives, learning experiences and evaluation procedures in school education.

9. Guidance and Counselling Facilities Inadequate. Little has been done in the matter of guidance services to secondary school pupils. To supply a trained guidance worker to every school is difficult. It would be unrealistic to think of providing qualified counsellors to all schools. Yet resources could have been mobilised during the 20 years that have elapsed since the setting up of a Central Bureau of Educational and Vocational Guidance in 1954.

Q. 37. The report of the Education Commission (1964-66) is the first serious attempt at evolving a comprehensive scheme of National System of Education. Discuss.

Ans. A national system of education is one which is established firmly on the basic values and traditions which a nation normally clings to. It tends to support national goal and tries to meet the national objectives.

The system of education that existed in the country prior to 1937 had been a foreign plant forced to grow on Indian soil. It was transplanted in India by British rulers and we had to cling to it for more than a century 'because it happened to be in tune with the traditional hierarchical structure of our society'. Else, it had no right to exist. The English people did try to improve the system from time to time but failed to evolve a system that could satisfy people's aspirations.

Many commissions and committees were appointed to suggest improvements in the system of education prior to 1947. But problems studied by them were specific in nature. They examined the issues one by one. The entire field was not surveyed and viewed. The significant role that education could play in the economic and social development of the country, in the building of a truly democratic society, in the promotion of national unity could not be realised before 1960, because the conditions were different. The Education Commission 1964-66 was charged with the responsibilities of examining the entire field of educational development and of advising the Government on the national policies of a fresh educational reconstruction. The Report that the Commission submitted on June 28, 1966 has been the most comprehensive piece of work on education published so far.

The First Service Attempt to Review all Aspects of Education. It contains recommendations on all aspects of education. It covers education at all levels from the pre-primary through the secondary to the higher. It highlights not only the existing defects in the system at each level, but also offers practical suggestion for eradicating them.

The width of scope covered can be gauged through a review of the sections of the report itself. The Report is divided into three parts. The first part deals with general problems of Indian education. Some of these are : How can a national sysem of education contribute to national development? What should be national pattern of education? How can teacher's socio-economic status be raised? How can qualitative improvement of education be achieved? How can social justice be achieved in the field of education?

The second part of the Report covers different stages and sectors of education. Stages are related to school and university education and sectors are concerned with agricultural, technical and vocational education. The aspects of school education covered are the problems of expansion, curriculum, teaching methods, text-books, guidance, evaluation, administration and supervision. Some of the problems relating to higher education are those that are connected with the establishment of major universities, programmes of qualitative improvement, enrolment and university governance. The second part deals with problems of agricultural, vocational, technical and engineering education, and those of science education and research and of adult education.

The last part of the Report deals with the problems of implementation, namely, educational planning and administration and educational finance.

It is the first serious attempt to examine all aspects of education (at all levels). Shri M.C. Chhagla did not exaggerate when he remarked that the Report is 'a unique document'. It provides realistic and categorical answers to questions in education. Controversial problems have been examined from all possible angles and definite solutions have been suggested. For example, the Report gives an exact answer to the language question for the first time. The answer has satisfied all. It says that by 1975 Regional languages should become the media of instruction at all stages including the university stage, that English may continue to be the link language of the intellectual people for some time, that it may be replaced by Hindi (the language of the Centre) sooner or later, and that Hindi should not be a compulsory subject in non-Hindi speaking areas.

The Report is a serious attempt, because whatever suggestions or recommendations it presents are practical and can be implemented. When the Report was published, doubts were raised and the following questions were asked :

'Is the game worth the candle?"

"Is it not going to meet the same fate as its predecessors?"

"Will it not be devaluated in course of time?"

Impact of Education. But even after a decade of the publication of the Report, it appears that it had stood the test of time. Government is pledged to promote the development of education in the country on the lines suggested by the Commission. It has done its utmost in implementing the national policies and is still bent upon doing so. Strenuous efforts have been made to provide free and compulsory education for all children upto the age of 14 ; economic and social status of teachers has been raised : languages are being developed; regional, social and sex imbalances in the provision of educational opportunities are being corrected; work experience is being introduced from the primary stage upwards in the school education; the educational structure of 10+2+3 is being adopted ; the quality of higher education is being improved.

Q. 38. Explain the National Policy on Education declared by Govt. of India in 1968.

Ans. NATIONAL POLICY ON EDUATION (1968)

The Education Commission 1964-66 recommended that the Government of India should issue a statement on the National Policy on Education which should provide guidance to the State Governments and the local authorities in preparing and implementing educational plans. In 1967 the Government of India constituted a committee of Members of Parliament on Education to prepare the draft of a statement on the National Policy on Education. The Committee prepared a draft which was considered by the Central Advisory Board of Education. A general consensus on the national policy on education emerged in the course of the Board's deliberations. Thereafter the Government of India issued the Resolution on National Policy on Education in 1968. Since then the Resolution has become the basis of education reforms in India.

PRINCIPLES OF DEVELOPMENT OF EDUCATION

1. Free and Compulsory Education

(a) Strenuous efforts should be made for the early fulfilment of the Directive Principles under Article 45 of the Constitution seeking to provide free and compulsory education for all children up to the age of 14.

(b) Suitable programmes should be developed to reduce the prevailing wastage and stagnation in schools and to ensure that every child who is enrolled in school successfully completes the prescribed course.

2. Status, Emoluments and Education of Teachers

(a) Teachers be accorded an honoured place in society.

(b) Their emoluments and other service conditions should be adequate and satisfactory having regard to their qualifications and responsibility.

(c) The academic freedom of teachers to pursue and publish independent studies and researches and to speak and write about significant national and international issues should be protected.

(d) Teacher education, particularly in-service education, should receive due emphasis.

3. Development of Languages

(a) Regional Languages. The regional languages are already in use as media of education at the primary and secondary stages. Urgent steps should now be taken to adopt them as media of education at the university stage.

(b) Three-Language Formula. At the secondary stage, the State Governments shuld adopt, and vigourously implement the three-language formula which includes the study of a modern Indian language, preferably one of the southern languages, apart from Hindi and English in the Hindi-speaking States, and of Hindi along with the regional languages and English in the non-Hindi-speaking States. Suitable courses in Hindi and English should also be available in universities and colleges with a view to improving the proficiency of students in these languages up to the prescribed university standards.

(c) Hindi. Every effort should be made to promote the development of Hindi as the link language, due care should be taken to ensure that it will serve as provided for in Article 351 of the Constitution, as a medium of expression for all the elements of the composite culture of India. The establishment in non-Hindi States, of colleges and other institutions of higher education which use Hindi as the medium of education should be encouraged.

(d) ***Sanskrit.*** Considering the special importance of Sanskrit to the growth and development of Indian languages and its unique contribution to the cultural unity of the country, facilities for its teaching at the school and university stages should be offered on a more liberal scale. Development of new methods of teaching the language should be encouraged, and the possibility explored of including the study of Sanskrit in those courses (such as modern Indian languages, ancient Indian history, Indology and Indian Philosophy) at the first and scecond degree stages, where such knowledge is useful.

(e) ***International Languages.*** Special emphasis needs to be laid on the study of English and other international languages.

4. Equalization of Educational Opportunities

(a) Strenuous efforts should be made to equalize educational opportunity.

(b) Regional imbalances in the provision of educational facilities should be corrected and good educational facilities should be provided in rural and other backward areas.

(c) To promote social cohesion and national integration in the Common School System as recommended by the Education Commission should be adopted.

(d) All special schools like public schools should be required to admit students on the basis of merit and also to provide a prescribed proportion of free studentship to prevent segregation of social classes.

(e) Thc education of girls should receive emphasis, not only on grounds of social justice, but also because it accelerates social transformation.

(f) Efforts should be made to improve the standard of education in general schools.

(g) More intensive efforts are needed to develop education among the backward classes and especially among the tribal people.

(h) Educational facilities for the physically and mentally handicapped children should be expanded and attempts should be made to develop integrated programmes enabling the handicapped children to study in regular schools.

5. Identification of Talent

For the cultivation of excellence, it is necessary that talent in diverse fields should be identified at as early an age as possible, and every stimulus and opportunity given for its full development.

6. Work-Experience and National Service

The school and the community should be brought closer through suitable programmes of mutual service and support. Work-experience and national service including participation in meaningful and challenging programmes of community service and national reconstruction should accordingly become an integral part of education. Emphasis in these programmes should be on self-help, character formation and on the developing sense of social commitment.

7. Science Education and Research

With a view to accelerating the growth of the national economy, science education and research should receive high priority. Science and mathematics should be an integral part of general education, till the end of the school stage.

8. Education for Agriculture and Industry

(a) Special emphasis should be placed on the development of education for agriculture and industry.

(b) There should be at least one agricultural university in every State. These should, as far as possible, be single campus universities; but where necessary, they may have constituent colleges on different campuses. Other universities may also be assisted, where the necessary potential exists, to develop strong departments for the study of one or more aspects of agriculture.

In technical education, practical training in industry should form an integral part of such education. Technical education and research should be related closely to industry, encouraging the flow of personnel both ways and providing for continuous cooperation in the provision, design and periodical review of training programmes and facilities.

9. Production of Books

(a) The quality of books should be improved by attracting the best writing talent through a liberal policy of incentives and remuneration.

(b) Frequent changes of text books should be avoided and their prices should be low enough for students of ordinary means to buy them.

(c) The possibility of establishing autonomous book corporations on commercial lines should be examined and efforts should be made to have a few basic text books common throughout the country.

10. Examinations

A major goal of examination reforms should be to improve the reliability and validity of examinations and to make evaluation a continuous process aimed at helping the student to improve his level of achievement rather than at 'certifying' the quality of his performance at a given moment of time.

11. Secondary Education

Educational opportunity at the secondary (and higher) level is a major instrument of social change and transformation. Facilities for secondary education should accordingly be extended expeditiously to areas and classes which have been denied these in the past.

There is need to increase facilities for technical and vocational education at this state. Provision of facilities for secondary and vocational education should conform broadly to requirements of the developing economy and real employment opportunities. Such linkage is necessary to make technical and vocational education at the secondary stage effectively terminal. Facilities for technical and vocational education should be suitably diversified to cover a large number of fields, such as agriculture, industry, trade and commerce, medicine and public health, home management, arts and crafts, secretarial training, etc.

12. University Education

(a) The number of whole-time students to be admitted to a college or university department should be determined with reference to the laboratory, library and other facilities and to the stength of the staff.

(b) Considerable care is needed in establishing new universities. They should be started only after an adequate provision of funds has been made for the purpose and due care has been taken to ensure proper standards.

(c) Special attention should be given to the organization of post-graduate courses and to the improvement of standards of training and research at this level.

(d) Centers of advanced study should be strengthened and a small number of 'clusters of centers' aiming at the highest possible standards in research and training should be established.

(e) There is need to give increased support to research in universities generally. The institutions for research should as far as possible; function with the fold of universities or intimate association with them.

13. Part-Time Education and Correspondence Courses

Part-time education and correspondence courses should be developed on a large scale at the university stage. Such facilities should also be developed for secondary school students, for teachers and for agricultural, industrial and other workers. Education through part-time and correspondence courses should be given the same status as full-time education. Such facilities will smoothen transition from school to work, promote the cause of education and provide opportunities to the large number of people who have the desire to educate themselves further but cannot do so on a full-time basis.

14. Spread of Literacy and Adult Education

The liquidation of mass illiteracy is necessary not only for promoting participation in the working of democrating institutions and for accelerating programmes of production, especially in agriculture, but for quickening the tempo of national development in general. Employees in large commercial, industrial and other concerns should be made functionally literate as early as possible. A lead in this direction should come from the industrial undertaking in the public sector. Teachers and students should be actively helped.

Q. 39. What is the relation between Education and National Development? Discuss it in the light of recommendations of the Education Commission 1964-66.

Ans. Education as a Powerful Tool for Social, Economic and Political Changes. Education determines the level of prosperity, welfare and security of a nation. It is the most important instrument of economic, social and political change. The power and efficacy of education in bringing about a revolution in the life of the country have been realised ever since the attainment of Independence.

The country has launched a planned programme of economic development. National economy is expected to be developed to the desired extent through a series of Five Year Plans. It is believed that the pace of economic development may be quickened if the nation adopts a bold and imaginative policy of educational reconstruction.

If education has to serve as a powerful instrument of economic, social and political change, it has to be planned in relation to the programmes of national development. It has to be related to the problems of National Development. It has to be related to the life, needs and aspirations of the people.

Problems of National Development

We are facing a number of problems of varying degree of importance, and complexity. Of these there are some to which education is directly related. "The first and the most important is the Problem of Food", says the Education Commission. Food problem is perhaps the most acute one and in spite of having laid an increasing emphasis on its solution during the last four Five Year Plans, we are still in the grip of starvation.

2. The second problem of National Development is economic growth and full employment. The rate of economic growth has not been satisfactory during the last two decades. Per capital National income has been increasing at an insignificant rate. Population is growing fast. People are suffering either from unemployment or from underemployment.

3. The third problem related to National Development is that of social and national integration. Social distance between the rich and the poor, the educated and the uneducated, the elite and the masses is increasing. Loyalties, local, regional, linguistic, and state are showing a tendency to grow. National unity is being threatened. Social progress is blocked. People are forgetting 'India'. Old values and traditions are fast dying out.

4. The last but not the least significant problem of national development is related with strengthening of Indian democracy. Parliamentary democracy has not yet taken firm roots, perhaps, because an educated electorate has not yet been created or because a dedicated competent leadership has not yet been produced, or because we have not been able to cultivate in the people essential democratic values like those of self-control, tolerance and mutual goodwill.

Solving National Problems through Educational Reform. Problems of national development and especially those listed above can be solved through a well-thought out programme of educational development. For example, we can give supreme importance to agricultural education if we want to solve the food problem. The top talent in the country may be attracted to it. Agricultural colleges may be developed and a separate agricultural university may be established. Similarly, if we want to accelerate the pace of economic development, we can relate education to productivity and the following programmes as suggested by the Education Commission (1964-66) may be given high priority in the educational reconstruction:

(a) We may make science a basic component in the education of the child. With a view to accelerating the growth of national economy, science education and research should receive high priority, says the Commission.

(b) We may vocationalise education especially at the Higher Secondary level, so that we may inculcate vocational competence at least in the 50% youths who join the Higher Secondary stage (XI-XII). The manpower may then be directed to industry, agriculture and trade.

(c) We may improve scientific and technological education and research at the university stage.

(d) We may make work experience an integral part of general education.

The problem of social and national integration can be fought at the same educational front. Gandhiji's scheme of basic education was designed to eliminate the social distance between diverse sections of the society.

We may carry out the suggestions made by the Education Commission (1964-66) which run as follows:

(a) We may introduce a common school system of public education to get the different social groups together.

(b) The common school system of public education will be a powerful instrument of national development in general and social and national integration in particular, because it will be open to all children irrespective of caste, creed, community, religion, economic conditions or social status.

The last problem of National development concerning strengthening of democracy can also be grappled with through educational pogramming.

A Need of Educational Reform. If education has to serve as a powerful instrument of social, economic and political change it should be properly organised. No scheme of national development will bear fruit unless there is an educational revolution. Not all the systems of education can achieve the national objectives. 'It is only the right type of education provided on an adequate scale that can lead to national development', says the Education Commission. For example, a system of higher education if properly organised to meet the aspirations and needs of the people can promote economic development by emphasising on the production of competent professional manpower.

Q. 40. 'For National Integration education has a great role and objectives.' Discuss in reference to the Education Commission Report (1964-66).

Ans. A nation is said to be strong and united when devisive forces causing distintegration are totally absent in it. A nation is socially integrated when all its members enjoy a sense of equality of opportunities in political, economic and social spheres of activity and when they have mutual understanding of and respect for each other's ways of life. A country is said to be nationally integrated when its people rise above sectional loyalties and identify themselves with the nation as a whole and have faith in the nation's future.

Gravity of the Problem. The attainment of social and national integration as one of the objectives of the national system of education is a challenging problem. For a country like ours, it is difficult to achieve this objective because there is already a wide gulf between the rich and the poor, the urban and the rural, the elite and the masses. Besides, people are bound by local, regional, linguistic, religious and other sectional ties. Old traditions and values are fast disappearing. Education is promoting devisive tendencies. The schools for the rich and the poor are segregated. There is a lack of national consciousness everywhere. Communal riots, corruption, strikes, lawlessness, disregard for public property are some of the symptoms of social distingration.

Steps Suggested. The Education Commission (1964-66) suggested certain steps to create a strong and united country to make people conscious of what 'India' is and to create an integrated society. This could be done by the introduction of the common school, by making social and national service an integral part of education at all stages, by adopting a proper language policy and by promoting national consciousness.

1. The Common School System. The educational system as it exists even today is undemocratic and harmful for national unity and social solidarity. It is undemocratic because under this system good education is not available to all children. The children of the masses are sent to schools managed by the government or by the local authorities. The schools charge either no fees or normal fees. They provide sub-standard or poor quality education. The children of the privileged class are sent to the private, fee-charging, better schools. The present system of education is harmful for the country not only because 'the identification and development of the total national pool of ability is greatly hampered', but also because it weakens social cohesion.

The common school system of public education has been suggested by the Commission as a powerful instrument for achieving social and national integration, because the schools under this system would be open to 'all children, irrespective of caste, creed, community, religion, economic conditions or social status'. As these schools would maintain adequate standards the rich people will tend to send their children to them and as they will not charge any fees, they would meet the needs of average parents too.

2. Social and National Service as an Integral Part of Education. The Commission suggested that programmes of social and national service should be incorporated in the education of children at all stages. The programmes should run together with academic studies in schools and colleges and start from the upper primary stage (V-VII) and continue up to the university. Social service may take the form of participation in community living on the school or college campus or in programmes of community development. Every school and college should try to develop a rich community life for its students and should provide adequate opportunities to them to participate in it; for example, much of the work done by hired labour or menial servants can be done by students themselves. Money so saved may be used for providing amenities to them. Programmes of community service may also be integrated in school and college education. At the higher primary stage students may be encouraged to serve the community in a number of ways. At the secondary stage suitable forms of service to the community may be sought after. At the college level participation in Labour and Social Welfare camps or the N.C.C. may be made obligatory and programmes of community development may be developed agreeing with the available resources, age and competence of students.

Social and national service so organised and made obligatory for all students at all stages would certainly lead to a decrease in the social distance between the educated and the uneducated, the intelligentsia and the masses. It will also help up in evolving a united nation.

3. Evolving a Language Policy for National and Social Integration. The Emotional Integration Committee regarded the use of regional languages from the primary to the college level as media of education, 'a matter of profound importance for national integration'. The National Integration Council (1962) spoke in support of the same view. The Education Commission (1964-66) also agreed with these observations. The Commission recommended that regional languages should be made media of instruction at all levels, that Hindi should be so developed that it becomes the link language of the people in the shortest time possible, and English may continue as the link language of the intellectual people or it may function as library language at all stages of education. The language question which had been very 'complex and intractable' so far has been solved by the Commission to the satisfaction of all.

4. Promoting National Consciousness. The schools under the English regime taught loyalty to the English people by giving instruction to our students in their literature, history and culture. Love for the motherland was never developed before 1937. It was the struggle for Independence between 1900 and 1947 that made people nationally conscious. The development of national consciousness was effected outside the school walls.

After the attainment of Independence in 1947, the people began to forget 'India'. Sectional loyalties grew up. Schools remained sleeping. The unfortunate international conflicts—the Chinese invasion of 1962, the two recent aggressions by Pakistan--did something to unite us. But such happenings could never be regarded as a right solution. Can education be not used as an effective tool for promoting national consciousness? Schools and colleges in other countries have done so.

The Education Commission believed firmly in the efficacy of formal education for promoting national spirit in the educand. It suggested that the Indian youth could be made to understand his cultural heritage by a well-organised instruction in Indian languages, literature, history and philosophy, and that he could be helped to instil faith in the future of the nation through a systematic course in civics and politics and political economy.

Q. 41. What circumstances led to the setting up of the Education Commission (1964-66)?

Ans. A Need for Social Change after Independence. Education, all the world over, has been used as a powerful tool of social, economic and political change. The political upheaval that took place in our country in the beginning of the century brought in its train a set of changes in the life of the nation. A need began to be felt to bring about a multiphased revolution within the shortest possible period. The whole government machinery was set in motion for making an effort at economic growth, social change and cultural advancement. As the government was convinced that education is the key to national prosperity and welfare, an all-out attempt was made to transform the education system.

A Need for Evolving a National System of Education. In spite of much valuable thinking and considerable implementation of educational ideas during the 15 years that followed the attainment of Independence, the nation could not develop a system of education which could meet the needs of the newly born democratic state. The Government of India expressed its grave concern at the state of affairs in 1964 in the following words, "While some advances have been made in (certain) directions, the education system has not generally evolved in accordance with the needs of the times, and a wide and distressing gulf continues to persist between thought and action in several sectors of this crucial field of national activity." The views expressed by eminent educationists to evolve a national system of education or the recommendations made by Committees and Commissions (especially appointed ever since the achievement of Independence) were either ignored or partially implemented. For example, the Higher secondary (three years) pattern was not given a fair trial in most of the states. The scheme of basic education could not achieve desired success. The multipurpose scheme of diversified courses have to meet the same fate.

Realising the importance of education in the bringing about of the desired economic and social development the Government of India in 1964 considered the urgency of surveying and examining the entire field of education. Problems of educational reconstruction had been reviewed by a number of Committees and Commissions which attempted to solve difficulties faced in specific areas only. For example, the University Education Commission (1948-49) and the Secondary Education Commission (1952-53) surveyed the fields of university and school education respectively. Towards the end of the Third Five Year Plan, a need began to be felt to make a review of the present education system so comprehensive that it may cover the entire field.

During the three Plan periods education at all levels had expanded tremendously. Yet people were not happy about a number of educational aspects: for example, the nation was not yet able to provide free and compulsory education for all children of 14 + ; nor could it solve the problem of educated unemployment throught diversification of courses nor could it produce an adequate supply of manpower in many sectors of economic life nor could it raise the status of the teaching community. Quantitative expansion of education did take place, but qualitative improvements suffered.

A Need for Improving Quality of Education. The need for appointing a fresh Education Commission in 1964 arose out of a grave concern for the improvement of quality of education. The Government wanted an expert advice on the evolution of the much desired national system of education and on the formation of 'general principles and policies for the development of education at all stages and in all aspects.' The Resolution of the Government of India in 1964 said, "It is desirable to survey the entire field of educational development as the various parts of the educational system strongly interact with and influence one another. It is not possible to have progressive and strong universities without efficient secondary school and the quality of these schools is determined by the functioning of elementary schools. What is needed, therefore, is a synoptic survey and an imaginative look at education considered as a whole and not fragmented into parts and stages. In the past several commissions and committees have examined limited sectors and specific aspects of education. It is now proposed to have a comprehensive review of the entire educational system."

Q. 42. Examine the National Policy of Education, 1986.

Ans. On April 20, 1986 a new Educational Policy was placed before the Indian Parliament for consideration and approval. The following objectives of education were particularly emphasized in this policy:

1. Vocationalization of Education. Particularly, at the secondary stage of education the curriculum should be job-oriented.

2. To awaken the people about the various scientific and technological developments and to make the students at the various stages of education aware of the same in order that they may utilize them in their future life.
3. To encourage the governmental and non-governmental efforts for wiping out illiteracy and to emphasize the necessity of adult education, formal education, farmers' education and 'open' schools.

Onwards we shall look into some basic details of this new policy:

1. National form of Education. At least 75 per cent of the curriculum should be identical for all the States. The remaining 25 per cent may be related to the particular local conditions of a State. The purpose of incorporation this basic feature is to acquaint all the citizens of the country with their basic rights and duties, history of the freedom struggle, the common cultural heritage and national identity.

2. More Emphasis on Learning. The teacher must not harbour the notion that the child learns through his teaching alone. In fact, the child learns many more things by himself. Therefore, the teacher must not emphasize only by teaching procedures in the class-room. Essentially, he should also try to create such an environment in the class and school in general that the children may learn many things through their own creativeness. The prescribed curriculum for children do not contain the latest informations of the concerned subject. Generally, they are four or five years old. So they are not very useful, because they contain incomplete informations. Therefore the teacher must inspire the students to learn things on their own as far as possible. The mental development of children should be so guided that they make understand the utility of knowledge themselves. The Education Policy of 1986 has particularly emphasised this point.

3. Delinking Degree for any Service. If the compulsoriness of a degree for securing a job is done away with, many youths will automatically refrain from obtaining higher education. Thus crowding of aspirants for admissions to colleges and universities will be reduced. In fact, a degree should not be considered as a pre-requisite for a job which has not direct relationship with it. In many foreign developed countries a degree is not considered as a condition for obtaining a job. According to the 1991 Census Report a degree is considered in our country as a requisite for securing a service. At the T.V. centres for the Chaupal or Krishi Darshan Programmes, B.Sc. (Agr.) has been made as compulsory for a person conducting them. Similarly, in our country a degree has been made compulsory for a job. In fact, many students of our colleges and universities have absolutely no interest in their studies.

4. Importance of Moral Values. The importance of moral values has been recognised by this new policy. The development of healthy moral values in an individual will help him to depend upon his own efforts and not on his self-imposed destiny. Education is a tool for bringing in desirable changes in a society. Therefore importance of moal values in life should be pointed out wherever possible in teaching. This method of teaching moral values will be more helpful to students.

5. Vocationalization of Education. Vocationalization of education has been particularly been emphasised in this new education policy. As far as possible, education should be given in a natural environment. The child must acquire some skill in some area of his interest. This is necessary for a happy life in future. With this end in view this new education policy has advocated for inclusion of scientific and technical subjects in the curriculum. It has been specifically stated in the policy that in the tenth class not more than 50 per cent students should opt for literacy subjects and the rest should be encouraged to study vocational courses of various types according to their interests. This kind of vocationalization of education will minimise the unemployment problem, because then the educated person will not depend on some service alone and may utilize his acquired skill for earning his bread.

6. Emphasis on Reforms in Examination System. It has been suggested in this new policy that 'grade' should be given in examination in place of 'division'. In the current system of examination the student scoring between 45 to 48 per cent of marks is placed in the second class and those sixty or above are placed in the first class. In this situation the students getting within the range of 44 and 47 and also only 59 think that they have lost their higher division by one mark only. This feature develops a kind of frustration and anguish in them. In order to do away with this situation, this new policy has suggested giving of "grades" and not "class" or "division". According to this new policy those coming within the range of 40 to 50 or of 45 to 55 will be given "B" or "C" grade. A determination of assigning "B" or "C" grade will depend upon the nature of achievements of all the students taking up an examination. Suppose in a certain difficult test no student scores more than 45 per cent, then it is just possible that it may be considered desirable that those scroing 45 per cent or above may be given "A" grade and those getting 40 may be grouped under "B" and those 35 may be assigned "C" grade. Thus assigning of "grades" will depend upon the nature of a test and how all the students as a whole show performance on the same. Periodical tests have also been recommended in this new policy, because the determination of merit of a student on the basis of only one examination has not been considered as just. Similarly, appointment of external exeminers, too, has been considered as undesirable. Thus the teachers have been made solely responsible for evaluating the merits of his students. It has been felt that this method will increase the importance of teachers and marks of indiscipline in students will also be gradually minimised.

7. Ever-Continual Primary School. According to this new education policy each primary school will have at least a two-room-building with at least two teachers. Of these two teachers, one will be a lady. Each primary school will function throughout the twelve months a year. Thus all the young children in an area will be receiving primary education.

8. Education for the Weaker Section of the Society. The education of scheduled castes, scheduled tribes, handicapped and girls has been greatly emphasised because in the interest of national progress, their development has been considered necessary. Hence reservation for such persons has been recommended in various types of educational institution.

9. All India Educational Service. In order to tone up educational administration, this policy has emphasised the necessity of starting an All India Education Service cadre. Under this scheme any education officer may be transferred any where in the country. It has been felt that this kind of transfer will weaken the undesirable bond of regionalism and will bring dynamism in the educational administration. The policy of transfer will dissuade the education officers from coming into the pressure of politicians in the sphere of their work and as a result they will be more honest in the performance of their duties.

10. Importance of Sports and Games. In this new policy importance of sports and games has been recognised because participation in them will maintain the health of children. With this end in view forming of active committees of sports and games has been particularly emphasised. Framing of curriculum of small sports and games has also been suggested.

11. Open University. In this policy starting of Open universities has been emphasised. These universities are meant for those persons who have not been able to obain higher education, but are desirous of receiving the same in order to better their prospects. The necessity of open universities has been recognised also for expansion of higher education. In an open university any person may obtain higher education according to his own speed. A certain examination may be passed in parts in an open university.

12. Modernization of Education. Computerisation has been suggested in this policy. This method will be employed in the expansion of literacy. The utility of correspondence courses, T.V., Radio and Satellite, and Video-cassetts has been accepted for education in this policy.

13. Right Persons Alone to be Teachers. This education policy has considered the training of teacher as very important for raising the falling standard of education. Hence, some very useful suggestions have been given for improving the condition of teachers. According to this policy the teachers of a certain cadre should enjoy identical scale of salaries and all of them should be given residential facilitis. The society should be well awakened for giving due respects to teachers. Refresher course for teachers after every five years period has been considered necessary in order to acquaint them with the latest developed teachnique of teaching.

14. New Educational Institutions. In the education policy of 1986, it has been recommended that "District Institute of Education and Training" and "District of Education" should be established in the various states of the country. These institutions will survey the educational needs of people of various areas separately and will inform the concerned education officers about the same from time to time. The constitution of a national institute has also been proposed with a view to raise the standard of education. The main purpose of the new policy has been to prepare such citizens for the coming twenty-first century who may be responsive to their basic duties in consonance with human values and democratic ideals.

15. Establishing Navodaya Schools. Students in these schools will be admitted to class VI on the basis of an admission test. In the admission process pre-determined ratio for boys and girls of both urban and rural areas will be observed. In admission to these schools no financial criterion will be observed. All these boy and girl students will have to reside in the respective associated hostels after being admitted to the Navodaya schools. Such students will be given free boarding and lodging and free education. Twenty per cent of the students after passing 8th class in a Navodaya school will be transferred for education to other States with a view to promote national integration.

16. Protection of Environment Necessary. Protection of environment has been emphasised in the new policy of 1986. The students and teachers will be urged to protect rivers, lakes, hills, mountains, forests, and pasture lands. They will also see that the existing mills and factories do not pollute the surrounding environments.

17. Adult Education. A literacy programme will be organised for making illiterate persons literate within the age group of 15 and 35. For this purpose Continuing Education Centres will be established in rural areas. It will be a duty of a Project Officer to spread literacy amongst labourers. Distance education will be given through Radio, T.V. and films. These media will be utilized for vocational programmes as well.

18. Women Education. According to this policy the standard of education of women should be raised. In vocational and technical education, women will be assigned their proper place in order to equate them with men as far as possible. An attempt will also be made to minimise the difference existing in the curriculum meant for women and men.

19. Operation Black Board. In this new policy the term "Operation Black Board" has been used for conveying the ideas that minimum facilities will be provided to a primary school. These minimum facilities will include at least two rooms, some necessary charts and maps, a black-board, Tatpatti (about one metre wide and 10 metre long pieces of carpet) for seating children and other essential material equipments. In the beginning at least two teachers will be appointed for each primary school. Afterwards more teachers may be appointed as new classes are added. In the "Operation Black Board" the co-operation of voluntary organisations, local bodies and desirous persons will be enlisted. At first-some building will be provided to a primary school if it does not have any.

20. Preservation of Own Culture. There appears to be a wide gulf between the modern formal education and our cultural traditions. This new education policy wants to bridge this gulf, because the scientific and technical developments have to be associated with our proud history and culture. Our system of education should be related with our Fine Arts, Architecture and Oriental Studies. Hence we shall have to pay particular attention on organisation of museums, folk arts and literature. This policy urges us to do the needful in these directions. Modern education has led many of our youths to drug-addiction and it has not taught many of them how to be respectful to teachers and other elders in the society. As a result, deplorable marks of indiscipline in these usually stare at us.

Q. 43. What is the Philosophy of Educational Policy, 1986?

Ans. EDUCATIONAL PHILOSOPHY OF NEW POLICY

1. New Acculturating Role of Education. One of the most important contributions of New Policy of Education is that it has provided a comprehensive educational philosophy covering the new acculturating role of education by way of refining sensitiveness, building scientific temper and cultivating independence of mind and spirit.

2. Natural Perspective. Manpower planning and its educational investment has brought in a national perspective to our development needs. A unifying policy in the development of human resources provides a social dimension to an area of personal perception. The pooling of resources in the area of personnel and research at the national level with the provision for interregional mobility with equal access for every Indian of requisite merit is a most welcome and timely policy statement.

3. Universalisation. The universalisation of education upto a given level with access of education of a comparable quality is another positive aspect of the policy.

4. Equalisation. The special emphasis laid on the removal of disparities and equalization of opportunity by attending to the specific needs of different groups of distressed people including women, scheduled castes, minorities and the handicapped, should enhance the sense of social responsibility and a fair distribution on justice to all concerned.

5. Efficiency. The policy determination to promote efficiency and effectiveness at all levels (though easier said that done) brings in new dimension in the performance of teachers, students, administrators, Government officials and institutions.

6. Beneficial. The realisation of education needs to be managed in an atmosphere of ultmost intellectual rigour, seriousness of purposes with adequate freedom for innovation and creativity should bear beneficial fruits.

7. Value Education. The focus on value education and work experience as an integral part of the learning process will enable us to uphold human values necessary for raising the quality of life for all. The document speaks about combating certain negative values and promoting positive ones from our heritage. It mentions social, ethical and moral values which have to be cultivated.

8. Cultural Perspective. Another special feature of the policy is the concept of providing a cultural perspective in the formal system of education.

The Essence and Role of Education

The policy envisaged the role of education as follows—

1. Education is fundamental to our all-round development, material and spiritual.
2. Education is the highway to derive the maximum benefit from the areas already created by the economic and technical development and a means to ensure that the funds must reach all sections.
3. Education needs to be planned meticulously and developed with great sensitivity so as to make the best use of the human being who is a positive asset and precious national resources.
4. Education should be an effective instrument of reducing rural-urban disparities.
5. Spread of literacy and education among women in the largest single factor in bringing down the growth of population in India.
6. Education must prevent the erosion of long-cherished values.
7. Education should assist in the realisation of goals of secularism, socialism and professional ethics.
8. Education should develop the activity of the coming generation to internalize new ideas constantly and creatively.
9. Education should imbibe the coming generations with a strong commitment of human values and to social justice.
10. Education has an acculturating role. It refines sensitivity and perceptions that contribute to national cohesion, a scientific temper and independence of mind and spirit.
11. Education develops manpower of different level of the economy.
12. Education is unique investment in the present and the future.

Q. 44. Describe features of National System of Education envisaged by NPE, 1986.

Ans. THE NATIONAL SYSTEM OF EDUCATION

The National Policy on Education, 1986 has envisaged the following main features of the National Systems of Education:

1. Based on Constitutional Principles. It derives its inspiration from the ideals and values of democracy, secularism and socialism enshrined in our Constitution.

2. Access of Education. It implies that upto a given level all students, irrespective of caste, creed, location, sex, have access to education of a comparable quality. To achieve this, the Government will initiate appropriate funded programmes. Effective measures will be taken in the direction of the Common School recommended in the 1968 policy.

3. Common Educational Structure. It envisages of common educational structure. The 10+2+3 structure has now been accepted in all parts of the country. Regarding the further break-up of the first 10 years efforts will be made to move towards an elementary system comprising five years of primary education and three years of upper primary, followed by two years of High School.

4. National Curricular Framework with a Common Core. It will be based on a national curricular framework which contains a common core along with other components that are flexible. The common core will include the history of India's freedom movement, the constitutional obligations and other contents essential to nurture national identity. These elements cut across subject areas and will be designed to promote values such as India's common cultural heritage, egalitarianism, democracy and secularism, equality of the sexes, protection of the environment, removal of social barriers, observance of the small family norms and inculcation of the scientific temper. All educational programmes will be carried on in strict conformity with secular values.

5. Education for International Understanding. India has always worked for peace and understanding between nations, treating the whole world as one family. True to this hoary, tradition, education has to strengthen this world view and motivate the younger generations for international co-operation and peaceful co-existence. This aspect cannot be neglected.

6. Equality of Opportunity in Education. To promote equality it will be necessary to provide for equal opportunity to all not only in access, but also in the conditions for success. Besides, awareness of the inherent equality of all will be created through the core curriculum. The purpose is to remove prejudices and complexes transmitted through the social environment and accident of birth.

7. Minimum Levels of Learning. Minimum levels of learning will be laid down for each stage of education. Steps will also be taken to foster students an understanding of the diverse cultural and social systems of the people living in different parts of the country.

8. Universal Character of Higher Education. In higher education in general and technical education in particular, steps will be taken to facilitate inter-regional mobility by providing equal access to every Indian of requisite merit, regardless of his origins. The universal character of universities and other institutions of higher education is to be understood.

9. Promotion of Languages. Besides the promotion of the link language, programmes will also be launched to increase substantially the translation of books form glossaries. The young will be encouraged to undertake the rediscovery of India each in his own image and perception.

10. Priorities in Educational Reform. The Nation as a whole will assume the responsibility of providing resource support for implementing programmes of educational transformation, reducing disparities, universalisation of elementary education, adult literacy, scientific and technical research, etc.

11. Open and Distance Learning. Life-long education is a cherished goal of the education process. This presupposes universal literacy. Opportunities will be provided to the youth, house-wives, agricultural and industrial workers and professionals to continue the education of the choice, and the pace suited to them. The further thrust will be in the direction of open and distance learning.

12. Strengthening of National Institutions. National institutions which will be strengthened to play an important role in giving shape to the National System of Education, are the University Grants Commission. The All India Council of Technical Education, the Indian Council of Agricultural Research and the Indian Medical Council. Inegrated Planning will be instituted among all these bodies so as to establish functional linkages and reinforce programmes of research and post graduate education. These, together with the National Council of Education Research and Training, the National Institute of Educational Planning and Administration and the International Institute of Science and Technology Education will be involved in implementing the Education Policy.

13. Meaningful Partnership. Concurrence signifies a partnership which is at once meaningful and challenging. The Centre and the State shall give effect to it in letter and spirit.

Q. 45. What are eight bold steps suggested by NPE, 1986? Point out its missing links and limitations.

Ans. EIGHT BOLD STEPS OF NPE, 1986

1. National System of Education. National system of education to provide access to education of a comparable quality to all students, to have a common educational structure with national curricular framework containing a common core.

2. Navodaya Schools. Pace setting Navodaya Schools to be started which will be residential and free of charge.

3. Vocational Targets. Vocational courses to cover 10 per cent of higher secondary students by 1990 and 25 per cent by 1955.

4. Delinking Degree from Jobs. Beginning to be made in delinking degrees from jobs in selected areas.

5. Performance and Accountability. To ensure that all teachers should teach and all students study.

6. The Management of Education. Evolving a strategy of decentralization and the creation of a spirit of autonomy for educational institutions.

7. Indian Education Service. Constitution of this Service is likely to bring a national perspective in education.

8. Raising Resources. Resources to be raised through:

(i) Asking beneficiary communities to maintain school buildings,

(ii) Raising fees at the higher levels of education, and

(iii) Levying cess or charge on the user agencies.

Missing Links and Limitations

1. Confined to Privileged. A lion's share of the benefit of education is cornered by about six per cent of students who have been fortunate to join colleges. It is this privileged section which corners 99 per cent of Government jobs. Educational expenditure has become a mechanism of transferring resources from rural sector to urban sector or in other words from poor to the rich.

2. Neglect of Neighbourhood Concepts. The New Education Policy has completely ignored the 'neighbourhood' concept of school system advocated by the Kothari Commission. It is interesting to note that the Kothari Commission considered that the 'neighbourhood School' was a step towards eliminating the segregation that now takes place between the schools for the poor and the underprivileged classes and those for the rich and the privileged one.

3. Wrong Basics of Reservation. The New Education Policy should have suggested reservation not on the basics of merit but on the basics of economic conditions.

4. Need of Basic Education. The Education Policy does not refer to Basic Education although it has an important place in the ideology of freedom struggle and procedures were finalised as long back as 1937.

5. No Reference to Working Days. The New Education Policy should have recommended increased number of working days in educational institutions. There should be about 300 working days instead of about 200 at present.

6. No Check on Minority Institutions. Some suitable checks on the working of the schools run by the minority communities should have been proposed so as to prevent them from exploiting the staff working in these institutions.

7. No Check on Nursery Schools. The New Education Policy has not mentioned concrete steps to curb the mushroom growth of nursery schools charging high fees and meant only for the rich.

8. Lack of Teachers and Equipments. The emphasis on teaching and learning through discovery has little meaning as the nation has thousands of schools without adequate teachers and equipment.

9. No Research Basis. There is practically no proposal in the documents which is based on authentic research.

10. No Check on Public Schools. The New Education Policy has, by and large, evaded the issue of the 'loot' by so-called public schools which take money only and do not give good education.

11. No Supervision. The New Education Policy does not include specific measures for supervising and monitoring Government and Central schools properly. There is an urgent need to ensure that, 'All teachers should teach and all students study'.

12. Multiplication of Authorities. Setting up State Advisory Boards of Education, District Institutes of Education and District Boards of Education is not likely to serve any useful purpose. Already there is multiplicity of authorities in the field of education.

13. Lack of Funds. There is very little hope of obtaining community funds for educational purposes as there is a growing tendency on the part of the rich members of the community to contribute liberally to political parties due to obvious reasons. People, in general, are not motivated to donate funds for welfare services.

14. No Fixed Target. It is very unfortunate that no target has been fixed in different areas of reforms.

Q. 46. Write short note on Revised Policy Formulation, 1992.

Ans. REVISED POLICY FORMULATIONS, MAY 1992

The National Policy of Education (NPE), 1986 is a landmark in educational development of the country. A review of the NPE, 1986 was conducted during 1990-92. The Central Advisory Board of Education (CABE) in its 47th meeting held on May 5-6, 1992 considered the report of the CABE Committee on policy set-up to make an in-depth study of the report of the Committee for review of NPE, 1986. While broadly endorsing the policy, it recommended certain modifications in the light of the developments during the last few years and the experience gained in the implementation of the policy. The revised policy formulations containing these modifications recommended by the CABE were tabled in the Parliament on May 7, 1992.

Following the adoption of the revised policy formulations in May 1992, a revised POA was prepared. The POA 1992 was tabled in the Parliament on August 19, 1992.

Universalisation of elementary education, equalization of educational opportunities, women's education and development, vocationalisation of school education, consolidation of higher education, modernization of technical education, improvement of quality content and process of education at all levels continue to be the themes of national endeavour in the field of education.

Q. 47. Describe Committee for Girls Education and Public Corporation 1963-65.

Ans. Committee for Girls' Education and Public Co-operation (1963-65). At its meeting held in April, 1963 the National Council for Women's Education endorsed the suggestion made by the Union Education Minister that a small committee be appointed to look into the causes for lack of public support, particularly in rural areas, for girls' education and to enlist public co-operation. The Chairman of the National Council for Women's Education accordingly appointed in May 1963, a Committee with M. Bhaktavatsalam, Chief Minister, Madras as Chairman the Committee in this field. The Committee submitted its report in 1964 and the report was published in 1965.

Recommendations

It is only through a willing, educated and informed public that any progress can be made at all. Not only is the need urgent, but the ground is also ready for a comprehensive programme for mobilizing public co-operation to promote girls' education and giving it constructive channels for expression. It is essential that official action and the programme based on public initiative must move forward in close foremen. There has to be a sense of partnership and shared responsibility between official and voluntary agencies. There is also the need for a systematic and sustained programme with an adequate organisation for mobilizing community efforts.

1. Public Co-operation. Direct co-operation of the public should be encouraged in the following fields :

(i) Establishing private schools;

(ii) Putting up of schools buildings;

(iii) Contributing volunatary labour for construction of school buildings;

(iv) Helping in the maintenances of school buildings;

(v) Helping in providing suitable accommodation for teachers and students, particularly in the rural areas;

(vi) Popularizing co-education at the primary stage;

(vii) Creating public opinion in favour of the teaching profession and to give greater respect to the teacher in the community;

(viii) Initiating action and participating in educative propaganda to break down traditional prejudices against girls' education;

(ix) Setting up and organizing school betterment committees, improvement conferences;

(x) Undertaking necessary propaganda to make the profession of teaching for women popular;

(xi) Encouraging married women to take up at least part-time teaching in village schools and to work as school mothers;

(xii) Supplying mid-day meals;

(xiii) Supplying uniforms to poor and needy children; and

(xiv) Supplying free text-books and writing materials to needy children.

2. The State Council for Women's Education. These are the most suitable agencies for providing the organisation and leadership for mobilizing community effort. They should function as a part of the network of which the district Councils at the district level, and the Mahila Mandals and similar voluntary bodies at the town and village levels would be strong and active links. These agencies should look upon mobilising of community effort and educating public opinion to promote girls' education as their main and primary responsibility. They should aim at building up in villages and towns' teams of volunary workers, men and women, who are willing to devote themselves to this cause and work actively for its promotion.

3. State's Responsibility. The State should educate public opinion in favour of girls' education through:

(i) School improvement conferences;

(ii) Seminars;

(iii) Radio talks, audio-visual aids and distribution of informative pamphlets;

(iv) Enrolment drives, generally in June and special additional drives for girls' education during Dussehra; and

(v) Assisting voluntary, welfare and other organisations, private individuals and associations engaged in the field of education of girls and women.

4. State Help. The State should continue to help in an abundant measure in providing necessary schooling facilities in all the areas and in the habitations, however, so that the local population can make use of them.

5. School Improvement Conferences. These should be arranged widely throughout the State and particularly in the less advanced States in order to encourage people to contribute to educational awakening and advancement.

6. Pre-Primary Schools. It is necessary that in rural areas paricularly, pre-primary schools should be attached to primary schools so that children get accustomed to shcooling even at the tender age.

7. More Attractive. School work should be made more attractive and should present education in terms more acceptable to pupils.

8. Reform and Inspection. The existing functional deficiencies of schools should be remedied by replacing buildings which are totally inadequate to modern educational needs. There should be periodical inspection of school buildings and hostels so as to ensure their structural soundness and suitable sanitary facilities.

9. Recruitment of Women Teachers. Concerted efforts have to be made to recruit as many women teachers as possible. Women are by general consent the best teachers forth primary classes in all schools. It should be the aim of all states to appoint women teachers in primary schools and a greater number of women teachers in mixed schools. A school staffed by women will inspire greater confidence in the parents and make them willing to send their children to mixed institutions.

(i) ***Conditions of Recruitment.*** The basis of recruitment of women teachers should be widened and their conditions of work should be made more attractive. Financial incentives like special allowances for hilly, isolated or any other specific backward rural areas should be given to teachers. Each State may specify areas where such allowances would be available.

(ii) ***Married Women Teachers.*** Attempt should be made to bring back to the teaching profession married women who have left it in recent years and to bring women from other occupations to supplement the teaching staff.

(iii) ***Recruitment Age Limit.*** In order to attract more women teachers the age limit for the unmarried and married women teachers should be relaxed in the case of those working in village schools. The service conditions of such married women who do part-time teaching work should be made more attractive.

(iv) ***Condensed Courses.*** Condensed courses should be organised on a large scale foretold, women particularly from rural areas so that they could take up teaching jobs in the villages.

(v) ***Training Schools.*** Training schools with hostels need to be located in the rural centres and near 'different' areas where girls from the villages are trained and sent back to work in their own or neighbouring villages.

(vi) ***Posting.*** As far as possible women teachers should be posted in or near their own villages.

(vii) ***Pay Scale.*** The pay scales of all teachers should be improved and the teachers should be paid an economic wage, so that they may be retained in the profession.

(viii) ***Special Attention.*** Special drives should be organised to as the best form of social service needed for the upliftment of the villages.

(ix) ***Sufficient Facilities.*** The training facilities available in each State should be of such a magnitude that the annual output of trained teachers would be equal to the demand for additional teachers.

(x) ***Training.*** During selection of trainees for training schools and colleges, special preference should be given to women from rural areas seeking admission.

(xi) ***Lodging.*** It is only by providing women teachers with quarters near the schools that we can attract many educated women to the teaching profession.

(xii) ***Inspection.*** The inspecting staff should be adequate and strong if improvement into be secured and waste reduced. A separate women inspectorate will help to bring in more girls to school.

(xiii) ***Hostels.*** The absence of hostel facilities as also the slow progress in the construction of those that have been undertaken, have affected the hostel. The construction of hostels should be included as one of the priority objectives in the Plans of the States and necessary financial assistance for the construction of hostels and maintenance stipends be made available more liberally to local authorities and voluntary organisations working in the field of education of girls and women.

10. Building and Equipment. Local bodies should be made responsible for the provision of school buildings, equipments, playing fields and the like and observance of the educational code in the State.

11. Social Education. In the field of social education, a determined effort should be made to increase the number of literacy classes for women in rural areas and to carry out intensive campaigns for the spread of literacy amongst women. Activities in this field should be administered by the education departments of the State Government.

12. Central Assistance. Such Central assistance should be—

(a) At the elementary stage for:

(i) preparation and employment of women teachers;

(ii) grant of free books, writing material and clothing to girls; and

(iii) twin quarters for women teachers.

(b) At the secondary stage for:

(i) provision of separate schools for girls;

(ii) hostels;

(iii) grant of free books, writing materials and clothing to girls; and

(iv) preparation and appointment of women teachers in increasing numbers.

13. Curriculum. While the curriculum can be the same for both boys and girls at the primary and middle stages, provision should be made for offering of electives comprising subjects which would be of special interest to girls and which would help them later in their fields of activity.

14. Shift System. In schools that lack accommodation but have a rich of admission, the double shift system may be tried as a temporary measures.

15. Seasonal Adjustment. Changing of school hours and school holidays to seasonal requirements has been found in some places to be a helpful concession to parents who would otherwise not be in a position to spare the children for attending classes.

16. Compulsory Education. Compulsory Education Act should be introduced in States where it does not exist. In addition, State Governments should provide sufficient incentives and carry on propaganda to attract all children to school.

❐

PAPER-IV

Essentials of Educational Technology and Management

Q. 1. Define Educational Technology, its characteristics, nature, objectives and components.

Ans. Modern age is the age of science and technology. The world of today is very dynamic. The life of man in the primitive age was altogether different from his life in this sputnik age. There have been tremendous changes in the life style of human beings which may be attributed to the contribution of science and technology, science has extended the frontiers of our knowledge in various ways and directions. Science is considered to be a blessing to mankind. Nothing better has happened than the advent of science in man's life. The contribution of science and technology has been experienced in almost all the spheres of human life including education.

Before understanding the meaning of educational technology it is essential to know the meaning of technology. The word 'technology' has been taken from the Greek word (technikoes) which means an art and which is related with skill and dexterity. The term 'technology' implies the application of science to art. The concept of technology has developed during the last few years. It is a new area in the discipline of education. Educational technology is comprised of two words education and technology. When we apply the science of learning and communication to teaching we evolve a technology. There are three major factors that emphasize the linking of education with technology.

— Explosion of population.

— Explosion of new knowledge.

— Explosion of scientific and technological development.

Meaning and Concept of Educational Technology

Educational Technology is concerned with the development, application, and evaluation of system, techniques and aids to improve the process of human learning. It could be conceived as a science of techniques, methods and media by which educational goals could be realised. Generally the term "Technology" denotes the systematic application of the knowledge of science to practical tasks in industry. Hence, "Educational Technology" may be roughly defined as the systematic application of the knowledge of sciences to practical tasks in Education. It is not primarily concerned with the task of prescribing the goal although it does help in specifying the goals and translating them in behavioural terms. It is a communication process resulting from the adaptation of the scientific method to the behavioural science of teaching/learning. Educational Technology widey accepted as the application of system approach in the systematic design of a learning system to bring about improvement in teaching-learning evaluation process.

It is not an end in itself but a means to accomplish some educational and instructional objectives already determined and clearly defined. It tries to make the whole teaching-learning process more and more meaningful for both the teachers and the learners. It modifies teacher's method of teaching and learner's behaviour for their own betterment and for the betterment of the mankind. It is not the same thing as instruction or education or learning but an aggressive invention which includes in itself every thing that helps in shaping personality.

Earlier the Concept of Educational Technology was used as a synonym to audio-visual aids like pictures, charts, maps, and models meant for direct teaching-learning. With the advent of physical science and electronic revolution there came an era of hardware and software like projectors, tape-recorders, radio and T.V. etc. Then came the age of mass media which led to massive communication revolution for instructional purposes. With the advent of programmed instruction and programmed learning, a new dimension of educational technology came into existence. It has individualized the process of education and introduced a system of self-learning in the form of self-instructional material and teaching machine. The concept of programmed learning added another dimensions to the meaning of educational technology when some new devices and approaches such as Micro-teaching.

In other words we can see one aspect of Educational Technology related to the use of specific techniques such as educational television, radio, programmed learning and other audio-visual aids. In another aspect, Education Technology is seen as the application of scientific and other organised knowledge to the practical problems of education. In the particular context of the developing countries, the emphasis is on the application of techinques and knowledge with a view to mobilising and optimising the available human as well as technological resources. Educational technology is seen both as a means as well as service to effect and facilitate better and more productive learning systems. It may be defined as a separate field in the theory of education dealing with the development and application of the use of educational resources.

Educational Technology should not be confused with teaching or instruction or education or learning or engineering but it should be taken as a sum total of all such aspects which go a long way in shaping the personality of the learner in a meaningful context.

It is neither technology in education nor technology of education but both and all pervasive which pervades the whole teaching-learning process to make it meaningful for the teacher who teaches and the learner who learns and modifies his behaviour for his own betterment and the betterment of mankind.

DEFINITIONS OF EDUCATIONAL TECHNOLOGIES

G.O. Leith, "Educational Technology is the application of scientific knowledge and learning and the conditions of learning to improve the effectiveness and efficiency of teaching and training."

Robert A. Cox, "Educational Technology is the application of scientific process to man's leraning conditions."

John P. Dececco, "Educational Technology is the form of detailed application of psychology of learning to practical teaching problems."

E.E. Hadden, "Educational Technology is that branch of educational theory and practice concerned primarily with the design and use of messages which control the learning process."

Richmond, "Educational Technology is concerned to provide appropriately designed leraning situations which, holding in view of objectives of the Teaching of Training, being to bear the best means of instruction."

S.S. Kulkarni, "Educational Technology may be defined as the application of the laws as well as recent discoveries of science and technology to the process of education."

S.K. Mitra, "Educational Technology can be conceived as a sicence of techniques and methods by which educational goals could be realized."

Robert A. Cox (Article : The Process of Educational Technology : A Tool for Development 1970). "The application of scientific process to man's learning conditions is what has come recently to be called 'educational or instructional' technology."

D.E.S. Working Party (U.K.), "Educational Technology is the development, application and evaluation of systems, techniques and aids in the field of human learning."

Robert M. Gange defined Educational Technology as "The Development of a set of systematic techniques and accompanying practical knowledge for designing, testing and operating schools as educational systems."

Characteristics of Educational Technology

Characteristics of Educational Technology are as follows:

1. It is based on scientific and technological advancements.
2. It is more a practical discipline and less a theoritical one.
3. It is a fast growing modern discipline.
4. It makes use of the research findings of psychology, sociology, engineering, sciences and social psychology etc., and applies the same to the field of education.
5. It brings pupils, teachers and technical means together in an effective way.
6. It is the science of techniques and methods. It locates the problems in the field of education, remedies them and ultimately aims at improving the education system.

7. It is bound to improve the teacher, the learner and the teaching learning process.

NATURE OF EDUCATIONAL TECHNOLOGY

1. The basis of educational technology is science.

2. Educational Technology studies the effect of science and technology upon education. In other words, science and technology are used under educational technology. Hence, it is the practical aspect of science.

3. Educational Technology is a continuous dynamic, progressive and effect-producing method.

4. New conceptions are prossible only due to educational technology such as programmed learning, micro-teaching, simulated teaching, interaction analysis, video-tape, tape-recorder, projector and computer, etc.

5. Educational Technology accepts schools as a system. In this system, the school-building, furniture and teachers act as input while various methods, techniques, strategies and the teaching and examination with the help of audio-visual aids function in the form of a process. Lastly, the output is in of form of ability of the pupils.

6. Audio-visual aids cannot be termed as educational technology. It is because its concern is only with the process-aspect of educational technology and not with the input and output aspects. But if these A.V. aids are used to achieve educational objectives, then it can be put in the category of Educational technology.

7. Programmed Instruction is also different from Educational Technology. Its main cause is that the student learns himself during the programmed instructions. It does not allow interaction between pupil and teacher. Hence, it can be used only for limited objectives and limited subject-matter. Therefore, programmed instruction is merely a part of educational technology.

8. Engineering Technology is not the educational technology because the engineering technology has manufactured radio, tape-recorder, video-tape and T.V., etc., which are used in teaching as audio-visual aids, but still engineering technology is different from educational technology. In education, it is accepted as hardware approach only.

9. Educational Technology cannot solve each and every problem of education. It can be used successfully in teaching and instructional system only.

10. Some people assume that educational technology will replace the teacher which will make the teacher unemployed one day. It is their mistake. Educational technology can never replace the teacher. It is because of three aspects of educational technology. These are—*1*. Input, *2*. Process and *3*. Output. Input is the teacher's job and therefore, educational technology cannot snatch the place of a teacher. In spite of this, educational technology develops cognitive domain only and not the affective domain. Affective domain can only be developed when an interaction between teachers and pupils takes place. Hence, educational technology cannot replace the teacher.

GENERAL OBJECTIVES OF EDUCATIONAL TECHNOLOGY

The objectives of Educational Technology at macro level or broad level are as under:

1. To identify educational needs of the community.
2. To determine the aims of education.
3. To develop a suitable curriculum.
4. To determine appropriate strategies.
5. To identify the resources—human and non-human.
6. To locate the major obstacles in the way of proper development of learners.
7. To suggest remedies to overcome the above traced out obstacles.
8. To manage the whole system of education.

SPECIFIC OBJECTIVES

The objectives of educational technology at micro-level *i.e.*, in view of specific class-room teaching are as under :

1. To identify the educational needs of the pupils.
2. To determine the class-room objectives in behavioural terms.
3. To analyse the contents of instructions and organise them.

4. To plan the teaching strategies.
5. To identify the resources—human and non-human.
6. To evaluate class-room teaching in terms of students' performance.
7. To provide feedback to the teacher and the students for betterment of teaching-learning process.

Regarding objectives of Educational Technology, Hilliard Joson has given the following objectives :

1. Transmission of Information.
2. Serving as role model.
3. Assisting the practice of specific skills.
4. Contribution to the provision of feedback.

MAIN OBJECTIVES OF EDUCATIONAL TECHNOLOGY

1. To help in the environment of facilities required in the teaching learning process.
2. To make the class-room teaching more effective.
3. To modify the behaviour of the teacher and the learner.
4. To improve and update the methods of leraning.

TECHNOLOGIZING EDUCATION IS TO OPTIMIZE LEARNING ENDEAVOURS

In Educational Technology, both hardware and software mechanisms are involved.

Garrison (1989), opines "technology will be viewed here as having both a process (software) and a product (hardware) component, where process is the creative application of knowledge of purposeful activities. A subset of hardware is media, where media are the devices used to distribute information."

In Educational Technology, hardware covers TV, Computer, Overhead projector, Tape Recorder, Teaching machines etc. Software includes audio/video cassettes, Filmstrips, micro films, slides etc.

Educational Technology is comprehensive. It is associated with all aspects of educative process-methods, teaching strategies, learning materials, handling of various equipment etc.

COMPONENTS OF EDUCATIONAL TECHNOLOGY

The following 4 M's are the major components of Educational Technology :—

(i) Methods, (ii) Materials, (iii) Media, (iv) Manpower.

(i) Methods. It is concerned with the devices such as Programmed Learning Team Teaching, Micro Teaching, Personalized System of Instruction in Teaching Learning situations.

(ii) Materials. Instructional materials such as Programmed Text-book. The material of this type may be handwritten or printed.

(iii) Media. The media used here are audio, or visual or audio-visual. A few examples are—radio, tape recorder, charts, films, educational television etc.

(iv) Man Power. Man power controls educational technology in every way. Educational Technology without man is zero.

Q. 2. Discuss the scope and functions of Educational Technology.

Ans. SCOPE OF EDUCATIONAL TECHNOLOGY

By scope of educational technology we mean the jurisdiction, the limits or the bounderies within which it works. It needs demarcation of the boundaries within which the process of education can go on. Being a fast growing modern discipline it is almost practical all through and is expading with a tremendous speed, aiming at all-round development in the area of education.

National Policy on Education (1986), recommends that, "Educational Technology will be employed in the spread of useful, information, the training and retraining of teachers, to improve quality, sharpen awareness of art and culture, inculcate abiding values etc., both in the formal and non-formal sectors. Maximum use will be made of the available infrastructure."

The scope of Educational Technology can be assessed from the following points:

1. Determination of Objectives. Educational Technology provides different methods and techniques for writing instructional objectives in behavioural terms such as Bloom Taxonomy Magar's Approach and RCEM Approach.

The needs and requirements of the people and hence education need be revised from moment to moment. Educational technology helps in fixing-up the right objectives in the light of the changed circumstances and changed environment.

2. Improvement in Teaching Learning Process. It helps in improving the teaching learning process and makes it more purposive. It tries to discuss the concept of teaching, analysis of teaching process, variables of teaching, phases and levels of teaching, principles of teaching, maxims of teaching and relationship between teaching and learning.

3. Development of Teaching Learning Material. Teaching learning materials are also as important as anything else in the teaching learning process. In this age of science and technology, the materials of teaching can not be unscientific. Everything of the society including values of life need be reflected in the materials. Only right type of material will be able to modify the behaviour of the learner suitably making him a fit person for the society.

4. Improvement in Teaching Training. The change of environment with new curriculum and new materials need be handled by the teachers. The teachers equipped with old strategies and methodologies of teaching will remain misfits. Right type of training to the teachers is the need of the hour. Educational Technology can render its valuable help in the training of teachers also. The use of video tapes and close circuit T.V. will help the teachers to remodel and reshape their teaching behaviours suitably.

It includes micro teaching, simulated teaching, term-teaching, teacher effectiveness, modification of teacher-behaviour, class-room interaction and interaction analysis, etc.

5. Development of Teaching Learning Strategies. A strategy plays an important role in the hands of a teacher in every learning situation. The strategy has to be the right one which should be according to the materials and is able to bring about effective teaching-learning. The differnt strategies are being evolved by educational technology. The knowledge of those strategies is a must for every teacher. Then only the teacher will be able to do justice to their jobs.

It tries to describe the ways and means of discovering selecting and developing suitable startegies and tactics of teaching in terms of optimum learning and available teaching-learning resources; the availablity of the different types of teching methods, devices and models of teaching—their appropriate selection and use—for the optimum results.

6. Proper Use of Audio Visual Aids. Audio Visual aids have always played an important role in the teaching-learning process. They need be used according to the times. The software aids, the hardware aids, the computer and other such appliances, equipment etc., have to be used in the present type of teaching-learning environment. Computer assisted instructions will help the learner as well as the teacher to achieve the goals of education more conveniently.

7. Utilization of the Sub-System of Education. Educational Technology considers education as a system operating in a systematic and scientific way for the achievement of educational objectives. For the coverage of its systematic approach, it tries to include the topics dealing with the theory and principles of a system approach, explaining education as a system, its different sub-systems in terms of input and output. It is helpful in solving scientifically educational administrative problems with the help of system analysis.

8. Development of Curriculum. Educational Technology is concerned with the designing of a suitable curriculum for the achievment of the desired objectives. It is helpful in describing the ways and means of the selection of suitable learning experiences, organisation of the contents in a suitable framework in order to bring better results. It provides the scientific foundation to education as well as develops theories of teaching and learning.

9. Proper Use of Hardware and Software. These days hardware and software are playing an effective role in the attainment of educational objectives. Educational Technology helps in the proper use of these aids. It tries to describe these resources in terms of their specific functions, their solution, proper handling and maintenance.

10. Provides Feedback. It provides an appropriate feedback to the learners as well as teachers for bringing necessary improvement at the preparatory and implementation stages of their specific acts. For this purpose, educational technology discusses the ways and means of suitable evaluation techniques, their planning, development selection and appropriate use in relation to the objectives of teaching-learning system.

In this way Educational Technology is concerned with all those who are connected in any way, directly or indirectly, to the processes and products of education. It teaches the teachers the art of teaching, the learners the science of learning the educational planners the structure of planning and administrators or managers the skill of managing or administering the task of teaching and learning. It works for the individualization of instructions as well for improving the group dynamics of the class-room.

Therefore, in any way, the scope of the educational technology should not be confined to the limited boundaries, but it should be left free for the necessary expansion and development for carrying out its mission, tasks and objectives.

FUNCTIONS OF EDUCATIONAL TECHNOLOGY

Important functions of educational technology are briefly explained here:

1. Improvement of Teaching. Educational Technology analyses the process of teaching throughly. It tries to find out the different variables of teaching, their interlinks, effects upon each other, relationships, theories of teaching, phases of teaching principles of teaching, maxims of teaching etc. By developing the theories of teaching, it helps in improving the quality of education.

2. Analysis of the Teaching-Learning Process. Educational Technology aims at analysing the process of teaching-learning thoroughly. It tries to find out the different variables of teaching, their interlinks, effects upon each other, relationship etc. It is also concerned with various phases of teaching. The principles of teaching and the maxims of teaching are also analysed by it. Over all, it tries to establish better and better relationship between teaching and learning.

3. Improvement of Learning. Educational Technology analyses the process of learning and the related theories. It facilitates more and more of learning in less time. It takes the help of various empirically established generalisations from psychology, sociology, physical sciences, engineering etc.

4. Fixing up Goals of Education. The objectives of education are being reviewed and revised with the passage of time. Educational technology helps in finding out the right objectives. Everything in this universe is undergoing tremendous changes and with a very fast speed. The needs and requirements of the people and hence education need be revised from moment to moment. Educational Technology helps in fixing up the right objectives in the light of the changed circumstances and changed environment.

5. Training to Teachers. The changed type of environment with new curriculum and new materials is to be handled by the teachers. The teachers equipped with old strategies and methodologies of teaching will remain misfits. Right type of training to the teachers is the need of the hour. Educational Technology can render its valuable help in the training of teachers also. The use of video tapes and close circuit T.V. will help the teachers to remodel and reshape their teaching behaviours suitably.

6. Development of Curriculum. Keeping in view the objectives of education which have been finalised by education technology, thereafter comes the question of developing right type of curriculum. Only a suitable type of curriculum will help in the attainment of goals. Curriculum is the total teaching-learning environment which has to be modified and remodelled in the light of latest thoughts. Only educational technology can do this job of developing a suitable curriculum appropriately.

7. Development of Teaching-Learning Materials. Teaching-learning materials are also as important as anything else in the teaching-learning process. They have to be in accordance with the environment of the learners. In this age of science and technology, the materials of teaching cannot be unscientific. Everything of the society including values of life need be reflected in the materials. Only right type of materials will able to modify the behaviour of the learner suitably making him a fit person for the society. Only educational technology can develop the required and the desired type of teaching-learning materials.

8. Teaching-Learning Strategies. A strategy plays an important role in the hands of a teacher in every teaching-learning situation.

The strategy has to be the right one which should be according to the materials and is able to bring about effective teaching-learning. The different strategies are being evolved by educational technology. The knowledge of those strategies is a must for every teacher. Then only the teachers will be able to do justice to their jobs.

9. Development of Audio-Visual Aids. Audio-Visual aids have always played an important role in the teaching-learning process. They need be used according to the times. The software aids, the hardware aids, the computer and other such appliances, equipment etc., have to be used in the present type of teaching-learning environment. Computer assisted instructions will help the learner as well as the teacher to achieve the goals of education more conveniently. There is need of deriving maximum benefits out of educational technology.

10. Help in Over all Improvement. Educational technology helps in locating the problems in the different areas of education. It also helps in remedying the draw-backs. Evaluation of the teaching-learning process is also made better because through feedback, things are improved thoroughly and there is better control over the process of education. Thus, educational technology can revolutionise the whole process of teaching-learning.

11. Identification of Needs of the Community. Educational Technology identifies the needs of the community. It helps in providing equal education opportunities to backward people, disadvantaged students and deprived sections of the society. It helps education to reach the remotest corner of the country. The needs and requirements of the community are fast changing. Educational Technology aims at identifying the needs of the community from time to time. Then it tries to improve the community in every possible way.

12. Identification of the Needs of Class-Room Behaviours. Educational Technology identifies the needs of class-room behaviour. As the mass education has reduced the standard of education, the use of educational technology can maintain and improve the standard by the use of teaching aids and programmed instruction material. Educational Technology can inspire the students in the class-rooms for self-learning.

Q. 3. Discuss the different types of Educational Technology, their feature, characteristics and assumptions.

Ans. The scientific, inventions and technological developments have influenced every walk of human life. There is rapid mechanization in the field of industries, defence, trade, administration, etc. The educational process does not remain untouched by these advances. It has necessitated introduction of technology in the field of education.

Hence Educational Technology came with its various forms which are as under :—

1. Teaching Technology,
2. Instructional Technology,
3. Behavioural Technology,
4. Instructional design Technology.

Teaching is purposeful activity. The ultimate goal of teaching is to bring allround development of a child. The knowledge and practice which help in realizing the goal is the content matter of teaching technology.

Teaching is an art as well as science because teaching can be studied objectively an scientifically. Teaching has the scientific foundation. This has evolved the concept of 'teaching technology.'

Teaching technology is the application of philosophical, sociological and scientific knowledge to teaching for achieving some specific learning objectivies.

I.K. Davies, N.L. Gange, Robert Gánge, Burner and Robert Glaser have contributed significantly in this area of education. Silverman has termed it as constructive educational technology.

Assumptions of Teaching Technology

'Technology of Teaching' is based on the following assumptions:

1. Teaching is a scientific process and it has two major components : Content and communication.
2. The teaching activities can be modified and improved.

3. Teaching skills can be developed with the help of feedback devices.
4. A close relationship may be established between teaching and learning.
5. The learning objectives may be achieved by performing teaching activities.

K. Davies and Robert Glaser (1962), have developed the content of Technology of Teaching and classified it into four elements :

1. Planning of Teaching,
2. Organization of Teaching,
3. Leading of Teaching,
4. Controlling of Teaching.

Main Features of Teaching Technology

1. All the three types of objectives: cognitive, affective and psychomotor can be achieved by this technology.
2. The philosophical, sociological and scientific knowledge can be applied to teaching process.
3. The teaching process can be made effective with the help of Teaching Technology.
4. The teaching can be organized from memory level to reflective level.
5. Teaching technology implies the input, process and output aspects side by side.
6. The content structure can be related to communication structure for achieving the learning objectives.
7. The teaching theories can be formulated by the use of teaching technology.
8. The pupil-teachers and in-service teachers can improve their teaching and make it more purposive.

Instructional Technology

The instruction has significant role in human learning. The systematic actions which induce learning is known as instruction. The instruction stands for development of knowledge and beliefs.

Instructional technology means a net work of techniques or devices employed to accomplish certain defined set of learning objectives. It implies the application of psychological and scientific principles and knowledge to instruction for achieving the specific objectives of learning.

The origin of instructional technology is from psychological laboratory experiments. The most important example of instructional technology is 'programmed instruction'. The programmed instruction and instructional technology can be used inter-changeably.

Assumptions of Instructional Technology

The instructional technology involves the following assumptions:

1. Reinforcement can be provided continuously by the use of instruction.
2. The content matter can be divided into its elements and each element can be presented independently.
3. The external learning conditions can be created by arranging the elements in a logical sequence.
4. The student can learn successfully with out the physical presence of a teacher.
5. The strategies and tactics of instruction can be used for achieving certain well defined set of instructional objectives.
6. The student can learn according to his needs and rate of learning.

Characteristics of Instructional Technology

1. The cognitive objective can be achieved successfully by the use of Instructional Technology.
2. Reinforcement is provided with the help of right responses.
3. Individual differences are taken care of in his technology.
4. The students can learn at their own pace.
5. It makes use of the psychological learning theories and principles.
6. It provides deep insight into the content structure.

Behavioural Technology

Psychology is the science of behaviour. It studies the nature and structure of behaviour of the organisms. The learning is the modification of behaviour through activities and experiences. The educational activities are designed to bring desirable changes in the behaviour of the students. The psychology deals with every type of human behaviour. Thus, the behavioural technology has wider scope. It covers the area of industry, defence, commerce, communication, administration, health, motivation, training education, teaching and instruction.

The teaching and instruction activities are organised to achieve sepcific learning objectives by bringing desirable behavioural change among the students. Thus, teaching and instructional technology are two forms of behavioural technology. But in the field of education it refers mainly to the teacher behaviour. The behavioural technology is the application of scientific knowledge in modifying the teacher behaviour. Thus it is also termed as training technology.

Assumptions of Behavioural Technology

The behavioural technology is based on the following assumptions:

1. Teacher behaviour is observable.
2. Teacher behaviour is measruable and quantifiable.
3. Teacher behaviour is relative.
4. Teacher behaviour is social and psychological.
5. Teacher behaviour is modifiable.

Characteristics of Behavioural Technology

1. The specific teaching skills can be developed.
2. It helps in developing the theory of teaching.
3. The achievement of teaching can be evaluated objectively and in a systematic manner.
4. Feedback devices can be used for the improvement of communication skills.
5. The individual differences of pupils and teacher can be tackled.

6. The knowledge and practice of behavioural technology may be an important instrument for training colleges to produce effective teachers.
7. In class-room, behaviour technology concentrates on elements of behaviour.
8. In behavioural technology the theory and practice of class-room teacher behaviour are included.
9. In it mechanism of feedback devices for modification of teacher behaviour are also employed for developing teaching skills.

Q. 4. What are the different approaches of Educational Technology?

Ans. Approaches of Educational Technology are as follows:

I. Hardware Approach. Hardware Approach has physical science and applied engineering as its basis. They have mechanised the whole teaching-learning process. There is even reduction in the cost of education. Educational Technology that way, has almost revolationised the total teaching-learning. The new mechanism of teaching-learning with improved technology as its basis is suggesting innumerable new ways of doing things to the class-room teachers. A good many gadgets of teaching-learning find their place in the class-room situations and many more of that type are expected to enter into the class-rooms in the near future. The job and the duties of the teacher are likely to have multifaceted changes.

As a result of Hardware technology, electro-mechanical equipments have been developed which are used for instructional pruposes. In the overcrowded class-room, the teacher uses microphones for making his voice fully audible to the learners. Radio, T.V., tape recorder, epidiascope, projector, closed circuit television (C.C.T.V.), teaching machines, computers are used for teaching the students. Silverman (1968), called this type of educational technology 'Relative Technology'. According to Marilym Nickson (1971), educational technology deals with the application of many fields of science to the educational needs of the individual as well as of society.

Davis (1971), thinks that the hardware approach is based on the application of physical science to the education and training system which mechanizes the process of teaching gradually so that teachers would be able to deal with more students, resulting in less cost and economy in finances.

Hardware approach, undoubtedly, is bound to work wonders in the area of education. It has a few draw-backs which are given below:

(a) Hardware material, equipment were devised by science for use in science but now they have been borrowed from there and are being used in education.

(b) While operating in the field of education, it works in isolation and not as an integral part of that system where it existed earlier.

II. Software Approach. In software approach, the basis of all thinking and working is behavioural science and psychology of learning. The scholar can exploit psychology of learning to any extent to attain the different objectives. With every new thinking he can evolve something new for teaching purposes. The teacher with added knowledge of software approach can use the films, flash-cards, tapes etc., for various purposes. There is not end to his thinking. Decidely he can plan better teaching which results into better learning.

Software approach uses the principles of psychology for the purpose of behaviour modification. In this connection, Davis (1971), observes, "This view of educational technology is closely associated with the modern principles of programmed learning and is characterised by task analysis, wirting precise objectives, selection of appropriate learning strategies, reinforcement of correct responses and constant education."

Silverman (1968), termed this educational technology as 'constructive educational technology.'

Both software and hardware approaches are so interlinked that they cannot be sparated from each other. One without the other is incomplete. It is software approach which makes the hardware approach function well. Mitchell (1973), writes, "By directing attention to the achievement of educational aims of standards through knowledge and control relation between inputs in man-machine systems and organisations, educational technology can be expected to make more contributions to behavioural science than science has made to educational technology."

III. System Approach. This new technology has influenced the educational administration and organisation to a great extent. This is the modren approach. It acts as a link between hardware and software approach. It is also known as 'Management Technology'. It has brought to educational management a scientific approach for solving educational administrative problems.

It is essentially a new management approach, influencing management decisions in business, industry and education. Education is regard as a system and system approach is a systematic way of designing an effective and economical educational system.

System is defined in the dictionary as "an assemblage of objects united by some form of regular interaction or inter-dependence; as organic or organised whole as the solar system or a new telegraph system". System may be divided into three broad categories. For instance, there are natural systems as solar system; there are systems which have been designed by man as telegraph system and lastly, there are systems which are combinations of natural and man-made systems like hydro-electric plants or modern dairies.

Aspects of System Approach

System approach has three major aspects :—

— Input
— Output
— Precess

Input. It involves the entering behaviour of the learner.

— It involves previous achievements, abilities of student and level of motivation.
— It concerns with the comprehension level of the learner.
— It includes the skill of teaching and awareness of teaching and training methods.
— It considers availability and skill for teaching aids.

Teaching Learning Process. It involves the means and devices of learning experiences.

— To generate situation for presenting the subject-matter systematically.

— To select and use appropriate teaching strategies and tactics for desired learning structures.

— To employ appropriate teaching aids for desired behavioural change.

— To ideantify and use suitable communication techniques for the comprehension of the sub;ect-matter.

— To use suitable schedules of reinforcement for effective learning.

— To establish rapport with students for effective teaching.

— To evolve appropriate school environment by developing good relations among students.

Output. It includes mainly the terminal behaviour of the learner.

— To identify the characteristics of content.

— To clarify the objectives achieved through are content.

— To analyse the stimuli.

— To determine the characteristics of students' desired activities.

Advantages of System Approach

— It provides conceptual framework to build plans for implementing change for education.

— It helps to identify the suitability of the resource material to achieve the specifc goal.

— It hepls to assess the resource needs, their sources and facilities in relation to quantities, time and other factors.

— Technological advance could be used to provide integration of machines, media and people for attaining the defind goals.

— It permits an orderly introduction of components demonstrated to be required for systems success in terms of student learning.

Q. 5. Discuss the role of Educational Technology in modern educational practices and its features.

Or

Discuss Educational Technology today and tomorrow.

Ans. Educational Technology is bound to improve the teachers considerably. In the absence of working knowledge of this growing discipline, the teacher will find himself lagging far behind in the modern system of teaching-learning. In fact, the teacher with his upto date knowledge of educational technology can work wonders in the discharge of his duties.

Utility of the subject of Educational Technology for the teachers is briefly explained below:

1. Knowledge of technological advancements in the field of education is needed awfully by all the teachers. Only then they can come upto the expectations of all concerned. It is educational technology which provides clear cut information and knowledge to the teachers.
2. The teachers become more efficient academically, professionally and technologically.
3. The teachers are able to learn how to prepare Modules, Programmed Learning Materials etc. That way, they are able to contribute handsomely to the field of education.
4. In the discharge of class-room duties, the teachers are able to handle their techniques more confidently.
5. Some teachers develop more interest in software. They are able to create materials for their students. Thus, the teachers learn how to make maximum use of the hardware aids.

EDUCATIONAL TECHNOLOGY TODAY-AND-TOMORROW

Impact of educational technology for over all development in different fields of life has been realized. The Green Revolution in agriculture; Hydro-electric projects in irrigation; production of heavey machinery and tools in industry and electronics are the result of technological advancement. Our technocrats and other experts are able to go abroad showing their far advancing excellences. This is one of the picture, on the other side of the picture we have poverty, illiteracy, rapid increase of population growth which continue posing challenges to every one.

To promote the use of mass media and instructional technology, the Government of India launched an educational technology project in 1972-73. The project was implemented with the collaboration of the United Nations Development Programme (U.N.D.P.) The Educational Technology Centre was set-up in NCERT and its units were set-up in some states. The chief purpose was to improve education by the proper use of educational technology.

National Policy on Education (1986), has stressed the important role of Educational Technology in the following ways :

(a) establishment of National Open University,

(b) establishment of Navodaya Schools in some areas to train rural talents,

(c) unviersalisation of Primary Education through non-formal systems,

(d) developing effective systems of life long education encompassing agriculture, health, literacy and other forms of adult learning needs, and

(e) more effective use of educational technology in the qualitative improvement of education in existing school systems and universities.

Now technology is used in education in almost every country of the world. Today it has become the pillars of education giving support and lending guidance and direction to it. It has simplified the process of education, made the process of teaching-learning easy and economical. Application of hardwares and softwares systems approach etc., have revolutionised education and training in the world.

Q. 6. What do you understand by Hardware? Describe the use and educational significance of audio-visual aids characterised as hardware.

Ans. Hardware is that part of educational technology which refers to tools and instruments. With the advancement of science, we find that the process of teaching-learning has been gradually mechanized through the use of teaching machines, languages laboratory, television, radio, computer, epidiascope, slide, projector, over head projector and opaque projector etc. All these sources are involved in hardware. Hardware approach has physical science and applied engineering as its basis.

Characteristics of Hardware in Teaching

- — Hardwares are generally electronic and mostly depend on mechanical system.
- — The outcome of hardware is direct and immediate because they can be seen in concrete form.
- — New techniques and research is being done of evaluating the effect of hardware
- — Hardware are media of communication. Some commercial agencies are manufacturing hardware from business point of view.

Need and Importance of Hardware

The proper use of hardware helps in maintaining the tempo of motivation and attention in the process of teaching and learning.

By using hardware, subject matter becomes clear and simple.

The proper handling of hardware contributes to the economy of time, resources and energy of teacher and students.

Educational Hardware are as follows:

Overhead Projectors

By the name of the equipment itself it would be evident that in overhead transparency projector, the projected image is obtained behind and over the head of the instructor. The OHP reflects images coming from a powerful light that shines through a transparency on a screen by means of a tilted highly polished mirror and lens assembly.

The screen image is brilliant enough to be seen even in a lighted room. The projector area ranges from 3" ×3" to 10" ×10".

Normally overhead projectors are composed of a projection lamp to act as a source of light condensing lenses to concentrate all the light into usable beam, a polished mirror and lens assembly and a blower for cooling the system.

Epidiascope

Epidiascope as the name suggests is the combination of episcope and diascope. With its help a picture, chart, map, diagram photograph or printing material can be projected in an enlarged size. For showing these materials there is no need of any slide, they can be shown on the screen as it is. When it is used to project an opaque object it works like an episcope and when it is used to project slides then it works as a diascope. Thus, it serves both as a disaçope and as an episcope and therefore it is rightly called epidiascope. In epidiascope different types of pictures as well as slides can be presented on the screen, where as in diascope only slides can be projected. Plane mirror, projection lens and horizontal straight line projection with a lamp are essential requirements for epidiascope. A plane mirror is placed at an angle of 45° over the object. It reflects the light so that it passes through the projection lens forming a magnified image on the screen.

Utility of Epidiascope

Use of epidiascope makes teaching learning process more interesting, easy and impressive. Small pictures can be enlarged with its help. This instrument helps in enlarging those prictures which can not easily be enlarged by artists. Written lesson, map, cartoons, posters, diagrams and photographs can easily be shown to the students in the class with the help of epidiascope. A model of good handwriting can also be shown with its help to encourage the students to improve their handwriting. General mistakes committed by the students can be shown with its help to enable the students to make corrections. Teacher can explain the difficulties of the students simultaneously while showing the picture with the help of projector. Students become more attentive, active and disciplined in the class. Use of this instrument in teaching learning process makes teaching and learning more interesting and effective as students derive more pleasure in learning by seeing pictures. It also makes teacher active as he has to plan and prepare in advance all that he has to show in the class.

Radio

Radio is considered to be an improtant media for effective education. It is a powerful audio aid. It was invented by Marconi in

1895. It is considered to be the most effective means to impart education to the masses. Its popularity as a means to education is fast increasing in both developing and the developed countries. Invention of radio has brought about a great revolution in the world of educations. Radio helps the students to listen to the lesson. It was the only popular means to impart education in schools and colleges in different countries of the world before the invention of television. It holds fascinating opportunities for the world of education. In this era of constant change it has opened a new vista of an instructional media to alleviate the difficulties and problems of critical shortage of school facilities for ever growing school population. It is of great help to poor countries of the world in the field of education where school going population is large and where there is acute shortage of qualified teachers, well equipped laboratories and other necessary infrastructure for growth of education. It can reduce the mounting cost of education in underdeveloped countries.

Tape-Recorder

Tape-recorder is an important audio-aid. The invention of tape recorder has brought about a revolution in the teaching-leraning process. Its main function is recording and reproducing of the sound. Microphone, amplifier and reproducer are its three parts. It is an instrument which is used to record speeches, songs, music etc. and which may be played back at any time and any number of times. Teaching with tape recorder is extention of a teacher work. Talks and leactures of great educationists of the world can be recorded permanently. Different types of errors especially related to language can be recorded with its help. If the tape recorder is handled properly and carefully, the matter recorded on it can be repeated 100 times. The same lesson can be heard again and again in the class. Children feel happy when they listen to their own voice and feel encouraged. Tape recorders are available in all sizes and it is not at all difficult to handle them.

Educational Utility of Tape Recorder

1. Like radio programme we need not fix time for tape recorded programme and no change is required in the time table of school. Tape-record as a teaching device can be used any time and any where.

2. It helps in supplimenting the educational output of radio and television broadcasts and guest lectuerers.
3. It can help in preparing recorded educational programmes to be used for instructions in schools and colleges.
4. It is of immense use in developing conversation skill, expression power and techniques of effective dramatization.
5. Educational material related with film strips and slides is recorded in the tape recorder. Thus, it is helpful in preparing commentary, display of slides and filmstrips.
6. Tape recorder is helpful in bringing social awareness among people and can be used for canvassing in the elections.
7. It helps students in developing the skill of oratory by practising again and again on it.
8. It is very useful for improving the pronunciation of different languages.
9. Sometimes students can not be taken to real life situations *e.g.*, in Delhi on the occasion of 15th August and 26th January. Students remain deprived of speeches and ideas of the President and other great patriots of the country. Tape recorder can be used in recording the speeches of these great men which can be heard later on by the students. Thus, tape recorder helps in overcoming this shortcoming.
10. The teacher can record talks and lectures related to various subjects like science, maths, religion, music, morality, dance, social-studies, drama, poetry, economics etc., on tape recorder can be presented before the stduents whenever need arises. Thus, by presenting the recorded talks to the students and by listening to it again and again, the students can enhance their knowledge.
11. Use of tape recorder in teaching learning process gives more emphasis on learning by doing. Students can practice on tape recorder again and again till they become perfect. Thus, tape recorder helps students to learn things by trial and error method.

Television

Television is the most powerful media which has revolutionised the world. It can reach enormous cross-section of population with simultaneous presentations. It is helping learners and viewers to overcome the social deficiencies and cultural obstacles. It has immense attraction and potentiality in moulding characters, forming attitudes and shaping values.

According to **M.J. Apter.** "Television is the most powerful medium of mass-communication which has ever existed and it has revolutionised our life in many ways. It appears that the future television is going to have definite positive contribution to make childrens' life in the class-room happy. Television is already being used in schools more and more widely."

Through a television programme the audience not only hear but also see an event happening. Television is both audio and visual media. It is an improvement upon radio broadcast. It is fast becoming an integral part of school education. Invention of television has brought about a great revolution in the world of education. Today, television is considered to be really an important means for effective education. It is a powerful medium of communication through both auditory as well as visual channels. It helps the students to listen to and directly see the lesson on the television screen ensuring teaching learning to be durable and everlasting.

It is rapidly becoming the centre of the audio-visual approach to education. It is an important aid to teachers, supervisors and educational planners. It is utilized for informal and formal education and for distance and correspondence education.

Educational T.V. was first telecast by AIR in 1960. The regular T.V. service was inagurated in Delhi on 15th August, 1965. The famous satellite Instructional Television Experiment (SITE) was implemented during the year, 1975-76. The T.V. programmes produced by Doordarshan and Space Application Centre were telecast for primary school children in the day time and for the community during evening hours. Educational Television has been made available in most of the important cities of the country with the help of the satellites. Besides education other subjects like health, family planning, agriculture and technology were provided through educational television programme in six states—Andhra Pradesh, Bihar, Karnataka, M.P., Orissa and Rajasthan.

The Educational Television Programmes were telecast through Indian Nations Satellite (INSAT-1A) during 1982, and then (INSAT-1B) from 1983. More than 200 transmission centres have been set-up throughout the country. Each and every corner of the country is being linked with the television services. For spreding more television programmes National workshops are being organised by NCERT. More T.V. sets are being supplied to primary schools and non-formal centres for better education and awakening.

Video

The Video helps to increase the educational and entertainment values of Television. It can not only play pre-recorded cassettes, but also record any programme and replay it. Thus, the educational T.V. programme telecast can be recorded and later on shown to the pupils as per requirement. With the help of Video cassette recorders educational and other useful events can be recorded for the teaching purposes. The replay of those programmes in colour makes viewing very interesting and its impact on the viewers leaves a cosiderable impact.

Operation of Video cassette recorder is very easy and simple.

It is quite portable and can be moved from on place to another easily.

— Knowledge acquired by video is permanent.

— It is helpful to the students in providing them the knowledge of social and political conditions of different countries.

— It is helpful in developing thinking and reasoning power of the students.

— It is equally helpful in educating and entertaining both backward and gifted children.

— Teacher hold control over video presentation.

— It can be used anytime and anywhere.

— With the help of video, teacher can remove the doubts of the students side by side, which is not possible in T.V. lesson.

— We can put the picture on the screen as long as we want.

— Picture can be repeated as many times as one wants.

— These days the use of video is on the increase in the education and recreational field due to the expensive use of T.V.

— Video films are easily available on different teaching subjects.

Computer

The advent of the computer and the educational technology related to it, clearly points to the way to major changes in education that will free the individual both teacher and student, to interact in more human ways than ever before.

The computer is one of the most wonderful inventions that man has made. At present the computer is used in almost all the fields where very complicated functions are to be performed. The computers are guiding the sophisticated rockets and satellites to the moon and to the distant planets. The computers are also guiding the submarines jet engines etc., for safe voyage. Computers are also used in large business concerns offices, banks etc. Now the computers have also entered schools and colleges.

"A computer is an electronic device which stores information on discs or magnetic tape, analyses it and produces information as required from the data on the tape etc". (A.S. Hornby). Computer is essentially a device for storing large amounts of information and handling this information in specified ways in extremely short period of time.

"Now education is, at least partly, about information. Sometimes the learning of this information is regarded as an end in itself, at other times it is regarded as the means to more general educational objectives. But even to merely learn information, more must be provided by an educational system than the mere presentation of information. Information must be processed to and from the student in order to provide the right information to fulfil particular needs. The amount of information processed in any educational system, taking into account the needs of all students at all times in all subjects, is enormous; and at its best, the processing of this information must be fast and accurate".

We see that the computer can handle and process enormous amount of information accurately and at tremendous speeds. If we put the computer at the disposal of teacher and pupil we open up the possibility of a revolution in education.

Many teachers oppose the instruction by computer on the assumption that it will them unemployed. But actually computer cannot replace a teacher, but it will simply release him from some of the chores of infomation processing. Acutally computer is only an aid to the teacher. That is why now we talk of "Computer Assisted Instruction". The overal control of computer assisted instruction is in the hands of the teacher. It should also be noticed that the computer is not being used to treat all pupils in an identical way.

Q. 7. Discuss design of the Over Head Projector (OHP), its advantages and, Method of using.

Ans. THE OVER HEAD PROJECTOR

The name comes from the fact that the projected image is behind and over the head of the speaker. In overhead projection, a transparent visual is placed on a horizontal stage on top of light source. The light passes through this transparency and then is reflected at an angle on to the screen at the back of the speaker. Using OHP is not a new concept. It dates back to World War II when the armed services employed this equiment for teaching recruits.

The Design of OHP

Overhead projectors are designed for direct or indirect projection. The projectors designed for direct projection use either Halogen lamps, linear or pea (650W) or in some cases 30 volt locomotive head lamp, worked with a transformer.

The overhead projectors designed on principle of indirect projection use the tubular projection lamps (750 or 1000 W) as in a film projector.

In all the overhead projectors, the lamp enclosure is blower cooled. In some overhead projectors, the blower is kept working till the enclosure cools to normal outside temperature by using thermostat (bimetallic) switches which switch off the blower. In such projectors only the lamp should be switched off and the power supply should be on to enable the blower working.

A fresnel lens is used to form a convering beam of light which illuminates the stage area uniformly and converges to the projection lens. The projection lens is a combination of two lenses with their principal axis at right angles. A surface silver or surface aluminsed mirror or very thin flat mirror is serves to rotate the path of light by 90. The lens head could be rotated to form the image at any height. In some projectors, the mirror rotated to do the same function. The screen usually of 1 cm thick joly board or plywood (.5cm) or hardbound (3mm) is painted with non-glossy white paint and fixed to the right side corner near ceiling at an angle of 30-45 degrees to the vertical. This tilting is necessary to prevent keystoning. The OHP should be kept ncessarily in a fixed place so the that rotated projection axis meets the screen normally and the teacher does not cast a shadow on the screen.

The general precaution to be observed for use of any projector should be observed when suing the OHP projector. The projector should not be subjected to mechanical vibrations. Provision for voltage fluctuation should be taken care of by using a voltage stabiliser or by having a suitable choke in series. Halogen lamps particularly will not withstand heavy surge in voltage. The lamp should not be touched by hand. OHP should not be kept on continuously for long periods. To use it as one would use a chalkboard is a very costly procedure. The fresnel lens is protected by a glass plate on top. It is necessary to remove dust or dirt on the protecting glass and also from the outside lens surface by flat camel hair brush. Surface silvered or aluminised reflector should not be cleaned.

Advantages of OHP

1. Large Image. A very large projected image in a minimum of projection distance is obtainable.

2. Face the Audience. The teacher can always face the class, maintaining eye contact with the pupils. There is no "back and forth" action when using the OHP as in the case of chalkboard.

3. Flexibility and Versatility. The ""user operated" visualisation may be integrated into the total presentation with complete flexibility.

The teacher maintains complete class control and interest in a lesson by turning a switch on or off.

4. Identity with the User. Whether in a teaching or a presentation situation, the aduience sees the visualisation from the same point of view as the communicator. The feeling of oneness with the communicator is created.

5. Lighted Room. This equipment can be used in a well-lighted room which enables the teacher to develop a sort of 'circuit of understanding' by watching the expression of others.

6. Light Weight. The comparative lighter weight to the equipment makes it portable.

7. Home-made Materials. Effective visuals can be made in a minimum of time and at low cost. Once a transparency is made, it is permanent. It need not be erased as in a chalkboard.

Method of Using OHP

A tri-acetate film of minimum thickness is available as continuous roll. This roll could be constantly rolled over the illuminated stage. Matter clearly wirtten or continuously created over the surface could be presented on the screen. This method of using the OHP requires the projector to be continuously working during the entire period. This procedures is costly as the lamp has a limited life and the projector may also get very hot in spite of the cooling arrangement. Matter can be permanently written on acetate sheets using quill or ruling pen or rapidomat pen with special Indian ink or acrylic markers with special inks. Temporary, erasable impressions may be created with Chinagraph pencils, also called glass marking pencils (wax pencils), and water colour markers with special inks. These impressions can be removed by wiping with a dry cloth or cotton waste. Acetate sheets may be cleaned with sponge dipped in detergent or soap solution.

Tri-acetate sheets are available in large rolls of 75 cms width which could be cut into sheets of dimensions 20×25 to 25×25 cms. They can be suitably mounted on suitable cardboard mounts. Poster boards make attractive mounts.

Specific Uses of OHP

The real advantage of OHP lies in the different uses to which it can be put. Instead of presenting static pictures on the screen, the teacher can develop the diagrams. The teacher, by moving an opaque or coloured pointer on the stage, can very easily focus the attention of the class on the screen, on the required aspect. The teacher can cover the completed visual on the stage and by sliding an opaque cardboard can progressively disclose one item at a time in stages.

One of the most effective ways to teach with overhead projector is using overlays. This is an effective technique for persentation of material in a step-by-step fashion. The information that is to be presented can be broken down into component parts. A transparency is made of each component and then the component transparencies are taped together. The basic transparency is mounted on a frame and three overlays can be hinged to the side of the frame. The series of components are then flipped into place on the stage of the projector as the information is develped in the class. For example, a geography teacher may wish to show a country depicting its rivers, mineral deposits and major cities. The first overlay transparency would have lines representing rivers; the second would depicit only the mineral deposits, and the third overlay would show only the major cities.

Sectional Models. To explain the working of certain machines lift-pump may be made with tinted acrylic sheets cemented by chloroform on a clear acrylic sheet, along with pieces which can be moved in slots or rotated about rivets. This will be highly effective.

Small live aquatic animals may be kept in a flat glass dish and get projected. Leaf profiles, flower petals and details can be projected. Silhouttes of small flat objects may also be projected using sectional models. Even dynamic demonstrations like rotation of a magnetised needle when a magnet is brought near could be shown.

Q. 8. Write short note on Motion Picture Projector.

Ans. MOTION PICTURE PROJECTOR

Motion picture as an aid to teaching is inferior to direct experience. But in some cases motion picture will be able to provide the expected learning outcome better than even direct experience.

The bright image on the screen with the associated sound is more realistic if it is in colour.

Tepe-recorders and the mixed re-recording of the final tape done on a thired recorder. All recordings should preferably be made during night time, when disturbing sounds will be minimal. When sound a material for use with a particular slide has been recorded, a single short peal from a bell will indicate to the operator of the slide projector that the side being shown should be changed and the next one brought on. Many projectors with automatic slide changing mechanisms are now available and a high frequency sound pulse from the tape acts as a cue for automatic slide change in some of these.

Present day slide projectors are more compact and efficient than those of the past and are fitted with low voltage halogen lamps and utilise a large percentage of light output. The slides produced using a camera with near focussing attachment, are made using 35m.m. perforated film with a picture size of 36mm × 24mm. Slides can be made with black and white film and then coloured or could be made using the costlier colour film. The slides are mounted on cardboard or plastic mounts. For line drawings, black and white film is more suitable than coloured film. From the resulting negative, a positive film print is taken and this positive could be used to get further prints which would display the diagrams clearly as bright lines on dark backgrounds. Such lines of diagrams can also be toned to suitable colours using required dyes (dye toning).

The mounted slides are kept in the required sequence in a linear or circular magazine for use. With non-automatic slide projectors, the operator should change the slide on hearing the cue-bell from the recording in the cassette tape recorder. The same set of slides could be used for instruction in different languages with suitable sound tracks recorded in different languages in spearate cassettes. The recorded sound could be easily changed by recording if needed. The slide-tape sequence, suitably produced can be almost as effective and dynamic as a motion picture and it appeals to the eye and ear of pupils.

Q. 9. Write short note on Video-Tape, methods and guidelines for its preparation.

Ans. **VIDEO TAPE**

Storage of instruction for repetitive use is easily accomplished now with the use of video tapes. They may be played back through monitors in a studio or class-room. Video tape can provide virtually instantaneous reproduction and in that sense, it is superior to films. Video cassettes are also available now-a-days. The user simply attaches the cassette player to his own television set, inserts a cassette and presses a button. The obvious advantage of the cassette is that it is portable and can be used and reused at will.

Suggested Lessons for Instructional Video

Video materials can be used from mass lectures to individualised learning; from primary classes to open university systems. Any subject can be presented in a video format. Many processes and procedures, techniques and skills lend themselves to video presentation, such as the following :

— For reproducing rare field trips in Earth Sciences like tectonics, minerology, creation of geysers and natural springs, volcanoes, oil retireval, oceangraphy, paleontology, meteorology.

— For demonstrating basic priciples of Physics and Mechanics, like machines, energy, force, gravity, Newtonian laws and the applications of these principles to human development.

— For demonstrating a process or procedure using laboratory facilities in Physical Science.

— Showing aspects of plant life in Biology, photosynthesis, relation between plant life and animal and human development, ecological aspects.

— Demonstrating vocal inflections, lip movements and body gestures in learning foreign languages.

— In Physcial Education, the effects of different exercises on the basic anatomy of body, health education, athletic skills, gymnastic demonstratins, games techniques.

Modes of Using Videos

There are many ways that learners can use the videos. The following are some ways for using a 30-minute video programme in learning situations:

— The video can be played continuously to a large group in a lecture room as a prelude to discussion and a question-answer session.

— The 30-minute video can be played as a series of half-a-dozen shorter 'clips' during the 1-hour-long discussion.

— The video can be used in tutorial groups, either played continuously or as a series of clips.

— The video can be given to individual learners supported by handout or workbook material.

— The video can be part of an open learning package, where learner individually or collectively in small groups use it at their own pace.

Guidelines for Preparing a Video

The following list of guidelines is not a rigid prescriptive 'recipe' but contains only suggestions.

1. Objective. For the grade level, subject area and nature of the lesson, keep goals to a minimum. Fomulate the specific behavioural objectives in terms of learning outcomes.

2. Content Outline. Determine the content of the lesson by gathering materials and extracting the most important elements.

3. Audience. Identify who will use the lesson. Specify age and subject knowledge.

4. Treatment. Determine the style or combination of styles, *viz.*, lecture, demonstration, interview, dramatic form, field observations. Decide on the specific visual and aural materials like title, charts, models, sound and music. Video is essentially a visual medium. Narrative should play a supportive role rather than a central role. When planning the sequences to be filmed, think visual at all times. The TV camera makes use of four types of lens, normal, wide angle, telephoto and zoom. A wide angle lens helps to create illusion of objects being further apart. Telephoto lens narrows the angle and compresses distance and creates illusion of objects being closer than they are. The zoom lens changes the focal length from the telephoto to the wide angle usually in the ratio of 4:1.

5. Review. To focus attention, a brief review of materials covered may be given, summarising main points at the end, or one review in the middle.

6. Continuity and Pacing. While preparing the script, let the sequences be logical. Determine how much time each point should take. Provide variety and pace for difficult points. Avoid emphasis on subpoints at the expense of major ones.

7. Instructional Guides. To clarify materials and methods and reinforce concepts. Instructional guides may be designed to accompany the video cassette.

8. Evaluation. Evaluation will give information concerning the value of the tape in instructional process. A few questiones can be arranged with reference to achievement of goals, the relevanoy and accuracy of the subject matter, effectiveness of the graphics used, etc.

9. Validation. On the basis of the evaluation, the cassette material may suitably be revised, reused, re-evaluated and validated for wider use.

The film projectos in schools have became obsolete as result of the advent of camcorders, video-players and TV sets. The camcorder consists of a camera and a recorder and is very easy to handle. Video tapes are also cheap and can be used over and over again. Hence, it costs very little to practise taking shots with the camcorder. The art of making good videos is learned by trial and error. If zoom facilities are to be used, it is better to use a simple tripod to avoid camera shake. When capturing sounds, it is desirable to use a suitable separate micorphone instead of the built-in microphone in the camcorder.

Three basic types of shots form the bulk of most sequences in cine and video programmes. The long shot provides a general view of the subject taken from a distance so that the subjects is seen in the context of the background. The medium shot provides a closer view of the subject and eliminates most of the background details. The close-up provides a closer view of the subject or a specific part thereof. When the readings of a small meter are to be shown clearly, a close-up shot is used.

Educational Value of TV

1. Communication by TV is effective because it can bring very good demonstrations and audio-visual materials to the class-room.
2. TV can bring the world to reality of the home and to the class-room.
3. TV permits everyone to look through a microscope at the same time.
4. TV can save the time and effort of the student and teacher.
5. TV facilitates a school or college to share its best teachers rather than rationing them.
6. The concrete nature of TV makes some programmes understandable, appealing to a wide variety of age and educational levels of people.
7. TV can be both instructive and enjoyable.

Limitations of TV

1. TV is one-way communication. It does not stop to answer question. It does not permit class discussion.
2. There is no personal contant with the teacher. The programmes do not adjust well to individual differences.
3. TV encourages a passive form of learning rather than an active seeking. It cannot provide for individual and group activities. It does not provide for laboratory experience.
4. TV screen is small in size as compared to projected pictures.
5. The equipments necessary for TV is costly and complicated. A properly designed studio with controllable lighting facilities and with acoustic proof walls is necessary. It should be maintained by competent staff all the time.

Q. 10. What are Audio-Visual Aids of Hardware-Software? Discuss their need and importance in education.

Ans. Today's education system is not the same as it was in the past and witness lot of changes in it. Even the current education system is fast changing and we expect this system to be entirely different in the years to come as a result of the impact of continuous research in the field of education. The object of teaching is to make teaching learning more effective, permanent and long lasting by focussing the attention of the students at the communication. For realising these objectives, it is essential for the teacher to make use of different types of teaching aids and materials such as models, films, tapes, charts, diagrams, maps, television, radio, projectors, epidiascope, filmstrips concrete objects and similar other resources. All these materials, instruments and resources are termed as teaching learning aids as they supplement class-room teaching and come to the help of a teacher in making his communication clearer, class-room inter-action healthier and teaching popular and effective.

These aids are also known as audio-visual aids as they influence the auditory and visual senses of the learners and permanently imprint teaching upon the minds of the students. These aids provide real experiences to the learners. It is well understood that a student can better understand, appreciate and preceive by touching, seeing, smelling and directly tasting an object. For example a child can better understand the difference among an orange, an apple and a banana by seeing, touching, smelling and tasting these fruits, thus by applying his senses rather than by simply being told about them. These aids are sort of means which provide real and valuable learning experience to the students. A learner with the help of these aids successfully makes better utilisation of his senses in making learning more permanent, interesting, effective, meaningful and clearly understandable. According to an old saying, 'A thousand hearings are not as good as one seeing.' So strong is the influence of our senses on understanding that according to Joseph J.Weber, "We get 40% experiences from vision, 25% from auditory. 17% from touching, 3% from smelling and rest 15% from other physical experiences. According to Dr. Kenneth B. Hass and Dr. Harry Q Packer, "It is natural that in education, we should appeal to the mind chiefly through the visual and auditory sense organs since it is possible that 85% of our learning begins at those terminal points. "Audio visual aids are being increasingly used at all the stages of education—primary, middle, secondary and higher secondary. In the process of learning, greater is the involvement of senses more permanent and effective is the learning as senses are taken to be the gateway of knowledge. Audio visual aids are better means for drawing the attention of the students towards their studies. By creating attention and arousing curiosity of the students these aids help and prepare the students for teaching learning.

Following points highlight the need of audio-visual aids in teaching-learning process:

1. To Develop Educational Interest. These aids motivate the children to learn efectively and thus to acquire permanent knowledge. In this way audio visual aids develop educational interest among the students to attain knowledge about some subject.

2. To Supplement Direct Experiences. These aids help in getting direct experiences from real things. Children always get pleasure in getting direct experiences by touching, tasting or seeing a particular object. By using these aids the students give practical shape to their ideas. When a teacher teaches with the help of a model or a picture about a particular animal and when the child sees the same animal in reality in the zoo, his acquired knowledge about that animal is reinforced and becomes permanent. The direct experiences of the students can be supplemented by showing models and charts in the class. It will also reinforce the knowledge of the students.

3. Attraction Towards New Things. Audio-visual aids develop attraction and interest in the process of teaching learning. Children have great attraction towards new things. If the teacher teaches with the help of audio-visual aids, he arouses the interest and attraction of students towards learning new things.

4. To Help in Meaningful Experiences. These aids provide meaningful experiences with the use of more and more senses, which is the foundation of educational process. The senses are gateway to knowledge. When knowledge is imparted to the students with the help of various senses and more the senses are involved, the stronger is the foundation of knowledge.

5. Educational for Life. It is said 'life is for education and education is for life.' Education makes the life happier and meaningful. An educated man is generally said to be more rational compared to an uneducated man. Thus, these aids become the part and parcel of the life of children and help them in solving various problems related to life.

6. Direct Experiences. The knowledge which the students get through direct experiences is everlasting because of involvement of the sense organs like eyes, ears and nose etc. Similarly when a student sees for himself the process of manufacture of various commodities like vanaspati ghee, soap, oil etc., in factories, it gives him direct experiences and his knowledge about manufacturing process of these commodities which he has acquired from books and teachers, is reinforced and becomes permanent.

7. To Develop Reasoning and Logical Power. Use of audio-visual aids develops the imaginative reasoning and logical power of the students. The children become capable of differentiating between effective and ineffective teaching.

8. To Make the Students Active. Use of audio-visual aids makes children more active in learning and motivates them to actively participate in teaching learning process. Such activities as turning of globe, to see seven colours in Newton's disc, to make a picture, to prepare gas in the laboratory, to draw and fill the maps with colours etc., provide ample opportunities to the children to learn by doing.

9. For Clarity in Educational Process. It is here that audio-visual aids play their role to make educational process simpler, clearer and more understandable for students. Some times due to inherent shortcomings of lecture method students feel bore and lose interest in studies. It is here that these aids come to the help of teachers in reviving the interest of students in teaching learning process.

10. Useful for Slow and Backward Learners. The use of audio-visual aids is specially helpful for backward and slow learners in teaching learning process. Due to low level of intellect and understanding some times they fail to understand from books and class-room teaching. But when the same thing is taught by teacher with the help of pictures, charts, models and other aids, it facilitates their learning and helps the students to understand abstract things more clearly.

Thus, it can be concluded that audio-visual aids play dominant role in the process of education. In the present modern scientific age, audio-visual aids are those effective tools in the hands of the teachers which enable him to perform his duty more effectively and efficienty. These aids help him in imparting education properly. Such aids are also very useful in providing direct experiences and in imparting education related to life and profession. These aids motivate the interest, aptitude and capabilities of the learners and by actuating the senses help students to take active part in teaching learning process.

Main Principles in using Audio-Visual aids :

Use of audio-visual aids in teaching is increasing day by day. Its use has been recommended in all subjects like science, arts, commerce and other humanities. These aids are of immense help in making lessons and teaching learning simple, clear, interesting and comprehensive. The utility of these aids is relatively greater for younger children and in lower classes. While using these aids we should bear in mind that following principles must be emphasised as suggested by eminent educationist Maurice P. Moffat.

1. Principle of Effectiveness. In the selection of audio-visual aids the principle of effectiveness is very important. It implies that the aids should be chosen carefully so that they prove meaningful, important and effective for understanding the lesson. Selection and effective use of these aids depend upon ability, foresightedness and capability of the teacher.

2. Principle of Means. Principle of means implies that these aids should only be taken as means to achieve certain ends. They are neither the ends in themselves nor can they replace the teacher and the books. They serve only as helping aids in the process of teaching learning, use of which makes the lesson and the teaching interesting, easy, clear, uderstandable and durable, which is the main aim and objective of using aids.

3. Principle of Selection. The principle of selection implies the need for carefully selecting these aids for use in teaching. The chief aim of their selection should be to achieve the desired and pre-determined objectives of teaching learning. While selecting these aids the teacher should ensure that they are in accordance with the age, mental level of students, interests and objectives of the lesson.

4. Principle of Stimulation. These aids provide direction, motivation and stimulation to the learning process. Audio-visual aids actuate the learners and make them participate in the process of learning by influencing their sense organs and thus help them in remembering the learning for a longer time.

5. Principle of Purposiveness. The teacher always has certain definite purpose in mind while making use of these aids. In other words aids should not be used without purpose. The purpose of using aids should be explained by the teachers to the students beforehand. The objectives of lesson should be pre-determined for which these aids are to be used. It will create interest among students and they will actively participate in teaching learning activity. Thus, it will help in making learning process more useful for learners.

Concludingly we can say, while using these audio-visual aids, the efficient teacher should keep in mind and practice above mentioned principles, if he wants to succeed in making his teaching and lesson forceful, meaningful and really effective. These aids act as motivators in the exchange of ideas and view points, which finally make teaching process more interesting and dynamic.

Some Precautions in the Use of Audio Visual Aids

These aids are use only for fulfilling certain aims, objectives and purposes. Efficient and right use of these aids calls for a teacher to be efficient, skilled and trained accordingly. Even an efficient and trained teacher should keep in mind the following precautions in using these aids in teaching learning.

1. These aids should be proposive and educative and should not be allowed to become means of amusement, joke and fun for students.

2. They should be according to grade, age, and mental level of the pupils. Before using these aids it is essential that a teacher should prepare himself mentally to do so and he should have the necessary capacity and ability of using them.

3. The utility of these aids should be according to the needs and objectives of lessons. Some times in some lessons they do not prove useful. Every type of topic being taught in the class does not need to be illustrated by every type of audio-visual aid.

4. Due Emphasis should be placed on the educational value of these aids. They should be true, authentic, accurate and real substitute for the first hand experience.

5. They should be capable of providing more and more learning experiences so as to make teaching learning effective. Also, an aid to be effective must be capable of representing whole idea in a concise but comprehensive manner.

6. These aids should be used in proper class-room environment ensuring lighting, space and other facilities.

7. To make these aids more meaningful, useful and effective in understanding the lesson the teacher should make supplementary comments at the time of using the aids. Mere display of an aid is not sufficient.

8. Before using the aids, the teacher should explain their utility and relevance for the lesson in order to arouse interest, zeal and curiosity of students about these aids and their use in making the lesson effective and clearly understandable. The teacher should be clear in his mind about the exact point in the lesson which the aid is expected to illuminate and the way it could do it. The teacher should see that audio visual aids are not too numerous and over used.

Q. 11. Discuss the use of Computer, its Advantages and drawbacks.

Ans. COMPUTER

Progress in the field of science and technology has worked wonders in the different walks of life. The latest advancement is of computers and their successive use for instructional purposes. In the developed countries like U.S.S.R., U.S.A., Canada etc. Computer facility has reached every educational institution. But in our country, its need and importance has been recognised increasingly and efforts are afoot to have it and make use of it in different facets of life. Only in limited institutions, computers are being used for the instructional purposes. Computer can work wonders almost in every field of human activity. Countless number of calculations within a second are possible with the help of a computer.

What is a Computer

A Computer is a power-driven machine equipped with key boards, electronic circuit, storage compartments and recording devices for the high speed performance of mathematical operations. It his also a capacity for storing of memorising a large amount of information and producing any of them when called for. We may say that the computer is a box loaded with information. It has its own symbolical language. In order to work on a computer or to derive benefit, we shall have to familiarise ourselves with the language of the computer. So we shall have to feed the computer first. Then it interacts and manipulates the information, translates the answer and types it on a tele-type-writer.

Basic Parts of a Coumputer

There are five important parts of a computer which are briefly explained below:

1. The input equipment of the computer is in the form of key board and cassette recorder. It receives the outside information so that it may work accordingly.
2. The output equipment translates information back into understandable form.
3. The memory part contains all information which has been fed into the computer. It helps in storing information and retaining it. Further it can be used whenever needed.
4. The processing unit is the arithmatic and logic mind of the computer which is responsible for all types of date manipulation and computation work.
5. The control sub-system controls the execution of the programme and co-ordinate all the activities of the sub-system of the computer.

The computer is a hardware machine. The software used in it is in the form of written programme which is prepared by the computer programme writer. The computer works as the programme writer directs it. The computer in itself is not an independent thinking machine.

Computers have their own languages. They are known by different technical names Basic, Logo. Pilot, Cobol etc. We should understand the languages of the computers if we want to communicate with them. Most of the computers make use of binary system, where two digits symbol O and 1 are used for expressing any number.

For Example,

Step I. Number	**Computer Language**
0	0000
1	0001
2	0010
3	0011
4	0100
5	0101
6	0110
7	0111
8	1000

Step II. Then the operations are given code numbers as given below :

Operations	**Code Number**
Add	1
Subract	2
Multiply	3
Divide	4
Read a card	5
Square	6
Draw a line	7
Transform	8

Step III. At this stage, the code numbers are transformed in computer language as suggested above in step I.

According to J. Bruchner, there are two systems for computerized instruction:

1. In computer assisted instruction, the student participates with the computer system on a direct basis and the instructional materials are stored in the computer system.

2. Computer managed instructions are used to help the teacher to administer and guide the instructional process but relies on separate

hardware and learning materials; the student is usually not on line with the computer system and the processing need not be in real time. Instructional materials are not stored in the computer system.

Advantages

We can use the computer as an effective and indispensable aid in the teaching-learning process. Here below are given a few advantages:

1. It helps the learners in the development of variety of skills. It can also be used for providing drill and practice to the learners.
2. It can serve the role of an inquiry officer. The students put questions and it gives response with the help of answers it has already stored.
3. The computer can play efectively the role of a tutor by maintaining perfect interaction and dialogue with the individual students.
4. They can be used to develop problem solving ability and creativity among the students.
5. The computers can be used to give training to the students through simulated and gaming techniques.
6. They can supplement laboratory and other practical work specially in science subjects.
7. They can be used in providing education to the handicapped children like deaf and dumb.

Limitations or Drawbacks

The computer assisted instructions suffer from some drawbacks which are given below:

1. The use of computers in the class-rooms is very expensive and uneconomical in terms of educational returns.
2. Handling the computer is rather technical. There is always the danger of damaging the costly machine by the students.
3. It is rather difficult to teach all subjects and all topics with the help of a computer. There is dearth of computer programmes for teaching purposes.

4. Being auto-instructional, it may lead to indiscipline, truancy, carelessness and wastage of time on the part of some students.
5. The repair work or its servicing causes a serious problem to the institutions.
6. Heavy school curriculum and shortage of trained personels pose a threat to the introduction of computer assisted instruction in the educational institution.

Q. 12. Describe the Role of Computer in Education.

Or

Undoubtedly this is the time of Computer Education. What kind of Computer would you suggest for a Class-room Teacher?

Or

Discuss the role of Computer in Education. What are the limitation of use Computers in India now-a-days?

Ans.ROLE OF COMPUTER IN EDUCATION

In 1965, Lorence Settlor and Daniel Davis developed most complicated teaching processes in which computer was used for presenting instructions in place of teacher. They divided the teaching process of the computer in two parts :

1. Pre-tutorial phase.
2. Tutorial phase.

In the first phase, computer assisted instruction is given to the pupils to achieve the specific objectives on the basis of his entering behaviour. In the second phase, instructing material is presented accordingly. The pupil studies it. Then, the achievement of the pupil is evaluated. After presenting the instruction, computer also controls it. It also provides reinforcement to the pupils.

In the modren age, the use of computers in the field of education, made in following areas :

(i) All the researchers do all analytical tasks with the help of computers in the research work.

(ii) Computers are also used in educational guidance and counselling.

(iii) Computers' help is sought for preparing the results of the examinations.

(iv) Remedial teaching of the pupils is also done by the computers.

Computer Programmes

While observing groups of students working with the computer, you would notice that students enthusiastically participate in the learning programme. The computer's novelty, the challenge involved in the programme, the wonderful display of tasks-all help in creating and sustaining their motivation. Learning with the computer is never full and monotonous. Some illustrations given below would reveal a few more qualities.

1. Codebreaker. It is a programme which keeps asking questions and the students supply the answers. In pedagogic terms this question-answer sequence provides an opportunity for useful interaction which is essential for successful learning.

2. Varietext. It is part of the text with blanks for the students to fill in. For each blank four alternative appear one after another and the student has to choose the most appropriate one. Whenever necessary, the student can get the computer to display the correct words. This instant feed-back is apart of the progarmme and no other technological instrument can be faster than the computer in providing such instant feedback.

2. Yellow River Kingdom. It is problem-solving activity. The computer displays a vast kingdom with a lot of resources. The Computer is capable of simulating such complicated situations for the purpose of teaching learning. It can be simulated dangerous situations such as burning forest or division of atom.

Pedagogic Qualities of the Computer

1. Motives the learners.
2. Interacts with the learners.
3. Stimulates situations which are difficult and dangerous.
4. Provides instant feedback.
5. Distance Education.

Such a powerful instrument has several uses in the field of distance education where technological media are a basic necessity. There is hardly any distance education institution in the world which does not make use of media such as radio and T.V. Regular, though in a small scale, radio broadcasts and TV telecasts are a part of distance education courses in India too.

Some of the major advantages of using computers in distance education are as follows :

(i) Computer brings flexibility and individuality to the study process.

(ii) Computer reduces the isolating of distance learners.

(iii) Computer stimulated students to experiment, design and create solutions to the problems.

(iv) Computer-based study materials are cost-effective when produced on a large scale.

The increasing availability of micro-computers in the developed countries offered major new opportunities for distance education. The computer has various applications for distance learning. It can be used as a teaching medium, a learning tool, a manager of learning or as an aid to educational administration.

Administrative Applications of Computers

1. Budgeting and monitoring of finances.
2. Keeping students records.
3. Maintaining statistics.
4. Mailing of rest score.
5. Monitoring materials production register and so on.
6. Student billing.
7. Preparation of payroll, bills and debts ledger.

Instructional Situations of Computer Application

1. Pretesting of students knowledge on enrolment.
2. Planning and printing individualized programmes.
3. Compilling tests and scores erc. A number of such data files can be stored in the computer.
4. Monitoring students progress.

Other contributions of computers are word processing to aid course development and data processing to aid administration. In addition, electronic mail is also used to communicate, change and exchange materials. The course teams can also use computers for conferences, establishing a communication channel among multiple writers and other professionals.

'ON-LINE' AND 'OFF-LINE' COMPUTERS

Computers can be used in distance learning in two modes—local mode and transmitted mode—local mode or 'off-line' computer stands on its own as an independent system helping the learner to work on his own. In transmitted mode, one computer is connected to another computer which is 'on-line' and then the operation depends upon communication between these devices. By inter-connecting the computers, a complex learning Network can be created which could link all distance learners with their teacher and with a central institution.

Q. 13. Discuss the new Technologies in Educational Technology taken in the field of NETWORK (Internet, e-mail etc.).

Ans. Information Technology broadly deals with the application of technology in the field of information. In this process, media, computer, operations related to hardware and internet play a vital role in education especially in class-room instruction. New technologies which are emerging need to be integrated in order to provide meaningful and complete information. An effort to this direction has led to constitute a NETWORK. It makes the flow of information very simple, easy, and effective on the part of transmitter (teacher) and receiver (student).

The basic structure involved in NETWORK is :

(i) Interlinkages. Defferent components involved in Information Technology are interconnected. The relevant information is passed on from one channel to another. The whole NETWORK is based on the nature and type of interlinkages (interconnectivity).

(ii) Communication. The second component in INTERNET is effective communication. Messages are passed on from one place to another. Information reaches from one point to another. Without any loss of information, complete message is commnunicated.

(iii) System. NETWORK operates through a system. There are sub-systems. Each sub-system performs its function. The integrated one whole of sub-systems leads to work as much expanded and multiple functions.

NETWORK is a vast cyberspace where one can gather, disseminate and exchange all types of information. An arrangement consisting of two or more computers is called NETWORK. It is a physical medium used to transport the data. A computer network is created when several computers are linked by data communication channels. Each computer in a network can have its own processing capabilities and can also share hardware, data files and programmes. Following are the types of Computer Network:

1. Local Area Network. A local area network is two or more computers directly linked with in a small well defined area such as a room, building or a group of closely placed buildings. A LAN may be made up of only microcomputers or any combination of microcomputers and large systems.

A Local Area Network usually consists of the following :

(i) Two or more computers.

(ii) Peripheral devices such as printers and hard-disk drives.

(iii) Software to control the operation of the computers.

(iv) Special cables.

(v) A plug in board to handle the data transmission.

2. MAN (Metropolitan Area Network). Man is basically a bigger version of a LAN, and normally used similar technology. It might cover a group of nearby corporate offices or a city and might be either private or public. A MAN just has one or two cables and does not contain switching elements. A MAN can support both data and voice and might even be related to the local cable television network.

3. WAN (Wide Area Network). A WAN is two or more computers that are geographically dispesed, linked by communication facilities such as telephone system or microwaves relays. This type of network is usually limited to use by large corporations and government agencies because of the high costs involved in building and manitaining them.

The main difference between a WAN and LAN is that, the LAN is under the complete control of the owner, whereas the WAN needs the involvement of another authority like telecom department.

— LANs are successful and capable of handling very high data transfer rates at low cost because of the small area covered.

— LANs have a lower error rate than WANs.

Types of WAN—

There are mainly two types of WAN :

Public Networks.

Private Natworks.

Public Networks. Public Netowrks are those Networks which are installed and run by the telecommunication authorities and are made available to any organisation or individual who go for their subscription.

Private Networks. The basic technique used in all forms of Private WAN is to use private circuits to link the locations to be served by the network. Between these fixed points the owners of the network have complete freedom to use the circuits in any way they want.

INTERNET

Internet is a World-wide Computer Network that contains a large collection of information which could be made avaliable to you on your computer. The person having internet connection can retrieve any information of individual interest.

Internet is the abbreviation of Inter-network System. The Internet is the name for a vast, Worldwide system consisting of people, information and computers. It is also described as a network of networks because these are more than one lakh readily accessible through the Internet. Internet is the largest and most complete learning tool for a group of people with varied educational backgrounds and interests. Teachers, students, businessmen and other educators can share ideas instantly across vast distances. For scientific and research community, internet is an essential and indispensable tool.

Through Internet Scientists can gain and enjoy instant access to the world's most advanced research facilities and discuss their research problems with others, working in the same field.

It also serves as an encyclopaedia since one can get the desired information in detail on any subject of his interest.

History of Internet

ARPANET (Advanced Research Projects Agency Network) laid the foundation of today's Internet almost three decades ago. It was establised to test the security of a network.

Advantages of Internet

Internet is playing a very important role in the National Development by giving the following major benefits to the citizens world-wide :

—Education
—Advertising
—Government
—Shopping
—Financial Services
—Careers and so on.

Using the Internet's Vast resources, one can communicate with people from all over the world and about any desired subject of choice.

APPLICATION OF INTERNET

Internet being a network of networks spread world-wide is capable of offering the following major services :

(a) E-Mail

(c) WWW (World Wide Web)

Electronic-mail

E-mail is an application in which any user as a network can send/receive letters on his computer terminal to/from any person in the world who has an electronic mail address. Internet provides a world-wide electonic mail facility.

The gerneral format of Internet e-mail address is :

< name of addressee > @ < identity of his dept. >

< Institution > < identity of Indian Network > < country code >.

Mail can be sent only to individuals but to groups, by using group identity. The Network takes care to see that the mail is delivered safely if it leaves the user's terminal.

WWW

World-wide web offers facilities to the users to share information with others. This is the fastest growing part of the internet. The web is a vast network of documents and it also gives access to every internet service. The Web server can publish text and graphics including sound and video.

Website

Website makes a user as a node of internet. This means that if a university decides to float its own website, then all information regarding admission, scholarships, rules and regulations, courses it offers, department, staff and their profiles, workshops, conferences, seminars to be conducted etc., can be kept at university's computer centre. This computer can be accessed by any member on Internet for any particular course: it will be automatically listed with all its details. This website is important to a university or a company to offer 24 hours services and on line help to international clients.

Developing a website on Internet is a costly affair as far as hardware and other costs are concerned.

Q. 14. Describe the History of Computer development and mention different types of computers.

Ans. HISTORY OF COMPUTER DEVELOPMENT

The need for counting and calculating was felt as early as The Stone Age. The primitives used pebbles to count their cattle and other food stuff. Later, with the production of surplus goods, goods started getting exchanged for rice and other similar commodities, resulting in the Barter System.

Still later, people used to count by putting tally marks on sand or stone. A need for counting became more urgent giving rise to the development of various counting systems and devices.

Abacus. The Chinese developed the Abacus, a manual calculator of sorts. in as early as 3000 BC. In about 1000BC, Greeks and Egyptians improved upon it. The final version, can still be seen being used in Hong Kong and other parts of China.

Leibnitz Machine. In 1964, Gottfried Wilheim Leibnitz improved Pascaline and called it Stepped recliner or Leibnitz machine, it could multiply and divide as well as find square roots.

Pascal's Calculating Machine. In 1642 AD, Blaise Pascal, a young French scientist, developed a mechanical calculating machine, known after his name and called Pascal's Calculating machine. This machine was capable of performing only addition and subtraction. It was also called Palestine.

Analytical Engine. In 1833 AD, Charled Babbage, invented a Difference Engine to generate logarithmic and stromatal tables of numbers upto 6 places. The technique he used was the computations of successive differences. Later he developed, the concept of Analytical Engine, a calculating machine, which still forms the base of all computers. He however, could not complete his work during his lifetime. For his fundamental research he is known as the father of computers.

His work was completed by Lady Augusta Add loveless, daughter of Lord Byron, the English poet. She developed the essential ideas of programming the analytical Engine. For her contribution she is known as the first Computer Programmer.

5. Hollerith's Machine. Herman Hallerith, an American statistician developed a punch-card machine in 1887 AD. This machine could store the results in the form of punched cards and read them later on. Hollerith formed a company called Tabulating and Calculating? Company of America. It combined with other companies to form what is now known as IBM (International Business Machines Corporation, USA). IBM is among the largest manufacturers of computers in the world.

6. Mark I. In collaboration with IBM Howard Aiken of Harvard University developed 'Automatic Sequence Controlled Calculator' or Mark I. This was the first commercial computer available in the market. IBM marketed it in 1944. It was the fastest electro-mechanical machine, capable of multiplying in 4 seconds and dividing in 10 seconds. It was a huge structure, 15 meters long, 2.5 meters high and weighing 31 tons, having around 750,000 parts. At the same time came into existence the use of electronics in computers. Computers like ENIAC, EDVAC, and UNIVAC were developed. These were all huge and very expensive machines mainly used for research and development work.

7. Three Generation Computers. The principle of On Switch and Off Switch, that is the two states represented by 1 and 0, was used here. First, electronic devices, vacuum tubes were used to provide On and Off conditions. This formed the 1st Generation of Computers (1940-52). Then transistors replaced vacuum tubes forming 2nd Generation (1952-64) reducing overall size of components required for the computers. Next were Integrated Circuits or ICs also called the Chips. These were made of a material called silicon. A small silicon chip had hundreds of transistors forming ON (1) or Off (0) conditions in a very small space. This was third generation computers (1965-71).

8. Around 1972 to Till Data. Several more transistors and other electrical components like capacitors were added on to this IC to make large scale integration (LSI). In fact, a chip had an entire CPU on it and was called a micro processor resulting in smaller size, faster speed and lower cost of operations. Our present day ICs belong to 4th Generation.

Research is going on for increasing the speed of operations, decreasing the size and adding more components on a chip to give human like intelligence to computers.

Kinds of Computers

1. IBM 650. In 1955, this was launched by IBM. It was one of those big computer requiring full room to store with cables running underground to connect the various components of the machine.

This machine actually madethe scientist sit back and think of crating new machines, which could work faster and would take less space.

2. Aple PC. In 1977, this computer was developed by two young men in their twenties, named Steve Worzniak and Steve Jobbs. It became vary popular for home and small business use. They formed, Apple Computers the company which manufactured more small computers than any other computer manufacturer of the time. Over the years the company has grown tremendously and has McIntosh brand of computers available throughout the world. Their computers are better than those manufactured by IBM.

3. Personal Computers (PCs). In 1981, the IBM launched its first Personal Computer called IBM-PC, since then, manufacturers other than IBM have also developed PCs which are of the same standard as that of the IBM. While IBM-PC remains the trademark of IBM, the other manufacturers market their small computers as PCs, which are also called IBM-PC compatible machines. PC has become a general term including all kinds of personal computers from IBM and other companies. PC has been improved over the years as per the following development stages:

(i) PC-I. A PC with a single floppy diskette drive. This PC had a 51/4" double sided diskette can could store upto 360 kilobytes of data. It was based on Intel 8088 IC chip. The computer operated at 4.77 Megahertz speed and had a memory of 640KB.

(ii) PC-II. A sort of extension of the PC-I computer mentioned above. Instead of single floppy drive, it had two of them. Rest of the features remained the same.

(iii) PC-XT. Developed in 1982, Personal Computer with extended Technology, had an additional fixed hard disk drive and a floppy disk drive. The microprocessor used was Intel 8088; however, the speed was increased to 8 megahertz. The usual capacity of hard disk was 20 Megabytes.

(iv) PC-AT. Developed in 1984, Personal Computer with Advanced Technology, also had a floppy drive and a hard disk drive in a minimum configuration. It could also have, within the system box, a maximum of 2 floppy drives and 2 had disk drives. The floppy diskette used were of Double sided High Density and could store data upto 1.2 Megabyt. The capacity of a hard disk also increased from 20 to 80 Megabytes and been beyond that. The speed was also increased to 13Mhz (Megahertz) because of use of new Intel 80286 chip. The memory also increased from 640KB to standard of 1 MB but could be increased to 16 MB.

(v) PC-AT/386, 586. Form 1985, through 1997, and beyond, advancements in computer technology has brought about Intel processor chips in market ranging from 80386 to 80585 in such a short span of time. Now a days 80586 chip which is also known as Pinetum is used in the computer system.

AT/386 introduced 1.44MB mini floppy of 3½", which revolutionized floppy system to such an extent that the new computers now do not have 5¼" floppy drives.

Hard disk capacity also went on increasing from 80MB to 1.2GB, in between experimenting with 256MB, 512MB and 800MB etc. Even 1.2 GB is now replaced with 2.1 GB and even 4.3 GB are available presently.

The memory chip which was IBM in case of XT, increased to 4MB, 8MB, 16MB, 32MB and even higher.

Speed of processing also kept on increasing. It was 4.77 Mhz in case of XT and then went on to 50Mhz and then on to 133Mhz and now 200MHz is the standard. PCz with speeds of 400MHz are also available.

(vi) Pentium PC. The optimum machine these days, it has a hard disk of 2.1 GB. The memory is of 32MB. It has one floppy drive of 3½", 1.44MB capacity. The clock speed is 200MHz and is based on latest Intel chip called Pentium.

(vii) Pentium MMX. The new version of Pentium chip which supports the multimedia operations like audio speakers, video card capabilities and has all these features built-in on to the single chip of the system is called Motherboard.

(vii) Pentium II-Processor. A new, more powerful processor has been developed by Intel Corporation. In its competition, Cyirx Corporation, US has produced equivalent micro-processors. K-6 and K-7.

Another American Company—Motrolla has developed another series of micro-processors-68000 series, which are mainly used in the Apple-Macintosh computers.

(ix) Power PC. There is also consortium of Apple. IBM and Motrolla which manufactures Power PC. Power P/C is supposed to take advantage of all the features of the IBM-PC compatible machines (PCs) and the MacIntosh (ac) machines. Programmes written both or the PC and the Macwill run on the Power PC machines.

Q. 15. Discuss the meaning, concept, characteristics phases, procedures, merits and demerits of Micro-Teaching. Discuss the steps or procedures of Indian Model of Micro-Teaching.

Ans. MICRO-TEACHING

Micro-Teaching is one of the most recent innovations in teacher education programmes which aims to modify teacher's behaviour according to the specified objectives. Educationists in our country have recently recognised the importance of Micro-Teaching in preparing efficient class-room teachers. A beginning has been made at some centres in the country, in the direction of conducting researches on Micro-Teaching to replace traditional methods of class-room teaching in teachers' training institutions. It is assumed that if a person is trained to acquire the sub-skills of teaching one by one, and then if all these sub-skills are integrated together he becomes an efficient teacher. The systematic training that a would-be-teacher or a practising teacher, receives for each sub-skill of teaching is called MICRO-TEACHING.

Micro-Teaching was developed by Professor Dwight Allen and Robert Bush in the teacher preparation programme at Stanford University between 1960-1967. It can be used for pre-service and in-service teacher training programmes.

It is a laboratory technique of teacher training in which the complexities of normal class-room teaching are simplified. It is based on Skinner's operant conditioning. It is not a teaching technique. It is a training technique. It is described as a 'Scaled down teaching encounter in class size and class time (Allen and Ryan 1969). The student-teacher teaches a class of 5 to 10 pupils for 5 to 10 minutes. It is also scaled down with respect to teaching complexity.

Teaching is considered to be made up of skills and each teaching skill is a set of related teaching behaviour which tends to facilitate pupils' learning. Such skills can be defined, practised, controlled, observed and evaluated. A particular lesson may involve any number of skills.

A teacher should be trained in all these skills for developing the ability to teaching. These skills are developed by Micro-Teaching.

According to **Allen and Eve (1968),** "Micro-Teaching is a system of controlled practice that makes it possible to concentrate on specific teaching behaviour and to practise teaching under controlled conditions."

According to **N.K. Jangira and Ajit Singh,** "Micro-Teaching is a training setting for the student teacher where complexities of the normal class-room teaching are reduced by:

— Practising one component of skill at a time.

— Limiting the content to a single concept.

— Reducing the size to 5 to 10 pupils, and

— Reducing the duration of the lesson to 5 to 10 minutes.

According to **L.C. Singh (1977).** "Micro-Teaching is a 'scaled down teaching encounter' in which a teacher teaches a small unit to a group of 5 pupils for a small period of 5 to 20 minutes. Such a situation offers a helpful setting for an experienced or inexperienced teacher to acquire new teaching skills and to refine old ones".

MICRO-TEACHING IN INDIA

Micro-Teaching was introduced in India in 1967, with the humble attempt made by D.D. Tiwari of Government Central Padagogical Institute, Allahabad.

In 1970, G.B. Shaw experimented with Micro-Teaching at M.S. University, Baroda. Then the Technical Teachers Training Institute, Madras introduced Micro-Teaching to train the technical teachers. In 1947, Dr. N.L. Dosajh used Micro-Teaching as a teaching device in Teachers Training Institute, Chandigarh. He also wrote a book namely : Modification of Teacher Behaviour through Micro-Teaching'. NCERT, SCERT, in the different states have been propagation this concept.

A FEW DEFINITIONS OF MICRO-TEACHING

D. W. Allen (1966), "Micro-Teaching is a scaled down teaching encounter in class size and time."

Buch (1968), "Micro-Teaching is a teacher education technique which allows teachers to apply clearly defined teaching skills to carefully prepared lessons in a planned series of five to ten minutes encounters with a small group of real students, often with an opportunity to observe the result on video tape."

Allen and Eve (1968), "Micro-Teaching is defined as a system of controlled practice that makes it possible to concentrate on specific teaching behaviour and to practise teaching under controlled conditions."

David B. Young defined Micro-Teaching as "a device which provides the novice and experienced teacher alike, new opportunities to improve teaching."

Clift and Others (1976), "Micro-Teaching is a teacher training procedure which reduces the teaching situation ot simpler and more controlled encounter achieved by limiting the practice teaching to a specific skill and reducing teaching time and class size."

MC Alleese and Unwin (1970), "The term Micro-Teaching is most often applied to the use of Closed Circuit Television (CCTV) to give immediate feedback of a trainee teacher's performance in a simplified environment."

Passi, B.K. (1976) says, "It is a training technique which requires pupil-teachers to teach a single concept using specified teaching skills to a small number of pupils in a short duration of time."

According to the **Encyclopaedia of Education (Ed. DeigHton),** "Micro-Teaching is a real, constructed, scaled down teaching encounter which is used for teacher training, curriculum development and research."

Nature of Micro-Teaching

On the basis of these definitions, the nature of Micro-Teaching can be concluled as follows :—

— Micro-Teaching is an innovation in the field of teacher education.

— It is a techer training technique.

— It is micro in the sense that it scales down the complexities of real teaching.

— In Micro-Teaching only one skill at a time practised.

— The size of the class is reduced and the number of the students is just 5 to 10.

— Duration of each micro lesson is 5 to 10 minutes.

— It is a highly individualised training device.

— In Micro-Teaching 'feedback' is provided immediately after the complextion of the lesson.

— The use of video tape and CC TV make the observations very objective.

Characteristics of Micro-Teaching

A few characteristics of Micro-Teaching are as under :

1. It is a teacher training technique and not a method of class-room instruction.
2. It is micro in the sense that if scales down the complexities of real teaching.
   (a) Out of contents, a single concept is taken up at a time.
   (b) Only one skill at a time is practised.
   (c) Size of the class is reduced and thus the number of students is just 5 to 7.
   (d) Duration of each micro lesson is 5 to 7 minutes.
3. Feedback is provided immediately after the completion of the lesson.
4. The use of Video Tape and Closed Circuit Television makes the observation very objective.
5. It is highly individualized training device.
6. There is a high degree of control in practising a skill when this technique is used.
7. Micro-Teaching is an analytic approach to training.

Micro-Teaching involves actually teaching a real lesson to real pupils with none of the role-playing of earlier modelled teaching situations.

— Micro-Teaching lessons are constructed for the benefit of the teacher and student's learning is incidental.

— Micro-Teaching provides a significant way to bring specific educational problems into manageable focus.

Components of Micro-Teaching

The components of Micro-Teaching are :

(i) a teacher,

(ii) the pupils (usually 4 or 5),

(iii) a brief lesson,

(iv) the objectives of the specific Micro-Teaching occasion,

(v) feedback by the supervisor, or by using audio tape recordings, video tape recordings and closed circuit television.

Assumptions of Micro-Teaching

The assumptions on which Micro-Teaching is based are as under :

1. Teaching behaviour of a teacher can be observed in class-room situations.
2. Drawbacks in the teaching competency can be traced out and then they can be improved upon.
3. Complexities of normal class-room situation can be reduced. The size of the class, the duration of teaching, teaching contents etc., can be reduced for giving training to the beginner teachers.
4. Training of specific skills can be given very well by taking up one skill at a time.
5. Practice of teaching can be controlled by providing regular feedback.
6. Teacher training programme can be highly individualised.
7. In-service teachers can also be better trained through Micro-Teaching technique.
8. Observation of teaching can be done objectively by using video-tape and Closed Circuit Television.
9. Feedback to the teacher trainee can be possible immediately. The earlier the feedback to the teacher trainee, the better is his learning the different skills of teaching.

PROCEDURE ADOPTED IN MICRO-TEACHING

The following steps are used for conducting a micro lesson successfully :

1. There is general discussion about Micro-Teaching. Theory of Micro-Teaching with all details is discussed. The teacher under training reads related literature and through discussions, clarifications are sought.
2. Different skills involved in teaching are explained to the pupil-teachers.
3. Out of the various skills, one skill for mastery purpose is selected. Full details of that skill are given to the pupil-teachers.
4. An expert the subject gives a demonstration lesson on that particular skill.
5. The demonstration lesson is followed by discussions in which the learner teachers discuss things and seek all type of clarifications.
6. The pupil-teacher writes the micro lesson plan on the skill already selected. He does this in consultation with the supervisor.
7. The pupil-teacher teaches the lesson to a small group of students (*i.e.*, 5 to 10 students). The lesson is observed by the supervisor (the teacher) or by the peers or video tape.
8. Immediately after the lesson, feedback is proved. All type of suggestions are given for the improvement of the lesson.
9. In the light of discussion and suggestions, the pupil-teacher replans the lesson. It is done again under the guidance of the supervisor.
10. The lesson replanned, is retaught to the small group of students.
11. After the lesson is over, again feedback is given and thus improvement in teaching is made.

Thus, we find that through Micro-Teaching, the pupil-teacher is able acquire 5 R's *i.e.* Recording, Reviewing, Responding, Refining and Redoing.

PHASES OF MICRO TEACHING PROCEDURES

According to Clift and Others (1976), Micro-Teaching procedure have the following three phases :

1. Knowledge Acquisition Phase. At this stage, the student teacher tries to get knowledge of the skill to be practised. He reads revlevant literature concerning that skill. He is also made to observe a demonstration lesson in which that skill figures prominently. The person who demonstrates the skill is an expert of the subject and the skill. By observing that lesson, the teacher under training gets theoretical as well as practical knowledge of that skill.

2. Transfer Phase. At this stage, teacher integrates the different skills. Instead of artificial situation he teaches in the real class-room where the number of students full class. His lesson is of 30 to 35 minutes duration and there he tries to integrate all the skills for which he made efforts in Phase Nos. I and II.

3. Skill Acquisition Phase. The student teacher acquires the skill in hand through a lot of practice. He prepares the micro-lesson, teaches it to have practice and then through feedback the evaluates his performance. Then he replans the lesson with modifications and improvement and then reteaches that lesson. Again there is re-feedback in order to enable him to have mastery of the teaching skill. In this way, different skills are learnt by the student teacher one by one.

PRINCIPLES UNDERLYING MICRO-TEACHING

Micro-Teaching is based on a few sound principles which are briefly explained below :

1. Principle of One Skill at a Time. In Micro-Teaching, training of one skill is given till the person has acquired mastery over it. Then the second skill is taken up and so on. Thus, we find that Micro-Teaching is based on the principle of giving training of one skill at a time.

2. Principle of Limited Contents. In Micro-Teaching, limited contents are taken up and the teacher is required to use those contents only. It helps the beginner teacher teach that limited material easily and confidently.

3. Principle of Practice. Micro-Teaching is based on the sound principle of practice. Here lot of practice is given by taking up on skill at a time. Practice makes a man perfect. It helps the pupil-teacher in becoming better and better.

4. Principle of Experimentation. A lot of Experimentation is involved in Micro-Teaching. The experiment consists of objective observation of actions performed under controlled conditions. The pupil-teacher and the supervisor conduct experiment on teaching skills under controlled conditions. Variables like time duration of the lesson, contents of the lesson to be taught, number of students sitting in the class etc., can be easily controlled.

5. Principle of Immediate Feedback. The micro lesson lasts for four or five minutes only. Thereafter, feedback is provided to the pupil-teacher. It helps the pupil-teacher to know his drawbacks and improve them effectively without any delay.

6. Principle of Evaluation. In Micro-Teaching, there is continuous assessment of the performance of the pupil-teacher. Evaluation helps the learner know his drawback and then he is able to improve it. In Micro-Teaching, each micro lesson is supervised by the supervisor or the peers. Drawbacks in teaching are pointed out and suggestion for improvement are given. Self-evaluation is also possible. Thus, evaluation ensures good learning by the pupil-teacher.

7. Principle of Continuity. Learning of different skills of teaching is a continuous process in Micro-Teaching programme. The pupil-teacher is learning one skill at a time and learning continues till he has mastered the skill. For each skill, the principle of continuity is implied. It makes the teacher good and effective.

8. Principle of Individualised Training. In Micro-Teaching, each trainee is given training very thoroughly. There is individual attention by the supervisor. The drawbacks in teaching are pointed out, suggestions given one by one and thus improvement is brought about.

Micro-Teaching Procedures/Steps of Micro-Teaching

A Micro-Teaching programme is organised to expose the trainees to an organised curriculum of miniature teaching encounters, moving from the less complex to the more complex. At each step along the way, a teaching strategy is discussed until it can be incorporated into a short teaching lesson of approximately 5 minutes duration. The trainee then teaches this lesson with a small group of four to six pupils in front of a video camera (if it is available), a supervisor, and often some trainee peers. The pupils are sent out after filling a short rating form, and the video recording is replayed and criticised by the supervisor and trainee peers. Then the trainee is given time to think about this criticism and to make modifications in his teaching strategy.

Micro-Teaching process includes the following steps:

Orientation. In this step teacher provides orientation *i.e.*, lectures on Micro-Teaching, its process, aspects, merits and limitations, to the popil-teachers.

Discussion of Teaching Skill. Under this step the pupil-teachers should be introduced with various teaching skills. Teacher discusses and explains the psychological rationale behind a particular skill under use.

Presentation of Micro-Teaching Model. The teacher educator gives a model Micro-Teaching (5 to 10 minutes) for the particular skill. His model-examplifies the use of the particular skill and its components. There are following different ways for providing the model lesson :

— The teacher himself can present the model-lesson.

— The model-lesson can be given with the help of a film or video-tape.

— It can be provided with the help of a audio-tape.

— Written or printed model-lesson can be distributed among the pupil-teachers.

Observation Schedule. The pupil-teachers should be provided the 'Observation Schedule' for the observation of the specific skill. Each skill has different observation schedule. The observation and criticism of the model lesson provide feedback to the demonstrator.

Preparation of Micro-lesson-Plan. Under this step pupil-teachers are required to prepare micro-lesson-plan related to the specifically selected teaching skill. The pupil-teacher should preferably select one unit concept for micro-lesson.

Teaching Session. The teacher teaches a group of four or five pupils (or his own peers). The teacher educator or a peer can observe the micro lesson by the trainee and note down the observations in a specially developed proforma. The micro lesson may be video taped or atleast recorded using cassette recorder.

Feedback. Under this step, immediate feedback is provided to the trainee for his micro lesson. This feedback is provided by playing the video or audio-tape. The trainee observes his own lesson and analyses it with the teacher educator and his peers. If video and audio tape recorders are not available, the observation schedule maintained by the teacher educator and the peers can serve as a good basis of the feedback. This feedback session helps the trainee to know what acts of his teaching are to be consolidated and what acts be eliminated.

Replan. In the light of the feedback and the educator's comments the trainee re-plans the micro lesson. Duration of this session is 12 minutes.

Re-Teach. The trainee re-teaches the micro lesson to a different but comparable group of pupils. This time also the micro lesson is video or audio-taped and the observations are noted in the proforma. Feedback is again provided on the re-teach lesson.

Re-Feed Back. After re-teach, re-feedback is provided to the pupil-teacher. The duration of re-feedback is 6 minutes.

Repetition of the Micro-Teaching Cycle. The Micro-Teaching cycle is repeated till the pupil-teacher acquires the mastery in the teaching skill. The Micro-Teaching cycle consists of planning, teaching, feedback, re-planning, re-teaching and re-feedback.

Creation of Micro-Teaching Setting. Under this step, consideration is made for creating proper conditions and providing appropriate facilities for the practice of a teaching skill. In the Indian model of Micro-Teaching developed by NCERT the standard setting for a micro class as below:

(a) Number of pupils : 5-10

(b) Type of pupils : Real pupils or preferably peers.

(c) Type of supervisor : Teacher educators and peers.

(d) Time duration of a micro lesson : 6 minutes.

(e) Time duration of a Micro-Teaching cycle : 36 minutes.

This duration is divided as under:

Teaching session : 6 minutes
Feedback session : 6 minutes

Replan session : 12 minutes

Re-teach session : 6 minutes

Re-feedback session : 6 minutes

Total : 36 minutes

Merits of Micro-Teaching

Micro-Teaching is an innovation which has sound basis of principles of learning and application of technology. The advantages of Micro-Teaching are as follows :—

1. It is an effective feedback device for the modification of teacher's behaviour.
2. It is highly individualized type to teacher training.
3. It is useful for developing teaching efficiency in pre-service and in-service teacher training programme.
4. It helps in systematic and objective observation by providing specific observation schedule.
5. It helps in acquiring various types of skills which ultimately form the basis of successful teaching.
6. It reduces the complexities of normal class-room teaching such as size of class, time and problem of discipline.
7. It is a training device for improving teaching practice and to prepare effective teachers.
8. Teaching is a complicated type of activity. Micro-Teaching simplifies it so as to make it suitable for the beginner teachers.
9. It develops the feeling of confidence among the teachers.
10. It provides economy in mastering the teaching skills. The use of video-tape enables the trainee to analyse his own teaching performance.
11. It can be done either in real class-room conditions or simulated conditions.

12. It focuses on training for the acomplishment of special tasks such as practice of instructional skills, mastery of certain curricular materials and practice of techniques of teaching.
13. It permits increased control and regulates teaching practice.
14. It enables the trainee to make progress in developing teaching skills at his own rating depending upon ability.
15. Trainees get staisfaction when they hear and see themselves through audio-video-tapes.

Demerits of Micro-Teaching

The drawbacks of Micro-Teaching are as follows:

1. Through Micro-Teaching one trainee is trained at a time.
2. It is more time consuming as a trainee will take 35 minutes to practice one skill only.
3. It presents fragmented view of teaching.
4. It may enable a trainee to seek mastery over the isolated teaching skills but hardly trains him to meet the needs of the real teaching encounter.
5. The immediate feedback which is a must, may not be feasible in all conditions.
6. Due to short lesson of 6 minutes, a trainee cannot get training in evaluation, diagnostic and remedial skills.
7. It can not fit in Indian conditions and situations due to its short practice period which may create academic and administrative problems in the schools.
8. It depresses the creativity of teachers. During teaching a teacher evolves something new but he has to stop as the micro lesson ends.
9. Micro-Teaching can be carried on successfully only in controlled environment but generally it is found class-room situations are flexible.
10. It wastes a lot of time of students. Each micro lesson goes on for 5 to 10 minutes where the main emphasis is on teaching technique, learning by students is almost ignored.

11. Micro-Teaching alone may not be sufficient. There is need of integrating it with other teaching techniques.

MICRO-TEACHING AND TRADITIONAL TEACHING—A COMPARISON

Micro-Teaching is a new idea in the field of teacher education. People who have traditional outlook don't want to change their ideologies. They face problems in accepting the innovation of Micro-Teaching. This type of situation always arises whenever new things will come up. The old nations need be converted into the modern ones because the modern ones are undoubtedly unique. The comparison of the two teachniques-brings home clearly the view point that Micro-Teaching is an inproved teachinque in every way and is better as compared to the traditional teaching :

Micro-Teaching	*Traditional Teaching*
1. Teaching is relatively simple.	1. Teaching as experienced by the teacher is complicated and difficult.
2. It does not pose a big threat or fear to the teacher.	2. It poses a big threat and a challenge to the teacher.
3. It usually encourages the beginner teacher for better job performance in future.	3. It may lead to failure and cause frustration.
4. Here the objective are given in behavioural terms.	4. The objectives are not stated in behavioural terms.
5. The number of students in a class is less. It is rather a small group of 5 to 10 students.	5. It is an over-crowded class where the number of students is 60 to 90.
6. There is provision of immediate feedback. That helps the teacher to know his drawbacks and improve upon them.	6. Mediate feedback is not provided.
7. Teaching is carried on under fully controlled situations. The supervisor is there who is determined to improve teaching.	7. There is no control as such over teaching. There is no supervision.

Contd.

Micro-Teaching	Traditional Teaching
8. The teacher practices one skill at a time. He continues the practice till he is able to have mastery of it.	8. The teacher practices the whole teaching behaviour which consists of many skills.
9. Duration of time for teaching is 5 to 10 minutes.	9. Time duration is 35 to 40 minutes.
10. Patterns of class-room interaction can be studied objectively.	10. Patterns of class-room interaction cannot be studied easily.

Q. 16. What do you mean by teaching skill? How is their integration planned and a pupil-teacher trained for this work?

Ans. **TEACHING SKILLS**

Teaching is a complex phenomenon that comprises of various specific teaching skills. Through Micro-Teaching, complexities of class-room teaching are reduced. The different skills are identified and then mastery of each skill is acquired. Here two important questions crop up which need consideration. The first one is to know what is a skill. The second one is how many skills are involved in the teaching process.

What is a Teaching Skill? N.L. Gage (1968) says, "Teaching skills are specific instructional activities and procedures that a teacher may use in his class-room. These are related to the various stages of teaching or in the continuous flow of the teacher performance."

To know how many skills are involved in the teaching process is rather an interesting study. A few research workers have tried to identify several sets of component teaching skills. Some of them are common with a little different terminology.

Allen and Ryan (1969), of Stanford University put forth the view that fourteen skills are involved. Borg and his associates (1970), increased the number to eighteen.

In India, B.K. Passi (1976), on the basis of work done in CASE, Baroda has given a list of twenty one skills. Jangira and his associates (1979), gave a list of twenty.

None of the lists suggested by the researchers are exhaustive and final. We can add or subtract from the lists as per need of the situation. The list of skills given by Allen and Ryan (1969), is as under :

1. Stimulus Variation. Teaching depends upon the stimulus provided by the teacher during teaching. A good teacher goes on varying the stimulus in order to bring in variety in his teaching. That way he is able to attract the attention of the students. Thus, the teachers are trained in movements, gestures, focussing, interactional styles etc.

2. Closure. It is related with the finishing up of a stage in teaching. It helps the students to relate the new knowledge with the previous one.

3. Set Induction. Set induction helps the students to induce maximum. The teacher uses their present knowledge and skills and tries to involve them in the lesson.

4. Silence and Non-Verbal Cues. During teaching, the teacher provides cues to the students in order to encourage them. Sometimes he puts a thought provoking question. The students speak on it. The discussion goes on and on when the teacher does not give his personal comments. He rather remains silent. It makes many other students to come forward and speak.

5. Higher Order Questions. In every good lesson, the teacher puts some questions which are of higher order. This type of questions enable the students to form generalizations or to reach some definite principles.

6. Reinforcement of Student Participation. The pupil-teacher in every way tries to encourage students's participation in the lesson. As fas as possible, he accepts their responses with a smile. Only positive reinforcers are used by him. He makes every effort to avoid the use of negative reinforcers which may result into any type of discouragement for the students.

7. Divergent Questions. Putting divergent questions is another skill which makes the students think creatively.

8. Probing Questions. The teacher puts such questions with the help of which he is able to dig out something from the students.

With the help of probing questions, the teacher is able to lead the students to correct responses.

9. Fluency in Making Questions. While putting questions to the class, the teacher should have fluency. He tries to have as many questions as possible in the scheduled period of teaching.

10. Recognising Attending Behaviour. Every good teacher has the ability to judge while teaching how far the students are taking interest in the lesson. The teacher is able to do so through visual cues.

11. Planned Repetition. Sometimes during teaching the teacher repeats things in a planned manner. He does so in order to focus the attention of the students over some important points.

12. Illustrations and use of Examples. A good teacher has the skill of clear teaching. For this purpose he is able to give good examples. Through illustrations, he is able to capture the attention of all.

13. Lecturing. The teacher is able to present the material effectively by using the right type of techniques.

14. Completeness. Communication of teaching is a two way traffic. Through teaching, the teacher is able to communicate himself fully. He is able to give knowledge, develop attitude and interest of the students.

B. K. Passi (1976), described 13 skills in his book 'Becoming Better Teacher—Micro-Teaching Approach.' The different skills are as under :

(i) Writing instructional objectives.
(ii) Introducing a lesson.
(iii) Fluency in questioning.
(iv) Probing questions.
(v) Explaining.
(vi) Illustrating with examples.
(vii) Stimulus variation.
(viii) Silence and non-verbal cues.
(ix) Reinforcement.

(x) Increasing pupil participation.

(xi) Using blackboard.

(xii) Achieving closure.

(xiii) Recognising attending behaviour.

The Baroda General Teaching Competence Scale (BGTC) has divided teaching skills into three categories :

(a) Pre-instructional Skills.

(b) Presentation Skills.

(c) Closing, Evaluation and Managerial Skills.

LIST OF PROBABLE TEACHING SKILLS FOR DIFFERENT STAGES OF A LESSON

Below is given a list of probable teaching skills which are required at different stages of a lesson :

I. Planning Stage

This stage involves the following skills.

1. Writing Instructional Objectives.
2. Selecting the content.
3. Organising content.
4. Selection of Audio Visual Aids material.

II. Introductory Stage

1. Creating set induction.
2. Introducing the lesson.

III. Presentation Stage

The Presentation Stage has four sub-stages. Each sub-stage needs different type of teaching skills which are given below :

(a) Questioning Skills

(i) Structuring Class-room questions.

(ii) Fluency in asking questions.

(iii) Probing questions.

(iv) Question-delivery and distribution.

(v) Higher order questions.

(vi) Divergent questions.

(vii) Responses Management.

(b) Presentation Skills

(i) Packing of the lesson,

(ii) Lecturing,

(iii) Explaining,

(iv) Illustrating with examples,

(v) Discussing,

(vi) Demonstrating.

(c) Aid Using Skills

(i) Using teaching Aids.

(ii) Using blackboard.

(iii) Stimulus variation.

(iv) Silence and Non-verbal cues.

(v) Reinforcement.

(d) Management Skills

(i) Promoting pupil participation.

(ii) Recognising attending behaviour.

(iii) Management of the class.

Teaching is a very complex activity having atleast three levels of teacher behaviours *viz.*, component teaching skills, component teaching behaviours having the component skill and atomistic teaching behaviours. This is primary level of teaching skills. These component teaching skills can be classified into individual sets of component teaching behaviours at the secondary level. The component teaching skills can be defined as a set of inter-related component teaching behaviours for the realisation of specific instructional objectives. To help the student teachers at the beginning stage to prepare the lesson, a component teaching skill and its component teaching behaviours are selected as units and not the complex teaching as a whole. Thus, we may say that the Micro-Teaching is an analytic approach to teacher training.

There is a feeling that teaching cannot be broken into pieces in the form of various teaching skills and component behaviours. Teaching is not just a combination of these isolated bits and therefore mastery over the different teaching skills does not make one an effective teacher.

There should be some bridge between training in isolated skills and the real teaching situations. The concept of integration of teaching skills may perform the role of such bridge.

Inegration of skills means a process of selection, organistation and utilization of different teaching skills to form an effective pattern for realizing the specified instructinal objectives in a given teaching-learning situation.

Objectives. The major objectives of the integration of teaching skills are as follows :—

1. Helping in the transition from Micro-Teaching situation to real teaching situation.
2. Providing practice in making decision regarding the synthesis of teaching skills in view of the teaching situation and instructional objectives.

Integration in parts and integration as a whole are the strategies for the integration of skills.

Integration in Parts. First of all decision is made with respect to the number of individually mastered skills required to be integrated. The time duration of the teaching excercise for integration depends upon the number of teaching skills to be integrated. It is increased four time if there are four skills to the integrated and five times in case of five skills and so on. All the steps like teach, feedback, re-plan, re-teach, re-feedback are planned and carried out in the controlled setting (as in the case of Micro-Teaching) and this process continues till the student teacher acquires a reasonable level of mastery in the integration of the skills in hand. After acquiring mastery in the integration of these skills he is required to apply it in a real class-room setting and have sufficient practice in such real teaching.

Integration as Whole. In this approach, opportunity is provided to integrate all the individual teaching skills by taking them as a whole and not in parts. It is a sort of mini-teaching, bridging the gap between Micro-Teaching and teaching in real situation.

Student teacher should have full knowledge of the content, instructional objectives, teaching learning situations and scope of utilization of the learned individual teaching skill.

Q. 17. Write an essay on Computer Assisted Instruction (CAI).

Or

What is Computer Assised Instruction? What is its theory and what are the limitations of CAI?

Ans. "Computer Assisted Instruction has now taken on so many dimensions that it can no longer be considered a simple derivative of the teaching machine or of the kind of programmed learning that Skinner introduced. The teaching machine and the linear or branching programmes are to be sure, its immediate ancestors, but it has evolved rapidly." (Hilgard and Bowar, "Theories of Learning" Prentice Hall of India, New Delhi, 1975.)

The impact of the computer on education will be in the area or clerical and accounting efficiency because the great advantage of computer over other kinds of educational technology lies in the nature of the device it computes. Therefore the computer provides a flexible presentation of materials to the learner and also keeps track of the progress of the number of learners at the same time. In the earlier chapter a detailed description of C.B.T.M. is given. Evidently a C.B.T.M. has three capacities.

1. In a given subject area, it must have at its disposal a number of different programmes.

2. It must be able to change programmes during the course of instruction.

3. When specifying a programme for each student, it must make use of the student's entering behaviour, general ability and personality characteristics.

Modes of CAI

1. The first mode is the tutorial drill and practice procedure which is an outgrowth of programme learning.

2. The systems developed by Atkinson and Suppes at Stanford is commonly used by teachers without the computer. The computer has the advantage of individualization the activities and of introducing greater learning efficiency through the management of the learning by the computer.

3. Another use is in connection with games that stimulate actual problems whereby complex decisions in relation to metropolitan problems of political control systems can be made and their consequencies studied.

4. Another method has been used in the teaching of statistics at the University of California at Los Angeles. The student learns a computer language through which he can manipulate large bodies of data, and hence come out of the statistics course able to handle data.

Devices Used in CAI

Visual Communication. Ronald Gentile describe some of the following devices used in CAI:

1. Type-writers ask a question under computer control and answer a question under student control.

2. Film projection devices, on the basis of student responses, select films, present auditory and visual materials and automatically score students responses.

3. With Cathode-ray tubes a pen can be used for drawing curves indicating answers on a screen. These answers can then be evaluated by a computer.

4. Display superimposed on films highlight certain excepts on the films.

5. Random-access slides and films are available. The area of auditory communication presents many unsolved problems. There are two devices developed for auditory communication. They are:

(i) Compiled Speech. Here the computer has random access to pre-recorded phrases which can be arranged on the basis of student response. For example, the computer can tell the student a chemical formula.

(ii) Synthetic Speech. Here the computer uses a set of rules to convert stored speech, sounds into meaningful speech patterns.

Theory of CAI

1. CAI was developed on some sound assumptions. Therefore, it is popular in the training for different levels and areas of education. This instruction can be arranged for a large number of students with scope for maintaining quality and quantitative education. Computer based programmes provide the maximum amount of flexibility (flexible kind of branching including alternative parts and different examples for the students who may need them. Therefore the learner goes at his own pace, receives immediate personalized feedback and freely chooses the content, sequencing and degree of difficulty of instruction. CAI has completely individualized section.

2. Any lesson material in any subject can be programmed for CAI with explicitly defining the strategy to be used and the lesson material to be presented in the form of words, pictures and experiments. Becauase of the variety and versality, CAI serves as an effective educational tool to meet the varied problems of students on a sound educational basis. In advanced countries the introduction of CAI has created a fear in the minds of teachers that CAI will relicate the people of the teacher and to some extent eliminate teachers from the teaching scene. From experiences it is found that the truth is otherwise, since CAI has become a powerful tool for the teacher in his instruction. The Teacher has a changing role or play in the new technological society and goes out of his conventional assignment of delivering lectures alone. The teacher takes an active role. It is significant that CAI directly interacts with students individually and with the teacher.

3. In CAI the performance of the learner during the course of instruction and his performance on the test are automatically recorded. Therefore, his performance can be evaluated by the teacher enabling to evolve or design the appropriate teaching strategy for the learner in future.

Limitations of the Theory

Dececco and Crawford (1977), observed : "considerably more progress has been made with the technical development of CAI than with the problem of writing instructional programmes. The chief unsolved technical problem is how to reduce the cost sufficiently to prevent bankruptcy of local school districts. As in the case of the general development and use of the instructional media, the temptation has been to dazzle the student with an array of visual and auditory stimuli which serve more to impress him with the capabilities of a computer than to provide him with the necessary instruction."

1. How to provide for individual difference is not specified clearly. The individual differences are varied in nature depending on the individuals. Therefore, all the differences cannot be accommodated by allowing the computer to generate sequences on the basis of student response.

2. The expectation to eliminate the individual differences by any teaching method becomes unrealistic because of "prior differences in student verbal abilities and mental sets".

3. We need a classification of individual difference variables especially in terms of learning variables.

4. Adaptation to individual differences most prove to be superior to teaching which is aimed at the group mean.

CAI and Evaluation

There are many appropriate approaches to the evaluation of educational endeavours, which are evolving in adding to the usual individual measurement approach, Scrivan (1967), states clearly that "As a matter of terminology, I think that novel terms are worthwhile here, to avoid in appropriate connotations, and I purpose to use the terms "formative" and "summative" to quality evaluation in these roles. "These roles" refer to the role of evaluation in improving a course while it is still fluid—being developed and its role finding the worth of a completed product course, text, instructional package, and so forth. (Serivan J.C., The Methodology of Evaluation. AERA Monograph Series on Curriculum Evaluation, Chaicago, Rand Mc Nally Co 1967, No 1, pp 39-83). Formative evaluation refers to a student's learning during a course, when changes can be made in the transactions of subsequent instruction on the basis of current attainment. Summative refers to evaluation of a student's assessment at the end of a course or topic or unit, that is, when no subsequent changes in treatment for that learning will be made, therefore, in the former, the focus is upon the alteration of course or other unit during its development.

A taxt-book author, a teacher in the class-room or a team of curriculum developers are called the 'developers'. Here CAI is an instrument for change. We know CAI is the result of the convergence of two technologies: programmed instruction technology and computer technology. The basic ingredients in CAI may be described briefly. A lesson to be taught is analysed into the essential message to a student. These message may be delivered through words, graphs, pictures of any combination, Some messages may be auditory. As materials are presented the student reacts to them by answering questions, working problems identifying points on a graph or objects in a picture giving examples, requesting more information or a change to review messages presented previously, and so forth. Depending upon the student's response, the computer presents the next messages in the lesson, additional messages, ideas given earlier, a review of earlier messages or additional 'developing' questions. These operations can be part of any programmed instruction. However, these operations are controlled by a computer in CAI. Therein lies the special application of CAI to formative evaluation. We know the computer can be used to analyse data very rapidly. Besides, the same computer which controls the instruction can be used to collect information concerning the following variables in the learner's responses :

(a) Length of time between presentation of questions and student response.

(b) Requests by the learner for review and the material reviewed.

(c) Requests for additional information of examples.

(d) The computer can store in its memory any 'legal' move.

(e) The computer can be requested to summarize such veriables over students or sub-groups of students.

(f) Number of times the learner reviews an item or responds incorrectly after review.

Consider an example of the CAI—Lesson concerning the concept of their relation between volume and pressure in gases. Illustrations and definitions are presented. The student is asked to respond to some questions. He applies the concept to a problem. The students are progressing at different rates in reading the messages (words, pictures, graphs) and in responding to request. The computer keeps track for each student of each of the kinds of variables listed above. Then the computer can summarize the number of 'correct' or 'incorrect' responses across the students. The teacher has sub-grouped the students, for example, by vocabulary level of achievement of marks in science in the previous class, the computer can be requested to summarize each group separately.

There are at present some CAI system in which the author can change materials in a lesson—the messages, the questions, and so forth,—through the use of one of the student stations with a special control. The mere collection of the group data would allow a class-room teacher or curriculum development team to revise lessons in a much better way than is customary today.

Q. 18. Describe the characteristics of Computer Assisted Instruction. Discuss the importance of awareness of Computer Software in Teaching Children in School.

Or

Is there any difference between Computer Assisted Instruction amd Computer Managed Instruction? Discuss their relative merits and demerits in teaching.

Ans. COMPUTER ASSISTED INSTRUCTION

Amongst the important hardware devices of educational devices, computer occupies an important place. Computer is used for individualized instruction. It is based on self-instructional system. The use of the computer has increased not only in education, but it has also affected the trade, industry, war, administration and research work etc. In the field of education, the influence of computer can be seen maximum in research work, examination system and instructional system. Hence, it is also known as electronic brain. By considering entering behaviours by the computer, instruction has to be selected.

Functions of Computers

In teaching process, the computer has the following functions:

1. Instructional material can be collected by a computer. It can have 32 types of instructional material for a single topic.

2. Informations on cards can be collected by the computers.
3. Computers can communicate the informations.

COMPUTER MANAGED INSTRUCTION AND COMPUTER ASSISTED INSTRUCTION (C.M.I. AND C.A.I.)

In the domain of instruction, there are two major applications of the computers:

1. Computer Managed Instruction (CMI). In CMI the computer gathers, stores, and manages information of guide students through individualist learning experience.

It gets a student move through check-points (in the form of definite activities) in the education process at different times via different paths matching the individual capabilities. It achieves this individualized instructional processes by a series of activities—administering diagnostic tests, scoring them, prescribing appropriate next steps and monitoring the progress of the individuals all the along the route.

2. Computer Assisted Instruction (CAI). In CAI the computer interacts directly with the learners while presenting lessons. It delivers instruction directly to students and allows them to interact with the computer through the lessons programmed in the system. The computer's ability to engage in instructional 'dialogue' with the student while delivering information makes it adaptable to any number of instructional situations. It can facilitate various instructional modes. These modes are as follows:

(i) Tutorial Mode. In the tutorial mode, as in programmed in subtraction, information is presented in small units followed by a question. The student's response is analyzed by the computer and appropriate feedback is given. A network of 'branches' or pathways can be programmed to teach and to allow students to work on their own pace. The more alternative programmes available to the computer, the more adaptive the tutorial can be to individual differences.

(ii) Drill or Practice. This mode is to make sure that concept, rule and procedure has already been learned by the learner. The programme leads the learner through a series of examples to develop dexterity and fluency in using the kill. All correct responses are reinforced. The computer goes ahead only when mastery is achieved by the learner.

(iii) Discovery Mode. In this mode inductive approach to learning is taken up, that is, the problems through trial and error. It approximated to laboratory learning and the real-life-learning outside the class-room. The aim of this approach is the deeper understanding that results from discovering and solving a complex problem.

(iv) Gaming Mode. Gaming mode can or cannot be instructional. It is mostly recreational in purpose, while sometimes it teaches through games. It is specially suitable for young children.

(v) Simulation Mode. In simulation mode the learner confronts a scaled down approximating of a real-life situation. Thus, this mode allows realistic practice without the expense of risks otherwise involved.

Q. 19. Write down a brief note on Programmed Instruction strategy, its characteristics and need.

Or

Discuss the advantages and disadvantags of Programmed Instruction.

Ans. Before beginning to explaining Programmed Instruction, let us first see the differences between Teaching, Instruction and Programmed Instruction. According to Edgar Dale, " 'Teaching' is a broad, vague, ill-defined term and 'Instruction' is a purposeful orderly,

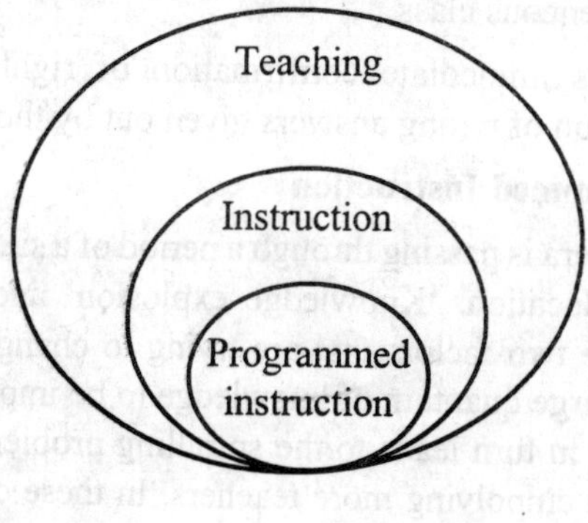

controlled sequencing of experiences to reach a specified goal." All instruction involves teaching, but all teaching cannot be instruction.

Programmed instruction is a sub-head under instruction and represents a more rigorous attempt to develop a mastery over specified goals to secure "insured" learning. Programmed Instruction involves controlled, carefully specified and skilfully arranged learning experiences. They are self-instructional and self-corrective.

The fundamental idea of programmed self-instructional materials was described in 1912, by Edward L. Throndike in these words: "If by a miracle of mechanical ingenuity, a book could be so arranged that only to him who had done what was directed on page one, would page two become visible and so on, much that now requires personal instruction could be managed by print." Programmed instruction is a technique of self-instruction in which all of the instructional load is carried by teaching machines or programmed tests. Programmed Instruction is a new path towards automation and individualised instruction.

Major Characteristics of Programmed Instruction

1. The subject-matter is broken down into small steps called frames and arranged sequentially.
2. The content and sequence of the frames are subjected to actual try out with students and are revised on the basis of data gathered by the programmer.
3. Frequent response is required of the student.
4. Each student programmes at his own pace without any threat of being exposed to any humiliation in a heterogeneous class.
5. There is immediate confirmation of right answers or correction of wrong answers given out by the student.

Need for Programmed Instruction

The present era is passing through a period of a silent revolution in the field of education. 'Knowledge explosion' and 'population explosion' are the two factors that are trying to change the web of life. They mean large quantum of knowledge to be imparted to large population which in turn leads to the spiralling problem of opening more schools and empolying more teachers. In these circumstances what is needed is an 'education explosion'. Technology or automation is the only solution to solve all these problems. Programmed instruction is an innovative step in this direction towards automation and individualisation of instruction. Programmed learning is an application of principles of behavioural sciences and technology in the field of education. It emerged from the efforts of American psychologists during the present century. Significant contributions have been made to the theory of programming by Sidney L. Pressey, Robert M. Gagne, Robert Mager and B.F. Skinner.

Contributions of Pressey

Sidney L. Pressey, a psychologist of Ohio State University, is credited with developing, in 1920, a self-teaching machine called 'Drum Tutor' which could teach as well as test. The machine presented a series of questions to the student until the student responded correctly. When the particular criterion was reached, the item was skipped. When the question was set, the student selected his response from the multiple choice alternatives by pressing one of the keys corresponding to the answer. When all the items in the lesson were learned, the machine stopped and hundred per cent mastery of the lesson was taken for granted. Pressey's type of machine was a testing machine and not a teaching machine. This adjunct auto-instructional programming had the advantages of fitting conveniently with all the instructional materials. After teaching the subject-matter in any one of the conventional methods, this self-testing machine can be effectively used as a diagnostic tester.

Pressey described the period as the coming of "industrial revolution" in education. In an era of economic depression marked by rising unemployment. Pressey talked of saving material and labour and hence his remarks were not well-received by educators. Pressey received recognition he sought for his work only in 1950.

Robert Mager

Mager developed a new concept known as "Learner Controlled Instruction" which is a kind of Socratic dialogue in reverse, where the learner led the instructor. The main theme of the learner controlled instruction is that the learner is one of the best sources of information about himself. The task of the instructor is responsive rather than directive. The instructor remains silent until the learner stimulates him with questions that suggest the needed illustrations, demonstrations or some other help.

Mager conducted studies to find out whether the learner-generated sequence was more efficient than the instructor-generated sequence. It was concluded that learner-controlled instruction was very effective. The programmer develops a unique programme for each learner. It is wrong to claim that learner-controlled instruction is a panacea; it simply reminds one that the learner deserves consideration. The attempt to impose order on learning is futile. In programming sequence, the observation of learner's behaviour should begin early, followed by the determination of objectives before proceeding to write the frames. Mager's studies also emphasise that the experience of the learner can possibly be used as basis for further understanding.

Mager is also remembered for his stress on the formulation of instructional objectives in a clear and specific manner before proceeding to organise instruction. Such objectives are at the bottom of programming too. Mager states, "once an instructor decides he will teach his students something, several kinds of activity are necessary on his part if he is to succeed. The first among these is to decide upon the goals he intends to reach at the end of his course or programme. All other activities stem from the selection of objectives and goals. A statement of instructional objectives is a collection of words describing one of our educational intents." The objective clearly specifies the terminal behaviour of the learner at the end of instruction. Description of such a terminal behaviour will include identifying and naming the overall behaviour act, defining the important conditions under which the behaviour is to occur and defining the criterion of acceptable performance. Though some educationists have criticised the spelling out of such specific behavioural objectives of instruction, research conclusions say that such objectives are useful and almost never harmful. They give direction to teaching and help in curriculum development and also provide guidance for evaluation.

Advantages of Programmed Instruction

1. The student is continually active when he is using a programme. In other methods of teaching he is active only sometimes and practically nil in a lecture.

2. Programmed instruction is basically individual instruction. Every student proceeds at his own pace. In a conventional class, the teacher attends to only children of average abilities with the consequence that the intelligent get bored and the dull have no extra help. But programme instruction helps the dull with extra information where it is needed and no stigma is attached to the making of mistakes. At the same time, it does not hold up the progress of a fast learner as he goes along and completes the task at his own pace of learning.

3. A programme is planned and prepared much more carefully than a teacher would do for a conventional teaching programme. Mostly programmes are written by experts in the field.

4. Immediate reinforcement helps a child to know whether his answer is right or wrong. In normal class feedback takes a long time.

5. Each programme has to prove itself to be effective during the process of validation and must be re-written as many times as is necessary. If proper learning does not take place, it is only due to the fault of the programme and not of the learner. This positive attitude is quite distinct from what we normally witness in normal class situations where there is always the tendency to blame the pupils rather than the teacher when there are failures in examinations.

6. A programme is not a human being and hance can be used at any time of the day. Programmed materials or teaching machines are never tried and never lose their temper or patience. Hence programmed materials are very useful in the field of non-formal education.

Limitations of Programmed Instruction

The following are the limitations of programmed instruction :

1. Programmed learning does not eliminate competition or grades as often claimed.

2. Mere manipulation of machine is not rewarding to children as Skinner seems to think. Once the novelty wears off and if, at the start, too many errors appear the pupils loses interest and motivation. Later reinforcements often do not accelerate learning.

3. Operant conditioning is found successful only with some pupils, in some cases and not in all. Programmed instruction ignores

or makes inadequate provisions for variables like cognitive variables, personality variables and motivational variables.

4. Programmed instruction restricts the learner's freedom of choice resulting in cramping of his imagination and initiative.

5. The teacher-pupil contact which is so vital for development of human personality and relationship is completely lost.

6. In language learning, speech is equally important as development of reading and comprehension skills. But there is no scope for providing this experience.

Q. 20. Discuss briefly the language Laboratory, its need, functions, features and advantages.

Ans. The language laboratory is a very popular technical innovation. It is derived from America, although its use had gained ground rapidly in the United Kingdom in 1960s. Language laboratory affords opportunity for the students to hear the language spoken by a native and to practise speaking the language themselves. Traditional language teaching does not allow much time for oral and auditory experience and in this respect, the language laboratory is an innovative technique.

Objectives. The function for language is to communicate ideas. Today, the aim of the good language teacher is to teach his students to communicate successfully with the native speaker of the language. Otherwise stated, language is a medium for communications and hence the ability to communicate in the language concerned is now emphasised in language instruction.

The purpose of language teaching is to enable the students to understand, speak, read and write the foreign language with the native speed, The order in which the language skills are presented is hearing, speaking, reading and writing. This sequence emphasises the essential feature of language, *i.e.*, reliance on printed words is eliminated unitil mastery of sound is achieved.

Need for Language Larboratory. The most important advance made in language teaching is the language laboratory. Language laboratory recognises the prevalence of widespread individual differences in language aptitude even among pupils of average and superior intelligence. It is esentially individualistic in its approach.

The language laboratory recognises that the spoken form of language is central to effective communication. Spoken form should have a large share along with written forms in language teaching. The language laboratory implements this programme by supplementing the sound recording of native speakers with the text-book.

The only realistic purpose of the language laboratory is to provide a convenient means of hearing and responding to audio-drills. Well designed and carefully produced pattern drills can be easily recorded and used in the laboratory. The language laboratory thereby relieves the teacher of endless repetition of patterns.

Functions of the Language Laboratory. A language laboratory is fully equipped if the students can :

(a) hear the tape distrinctly,

(b) stop, rewind and replay the tape at any time,

(c) work at his own pace,

(d) select his materials freely,

and if the teacher can :

(e) listen to individual students without disturbing them,

(f) communicate with the students,

(g) control the programme when he so desires.

The typical complete language laboratory provides separate booths, one for each student in the class. Each booth is equipped with earphones, a micro-phone and tape-recording and playing equipment. The teacher controls the class from a *console.* The console has one or more tapes with master tapes and special equipments of 'monitor' any student and thereby two-way communication is ensured.

The normal teaching sequence is as follows : The teacher first plays a master tape. The sounds are picked up and recorded on the separate tape-recorders kept in each booth. There is no possibility to stop the tape and repeat the difficult parts. This is called *lockstep* learning and has no opportunity for individualisation or programme selection or control.

The student then listens to his copy of the tape and at specified stages makes oral responses to it. These responses are recorded by the recording equipment in the sutdent's own booth. Each student can go back over his copy of the tape as many times as he requires, listening to both the pre-recorded material from the master tape and also to his own responses. If he is not satisfied with his own response, he can also record and improve his previous performance.

The student's tape-recoder uses *twin track* tape. The master tape is recorded on one of the tracks and the student's responses are recorded on the other. The material on the master tape has pauses left in it which give him enough time to respond. In playing back, the student listens to the original material and also his own recording responses. In both recording and re-recording by the student, the master track remains untouched and cannot be recorded over. This type of programme is normally used in the initial stage for correcting pronunciation. The exercise is called *speech drill.*

In all the speech drills, the following order is observed :

Master Track	Stimulus 1		Stimulus 2	
Swdent track		Repetition 1		Repetition 2

FEATURES OF THE LANGUAGE LABORATORY

(a) Retracing. Language consists of a set of habits which have to be acquired through much imitation and practice. Hence, in intensive drill practice, students should be able to stop the tape, hear again the sounds and to practise them by imitation as often as desired. In programmed instruction, the student cannot advance until he has mastered the previous. But in language laboratory, although the programme is linear, the next step automatically appears irrespective of the success of the student in the previous frame. The student must himself determine whether he has performed accurately. If he decides that he has not, the student must be able to repeat the defective frame until he succeeds. This is called 'retracing'.

(b) Self-Pacing. In a language laboratory, every student works at his own speed. A slow worker would be one who does much retracing and who spends much time on a tape. A fast worker would do less retracing.

(c) Material Selection. In a basic language laboratory, no selectivity is provided to the student. In other laboratories, the student may select and use tapes individually as explained in library operation.

(d) The Console. This is the control centre where the instructor's equipments are located. It has the following switches :

(i) Dirtribution Switches. To direct the recorded programmes to the selected student booths.

(ii) Monitoring Switches. Monitoring enables the teacher to listen to any individual as he works with the tape. It is done for:—

(a) correcting errors in procedure

(b) correcting linguistic errors.

(c) evaluating and grading the students.

(iii) Intercom Switches. to permit a two-way conversation with any individual student.

(iv) Group-call Switch. Enables to make announcements to all students who are listening to a particular tape from a console source.

(v) All-call Switch. For making announcement to all students in the laboratory, regardless of the nature of the programme.

Advantages of a Language Laboratory

The following are the specific advantages claimed for language laboratory over conventional class-room method :

(a) The student listnes to perfect native speech rather than the less-then-perfect speech of the teacher.

(b) The students' active speaking time is increased considerably.

(c) The teacher, by monitoring the programme, can give individual instruction without disturbing the whole class.

(d) Since the student is not being listened to by other students when he is practising, he is likely to be less inhibited than in a normal class-room.

(e) The student can hear his own mistakes for himself.

(f) The teacher is relieved from the chose of presenting routine and repetitive practice material. He has now more time and energy to devote to the particular needs of individual students.

Q. 21. Discuss the Case of Experience by Edgar Dale.

Or

Discuss Edgar Dale's Cone of Experience.

Ans. There are three sources to gather human experience:

1. Direct sensory contact which involves *doing*.
2. Oral and printed words which involve symbolising.
3. Pictures or some other forms of representation of objects which involves *observing*.

Or these three, the symbolising is of least importanace while teaching young learners. Edgar Dale represents this in a pictorial device—pinnacle form—which is called Cone of Experience. Let us travel up the cone from the base. The order will be that of increasing abstractness. The experiences included in the cone are as indicated below:

1. Direct, Purposeful Experience. That is seen, felt, touched smelt, *i.e.*, experience gained through senses. These are direct purposeful experiences. Objects are reality. They are preferred in teaching. They help to develop concepts in the minds of students.

2. Dramatic Participation. When we talk of dramatic participation, we mean that we can get as close as possible to the realities of the past. Dramatisations are available in a variety of forms. You have to rehearse before hand. You can be an observer. You can be a participant. You have to wear a costume. Proper costumes heighten the effect of dramatisation in three ways :

(i) It compels attention.

(ii) It helps to identify the actor—young, old, type of work or character.

(iii) It enables the actor to feel and play his role better.

The types of dramatised play are—the play, the pagent, tablean etc.

3. Contrieved Experience. Like working out a mode. A model is a miniature form of reality. A model helps in understanding.

4. Field Trips. With the help of field trips, you can get *first hand* experiences with the things and phenomena which cannot be brought into the class-room. Only when this is not possible, the teacher should resort to other visual aids.

5. Demonstration Experiments. Complicated processes can be performed by the teacher for the benefit of pupils who are reduced to the position of passive observers. You can demonstrate on a demonstration table.

6. Exhibitions and Museums. By means of exhibits, we can bring the outside world into the class-room and there is concrete representation of things.

7. Television. Television can bring the real experience in the class-room. It is beyond motion picture. In a television, event is seen as it happens.

8. Motion Pictures. Things are filmed elsewhere and are brought into the class-room. Motion pictures with sound system yield good results in teaching all the subjects in the school curriculum.

9. Designed Materials. Such as maps and charts.

10. Verbal Symbols. Here it is use of 'chalk' and 'talk' method. It requires great thinking. There is spoken word 'talk' and written word 'chalk'. A distinction has to be made between chalk and talk or written word and spoken word. Spoken word is always placed lower than the written word in the cone.

11. Radio and Recordings. The advantages of radio are many. The only drawback is that it is "one way communication" only.

12. Still pictures, pictures, illustrations are there and these can be projected.

K. Sampath states, "It can thus be seen that the opportunities afforded by the sensory aids are very great and that it all depends upon the ingenuity of the teacher as to how he could exploit the learning situation by the right use of the proper aid. Nevertheless the richer the teaching materials, the more will be the teacher's responsibility correlate and plan his teaching. The following general principles may however serve as guides to the use of these aids:

1. There are three stages in a leraning process when an educational aid is used to supplement the ordinary teaching, *viz.*, *(i)* preparing the pupils for the learning experience; *(ii)* reinforcing

the values while the pupils are sharing the experience, and relating the experience with the lesson and thus stimulating further learning.

2. The aids must be adapted to the intellectual maturity of the pupils and to the nature and extent of their previous experience.

3. There is no best aid which has all the advantages. Most visual aids suffer from some psychological limitations. The teacher should be familiar with the advantages and limitations of the various types of sensory aids.

4. Visual instruction in the class-room should not be confused with entertainment. The effective use of an aid depends primarily on careful planning by the teacher.

5. Visual aids should not be considered us substitutes for oral and written methods of acquiring knowledge. They should be used to supplement the class-room teaching.

6. In all cases, the time and effort on the use of a particular aid in preference to others must be justified.

A Practical Cone Classifying Different Aids

The 'Cone' proposed by Edgar Dale was the earliest attempt to classify the audio-visual aids according to their effectiveness in communicating ideas. The cone classifies sensory aids in terms of greater or less concreteness and abstractness as learning experiences. The cone device should not be constructed as an accurate arrangement of the learning experiences systematically from base to pinnacle. Field trip has been classified as an experience involving only observation and hence has been placed much high in the ladder. Actually, field trip provides rich, first-hand experiences in some instances and hence should be classified under 'Direct, purposeful experience'. Similarly, projected aids are considered to be more effective in teaching than the non-projected aids. But projected aids occupy a top position in the pinnacle, signifying thereby that they are comparatively abstract experiences in relation to direct experience.

Q. 22. Explain Simulated Teaching.

Ans. Simulation means to copy. It is away from real. It is another innovation in teacher education.

Simulation offers opportunities for compensating the trainee for lack of actual time spent in practice teaching.

Simulation is a "controlled representation of reality involving role-playing" and a simplified but minimally distorted reflection of class teaching."

Some other difinitions of simulated teaching and simulation are as under :

Webester's Dictionary, "Simulation is defined as giving the appearance of or effect of to have characteristics of."

Views of Fink, "Simulation is the controlled representation of reality.

Tansey's definition, "Simulation is the all—inclusive term which contains those activities which produce artificial environments or which provide artificial experiences for the participants in the activity. It is reproduction of the reality.

What Constitutes Simulated Teaching?

There are three important ingredients of simulated teaching :

1. Simulated teaching implies an analysis of teaching act and of the teaching learning situation from the point of view of the learner.
2. It is dependent upon empathetic understanding of the reality content on the part of participant, the practising teacher.
3. It is ploting of the real situation and capturing the essential which forms part of it.

Properties of Simulated Teaching

1. It is imaginative handling of the situation, playing the role and evaluating the utility of such an exercise in terms of fluency and facility shown in dealing with the actual class-room problems.

2. It is made up of the actual role playing operation by the teacher.

3. Evaluation of the effect of simulated teaching is the third property of simulated teaching. If the teaching behaviour does show some changes in the structuring devices of the practising teacher, it may be considered to be the effect of simulation practice.

Procedure of Simulated Teaching

It was developed by Cruick Shank in 1968. It is a teacher training system based on the technique of simulation. This could present the students will upto thirty one different simulated problems related to teaching. The aim of his 'Teaching Problem Laboratory' is for the participant to assume the role of the teacher and to practise solving the teaching problems he has identified.

Simulation technique is usually employed before sending the student teachers to actual teaching practice. Concrete examples of teaching problems and activities are presented in a structured way so that the student teachers are able to abstract the common general features from the specific examples.

According to Cruick Shank, there are three roles—1. The Teacher, 2. The Pupil, 3. The observer and three elements—Diagnosis, 2. Prescription, and 3. Evaluation in the Simulation Training Techniques.

Diagrammatical Representation of the Roles :

1 Pupils Diagnosis

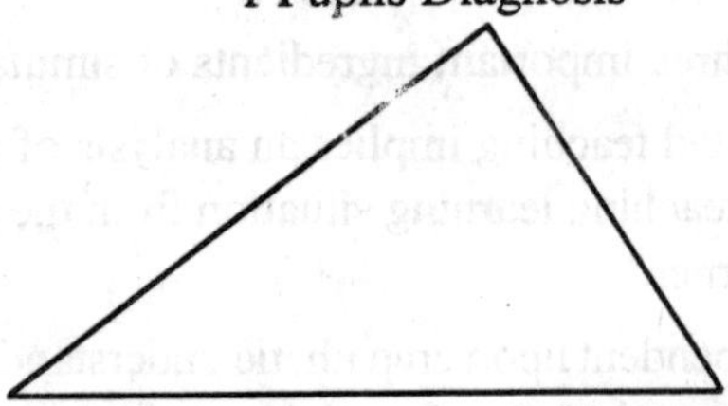

2 Teacher Prescription 3 Observer Evaluation

STEPS IN SIMULATED TEACHING

The following steps or procedure have been recommended in simulated teaching :

1. Selecting the Role of Players or Pupil Teachers. A small group of pupil-teachers is selected. They are assigned different letters in an alphabetic order such as A through D or E. The role assignments are rotated within the group to give chance to everyone. Thus, every member of the group gets an opportunity of playing the role.

2. Selecting and Discussing Skills. The skills to be practised are discussed and the topics that fit in the skills are suggested. One topic each is selected by the group members for exercise.

3. Deciding the Procedure of Evaluation. This step is undertaken to speculate the procedure of evaluation and deciding what kind of data and opinions can best be presented to the actor when the interaction stops.

4. Deciding Considerations. This refers to deciding who starts th conversation, who will intervene, who will stop the interaction and when it will be stopped and so on.

5. Prepared to Change the Procedure. Be prepared to change the procedure, change topics and move on to the next skill so as to present a significant challenge to each actor and to keep the interest to the maximum.

6. Conducting Practice Session. First practice session is conducted and the actor is provided with feedback on his performance. As soon as the practice sessions are working smoothly and each person has had an opportunity to be actor, the difficulty of the task should be increased.

Advantages of Simulated Teaching

The merits of simulated teaching are:

1. Simulated teaching is a like between theory and practice.
2. Simulated teaching is an innovation. It keeps one motivated and amused.
3. As a result of role playing, critical thinking is developed in the students.
4. The behaviour problems of the class are better understood.
5. New vistas for teaching and learning are opened.
6. Simulated teaching is a social laboratory. It leads to the development of social skills.

Demerits/Limitations of Simulated Teaching

1. Simulated teaching is away from reality. After all it is a copy of reality.
2. The feedback provided is not total but only the most likely feedback.
3. It requires a lot of preparation on the part of teachers.
4. It is a sheer waste of time.

Q. 23. Discuss the different styles of developing programme material.

Or

Explain the various Styles of Programming.

Ans. Modes of preparation of programmes are known as styles of programming. The advancement in the field of science and engineering have affected it in many ways. Various styles of programming have emerged. In 1950's B.F. Skinner developed a style which is known as Linear Programming. It was followed by another model namely 'Branching' given by Normal A. Crowder. In 1962 T.F. Gilbert developed a new system of programmed instruction which is known as Mathetics.

These Styles are—

(1) Linear of Extrinsic Programming.

(2) Branching or Intrinsic Programming.

(3) Mathetics.

Linear Programming. B.F. Skinner was the chief originator of this style. He was concerned with shaping and conditioning of behaviour. His view point was that every creature can be guided to a desired behaviour by means of a series of carefully structured small steps on the condition that each correct step is immediately reinforced by some kind of reward. For complex behaviour, each response becomes the stimulus for the next response.

A linear programme is called a straight line programme as the learner starts from his 'initial behaviour' to the 'terminal behaviour' in a straight line. The learner proceeds from one frame to the other till he completes the programme. Subject matter is broken down into very small steps and each step is presented in a proper sequence. The responses of the pupils are immediately reinforced in the succeeding frames. In each frame a small amount of information is provided. The pupils then will be required to make an active response, positive reinforcement or feedback is given and cuse or prompts are provided that increase the probability of correct responses and eliminate the chances of errors.

It is called 'Extr insic' because the learner has no choice of his own in following the path of learning. It is decided by the programmer extrinsically.

In this style of programming following steps are taken:

(a) The subject matter is presented in small steps or frame.

(b) The student is required to make response to one frame at a time and receive immediate confirmation (feedback) to his answer before proceeding to the next frame.

(c) There is self-pacing among different learners.

(d) The learner compares the constructed answer with the correct answer provided immediately there after.

Format of linear Programme is as follows :

Frame 1................

Response...............

Frame 2................

Response...............

Frame 3................

Response...............

Frame 1 → Frame 2 → Frame 3 → Frame 4

Entry behaviour—path of learning—Terminal Behaviour.

The response is made within the instructional sequence. The correct answer is found by the side of the next or succeeding frame. The answer is carried over until the learner is ready to proceed to this item.

The author of linear programme tried to make each successive step small enough to avoid student error. If the student does error, he is merely exposed to the desired answer and no other action is taken to correct his response. As the steps are small, a linear programme typically moves slowly in progressive manner towards its goal.

Skip Linear. This is the same as the basic method but at certain points in the programme, the learner is given a test question(s). If his response is correct he goes further to another part of the programme, skipping or jumping a few frames. If 'not' he goes through the normal sequence in order to obtain further piece of information.

Characteristics of Linear Programming

Characteristics of Linear Programming are as follows:

- Linear Programme is a single track programme or straight line programme.
- It consists of small steps.
- In this programme every learner follows the same path.
- Learner has to respond actively to each frame.
- In it the responses of the learner get immediate reinforcement.
- In this programme one can learn according to one's own speed.
- In it programmer controls the response of the learner.

Branching Programming

Branching Programming was developed by Norman A. Crowder. It is an improvement over linear programming. In this progarmming the student proceeds to the next frame, until he makes an error. The error branches him to supplementary material designed to give him remedial instruction. This can be achieved by giving the students some information, and asking a multiple choice question and then providing a different response for each answer chosen. Thus, the students proceed through a programme along different routes or branches. This type of programme is called branching programme.

Branching programming is represented as follows:

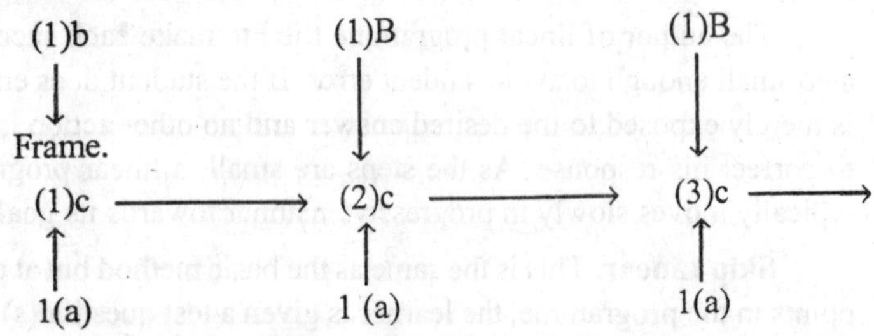

For response three alternative a,b,c have been given at the first frame. It the learner selects I(c) alternative he can go straight but if he goes for (1a) or (1b) he has to follow the instructions, only then he can move onwards.

Here the learner is independent to choose any alternative that is why if is also called intrinsic programming. Here all the learners do not follow the same path.

In other words we can say that in this style each frame is of bigger size and contains two or three choices. This programming employs multiple choice type of questions. The student is required to choose the one right answer out of the choices. If the student selects the correct answer, he is taken to the next frame in the main teaching sequence. If this response if wrong, he is taken to a remedial frame where his mistake is explained. The topic under consideration is further explained with the help of examples. After remedial work he is directed to the original frame for making new attempt. According to the alternative selected, the pupil is asked to proceed to a particular page.

Assumptions of Branching Programme

This programme is based on the following assumptions:

(a) Multiple choice items help more in the learning process.

(b) The learner learns better if matter is presented in totality.

(c) It is based on the possibility of detecting and correcting errors.

(d) By his ability the learner controls the exact sequence.

Characteristics/Merits of Branching Programming

(a) It is helpful in the development of the power of discrimination.

(b) It helps in practising creativity.

(c) It gives training in problem solving.

(d) The large size of frames maintain the interest of the students. The programmer may further enrich his style an expand his ideas.

(e) The students come to know about their mistakes.

(f) Big size of frame reduces unnecessary repetition and responding.

(g) The programmed material in this style may be employed in the form of programmed test or teaching machines.

MATHETICS PROGRAMMING

Thomas Gilbert originated this concept in 1962. The word 'Mathetics' has been derived from the Greek word 'Mathein' which means to learn. Mathetics is defined as, "The systematic application of reinforcement theory to the analysis and construction of complex representories which represent the mastery of subject matter.

'Gilbert's main interest lies in building a system that guarantees effective teaching. For this purpose he has used only those aspects of reinforcement theory which he found suitable for building the technique of teaching.

It is eclectice in nature and unique in application. It analyses the deficiencies and tries to make it up. As a technique of teaching, it may be applied to any subject but it is more suitable for teaching of skills. It is a complete training system that gives the programmer—

A guide for determining what to teach.

A basis for making teaching strategy decisions.

A detailed procedure for constructing a programme.

It uses backward chaining as a method of teaching. It is also known as retrogressive chaining. In this programming an exercise is the technical unit of learning instead of a frame of linear type.

In this programming the pupil learns the last step first, then he goes to the next one before it and thus to the introductory step. This system where the tasks are connected from the last to the first is called chaining.

There are three steps in designing a mathetics programme.

– Demonstration.

– Prompt.

– Release.

Example of Mathetics Programme

1. To find the square of any two digit number ending in 5.

(i) Multiply the first digit number by the next higher consecutive number.

(ii) Write 25 to the right of result (No. Response required). Programme.

Page 2

2, To find the square of 35.

(i) Multiply first digit (3) by the next consecutive number (4), $3 \times 4 = 12$.

(ii) Write 25 to the right of the result 12 = 1225 (no response required.)

Programme 3

3. To find the square of 55.

(i) Multiply the first digit (5) by the next higher consecutive number.

(ii) Write . . 25. . .to the right of the result.

(iii) The square of 55 is . . . .

Ans. Write 25, $6 \times 5 = 30$

The square of 55 is 3025.

Merits/Features of Mathetics Programming

1. It is a complete training system that guides the trainer to describe mastery of skills and knowledge to be acquired.
2. It clearly identifies the task operations involved and gives the student exercises to perform those operations.
3. It is a scientific teachnique of programme construction and is the systematic application of concepts and rules.
4. It is prescriptive rather than descriptive process.
5. It is a job-oriented technique.
6. It uses the principle of motivation in task analysis.
7. It emphasises on the student success, mastery, learning which means that the student is constantly motivated and reinforced by the consequences of mastering the knowledge.

Q. 24. Write note on Development phase of Programme writing.

Or

Write down the evaluative phases of programme.

Ans. DEVELOPMENT PHASE OF PROGRAMME WRITING

The writing of the programme involves the following steps :

Writing the Draft Frames. The progammer should have a clear idea about the programme to be taught to the pupils. First he analyses the subject matter and then the frames are writien in a sequence. Easy and simple frames should be placed in the beginning and complex frames should follow later.

To help learners to proceed correctly and with minimum error rate from one frame to the next, programmer has to make use of priming and prompting. In priming, information is poured into the minds of the learners for facilitating active responding, whereas in prompting, some help in the form of an additional stimulus is provided.

Sequencing of Frames

For sequencing, the frames are to be arranged in a systematic order (remembering the logical and phychological principles) to lead a learner from his entry behaviour to terminal behaviour. Three approaches are followed for sequencing frames which are as follows :

(a) Matrix Approach. A matrix is prepared in the shape of table; on one axis, the major concpets and sub-concepts are placed and to the other axis, the frames of the programme that lead to the behavioural changes in learner, are placed.

(b) Ruleg Approach. In this approach the frames which present the rules are placed earlier in sequence followed by frames that illustrate examples. This approach is followed by deductive reasoning logic for sequencing frames.

(c) Egrule Approach. In this approach frames representing examples are placed earlier followed by frames that depict the rule. This approach is followed by inductive reasoning logic for sequencing frames.

Editing of the Programme

The draft of the programme developed in the form of frames is subjected to a thorough review and editing process.

— Editing is done at the following levels.

— For technical accuracy, editing and to remove inaccuracies of the programme, help of the subject expert should be taken.

— With respect to designing and sequencing of frames, style and format of programming help of the educational technology expert should to taken.

— Assistance is taken of some language experts to remove inaccuracies in language especially with respect to spelling, grammer and punctuation etc.

Evaluative Phase

This is the last phase of the development of programmed instruction material, where activities are undertaken to test effectiveness of the programme and in the light of results proper modifications and improvements are brought about. The activities undertaken in this phase are as follows:

Individual Try-out. In the individual try-out, the programme is administered on a few learners one at a time. In practice the learner is presented with the material of the frames one by one and asked to write down his responses on a separate sheet of paper and then tally them with the correct responses written on the back page of the frames. Here the informal face to face contact with a single learner at a time provides a valuable opportunity to the programmer to study the reactions of the learner regarding the difficulties faced and inadequacies of the programme. Thus, the draft of the programme is improved on the basis of the result of the individual try-out.

Small Group Try-out. The modified draft is next try-out on a small group of learners. Again each learner is provided with a sheet of paper to record his responses and suggestions for modification. Time taken in completing the programme is also carefully noted. Pre-tesat and post-test are conducted. The differences in the attainment scores of pre-test and post-test ar employed to ascertain the effectiveness of the programme.

Field Try-out. On the basis of the finding to a small group try-out, the programmer does a field try-out in order to test the validity of the programmed instructional material in real setting. It differs from the above two try-outs in that the field try-out is undertaken by teachers with real students in a school. Otherwise, the method of try-out is similar. Pre-test and post-test are administered to the students and the scores are analysed to determine effectiveness of the programme. Suggestions and responses of students to each frame are noted and incorporated to improve the programmed material.

Validation of the Programme

Finally, the programme has to be validated in the natural conditions of its use. Following tools are helpful in validating a programme.

(a) Criterion Test. This test helps to determine the extent to which objectives have been realized.

(b) Gain Ratio. The effectiveness of a programme can properly be measured with the help of a concept known as gain ratio. It is defined as the ratio between the amount learned and the amount that could possibly be learned. The gain ratio can be computed with the help of the following formule :

$$\text{Gain Ratio} = \frac{\text{Mean of (Post - test scores minus Pre - test Scores)}}{\text{Mean of (Total scores of Post - test minus pre - test scores)}}.$$

Q. 25. Define the meaning of Guidance and its nature.

Ans. In order to understand the meaning of guidance, it is to be accepted that the focal point of guidance is 'an individual, not his problem'. From this point of view, before starting guidance, the potentialities and abilities of the individual are studied. Then that individual is made capable of solving his problems. This is known as an act of guidance. In this way, guidance is a process of all-round development. Hence, we can say that the guidance is that process which makes an individual aware of those methods for knowing his natural powers.

Jones, Stefflre and Stewart have defined guidance as "the help given by one person to another in making choices and adjustments and in solving problems."

"Guidance is a continuous process of helping the individual to develop to the maximum of his capacity in the direction, most beneficial to himself and to society."

Guidance is not a direction. It is also not imposition of one's ideas on others. Guidance is not making decision for others. Decision should be made by an individual himself. To carry over the bruden of an individual is also not guidance. In such situations, to what we can call guidance? Keeping in view these ideas, the definition suggested by Crow and Crow bears very comprehensive meaning :

"Guidance is assistance made available by competent counsellor to an individual of any age to help him direct his life, develop his own point of view, make his own decisions and carry his own burden."

In the context of dynamic interpersonal relationships, Carter V. Good has said in Dictionary of Education (1959), while defining guidance, "Guidance is a process of dynamic interpersonal relationships designed to influence the attitudes and subsequent behaviour of person."

Knapp has given the definition of guidance as "Learning about the individual student, helping to understand himself, effect changes in him and his environment which will help him to grow and develop as much as possible."

G.E. Smith, by considering the group of various services for helping an individual, has defined guidance as, "the process consists of a group of services to individuals to assist them in securing the knowledge and skills needed in making adequate choices, plans and interpretations essential to satisfactory in varieties of areas.

"Guidance is a help to the students in making the best possible adjustment to the situations in the educational institutions and in the home and at the same time facilitates the development of all aspects of the personality."

According to Skinner, "Guidance is a process of helping young persons learn to adjust to self, to others and to circumstances."

NATURE OF GUIDANCE

We familiarize ourselves with the following characteristics after analyzing the various definitions of guidance. This analysis also throws light on the nature of guidance.

(1) As a Process. Guidance does not occupy independent place. The chief aim of this process is to assist in the development of an individual keeping in view the social needs.

(2) A Continuous Process. Guidance is a process. Here, it is important to point out that the process of guidance never ceases. It remains dynamic. In this process, an individual understands himself, learns to use maximum his own capacities, interests and other abilities. He continues his struggle for adjustment in different situations. He develops his capacity of decision-making. Hence, we see that it is a non-stop process.

(3) Related with Life. The process of guidance is related to life. This guidance contributes formally or informally to life because life experiences both formal and informal occasions. A person gets informal guidance from his friends and relatives while formal guidance is sought from organised school guidance services and other organised guidance services.

(4) Development of Capacities. During the process of guidance the individual is assisted in such a way that he makes himself enabled to develop his capacities maximum from all angles. Hence, guidance stresses the complete development of possibilities present in an individual. An individual becomes familiar with his real image. Hence, guidance is helpful in self-realization.

(5) Individual Assistance. Guidance is accepted as individualized help. Through guidance an individuals personal development is provided a direction and not to a group. Hence, it is process of individualized assistance.

(6) Task of Trained Persons. Providing guidance is not the function of all persons because various techniques and skills are to be used in it. Everybody does not possess the knowledge of the same. For this task, trained persons psychologists and counsellors are required. Hence, guidance is a skill-involved process.

(7) Wide Scope of Guidance. The scope of guidance is too wide. Any needy person can be guided. This can include the persons of different age, different interests, various characteristics and persons of different nature. Hence, we cannot draw boundaries around the process of guidance.

(8) Helpful in Adjustment. Guidance helps th person in his adjustment in different situations. This process allows to learn to adjust with different types of problems. In this way, the main characteristic of the nature of the guidance is to provide new energy to the demoralized person by adjusting himself in the problematic situation through the process of guidance.

(9) Helpful in Developing the Ability of Self-Guidance. The nature of guidance also includes the characteristic of developing self-guidance in a person with the help of guidance process. This enables him in achieving self-dependence by searching out the solution of problems of life.

(10) No Imposition of One's View Point. It is also the main characteristic of guidance not to impose one's view-point on others. It depends upon the wish of an individual how he acquiries benefit by accepting the decision of the guidance worker. If he wishes, he may deny to accept such decisions of the guidance workers. Hence, it is not a process of imposing the decisions.

(11) Helpful in Preparing for Future. The process of guidance is helpful in preparing a person for his future. Hence, a person can succeed in preparing himself for future activities. In this way, guidance is a well-wisher of an individual's future.

Q. 26. Define the objectives of Guidance at different stages.

Ans. OBJECTIVES OF GUIDANCE

Guidance process is purposeful process. Without determining the objectives, this process cannot be completed or concluded. Due to the variations in the scope, guidance has a variety of objectives. If we start guidance process without any objective it cannot be concluded because various sub-processes involved in the guidance cannot be given any direction and these activities ramain meaningless.

Objectives of guidance change at each level of education. Every stage of education enjoys different objective of guidance. For example, the functions and objectives of guidance at primary level will be different from those of middle stage. Similary, objectives of guidance at high school or higher secondary stage will be different from those of middle stage :

(1) Objectives of Guidance at Primary Stage. Every activity at primary stage includes guidance. At primary stage, there is need to pay special attention towards the health of the children. At this stage there is great need to coordinate the functions of a teacher, guidance worker, school, staff members of medical service and school social service workers. All these persons help in learning properly essential skills for primary education, for acquiring basic knowledge, for adapting according to the social traditions and for developing proper attitude towards school activities. These too are the objectives of guidance at this stage.

When a child leaves home and enters into the school environment, he has to make many coordinations. School environment is very comprehensive for a child. In school, the child comes in contact with various types of persons, children and teachers. Also he lacks security in the school and he becomes very fearful, hesitating and remains suppressed in the school. Those children are more in difficulty who are fully dependent on their parents.

Primary stage ranges upto fifth class. During this period, children make their place in the school. Gradually they get themselves established in the school and they consider themselves an honourable member of the school. When these children cross over from primary stage to higher stage, they feel suffocated. Behaviours of primary stage sometimes look like a joke. The traditions of new school, rules, administration, curriculum etc., are all new. In such situations, the guidance worker plans the guidance programme in order to prepare the children of primary stage, for next higher school stage, such as arranging the visits of primary stage children to high schools, inviting high school teachers to primary schools, explaining the procedure for getting admission to high schools after leaving the primary schools, making them familiar with the curriculum of high schools etc.

In nut-shell we can say that the following are the objectives of guidance at the primary school stage:

1. To coordinate all the activities of all the workers such as a teacher, medical service staff members, school social-workers and the activities of a person providing guidance etc.

2. To assist developing higher attitude towards school activities.
3. To assist children adapting according to the school traditions and rules-regulations of the school.
4. To assist children in developing their physical and emotional stability.
5. Objective of finding out problems regarding adjustment in the school and to control them.
6. Objective of making children self-dependent.
7. Objective of creating the feeling of cooperation in the children.
8. Objectives of making children ready for crossing over from primary school to next higher stage.
9. Objective of supplying various informations to children regarding higher stage such as curriculum of next higher classes and distribution of booklets regarding various school functions among the children and their parents.

(2) Objectives of Guidance at Secondary Stage. The child leaves primary stage and enters secondary stage. At this stage the scope of guidance becomes more comprehensive as compared to the scope of guidance at primary stage. At this stage, guidance becomes more important as a result of multiple reasons. At this stage, teachers too teach according to the subjects. Therefore, all the children cannot contact all the teachers. At high and higher secondary schools, only subject specialists teach. At these stages, personal, social and vocational problems of the children come into light and solution of these problems is necessary. In order to achieve this objective, a comprehensive and organized guidance service is continuously required.

In this way, we see the following are the objectives of guidance at secondary and higher secondary stages:

(i) Objective of familiarizing with New School Life. A child is not familiar with the life of new school when he leaves the primary school and enters to a new higher school. He has to face a number of problems regarding admission. Also, it may become difficult for him to coordinate with new classmates and new friends. Hence, the objective of guidance service existing in the school should be to eliminate such problems of the pupils.

(ii) Objectives of Helping in Selecting the Subject. After reaching at this higher level, the selection of subject becomes necessary. In this task, the pupil may face difficulty. He is unable to understand in which subject he is competent and which subject he should not opt. The selection of subjects has become very difficult task due to the variety of subjects. Hence, the objective of guidance should be to understand this type of problem and the same should be solved.

(iii) Objective of Co-curricular Activities. Co-curricular activities are being considered very important for the physical development of the children, such as debates, sports, cultural activities, programmes of social service etc. Hence, the important objective of guidance services is to guide the children for such activities so that their physical development may be given proper direction.

(iv) Objective of Fulfilling the Needs, related to Students Health. The objectives of guidance service existing in the school is to take care of needs related to the health of the children and to inform timely the relevant persons regarding those health deficiencies so that the necessary action can be taken.

(v) Objective of Maintaining the Records. In schools it is important to maintain the records regarding the development of the pupils, education, psychological development, cultural activities, because the entire guidance programme is to be conducted on the basis of these records. Hence, the objective of guidance programme workers should be to maintain such record so that the counsellor may feel convenience during counselling.

(vi) Objective of Emotional and Individual Needs. When an individual enters adolescence, an individual experiences emotional and personal needs. Therefore, the objective of guidance services should be to solve the problems related to such needs.

(vii) Objective of Cooperation. In solving the problems of the children, cooperation plays an important role. This cooperation is desirable in guidance at all levels. The objective of guidance services should be to create a feeling of cooperation among all the workers involved in this service. This cooperation acts as a substantial base for guidance at the next higher level.

(viii) Objective of Creating Environment. According to Crow and Crow, the creation of academic environment in accordance with the adolescent stage is very essential so that the pupils may be motivated in order to acquire higher education and they may be helped in selecting the subject according to abilities.

(3) Objectives at College and University Stage. When a child enters the college he becomes a complete young man and his personality acquires has own pattern. Some of them have clear objectives. Some start feeling their responsibilities. They are also very serious in their studies because they know the meaning of success and failure. But there are some persons who fail to understand what the college education means. They come to college without knowing what they can do. After securing admission to the college they face multiple difficulties. They consider their studies meaningless. That is why they go to college without any objective.

In such situations, the objective of college guidance programme is that the needs of such students should be looked into immediately who are unable to make progress in the college affairs and who can use their telent in their activities on providing proper educational facilities.

In college, the objective of guidance service should also be to help the pupils in selecting the subject so that they can acquire specialization because such specializations help the pupils in their future vocational plans.

Similarly other objectives of guidance service include organized programmes of tutorials and providing help to the pupils for making progress by studying the books existing in the library. It would be very meaningful if the students are made aware of objectives, nature and scope of college educations before its commencement in the college. According to other objectives of guidance service, the pupils should be informed regarding the various facilities existing in the college such as library facilities. If such is not informed, it would lead towards the wastage of pupil's time.

In this way, we see that there is no much difference between the functions and guidance objectives of high, higher secondary and college stage. Hence, the guidance objectives at college and university stage can also be presented in the following manner:

(i) To make available informations regarding admissions to college and university.

(ii) To provide informations regarding co-curricular activities in the college and university.

(iii) To help pupils selecting subjects so that they may achieve their future programme and objectives.

(iv) To provide vocational informations to the pupils so that they may take decision regarding their future.

(v) To arrange for testing the pupils.

(vi) The help the children eliminating their financial difficulties.

(vii) To make aware the pupils regarding the existing hostel facilities so that the problems of their boarding and lodging can be removed.

The objectives of guidance can also be expressed as follows:

(a) Objectives from pupils' point of view.

(b) From institution's point of view.

Q. 27. Define Counselling, its characteristics and basic principles.

Ans. The scholars have exhibited variations in their view-points regarding defining the term "counselling". One major cause of these variations is—occurrence of historical changes in the perceptions of the persons. Inspite of this, there was a lot of variation in the philosophy of experts.

According to Shostorm and Brammer (1952), "Counselling is a purposeful reciprocal relationship between two people in which one a trained person, helps the other to change himself or his environment."

According to Wrenn (1951), "Counselling is a dynamic and purposeful relationship between the people in which procedures vary with the nature of the students' need, but in which there is always mutual participation by the counsellor and the student with the focus upon self-classification and self-determination by the students."

Ruth Strang, emphasizing mutual relationshps of persons, has said, "Counselling is a face-to-face relationship in which growth takes place in the counsellor as well as the counsellee."

Wolberg (1954), has considered counselling as a form of interview. He has defined it as, "Counselling is a form a interviewing in which the client is helped to understand himself more completely in order to correct an environment or adjustment difficulty."

Myers has written as, "Counselling means a relationship between two persons in which one person provides special assistance to the other."

Rogers says about counselling that, "Counselling does not mean providing a service by means of which specific problem of an individual may be solved. The process should help the counsellee in gaining claer insight into the problem and in achieving the self-confidence."

Considering counselling as a problem-solving effort, Hamrin and Erickson have said that, "Counselling is an attempt made by the counsellee to think through and solve the problem that confronts him. It is an experiment in cooperative thinking, who two individuals (the counsellor and the counsellee) srtike to solve a problem."

Considering counselling as a mutual learning process, Willy and Andrew have said, "Counselling is a mutual learning process involving two individuals—one seeking help and the other a professionally trained person helping the first to orient and direct himself towards a goal which leads to his maximum development and growth in his environment."

CHARACTERISTICS OF COUNSELLING

The following facts become distinct about counselling after studying and analysing the above mentioned definitions:

1. Counselling is a conversation with some one regarding some problem.
2. Nromally, not always, one of the two persons possesses facts or experiences or abilities which the other lacks.

3. In the process of counselling, the problem is made clear through discussion. The counsellor explores the problem and its importance through his skilful questioning.
4. Counsellor draws out the facts from the pupils through counselling process.
5. Counselling helps the pupil in making selections and following those selections.
6. Counselling is an assistance to the persons in their behaviour related problems in which their emotions and motivations are main.
7. Counselling involves interactions in which the counsellor accepts the responsibility of positive contribution in the development of other person's personality.
8. He also informs the pupils certain facts.
9. Counsellor guides the pupils to establish contacts with various factors in the counselling process. He explains the importance of those facts which the pupils consider unimportant.
10. Counselling is a vital part of the entire guidance programme.
11. Counselling is only one aspect of guidance.
12. Counselling is a learning oriented process.
13. Counselling is a face to face relationship with a person. This' relationship is between a counsellor and a client.
14. Counselling is democratic. It lays down the democratic system. The client can behave as he wishes.
15. Counselling is a professional service.
16. Counselling is problem-oriented.
17. Counselling is based on the appropriateness of counsellor's prediction.
18. Best counselling is in the form of the decision made by the counsellee.
19. Counselling is possible in humorous and cooperative environment only.

(20) Counselling is completely based on self-guidance.

BASIC PRINCIPLES OF COUNSELLING PROCESS

According to Mc Daniel and Shaftal, the counselling process is based on some basic principles:

(a) Principle of Acceptance. According to this principle, each client must the accepted as an individual and dealt with as such. The counsellor should give, due regard to the rights of the client.

(b) Principle of Permissiveness. Counselling is such a relationship which develops optimism and the environment shapes according to the person. All the thoughts accept the relative relationship of counselling.

(c) Principle of Respect for the Individual. All the schools of thoughts of counselling advocate for the respect of the individual *i.e.*, respecting an individual's feelings must be an integral part of counselling process.

(d) Principle of Thinking with the Individual. Counselling emphasizes thinking with the individual. It is essential to differentiate think for whom? And 'why to think'? It is the role of the counsellor the think about all the forces around the client to join client's thought—process and to work collectively with the client regarding his problem.

(e) Principle of Learning. All the assumptions of counselling accept the presence of learning-elements in the counselling process.

(f) Principle of Consistency with Ideals of Democracy. All the principles are associated with ideals of democracy. The ideals of democracy desire to accept a person and want to respect the rights of others. The process of counselling is based upon the ideals of a person's respect. It is a process with accepts individual differences.

Q. 28. Discuss the Directive or Prescriptive Counselling, its basic assumption, steps, Advantages and Disadvantages.

Ans. Directive or Counsellor-Centred or Prescriptive Counselling. Counseller-centred counselling revolves around the counsellor. He tries to establish good relations through the friendship and assistance. In this, the counsellor is very active and he expresses his ideas and attitudes independently. He evaluates the expressions of the client. According to this view-point the counselling leads the interview. In this, the counsellor asks a series of standardized questions. Each question carries a short answer. The counsellor does not allow the development of client's expression and feelings. He leads as an expert, evaluates and gives suggestion or advice.

The chief advocate of this school is E.G. Williamson of the University of Minnesota. Hence, according to this school of thought, the counsellor owns entire responsibility of solving client's problem. In this procedure, the counsellor explores the problem and defines it, diagnoses it and tell about the remedy of the problem.

BASIC ASSUMPTIONS OF DIRECTIVE COUNSELLING

According to Andrews and Willy, the following can be the basic assumptions of directive counselling:

(i) Counselling as an Intellectual Process. Any client's intellectual capability is not destroyed as a result of his mal-adjustment. Hence, counselling is primarily an intellectual process. It stresses upon the intellectual aspects of a person instead of his emotional aspects of the personality.

(ii) Competency in Giving Advice. The counsellor possesses the best training experience and informations. He is more competent to provide an advice to solve the problem.

(iii) Counselling Objectives as Problem Solving Situation. The objectives of counselling are achieved through problem solving situation.

(iv) Client's Incapability of Solving the Process. The counsellor assumes that the client does not possess the capability for solving the problem always.

Hence, we observe that the direct and explanatory methods are suggested. In such a counselling focus should be on the problem instead of the person and the client should cooperate in the entire process. The client is to act under the counsellor, not along with him.

STEPS IN DIRECTIVE COUNSELLING

Williamson has described the following six steps of directive counselling:

(i) Analysis. In this steps, data and informations are collected regarding the situation or the client which can be used in the counselling process as a valid and reliable base. For this counselling step, the following tools are used:

(a) Cumulative records.

(b) Interview.

(c) Time distribution form.

(d) Autobiography.

(e) Anecdotal record.

(f) Psychological tests.

For the integration of entire data, case-history method is used. It includes family-history, recreational interests and habits etc.

(ii) Diagnosis. Diagnosis consists of the interpretations of the data in terms of the problems indicated and assets and liabilities, the strengths and weaknesses of the students.

Diagnosis has the following main three stepes:

(a) Identification of Problem.

(b) Discovering the cuase.

(c) Prognosis.

(iii) Synthesis. Williamson has defined synthesis as—"The process of summarizing and organizing of the data from the analysis in such a manner as to reveal the student's assets, liabilities, adjustments and mal-adjustments."

(iv) Prognosis. This step can be a part of diagnosis and can be a separate step too. It depends upon the available specfic information. Where the result of the problem or knowledge of the situation occurs then the prognosis becomes the part of the diagnosis. Both, prognosis and diagnosis are cooperative processes in between the counsellor and the client.

(v) Follow-up. In this step, the evaluation of the effectiveness of the counselling procedure is done and in this, it is observed what the client could achieve through counselling?

(vi) Counselling or Treatment. It is that step when the counsellor helps the client. In this, various questions are answered. Client answers these questions for himself, such as, How I can make changes in self? What can be its alternate? If such goes on, how the progress will occur in future?

ADVANTAGES OF DIRECTIVE COUNSELLING

1. This method is useful from the time-consumption view-point. It saves a lot of time.
2. In this type of counselling, there is more focus on the problem and less on the person.
3. Counselling focuses more on the intellectual aspect of the person than his emotional aspect of the personality.
4. The counsellor can look the client directly.
5. In this process, the counsellor becomes readily available to help the client which makes the client very happy.

DISADVANTAGES OF DIRECTIVE COUNSELLING

1. In this process the client is more dependent. He is also unable to solve the new problems of mal-adjustment.
2. As the client is never independent of the counsellor, it is not an effective and best guidance.
3. Unless and until a person does not develop some attitudes through experiences he cannot make any decision himself. This type of guidance always lacks such experience and development of attitudes.
4. The counsellor fails in saving the client to commit the mistakes in future.
5. There is scarcity of informations regarding the pupil which creates the possibility of wrong counselling.

Q. 29. Explain Non-directive or client-centred Counselling its basic assumption, steps, characteristics advantages and disadvantages.

Ans. Non-Directive or Client Centred or Permissive Counselling. The main advocate of non-directive or client-centred or premissive counselling is Carl R. Rogers. This principle was developed in many years. Hence, various areas got included in such type of counselling such as, the development of personality, group leadership, education and learning, creativity, interpersonal relations and the nature of an entirely active person. This theory was developed in between 1930 and 1940. This theory believes that the sufficient means of solving a person's problem are present within the person himself. The function of the counsellor is to provide such an environment in which the client is independent to grow so that he may become what he likes to become. This school of thought gives importance to the emotional aspects of vocational and emotional problems and disapproves the diagnostic information as a part of counselling process.

The client-centred counselling revolves around the client. In this, the client is encouraged to leadin conversation and to express his own attitudes, feelings and ideas. The counsellor mostly remains passive. He never interferes the client's ideas, thoughts, feeling, flow of expressions. The counsellor helps the client in completing his conversation, basically the counsellor makes his efforts to develop rapport and mutual feeling of confidence in both the parties.

In this approach, open-end questions are asked. These questions are loosely structured. In the answers of these questions, the person projects his own personality. The main concern of the counsellor is with the summarization of emotional contents told by the client.

When the client is answering, he should be encouraged to speak in detail through proper methods. The client feels that the counsellor really respects the client's ideas. He gets the impression from the types of questions which a counsellor asks from the client and the interviewer is taking interest in the client. The counsellor does not ask the questions merely to explore the facts. In the non-directive counselling, every person has the right to be independent as a specialist psychologist. In such type of counselling, diagnostic instruments are used either infrequently or completely not used.

BASIC ASSUMPTIONS OF NON-DIRECTIVE COUNSELLING

1. Tendency Towards Actualization. In the earlier writings of Rogers, it was emphasized that the person's or client's growth and developmental capacity is that person's characteristic on which the methods of counselling and psychotherapy depend. Even after so many years, his this opinion got strength that a persons' inherent tendency includes growth, adjustment, socialization; freedom etc.

This directional tendency is termed as 'Actualizing Tendency' these days.

2. Belief in the Dignity of Man. Rogers believes in the dignity of the man. He considers the person capable of taking decisions and he accepts his right to do so.

3. Man is Trustworthy—Rogers considers the person basically good and reliable. He also knows that the person behaves in an unreliable manner too. A person is born with some urges which must be controlled if healthy personality development is desired.

4. Man is Wiser than His Intellect. When some organization is functioning independently and effectively, then the 'awareness' is a very small part or component of the entire process. When the organization feels some difficulty in its system of functioning, this awareness becomes more sharpened and focussed.

Snyder has also mentioned the following assumptions of non-directive counselling:

(i) The client has right to select the goals of his life.
(ii) If the client is given an opportunity, he will select those goals which may possibly provide him great happiness.
(iii) Emotional disturbance inhibits a person's proper adjustment intially.
(iv) In the counselling situation, one should reach very quickly at a point from where the client may be able to start functioning independently.

STEPS IN NON-DIRECTIVE COUNSELLING

Carl Rogers has given the following steps of this non-directive counselling:

1. Defining the Problematic Situation. First of all the counsellor should define the problematic situation.

2. Free Expression of Feelings. After the first step, the client is made aware of the fact that he can express his feelings freely and the counsellor approves this.

3. Development of Insight. The counsellor goes on thinking regarding the client's new feelings along with the development of client's insight and he goes on classifying all those new feelings.

4. Classification of Positive and Negative Feelings. After the free expression of feelings by the client, the counsellor identifies his negative and positive feelings and he classifies them.

5. Termination of Counselling Situation. The counsellor looks for a point where he can terminate the counselling situation after all the above steps. According to this school of thought, either the client or the counsellor can suggest for such termination of counselling situation.

CHARACTERISTICS OF NON-DIRECTIVE COUNSELLING

1. It is a client-centred counselling.
2. It is based on the principle that a person has so much capacity and drive that he can grow and develop so that he may face the situations in reality.
3. In this school of thought, the counsellor is passive to the maximum.
4. Its use reduces psychological tensions.
5. In this type of counselling, defensiveness falls down.
6. In this type of counselling, there is closeness betwen the picture of the self-drawn by the client and a desirable or an ideal picture of his own.
7. Through this counselling his psychological adjustment improves.
8. Client's behaviour is considered more matured emotionally.
9. A person is accepted in his originality and he is free to express his any attitude.
10. In his research Axlines (1947) has shown that the reading improvement speeds up as a result of client-centred play way-methods in the primary schools even if special reading instructions are not given.
11. This school of thought is just reverse to that of directive counselling.
12. In this counselling, the entire responsibility is of client or the person.

DISADVANTAGES OF NON-DIRECTIVE COUNSELLING

1. This counselling is not so deep like psycho-analysis.
2. This counselling has a drawback of lack of permission for flexibility to the counsellor.
3. The client is allowed for the free expression of his present attitudes but it is not attempted to explain why these attitudes occur? There is no research regarding the past, no suggestion, no attempt of re-education.
4. It is a time-consuming process. Once the client strats his conversation, he does not cease to speak. This makes the other's turn for seeking counselling impossible.
5. This client-centred theory suffers the basic defect that it does not care how the behaviour is affected by the stimulus-situation and the nature of the environment.
6. The client cannot depend on his resources, decisions and intellect.
7. Many counselling situations do not arise successfully in this client-centred counselling.
8. All the problems cannot be solved orally or verbally or by talks only.
9. Sometimes, due to the counsellor's passiveness, the client hasitates in expressing his feelings.
10. It is not possible in all the schools because the counsellor has to attend many pupils.

ADVANTAGES OF NON-DIRECTIVE COUNSELLING

1. The development of the problem-solving ability in the client through this school of thought is definite.
2. Being client-centred school of thought, other unwanted activities and tasts can be avoided.
3. This type of counselling leaves its impressions for a longer period.
4. This school of thought shifts the person from his unconscious state of mind to the conscious state of mind and releases tension.

Q. 30. Discuss the basic considerations for organizing school guidance service.

Or

Discuss forms of organisation of Guidance services.

Ans. BASIC CONSIDERATIONS FOR ORGANIZING SCHOOL GUIDANCE SERVICE

In order to organize school guidance services, certain principles should essentially be followed. Jones has insisted not to separate guidance from the normal school life. According to him, this can be focussed in some specific part of the subject. It cannot be restricted to the office of the counsellor or a headmaster. Jones has assigned the responsibility of providing guidance to every teacher. In this exercise, co-operation of all is desirable. Hence, for organizing school guidance service, application of certain principles is must.

Humphery and Traxler, in their book entitled 'Guidance Services,' have mentioned some basic things for organizing school guidance service, which are as follows—

Defining the Objectives Clearly. The objectives of entire guidance programme should be clearly defined at the time of organizing school guidance service. While defining these objectives, the school ideals and needs of the pupils must be kept in mind.

Defining the Tasks. All the activities to be performed through the guidance programme must be enlisted beforehand.

Allocation of Duties. The success of the guidance programme depends upon the allocation of duties to the persons involved in this job in advance so that every person should have a clear idea what he is to perform. The allocation of these duties should be according to the abilities of the persons or workers.

Defining the Powers. The workers should be made aware of their powers just like their duties.

Defining the Relations. The relations of employees working in the guidance programme, whether full-time or part-time, must be defined clearly. Inspite of this, their relations should be defined in accordance with their guidance responsibilities with other employees.

Nature of Guidance Organization. It is proper to decide about the structure of school guidance service prior to its beginning such as number of its employees, finance, size etc. The basis of its composition should be the objectives of the institute, financial resources and the number of students in the school etc.

Simplicity. The organization of school guidance service should not be of complicated nature. The framework of its structure should remain simple as far as it is possible, because every person will start taking interest in such a simple framework of the organization.

Crow and Crow, in his book, has also suggested the following points to keep in mind before executing the plan of guidance programme:

(i) First of all it should be decided the number of persons to be involved in executing the guidance programme and the time required for the same.

(ii) How much increase in the workers' strength is required.

(iii) Is the building and the space are enough for conducting the various activities of guidance?

(iv) Which teachers are available to provide various proposed services?

(v) Do the parents too show interest in the guidance related planned programme and will they cooperate in this programme?

(vi) Are the teachers and other employees available in the school capable of devoting expected time and energy in the guidance programme?

(vii) Do the employees exhibit interest in the programme? If yes, to what extent?

(viii) What is the viewpoint of schools and the society regarding the expansion of guidance services?

(ix) To what extent other community agencies can be associated with the guidance programme?

(x) How the pupils can be motivated to understand for themselves the value of the guidance programme?

(xi) In which experience areas the pupils are required to serve?

(xii) Would the provision of finance in the school budget be possible?

FORMS OF ORGANISATION OF GUIDANCE SERVICES

The following can be the forms of organisation of guidance services:

1. The Centralised Form. The guidance work should be performed by the experts because the teachers are not trained in this guidance job.

The teachers cannot provide properly any assistance to the pupils who need the same to solve their problems. the central form of the guidance programme means conducting and controlling most of the guidance activities from the central guidance office. All the teachers also perform their duties according to the supervision of Central Guidance Bureau and its orders.

2. Decentralized Form. The decentralized form of the guidance means providing guidance as a responsibility of the teachers. The teacher remains in close contact with the pupils of his class. He understands the needs and problems properly of his pupils. Due to this reason the teacher can help the pupils in a better way. Some people also believe that if a separate department is opened for guidance in the school, the teacher will not show any interest in guidance work and also he will not consider guidance as his responsibility. Hence, it would be better if the responsibility of guidance work in schools lies with the teachers.

3. Mixed Form. The centralised and decentralised form of the guidance have their own merits and demerits. No form of guidance is practically possible independently. Hence, some experts express their views that the form of guidance programme should be mixed one. The mixed form means—guidance provided by the teachers and experts collectively. Crow and Crow also said, supporting the mixed form, that the school guidance programme includes the coordinated services of administrators, teachers, employees and social institutions etc. There are certain jobs in guidance programme which the teachers can do better, such as, collection of informations related to the pupils. There are certain jobs which can be done better with the help of experts.

The designs or forms of school guidance service organization can also be described in the following terminology:

(i) The Line Organisation.

(ii) The Staff Organisation.

(iii) Mixed Line and Staff Organisation.

In the line organisation, the employees are arranged in an order with regard to their duties or rights. The top position occupies by the administrative officer *i.e.*, head of the administration. There other assistant officers and the officers and employees working under them come in the sequence. Being head, the administrative officers supervises and examines the performance of other officers and employees.

The administrative officer controls both the line and staff organisation. The staff members deputed in certain areas have their definite responsibilities. The specialist employees play a special role in the process of guidance management and policy making even they work under the administrative officer.

The mixed form of line and staff organisation is known as 'line-staff mixed organisation'. Such organisations have the elements of both types of organisations. The provision of such form of the organisation is possible only in big institutions and occurs there.

PERSONS WORKING IN SCHOOL GUIDANCE SERVICES AND THEIR FUNCTIONS

As it has already been made clear that the guidance job is a specific task. To run this programme in schools, a specific category of staff members and officers is required. In the school guidance service organisation, the participation of the following persons is mainly involved:

1. Headmaster.
2. Class Teachers.
3. School Psychologist.
4. Counsellor.
5. School Doctor.
6. School Activities Coordinator.

7. Placement Officer.
8. School Psychoanalyst.
9. School Social Worker.
10. Child Welfare Worker.

Q. 31. Explain the characteristics of well-organised guidance programmes.

Ans. The following should be the characteristics of a well-organized guidance programme:

1. Child Centredness. The main characteristic of guidance programme should be its child centredness *i.e.*, the organisation of guidance services should be in accordance with the needs, interests of the children and objectives.

2. Specialisation. The role of specialists is very important in the organization of guidance services. Hence, for the success of guidance service, the presence of specialists in the guidance service is essential, such as the counsellor, psychologist, psycho-analyst, social worker of the school, doctor etc.

3. Continuity. Continuity of each guidance service is very essential. Continuity of problems occurs in the life of each person. Therefore, the continuity of these services is needed.

4. Coordination. There should be another characteristic of guidance service that it should maintain coordination between all the associate agencies and the community for the guidance of youth for a longer period.

5. Cooperation. The characteristic of a good guidance service organisation is that it should seek the cooperation of the parents. The guidance service can be made better by seeking the interest and cooperation of each staff member.

6. Budgetary Provisions. Budgetary provisions are also necessary to make the guidance service better. Budgetary provisions are made before starting the programme.

7. Proper Information and Record. The superiority of the services also depends upon the proper information and record. The guidance service should be used to collect the informations about educational and vocational needs and tests and to record them.

8. Guidance for All. The principle of guidance for all is followed in a good guidance service. In a democratic country each pupil has a right to get guidance. In school, all the pupils should be provided with guidance.

9. Confidential. It is very important to maintain confidentiality of the collected informations for the guidance in guidance service so that the confidence of the pupils on the guidance workers may be maintained. After winning the confidence of the pupils, true informations about them can be collected. Only the counsellor should have access to the confidential informations.

10. Opportunity for Final Decision to the Client. In a good guidance programme, the opportunity for final decision should be provided to the client. There should be no compulsion on them.

11. Sufficient Time for Guidance. The guidance workers should be allotted sufficient time to provide successful guidance in the guidance service, such as time for testing and time for counselling. In time-table too, the sufficient time should be allotted for guidance.

12. Selection of Guidance Workers. For a good guidance programme, the guidance workers should be selected on the basis of their abilities, training and experiences. It is not possible to perform all the duties related to guidance by the teacher alone. Hence, for specific duties in guidance, persons with special abilities in guidance are needed to be appointed.

13. Use of Various Methods. It is not possible to apply a single method for collecting informations meant for guidance. Also, it is not proper to use single method for the same purpose. Only one method cannot collect reliable informations. It is essential to apply various methods on one person at the different occasions and in different situations. It increases the reliability of the programme.

14. Finding Solution. The utility of guidance service increases when it is organised for finding the causes of the problems. These problems should not be allowed to arise and preparation should be made to solve them if the same arise.

15. Simplicity. If the guidance programme is simple, it will be interesting and successful. In such simple programmes, all the persons show more interest.

16. Providing Opportunities for Acquiring Abilities. The opportunities should be provided to the guidance of workers and other persons associated with such programme to increase their abilities. It is essential because new methods are innovated in the field of guidance every year and old methods are modified and improved. Every year new tests are constructed. The guidance worker should be given an opportunity to remain in-touch with all these modifications or changes.

17. Responsibilities According to Abilities. A good guidance organisation is that where all the persons are assigned their responsibilities according to their abilities and capacities. If they are not assigned the responsibilities according to their abilities, then the success of the entire guidance programme cannot be expected. However, the client can experience some harm.

Hence, we see that the above characteristics are responsible for the success of guidance service in an organisation.

Q. 32. Discuss the types of Guidance.

Or

Write briefly about Educational Guidance, Vocational Guidance and Personal Guidance.

Ans.

EDUCATIONAL GUIDANCE

The most important type of the various types of guidance is educational guidance. Educational guidance is directly concerned with the pupil. In the student life, educational guidance is very important. The chief aim of educational guidance is to develop the ability of coordinating with the school environment in the pupils and to create necessary awareness and sensitivity so that they may select themselves proper learning objectives, devices and situations. If we study and analyse Indian conditions, then we shall find the educational guidance is more needed in Indian conditions. Therefore, guidance is considered an integral part of education because educational guidance is viewed in the context of child's growth.

According to Jones, educational guidance is concerned with that assistance to be provided to the pupils which is expected for their adjustments in the schools, selection of curricula and school-life.

Four Main Functions of Educational Guidance

(i) To plan education according to the capacity, interest and resources of the pupil.

(ii) To collect information regarding the future possibilities of the pupils.

(iii) To be helpful for necessary progress in educational programme.

(iv) To fulfil the needs of the pupils.

Myers has also described educational guidance as a process of creating favourable conditions for the pupil's development or education. From this point of view, educational guidance is required at each level during the pupil's education. For example, educational guidance at primary level, secondary level, at higher secondary level and at college level. Psychological research has also proved that the educational guidance must be given to the pupils at each level. In order to study educational guidance, we shall have to go through its various aspects. Various aspects of educational guidance have been described in detail in the next units.

VOCATIONAL GUIDANCE

Vocational guidance is not a mere technical process by which a person can be fitted in some vocation. Also he is not born for some vocation. The persons having normal intelligence can be adjusted in various vocations. In vocational guidance, a person is evaluated with regard to his capacities, capabilities and the changed conditions in the vocational areas and needs. In the vocational guidance the help is included in order to solve various problems related to the selection of a vocation, which is provided keeping in view the expected capabilities.

According to Super too, the main aim of vocational guidance is to enable a person for coordination with his vocation, he can use his energies properly and can develop the society financially by the existing facilities.

Crow and Crow have also given the objectives of vocational guidance. The process of vocational guidance is organised by keeping in view these objectives. In the process of vocational guidance, vocational charts, vocational information booklets, talks can provide information to the pupils relating to the vocations.

In nut-shell, we can say that vocational guidance helps the persons to adjust in the various vocations. The function of guidance is not only to help in selecting the proper vocation, but also to help in placement and progress. If all the persons possess same powers and abilities, then no guidance is required for various guidance processes. Hence, in all the vocations, same abilities are not required. Every vocation has its own needs. Persons are selected who are fit for those vocations. Hence, vocational guidance is needed. Therefore, vocational guidance is:

(i) a process.

(ii) must for selection of a vocation or adjustment in a vocation.

(iii) to know the necessary features of various vocations and abilities.

(iv) a process of introducing with various vocations.

A detailed description of vocational guidance has been given in other unit.

PERSONAL GUIDANCE

Personal guidance includes personal-psychological or emotional relationships which a person develops himself. Paterson has included social, emotional and leisure time guidance in personal guidance. In fact, the problems regarding health, emotional adjustment, social adjustment and leisure and recreational problems are included in personal guidance for solution. Under social adjustment, an individual's economic problems are included. The aspects of the life's character and spiritual fields can also be included in the personal guidance. In other words, the problems which cannot be included in educational and vocational guidance, we can include them in personal guidance.

In this way, the main aim of personal guidance is to establish balance between the individual's mental, social and physical aspects, because it is often seen that a person sometimes is surrounded by abnormal behaviours and social demerits even though they possess educational competencies and satisfactory progress in the professional areas. Such persons lead neglected life among their families, neighbourers and members of the community. Due to lack of balanced personalities in the families and neighbourhood and due to vague identification of mental and emotional deficiencies, the resultant conditions do not allow the person to imagine a peaceful and progressive life. In such conditions, personal guidance can prove helpful in solving such problems.

Hence, the solution of the following types of problems is possible in personal guidance—

(i) Problems related to the health and physical development.

(ii) Problems related to emotional behaviour.

(iii) Problems related to home and family relationships.

(iv) Problems related to sex, courtship and marriage.

(v) Problems related to religion, morals, ideals and values.

(vi) Economic Problems.

(vii) Problems related to social relationships.

Q. 33. Define Vocational Guidance. What is its scope? What is its need? What is the difference between educational and Vocational Guidance?

Ans. The vocational guidance is a long continuous process which begins in the school and is needed throughout the working life of the individual. It is aimed at wise use by person of priceless native capacity and the results of costly training provided by the school for the good for the individual and the society.

According to the National Vocational Guidance Association of America 1973, "The vocational guidance is the process of assisting the individual to choose an occupation, prepare for it, enter upon and progress in it. It is concerned primarily with helping individuals make decisions and choices involved in planning a future, and building a career decision and choices necessary in effecting satisfactory vocational adjustment."

The general conference of the International Labour Organisation in 1949, described Vocational Guidance "as assistance given to an individual in solving problems related to *occupational choice and progress* with due regard for the individual's characteristics and their relation to occupational opportunity."

Scope of Vocational Guidance

The scope of vocational guidance may be understood better, perhaps, by a consideration of the general activities which comprise it. These are as follows:

(a) Analysis of the Individual. Without extensive knowledge about the individual desirous of getting vocational guidance, it would be impossible to effect his matching with the vocation. Competent men do this appraisal through various tests.

(b) Occupational Information. Next to the analysis of the individual is the collection and dissemination of information about an occupation. This is done by career talks, career conferences, visits to factories, establishing career corners, career clubs, career news-letters etc. Then only we shall be able to match the individual with the job.

(c) Community Occupation Surveys and Follow-up Studies. Most of us find jobs in the immediate neighbourhood. Other than national occupational information, vocational information should be focussed upon local conditions. Community occupational surveys and follow-up study of school-leavers wilol provide data on local training and employment conditions, labour turnover and job opportunities. This is to be done by a vocational guidance worker.

(d) Counselling. Counselling is a technique of guidance—any type of guidance. Herein we give individual help to students.

(e) Group Activities. Much of the work of self-appraisal and occupational study is handled most efficiently through group approach. Group activities in vocational guidance be done by the properly educated and trained teachers. These activities stress the methodology of vocational selection, preparation, job-getting and advancement. They provide occupational motivation and information through field trips, career conferences etc.

(f) Placement. This is the last and most important activity of vocational guidance. It cannot be left to chance. Herein the school places the individual in a job vocation and watches his progress.

Need of Vocational Guidance

According to Myers, vocational guidance is needed because :

1. If an individual stays in wrong profeesion for along time, he suffers economically. There is financial loss.
2. If an individual stays in a wrong profession, he suffers from a psychic loss. The individual is not happy. He is frustrated. His family life is affected.
3. There are a large number of *personal and social values* of vocational guidance. Leaving aside financial considerations, the worker's happiness, his personal development, his value as a social unit and contribution to human welfare are all involved. Right vocational guidance helps us achieve that.
4. Vocational guidance provides many economic advantages to the employers. Their labour problems are less because these workers enjoy job satisfaction.
5. It is needed from the point of view of health of the workers. If the profession is such where health of workers breaks down, production suffers and morale of workers goes down.
6. Human potentialities are utilised to the maximum with the help of vocational guidance. We are then truly benefited by it.

Q. 34. Discuss the forms of school management and the features of ideal management.

Or

Discribe the various forms of school management in our country. Suggest steps to make school managements ideal.

Ans. Schools in our country are managed by the Centre, the States, local bodies, municipal boards, district boards, religious organisations, private bodies, registered trusts, and individually:

(a) Schools Run by the Centre or States. As education is the responsibility of the Central and State Governments, these Governments run and manage some schools. In the C and D lists of States the Centre manage the schools.

(b) School Managed by Religious Organisations. Christian missionaries were the first religious bodies that began to control education in the country. Other religious bodies like Arya Samaj'

Sanatan Dharma Sanstha, Sikhs, Parsis and other religious people began to run schools and manage them.

(c) School Managed by Local Bodies. Primary schools are managed by the local bodies—the District Boards, Municipalities and Corporations manage primary education in the country.

(d) Privately Managed Schools. Private bodies have played a great role in the education of the masses because the Government did not find enough finance to run and control school education since the early days of East India Company.

(e) Individual Managements. Some individual run and manage their own schools and do not like to take grant-in-aid from the Government.

Thus, there are government schools wholly managed by the government the private aided schools run by different types of management, and private unaided schools.

Features of an Ideal Mangement. A good management has its own constitution. There is a managing committee consisting of elected or nominates these members. The General Body elects or nominates members. A management committee has on its roll the representatives of teachers and of old pupils, the Principal and the members from the General Body. Some management bodies have seats reserved for guardians also.

The Manager is the Chief Executive of the Management Committee. He is the boss. He is responsible for:

(a) solution of all financial problems of the school.

(b) distribution of salaries in time.

(c) in maintenance of provident fund accounts of the members of the staff, and other accounts of the school.

Funds are kept in the name of the Manager. All moneys from fees, grants, donation, subscription are deposited in his name. The payments to teachers are made by him direct or through the Principal or through a bank. The accounts are auditable.

The Management Committee is responsible for all educational matters of the school. It appoints teachers and headmasters or Principals under rules laid down by the Education Department. Its orders are final. It sees that the relations between the Headmaster and the teachers, are happy, and where there are differences, the Management Committee tries to make the relations smooth.

A good Management Committee takes a keen interest in the school affairs and does not leave all matters for the managers to look after. All the members try to see what is going on in the school and pay visits in the right spirit for school progress.

The Management Committee sees that there is a proper accomodation in the school, that equipments are sufficient and adequate, that the sanitary arrangements are satisfacting, that library and laboratories are properly maintained, that games and other co-curricular activities are organised well. A good management has an eye on every aspect of school life and a wish to see the school developed.

But there are managements whose working is not satisfactory. The Managers and other members of the committee are illiterate, money-minded and have no interests in the school education. Some Managers use schools for their own benefit and the members of the committee connive at their actions.

The lack of interest in school affairs by members of the committee is a general complaint of private management.

Q. 35. Discuss the co-curricular activities organised by school and their main objectives.

Or

Why should a school organise co-curricular activities? Disucss their main objectives.

Ans. The personality of the child can be developed when he is provided with manifold activities inside and outside the school under its own control and supervision. All co-curricular activities are organised with specific purposes which vary according to the nature and form of such activities. The main objectives are listed below:

1. Physical Development.

2. Development of literary and academic interests.

3. Social Service.

4. Civic Training.

5. Cummunity Living.

6. Development of 4 H's—Head, Heart, Hand and Health.

1. Physical Development. Games and sports, mass physical training, athletics, mass drill are organised to produce healthy human beings.

2. Development of Literary and Academic Interests. Schools want pupils to become intellectually alive; hence they organise debates on burning topics of everyday interest. Group discussions are held to solve some problems of the society and community in which they live. Writing and enacting of short one act plays develop literary tastes. School magazine, wall magazine, and school publications on topics of public interest are meant for development of literary disposition.

3. Development of Civic Sense. Co-curricular activities like organisation of student councils, opening of student cooperative stores, self-government, are organised to develop civic sense in pupils. They promote a spirit of self-discipline, tolerance, good temper, fellow feeling, patience and character. Lessons in cooperation are got in managing cooperative stores or in conducting students councils. Boys learn how to share responsibilities and perform duties assigned to them. They come to common decision through cooperative thinking and try to implement it because it is theirs. Games and sports are also valuable because they develop team spirit. The boy, who takes an active part in any organised game, *e.g.*, football, hockey, volleyball, ro cricket, learns that if he is to win he must play in a team. To become a good member of the group, he sacrifices his own immediate interests. He develops a spirit of give-and-take as he participates in group activities.

3. Development of Sense for Social Service. Society wants its members to serve its needs and purposes. There are occasions when social service from voluntary organisations is required. Schools send their boys and girls out to help the organisers of Melas, and exhibitions. Scouts and Guides do useful service to the society on such occasions. Activities such as these are organised to develop a sense of social service in the individual child. Organisation of social service camps tends to create happy relations between the school and community.

5. Development of Community Life. Community living on the càmpus helps develop the art of living together. Cleaning the school premises, beautifying the class-room, levelling the playground, preparing and maintaining the school garden, polishing furniture, whitewashing walls, painting doors and windows, are some very useful activities which help to develop a sense of living together.

6. Development of Four H's. Cultural, creative and productive activities are supposed to develop qualities of Head, Heart and Hand. They also develop Health. They provide an elementary knowledge and basic training for some future vocation in life. They meet individual interests.

Such activities are now being proposed under the scheme of work experience. In lower primary classes for example, we are trying to introduce paper cutting, card-board cutting, and folding, modelling in clay or plasticine, spinning and simple needle work, planting in-doors or on plots. The main objective behind their introduction is to trained school children to make use of their hands and thereby to help their intellectual and emotional growth.

In the senior class-work experience will take the form of some craft. The objective behind the compulsory introduction of a craft is development of technical thinking and creative capacities.

Q. 36. Discuss the features of various co-curricular activities that can be organised in a school.

Ans. KINDS OF CO-CURRICULAR ACTIVITIES

The number and kinds of co-curricular activities that a Principal can organise is his school will depend upon the size and the financial position of the school, the type of the school, the size and qualities of the staff, the support of the local community and the parents. However, a list of co-curricular activities that can be organised in a school is given below and the Principal will have to make a choice from among them. The following are the activities which are generally organised in schools :

1. Physical Activities. Every school can organise mass-dri and mass-P.T. in the morning assembly or at some other suitable time, games and sports in the evening or on holidays and Sundays.

2. Literacy and Academic Activities. Debates, group discussons, mock parliaments, elocution contests, wall magazines, visits to historical buildings, and civic institutions like the Parliament House in State Legislative when in seesion, dramatics, art, music, publication of magazines are some of the activities by which instructional programmes can be enriched.

3. Civic Training Activities. Student councils, students cooperative stores, are organised to develop a spirit of citizenship. School, itself, when organised an democratic lines, provides a training ground for democratic way of life, yet various other activities can be organised to give students lessons in the act of governing and of being governed.

4. Social Service Activities. Social service work in special occasions like fairs and exhibitions through NCC, ACC, Scouting and Girl Guiding and Red Cross can be performed by school students.

5. Community Life Activities. Celebrating community functions, conducting work connected with school sanitation, cleaning village wells and streets, mass-cooking and serving are sense of the activities that are organised to trained children in the art of living together.

6. Creative and Productive Hobbies. School are trying to start clubs connected with photography, science, philately (stamp collecting), leather and wood-work, and such other productive hobbies. However, hobbies satisfying following interests of pupils can be safely organised :

(a) academic interests pertain to Languages, History, Geography, Mathematics, Radio, etc.

(b) artistic intersts such as painting, dancing, singing orchestra.

(c) social interests such as starting cooperative societies, Junior Red Cross, Social Service Leagues ACC, NCC Scouting and Guiding.

(d) interests showing love of nature such as cycling, hiking, gardening.

7. Work Experience. At all school stages, from the Primary to the Higher Secondary, some form of productive work can be organised by every educational institution to provide a much needed corrective to the extremely academic and bookish character of education.

Q. 37. How to organise co-curricular activities without disturbing the curricular programme? Democratic organisation demand coordination. How?

Ans. Co-curricular activities have to be planned, organised and co-ordinated. In the planning of these activities the Principal and the teachers will have to keep certain points in view. Activities should be as varied as the school resources permit. Academic activities like debates, discussions, dramas, school magazines, social activities like the organisation of different functions in the school as well as in the local community, sports activities, manual and practical activities, social service projects, art projects, all have to be woven into a rich and unified pattern within which every one of the members of the staff and each one of the pupils in the school will be able to find something to suit his tastes and interests. Thus, the first aim of planning co-curricular activities is the maximum participation of all the members of the school.

In the actual working out of these activities listed under different heads as academic and literary, social, practical and productive, games and sports, hobbies and clubs, the organisers will find that there is unity and cohesion. There are no boundary lines between, for example, those which are aimed to achieve social and community life development. By planning a coherent programme of different activities, rich in stimuli, the school will not be frittering away either the time or the energy of pupils but will be highlighting their intellectual powers besides training them in other finer qualities. Nor will the organisation of these activities be deemed as a disturbance to curricular programme.

Before an activity is launched it should be approved democratically by the staff. Before approving a new activity the following things should be kept in mind.

1. Does the activity proposed meet the needs of the school?
2. Are pupils sufficiently interested in it?
3. Is there a teacher in the school who is qualified, has time, and is willing to direct the proposed activity?

All the members should be democratically taken into confidence before introducting an activity in the school. Coaches or sponsors of school activities should be the members of the staff and not outsiders.

The introduction of the programme of co-curricular activities should be a gradual one. An activity should be introduced only when the school has a need for it and when its pupils are interested in it. For example, when there is a fully developed department of History in the school, a History club may be started.

The number and type of activities to be developed in any school should be determined by the size of enrolment, and the needs of the school. Activities should not be overorganised even in larger schools. Smaller schools should not waste time and energy and squander money in an attempt to ape the larger ones.

Activities that are organised in the school should as far as possible aim at achieving civic, social, moral, and other worth-while values as indicated in a previous section. Activities for enjoyment are useless though they may be harmless.

The nunber of activities which a student should be allowed to take part in during an academic year should be according to his needs. A limitation on participation is required because it will check the over-ambitious lad from over-loading himself with activities to the possible detriment of his health and regular studies and because a larger number of pupils will be able to participate in the activities organised in the school.

Since it is desired that the maximum possible number of students shall participate in each activity there should be democracy in the activity. Participation in each activity should be open to all. It does not mean that there should be no consideration for reasonable standards of achievement, or for eligibility to take part in it.

In order that each student should have a well-rounded development in both curricular and co-curricular activities, the plan of educational guidance of the school should consider both types of activities in advising pupils regarding their total school programme.

For democratic organisation the following other points should also be kept in mind:

(a) an activity should be organised in school time as far as possible. If there is no provision for such facilities as are required for the organisation of an activity in a single shift school, it may be organised in after-school hours or on holidays.

(b) regular time should be given to an activity.

(c) the teacher should play the role of an adviser and not dominate.

(d) the activity should not be too expensive.

(e) there should be a close supervision of all co-curricular activities, funds and accounts. Pupils Funds should not be misappropriated or squandered.

Supervising Co-curricular Activities. All co-curricular activities should be supervised by the school. They should be amenable to school control and discipline. Too much supervision is, of course, not required, nor is it desirable, because it stifles spontaneity and makes it difficult for pupils to develop initiative. The amount of supervision will depend upon the type of the activity and the maturity level of students. For example, you will need a greater quantum of supervision for athletics and dramatics. Similarly, in lower classes the work will have to be closely supervised, but here supervision will have to be of mother-type. In higher secondary schools and colleges where students are quite mature and grown-up the supervision will have to be of brother-type. But the essense and supervision should be democratic.

To plan the activity programme the school administrator will have to delegate powers to a director to coordinate the various activities to be organised in the school. The teaching load of the coordinator shall have to be kept to the minimum if an ambitious plan of organising co-curricular activities is adopted. The coordinator will be required to devote sufficient time to the planning execution of various activities in the school. His duties will be to plan the schedule of the year's activities, to select those which relate to school curriculum and satisfy school needs, to think of the ways and means to finance activities, to conduct research on the values of all curricular as well as co-curricular activities to keep touch with transportation services to take students to various places of interest, and to evaluate pupils performance in these activities.

Q. 38. Write note on the managing School Discipline.

Ans. SCHOOL DISCIPLINE

Every phase of school management is closely related to school disciplinary. A well-ordered class-room is likely to be from discipline problems. According to Hansen, "Discipline becomes a problem when students are not productively busy." Discipline must not be confused with stupid forms of punishment. Discipline is associated with wholesome class conduct. Discipline is always connected with a goal. The attainment of a goal which is bigger than that which can be reached immediately by the individual involves discipline. Thus, discipline may be thought of as an orgnization of one's impulses for the attainment of a goal. Modern educators think of discipline as primarily concerned with meeting the causes of maladjustments in the school so that right thinking and right conduct may be firmly established. Often-times, disciplinary problems grow out of poor class-room procedures and the teacher's weak personality. The teacher who really teaches will generally be able to maintain a fairly good order, and one may be quite certain that continuous disorder is the result of faulty organization and technique in the treatment of the lesson. Studies have shown that one chief cause of the teacher's failure is his inability to maintain order in the class-room.

Good teaching is made possible by good discipline. Likewise, Grim and Michaelis state that, "good discipline is a result of good teaching, a by-product, as it were." Good discipline implies obedience on the part of every pupil to class-room rules and regulations with the aim of achieving success in learning. It has been said that discipline is best when it is least in evidence. Ability to secure good discipline is one of the qualities of a good teacher. Psychological studies have revealed that poor discipline is one of the causes of failure in teaching. The correct techniques of management and method must be regarded as the principal agency of good discipline within the school. Good discipline is enforced not merely for regulative purposes; it has also important educational values inherent in itself.

Modern Conception of Discipline

The modern conception of discipline is that it is both regulative and educative wherein the attention of the teacher is directed to the development of constructive attitudes and habits of conduct, rather than to regulations of control negative in nature. It is regulative because without quiet and order, effective teaching on one hand, and profitable learning on the other, are not possible. Pupils doing group work require a quiet and regulative class-room atmosphere in other that they may derive the maximum benefit from the exercises. The true function of class-room discipline is to create and maintain class-room conditions favorable to effective teaching and learning, or to create a desire to help establish and maintain good working conditions to further the accomplishment of the objectives for which the teacher and the pupils are working. The ideal conditions for teaching and learning depend largely upon the attitude of the learner, class-room conditions conducive to good teaching and learning, and the teaching skill of the teacher in setting the stage for learning.

The real purpose of modern discipline in school is to guide social development and adjustment. The problems of class-room discipline are problems for guidance and for education, not for coercion and punishment. And of course, the kind of guidance we give depends on what the teacher wants to produce. It has not been long since most parents and teachers sought implicit obedience—unquestioning docility and conformity as evidence of successful discipline. But unfortunately this criterion is rapidly giving way to the idea that initiative, self-direction, and social conscience are the normal indications of wholesome development.

The modern concept of discipline is based on rational approach. In a rational approach to discipline, mere compliance is subordinate to understanding. The pupils must be made to understand why certain modes of behaviour are to be followed, to question the reasonableness of things, to have the habits of finding out about things, and to make up their own minds. They must grow up as people who have had much practice in planing for the welfare of themselves and their communities. The teachers must see to it that discipline of the home and the school does not interfere with that development by inculcating an attitude of subservience to the ideas and demands of the older generation. The discipline of both the home and the school should recognize the dignity of each individual and his right to seek recognition and to direct his own activities. Modern discipline must be viewed with new insight and understanding.

The modern concept of discipline is based on the following democratic principles:

1. Discipline based on devotion of humanitarian principles and ideals such as freedom, justice and equality for all rather than discipline based on a narrower and more egoistic affiliation.
2. Discipline which recognizes the inherent dignity and rights of every human being, rather than discipline attained through humiliation.
3. Discipline based on understanding of the goal in view rather than discipline based on high authority.
4. Discipline which develops self-direction, self-discipline rather than discipline based on compulsion and obedience.

It can be said that modern concept of discipline is based on democratic principles. Discipline is not coercion through force but it is a spirit. And a spirit cannot be ordered, or punished into or regimented for. Democratic discipline is based on admiration and love of an ideal or good and the love of this goal must be so great that sacrifice for the attainment of this goal ceases to be sacrifices and becomes incidentals of a process. Those persons who complain about the softness of the modern schools and who demand that the school use "Army methods," do not understand the methods of education for a democracy. The teachers must bear in mind that democracy is built on respect, on confidence in each other and on cooperation. True discipline is based on willing cooperation, which springs from knowledge, idealism, and a sense of service.

One great task of the teacher in a democracy is to understand and accept principles of democratic discipline. However, by understanding and accepting the principles of democratic discipline does not mean that all disciplinary problems are solved, or will-disappear. The other great task which confronts the class-room teacher on his job is to translate the principles of democratic discipline into daily action in his class-room. It is with this idea in mind that the principles governing the handling of disciplinary problems are discussed in this Chapter.

Q. 39. Discuss the meaning of Evaluation and its importance for the Institutional Performance.

Ans. THE MEANING OF EVALUATION

If education were to become a science and an art, it must develop means of determining with accuracy the degree and kind of all the changes which it brings about. Teaching becomes more productive when followed by an accurate appraisal of its results. The teacher cannot of course determine accurately how much he has contributed to the education of the pupil at the onset of his teaching. Various studies have shown that opinions on all types of educational outcomes are unreliable. The more objective and refined the measures of educational products, the greater are the possibilities of determining and putting into effect improved educative procedures.

The success or failure of the teacher in applying the principles which have been discussed in this book is evaluated by the growth and development of the children. Of course, it is also possible that the validity of the principles which we sought to establish may be called in question by the same sort of evaluation. Teaching is, after all, the adaptation of our methods to the normal growth and development of boys and girls whose growth can be evaluated in terms of knowledge, habits, skills, abilities, attitudes, reasoning, and the like.

According to the Dictionary of Education, "evaluation is the process of ascertaining or judging the value or amount of something by careful appraisal." To Wiles, "evaluation is the process of making judgments that are to be used as a basis for planning. It is a procedure of improving the product, the process, and even the goals themselves" In education, the terms refers to the step taken in directed study in which the teacher and the pupils appraise the progress made in the study of a subject or unit. Likewise, the term evaluation also refers to the process of determining experimentally or subjectively the merits of a test on the basis of such characteristics as validity, objectivity, ease of administration and scoring, adequacy of norm, availability of duplicate forms, and ease of interpretation; Evaluation is closely related to educational measurement. However, it is a far more inclusive concept than measurement. "Measurement" implies the use of standardized tests, the results of which are expressed in quantitative terms.

IMPORTANCE OF EVALUATION

Evaluation is not just a testing programme or an administrative technique. It is not something to be resorted to at the close of the school term as a culminating activity, nor should it be viewed as an end activity to be done by the district and division supervisors of the Bureaus of Public and Private Schools. In the modern school, increasing emphasis on the personal and social development of the child, as well as his academic achievement, has called for the corresponding development of a variety of techniques fur appraising all phases of child growth and development, of pupil achievement, of behaviour and of the teaching-learning processes. Due to the large number of factors that enter into teaching and learning including such instructional variables as objectives, methods and techniques, and subject-matter on the one hand; and such human variables as pupils, teachers, and supervisors on the other, it has been difficult to appraise the validity of the pupil's achievement. There is, therefore, a comparatively large subjective factor in the evaluation of teaching and learning that needs to be taken into account together with its objective features.

It cannot be denied that the evaluation of teaching and learning is an exceedingly complex activity. However, the efficiency of the teacher and the growth and achievement of the pupil can be evaluated through the use of such devices as check lists, rating scales, tests of different aspects of teaching ability, interview, and questionnaries. Through the use of such devices much valuable data may be gathered relative to many of the important aspects of teaching and learning.

The importance of evaluation in teaching can be summarized as follows:

1. Evaluation is Important to the Class-room Teachers, Supervisors, and Administrators in Directing as well as Guiding Teaching and Learning. Evaluation, to be of importance to teachers and supervisors, should be diagnostic, *i.e.*, it should reveal the specific points of strength and weakness in teaching and learning.

2. Evaluation also Helps to Measure the Validity and Reliability of Instruction. The effectiveness and success of any phase of teaching technique can be demonstrated through the nature of the results obtained. From a purely methodical point of view, the measurement of effective teaching finds its great value in the prossibilities it offers for the the improvement of teaching and learning. All activities of the teacher should be evaluated in the light of their adequacy to promote the democratic way of life and on how nearly do the students realize the objectives of education.

3. Evaluation Aids in Devising more Effective Instructional Meterials and Procedures of Instruction. Current educational literature is filled with enthusiastic advocacy of various cooperative research, and if worked along this line, will determine the degree of success and effectiveness of evaluation.

4. Evaluation Helps Teachers to Discover the Needs of the Pupils. The purpose of any program of evaluation is to discover the needs of the pupils being evaluated and then to design learning experiences that will satisfy these needs. Traditionally, the results of evaluation have been used to compare one individual with another. It is an accepted fact that growth is a continuous process and that each individual grows at a rate that is unique for him.

5. Evaluation Stimulates Students to Study. A questioning teacher creates incentives for students to learn more. He sets up effective and definite goals for learning. Giving oral or written examination is a good incentive for the students to study harder or to do better work. It makes the learner familiar with his own results. Likewise, he needs to understands his own high and low potential for learning, but even more, he needs help in understanding the personal problems of human relations.

6. Evaluation Helps Parents to Understand Pupil-Growth, Interests, and Potentialities. The major responsibility of the school and teacher is to help the parents understand their children. Understanding a youth means understanding his progress in the various areas of the curriculum, his desires and motives and behaviour they lead to, his potentialities for learning, as well as his achievement.

7. Evaluation can be Used to Enforce External Standards upon the Individual Class or School. This method should be such as to encourage a flexible curriculum which is ever responsive to the changing needs of modern life and to the variations in local conditions. Local schools should be free to select and develop instruments for evaluation which are appropriate for their curricula.

8. Evaluation, Likewise, Helps to Provide Objective Evidences for Effective Cooperation Between Parents and Teachers. The increasing complexity of our present society has emphasized the importance of the cooperation of the school, the home, and the community in making significant educational progress.

9. Evaluation is Helpful in Securing Support for the School from the Government, Local or National. The people frequently complain that public schools in this country are inadequately supported.

10. Evaluation is Helpful to the Teacher. It enables him to see how he can make his contribution to the accomplishment of the total goals or aims of the school system. It helps the teacher to coordinate his efforts with the efforts of others who contribute to the general educational goals.

Q. 40. Discuss the types of tests useful in teaching and its value for institutional performance.

Ans. TYPES OF TESTS USEFUL IN TEACHING

Modern tests are so numerous that it is extremely difficult to classify them closely. Tests can be classified on the basis of their forms, their functions, and their content. The types given by the writer are classified as: function, educational intelligence, and personality tests.

1. Educational Tests. Educational tests have as their primary function the measurement of the results or effects of instruction and learning. They are intended to test primarily class-room learning. Educational test may be either standardized or non-standardized. A non-standardized test has no fixed norm and it is free from prescribed rules. The teacher-made test is a good example of the non-standardized test. Examples of educational tests are the following:

(a) Standard Survey Test, which aims to measure the attainment, progress or status of the pupils or the schools. It refers also to a test which measures the general achievement of the pupils in a certain subject or field.

(b) Informal or Teacher-made Test, which aims to measure the achievement, progress, weakness or defects of the individual pupils or class, or the effectiveness of the method used by the teacher. This may be either an essay or an informal objective test.

(c) Standard Achievement Test, which aims to measure the pupil's accomplishment as a result of instruction in a given subject or subjects.

(d) Standard Diagnostic Test, which aims to locate the weaknesses, and if possible, the cause of disability in performance.

(e) Aptitude Test, which aims to measure the specific intelligence as it operates in a certain field or area of performance. It may be used for prognostic purposes.

(f) Inventory Test, which aims to measure the degree of mastery exsiting before the teaching or the learning of the subject or subjects.

2. Intelligence Tests. The intelligence tests have as their purpose the measurement of the pupils intelligence or mental ability in a large degree without reference to what the pupil learned in or out of school. The two types of Intelligence Tests are :

(a) Individual Intelligence Test. This type of intelligence test can be administered only to one pupil at a time, like the Binet and Simon Intelligence Test (1904).

(b) Group Intelligence Test. This type of Intelligence test can be administered to a number of pupils at the same time, like the Alpha and Beta Intelligence Tests, or the Philippine Mental Tests.

Values of the Educational Test

Some values of the educational test worth considering are as follows:

1. The Educational Test Measures the Accomplishment and Progress of the Pupils. Any attempt to measure the achievement of the children would result in the discovery of the progress being made from week to week, or from month to month or from year to year. It would be advantageous to note the progress and deficiency at all periods if comparison is to be made with the work three weeks or a month later. Some tests are designed to serve this end. This results of achievement tests are widely used for classification and promotion.

2. An Educational Test Diagnoses the Strength and Weakness of the Pupils in a Subject or a Subjects. The test will serve both as a guide to teaching and as an enlightenment to the learner. When a pupil makes an error, the teacher needs to apply a diagnostic test to discover why the pupil made the error and to determine how the thinking of the pupil may be directed in order to build up a correct reaction in place of the incorrect one. Asking questions, the use of drill material, and the review are all forms of diagnostic tests. It is, therefore, a sound educational practice to use both oral and written tests for diagnosing what goes on in the pupil's mind.

3. The Educational Test Stimulates the Pupils to Study. Testing serves as a stimulus to daily preparation. The teacher, by giving an unannounced or announced test of some sort will, no doubt, stimulate the pupils to study the lesson assigned or the work covered. Giving a written examination is a good incentive for the pupils to study harder or to do better work. It makes the learner familiar with his own results. The final Examination given in the high school and in college at the end of the course or term furnishes a very powerful stimulus to review.

4. The Educational Test Measures the Validity and Reliability of Instruction. The effectiveness and success of any phase of teaching technique can be demonstrated through the character of the results obtained. The teacher should know how to measure the results of his work in order to adapt his procedure to the needs of the varying situations. From a purely methodical point of view the measurement of teaching effectiveness finds its greatest value in the possibilities if offers for the improvement of teaching.

5. The Educational Test Sets-up Standards of Performance for the Pupils. It increases the effectiveness of education by setting up standards of achievement in terms of varying capacities. A standard test can be used in comparing the merits of different schools, different class-room methods, different organisations of materials, and the different lengths and methods of assignment.

6. The Educational Test Opens the way to Remedial Work. Test results afford a basis for diagnosing the pupil's needs. Difficulties are prevented by the early discovery of the strength and weakness of the pupil. Knowing the defect of the individual or the general weakness of the class, the teacher will be able to select the right course or procedure to follow.

7. The Educational Test Can be Used for Educational and Vocational Guidance. Test results afford a basis for the guidance of pupils. The test first came into use in a general way. It can be used to guide the pupil in school in the selection of courses or of the vocation for which he is best qualified. It can be used to discover the unusual aptitude of pupils. The guidance function of education assumes a prominent place in the modern concepts of the aims of education. It is generally accepted that intelligence tests are necessary to supplement indices of achievement as a basis for guidance. The use of intelligence tests for guidance purposes has become so thoroughly accepted that no guidance can be considered effective which does not involve the use of these means.

8. Educational Test Results are a Valuable Part of the Pupil's Records. The meaning of the test data is widely understood, and when they are entered in the pupil's permanent record they can help other teachers understand him better. The test data should be used only as background information, not as a measure of present status.

9. Educational Tests can be Used in the Classification and Sectioning of Pupils. It has been proved that pupils learn most effectively when they are placed with other pupils having approximately the same abilities. This means that pupils of approximately the same intelligence and achievement levels should be grouped together for instructional purposes. For the accomplishment of this purpose intelligence and achievement tests can be utilized.

10. The Educational Test can be Used by Supervisors to Direct and Guide the Teachers. The supervisor who appreciates the value and limitations of tests can use the data to suggest changes and improvement in teaching procedures. However, tests should not be used as the sole criterion for evaluating teacher-effectiveness. The training of the teacher, the ability of the class, the materials and resources available to the teacher, are other factors that should be taken into consideration. The test data should be used as supplementary evidence.

Q. 41. Discuss in the light of teacher's roles in teaching, guiding children, community relations, and administration.

Ans. Good teachers make good schools. The quality of the school can be no better than the people who are responsible for its improvement. If the headmaster is the coping stone in the school structure, the teacher's role is no less important. If the nation's teachers are C_3, the nation itself cannot but be C_3 and let there be no doubt abou it: if we wish to be A_1 nation, our teachers will have to be A_1. We want a duly equipped living teacher—a teacher who realises his duties and responsibilities to the child, the parent, the community and the nation itself. As without a good Principal the best school is wrecked. So without good teachers the best system is bound to fail. With good teachers even the defects of a system can be largely overcome.

1. The Nation Building Role of the Teacher. The teacher's role in the society is vital. He acts as a pivot. He keeps the lamp of civilization burning. He guides the destiny of the nation. He is the architect of the future. He has a specific role to play in the reconstruction of the country.

India, which has planned for education reconstruction, is in need of really good teachers. It is the body of good teachers upon which the destiny of the nation depends.

2. Teachers Role in Guiding Learning and Building Character. The effective teacher develops broad outlines, and objectives to be attained for a subject, selects materials, teaching aids, uses efficient methods, makes judicious use of lectures, discussions, demonstration experimentation, projects and field trips:

maintains and develops pupil interests in the learning process; develops suitable study habits in children; evaluates pupil's progress with effective evaluation teachniques: in short, does all for pupil growth and development in the school.

He is responsible four judging pupil growth through evaluation. He collects evidence of specific nature about the child, judges it objectively, and makes unbiassed interpretation of the mass of data that he so collects regarding the child's intelligence, achievement and aptitude. He gets all information about the child from his health records, anecdotal reports, activity records, his creative writings, his interest inventories, and parent conferences.

The teacher is also reponsible for building character. It is he who can best infuse in the child the respect for what is good, what is right and what is just. It is he who can create leadership qualities in the children he guides. It is he who can encourage desirable traits of personality and character because he alone comes in direct contact with the pupil. No one exercise greater influence upon the mind of children than a teacher consciously or unconsciously, he is moulding the character according to his own model.

3. Teachers Role in Guidance. The changing concept of guidance, which associates it with the daily activity of the class-room teacher, gives a greater responsibility to him. It means that the teacher who is dealing with children should be given in-service education for discharging his responsibilities in personal, educational and vocational guidance. The necessity of such an inservice programme is felt because we are at present not in a position to employ special guidance personnel in each school. Many of the non-technical aspects of guidance can be taken up by every class-room teacher: and some aspects needing technical knowledge may be developed through in-service education. The functions of the school teacher for guidance include:

(i) Using of tools and techniques for intensive study of children, *e.g.*, intelligence, achievement, aptitude tests, interest inventories.

(ii) Developing a programme of study groups for parents so that they may be able to understand their children's problems.

(iii) Establishing and maintenance of record and reports.

(iv) Coordinating the work of special service related to guidance, for example, the work of school doctor, the dentist, the counsellor and the guidance officer.

4. Role of Teacher in Maintaining Community Relations. A good teacher understands the importance of good parent and community relations. He understands well that, however, good a proposal or an educational programme may be, unless the public understands and accepts it as good, he cannot hope to succeed. A good teacher therefore tries to make community ready for accepting a desirable change in the programme through parent teacher associations or parent study councils. He understands that, as the public has a tremendous investment in the public schools, participation of the community is essential in the development of schools policies. He also understands well that the role of education is not only confined to serve the needs of children and youth, but in a broader sense education has to contribute much to the community as a whole.

With this philosophy in mind, a good teacher tries to build good parent-community relations. He tells through his children what a good school is doing. He draws the attention of the parents to school's powers, service and cultural contribution by taking an effective part in the organisation of school functions. He impresses the public by showing the achievements or his boys in scholastic field in cultural programmes, and in games and sports. When parents come to school he welcomes their visits, respects their ideas and gives them help and confidence.

5. Role of the Teacher in Helping Administration. No administrator can be successful without the active and willing cooperation of the school teacher. The creative Principal knows well the power of cooperative process of using his staff and community resources. The creative headmaster improves an educational institution only through group approach. He believes that there is much greater chance of success when a group turns its creative power to the problem of school policy, making and executing it. He knows well that there is a greater support for him in the administrative work when he takes the group into confidence and shares with them his responsibility.

He helps the headmaster not only in administration but gives him enough support in his organisation which involves mainfold activities—classification and re-classification of pupils, framing of time-table, organisation of co-curricular activities, maintenance of building, maintenance of pupil records, management of school business, supervision of other colleagues, organisation of public function, building of head-community relations, etc.

Q. 42. Discuss the Pupils Ratings or School Grades.

Ans. PUPIL'S RATINGS OR SCHOOL GRADES

The discussion of the evaluation of results of teaching and learning is incomplete without a consideration of the real importance of test scores once they have been obtained. However, teachers and students must not consider evaluation solely as a means of obtaining grades. Basically, there are but two grading systems in use at present in this country. All other types of grading system are variations of these two. The first of these is called the Garrett Plan or the Percentage System; the other, the Missouri Plan or the Normal-Curve System.

1. The Garrett Plan or the Percentage System. The percentage system of grading assumes an absolute standard. The grades have some subjective concept of perfect performance for the particular exercise being graded. To this perfection standard he assigns the value of 100 per cent or 100-point scale. The exercise is then judged against this 100 per cent standard. This system is applied to examinations, test, and any other means used to measure the results of teaching and learning. If the outcome of the examination or test shows that three-fourths of the quantity or quality of the perfect exercise is covered satisfactorily, it is given a grade of 75 per cent; if it reaches nine-tenths of the way towards the perfection goal, it is assigned a grade of 90 per cent. The precentage system is used in all public elementary and secondary schools and some private school, college, and universities in the Philippines. The University of Santo Tomas and Far Eastern University use this system of grading.

As noted in the preceding illustration, the percentage system assumes a range of grades from 0 to 100. In other words, it is assumed that a teacher is able to distinguish 101 levels of achievement or ability. Psychology tells us, however, that the human mind, in rarely able distinguish more than five to seven classes in any situation.

We would all probably confirm this idea if we had experience in grading test papers. Those who advocate the curve system for grading purposes take cognizance of this fact inasmuch as they recommend that somewhere between three and seven grade distinction should be made.

A second serious mathematical formula that would apply to this stiuation is wherein a relatively small proportion of a class will receive grades scattered all along the way from 0 to 70, let us, say, and the much larger section of the class receives grades in the relatively smaller range of 30 points, from 70 to 100.

2. The Missouri Plan or the Letter-System based on Normal-Curve—The letters-system based on Normal-curve uses an entirely different point of reference. It is a system of distributing grades based on the normal probability formula and the law of chance. The average achievement or ability of the particular class taking the test is used as a standard against which each individual's performance of judged. The individual's test performance is graded in proportion to its distance from the average score. The group of scores clustering around the average score is given the middle grade symbol; the scores better than the average, another symbol; those lower than the average, another symbol; and so on out as far as the particular school system demands. This plan is based upon relative values, and marks are determined according to the rank or order of the merit. The distribution of grade is determined by some arbitrary scheme, such as the normal curve or some percentage distribution. Grades under such conditions are usally in letters or numbers, and the scales ordinarily used have four or five divisions. The University of the Philippines and Silliman University use this system of grading.

The real difference between these two systems is that the Percentage or Garrett Plan assumes that the standard of judgment can be applied reliably and validly by the teacher, while the Normal-Curve or Missouri Plan recognized that test vary in difficulty and that judgments vary in the marking; hence, marks can and should show relative ability only. According to Ruch "marks cannot be reduced into an absolute scale such as the percentage scale because no one knows what 100% means." However, reducing relative marks into percentage still persists in thePhilippines and in America.

...mal-curve system, on the other hand, originates from the ba... mathematical laws of chance, and is constructed according to the binomial expansion theorem. With such mathematical precision, one can face the grading problem with greater confidence that the results will be reliable.

A marking system based upon the normal probability curve indicated by the five letters with their corresponding areas computed on the basis of the M (median) and 6 (S.D.).

In a five-letter system based upon M and 6 or S.D., the areas representing the various letters are discribed as follows:

A is 1.50 or more above the Mean.

B is between +.50 and +1.50,

C is between -.05 and +.50,

D is between-.50 and -1.50.

E is 1.50 or more below the Mean.

The normal-curve pictures accurately what actually happens when a large, unselected group is measured for educational achievement and the results are presented graphically. Since this is what happens under controlled conditions, it gives us a guide as to what we might expect in a particular testing situation; hence, it might be called the expectancy curve. When the results of the particular test that we administer do not take the form of the curve, we are challenged to answer the question "Why?" Has the instruction been faulty? Has the test been properly constructed? Has the subject-matter been too easy or too hard? Just what has happened?

Q. 43. Discuss the principles to be observed in evaluating Teaching and Learning.

Ans. Evaluation, to be effective, must be based on the following general principles:

1. Evaluation must be based on the Clear Concept of the Aims of Education outlined in our Constitution, of the School, and of the Course of Study. Evaluation of the work of a school is made in terms of the philosophy of the school and the objectives which the school is expected to accomplish. The aims of the course of study must be formulated in terms of child growth and development. The ultimate purpose of evaluation is to improve the educational program of the school and to make it more effective.

2. Evaluation should be Comprehensive. It should not be limited to isolated goals, or educational objectives, but should include all the major objectives of instruction. It is concerned with all the aspects of pupil behaviour and with all the objective which the school and society hope to achieve. In other words, it should include all factors involved in the total teaching-learning situation.

3. Evaluation should be Continuous and must be made an Integral Part of all Teaching and Learning. While the usual program of evaluation in this country is periodic; on the order hand, evaluation in the modern program permeates the program of improvement, and is continuous. Gradual and continuous change is recognized as desirable and characteristic of a modern educational program. Evaluation, to be of value, must run parallel to education which is considered by John Dewey as life, growth, and re-construction of human experiences. If we consider education as directed growth, or a continuous modification of behaviour, only then can a continuous appraisal be adequate.

4. Evaluation should be Functional. Evaluation, which is part and parcel of the total teaching-learning situation, cannot help being functional. Evaluation of the teaching-learning situation, to be of value to all members of the teaching personel, must improve the existing situation and the conditions that affect them. The purpose of any program of evaluation is to discover the needs of the individual being evaluated and then to design learning experiences that will solve these needs.

5. Evaluation should be Cooperative. If evaluation is to be based on all aspects of the program of teaching and learning, it is only reasonable to suggest that all persons in the programme should participate in it cooperatively. Cooperative action by the teaching personnel and staff should be the outcome of evaluation.

6. Evaluation should be based on Accepted Criteria or Standard. The criteria which are used in the evaluation should be consistent with the accepted educational philosophy and objectives of education. Of several types of criteria to be used, those concerned with the pupil growth and development and the factors that affect such growth should receive first consideration.

7. Evaluation should be Diagnostic. Evaluation, to be of value, should serve as a guide to the teacher and as an enlightenment to the learner. When a pupil makes an error, the teacher must determine how to direct the thinking of the student in order to build up a correct reaction in place of the incorrect one. It is important that the teacher must be able to measure the extent and the degree of learning that results from study and teaching in order to note weaknesses and defects, as measured by the desired level of mastery.

❑